Charles William Boase

Register of the rectors, fellows and other members of the foundation of Exeter College, Oxford : with a history of the College and illustrative documents

Charles William Boase

Register of the rectors, fellows and other members of the foundation of Exeter College, Oxford : with a history of the College and illustrative documents

ISBN/EAN: 9783742858085

Manufactured in Europe, USA, Canada, Australia, Japa

Cover: Foto ©ninafisch / pixelio.de

Manufactured and distributed by brebook publishing software
(www.brebook.com)

Charles William Boase

Register of the rectors, fellows and other members of the foundation of Exeter College, Oxford : with a history of the College and illustrative documents

REGISTRUM COLLEGII EXONIENSIS

REGISTER

OF THE

RECTORS, FELLOWS, AND OTHER MEMBERS
ON THE FOUNDATION OF

EXETER COLLEGE, OXFORD

*WITH A HISTORY OF THE COLLEGE AND
ILLUSTRATIVE DOCUMENTS*

BY THE

REV. CHARLES WILLIAM BOASE, M.A.

FELLOW AND TUTOR

'Oh what contentment were it unto me to hear somebody that would
relate the customs, the countenance, the most usual words, and the fortunes
of my ancestors ! Oh how attentively would I listen unto it '

MONTAIGNE

A NEW EDITION

Oxford

PRINTED FOR THE OXFORD HISTORICAL SOCIETY
AT THE CLARENDON PRESS

1894

CONTENTS

———

LIST OF ILLUSTRATIONS

(at end of volume.

(See references, pp. 357–365)

HISTORY OF EXETER COLLEGE.

THE thirteenth and fourteenth centuries witnessed a great effort to improve the education given at Oxford, which had hitherto been largely in the hands of the monks and friars. The feeling against them had been growing for some time, and that for many reasons[1]; Roger Bacon says they withstood the progress of true knowledge. Hence Walter de Merton, Chancellor of England and bishop of Rochester, founded Merton College 1264–74, to train students for the service of God in church and state. Was he incited to it by Robert de Sorbonne having just founded his college at Paris to educate poor *secular* students of theology? No 'religious' person, i.e. monk or friar, was admitted by Merton. His aim was to establish 'a constant succession of scholars devoted to the pursuits of literature,' 'bound to study arts or philosophy, theology or canon law, or even civil law'; the students in canon law however were limited to four or five. To remedy the prevailing ignorance of grammar, which Roger Bacon so emphatically laments, one of the fellows was to devote himself to the study. He was to be provided with the necessary books, and regularly instruct the younger students, while more advanced scholars were to have the benefit of his assistance when occasion might require. English as well as Latin entered into his province of instruction. As the learned professions then practically belonged to the ranks of the clergy, most lawyers, doctors, &c. being in the minor orders, the clerical obligation at Merton, as far as it existed, was not at all a narrow limitation : in fact it did not exclude any of those professions that possess a

[1] Maxwell Lyte, *Hist. of Univ. of Oxford* 1886.

b

curriculum at either Oxford or Cambridge in the present day. Moreover, as the *Quadrivium* included arithmetic, geometry, astronomy and
music, the system implied a wider idea of culture than the modern
course which, until lately, was almost limited to classics, and even to
a very few classical authors. The statutes of Balliol, University,
Oriel, and Peterhouse (the earliest college at Cambridge) all borrowed
more or less from those of Merton; just as later colleges at Oxford
and Cambridge copied those of New College. By the statutes of
Exeter, the fourth college in order of foundation, only one fellow was
required to be in orders. In the earlier Colleges not even the Head
was required to be in orders of any kind, nor were students ordered
to go to church or chapel except on Sundays and holidays. It is clear
that the education of the laity was now thought to be as important
as that of the clergy. The colleges were, legally speaking, lay
corporations[1], and the religious services devolved on chaplains.

All students had been of course hitherto ' Unattached,' and discipline
was not much enforced. The creation of Halls, i. e. lodging-houses
let out by the owner to a group of students (artists or legists, Welsh or
Irish, &c.), each under a Principal, had been a first attempt to secure
discipline, but it had not been very successful. They became important however in 1420 when Unattached students were abolished, and
every scholar or scholar's servant was obliged to live in a hall under
a responsible Principal. The Masters, Bachelors, and students elected
their own Principal[2], i. e. consented to the transfer of the house by the
landlord from one Principal to another. A student might remove
from hall to hall at pleasure, until the statute passed between 1533
and 1547; and even then they might do so on just cause, or on the
death or cession of the Principal; their free choice of a Principal
tended to keep them in the hall. Each Principal had to give
security to the University for the payment of dues. The creation of
a College, a corporate body, for poor students, under adequate discipline, was a step in advance; and as Merton College soon acquired
influence in the University, Stapeldon and Wykeham were led to follow
the example. The improvement in discipline is shown by the special

[1] Huber i. 163, 187, 271, ii. 220, 240, 549; Rogers i. 22-4; Hook iii. 329.
[2] Laud's Chancellorship 35, 132; Wood's *City* i. 68. Laud's statute of 1636
gave the appointment of Principals to the Chancellor.

exemption of Merton *et aularum consimilium*—probably University, Balliol, Exeter, Oriel and Queen's—from the general rustication which followed the sanguinary riot on S. Scholastica's day 10 Feb. 135$\frac{4}{5}$. A matriculation oath was now imposed on students that they should keep the peace.

Merton, Stapeldon, and Wykeham (like Chicheley, Warham, Fox, and Wolsey, in later times) were statesmen as well as bishops. The Kings then paid their officials, and clerks in chancery, by church appointments, the only means at their disposal; this had one good result, of securing large-minded men for the Episcopate.

In 1314 Walter de Stapeldon, bishop of Exeter, founded Stapeldon hall for scholars from Devon and Cornwall; but the ground in and near Hart hall, which he bought for this purpose, not proving large enough, he removed the students next year to S. Stephen's hall, and gave them the rent of Hart hall, about £2 a year, that their rooms might be rent-free and kept in repair. Their new abode was at first also called Stapeldon hall, but was soon known as Exeter College[1].

Stapeldon[2] had taught Canon law at Oxford, and at the time of his election to Exeter 13 Nov. 1307 was precentor of the cathedral, rector of Aveton Gifford, and chaplain to Clement V. He was employed on service in France, before and after he became bishop; sent thither by Edward I 6 June 1306; Edward II sent him to Gascony in June 1310; on 6 Nov. 1312 he was ordered to defend the King's cause about Aquitaine before the Parlement of Paris, and again 8 Feb. 131$\frac{2}{3}$[3]. He was one of those who elected the Lords Ordainers in Mch 13$\frac{09}{10}$[4].

His predecessor Thomas de Bitton made several bequests to him. He was consecrated 13 Oct. 1308 and zealously pushed on the rebuild-

---

[1] Called Exeter hall in 1368, Lyte 181; Exeter college 1404. Wood (MS. D. 2, p. 94) says 'autoritate Innocentii vii,' but adds 'by a bull of Gregory xii, 15 Jan. 140$\frac{7}{8}$.'

[2] See Stapeldon's Reg., ed. Hingeston-Randolph, 1892. The bishop's brother Sir Richard m. Joan d. of Serlo Haye; their greatgranddaughter Thomasin m. Richard Hankford, and the heiress of Hankford [Stafford's Reg. 122, 142, 196, 337] brought the family estates to her husband Thomas earl of Ormond. Of the bishop's sisters Douce m. William Herward, Joan m. Thomas Kaynes of Winkleigh, Matilda m. [? Richard] Inwardleigh of Waghfield [Waysfeld, now Washfield]; William Walle, son of the fourth sister, was murdered with the bishop.

[3] Reg. 398, Close Rolls Edward II i. 269, 488, 496, 505, 567, 583, ii. 168.

[4] Close Rolls i. 253.

ing of his cathedral. The Fabric Rolls show that he was a benefactor to the amount of £1,800, an immense sum in those days.

He soon obtained high place under Edward II, was a collector of the Tenth imposed on the clergy in 1318 (Close Rolls ii. 551, 555, 561); Treasurer 18 Feb. 13$\frac{19}{20}$ and again 9 May 1322, after an interval of rest granted at his own request[1]. In 1324 he held Cornwall against the chance of a French invasion; he accompanied young Edward to France 9 Sep. 1325 when the prince went to do homage for Guienne, and probably saw enough to convince him that Queen Isabella was plotting against her husband. He had remonstrated strongly with the King about the Despensers, but when the revolution broke out the bishop was left by Edward, 2 Oct. 1326, in charge of London, and was murdered in Cheapside 15 Oct. 1326. 'The bishop of Exeter, riding towards his inn in Eldedeanes-lane [Warwick Lane] for dinner, encountered the mob and, hearing them shout "Traitor," rode rapidly to S. Paul's for sanctuary, but was unhorsed and taken to Cheapside, stript and beheaded. William Walle, and John Padyngton his steward, met with the same fate. About the hour of vespers the same day the choir of S. Paul's took up the headless body of the prelate and conveyed it to S. Paul's but, on being informed that he died under sentence, the body was brought to S. Clement's beyond the Temple, but was ejected; so that the naked corpse, with a rag given by the charity of a woman, was laid on a spot called 'Le Lawles Chirche' and, without any grave, lay there with those of his two esquires, without office of priest or clerk[2].'

---

[1] '27 Sept. 1323. *De custodia sigilli Scaccarii commissa,*—The King having appointed Hervicus de Stauntone, Chancellor of the Exchequer, to execute the office of Chief Justice, by which he is not able at present to attend to the said office of Chancellor,—"Custodiam sigilli nostri Scaccarii predicti venerabili patri, W[altero] Exoñ. Episcopo, Thesaurario nostro commisimus; habend. quamdiu nobis placuerit, percipiendo pro custodia predicta feodum consuetum. In cujus &c. Teste Rege, apud Skergill xxvij die Sept."' Rot. Pat. 17 Edw. II p. 1, m. 16.

[2] French Chronicle of London 52 (Camden Soc. 1844); see too Walsingham i.182; Leland Coll. i. 467; S. Paul's Documents (Camden Soc. 1880) 51, 177; Stubbs' *Chronicles of Edward I and II* i. pp. xcv, 316; ii. p. xcviii; Galfridus le Baker 23, 43, 198. For the grant of Cornwall see Rymer II.i. p. 569, and further mention of Stapeldon p. 19 (1307), 202 (1313) Stapeldon in France, 344 (1317) to the Pope against Stapeldon's enemies, 422, 428, 448, 520, 564, 565, 574, 584, 605 for going abroad, 617, 627; 603 the Sheriff of Cornwall ordered to proclaim the truce, and 610 to arrest suspected persons. See Index to Rolls of Parliament, Pat. Rolls

His remains were buried in S. Clements Danes, but transferred to Exeter cathedral 28 Mch 1327. The present epitaph on his monument there was composed by John Hoker in 1568, and put up at the expense of Bishop Alley; it has been repaired by the College[1]. His house, Exeter Inn, near Temple Bar, was sacked by the mob, his books—including his 'libri pontificales'—destroyed. His Register at Exeter ends 15 June 1325; that of his last sixteen months was probably destroyed in London. We might perhaps have found in it some account of his benefactions to his new foundation at Oxford. He also left funds to establish in S. John's Hospital at Exeter a grammar school to prepare boys for Oxford, and another at Ashburton[2]. His inventory shows that he possessed books valued at £201 10s 6d, which treated chiefly on Scripture and Canon law, with a few historical works such as the Letters of Frederic II and Peter de Vineis. He had previously given to the Cathedral Library a *Catholicon*, beginning with the words *Temporum summa*, valued at £5, and the Chronicles of Westminster *De gestis Anglorum* valued at £1 6s 8d.

As early as 21 Oct. 1312 Edward II granted a mortmain licence

1327 p. 27, 153; Gutch iii. 104; Hist. Comm. ix. 212 a; Stephens' *Chichester* 64; Hearne 17 Ap. 1712; *W. Antiq.* iv. 218. S. Clements Danes belonged to the Bishop of Exeter: it had previously belonged to the Templars, Eyton's *Henry II* p. 160. J. Diprose's *Parish of S. Clement Danes* 1868-76.

[1] Reg. 23 Jan. 173⅘ a sum of £7 2s was added to what had been given before for the repair of Bishop Stapeldon's tomb. Stapeldon's arms were argent, two bends wavy sable, on a bordure of the last 8 keys or. An older coat was without the bordure and the keys. Izacke says the elder coat was in the north side of the quire of Stapeldon's own chapel near the high altar. The College arms, as allowed by Portcullis in 1574, were Argent, 2 Bends nebulée, within a Bordure, sable, charged with 8 pair of Keys, addorsed, or; Visit. Oxon 5, 86, 100.

[2] It is touching to see what a number of bequests he had made to poor scholars. The accounts are for several years (Reg. 576), and the repeated payments show that some received so much a year. These names include Henry de Tuvertone, William de Heghes, and William de Polmorva; and others also may have been scholars, i. e. fellows. This may apply also to the *scholars* who have letters dimissory (536), though only Philip de Chalvedon is expressly said to come from Stapeldon Hall. One item is 'in expensis domini R. de Brayleghe eundo versus Oxoniam, morando ibidem pro edificiis et negociis scolarium de Stapeldone halle, et redeundo, per xv dies xxxvis.' Dean Brayleghe paid several visits as acting executor (578-9). The bishop's other agents in communicating with the College were Robert de Tauton (Stapeldon's Reg. 385); and Gilbert de Koldishall (R. of White Roding, Essex 26 Mch 1322, res. for Avely 1329; Rymer II. i. 605, Newcourt ii. 22, 500).

to the Bishop's brother Richard, allowing him to give an acre of land
at Draynek in Penwyth (Drannock in Gwinear, Cornwall), together
with the advowson of Gwinear, to the Dean and Chapter of Exeter,
to hold for the support of twelve scholars studying at Oxford and
their successors for ever; Sir Richard paid a fine of 100 shillings for
this licence, and on Friday before Lady day 131¾, at Crediton, he
transferred the property. The land and the advowson had been
conveyed to him by Reginald de Bevyle in a deed dated Walneston
5 Dec. 1312, after the Earl of Gloucester as lord of the manor had
authorised the gift at Westminster 24 May 1312. The licence of
mortmain for Stapeldonhall itself is dated 10 May 1314[1]. On 4 Ap.
1314 Bishop Stapeldon, after praise of Oxford where he had been
educated, says that on consultation with the Dean and Chapter,
M. John le Deneys rector of Gwinear, and Adam [de Carleton]
archdeacon of Cornwall, he gives the rectory of Gwinear[2] to the Dean

[1] Pat. 10 May 1314 licenses bishop Stapeldon to give 2 messuages in Oxford to 12
scholars studying in the University.

Pat. 4 Nov. 1315 confirms Skelton's charter of 6 Oct.

Pat. 30 Oct. 1318 confirms agreement with Godstow of 23 Ap.

Pat. 30 Nov. 1318 licenses Stapeldon hall to acquire lands and rents to value of
£20 a year, and advowson of a church, or of two, to value of 40 marks a year.

Pat. 20 May 1322 licenses bishop Stapeldon to give advowson of West Wittenham.

Pat. 18 June 1326 licenses bishop Stapeldon to give 5 messuages in Oxford to the
house of Stapeldon.

Pat. 20 June 1326 pardons the house of Stapeldon for acquiring without license
2 messuages in Oxford of bishop Stapeldon, 1 of Agatha d. of Henry Owen,
1 of Walter Siward, and 1 of Gilbert Beford.

Pat. 12 July 1351 licenses Warden of the King's free chapel Windsor to give
advowson of South Tawton in Devon to Stapeldon hall in exchange for West
Wittenham [Carta Custodis de Wyndesore 21 Sep. 1351 in Ashmole MS. 1125
fol. 24].

Pat. 12 Mch 1457 licence to acquire land to value of £11 14s 8d a year, and
advowson of 1 or 2 churches to value of 40 marks a year.

Pat. 18 June 1705 licence to purchase in mortmain advowsons of yearly value of
£500.

[2] On 28 Sep. 1319 at Clist the bishop arranged thus for the Vicarage of Gwinear
(Reg. 332): dominus Andrew de Tregiliou now Vicar and his successors are to
have the houses previously belonging to the rectory with the whole sanctuary
within the close, and the glebe of one acre, except a long building on the sanctuary,
with a curtilage of half an acre English adjoining, which the Vicar is to keep up
for the Chapter when they want it, to gather the harvest in. The Vicar is to have
the lesser tithes, oblations and obventions belonging to the altilage, and the tithe
of hay, mortuaries, flax, hemp, heifers, lambs, fowls, and 'blades' cultivated with

and Chapter, who are to pay the money arising from the rectory to
the use of the twelve scholars of Stapeldonhalle studying philosophy
'in municipio Oxon, vel alibi in eodem municipio ubi duxerimus
ordinandum dum ibi subsistit universitas, vel alibi in regno Anglie
si ad alium locum eiusdem regni eandem universitatem, quod absit,
transferri contigerit'; if the Dean and Chapter delay payment, they
are to pay forty shillings to the help of the Holy Land and forty more
to the Bishop's alms. But bishop Grandisson had to remonstrate with
the Chapter 28 Aug. 1329 because they withheld great part of the
money (Latin printed in ed. i. p. xliv), and again in 1354, and the
fellows petition Brantingham to the same effect 18 Sep. 1372[1].

spades in the present gardens. The Chapter is to pay the Vicar 40s yearly, but the
Vicar is to supply sufficient hay (literam 'litter,' et buscam) to the Chapter's agents
while on the spot. The Vicar is to pay the Chapter for the glebe two shillings of
silver yearly. And the Vicar is to pay all ordinary expenses of the church, keep
up the chancel, books, ornaments, belonging to the rectory, and the glass in the
windows of the Chancel at his own expense; extraordinary burdens however to be
paid by the Chapter. A receipt is preserved, dated Exeter 7 Oct. 1382, given to
the Chapter by William Slade rector of Stapeldon hall for £23 14s 8d received
through the hands of dominus Walter Compton seneschal of the exchequer of the
Chapter in presence of M. Hugh Hickelyng precentor and dominus William Fereby
canon of Exeter in payment for 1378-81. Extraordinary burdens probably refer to
voluntary subsidies, and to the tenths exacted by Legates and Nuncios &c., as in
the parallel arrangement made for the vicarage of Menheniot. The Vicarial glebe
now is 34 acres, ?=the sanctuary of 33 acres (after deducting the half acre) and the
one acre. For the Rectors and Vicars of Gwinear, see Lake ii. 146, N. and
Gleanings iv. 181. In the Taxation of Nicholas IV, 1288-91, Gwinear is valued
at 113s 4d, the tenth of which is 11s 4d.

[1] DOCUMENTS IN CHAPTER LIBRARY AT EXETER.

1162. Tuesday before S. Martin 15 Edward II. Joan who was wife of Philip
de St. Wynnoc and daughter and heir of William de Tregilla, widow, to Bishop
Stapeldon and Sir Richard de Stapeldon his brother, grant of an acre of land in
the vill of Menhenniot and the third part of the advowson of the church of
Menhenniot. [Year Books xii and xiii Edward III (Rolls Series 1885) pp. 282-98
A. D. 1339 Adam de Helygan v. Richard de Stapeldon and others. The advowson
of Mahynyet was alleged to be *appendant* to the manor of Tregilla. The descent
was from Adam de Tregilla to his daughters Emma Isabel and Joan, and from
Isabel to Adam Doygnel her son. Partition was made between Adam Doygnel,
Emma and Joan. Emma gave her purparty to Adam de Helygan. Richard
confessed Helygan's right to present in turn, and judgement was accordingly given
against him.]

1163. 12 Nov. 15 Edward II, letter of attorney to deliver possession of the
premises.

1177. 4 May 1478 appointment, by Nicholas Gosse chancellor of Exeter and
others, of proctors to obtain from the archbishop the confirmation of the appro-

On 7 Ap. 1314 Richard de Wydeslade precentor of Crediton quit-claimed at Oxford to the bishop his right over Hart hall ' now

priation of the church of Menheniot to the Dean and Chapter for the use of the fellows of Stapeldon hall.

1190. 23 July 1479 copy of composition for tithes of Menheniot, from original at Exeter College.

1191. Extracts from the Chapter Act Books, registers, &c., relating to Menheniot and Exeter College.

1487. Nov. 1316 Reginald de Beovyle knight to Richard de Stapeldon knight, grant of an acre of land in the manor of Drayneck, and the advowson of the church of St. Wynner.

1488. Nov. 1316 Laurence de Beovyle son of Ralph de Beovyle to Reginald de Beovyle, Release of the premises (see also no. 1499).

1489. 21 Dec. 1316 the same to Richard de Stapeldon knight, Release of the premises.

1490. 21 Oct. 6 Edward II (1312) Licence of Mortmain for Richard de Stapeldon to grant the premises to the Dean and Chapter of Exeter (see also no. 1500). Seal.

1496. No date, Memorandum of matters to be inquired of respecting a suit brought against the Dean and Chapter by the descendent of Reginald de Beovyle for the advowson of S. Wynner.

1497. Thursday after S. Andrew 5 Edward II (Dec. 1311) Reginald de Beovyle knight to John de Trejagu knight, letter of attorney to deliver seisin to Richard de Stapelton knight of the manor of Drennek in the hundred of Penwith, together with the advowson of the church of S. Wynner in the said manor [Seal, an ox, S.igillum) Reginaldi de Bevil].

1499. Friday after S. Andrew 5 Edward II (Dec. 1311) Laurence de Beovyle son of Ralph de Beovyle to Reginald de Beovyle, Release of his right to an acre of land in the manor of Drayneck *prope parcum prati rectorie ecclesie Sancti Wynneri in australi parte parci, et tendit usque regale iter de ecclesia de Wynieri versus Rudruth*, and the advowson of the said church.

1500. Friday before the Annunciation 7 Edward II (Mch 131¾) Richard de Stapeldone to the Dean and Chapter of Exeter, Grant of the aforesaid English acre of land and advowson of S. Wynner (Seal, a shield): Witnesses Robert de Stokhay, Richard de Merton, John de Valletort of Clist, Hugh le Prous, William le Espek, knights, at Criditon. No. 1501 Duplicate of same deed.

(MISCELLANEOUS DEEDS.)

2142. 24 May 4 Edward II Gilbert de Clare Earl of Gloucester to the Dean and Chapter, Grant of lands in Dreinok, Cornwall, in aid of the poor scholars of Oxford (injured by damp).

2215. 23 Nov. 1332 Ordinance of Bishop Grandisson for the foundation of the school in S. John's Hospital Exeter. It recites that Bishop Stapeldon after having founded Stapeldon Hall at Oxford had obtained the king's licence to acquire the advowson of the church of Erniscombe, &c.

2278. 24 May 1402 Agreement by Dean and Chapter to save harmless John Keynes and John Whityng the consanguinei and heirs of Richard Stapeldon knight for a suit brought against them concerning lands in Drennok belonging to the Chapter.

called Stapeldonhalle,' and Arthurhall (two messuages conveyed to them jointly by John de Dokelington), witnesses Sir Richard de Merton, Sir Richard de Stapeldon, Sir John de Treiaugu [1], Richard de Inwardlegh, John de la Pomeray. Hart hall lay within Smythgate, in S. Peter's in the East, between Black hall to the west and Scheld hall to the east; this Scheld hall was where New College cloister now stands. But Hart hall proving too small, the bishop moved his scholars to the site of the present College, where he obtained from Peter de Skelton for £50 on 6 Oct. 1315 S. Stephen's hall in S. Mildred's parish. Later on, a tower, part of which still remains in the rector's house, was built on the site of S. Stephen's hall [2], with a gate under it opening out into the lane inside the City wall. Skelton was very much favored by the bishop. Stapeldon's Reg. 12 Oct. 1315 'Apud Chuddelegh xii die mensis Octobris optinuit magister Petrus de Skelton [3] rector ecclesie de Esse [Saltash] in Cornubia licenciam commorandi in scholis per biennium in partibus transmarinis vel in Anglia prout elegerit, ita tamen quod singulis his annis si in Anglia fuerit semel in Adventu predictam ecclesiam suam visitet et per totam quadragesimam residenciam in eadem faciat personalem, proviso &c., et super hoc habet literas.' Stapeldon's statutes order that the Chaplain shall always pray 'pro salubri statu .. domini Johannis Tolliro [4] et magistri Petri de Skelton sacerdotum' &c. On 7 Oct. 1315 Skelton gave the bishop La Lavandrie lying east of S. Stephen's hall and containing two chambers and an area. On 8 Oct. Skelton further gave him a tenement lying east of La Lavandrie, between it and the Schools of Arts. This as well as La Lavandrie was held of the Abbess of Godstowe. A deed of

2872. Copies of documents relating to the grant of S. Wynner by Richard de Stapeldon 4–7 Edward II.

2922 and 2973. Copies of documents relating to the grants by Reginald de Bevil, and the mortmain licence.

[1] M.P. Truro 1304, Rymer II. i. 490, Bibl. Corn. 761.

[2] Gutch iii. 104, picture in Ingram (Ex. Coll.) p. 8.

[3] R. of S. Stephen's by Saltash 29 Dec. 1309, Stapeldon's Reg. pp. 344, 582.

[4] John de Tollir or Toyllero, R. of Morchard Bishop, exchanged for Poutone i.e. S. Breock 1 May 1310, canon of Crantock 1310–1, promoted to Crediton, d. 8 Ap. 1319; Stapeldon's Reg. pp. 11, 205, 214, 236, Bitton's Reg. pp. 420, 422, 432, Bitton's Will (Camden Soc.) 37, Eccl. Ant. iii. 48, Waters' Memoirs of the Chesters 623, Coll. Topog. et Gen. i. 383, R. I. C. 1871 p. 239. The name Toller occurs at Fowey.

23 Ap. 1318, with an Inspeximus of 30 Oct., recites that the Abbess
and Convent of Godstow grant the Rector and Scholars a tenement
adjacent to the former purchase, reserving a rent of 12s, for which
they may distrain on Hart Hall and Arthur Hall.

There were several persons connected with the foundation, and
their title-deeds are preserved. It is worth while quoting some of
them, since they help us to ascertain the sites of the Halls, and to
trace the history of early Oxford families. I give those of S. Stephen's
Hall in full. The first deed connected with S. Stephen's Hall is in
or about 1275 (but see other deeds in Bodleian Charters 288). By it
William Crompe gave M. William de Coudray a house in S. Mildred's
parish between the house which belonged to Hugh Rufus and that
which belonged to the Abbess of Godstow at a rent of two shillings
to himself and two pence to S. Mildred's, the sum paid down being
15 marks; witnesses N. de Kyngeston, mayor, Galfridus aurifaber
and N. de Coleshulle bailiffs; J. de Ho, P. de Ho, Ralph le seynter,
J. Culvert, W. Hastel, Simon Scotur &c. On 5 Feb. 128$\frac{4}{5}$, Thomas
de Merston quitclaimed to M. William de Coudray for a house in
S. Mildred's, which M. Thomas de Radenore bought of Geoffrey de
Merston his father, and which Thomas sold to William; and for
a *placea* behind the house which Geoffrey sold to William; Thomas
and William giving 2 marks to Thomas de Merston; witnesses H. de
la Grave, Hugh Cheche, J. de Fonte of Gersindon, Ralph le plumer,
J. Payn &c. In 1281–2 Geoffrey de Merston *allutarius* granted William
de Coudray a *placea* of land, of breadth, within William's walls, 6 royal
ells and a thumb, and a quarter of an ell; in length the whole space
between the land of M. Thomas de Radenore on the west and that
of the Abbess of Godstow on the east, between the land of William
on the north and Geoffrey's land on the south, at a rent of one clove [1]
at Easter, William paying down 40s; witnesses N. de Kyngeston
mayor, T. de Sowy and Ralph le plumer bailiffs, H. Owayn,
J. Culverd, N. de Coleshulle, J. de Eu, P. de Eu, Paulinus de
Eriditon &c. In 1281–2 Thomas de Sowy demised and quitclaimed
to William de Coudray a rent of 2s, which Thomas received from
a messuage between the land of the Abbess of Godstow and the land
of Lucia la Rede, William giving Thomas 2$\frac{1}{2}$ marks; witnesses N. de

---

[1] Cf. Hist. Comm. iv. 445; Rogers i. 628; Magdalen Muniments 139.

Kyngeston mayor, Ralph le plumer bailiff, H. Owayn, P. de Eu, N. de Coleshulle, J. Sewy, Paulinus de Eriditon[1] &c.   On 1 Aug. 1294 Alice daughter of H. de la Grave granted and quitclaimed to William de Coudray her right in the tenement which William had granted her, William giving her in exchange the tenement and mead given him by Sir H. Boveles and Henry his son in the vill of Curtelington; witnesses J. Culverd mayor, Andrew de Pyrie and J. Wyz bailiffs, P. de Ho, J. de Ho &c.   On 15 May 1296 Gilbert de Coudray quitclaimed to M. William de Coudray for his houses and land in Curtelington.   In 1296 W. de Coudray granted to William son of Thomas de la Rode of Cornwall and to Peter de Skelton 'my clerk,' 'and to whichever of them shall live longest,' the messuage granted me by W. Crompe, against the walls, between the land of the Abbess of Godstow, and a messuage once belonging to J. Culvert, with the lower court which he had from Geoffrey de Merschton.   After the death of both it is to go to the heir of William son of Thomas.   They are to pay him 40s a year for his life; witnesses P. de Eu mayor, Andrew de Pyrie and J. de Coleshull bailiffs, Robert de Wormenhale, Andrew Culvert, Symon le barbur, R. de Berkelc etc.   On 7 May 1297 Henry, son of *dominus* Henry de Boveles of Curtelinton [Kirtlington near Bicester] and Alice his wife, granted at Oxford to William son of Thomas de la Rode of Cornwall and Peter de Skelton clerk all his rights over the tenement which Alice his wife had of the gift of William de Coudray; witnesses Robert Jurdan, Richard de Canne, John de Codesford of Curtelinton, Symon barbitonsor of Oxford, Richard barbitonsor at the north gate &c.   In 1306 William son of Thomas de la Rode granted to Skelton his part of the messuage he had from Coudray, and his part in the lower court adjoining, between the Godstow tenement on the east and a tenement once belonging to John Culverd on the west; he further quitclaimed to Skelton the half of this property which Skelton held for life of the gift of Coudray; and to warrant the grant he bound his lands at Curtelington in Oxon and his lands at la Rode near Esse [Saltash] in Cornwall; witnesses J. de Dokelington mayor, Walter de Wicumbe and W. de Pennard bailiffs, Andrew de Pyrie,

---

[1] Hist. Comm. iv. 445, 468 (Cridilon).

Robert de Wormenhale, T. de Henexeye[1], Andrew Culverd, W. de
Burncestre, J. le sauser, Simon le barbur, T. clerk &c. On 11 June
1313 William de la Roede quitclaimed to Skelton his right in the
messuage with a court &c.; witnesses W. de Burncestria mayor, H. de
Lynne and Gilbert de Grenestede bailiffs, Robert de Wormenhale,
P. de Wormenhale, John Coleshulle, Andrew de Purie &c. About
1314 Gilbert de Coudray quitclaimed to Walter bishop of Exeter his
right in a burgage which he had from William de Coudray, which
burgage once belonged to William Crompe, witnesses John de
Karmynou, Otto de Bodrigan, Richard de Stapelton knights, Nicholas
de Ferrars, John de Rame, Peter de Bodrigan, Vincent de Poldrusek
and others. On 6 Oct. 1315 Skelton at the request of the Bishop
granted to the Rector and Scholars of Stapeldone halle a messuage
called S. Stephen's Hall in S. Mildred's parish, opposite the north
wall of the city between Northgate and Smythgate, for this the
Bishop gave him £50, witnesses Richard de Merton, Richard de
Stapeldon, John de Clifford knights, John de Gaynes, John de la
Pomeroy and others, dated at Chuddlegh in Devon on Monday the
feast of Saint Faith the Virgin 9 Edward II. On the next day,
7 Oct. 1315, Skelton granted to the Rector and Scholars two
chambers with an area, east of S. Stephen's Hall, called La Lavandrie,
which he had received from the convent of Godstow for his life;
witnesses James de Oxton, Richarde de Mertone, Richard de
Stapeldon, John de Clifford knights, John Caynghes and others, at
Chuddelegh in Devon Tuesday the morrow of S. Faith 9 Edward II.
On the next day 8 Oct. 1315, Skelton gave the Rector and Scholars
the rent and service of Joan de Bedeford for a tenement held by her
of Skelton for life, east of La Lavandrie and lying between it and the
'Scolae Artium,' with the reversion after Joan's death. On 7 Nov.
1315 John de Skelton, Peter's brother, quitclaimed to the Rector and
Scholars, at London on Friday the morrow of S. Leonard 9 Edward II.
Finally on 12 Jan. 133⁷⁄₈ Alice widow of William de la Rode quitclaimed at Oxford, Monday the vigil of S. Hilary 11 Edward II;
witnesses H. de Stodeleye mayor, R. de Selewode and J. Peggi
bailiffs, W. de Burcestre, R. Cary, Simon de Gloucestre, J. de Biburi

---

[1] Hist. Comm. v. 478.

&c. Enrolled on the plea-roll of the Hustings, Monday the Nativity of the Virgin for the first time, finally Monday after Epiphany.

No one, from looking at a modern College, with quadrangles and spacious chapels, halls, libraries, and gardens, could form any idea of how things looked in the Middle Ages. There were, it is true, small chapels, halls, and libraries, placed quite irregularly; but the rest of the area was occupied by small lodging houses, woodhouses, outhouses of all kinds, dotted about narrow lanes. Still less could any one standing in the Radcliffe Square (cleared of its population in 1749 by Dr. Radcliffe's executors) realise to himself a state of things when the Convocation house and Divinity School and Bodleian, All Souls and Brasenose and Hertford, did not exist, but there were on the west side rows of small houses used as *Schools* for disputations (Wood's *City* i. 89); on the east side the dwellings of the writers, bookbinders, parchment-makers, and illuminers all along Cat Street; and here and there a public house, among the two-storied halls and the *selds* or wooden booths used as shops; and when the dark lanes and the large cemetery of S. Mary's (Clark's *Colleges* 92) were so unsafe at night as the Coroners' inquests under Edward I show them to have been; when the University itself had no public buildings, but used S. Mary's for its Convocation house, its Library, and its Treasury; when the city wall ran from New College by the site of the Sheldonian, through Exeter, behind the present houses in Broad Street (where there are remains of the bastions), and Broad Street itself was the city ditch, 20 feet deep, with a few Halls on the opposite side, on the site of Balliol and Trinity, with Horsemonger Lane in front of them on the edge of the ditch.

Many Halls were named from some Saint, or from their owners, some from having a sign, some from having an elm by them, or a well, or from being at a corner of the street, or having a roof of stone or tile or lead, or having glass windows, or a chimney—a rare thing, when there was usually a charcoal fire in the centre of the room (after the fashion of the central fire in the huts of primeval tribes), with an opening above to carry off the smoke. The heat of the fire was thus all utilized while now most of the heat goes up the chimney. A procession of students sometimes marched round the central fire in a College hall. 'In these,' says Johnson jocosely, 'the fireplace was always in the middle of the room till the Whigs removed it on one side.' The early Halls were of wood, and thatched, with wooden shutters for the open windows, and mere latches for the doors (from the later use of staples came the name of Staple Hall).

Stapeldon Hall gradually absorbed several of the old Halls or lodging houses, Bataile hall in 1320, Fragnon hall 1323, Sheld hall 1325, Scot hall 1328, Bedford hall 1335, Culverd hall 1353, Hambury hall 1380, Castel hall (1358, finally) 1385, Checker hall 1406, Peter hall 1470. Besides some outlying property, it thus took in the frontage along the city wall to the north and that along S. Mildred's Lane to the south. Some of these grants were at first made to two or three of the fellows, who later on transferred them to the College—perhaps when a further mortmain licence could be obtained.

Bataile Hall[1] in S. Mary Magdalen parish, opposite the church, near the Curia Regis where the Carmelites lived (Peshall 237), lying between the tenement of Thomas Bost (Hist. Comm. iv. 446), and that of Thomas de Dodeford, was on 14 June 1303 given by Robert son of Robert Punchard of Garsington to M. Gilbert de Budeford clerk; witnesses Edmund de la More seneschal of the Hundred outside the North gate, Nicholas son of John de Eynesham and coroner of that Hundred, William de Ernesby, John de Dodeford, William de Clane-feld smith, Thomas Bost, Robert de Heyford, Robert de Brackele, Peter de Haneberg, Thomas de Dodeford, William Meke, Robert de Hamstalle clerk, and others. On 26 Aug. 1320 Gilbert de Bideford clerk granted it to the Rector and Scholars of Stapeldon Hall; witnesses Richard de Stapeldon and William Hereward knights, John de Pederton, John de Gaynges, Henry de Bokerel, and others. Gilbert de Bedeford made M. Robert Hereward clerk[2] and Roger de Doune bedell of Oxford his attorneys to deliver the seisin.

On 20 May 1323 Stapeldon granted them Ledeneporche[3] in

---

[1] Computus autumn 1365 'iiis iiiid de reditu de Battelhall in festo S. Michaelis.' In 1403 the College let Bataille hall to William Roll and Agnes his wife for thirty years at 6s 8d a year. There was an Oxford family called Bataile. On 10 Dec. 1803 the reversion of some houses in Magdalen parish, on lease to Mr. Welch, was sold to Worcester College for £141 16s, to improve its approaches.

[2] Stapeldon's Reg. 177, 255, 25 Dec. 1317 Robert Hereward deacon pres. to Mawgan in Kerrier by William de Whalesbreus; Le Neve i. 494; Rymer II. i. 443.

[3] Perhaps the same as Willoughby hall, Wood's City i. 66, 68, 636. It was on

Cornwall street, between North gate and Smythe gate, which the
Bishop had received from John (son of William) le Spycer and Alice
his wife; witnesses Richard de Stapildon, William Hereward knights,
John Kaygnes, John Prodhomme, John de la Slo, and others, at York
Friday after S. Dunstan 16 Edward II: the Bishop gave £60 for it,
and had on 10 May 1323 appointed 'Magister Stephanus' Rector of
Stapeldone halle to receive seisin of it; and on 21 May 1323 he
named Robert de Tauton or Thomas de Ston to give the seisin to
the Rector and Scholars. On 3 Nov. 1336 Alice widow of John de
Maydenstone [? her second husband] quitclaimed to the Rector and
Scholars for Ledeneporche, between Bruneshalle on the east and the
tenement of Robert de la Bache on the west [1].

---

the west side of Leadenhall or Aula Alba, and was at last turned into a garden.
It must therefore be distinguished from Leadenhall, which was sold to Jesus for
£400 in 1821 (Reg. 9 May 1821, and 1845). Leadenhall was also called Whitehall, but there was Great Whitehall in Cheney lane (Market street), and Little
Whitehall in Ship street (Wood's *City* i. index), besides half a dozen other White-
halls in the University, and it is not easy to distinguish them. Computi, autumn
1419 '12s 6d for repairs in Aula Alba'; winter 1419 '19d for 26 pounds (ponderibus) of lead bought for Aula Alba,' i. e. 3 farthings a pound; autumn 1420 '57s 9d
for repairs in Aula Alba'; autumn 1421 '17d for repairs at Aula Alba'; autumn
1425 '13d for the carriage *tabellarum* to Aula Alba'; '21d to John Edyngton
and his partners for repairing one *synk* at Aula Alba'; winter 1426 '12d to
Norton for a garden near Whytehall for last year'; summer 1438 '6s 8d from
M. J. Claydon'; Lent 1469 '4s received from Alice Berton for a garden called
Ledyngporche near Aula Alba'; Lent 1478 '3s 8d from John Rogger for a garden
near Aula Alba for last year,' so in winter 1504 'near Aula Alba, on *the west side*,'
and again autumn 1505 and autumn 1522 '2s'; winter 1539 '4d for repairing the
great gate which looks towards the garden of Alba Aula'; Lent 1544 '16d for
2 twysts for the back gate towards Wythall'; summer 1555 '18d to the Principal
of Whithall, as in bill'; autumn 1547 '6s received from M. Busbye for a garden
near Aula Alba for 3 years past.' Anstey 522 '1438 for Aula Alba in the Little
Bailey M. Claydone'; 600 '1450 Aula Alba under the walls'; 676 '1458 Aula
Alba in Chain street (vico catenarum, i. e. Cheney lane)'; 714; Wood's *City* i. 67,
71-2, 207, 258, 605; Wood's *Fasti* 61; Griffiths 14, 22, 29, 32, 53; State Papers
11 Ap. 1538.
  [1] In a deed of which the date is lost the Rector and Scholars granted to Richard
de Salisbersh of Oxford, Emma his wife and John their son a 'placea terre' once
called Ledynporche, between Richard's own tenement on the west and a 'placea'
which is called Fouks-yne (Wood's *City* i. 385; Hist. Comm. iv. 447) on the east, for
their lives at a rent of four shillings; Computus winter 1445 'iiiis a Thoma Barton
pro gardino ex antiquo vocato Lydenporche,' and a similar entry in autumn 1457;
compare Lent 1473 'xx^{ti}d Priori S. Frideswide pro ultimo anno, et pars residua
est ab ipso ablata propter negligentiam suam circa murum orti Aule Plumbee.'
See Gutch i. 172. A Richard Salesbury occurs 1381 (Wood's MS. D. 2, p. 466)

In 1299 Alice de Gorges Abbess of Godestowe and the convent granted for ten years to Peter de Skelton clerk a curtilage in S. Michael's parish near the North Gate, near a tenement once belonging to M. William de Coudray against the city walls, at a rent of two shillings, Peter to repair the 'muros bundales circa curtilagium.' This, says Wood, was a garden in S. Michael's, near White Hall. On 29 Sep. 1301 Peter let to Joan de Bedeford and her brother Richard (Godstow tenement i.e.) a 'placea terre' (different from the previous one) held by him under Godstowe, lying in S. Mildred's, between the land of the said Peter and the land of Thomas de Hengxeye for ten years. On 23 Ap. 1318 Margery Dyne, abbess of Godstow (Hist. Comm. iv. 467) granted to Stapeldon Hall in fee-farm for ever a tenement with a curtilage, between the tenement now belonging to Stapeldon Hall but previously to M. Peter de Skelton on the west, and a tenement of Thomas de Hengseye in S. Mildred's towards the city wall on the east, at a rent of 12 shillings a year, to be paid half-yearly : if the rent is not paid the Convent may distrain on Hert Hall situated between the University tenement called Blake Hall on the west and the tenement of the Prioress and Convent of Stodleye called Scheld Hall on the east in the parish of S. Peter in the east, and on Artur Hall in the same parish situated between the tenement of Osneye Abbey on the east and the tenement of Adam de Spaldheyk [Spaldyng, Bodl. Chart. 287] on the west, witnesses William de Burcestre mayor, Richard Kari and Gilbert de Grenstede bailiffs, John de Dokelynton, Henry de Lynne, John de Hampton, and others ; there is a receipt for 6s on 1 Oct. 1451 from Alice de Henley abbess of Godstow.

Fragnon[1] Hall lay between a tenement once belonging to Godstow on the west and a tenement belonging to Baliol hall on the east [i. e. S. Hugh's Hall] 'lying lengthways between the King's road and Scothall.'

Scheld Hall was within the present College, Gutch i. 369, iii. 182 ; Wood's *City*, index ; Hist. Comm. v. 477. In 1285 M. William de Coudray gave William de Paris and Yllaria his wife a messuage

---

as holding a tenement in Bedford's Lane, i. e. Cheyney or Somnor's Lane ; and Wood dates the deed ' in time of Richard II.' For Bruneshalle *see* Wood's *City* i. 66.
[1] Wood's *City* i. 112, deed of 1327.

situated in S. Mildred's parish between the messuage of Richard de
Hambury on the north and that of William and Yllaria on the south,
they paying annually the chief lord of the fee five pence, and a penny
to the lights of S. Mildred, and a clove to Coudray himself; for
this grant they gave him nine marks : witnesses John Culverd mayor,
Nicholas the goldsmith (aurifaber) and Thomas de Sowy bailiffs,
Henry Owayn, John de Eu, Philip de Eu, John Sewy, Thomas Pope,
Paulinus de Eriditon and others. Yllaria was a widow when, on
27 Oct. 1316, she gave this messuage to John de Perschore of
Oxford and Joan her younger daughter [Pershore's wife]. On
17 Mch 132⅖ Perschore gave it under the name of Sheldhall to
William Syward citizen and fishmonger of London, at a rent of 40s;
and on 6 June 1325 quitclaimed to him for the messuage and the
rent. On 16 June 1325 Syward gave it to the Rector and Scholars
of Stapeldonhall, and named M. Robert Hereward or John de Bury his
attorneys to transfer the seisin. On 23 July 1344 Joan widow of John
de Peshore quitclaimed to the Rector Masters and Scholars of Stapul-
done halle for a messuage between the tenement of John de Davyntre
Manciple [called *Spenser*, elsewhere; i.e. Hambury Hall] on the north
and a tenement of the Hospital of S. John on the south ... Recognised
before Mayor and Bailiffs at the Hustings held on Monday after
S. Peter ad Vincula 18 Edward III [i.e. 2 Aug. 1344]. On 2 Aug.
1344 there appeared before the Chancellor M. William de Bergeveny,
in the house of Joan widow of John de Pershore, Joan herself on the
one part and on the other M. John de Blatcheswall Rector of
Stapeldonhall, M. John de Landreyn, John Estcolme and Robert
Fromonde, and they acknowledged themselves indebted 40 marks to
Joan, but the next day this was reduced to 19 marks [1].

Hambury Hall, named from Richard de Hambury, was near Turl
gate [2], where the west part of Exeter College Chapel now is (Reliquiae
Hearnianae 7 July 1712). Hambury had it about 1288 for thirty
marks down and a rent of 8s 2d, from John de Hankinton and
Edith his wife, when it is described as in the parish of S. Mildred's
'that angular house extending towards the city wall and situated

---

[1] Wood's *City* i. 117.
[2] Not yet built; there was as yet only a small postern gate, Wood's *City* i. 111,
257, Hearne 3 June 1722.

between the tenement of William le Sauser and the tenement of Hugh Ruffus'; witnesses Henry Oweyn mayor, Nicholas de Kingeston, Elyas le Quilter and Philip de Eu bailiffs, Walter the goldsmith, William de Eu, William the apothecary, Andrew de Durham, John de Eu and others. On 16 Dec. 1331 Thomas son of Philip de Wormenhale quitclaimed Hambury Hall to John Leyre and Margaret his wife. (Seal of mayor of Oxford, 'my seal being unknown to most.') Wood D. 2, p. 81 'In a writing of R. Cary, mayor 15 Edw. III it is said that R. de Melton chapeleyn had purchased Hambury hall of J. Leyre of Berugby and Margaret his wife 14 Edw. III, and that Leyre did purchase this tenement of W. Burchestre and Alienora his wife 1 Edw. III. Where also tis said that Hugh de Stratton gave it to Philip de Wormenhale and Alienora his wife, in S. Mildred's, at the corner between the tenement once belonging to Richard de Parys on the south and the tenement once belonging to John Culvert on the east. Hugh also gave Philip and Alienor a tenement with a curtilage in S. Peter's in the east, lying between a tenement of the nunnery of Stodeley on the west, called Mayden hall, and the cotages called le vicoures court on the east; W. de Berncestre mayor, J. de Hamptone and R. de Berkele bailiffs' [i. e. 1311–2]. On 17 Feb. 134¾ Richard de Melton chaplain (parson of S. Ebbe, Bodleian Charters p. 308) granted a messuage called Gramerscoles alias Hamburyhall, situated in a corner between the tenement of 'dominus' John de Shordich called Culverdeshall and a toft of Stapuldonhall, to John elder son of Richard Martyn of Daventre 'spenser' of Merton Hall. John Davyntre junior by his will dated 30 July 1361 (proved 11 Dec. 1361 before J. de Stodle mayor), gave Matilda his wife power to sell a tenement in the corner near [west of] Stapuldonhalle, and an empty place (placea) lying between that tenement and the college called Stapuldonhalle. On 23 Dec. 1361 she sold them both to M. William de Daventre parson of Pytchecote [near Aylesbury; Wood's City i. 147] and M. John de Middleton clerk; and John de Benham quitclaimed to them on 14 Jan. 1363, Robert Tresilian being one of the witnesses. On 3 Nov. 1364 William de Daventre quitclaimed to John de Middleton [land between tenements of the college called Stapildonhall on either side]. On 21 Dec. 1366 Middleton granted to John Otery, Lucas Helland, Robert Lydeford, and Richard Rouland clerks a vacant plot (placea) at a corner near Stapeldonehall on the East, on which there were formerly two messuages, one called Hambury Hall, the other Culverd Hall (24 feet in breadth and 54 and an half in length), John de Benham and John de Northampton clerk were two of the witnesses ['ista carta registratur in papiro GildAuleOxon fol xli. ad requisicionem Johannis de Middleton']. Finally on 26 July 1380 John Otery, Robert Lydeford and Richard Roulond clerks gave this land to the Rector and Scholars of Stapeldonehalle. Permission for this was given 4 Richard II 24 July 1380, Statutes iii. App. p. 36 'a piece of ground in the parish of S. Mildred, 90 feet wide and 57 and a half feet long' [but see Wood's *City* i. 118].

Culverd Hall, 'Kulverdes hall,' was granted on 9 Feb. 135½ by Roger de Lodelawe cook of Oxford to Stephen de Bantre bedell of the University; it lay between 'Excestre Hall' on the east and a tenement of John de Daventre on the west. On 13 June 1353 Stephen de Bantre granted to John Martyn junior of Daventre and Alice his wife a spot (placea) lately built over, called Kylverde Hall, in S. Mildred's parish, between Excestre Hall on the east and a tenement of the said John on the west, which 'placea' he had from Roger de Lodelawe. On 28 Oct. 1353 John Martyn junior of Davyntre and Alice Pulteneye his wife granted to Robert Trethewy and John Cergeaux clerks a 'placea' in S. Mildred's, near Stapeldonhall, on which 'placea' a stone wall is built extending from the King's highway on the North to the corner of the said hall on the South, 23 feet long and 2 wide; they also gave the said Robert and John another 'placea' near Stapeldon hall, on which a stone wall is built, the 'placea' being in length 46½ feet from the west wall of that hall on the north of the kitchen of the said hall to their (Martyn's) tenement, and 2 feet broad. But they were to keep the right of building on the wall. (In dorso) presens carta recognita fuit coram Maiore et Ballivis infranominatis in pleno Hustango Oxon tento ibidem die lune proximo post festum S. Mathei apostoli anno regni regis &c., et super hoc Alicia uxor Johannis Martyn infranominati examinata fuit et confessa et donacioni concessioni et confirmacioni infra specificatis omnino concessit et forum Affis (?), &c. Et ista carta irrotulatur in Hustengo predicto [1].

---

[1] For another Culverd hall, in S. Giles, see Appendix.

Bedford Hall, in S. Mildred's (Wood MS. D. 2. 418, Wood's *City* i. 113, 227, 506, 513), had its name from a family so called, from whom it passed to the Chalfunts. In 1288 it is said to be a *placea* 8 feet broad and 20 feet long, and a wall dividing it from the tenement of Henry de Bedeford. In 1330 it is described as lying between Chekerhalle which belonged to Philip de Eu and Castellhall which belonged to John de la Wyke. On 20 June 1334 Walter de Chalfunt disposed of it to Stephen de Hereweldesore and William Liskerd; and on 4 July they gave Emma widow of Henry de Bedeford a messuage in S. Mildred's, between the tenement of the Abbot of Oseneye and that of John de la Wyk, at a penny rent, and on 25 Sep. 1335 John son and heir of Henry de Bedeford quitclaimed at Winchester to Walter de Chalfhunte and Emma de Bedeford his mother, to Richard de Gloucestre and Thomas le Irmongere executors of Henry's will, all the actions and demands which he had under the will. But in Sept. 1335 Walter and Stephen gave it to the Rector and Scholars of Stapeldonhall, and in June 1337 John de Bedeford son of Henry and Emma de Bedeford quitclaimed it to them at Winchester, as a tenement of Walter de Chalfhunte and Emma his wife by gift from Walter's brother Henry; and on 15 Dec. 1348 John de Littlemor Prior of S. Frydeswyde as chief lord remitted to them two shillings of rent due from Henry de Bedeford's property, which is defined as lying between S. Peter's Hall belonging to the Abbot of Oseneye and Castelhall belonging to John de la Wyk.

On 18 Nov. 1358 John son and heir of John de la Wyk granted to John Halle and John Wyseburgh, Castelhall which was *opposite the Chapel of Stapeldonhall on the south side* (see computus Lent 1357); and on 19 Nov. he bound himself to them in £20 to hold them safe in its possession. On 1 Aug. 1360 John Wyseburgh granted to Thomas Kelly, William Aleyn, John Restaurok, John Crabbe, Thomas de Hanneye and John Bremdon chaplain a toft (i.e. a place where a messuage has stood but is now decayed) formerly called Castelhall, once belonging to John de la Wyk: witnesses John de Stodele mayor of Oxford, John de Hertwell and Richard Wodehay bailiffs of Oxford, Robert Mauncel, Henry de Malmesbury, John de Olneye, John Bedeford, Roger Lodelowe, John le Sealer, John Cronk, John de Northampton clerk. On 21 Aug.

1385 John Restaurok clerk granted it to the Rector and Scholars of Stapeldonhall. Computus of Lent 1358 'iiii*d* pro vino dato Rectori de Seynt Holde et Johanni Wyke quando tractaverunt in aula de illo tenemento vocato Castelhall . . iiii*d* quando convenerunt in crastino dominice in ramis palmarum': summer 1358 'x*d* pro vino dato Radulpho Codeford et Johanni Seyntfresewyde[1] quando tractaverunt cum Johanne Wyke de Castelhall, presentibus Willelmo Stykelyng et Johanne Wysburg, iiii*d* pro vino dato Radulpho Codeford quando alloquebatur Rectorem de Seynt Holde in domo Johannis de Sancta Fredeswyda et quesivit de tallia illius placee de Castelhall': Winter 1358 'circa emcionem tenementi de Castelhall xi*li* traditis Johanni ate Wyke, iii*s* Johanni Norhamton pro factura munimentorum eiusdem tenementi, ii*s* pro impressione sigilli Maioris ad cartam eiusdem, iii*s* pro salario baliorum et Walteri Serjeaux, pro vino et speciebus datis Maiori et balivis et aliis qui fuerunt in seysina capienda iii*s* v*d*': the place became a 'disportum,' Lent 1360 'xii*d* uni operario qui paravit arbores in disporto, ii*d* pro *batellis* eiusdem, x*d* uni operario pro labore suo quando reparavit murum disporti inter nostram capellam et disportum Ybernicorum' (? S. Patrick's Hall); Winter 1360 'vi*s* operariis qui operabant in disporto ubi Castelhall fuit situata'; summer 1361 'ii*s* Priori S. Frideswyde pro quodam redditu annuali, iiii*s* eidem Priori pro duobus redditibus de Castelhall pro duobus annis proximis elapsis,' Lent 1362 'xlvi*s* viii*d* latomis qui erigebant murum ex parte disporti ubi aliquando situabatur Castelhalle.' Castlehall was 'standing about the corner at the west end of S. Mildred's Lane' (Wood's *City* i. 115, plan in 113). S. Patrick's Hall was on the north side of the Divinity school (Wood's *City* i. 111, 113).

Checker Hall had been given on 27 Jan. 137⁷⁄ by Thomas de Schepton (Bodleian Charters 292) R. of Melles in Somerset to the venerable Gregory Bottelee R. of Schepton Malet, Edmund Balrych or Barlych R. of Baudripp, and William Elys R. of Schepton Beauchamp, with some other lands with which they were to enfeoff some of his poor relatives; and on 14 Mch they empowered John Gabbere and John Person to receive the seisin. On 10 Dec. 1384 John atte Burgh, heir of Thomas de Shepton, required them to enfeoff his sister Agnes atte Burgh wife of Robert Draper of Wells in

---

[1] Gutch i. 463, 466, Bodl. Charters index.

frankmarriage, and they did so on 6 Feb. 138⅘; and on 3 Feb. 138⅞ Barlych certified that Thomas made no alteration in his lifetime. John atle Burgh, on 1 Aug. 1391, quitclaimed to Robert Draper, and on 19 May 1396 Draper granted Chekirhall to John Lewys, William Lirebck, Edward Elys and Adam Squier of Bytlysden in Northants, and made Thomas Thyngden of Thyngden in Northants and Gilbert Burton his attorneys to deliver the seisin, and on 20 May quitclaimed to the four. On 28 Oct. 1405 these four granted the Hall to Thyngden, who granted it on 31 Oct. to M. Thomas Noreys, M. John Gynne and M. John Cowlyng clerks for £20; and on 25 Nov. quitclaimed to them. On 27 Oct. Noreys Gynne and Cowlyng give up a statute merchant of £20 by which Thyngden secured them against any claim by himself or his wife Katerine (in right of dower), or by any of the previous owners, who are enumerated. On 12 July 1406 Noreys Gynne and Cowlyng gave two messuages to the Rector and Scholars of Stapeldonhall, viz. Chekerhalle in S. Mildred's, and Gyngyveres Place [1] in the Great Bailey in S. Martin's, after obtaining the King's licence 19 June 1406 (Comm. ed. of Statutes p. 50, Wood's *City* i. 78, 116, 220); Computus winter 1404 'iiii*d* pro oblacionibus mancipii de Chekerhall,' Winter 1405 'iiii*li* ex mutuo a cista Wynton ad solvendum pro Checerhall, vi*li* xiii*s* iiii*d* mutuatis a M. Henrico Bewmount pro eadem solucione: viii*d* pro iantaclo Johannis Honyngdon quando pervidimus munimenta de Checerhall, vi*li* xiii*s* iiii*d* Thome Thyngden in partem solucionis pro Checerhall, ii*s* iiii*d* Thome Hampton quando Maior ville Oxon sigillavit quoddam Statutum Mercatorium per quod nobis obligatus dictus Thomas Thyngden, iii*s* iiii*d* Nicholao Norton pro consilio suo circa dictam Aulam facto et pro factura indenturarum inter nos et predictum Thomam faclarum et statuti predicti, ii*s* vi*d* pro iantaclo dato dominis Johanni Castel, Johanni Honyngdon et Thome Sartery pro consiliis ipsorum, iiii*d* pro una bigata arene pro sporto de Chekurhall, iiii*d* pro exportacione fimi a pavimento [2] iuxta Checerhall': Winter

---

[1] Wood's *City* i. 116, 220. A William Gyngyare occurs in a Carole Hall deed of 1387. On 15 Aug. 1406 the College leased it to William Pecke baker and Alice his wife for 12 years at 12*s* rent. A bond to William Major, rector, 14 Jan. 147¼ follows (after the lease).

[2] On repairs of the pavement *see* Gutch i. 436; Wood's *City* i. 132; Lyte 121, 161; on repairs of the road Wood's *City* i. 122; Turner 166 (tax for it).

1406 'xxxviis xi*d* *q* pro reparacione in Aula Scacarii'; Winter 1408 'iis pro pencione gardini inter coquinam et Checkerhall,' summer 1410 'xiiis iiii*d* de Johanne Holand in partem pencionis Aule Scakkarii pro anno ultimo,' autumn 1411 'vis viii*d* de M. Edwardo Ros in finalem solucionem pencionis Aule Scakkarie pro anno ultimo,' autumn 1422 'xxiiis iiii*d* de executoribus M. Thome Bony in partem solucionis pensionis Aule Scackarii,' winter 1424 'iiiis a M. Johanne Bret [? Brent] in finalem solucionem Aule Scakcarii,' winter 1426 'iis iiii*d* pro tabula et formulis venditis de Chekerhall,' Lent 1459 'iiis iiii*d* a doctore Eggecomb pro redditu cuiusdam basse camere Aule quondam vulgariter dicte Chekkerhall,' winter 1459 'x*d* uni tegulatori et [? servienti eius] pro eorum labore, reparando novas cameras de Checkerhall ac etiam cameras Rectoris et doctoris Eggecomb et quosdam defectus apud Hertehall': see also summer 1457 and the Index.

Scot Hall[1] was close by. On 16 Ap. 1325 Richard de Tekne[2] of Norhampton and Joan his wife granted, to Walter Prodomme clerk, Scothalle with a garden adjoining; it lay in S. Mildred's between the tenement of the Prior of S. Frideswide which is called Patrichall on the east and the tenement of John de Wyke which is called Castelhalle on the west, and abutted on the King's street leading from Scol street to S. Mildred's church, and ran lengthways from the King's street to the tenement of the Rector and Scholars of Stapildonhalle on the north, the rent was 33s 4*d*. On 10 July 1325 William de Brabanzoun quitclaimed to Walter bishop of Exeter and Walter Prodhomme for Scothalle, witnesses John de Trejagu knight, John de Buri of Oxford, John Prodhome, John de la Slo, Ralph le Spek and others, at London. On 22 Jan. 132⁷⁄₈, 1st Edward III, William Prodhoume clerk granted to the Rector and Scholars of Stapeldonhalle a messuage called Scothalle in S. Mildred's street (Wood's *City* i. 112).

Peter Hall was near S. Mildred's lane. On 30 Sep. 1470 John Walton abbot of Osney and the Convent granted to John Philipp Rector of Exeter College and the Fellows, for £41 paid down, the toft

---

[1] Wood D. 2. p. 8, 'about the East end of the New Hall of Exon. Coll., and Castlehall where the kitchen now standeth, and Patrick hall where their *garden and mount* is'; in margin 'noe, further eastward.'

[2] Wood D. 2. p. 482 'John Tekene *son and heir of Joan Feteplace*.'

formerly called Peter Hall near the College on the south of it and
abutting on the lane (*venella*) leading from Lincoln College to
Scholestretys on the south, 59 feet long and 44 broad, at a rent of
fourpence; Computus autumn 1427 'iiiis iid recept. pro Aula Petri,
xs solut. pro Aula Petri,' summer 1515 'xxd Abbati et Conventui de
Osneye pro redditu superiori exeunte pro Aula Petri pro quinque
annis preteritis'; see Anstey 619, 678, 691, Wood's *City* i. 117,
598, 606; it had once been called Wyger's hall.

Black Hall lay about the N.W. corner of Hertford College, Wood's
City i. 91, 97, All Souls Archives 164, Bodleian Charters 355, Reliquiae Hearnianae 3 Mch 172⅞; the Acta Congregationis show that
on 8 June 1509 Convocation voted that a lease of Black Hall should
be granted to Exeter College for 99 years at a rent of ten shillings,
'omnibus reparationibus et oneribus quibuscunque deductis'; Univ.
Archives box H No. 19, 1 Aug. 1664 lease of Blackhall at 10s yearly
rent, and of Cathall at 20d to John Cross for 40 years : No. 22, 6 Ap.
1525 lease to Exeter College of Blackhall and a garden, once called
Cathall, next to Hart Hall, at 10s and 20d respectively for 99 years;
and at Lady Day 1513 Exeter let it to the Principal of Hart Hall[1].
The Principal however paid the rent for the garden direct to the
University until 1556. The Principal also paid the University in
the name of Exeter College 10s, over and above the 6s paid to the
College for Black Hall, until Michaelmas 1543 when 10s appears in
the College account as paid to the Proctors for the rent of Black Hall,
and at the foot of the account the Principal is charged with an arrear
of 56s for Hart Hall that year, which was afterwards paid, *i. e.* the
Principal paid 40s for Hart Hall (Rogers iii. 680), 6s for Black Hall,

---

[1] Computus autumn 1525 'xiid pro indenturis factis inter nos et Universitatem
pro quadam portiuncula terre iuxta Aulam Cervinam'; winter 1525 'viiid pro vino
dato M. Skewys, vis Collegio Cardinalicio pro annali redditu' (but Lent 1538 '6s
Porrett pro superiori redditu debito Collegio Regio Henrici VIII'); summer 1526
'xiiiid pro cerotecis datis M. Scuys et uxori eius'; Lent 1528 'xxiiiid pro cirothecis
pellitis datis M. doctori Smyth et M. Skewys, xiiid pro vino et ceteris rebus datis
M. Lubkyns, M. Wylson et M. Wylliams Collegii Cardinalis supervisoribus';
winter 1531 'xd pro pare cerotecarum pro M. Skewse.' The 6s was an old quit-
rent due to S. Frideswide's (mentioned Lent 1357) viz. 2s for the original Stapeldon
hall, and 4s for Castel hall; from 1363 the two rents are no longer kept separate.
A similar rent of 12s to Godstow merged in the 18s paid to Christchurch in this
century. For Wylliams, *see* State Papers 1533, p. 126. Was Wylson the W. Wilson who was B.A. 1630 after studying two years at Cambridge?

10s to the University for Blackhall and 1s 8d for the garden once known as Catthall, total £2 7s 8d (Wood's *City* i. index). Hart Hall sometimes cost more than the rent in repairs. The lease of Black Hall and Cat Hall had expired 1624, but the College continued to hold them without a lease till 1633 when payment ends. Part of Black Hall was long afterwards let out for dwellings and shops. The University leased Black Hall to John Cross an apothecary in 1664. Cross leased part of it to John Brickland tailor in 1669 (Peshall 28). Brickland's assignees sold it to Cutler a College servant. Exeter College appointed the Principals of Hart Hall until 1604, except for certain years during which New College was building, at which time some of that Society lived there (Gutch i. 488, iii. 640–1).

Hart Hall[1] anciently contained two messuages. One, in 51 Henry III, was the tenement of Henry Punchard butcher, containing his house and court and, at the head of the court, a piece of ground, about 18 yards long and 11 yards broad, which was for some years leased to the owners of Sheldhall adjoining. From Punchard all this passed through intermediate owners to Elias de Herteford, who let the place to Scholars and so made the place Hart Hall. He granted it 1301 to his son Elias, who on 17 June 1301 sold it, ' between Blackhall on the west and Micheldhall on the east,' to John de Dokelington[2]. The other messuage, consisting of a house and court, ' between the tenement of Osney on the east and that of Adam de Spaldyng on the west,' belonged to Alice wife of Giles de Stokwell; she conveyed it to Agnes widow of John de Staunton, who sold it, 25 Ap. 1308, to John de Dokelington, in whose time it was called Arturhall (documents printed in Bodleian Charters 287). On 12 Ap. 1312 Dokelington conveyed them both to Walter de Stapeldon and Richard de Wideslade clerk, or their assigns, for 80 marks. Hart Hall now took the name of Stapeldon Hall, and on 7 Ap. 1314 Wideslade sold his share of the joint ownership to the bishop. In the same year the king licensed Stapeldon to give all this property to twelve scholars residing in the University, viz. the Rector and Scholars of Stapeldon hall, to hold to

---

[1] Gutch iii. 640. The College book of Evidences pp. 37–41, 48–9, 53–4 gives extracts from the Computi, a summary of title with further particulars, an account of other claims made to the place, and the right of choosing Principals.
[2] Peshall 149, 356, App. 17; Wood's *City* i. 129, 174, ii. 37.

them and their successors. A license of alienation was procured
26 July 1314 from the Prior and Convent of S. Frideswide, the mesne
lords of Hart Hall, who reserved a rent of two shillings. The Rector
and Scholars, after they had removed from Hart Hall, usually let it
for 24*s* in Michaelmas term, and the same in Lent, for 12*s* in Easter
term (Trinity term does not appear). Arturhall was let at half those
sums. On 31 Oct. 1334 the College leased Arturhall to Walter
de Plescye, R. of West Wardon, for ten years at 9*s* rent, Walter
doing the repairs; witnesses M. Richard de Evesham, M. John de
Aylesbeare, M. Thomas Bradwardine, Peter de Aynho bedell of the
University, Nicholas de Seintefey and others; the lease expired at
Michaelmas 1344; Arturhall is only mentioned again by name in
the summer term of 1401, it had probably merged in Hart Hall
under one Principal since 1344. In 1544 owing to the Plague the
rent of Hart Hall was much diminished, but it was to be raised when
there were 30 students. In 1551 the rent was again revised. On
10 June 1559 'their tenement or house ordained for the advancement
of learning, commonly called Hart Hall,' was leased to Philip Randall,
Principal, for 21 years from the previous Lady-day at a rent of
33*s* 4*d*, the College doing the external repairs in slatt and slatting,
and the Principal the inward reparations of particyons windowes doors
flooring and glazeing, except it shall please the Rector and Fellowes of
their benevolence to give lime boards stones clay nayles as they had
accustomed to do before the making of this lease. The said Philip
shall not let &c. to any but one of the foundation of the said College,
and a bond of £6 13*s* 4*d* is added to secure this, by P. Randall and
John Collens M.A. and B.M. On 20 July 1572 Randall renewed his
lease. On 28 Oct. 1593 a lease was made, and sealed 3 Nov., to John
Eveleighe for 21 years on the same terms, except that he was to
undertake all repairs. After Eveleighe's death there was a lawsuit
about Hart Hall with Dr. Price the Principal, and the College evidences about it were sent to Archbishop Bancroft in 1608. Price had
to pay up 6¼ years' rent at £1 13*s* 4*d* since Eveleighe's death. In
1633 Laud named Dr. Parsons of S. John's Principal, on which
Exeter College protested. In Parsons' time the Principal could
dispose of eight habitable chambers, the University having resumed
possession of Black Hall and Cat Hall. The rent was paid to Exeter

College, and the College did not attempt to resume full ownership of
Hart Hall till 1723, when a dispute began with Dr. Newton the
Principal. In winter 1540 the College paid John French the Principal 20s 'pro exhibitione domini Bicknelli stabilienda in Aula
Cervina, concessio ex communi consensu sociorum.' This exhibition
issued out of certain lands given to the monks of Glastonbury by
Bicknell, knight (Gutch ii. 69, 80, iii. 642, App. p. 34; Wood's MS.
F. 28 pp. 256–7), and was appointed for the education of ten poor
scholars in the University, but by whom and in what manner it was
settled on Hart Hall, whether for ever or only as the Hall should be
applied to such uses, or with other limitations and conditions, does not
appear, the original settlement being lost. The crown granted part of
this exhibition to Emmanuel College at Cambridge on the dissolution,
so that apparently the gift to Hart Hall was not perpetual. See
Madan's *Materials* 88, Reg. of Congregation 14 June 1521.

The scholars of a College would at first be expected to attend the
parish church, but naturally soon tried to obtain a chapel of their own.
On 9 July 1319 John Parys rector of Stapeldonhall assures the
Rector of S. Mildred's, in the presence of Masters Richard Noreys,
Henry Bloyou, Stephen Pyppcote, John de Sevenasche, that if
a chantry should be held in the College chapel, it should not
prejudice the rights of that parish. In 1326 Henry bishop of Lincoln
allowed bishop Stapledon to consecrate the high altar of the chapel[1]

---

[1] The licence to build the chapel is dated 1321.

Register of Memoranda of Bp. Burghersh of Lincoln, fo. 14.

Cantaria Magistri	H. p. di. L. E.
et scolarium domus	[Henricus permissione
de Stapelton halle	divina Lincoln' Episcopus]
Oxon'.	dilectis in Christo filiis

Magistro et Scolaribus domus Aule de Stapeltonhalle in universitate Oxon'
nostre dioc' situate Salutem gratiam et benedictionem. Devotionem vestram qua
divinis cupitis officiis interesse in domino commendantes ac eam impedire nolentes,
vobis ut in oratorio infra mansum habitationis vestre constructo, dummodo decens
fuerit et honestum, ac eorum quorum interest consensus accedat, divina vobis per
sacerdotem vestris ipsis sumptibus exhibendum, absque prejudicio matricis ecclesie
et aliarum ecclesiarum vicinarum, hoc addito quod nec campanile illic aliquoliter
erigatur nec processio vel consimile ibi fiat nec ullimoda sacramenta vel sacra-
mentalia ministrentur ibidem, valeatis celebrare simpliciter sine nota et facere per
alios celebrari vobis licentiam de gratia concedimus, speciali proviso quod singuli
capellani in dicto oratorio celebraturi in primo adventu suo de restituendis matrici
ecclesie prefate universis oblationibus faciendis in eo ac indempnitate ipsius quo ad

in honor of the Blessed Virgin, S. Peter, and S. Thomas the martyr. On 25 April 1326, in the parsonage manse of S. Mildred's, John de Sovenassh Rector and William de Ponte Chaplain appeared with John the Rector of S. Mildred's before a notary to make the agreement, four of the parishioners being also present—Walter de Hamme, Richard de Burcestre, William Russel and Simon de Bristowe. The College however later on found it necessary to appeal against an interdict laid on the chapel by Thomas bishop of Lincoln, at the instigation of Roger de Faryngs R. of S. Mildred's, without the cause being heard. A library had been already built in 1383; but the chapel was afterwards turned into a library and the building was still standing in 1778, yet the fire in 1709 can have left little of the original work. Loggan's view in 1675 shows the Chapel as being on the first floor, with steps leading up to it. The Chapel at Lincoln was

alia in presentia Rectoris ejusdem seu locum suum tenentis vel tenentium ibidem prestent ad sancta dei Evangelia juramentum. Copiam autem presentium in dicta matrice ecclesia registrari et formam concessionis nostre hujus in omnibus et singulis volumus observari. Alioquin eadem concessio nullius penitus sit momenti. In cujus rei testimonium sigillum nostrum presentibus est appensum. Dat' apud Parcum Stowe ii Non' Januarij Anno Domini Millesimo CCC^{mo} vicesimo.

[Bp. Burghersh's Memoranda, fo. 35.]

Henricus permissione divina Lincoln' Episcopus dilectis in Christo filiis . . Rectori et scolaribus domus de Stapeltonhalle in universitate Oxon' nostre dioc' commorantibus Salutem gratiam et benedictionem. Literarum studia, que suorum fertilitate fructuum quos producunt cultoribus agri dominici verbi dei seminaria ministrare non cessant, quibus ad salutem universis consulitur, merito nos inducunt ut studentium desideriis favorabiliter annuamus, dum id a nobis petitur, per quod eorum devotioni prospicitur et divini numinis cultus recipit incrementum. Quamobrem fusis in hac parte nobis precibus inclinati ut infra septa domus vestre memorate le Stapeltonhalle vulgariter nuncupate oratorium seu capellam construere et in constructo seu constructa divina officia per proprium sacerdotem, cui de vite necessariis teneamini congrue providere, alta voce vel submissa prout temporis qualitas exegerit celebranda, cum familiaribus vestris et hospitibus licentiam audire vobis et successoribus vestris tenore presentium concedimus licentiam et liberam facultatem. Ita tamen quod de oblationibus et aliis juribus sibi debitis et consuetis ecclesie parochiali infra cujus parochiam vestra domus situatur patiatis prout jus exigit integraliter responderi, quodque singuli capellani in hujusmodi oratorio seu capella celebraturi in primo adventu eorundem de hujusmodi juribus et oblationibus . . Vicario seu . . Rectori ecclesie, in cujus parochia dicta domus ut premittitur existit, fideliter persolvendis ad sancta dei evangelia in ipsius . . Rectoris vel . . Vicarii presentia sacramentum prestent corporale, hac nostra concessione licentie non obstante, jure dignitate et honore ecclesie nostre Lincoln' in omnibus semper salvis. In c. r. t. s. n. p. [In cujus rei testimonium sigillum nostrum presentibus] est appensum. Dat' apud Newenton' juxta Lond' ix kal' Septembris anno domini Millesimo ccc°.xxj°.

similarly turned into a Library. The early College libraries had their sides facing east and west, the early morning light being so important; later on, when early rising was not so much in fashion, they faced north and south[1]. Men were glad to read in the Library, where there were many books, though chained to the desks, rather than in their stuffy little studies, where they had few or no books.

Besides the rectory of Gwinear, Stapeldon 12 April 1322 gave the College the rectory of Long Wittenham[2] or West Wittenham or

[1] Clark's *Colleges* 268, 428.

[2] John bishop of Exeter, to Roger bishop of Sarum, reminding him of the appropriation of West Wittenham to the scholars of both dioceses studying at Stapildon Hall, and asking him to favour the scholars' application to the Chapter of Sarum. At Chuddelegh 1 Sep. 1328 (Grandisson's Reg., the Latin of this and the next letter is printed in ed. i. p. xliii). Roger bishop of Sarum to John bishop of Exeter. I discussed the matter with your predecessor but we could not agree about it. We will talk it over in the Parliament summoned at Sarum. At Remmesbirie Park 27 Sep. 1328. (*a* John bishop of Winchester 'executor unicus ad uniendam parochialem ecclesiam de West Wittenham, Sarum diocesis, scolaribus domus de Stapeldonhall in arte dialectica studentibus ac presbitero in divinis deservienti eisdem, pro uberiori sustentacione et augmento numeri scolarium dicte domus, M. Roberto Hereward archidiacono Taunton.' We send you papal letters for this union and give you authority to carry it out, 6 Dec. 1333. (*b*) Robertus Hereward archidiaconus Taunton M. Thome de Braunton clerico nuncio nostro, Give notice to the bishop and chapter of Sarum and archdeacon of Barrocschyre and to M. Richard Pyn R. of West Wyttenham to appear before us at Wittenham &c. 8 Dec. 1333. (*c*) Roberto Hereward Thomas de Braunton, I have given the notices and I met R. Pyn in Oxford. There were present at Sarum and Wittenham M. H. Tyvertone clerk of Exon diocese, Walter le Honte of the same diocese, and at Oxford M. William de Hontyngdone Rector, and M. John Rotour clerk. (*d*) M. Roberto Hereward decanus Abendon et Ricardus capellanus ecclesie de West Wittenham, We have received your letter dated Oxon 17 Dec. 1333 about the union &c. directing us to summon the rectors of Dudecot, Est Wittenham, Hakebourne, North Morton, the Vicar of South Morton ; and Robert Lok, Thomas de Montfort, Simon de Pauleseye, Thomas Stoyl, John Hakkere of the parish of West Wittenham ; and John Moygne, John Brouns of Sutton, Thomas Payen of Appleford to give information &c. We have therefore summoned Thomas R. of Dudecote, Edmund de la Beche R. of Hakebourne, Richard V. of North Mortone, Robert Lok &c., but John de Appelford R. of Suthmorton, Alexander Hemmyngeby R. of Est Wittenham were not found at home. Abendon 21 Dec. 1333. (*e*) To the sons of holy mother church John bishop of Wynton. Pope John XXII. sent letters in the following form, Whereas Walter bishop of Exeter &c., We wish the union &c., a suitable income being reserved to the Vicar. Avignon 8 Aug. in the 17th year of our pontificate. We have therefore after full enquiry carried out the union. Farnham 31 Jan. 1333. (*f*) To all &c. William de Cranthorne canon of Exeter and official of John bishop of Exeter. Henry de Balrynton clerk, proctor of the Rector and scholars of Stapeldon hall announced to us the appropriation of West Wittenham to them. The tenor of their letter is as follows We appoint

Earl's Wittenham, in Berkshire, which he had obtained in 1320 from
Philip prior of Longueville-Giffard, a Cluniac monastery in the

M. Simon de Santfort canon of Criditon, William de Br[igge?] succentor of Exeter,
Henry de Balryntone clerk our proctors &c., Oxon 14 Ap. 1343. We therefore
have had copies made of all the documents lest the originals should be lost. Done
in S. Mary Major church Exeter 2 May 1343, present M. Richard Byschoplegh and
M. Robert de Peyle rectors of Clofely and Bykelegh, M. John Godeman and
M. Walter de Blakebroun examiners of the Consistory at Exeter, John de Northcote
and Walter de Wyke advocates of the Consistory &c. And I John de Piltone
clerk public notary &c. (g) On 9 April 1355 'in posteca' of the parish church of
S. Mary at West Wyttenham or Earl's Wyttenham in presence of one John Nikelyer
of Bodmin notary public and of witnesses, Robert de Trethewy clerk of the diocese
of Exeter showed that he was proctor for the Rector and scholars of Stapeldon hall
and, after showing the Pope's letters &c., took corporal possession of the church,
now vacant by the death of Richard Pyn the late rector, and celebrated and offered
three silverpennies for John Cerceaux, John Fleming and Nicholas Sapy of Exeter
and Lincoln dioceses. Done in the presence of dominus Nicholas de Aston
presbiter, Thomas Mountfort, William Assedene, Thomas Martyn clerks ; William
Blake, John Horsham, Robert Peyntour, John Birri, and Robert Walke and
Thomas Taylour of Lincoln and Sarum dioceses. (h) On 4 May 1355 in the
hospice of M. John de Letch official of the Court of Canterbury near the old
'piscariam' London in presence of me Michael Hauville clerk notary public,
Robert de Trethewy clerk of the diocese of Exeter and proctor of the Rector and
scholars of Stapeldon hall appealed against an attempt of the Sarum officials to
take possession of the vacant church of Wittenham, who sent thither as chaplain
Nicholas Mountfortes prest. Done [before] Richard Chude chaplain of the diocese
of Exeter and Richard de Drayton of the diocese of Ely clerks. (i) To the official
of the Court of Canterbury the Dean of Oxon. Your mandate of 12 May received
of this tenor. The official &c. to the Dean of Oxon and the Rector of Staunton
St. John's. You are to summon the Sarum officials to appear in the church of
S. Mary le Bow London on the second law day after Trinity. London 6 May
1355. I have therefore had them summoned through John Cergeaux clerk. Oxon,
28 May 1355. (j) To all &c. the official of Lincoln. There appeared before us
in Abyndon monastery Roger Cristemasse V. of S. Nicolas Abyndon, executor of
the late Richard Pyn R. of West Wittenham and stated that he had received from
William de Nassynton official of Sarum this letter. The official of Sarum to the
official of the Archdeacon of Berks, the Dean of Abyndon, the Rector of Dodecote,
the perpetual Vicar of S. Nicholas Abyndon, and John Berford lately chaplain of
Wittenham—you are to take into your hands the living and its profits &c. and cite
any that oppose to appear before us. Sarum 20 April 1355. We have added our
seal &c., present dominus John de Stapeldon monk of Abyndon monastery and
John Bouresyate clerk. And I Henry de Elsham notary public &c. (k) Robert
bishop of Sarum &c. We have seen the letters of Pope John XXII. and John
bishop of Winchester shown us by Robert de Trethewy proctor for the Rector and
Scholars of Stapeldon hall. We confirm the appropriation of West Wittenham,
reserving 3s 4d a year to the bishop of Sarum for the profit he used to have during
vacancies, and 40d to the Archdeacon of Berks, and 6s 8d to the Dean and Chapter
of Sarum for the same reason. We also order that the College shall within two
years elect two fellows from the diocese of Sarum and so on for ever. The Chapter

diocese of Rouen, but difficulties were made and the College did not get actual possession of it till 1355 and then only on condition that henceforth two fellows should be elected from the diocese of Sarum.

Stapeldon's Statutes bear date 24 April 1316 when they were accepted by the Rector and Scholars. There were to be thirteen Scholars, i.e. Fellows,—a mystic number which appears at several of the Colleges. Twelve were to study philosophy ; the thirteenth was to be a priest and chaplain studying scripture or canon law. Eight of the twelve were to be from Devon, four from the Archdeaconry of Cornwall, either born in the diocese or settled there. The Chaplain was to be appointed by the Chapter of Exeter and, if he should be declared unfit by two-thirds of the fellows, the Chapter was to appoint another. He was to celebrate and say the services and manage the choir. Candidates for fellowships were to be at least sophists, i.e. students in arts. They were to 'determine as B.A.[1]' within six years ; to determine meant disputing in the schools the Lent following the degree of Bachelor. Within four years of that time, or at least in the summer term next after the end of four years, they had to 'incept' as M.A. Then they were to 'read,' i.e. lecture, two years ; and

house of Sarum 1 Aug. 1355. The consent of the Rector and Scholars is dated Oxon 9 Aug. 1355. And we Edmond de la Beche archdeacon &c., Bradefeld 24 May 1356. (De la Beche and John Polyng had helped to procure the confirmation.) (*l*) Robert bishop of Sarum ordains thus. The Vicar of West Wittenham is to have the 'Aula' with the chambers annexed belonging to the Rectory and the open space on the east next to the ground of Richard le Skynnere extending in length from the public road on the south to the garden of Robert Kempe on the north, and in width 6 roods of 16½ feet each ; and further the open space near the former on the west near the gardens of Robert Kempe and extending to the Cemetery (so that the Vicar may construct a 'posticum' or 'posterna' for his entry to the church), containing in width from Kempe's garden to the ground remaining to the Rectory 4 roods less 3 feet ; and further 60 acres of arable, 2 acres of meadow, and pasture in 'le hurst' ; and further a tithe of mills, lambs, wool, calves, geese, flax, hemp, and oblacions—all in fact except the tithe of corn and hay. The Vicar is to keep up the books, vestments &c., and pay procurations sinodals &c., and a part of the tenth for Legates and Nuncios and voluntary Subsidies. Sarum 20 July 1358. See Ashmole's *Berkshire* i. 69, iii. 385–6, Clarke's *Wantage* 117, Peshall 47.

[1] The determining bachelors chose two *collectors* among themselves, who (1) arranged them into groups, so that each bachelor might dispute twice at least, (2) collected the fees. Determining ceased in Lent 1821 : see Ayliffe ii. 120, Gutch ii. 225, 254, 270, 291 ; Wordsworth 217, 317 ; Rawlinson MSS. class C. no. 421 fol. 66 ; Cox 143, 228 ; Wood's *Life* ii. 5 ; W. W. Phelps' *Life* i. 337 rule at Corpus ; Clark i. 50–63, *Reminiscences of Oxford* (O. H. S.) 95.

after one year more vacate the fellowship within fifteen days. The fellowships were therefore, at the outside, only tenable for rather less than fourteen years. They also ceased as soon as a fellow inherited or obtained sixty shillings a year, or any ecclesiastical benefice; and any one absenting himself five months in the year, or refusing to take the office of Rector, also lost his fellowship. Bishop Fox, the founder of Corpus, thought it sacrilege for a man to tarry any longer at Oxford than he had a desire to profit. Besides this, the fellowships in most Colleges were so poor, and the fellows were so crowded together, two in a room, with one or two students on truckle beds beside them, that they naturally left on any chance of promotion, and hence the succession to fellowships was often rapid.

The Rector was elected at the beginning of October, after the annual audit; the previous Rector was re-eligible and was not seldom re-elected once or twice. He was more like the Bursar than the Rector of our days; he looked after the money and rooms and servants but, if any two fellows demanded the removal of a servant, the Rector was to appoint another in his place. He was *Janitor*, as at most Colleges, and his rooms were over the Gateway.

Fellows were to be elected 'without regard to favor, fear, relationship or love, the electors naming men apter to learn, better in character, and poorer in means, or at least those who best come up to these three conditions.' The fellows were bound to dispute twice a week, but questions of natural science were to take the place of logic every third time. While sophists or bachelors, the fellows were also to read 'abstracciones, obligaciones, cynthategrammeta[1], circa signa (?), *necnon logicalia et naturalia.*' Men were not *educated* in College. They lived there, under proper discipline, and certain disputations took place there, but the College tutor was as yet undreamt of, and education was conducted by the Regent masters who lectured at the Schools. Osney alone had 14 out of the 32 schools in School Street, Exeter 4. All such schools were let out, when not wanted by the owners themselves. The statutes then relate mainly to domestic matters. They

[1] Perhaps syncategoremata, on which Robert or Roger Bacon wrote; Gutch i. 344, Grey Friars 197, Nat. Biog. ii. 374. The earliest existing copy of the statutes is of much later date than Stapeldon's time and the copyist has miswritten some words.

do not go into such minute detail as those of other Colleges, e.g. at Queen's in 1340 the use of musical instruments is forbidden because they lead to levity and distract men from their studies[1].

Under Stapeldon's system, the Rector and other officers were always young men. The fellowships, as in most colleges, were distinctly given for the children of the poor, and the number of the fellowships should have been increased as the revenues grew. But the Colleges did not carry out their Founders' wishes in this matter. In some it was ruled that personal property to any amount did not vacate a fellowship, and livings were estimated at the old value in the King's Books. And in most Schools and Colleges the richer classes have appropriated what the Founders gave to the poor. Students corresponding to servitors and battellars are now few, while in 1616 16 colleges educated between 400 and 500 poor students[2].

The regard paid to poverty brought forward some eminent men. Such for instance was Walter Lihert, a miller's son from Lanteglos by Fowey in Cornwall, who after being fellow of Exeter became bishop of Norwich and built the sculptured roof of the Cathedral; he supported in his troubles Reginald Pecock the author of 'The Repressor of over much blaming of the clergy,' whom he had probably known in his undergraduate days, when Reginald taught in one of the schools in School Street belonging to Exeter College[3]. Similarly long afterwards John Prideaux, Rector 1612, used to say 'If I could have been parish clerk of Ubber (Ugborough), I should never have been bishop of Worcester'; on his failing to become parish clerk, he had been advised to come as a poor scholar to the University. Benjamin Kennicott was master of a charity school at Totnes till by the assistance of some friends he was able to enter the University where

[1] Stapeldon's statutes were printed (with those of Sir W. Petre) in 1855 for the use of the Royal Commissioners. They were printed afresh from the MS. in Hingeston-Randolph's *Register of Walter de Stapeldon* 1892 p. 303, together with his two later ordinances—these last somewhat abridged from what I printed in ed. i. p. xl.

[2] Gutch Coll. Curiosa i. 196, Burrows 159, Heywood 14. Reg. 16 July 1656 'constitutum est ne numerus pauperum scholarium deinceps excedat viginti, ac praesentem eorundem numerum minuendum esse donec eo deventum fuerit; et interea temporis neminem in conditionem pauperis scholaris admittendum esse.'

[3] Autumn 1418 'xs a M. Regenaldo Pecok pro pensione scolarum suarum pro anno preterito,' Tanner 583.

d

he became a distinguished Hebrew scholar. Still later William
Gifford, after being a cabin boy on board a coasting vessel and then
at the age of 15 an apprentice to a shoemaker at Ashburton, was
helped to go to Exeter College by Mr. Cookesley a local surgeon and
gained a bible clerkship. This assisted him to complete the education
which gave him a leading position in the literary and political world.
He remembered his own rise in life and founded two Gifford exhibitions at Exeter College for poor boys from Ashburton school.
There was some narrowness in the old system, but the way to rise
was not closed to the poor, and the Universities had the character of
popular bodies in which learning and study were recommendations.

The Universities were a kind of High School, more like the Scotch
universities at present. The education given was practical and suited
to the wants of the country. Latin was necessary at a time when even
the accounts of a manor were kept in that tongue; it was the common
language of Europe and almost the sole language of literature, since
the vernacular tongues were as yet very imperfectly developed. The
number of boys or men at this High School was large, and the
chance of advancement was considerable. There was therefore as
keen an ambition among the small landowners to send one of their
sons to the University as there is now in Ireland to send a boy to
Maynooth. The number of ordinations in the Bishops' Registers is
very large. In Stapeldon's first ordination, 21 Dec. 1308 at Crediton,
he ordained 1,005 persons, viz.: 155 subdeacons, 77 deacons, 15
priests, beneficed clergy 42 (30 as accolites, the rest subdeacons,
deacons, or priests); 273 received the first tonsure, and there were
443 accolites. All the names are given. Mediaeval wills show that
almost every man whose circumstances made a will necessary had
sons or near kinsmen in orders. Livings are often given to mere
boys, who then have leave of absence for some years to study at the
University. Dispensations are often necessary on account of illegiti-
mate birth: some of them may be due to the extension of the degrees
within which marriage was prohibited to as distant relationships as that
of fourth cousins; while the births from 'a priest and an unmarried
woman' may represent what were really half-allowed marriages of the
clergy (Collier a. 1128, 1215, &c.). Of grown-up students there were
probably never so many as at present. The boys were brought up by

carriers, who had a regular route, which they took every year, about the beginning of October, when the University year commenced ; and this journey only cost 5*d* a day for each boy, and perhaps not more than 3*d* for the very poor. The boys could not go home so often as now, but had lectures in the Long Vacation on natural science. The rent of a room was about 2*s* 6*d* a term. Many of the students walked both ways. In modern times we hear of Thomas Carlyle walking 100 miles to Edinburgh. The Universities were Liberal in the Middle Ages, now they are largely Tory; the reason is that then most of the students were poor, now they mostly belong to the well-to-do classes. As to the age of taking the degree, Cavendish ed. Singer 1827 p. 66 says that Wolsey taking his B.A. at 15 was a rare thing and seldom seen.

Owing to this general poverty a number of *chests* were founded in the University for making loans to poor students. The money was lent on security of books, plate, or other property ; it was, in fact, a pawnbroking business which charged no interest. Thus in 1316 Ralph Germeyn founded a chest of £10 for making loans to poor scholars in the College ; Masters of Arts might borrow a pound, Bachelors a mark (13*s* 4*d*), and Sophisters half a mark, provided that they deposited pledges of greater value. The College was also allowed to borrow for its corporate needs. But all loans had to be repaid within 12 months. Some years afterwards Richard Grenfield founded a similar chest[1]; and Robert Rygge did the same towards the end of the century. In 1589 we hear of Bosisto, Helme and Eveleighe being appointed 'Keepers of the Germin Chest.'

We have occasionally a mention of the books that were studied. Thus Henry Whitefield, a former fellow, left the College money to buy books, with which ' Burley on the Ethics, on the Topics, and on

---

[1] See a. 1362 ; computus autumn 1511, Reg. 1645 ; Anstey pp. xxxvi–xliii and index; Gutch i. 374 a theft from S. Frideswide's chest; Merton Statutes p. 56 chests of Thomas Bodley and William Read; New College Statutes p. 86; All Souls Statutes p. 51. Mullinger 347, Ashley 203, Turner p. xix, Huber i. 169, *Flores Historiarum* i. p. xxi, Boase's *Oxford* 26, 79, 150. Germeyn was archdeacon of Barnstaple, then precentor of Exeter 1308, Stapeldon's Reg. 164, 210: Oliver's Bishops 50. Grenfield, 2 son of Sir Bartholomew, was R. of Kilkhampton 1308–24, Bytton's Reg. 426, Stapeldon's Reg. 168,226, 385—had leave of absence from his living (then M.A.) 3 Feb. 132⅔, and see 21 May 1324. The College kept his obit.

Logic' were bought and chained to desks in the Library. The two former cost 14*d* and 13*d* respectively for their binding. In summer 1389 £4 were given for the Problems of Aristotle and five marks for Boicius (Boethius) de Disciplina Scolarum and de Consolacione Philosophiae, and 20*d* for the stationer's services; while in winter 1445 fourteen pence were paid for repairs to a Concordance and to Boethius, and sevenpence for repairs to the book called Catholicon[1]. We also hear of the Liber Decretorum and the 'Sextum' and other law books, and even more frequently of medical books. Tullius in Rethorica occurs Lent 1391, a Corpus Juris Civilis winter 1375, the Clementines a. 1372, Gorham super Lucam Lent 1417, and autumn 1445. Other books mentioned are the Destructorium Viciorum[2], or Liber definitorius Viciorum, a Liber de Profetis, Liber de Proprietatibus[3], Liber de nomine Jhu; the names of many other books are quoted further on. The Library still possesses a splendid copy of Hugo de Vienna (d. 1263) in 18 volumes, given 1 Jan. 14$\frac{69}{70}$ by Roger Keys[4]. A curse is inserted at the beginning on any who shall

---

[1] The Catholicon of friar Johannes Balbus Januensis was printed at Mainz 1460. (Joannis' 'Balbi de Janua Summa quae vocatur Catholicon, sive Grammatica et Lexicon Linguae Latinae,' 2 vols. in 1 folio. Letters from Bodleian ii. 84, Tanner 118, supra p. v, Coxe no. iii. There were 4 stationers Gutch i. 441, Wood's *City*, i. 72, 139 &c., Anstey 52, 148-52, 176, 233, 253, 383, Ayliffe ii. 181, Hallam *Lit. Eur.* i. 243 ; A. Kirchhoff, *Die Handschriftenhändler des Mittelalters* ed. 2, 1853. The Ex. Coll. MS. no. 28 is Whatley's Commentary on (Pseudo-)Boethius de Disciplina Scolarum, perhaps by Thomas de Cantompré, from which Twyne made an excerpt on the behaviour of bachelors about to incept.

[2] See Waters' *Geneal. of the Chesters* p. 64. Coxe no. vii. Winter 1452 'vis viiid a M. Johanne Eggecomb ex dono pro copia libri vocati Destructorium Viciorum.' Destructorium Vitiorum ex similitudine creaturarum appropriatione per modum dyalogi, folio (122 woodcuts), Lugduni per Claudium Nourry 1509, is the second ed. of the Dialogus Creaturarum moralizatus (compiled 1429, printed 1479). The English ed., Paris 1540, with some of the woodcuts, was reprinted by Hazlewood. See Elyot's *Governor* ed. Croft i. 287, Alexander of Hales (Alex. Carpenter, Tanner 155), Hain's Repertorium i. 72 *v*. Alexander Anglicus, Fabricius Bib. Lat. i. 65, 353, Quetif's Bib. Dominicana i. 319, Wharton on Cave, Bodleian Cat. *v*. Alexander Anglus, *Collectanea* (O. H. S.) i. 154.

[3] ? Barth. Glanville (*floruit* 1248-60), see Coxe no. xxxv.

[4] Warden of All Souls 1442-5, preb. of London 1448, archdeacon of Barnstaple 1450, precentor of Exeter 1467-71, R. of Menheniot 1471, d. 11 Nov. 1477; famous as the architect of All Souls 1437. Henry VI brought him from Oxford to superintend the building of Eton, with a salary of £50 a year; Lyte 355, All Souls Archives 126, 289, 385, 396, All Souls Statutes p. 68, Gutch iii. 114, Clark-Willis *Cambridge* i. 397, 426, 468, Bentley's *Excerpta Historica* 45, 49.

take the book out without leave of the Rector and Fellows[1]. In 1446 the College bought parchment at Abingdon which it sent to the monastery of Plympton in Devonshire where a book was being copied for the College[2]. But when Bishop Fox founded Corpus, he expressly ordered his lecturer in theology not to use the interpretations of the Bible by Nicholas de Lyra or Hugh de Vienna, but those of the Greek and Latin doctors. Such was the spirit of the English Renaissance.

The fellows had their rooms free; and ten shillings a year as well, but the Rector and Chaplain received twenty. Each fellow was also allowed ten pence a week for his 'commons' but a proportion was deducted for each day that he was absent, and so of his yearly allowance if he was absent for more than four weeks in the year. We also find a sum of 3*s* 4*d* allowed for 'visiting friends,' and seeing to private business; and some clothes (liveries)[3] were supplied, apparently once in three years. In 1544 the arrangement about liveries is as follows. On the feast of All Saints every third year each fellow who

[1] Autumn 1480, 'uni scriptori pro pargameno et labore circa Sermones Hugonis de Vienna xiiii*s* i*d*'; Lent 1484 'xxvi*s* viii*d* a M. Johanne Combe pro complecione operis Hugonis de Vienna'; autumn 1484 'xxx*s* Johanni Bray pro ligacione et illuminatura 2ᵘʳᵘᵐ voluminum operis Hugonis de Vienna, xx*d* pro incathenacione eorundem in Libraria.' (See Rogers iv. 504.) The book was written at Oxford by William Salamon 'Leonensis dioceseos' in the years between 1450 and 1465; see Coxe no. li–lxviii. For Hugo, see Reg. Palat. Dunelm. (Rolls Series) iv. p. cxii. Magdalen bought his works in 7 volumes in 1502 for 46*s* 4*d*, Rogers iv. 600.

[2] Lent 1446, 'x*s* i*d* pro xii quaternis et duabus pellibus pargameni emptis pro quodam libro scribendo in monasterio de Plimpton, vi*d* pro expensis Rectoris apud Abindon pro eodem pargameno emendo, ii*d* pro reparacione Libri Sententiarum, ii*d* pro vectura pargameni versus Devoniam pro predicto libro'; summer 1446, 'vi*s* pro viii quaternis pargameni emptis pro libro nostro scribendo Plymptone'; autumn 1446 'iiii*d* vectori Cornubiensi pro pargameno misso Priori de Plympton.' Peter of Cornwall, prior of Trinity Priory London, d. 7 July 1221, wrote a Panthilogion; Tanner 694, Bibl. Corn. 461, 1310. Winter 1485 'xxii*d* pro vectura duorum magnorum voluminum unius operis theologici Panthilogion nuncupati nobis dati a M. Gwille canonici in capella regia S. Stephani in Westemonasterio per solas Rectoris industrias.' Will of William Brownyng canon of Exeter and rector of the parish churches of Uggeburgh and Byrynerberd, 15 Aug. 1454 (Lacy's Reg. III. 516ᵃ) 'lego collegio Exon in universitate Oxon ad librariam ibidem Librum Rubrum cum omnibus [illegible] quorum primus est liber S. Augustini de Retraccionibus in dicta libraria cathenandus' (proved 8 Mch 1455). For *quaterni* see Anstey 264, Peshall 45, Rogers i. 645, ii. 573 twice.

[3] Rogers vi. 549.

is M.A. is to receive 20s, each B.A. 16s 8d, others 13s 4d—subject however to the rule that £20 at least shall always be reserved in the College chest; at the same time an improvement was made in the commons, especially in what were called 'thirteenpenny commons' *i. e.* on 20 feast days[1]. The common chest had three keys kept by the Rector, Senior Fellow and Chaplain; there is still an old chest of this kind in the muniment room. The allowance of ten pence a week may seem small, especially as the arrangement was made just after the great famine of 1315, but Exeter was poor, and the sum allowed in the richer colleges was not much larger: it was raised to a shilling in 1408. In 1326 the Oriel statutes give twelve pence as the sum, which was to be made fifteen pence in times of scarcity. In 1340 the Balliol statutes allow eleven pence, which might be raised to fifteen pence when food was dear[2]. These allowances should be judged by the general rate of living. Thus, poor mass priests had 6 marks (£4) in the fourteenth century, Kellawe's Reg. Dunelm. 3 p. lxxxviii; and twenty nobles a year (£6 13s 4d) was a bare living for a priest just before the Reformation.

The average prices of the period 1261–1400 supply the explanation. Wheat was 5s 10¾d the quarter, and we must allow a quarter to each man in the year. Meat was a farthing a pound. Butter cost 7½d a gallon, but fluctuated much in price. 'Butter, I imagine, since it is so commonly sold by the gallon, was melted—a process which preserves it from becoming rancid, though at a great loss of flavour.' In other cases it is likely that it was pressed into earthenware pans, or into wooden tubs, the produce being salted in mass, as well as over each

---

[1] Reg. 1 June 1565 'decretum est hos sequentes dies perenniter fore limitatos ac nominatos dies minoris refectionis, Anglice appellatos xiiid gaudies, viz.: Circumcision, Purification, Matthias, Annunciation, Mark, Philip and James, Ascension, Corpus Christi, birthday of the Baptist, Peter and Paul, James, Bartholomew, birthday of the Virgin, Matthew, Michael, Luke, Simon and Jude, All Saints, Andrew, Thomas the Apostle'; see Clark's *Colleges* 186.

[2] At New College in 1400 it was ordered that the allowance of 12 pence might be increased to 13 or even 16 pence in seasons of scarcity, and even to 18 pence when the bushel of corn sold for more than two shillings. The Lincoln statutes of 1480 define a time of dearth as a time when a quarter of corn sells for ten shillings or more; ten shillings is also the limit fixed at All Souls in 1443; but in 1582 the Visitor of All Souls ratifies the change of the allowance from 16 pence to 2s 8d for a Master and 2s 2d for another Fellow; All Souls Statutes p. 90; Magdalen Statutes p. 71; Brasenose Statutes p. 22. See Waters' *Geneal. of Chesters* 25.

layer, just as in modern times. Salt was $6\frac{5}{8}d$. the bushel. Cheese
was a little over a halfpenny a pound. Eggs cost $4\frac{1}{2}d$ for the long
hundred *i.e.* 120 : there are other indications which show that poultry
must have been raised to a larger extent than at present. Vegetables
were scarce, and owing to the want of vegetables scurvy and leprosy [1]
were very prevalent: onions, leeks, mustard and peas occur, though
rarely [2]; turnips carrots and parsnips were not yet used. French
wine was a little over a penny a gallon. There are constant
entries for wine given to visitors, which we may suppose to have been
of a better quality than that usually consumed. In Lent 1361 3*s* is
charged for 3 flagons (lagena), in Lent 1375 2*s* 4*d* for 2 flagons, in
summer 1380 2*s* for 2 flagons, in summer 1401 21*d* for 3 flagons and

[1] Denton 207, Wood's *City* ii. 505, Rogers on Prices v. 764, Rogers' *Polltax*
(O. H. S.) 187, *Social England* 1893 p. 369.

[2] Rogers i. 17, 27, 66, 147, 187, 223; Hist. Comm. vi. 569. Autumn 1457 'x*d*
pro modio ceparum venditarum'; autumn 1372 'in porris ili*d* ad gardinum';
autumn 1425 'quinque *d* pro leke plantis ad ortum' [leac and gárleac and yneleac
and leaccerse *i.e.* leek and garlic and onion and nasturtium occur in Anglo-Saxon,
leactún is a garden and leacweard a gardener]; winter 1465 'xiii*d* pro duobus
duodenis ciphorum et duobus discis ligneis et una olla pro sinapis'; winter 1506
'x*d* pro sinapis'; apples are mentioned Lent 1360 'i*d* pro pomis'; autumn 1398
'iii*s* de vendicione pomorum in gardino'; pears in autumn 1356 'v*d* pro vino et
piris datis vicario de Blubry [Blewberry in Berks, mentioned again in winter 1485]
et Tome capellano de West Wyttenham quando idem vicarius venit pro emcione
lane nostre'; figs, grapes and almonds occur Lent 1358 'vs viii*d ob.* Alano Lenge
pro fructibus et speciebus viz ficis uvis amydol et aliis diversis fructibus et speciebus
positis in cervisia die S. Thome'; there is a doubtful mention of strawberries in
summer 1484 'x*d ob* pro vino zucara et fragris (?) datis doctori Aggecumb'
[probably John Edgcomb]; winter 1522 'x*d* preparando mala punica,' an incidental
mention of pomegranates (Rogers i. 632); 'graffing stockys' is mentioned Lent
1524. Gardeners occur Lent 1361 'xx*d* ortalanis pro seminibus'; Lent 1487 'xiii*d*
ortalano mundanti ortos nostros.' A gardener was perhaps only employed occasionally, the payments to regular servants were larger. Thus the manciple received
5*s* a term, the cook 2*s*, the barber 12*d*, the washerwoman 15*d*; sums which are
raised in Lent 1374 to 6*s* 8*d*, 40*d*, 20*d*, 2*s* 6*d*, respectively and in the sixteenth
century they receive in all 15*s* 10*d* a term. The amount of washing in the Middle
Ages was small. The tonsure of those who were in minor orders was shaved every
week. We may compare women's out-door wages : Winter 1408 'iiii*d* uni mulieri
que laboravit circa stramina, v*d ob* pro yelmyng [laying it in convenient quantities
for the thatcher] eiusdem straminis'; winter 1435 'duabus ylmestres xx*d*'; summer
1492 'iiii*s* iiii*d* pro 5 bigatibus straminis pro horeo nostro apud Wytnam, solvendo
pro bigatu viii*d* apud Suttun, xx*d* pro vectura eorundem, ii*s* vi*d* ly thakere ibi
5 diebus, servienti ei 5 diebus xx*d*, xv*d* cumulatrici Anglice a ylmer illis diebus.'
The ylmer had 3*d* a day, but a woman's wages were usually only a penny, Rogers
i. 273, 281, ii. 275, 710, H. Hall's *Elizabethan Age* ed. I. p. 23, Blomfield's
Bicester 47, Cunningham ii. 193. For yelming see Skeat, *v.* whelm.

one pottle. In 1395 a flagon of beer cost 1½d, and a ' quarter' 20d[1].
In Lent 1361 the ' quarter' of beer cost 2s 8d, but this was better
beer as it was bought for the feast of S. Thomas the martyr. The
account of the preparations for the feast runs on thus ' 12d for spices
in the 3 quarters of beer, 10d for a pound of wax candles, 1d for the
breakfast of two Carmelites who brought a "palleum" for the feast, 1d
to a poor man, 2d for incense (thimiama), 21d for loaves, 6d for
common beer, 12d for meat, 12d for 4 ducks (anatinis), 2s 10d for
capons, 17d for baking, 4s 4d for spices, 1d for ' salsamentis,' 8d for
rabbits[2], 22d for 6 ducks, 11d for two little pigs (porcelli), 3s for 3
flagons of wine, 7d for eggs, 1d for onions, 1½d for "gyncebrum"
(ginger was about 1s 6d the pound[3]), 6d for ducklings (aniclis), iiiid
for tallow candles (candelis de cepo), 12d for charcoal and faggots
(carbonibus et focalibus) in the kitchen, 11d for veal, iiiid for lard
(pinguedo), honey 6d, cheese 3d, flour 2d, the cook's services that
day 12d, 6d to the maidservant of Roger de Northwod, 5d for wine
given to the woman who keeps our public house (pandoxatrix nostra),
5d for wine to another woman who keeps a public house.' The
amount paid for spices on such occasions is remarkable (Rogers'
Holland 201, 1250). In the almost total absence of vegetables and
modern condiments, these were the choicest flavours which men
desired. Sometimes the fellows shared in greater festivities, for
instance in the Determination feast of Richard, the son of Thomas
Holland Earl of Kent, on the Monday and Tuesday before Ash

---

[1] Rogers i. 172 : ii. 644. The *lagena* or flagon of wine was 16 pints, the pottle
4 pints. The quarter of beer, i.e. 17 ' lagenae cum potello ' was an Oxford measure,
costing 1s 8d, 1s, or 10d according to quality. The gallon at 1½d is of better
quality than that bought by the quarter. But the *lagena* seems to have been
a variable measure. Besides wine, gloves were constantly given to visitors, as
now at weddings and funerals. See Index, Rogers i. 119, iv. 581, Blomfield's
Bicester 120. It was not till the 16th century that beer was distinguished from ale,
as ale to which hops had been added ; autumn 1559 ceresisia et birra.

[2] Probably rabbits were 4d or 5d each, as they were scarce; Lent 1360 'xd pro
cuniculis'; Rogers i. 33, 340-1 and index iv. 345, 582, 717, 34 D. K. Rec. p. 285,
Denton 164. There were rabbits on S. Nicholas' Island, Plymouth, in the 12th
century, Patent Rolls 3 Feb. 1324 p. 4. In the 15th century no inconsiderable
portion of good land was occupied by rabbit warrens. In 1431 a licence was given
to export 40,000 rabbit skins, 48 D. K. Rec. p. 220.

[3] Rogers i. 629. Compare the prices in Lord William Howard's Household
Books ed. 1878 (Surtees Soc.) p. lxxvi.

Wednesday, 21 and 22 Feb. 1395. The account of the feast is preserved among the archives of Merton, but several of the persons mentioned are fellows of Exeter, and Thomas Hendeman a fellow of Exeter was Chancellor[1]. It was in fact a University feast as liveries were given to the proctors and bedels. The charges are twofold, for liveries and an entertainment. The liveries were either of coloured cloth or of variegated pattern (stragulatus). The cloth was served out in various lengths, from nine, eight, and seven and a half yards to a yard and a half, the breadth being uniform. The hoods were trimmed with fur[2], the names of the material being various as miniver, bugeye, popul, and stanling (perhaps the winter fur of the squirrel). The pieces (panni) of cloth, containing 24 yards (virgae) each[3], were bought from John Hende a London cloth-merchant. The coloured cloth was given to academics, the cheaper variegated cloth to other persons and servants. ' To M. John Wykham 7½ yards, M. John Gylys 8 yards, each proctor 7½ yards, M. Ralph Rudryth 9 yards, Lentwardyn 7½ yards, Talkaron 7 yards, M. Thomas Hendeman 8 yards' (at the head of the list previously we find '12 yards of coloured cloth for M. Thomas Hendeman, price of the yard iis id,' probably given him as Chancellor), '29 determiners 7 yards each, 4 bachelors of law one piece 4 yards, 3 bachelors of arts 7 yards each, five fellows of the College 16 yards, 29 esquires 2 pieces 18 yards; 32 masters of arts pro furrura capuciorum xxxii furrurae de Menever, 29 determiners pro furrura capuciorum xxix furrurae de Bugey.'

The hall and kitchen are of course constantly mentioned. They were not on the site of the present hall and kitchen but more to the north. There was a large washing basin in the hall (lavacrum) with a pipe to it (fistula), and once we hear of a 'lavacrum[4] pendens

[1] Rogers i. 121, 582; ii. 643-7. M. John Gyles who managed the feast is mentioned in an Exeter Computus of autumn 1390 'viiis de M. Johanne Gelys pro pensione alte scole iuxta scolam ubi scamnum situatur in medio.' John Wykham is mentioned in summer 1393 'vis viiid a M. Johanne Wykam in partem solucionis unius alte scole pro A.D. &c. nonagesimo secundo,' and in summer 1398 'xvis iiiid de M. Johanne Wykham pro finali solucione scole sue.' Richard Lentwardyn, archdeacon of Cornwall 1395, R. of All Hallows, Lombard St. 3 Feb. 140⅘; but there was also Thomas de Lentwardyn, chancellor of London 1401, provost of Oriel 1414, Tanner 475.

[2] Anstey 301, 360-1, Patent Rolls 1 Mch 132⅘ p. 34.

[3] All Souls Statutes p. 42; Hist. Comm. v. 436.

[4] Clark's *Colleges* 331, Kirby's *Winchester College* 41.

in aula.' There are constant payments for towels[1]. There was a large expenditure for tablecloths and napkins (mappae and manutergia); winter 1417 '3s 2½d for linen for a tablecloth, 22d for 5½ ells for two towels to guard the tablecloth, 14d for two dozen cups in the buttery, 14d for a brass candlestick, 3½d for hemming (limbacio) a tablecloth two towels and two hanging napkins (manutergiorum pendencium), 2s 6d for three mats (storiis) for the hall.' A piece of linen for a tablecloth cost 3s 8d in the winter of 1382 and winter of 1406, 3s 1d in winter of 1411, while in winter of 1441 3s is paid for a tablecloth of 6 ells. In winter 1360 12d was paid for a case for the spoons of the House (casa pro coclearibus domus), and 5½d for a 'tankard'; 5 spoons cost 16d in summer 1394 and autumn 1394, while in summer 1361 7s 6d was given for making 18; a large kitchen spoon cost 3d in Lent 1404; silver spoons occur constantly, at Merton they were valued at 10d each (Rogers i. 647; ii. 569, 577, 579). The High Table (tabula alta) is mentioned in winter 1418 '6s for 11 ells of linen for a tablecloth and two towels for High Table.' The hall was lighted with torches, torticii, or rather large candles; a great torch of wax cost 3s 6d in Lent 1358, a torch for the hall 4s 7d in winter 1360, 10½d is given for making two torches in winter 1385[2]. Charcoal (carbones), often in an iron frame, was used for the fire. The University petitioned against cutting down the forests of Shotover and Stowe Wood, since it would ruin the University by destroying the wood necessary for fuel. Chimneys came into use in the fourteenth century[3]. The word chimney at first meant hearth or fireplace, and coal meant charcoal and collier charcoal-burner. In the computus of winter 1354 '23s 6d to a workman for making the wall of the chimneys (parietis caminorum) and a window,' autumn 1401 '5d for

[1] Tuellum, see Glossaries v. toella and toacula, Warton's *Life of Pope* 341: winter 1413, 6s 3d for 3 towels for the chapel; winter 1430 four shillings for four towels. For napkins, Rogers i. 574, iv. 554, 561, v. 552, vi. 522.

[2] There was a great consumption of wax. especially in churches, Rogers iv. 365, Roscher *Pol. Econ.* i. 289. The Cordwainers of Oxford paid 7d for a pound of wax 1483 (Cordwainers' Guild p. 14); cereus and torticius, Peshall 210.

[3] Rogers i. 421, iv. 370, 610, Magdalen Muniments 122, Southey's Commonplace Book i. 431, 536, ii. 619. Wood's *Life* i. 133, 304 'set up a chimney in the upper room looking Eastward,' ii. 98; Pepys 5 Dec. 1663 'a house so smoky that it was troublesome to us all, till they put out the fire, and made one of charcoal.'

a plank for the kitchen chimney (fumerali coquine), and 2d for "spiks" for the chimney and for an old *dressingboard*.' See a. 1384. Chimneys in the smaller rooms are mentioned Lent 1522 '9d for building a chimney (camini) in the chamber of M. Nycholls and M. Slad.' Lent 1547 '13s 4d to Jacson a mason (lapidario) mending a chimney (fumarium) in the chamber of M. Whiting.' The smoke of wood was of a fragrant character, and was thought to be medicinal and beneficial. With coal smoke it was different, and coal could hardly be used under such primitive conditions[1]. But by Tudor times wood was becoming scarcer and dearer, and owing to the need of using cheaper fuel chimneys came into use even in common houses. Previously, says Aubrey, 'ordinary men's houses, and copyholders' and the like, had no chimneys, but flues like beaver holes.' And Harrison in 1577 notes the use of chimneys in inland towns as one of those things that had marvellously altered within the recollection of old men, whereas in their younger days there were not above two or three in most *uplandish* towns, except in great houses. Students liked to remain round the fire in hall after dinner, partly for the warmth, or for the sake of an occasional drinking bout (bibesia); hence several Colleges have stringent rules against staying in hall after dinner. Thus at Magdalen[2] all are to leave the hall at curfew time, hora ignitegü, except on Saints' days when they may stay on and amuse themselves with ballads and read historical poems, chronicles, and the wonders of the world. At Balliol there was fire in the Hall on certain feasts and their vigils (*Early Balliol* by Mrs. de Paravicini 294). Candles were dear, nearly twopence a pound, that is two shillings of our money; men could not afford to read in their rooms after dark, they lacked the genial inspiration of good candlelight. In rude ages men have few amusements or occupations but what daylight affords them. Other students, besides Sixtus V, may have had to read by the light of the lantern hung up at the crossing of the streets. The French scholar Amyot read by the light of the charcoal in the

---

[1] Among Warden Clayton's misdeeds Wood reckons (*Life* i. 396) 'burning in one year threescore pounds worth of the choicest billet that could be had, not only in all his rooms, but in the kitchen among his servants; without any regard had to cole, which usually (to save charges) is burnt in kitchens, and sometimes also in parlours.'

[2] Statutes p. 71.

brasier.   Dr. Wood at S. John's, Cambridge, read by the rush light
on the staircase (Wordsworth 410). Alexander Adam in the last
century read his Livy in the early morning by the light of splinters
of bogwood.   The burning candle was sometimes protected by
a lantern[1].   In 1596 a fire occurred through one 'intempestive
studentis.'   Hence partly the 'ignitegium.'   It was noted that
at S. John's Cambridge some candles were lit before 4 in the
morning. A very old lantern is preserved in the Ashmolean museum;
it is of bronze and the light is transmitted through crystals.   The
wick of the better candles was made of cotton, which at that time
grew in Cyprus, Sicily and Italy; but rushlights continued in use
down to our own days (in 1662 Wood paid 6d for a pound of double
rush candles, in 1666 5½d for a pound of single rush candles).
Much use was made of rushes in other ways.   They were used to
strew the hall and chapel.   In summer 1358 1½d was paid for rushes
(cirpi) for the chapel (Blomfield's *Lower Heyford* 42), and in summer
1473 sixpence for the same purpose; straw was used at Christmas,
rushes at Whitsuntide[2].   The men too were much crowded in their
rooms.   Two fellows sometimes lived in one chamber.   John Hennok
was chamber fellow with John Dagenet in a room *ad ostium*; Lent
1415 'iiid pro emendacione sere in camera Hele et Yate'; and so
others, winter 1429 'iiis iiiid pro camera Pleasaunte et Martyn pro
ultimo anno': John Westlake fellow had a room in College with
Thomas Copleston sojourner in 1442.   The churches and castles
were splendid, but the inmates of collegiate houses were closely
packed and indifferently lodged, while the furniture was rough and
scanty.   The Magdalen statutes[3] order that in each of the better
rooms there shall be two chief beds and two beds on wheels, 'lecti
rotales, *Trookyll beddys* vulgariter appellati,' and in each of the other
rooms two chief beds and one truckle bed if the size of those rooms

---

[1] Rogers i. 415, iv. 367, Ayliffe ii. 241.

[2] Peshall 217 ; *Pictorial Hist. of England* iii. 474, Magdalen Muniments 88,
140, Elyot's *Governor* 121, Burgon's *Gresham* i. 12, Wood's *City* i. 478, Jusserand
p. 124, Eng. Cycl. *v.* Rush bearing, Ancient Charters (Pipe Roll Soc.) i. pp. 60, 63
'earliest notice at Tavistock 1386,' but at Ex. Coll. it is 1358 : for Rushbearing
day at Grasmere see *Pall Mall* 29 Sep. 1892 p. 3.

[3] P. 72, see statutes of All Souls p. 73, of Brasenose p. 34, of Corpus 81; Gutch
i. 597 this increased the plague.

allow of so many. The *musea*, or studies, were very small[1]. The services of a ratcatcher had to be called in sometimes, autumn 1363 '8*d* to a ratter (ratonarius) when he destroyed the rats in the rooms.'

The Chapel occurs constantly. A chalice is procured in winter 1413 which costs 34*s* 2*d*. Wine is bought, and wax candles, and incense. Thus in Lent 1334 'wine 5*d*, a quarter of oil 3*d*, 2 pounds of wax 13*d*, tallow candles 2.' Resin, called also 'thus,' was employed for ordinary incense[2]; it was about 1½*d* a pound, but in summer 1478 5*d* is paid for one pound. In summer 1334 and Lent 1355 1*d* is paid for 'thimiama,' and this is the more common name in the accounts; in summer 1507 we have 'thimiama et thus.' Thymiama was probably a composition. There was a 'sepulcrum' in the chapel[3]. Lent 1357 'thread for the sepulchre 1*d*,' Lent 1358 '6½*d* to John Walys for two days labour in whitening the chapel wall, 1*d* for tymiama at Christmas, 9½*d* for mending vestments and for wine, 1*d* for tymiama at the Purification, 40*s* for a silver turibule put up to sale with Richard the stationer and for his salary 3*s* 4*d*, 2*d* for the breakfast of a priest and clerk on two occasions who stood in the chapel and sang, nails and thread and repairing a hinge of sepulchre 1½*d*': summer 1404 '4*d* for the Lord's sepulchre, 10*d* to the bearer who brought us a black 'casula' with all belonging to it, a gift from Mr. Richard Mark.' The fellows sat near the door, summer 1372 'to John Lokier (*i. e.* locksmith) 20*d* for 12 *clitoriis* for the garden gate, for mending lock and for keys for the common chest and a lock for the chapel, and little iron hooks (hamis) where the fellows sit in chapel near the door, and drink for the same 6*d*, and for an iron chain for a book called Rabanus de Naturis Rerum 16*d*.' There were rooms under the chapel, autumn 1363 '8*s* 1*d* for beams to make doors to the chambers under the chapel'; and it had a porch, winter 1361 '8*s* to a plumber who repaired the porch of the chapel, 4*d* for tin (stagnum), 4*d* to another workman who stood with him when he covered the porch, 3*d* for nails for the work, 3*d* for drink.' Lead was in constant use : 6*s* 9*d* was paid for six stones of lead

---

[1] Wordsworth 413, 655, Return from Parnassus ed. Arber p. 33 'lay in a trundlebed.'

[2] Rogers i. 466.

[3] Warton's *Pope* 340, Cavendish's *Wolsey* ed. 1827, p. 309, Dixon's *Church Hist.* ii. 516, Kirby's *Winchester College* 52.

for a pipe (aqueductu) and for working it up in autumn 1401, *i.e.*
1*s* 1½*d* a stone or one penny a pound: winter 1419 '19*d* for 26
pounds (ponderibus) bought for White Hall,' *i.e.* three farthings
a pound. In autumn 1419 '15*s* to Thomas Plummer for melting
ten fotmelys of our lead and for 8 stones (petris) of new lead and for
melting it.' The fotmael, pedes, or pigs of lead each contained 5
petrae of 14lbs. each[1]. The pes or fotmael is one-tenth of a cubic
foot of lead. Thirty pigs made one fother, and melting or rolling
a fother cost 10*d*, but ordinarily the plumber was paid by the day.
The lead came mostly from the West of England, especially from
Devon. Autumn 1364 '2*s* for earth (terula) for repairing the chapel
porch and the stable, 4*s* 2*d* to workmen who repaired the chapel
porch, stable and chambers and cleansed the court (curia) and for
their bread and drink at the ninth hour[2] three days 6*d*, for lime 12*d*,
6*d* for wine in the chapel the whole term, 2*d* for skin to cover the

---

[1] Rogers i. 168, 596, 605: 600 tin used as solder: the average price in Rogers'
list is 11¼*d* a stone, and deduction must be made from the prices in the text for
labour.

[2] Hora nona, 'nunsyns,' constantly occurs; winter 1354 '15½*d* to a workman
working in the chamber of John Flemyn and for his dinner (prandio) one day *in
hall* and for his nunsyns 2*d*, 12*d* to a workman for labouring a week and for his
nunsyns, 10*d* to workmen for their nunsyns': winter 1402 '7*s* 2*d* to a mason
(lathomo) for his labour and noncynchys in repairing Hart hall': autumn 1457
'for removing earth from the well at Herthall 9*d*, for the drink of the labourers
s (seu) none segs 4*d*.' The nunsyns was often an allowance of beer, noncynchys =
noon-drink; Anglosaxon *scencan*, to pour out, is said to come from shank, the tap
of the barrel being a hollow shankbone. Such names came from the church
services. The sixth hour service, *sexta* (whence our *siesta*, for a sleep after a meal)
was at 12 o'clock, and the ninth hour service, *nona*, at 3. At 3, half way between
dinner and supper, a drink of beer and a hunch of bread were allowed, and
commonly named *bibesia* or *biberia monachorum*, and the custom of *bever* still
survives at Eton, Winchester and Westminster. A similar drink and hunch of
bread in the early morning came to be called breakfast (*jentaculum*) towards the
close of the fifteenth century, as the dinner hour was pushed on. Pepys constantly
mentions his *morning draught* (Wordsworth 126, 433). An old line (adapted
from Suetonius) runs Jentaculum, dein prandium, post cenam comessatio. But as,
on fast-days, it was a long time to wait till 3 o'clock, the nones were put back to
12 o'clock, and the *Sexta* disappeared; hence the words *noon* and *nuncheon*.
The second part of *nuncheon* means a drink, but the *lump* or hunch of bread that
accompanied the drink got mixed up with *nuncheon*, and the word is now spelt
luncheon. The Latin for nunsyns was *merenda*. *Nona* in Dante *Purg.* xxvii. 4,
meaning midday, is almost certainly the right reading, though most MSS. read
nova, but n and u (v) are constantly confused. See Gustav Bilfinger *Die
Mittelalterlichen Horen*, Stuttgart, 1892.

Legend (*i.e.* Lives of Saints), 1*d* for thimiama.' A cord for the chapel bell cost 1½*d* in summer 1359 : a small chapel bell cost 12*d* in winter 1363, another 4*d* in winter 1403. There were glass windows, Lent 1363 '8*d* to a workman who mended the glass windows in the chapel.' Glass[1] was also used for small vessels, autumn 1359 'ii*d* pro quodam vase vitreo pro hostiis conservandis.' Summer 1511 'v*d ob* pro parvis clavis circa aulam *et tabulam Kalendarii* in capella.' Tabula was a board on which were written the names of those who had to take particular parts of the services. See Henderson's *Processionale Sarum* p. ix.

Numerous exequies and obits were celebrated. Thus Thomas Barton canon of Exeter and R. of Ilfracombe, d. 1416 (Stafford's Reg. i. 327), says in his will ' volo quod exequie mee celebrentur per octavam post mortem meam inter socios aule Oxoniensis vocate Stapyldon hall, et habeant distribuendos inter ipsos xl. solidos, et celebrent presbiteri ibidem, et alteri socii dicant Psalterium.' Autumn 1477 'iii*li* vis viii*d* ab executoribus Wyllelmi Clerk *alias* Algod ad orandum pro anima eius'; winter 1477 'iiii*s* viii*d* in exequiis et missa Willelmi Clerk *alias* Algod.' Henry White, priest, fellow of New College 5 Nov. 1515, in his will 1538 (Probate Office) bequeaths ' to the company of Exceter College 10*s* to the amendment of their commons or to be bestowed at their pleasure, fyve shillings thereof to be delivered at my buriall, and fyve shillings at the moneth mynde ; . . . that Maister Rector of Excetur College have for his paynes taken with me a blewe glass the best; . . . I owe to Excetur College for my chamber one quarter rent, and to the mancyple for oon quarter.' Computus autumn 1520 'i*d* pro reparacione sere in camera domini White,' autumn 1538 ' 13*s* 4*d* ab exequtoribus doctoris White.'

The Library was thatched in autumn 1375 ' 3*s* 4*d* for straw and for covering the Library.' It had just received a donation Lent 1375 ' 40*s* for the use of the Library in part payment of 20 marks given by M. William Reed bishop of Chichester, but temporarily used for College payments.' Winter 1385 ' 3*d* for repairing two books, 1*d* for paper, 2*s* 5*d* for glass in the great window of the Library.' In the east window[2] was the picture of a man kneeling, with his gown and formalities on him, with this inscription, 'Pray for the soul of M. William

---

[1] Rogers iv. 591. [2] Gutch iii. 110, 116.

Palmer fellow of this place who caused this chapel to be lengthened.[*] Palmer's name was well known in the West, as he built Greystone bridge over the Tamar near Launceston, connecting Bradstone in Devon with Lezant in Cornwall, thus fulfilling a promise made in his schoolboy days, perhaps at Launceston school. In another window was a man kneeling with 'Orate pro anima Johannis Westlake quondam istius loci socii qui istam fenestram fieri fecit,' on a scroll issuing from his mouth 'Ibi nostra fixa sunt corda ubi [vera] gaudia[1].'

The books were chained to desks, and some of them kept in chests[2]. The account of the expenses of building a new Library in 1383 is printed below, where the masons' and carpenters' wages are given for each week. Bishop Brantingham gave £10 towards it, John More R. of S. Petrock's Exeter £20, Bishop Stafford enlarged it in 1404 (Gutch iii. 115). There was no architect, only a chief mason. In 1545 a notice occurs that a key of the Library was given to each fellow and that whoever lost one of the keys was to pay 5s[3]. The books had to be sometimes pawned to one of the loan chests of the University when the yearly expenses were too great (Coxe No. xxix, xxxvi). Autumn 1354 '6os for redeeming a Bible which lay in Langeton chest'; winter 1357 ' £3 for a Bible pledged in Chichester chest, 29s for a silver cup pledged in Goldeford chest, 13s 4d for a book on the prophets and the third part of Thomas de Alquino pledged in Tybeford chest': autumn 1358 ' £3 for a Bible redeemed from Chichester chest, 8s 4d for a missal pledged in Burnel chest, £3 for a Bible pledged in Winton chest'; summer 1374 ' 4 marks to our barber for a Bible which was pledged to him in the time of John Dagenet.' In 1446 a Psalter was ' redeemed.' In 1466 M. Chard

---

[1] Palmer was living 1460, Westlake gave the window 1488.

[2] Hist. Comm. ii. 126: *The Library* iii. 270 ; Winter 1392 'iiiis pro ligacione septem librorum et 1d pro cervisia in eisdem ligatoribus, vid erario pro labore suo circa eosdem libros, et iid Johanni Lokyer pro impositione eorundem librorum in descis': winter 1449 'pro una lamina ferrea pro magna porta et alia pro disco quodam in libraria iid ob'; Lent 1441 'iid pro una sera pendente pro cista librorum.' See Gottlieb's *Mittelalterliche Bibliotheken*, Leipzig, 1890.

[3] Reg. 8 Nov. 1545 'traditae sunt a Rectore 15 claves ad ostium librarii spectantes quindecim sociis, hac lege, ut quilibet eorum cedens vel decedens suam reddat clavem Rectori, aut solvat pro eadem'; 26 Mch 1562 'quicunque unam clavium (que nuperrime erant fabricate) forte librarii perdet, hac summa vs postea,' &c.

paid 2*s* 'pro renovacione unius libri positi in cista Cecestrie,' in 1470 he did the same for Avicenna. The Bibles were large and valuable. Summer 1390 '2*s* 2*d* for binding a Bible and mending two other books'; winter 1443 '2*s* for binding a Bible, and for parchment for its guards (custodibus).' In later times, when books were more common the Colleges[1] made special provisions in their statutes about the Library and the books[2].

The fellows devoted considerable time and pains to managing their property. It was difficult to get money carried safely from one part of the country to the other. Sometimes the Chapter of Exeter sent the Gwinear tithe to their bailiff at Bampton in Oxfordshire (the Bishop of Exeter had 6 hides of land at Bampton—Oxf. Arch. Soc. 1887 p. 129); but sometimes the rector or a fellow had to go to Exeter or Gwinear for it[3], and travelling was not easy nor was it always safe. Even in Risdon's time the roads in Devon were 'cumbersome and uneven, amongst rocks and stones, painful for man and horse, as they can best witness who have made trial thereof. For be they never so well mounted upon horses out of other countries, when they have travelled one journey in these parts, they can, in respect of ease of travel, forbear a second.' The roads were not meant for carriages or carts, goods

---

[1] Statutes of Brasenose p. 35, Corpus 90, Christchurch 112.

[2] For *electio librorum* (i. e. the fellows *chose* books, to be lent them for a year) see winter 1382 'vii*d ob* pro ligatura cuiusdam textus philosophie de eleccione Johannis Mattecote'; winter 1405 'id *ob* pro pergameno empto pro novo registro faciendo pro eleccione librorum'; winter 1457 'iiii*d* More stacionario pro labore suo duobus diebus appreciando libros collegii qui traduntur in eleccionibus sociorum'; autumn 1488 'iis id pro redempcione librorum quondam eleccionis domini Ricardi Symon'; All Souls Statutes p. 56; see preface to *Compotus Rolls of the Obedientaries of S. Swithun's Priory, Winchester*; and criticism on it in the *Tablet*, 29 Oct. 1892; *Collectanea* (O. H. S.) i. 76: Reg. 20 July 1650 'Agreed in the Chappell that thenceforth no man should take any booke out of the Colledge Librarie without the consent and allowance of the Rector, Sub-rector, and Deane; and then to leave it under his hand with the Keeper of the Librarie that hee hath in his possession every such booke or bookes; and lastly that hee restore all such booke or bookes into the Librarie again within the space of 8 dayes inclusive from the day on which they were taken out.' Reg. 12 Dec. 1684 'decretum est ad utilitatem Bibliothecae in usum juniorum institutae, quod quilibet socio-commensalis solvet decem solidos, suggenarius 7*s* 6*d*, battelarius 5*s*, pauper scholaris 2*s* 6*d*, a Bursario recipiendos, in usum Bibliothecae impendendos ex arbitrio Subrectoris et Decani.' Simon Cooper occurs as Bibliothecarius 1634.

[3] Summer 1407 'v*d* in gantaculo Coulynge quando portavit nobis aurum de Cornubia'; autumn 1431 'pro expensis Rectoris et famuli sui in equitando ad S. Wynnerum xxi*s* iiii*d*.'

were conveyed on mules, and even in the early part of the last century there was little but a system of bridle paths West of Exeter. In Lent 1400 John Jakys the rector was robbed of ten shillings on his way to Exeter. A horseman was often accompanied by a servant on foot to take charge of the horse, the distance travelled was about 20 miles a day; but messengers on foot at a penny a day seem to have accomplished a greater distance. Money and goods were sometimes entrusted to the Exeter carrier (cursor or vector)[1], when the Gwinear tenant had brought the money to Exeter; autumn 1460 '6d to the Exeter carrier for bringing us a " pannus depictus " given us by M. John Colyford prior of S. John's at Exeter to hang up in the Hall, and a table cloth of dyaper from the same M. John'; winter 1460 ' 50s from our tenant staying at the Taberd Inn at Exeter'; winter 1361 ' 15s from M. James de Molton by the hands of the prior of Abyndon for the fruits of S. Wyner, £4 which Thomas Kelly received in the treasury of the cathedral church at Exeter, 5 marks on the part of the Dean of Exeter from Leverton's prebend which the Dean received on our part for the fruits of S. Wynyr, £3 which Robert Clyst received in the treasury for the fruits of S. Wynyr when he last settled with the seneschal of the treasury.' The carrier even in 1707 went to Exeter only once in five weeks (Reliquiae Hearnianae 30 Jan. 172⅘ note). The cost of carriage in 1579 was fourpence a mile (Wood's *Life* p. iii; Rogers iii. 674). J. Taylor's *Carriers' Cosmography*, reprinted in Arber's *English Garner* i. 234 ' the carriers of Exeter do lodge at the Star in Bread street. They come on Fridays and go away on Saturdays or Mondays'; 227 ' the carriers or posts that go to Exeter may send daily to Plymouth or to the Mount in Cornwall' (Rogers i. 660; Boase's *Oxford* 194). The University carriers' stables were in Kibald street, which ran from Oriel backgate to Horsemulen Lane, and crookedly thence to the Angel backgate (Peshall 135, 141). The carriage up the Thames from London by water did not reach further than Maidenhead, and hence salt was dear, since it had to be brought from the coast (Rogers iv. 392). Lent 1422 ' 20d to the Devonshire carrier for carrying four

---

[1] Rogers i. 96; Reg. of Congregation 5 Mch 151⅚ ' decretum est quod Richardus Kybee debet admitti in vectorem in comitatu Somerzed.' Henry Slade the Exeter carrier was privileged 2 Dec. 1721; Hannah England was carrier to Devon 1722.

books assigned to us by the executors of Edmund de Stafford bishop of Exeter'; summer 1410 ' 4*s* 2*d* to the carrier (cursor) when he brought us gold from Exeter'; autumn 1414 ' 3*s* 8*d* to the carrier (cursor) for carrying £7 which he received from M. Thomas Hendeman'; winter 1469 ' 10*s* to the Exeter carrier (vector) for carrying books.' The gold (mostly in gold nobles, worth 6*s* 8*d*, first coined by Edward III 1343–4) received for the rents often required to be exchanged; summer 1358 ' xiii*d* circa camcionem auri '; autumn 1358 ' de camcione auri xvi*d*'; Lent 1409 ' iiii*d* pro cambicione unius nobilis defectivi.' The rector and fellows had constantly to ride to Wittenham and elsewhere to see about barns being mended, stone and slate being bought ; and more than once they had to get in their tithe in kind for themselves ; autumn 1363 ' 12*d* for hiring two horses when the Rector and John Trewyse were at West Wyttenham to arrange with the firmarii for making a barn '; autumn 1355 ' 2*d* for bread, beer, and cheese when our priest of West Wiham made his compact (convencio), 8*d* to Robert Clest and William Vatte when they went to Abindon on business, 7*d* for mending the rector's saddle (sella) which he broke when on the business of the house.' A pair of boots (ocreae) for these expeditions cost 2*s* 6*d* in Lent 1360, 3*s* 4*d* Lent 1362, 3*s* 8*d* Lent 1364, 3*s* 1*d* summer 1372 ; summer 1355 ' for shoeing (ferura) the common horse 3½*d*, 6*d* for victuals for the common horse, 7*d* for shoeing the common horse, 5*d* for his breakfast, 9*s* 10*d* to Cergeaux for going to Exeter and for mending his boots, 2*d* to Clest for mending his boots, 3*s* to Vatte for boots.' Suckling, in his address to Hales of Eton, tells his friend to ' bestride the College steed' and ride up to town. Oats cost 5*d* for 2 bushels (modii) in autumn 1444 [1]. In 1334 3½*d* was paid for a ' sum' (summa) of straw; the ' sum ' was usually equal to a quarter, but the ' sum' of oats was double this amount. The English were a nation of horsemen till the beginning of the eighteenth century.

Exeter College possessed four schools in School Street, which afforded a rent, as Determiners hired them to perform their

---

[1] Rogers i. 168; the glosses gives 'sumberinus' as a measure of oats on the Continent; in Lent 1455 ' loads ' of straw for the schools are mentioned, 2 loads (oneribus) costing 5*d*. Rogers iv. 423 stirrups in 1454; v. 688 tithe in kind; for horse hire see Jusserand 348.

exercises[1]. A composition with the City 16 Dec. 1384 exonerated Exeter Hall from the payment of Tenths, Madan's *City Records* p. 17. All transfers of houses had to be registered in the Hustings Court, and we hear of the Rector being present there, Turner 22.

In its early years the College had to pass through difficult times. The worst famine ever felt in England occurred in 1315–6 : 1320 was a year of pestilence, 1321 of famine, Wood's *City* i. 168. The Black Death caused many changes in the Colleges in 1349, and again 1361–2, 1370–1, Rogers i. 296 ; Gutch i. 485–6. The Computi too are missing for 17 years, 1337—autumn 1354. Was this owing to the plagues or to the great Riot on S. Scholastica's day, 10 Feb. 135$\frac{4}{8}$? On 3 May a special protection was issued for the master of the House of

---

[1] All Souls Archives index *v*. Oxford, Anstey 274 venella quae ducit a collegio Exonie usque ad Catstrete a parte boreali, 240, 520. School Street extended from the north side of S. Mary's under the west end of the Church to the City Wall; the ancient schools were to the east of it. To the west of it were a number of Halls *e.g.* Little Edmund Hall where the east part of Brasenose Chapel now is, with Salisbury Hall to the north of it; the lower rooms of these Halls were frequented by disputants in Lent and when they commenced for the degree of M.A.; see Wood's *City* i. 82–3, 112, 118, 140; Reliquiae Hearnianae 7 July 1712. On 15 Mch 1333 Robert de Grymmeston and M. William Dobbe gave two schools in Scolestrete to the Rector and Scholars of Stapeldonhalle, lying between the schools belonging to the Convent of Stodleye (Peshall 97, 98, 99, 100) and the 'scolas . . . Balliolo Oxon,' which two schools they had lately from William Atte Hole and Katherine his wife. In 1327 a Concord was made between the College and William Attehole of Botley, Wood's *City* i. 112. Exeter had two other schools as well, Wood's *City* i. 89. The 'Recepta' of autumn 1417 notice the four Schools in School Street belonging to the College, as well as Hart Hall and Checker Hall; 'iiii*li* xiii*s* iiii*d* de Johanne Chalener in partem solucionis fructuum ecclesie nostre de Wyttenham pro A.D. etc. xvi°; xx*s* de M. Willelmo More in partem solucionis pensionis pro Aula Cervina pro anno ultimo ; x*s* a M. Henrico Clerk in finalem solucionem pensionis sue pro scolis suis ultimo anno ; x*s* a M. Radulpho Morwyll in finalem solucionem pensionis sue pro scolis suis pro ultimo anno ' ; x*s* a M. Willelmo Ays in finalem solucionem pensionis sue pro scolis suis pro ultimo anno ; x*s* a M. Henrico Whyttehed in finalem solucionem pensionis sue pro scolis suis pro ultimo anno ; xx*d* a Willelmo Roll in partem solucionis redditus eius pro anno ultimo elapso ; xxiii*s* iiii*d* a M. Willelmo Andrew in finalem solucionem pensionis Aule Scaccarii pro anno ultimo ; Summa omnium receptorum xi*li* xi*s* viii*d*.' Summer 1549 'vi*li* xi*s* vii*d* diruendis scolis, pro vehendis lignis et tegulis ad Collegium et pro reparationibus'; winter 1552 'iis viii*d* ab Hurste pro horto in platea ubi scolæ nostræ sitæ erant'; Lent 1556 'iis iiii*d* a M. Collings pro redditu horti nostri ubi scolæ olim fuerunt.' Summer 1401 ' vi*s* viii*d* a M. Rodeborne procuratore in plenam solucionem pensionis scolarum suarum'; autumn 1527 'xl*s* a Bursariis pro scolis in quadragesima, et magistrorum Gyllet, Wyld, Lytlecot, Towchan, Colmer, Colyns ?, Pownset et Randall.'

Scholars of Stapeldon hall, his men lands possessions and goods (patent 29 Edward III part i memb. 7, in Statutes III App. p. 23).

The College was very poor, and in 1479 the advowson of Menheniot in Cornwall was given to it [1].

Clifton Ferry was given to the College by Roger Roper, draper, of Watlington, 1 Aug. 1493; see p. 327; Collect. Topog. et Geneal. i. 241, where many college documents are printed.

The bishops of Exeter were kind patrons. Bishops Grandisson [2], Brantingham, Stafford, and Lacy gave books. Bishop Stafford obtained a bull for the Fellows from Innocent VII. Copies of some of their rescripts to the College still exist. Thus on 2 June 1430 Bishop Lacy [3] orders as follows. 'To all sons of holy mother

[1] Winter 1479 'xxli xiiiis vd ob a M. Nicholao Gosse in pleusagio receptorum ultra expensas factas circa appropriacionem beneficii de Mayhyneot; xiid pro scriptura unius litere attornatorie misse magistris Johanni Combe, Wagot, et Johanni Philipp; xiid vi sociis presentibus in exequiis domini Fitzwaren.' A Latin deed says: 'To all . . . . . ., Owen Lloyd, doctor of laws, official of Thomas, Cardinal Priest of S. Ceriac in Thermis, primate and legate, having jurisdiction in the diocese of Exeter during the vacancy of the See : the Rector and Scholars of Stapledon Hall, now commonly called Exeter College, have petitioned that in consideration of their poverty, since M. Nicholas Gosse, chancellor, Walter Wyndesore subdean of Exeter, John Lyndon, dean of the Collegiate Church of Holy Cross at Crediton, patrons, have procured the glebe and advowson of Mahynyet in Cornwall, reserving a Vicarage, for the said Rector and Scholars, but in the name of the Dean and Chapter of Exeter . . . . . ., we decree the appropriation . . . . . ., with the King's license, reserving to the Vicar a fitting portion and house on the glebe ; and on the present Rector, M. Peter Courtenay, resigning or dying, the Rector and Fellows may take possession ; and they are to maintain a chaplain in the College, who at every mass shall utter a special collect for Fulk Bourchier Lord Fitzwarren and Elizabeth his wife, Edward Courtenay and Elizabeth his wife, Halnatheus Mauleverer and Joan his wife as long as they live, and for their souls after they die, as the original patrons of that church and promoters of this pious work, and there is to be an obit celebrated for them in the College every 20 Oct. ; and every Vicar of Menheniot is to be a B.D., or at least an M.A., and one who is [or has been : these words only occur in a copy of the deed] a Fellow of Exeter College, to be named by the Dean and Chapter. Exeter 28 Sep. 1478.' On 23 July 1479 the College gave up all the tithes, &c. to William Baron the Vicar, for an annual payment of £20, the Vicar to bear all expenses whatever (see College Reg. 1827 pp. 11, 15). The executors of Henry Webber, dean of Exeter, James Hamlin, canon of Exeter, and Richard Mounceaux, canon of Exeter, gave the College £60 for the expenses of the appropriation.

[2] I have printed a letter of Grandisson's about his own University career in *Oxford Magazine* 1892 xi. 122.

[3] Extract from Lacy's Register, vol. ii, folio 57, among the College muniments; summer 1391 'xs pro pensione unius alte scole a magistro Edmundo Lacy'; summer 1458 'xiid pro vectura unius cape pro capella, ac unius voluminis in

church, &c., Edmund bishop of Exeter patron and immediate ordinary of Stapyldon halle &c. Our predecessor Edmund Stafford gave the said College books for divine service in its Chapel and a chalice, and books for the library, and built a chamber 24 feet long under the Library (which had been lengthened, heightened and covered with lead), and rebuilt the porch of the chapel and covered it with lead, and built a new small chamber under the porch, and half covered the Hall and built the new west gate, all which cost him over 200 marks in money, not including the books, and his executors have also been liberal to the College [1]. Wherefore, after consultation with M. William Palmer, Rector of the College, and with the Fellows through M. William Fylham, S. T. P., authorised by the Rector and Fellows under their seal to act for them, at our manor of Chudelegh 2 June 1430 we have ordained as follows. The present Rector and Fellows, and any of their successors who are in priest's orders, and the chaplain are, when they celebrate, to say the collect or prayer which is usually said for bishops departed this life, on behalf of Edmund Stafford; and all Fellows both now and hereafter who are even in the lesser orders are to commemorate him in their prayers among other benefactors : and yearly on the morrow of S. Luke they are to keep his obit with Placebo and Dirige in the preceding night and mass on the morrow and he who performs the exequies and mass is to have six pence and the other Fellows present are to have four pence. And the rent of the two chambers mentioned above is to go to the repairs of the College Buildings. And this ordinance is to be kept like one of the statutes. The letters of authorisation to M. William Fylham are as follows' [space is left in the Register for the copy, but it is not inserted].

The Fellows also sometimes submitted Dubia to the Visitor as to the interpretation of the statutes, and these interpretations are preserved in some copies of the statutes. Besides regular commis-

---

Libraria cathenandi nobis transmissorum ab executoribus venerabilis patris ac domini, domini Edmundi Lacy nuper Exon. episcopi ; pro quodam anulo ferreo de novo facto ad ponendum in fine cathene dicti libri 1d.'

[1] Winter 1419 'iiii*d* uni preconisanti obitum domini Edmundi Stafford episcopi Exon et fundatoris nostri'; Lent 1422 'xx*d* cursori Devoniensi pro cariagio iiii librorum nobis assignatorum per executores domini Edmundi de Stafford episcopi Exon'; autumn 1431 ' xii*s* pro nova camera sub Libraria ad solvendum pro obitu Stafforde'; winter 1431 'iiii*s* x*d* sociis presentibus in exequiis et missa Stafford'; winter 1442 'ii*d* M. Johanni Code pro missa Stafford.'

sions to inquire into the state of the College, the Visitor interfered to see that their revenue reached them regularly, to increase the amount paid for commons in a time of dearth, and to help them to pay debts incurred under such circumstances, to protect them from oppression by the Chancellor, to restore a fellow who had been expelled, to remove an imbecile Rector, and to make that office tenable for life instead of annual.

It is worth while showing in some detail how the Visitors dealt with the College. The Latin of the following documents is given in ed. i. p. xliv, 233, 270.

Dispensation 20 June 1370.

Thomas (Brantingham) bishop of Exeter, to the scholars of our College at Oxford, commonly called Stapildon Hall. Since the famine has so burdened you with debt that you cannot be supported by your commons without some help, we allow you to take each 10s from the common chest to pay these debts, notwithstanding anything to the contrary in your Statutes or Customs. But you are not to do this again without our special license. At London.

Dispensation 13 Nov. 1370.

The Rector and Scholars of Exeter Hall in Oxford were allowed by the bishop (Brantingham) to take each 4d extra from the common chest weekly for forty weeks from the Saturday after Martinmas in the year 1370.

Commission for a Visitation 26 Oct. 1371.

Thomas (Brantingham) bishop of Exeter to our beloved Masters in Arts, Henry Whytefeld D.D. archdeacon of Barum, and Thomas Cary. We have been informed that Master William Franke, senior fellow of our College of Stapildon Hall, unjustly hinders his brother fellows in the election of a Rector. We therefore authorise you to visit the College and make them elect a Rector, and punish any who resist, and any offences of the fellows. At Esthorslegh.

Information for the seizure of William Frannk, an excommunicated person, 27 Jan. 137½.

To King Edward &c., we inform you that we have excommunicated William Frannk who pretends to be guardian of Stapildon Hall, but that

he has despised our sentence for forty days and more.   We therefore
ask you to use the secular arm against him.   At Far(ingdon ?).

Petition of the Scholars of Stapeldon Hall as to the Visitation, 18 Sep. 1372.

To the bishop (Brantingham) his devoted John Dagenet Rector of
the Scholars and of your College called Stapeldon Hall, John Dode-
more, Robert Lydeford, Richard Roulond, Richard Pestor, John
Hennok, John Henry, John Coly, Martin Archedekne, Laurence
Stephen, Thomas Worthe, Richard Broun, Thomas Fille, John
Skylling, Scholars of the College.   As regards your commission to the
reverend Masters Henry Whytefeld, Thomas Stowe, and Thomas
Cary for visiting the College, delivered to them by the Rector, the
said Thomas Stowe declines to act, and as the commission was directed
to the three jointly and not severally, the other two cannot act; we
therefore petition you to appoint three persons to carry out your commission, as also to charge the Dean and Chapter to pay us the
money due from S. Wynnery in Cornwall [1].

Commission for inquiring, correcting, and reforming, in Stapeldon Hall, 3 Oct. 1372.

Thomas (Brantingham) bishop of Exeter to Nicolas de Braybrok
and John Seys canons of Exeter.   We commission you jointly and
severally to visit our college or house of Stapildon Hall, and carefully
inspect their accounts as to the management of the goods of the
college, and entrust you with all our canonical powers of coercion.
At Clyst.

Letter of excuse from the Chancellor of Oxford, 3 June 1373.

To Thomas (Brantingham) bishop of Exeter the Chancellor of the
University of Oxford and the other Masters unanimously.   To coun-
teract the malice of some ambitious persons we inform you that as by

---

[1] Computus of summer 1374 '£11 13s 4d from the fruits of S. Wynery in
Cornwall, viz. £5 through M. Martin Lideford, and 10 marks through M. Nicolas
Braybroke; 10 marks from the bishop of Exeter our founder, 8 marks borrowed
from Winchester Chest on pawn of a Liber Sextus.'   Braybroke occurs again
Lent 1381 '5s 4½d for the breakfast of one who brought us books given by
M. Nicolas Braybrok'; and see Wilkins' *Concilia* 190.   He was archdeacon of
Cornwall 1377-81.

the Statutes of your college of Stapildon the Chancellor confirms the election of a Rector and in case of an equality of votes selects one of the two candidates, the commissary of the Chancellor finding that some had procured a commission from you, on pretence of which they tried to appoint an unfit Rector, forbad this being done, not with any intention of detracting from your jurisdiction. Nor do we wish to make your scholars hateful to you, whom we believe to be free from offence.

Certificate from the College of Stapeldon Hall, 30 *Oct.* 1373.

To Thomas (Brantingham) bishop of Exeter his devoted sons Robert Lideford, Rector, and Richard Roulond, John Dedimor chaplain, Thomas Worth, John Henry, John Coly, Richard Broun, John More, Martin Lerchedekne, Laurence Stevyn, Reginald Povy, and William Slade, Fellows. We have received your mandate to the following purport—Thomas bishop of Exeter to the Rector and Scholars of Stapeldon Hall; Whereas Henry Beaumond, clerk, of our diocese, whose character is certified to us by letters patent of William Rymyngton D.D., Chancellor of the University, has been unjustly deprived of his state and degree in the College, on your submission as contained in an instrument witnessed by Robert de Lideford, clerk, of our diocese, public notary, on 15 Jan. 1372 (137⅔) in the Chapter-house at Exeter, in the presence and with the assent of the Dean and Chapter, in the presence of Masters William Ryde our official, and Hugh Hikelyng canon of S. Crantock, and others, we have ordered him to be restored; We therefore command you to admit and replace him; On the authority therefore of this mandate we the aforesaid Robert Lideford, Rector, Richard, John, John, John, Thomas, Richard, Martin, Laurence Stevyn, John, Reginald, and William, have restored him to his former state and degree, on Sunday 30 Oct. A.D. 1373 in the Chapel in the presence of Master John Chayne your *confrater*.

Stapeldon Hall, 4 *May* 1374.

Simon (Sudbury) bishop of London, to the regent and non-regent Masters and Scholars of the University of Oxford. Know all that in the presence of William (of Wykeham) bishop of Winchester, and Thomas (Arundel) bishop of Ely, and Sir John Knyvet the King's Chancellor, and Nicholas Carru the Keeper of the King's Privy Seal,

Thomas (Brantingham) bishop of Exeter, visitor founder and patron of the College of Stapildon Hall, and Master William Wilton Chancellor of the University and Master Martin de Lideforde rector of the College and proctor for the scholars had certain complaints (given below) read, which the Chancellor of the University had brought against the Bishop and Rector and College, and after discussion referred the whole matter to our decision. And we have decided that the removal of the chaplain John Dedemor by the Rector and Scholars shall stand good, but that the bishop may cause him to be admitted to the first place vacant in the College ; that any persons aggrieved by the Chancellor's proceedings shall not be hindered in any scholastic act, and that the Rector and Scholars shall withdraw any proceedings against the Chancellor in the Court of Canterbury. The tenour of the complaints was as follows :

Hitherto the Rector had the free disposal of all the rooms, and with the consent of a certain part of the Scholars could punish and remove an incorrigible chaplain without appeal, and admit by election another chaplain on the presentation of the Dean and Chapter of Exeter, except during the Bishop's Annual Visitation. But when the Rector Master Robert Lideford had, with the consent of all the Scholars, removed the chaplain John Dedimor, Master William Wilton the Chancellor restored Dedimor to his chaplain's place and to his chamber and table ; and he excommunicated the Rector on his protesting, and suspended him and Master Richard Rowlond from all scholastic acts for three years, and forbad any advocate or notary, on penalty of imprisonment and banishment, to plead the case of the Rector or Bishop ; and he imprisoned Master Robert Worthe, notary public, for writing an instrument of the matter on the requisition of the Rector and Scholars ; and he banished Master Martin Lideford and Thomas Worthe for taking up the matter ; and when the Rector and Scholars made lawful resistance within the College and not without, he bound Master Robert Lideford the Rector, M. Richard Rowlond, John More, Reginald Povy, Philip Stonne, and M. Robert Worthe their notary by pledges, under penalty of £100 and over, not to hinder the peace of the University in that way ; all contrary to the Charters and Statutes of the College. Done in a great chamber in the south part of the inner cloister of the Friars Preachers in

London, 4 May 1374, in the 12th indiction, in the 4th year of Pope Gregory XI, in the presence of Masters John Wyliet D.D. Chancellor of Exeter, John Appulbi dean of S. Paul's, William Wyde canon of Sarum, John Blaunchard archdeacon of Worcester, and John Schilyngford[1] rector of the first portion of Wodesdon in the diocese of Lincoln, doctors of laws, and William Lorying canon of Bangor, inceptor in civil law, and Henry Persay, John Cary, and William Cary, and others. And I Robert Worthe saw and heard all this, and put it in this form, and being otherwise occupied had it written out by another and had it signed with my seal, and that of the bishop of London, and that of Master Edmund notary public. I the said notary had the words *et rectoris* interlined in line 39, *Robertum* in 40 and 45, *rectoris* in 50, which the writer had left out.

Commission for visiting the College of Stapeldon Hall, 13 *May* 1374.

Thomas (Brantingham) bishop of Exeter to Masters Henry Wytefeld, Thomas Montacute, William Todeworth[2], Robert Crosse, and William Middelworth, lawyers. We empower you to visit the College and examine the administration and last year's accounts of the Rector and the fourteen Scholars; and inform us of the result before the nativity of S. John the Baptist. At Horsley.

Stapildon Halle, 24 *Sep.* 1374[3].

Thomas (Brantingham) to the Rector and Scholars. Since the ten pence sterling allowed you for commons is not enough in the present scarcity, we allow you two pence each weekly extra. At Chuddelegh.

Commission for visiting Stapeldon Hall, 22 *Sep.* 1378.

Thomas (Brantingham) to Masters Henry Whitefeld D.D., and Thomas de Mountagu canon of Ottery S. Mary, Robert Rugge B.D., and Thomas Swyndon B.D. We empower you to visit the College and examine the administration and last year's accounts of the Rector and the fourteen Scholars. At London.

[1] Wilkin's *Concilia* ii. 620.

[2] R. of S. Tudy in Cornwall, exchanged for N. Alynton, Devon, 1371 (Todesworth); Maclean iii. 313; Ayliffe ii, App. p. lxiii; Tanner 717.

[3] Autumn 1376 ' xxviii*d* pro vino, quando Visitatores fuerunt hic.'

For the Restoration of a Fellow, 20 *June* 1379.

At London the Bishop entrusted his powers to the Rector for restoring, as a matter of grace, Master Henry Bewmond who was removed for his demerits by the last Visitors, on the said Henry swearing not to do the like again, but behave well and honestly.

Mandate for the Scholars of Stapeldon Hall, 23 *May* 1384.

Thomas (Brantingham) to the Rector and Scholars. Since statutes, like their makers, require change, as experience shows; whereas bishop Stapeldon ordered that the Rector's office should be annual, which causes quarrels about the election, and carelessness in the annual Rector, we now ordain that Master William Slade the present Rector, and future Rectors shall hold office continually unless proved to us by the fellows to be negligent or unfit, on which another shall be elected. At Sarum.

Commission for visiting the College of Stapeldon Halle, 24 *May* 1384.

Thomas (Brantingham) to Masters Roger Page D.Can.L., R. of Churiton Fyztpayn in our diocese, and Richard de Wykeslond B.L.L., V. of Colyton &c. At Sarum.

Commission to the Chancellor of Oxford to visit the College or Hall of Stapeldon Hall, 12 *Nov.* 1420.

To Edmund (Lacy) Bishop of Exeter, Walter Trengof Chancellor of the University of Oxford. We have received your commission to this purport. Edmund Bishop of Exeter to Master Walter Trengof D.D., Chancellor of the University of Oxford, our mother. Since our College needs supervision and reformation, we empower you &c. And as our seal is not at hand we use the seal of the Church of Hereford over which we lately presided. At Wyndsore Castle. On receipt of this commission, I sat on 20 November in the Chapel of S. Thomas in the College, when the Rector, Master Ralph Morewill, showed me a citatory mandate as follows. Although in the Statutes, which you are sworn to observe, it is expressly said that Scholars who are at least Sophists in Arts or at most Bachelors in Arts, born or resident in the diocese of Exeter, are eligible to the College, yet some of you, in the place of your colleagues lately removed, chose a man from the diocese of Sarum into the place of the first who was a

Devonshire fellow, though there are many sufficient scholars in the
University from the diocese of Exeter, and into the place of the
second, who was from Cornwall, a Master of Arts actually regent, to
the injury of the men of our diocese, who have nothing open to them
anywhere else in the University; hence we forbid such proceedings
for the future, and cite you all to appear before Master Walter
Trengof D.D., lately a fellow, whom we have deputed to act as our
Commissary on 20 November. And we send you this privately,
to avoid scandal, trusting to your prudence and obedience. At
Wyndesore Castle 20 November. On the reading of this mandate
Masters Ralph Morewill, Rector, William Andrew, John Brent,
Walter Davy, John Beaucomb, William Certyn; and Edmund Fychet,
William Collys, John Colyford, William Palmer, Bachelors of Arts;
Robert Stonard Chaplain, Walter Lyard and John Arundel, Sophists;
Scholars of the College, swore to yield canonical obedience to you and
your successors, and were examined by us singly and secretly, after
which we adjourned matters to 23 November. On that day John
Burwyk and Thomas Gourde, Scholars elected in the interim, swore
to canonical obedience in like manner; and we charged them to
abstain from such acts in the future, and suspended Walter Lyard
from commons for disobedience, after which we adjourned matters to
30 November and then again to 2 December, when we suspended
Masters William Andrew, John Brent, John Beaucomb; John Colyford
B.A.; Robert Stonard, chaplain, and Walter Lyard sophist, from
commons for five weeks, because of their naming for election Master
Thomas Bony, and Simon Row who was only resident in the diocese.
At Oxford 15 December.

Citation of Fellows, 20 *June* 1439.

At Bishop's Tawton. Edmund (Lacy) bishop of Exeter, patron
founder and ordinary of the College of Exeter or Hall of Stapuldon
Hall, to Master John Row, Rector. We hear that although Richard
Frensch of our diocese, a man of knowledge and character and poor,
was elected by the saner and senior fellows, and his election was
confirmed by M. John Carpenter the Chancellor of Oxford because
only a few fellows had voted for Richard Bokeler, nevertheless some
Masters, John Bulsey, Richard Bele, John Westlake, John Godeswayn;

and John Evelyng, William Sende, William Balam, John Andrew, Bachelors of Arts, hinder the said Richard from enjoying his election. We therefore command you to cite them to appear before us in the Chapel at our manor of Chuddelegh on Thursday after the feast of S. Anne, the mother of Mary.

Commission to visit the College or Hall of Stapeldon, 2 Oct. 1439.

Edmund (Lacy) to Master William Palmer, Precentor of Criditon &c. At Radeway.

Letter for reforming Stapeldon Hall, 19 *Nov.* 1442.

Edmund (Lacy) to Master Roger Keys, canon of Exeter, L.L.B., William Palmer, Precentor of Criditon, and John Rigge, Treasurer of Criditon, Scholars of Theology. Although the fellows elected John Bulsey Rector, being then quite competent, yet he has since become so ill and frantic that he cannot fulfill his duties. We therefore empower you to remove him from his office, which is only annual, and see that the fellows elect another Rector. At Chuddelegh.

Commission to reform the crimes and faults of the Rector and Scholars of Exeter College, 16 *Ap.* 1453.

Edmund (Lacy) to Master William Palmer, Precentor of Criditon, scholar of Theology. We empower you to visit the College, and correct all crimes and faults of the Rector, Fellows, and servants. At Chuddelegh.

Letter of Enquiry by Bishop Clagett, 28 *Oct.* 1742.

Good Mr. Dean,

It was signified to me some time ago by the Rector of Exeter College, that, in pursuance of the Powers given by an Act of Parliament made in the 7th year of the late King, the Rector and Fellows of Exeter had thoughts of selling a small Parcel of their Estate to Jesus College in your University ; to make which sale good and effectual the Act requires the Consent and Approbation of the Visitor.

The following is the description of the Parcel to be sold, as it stands in the lease now in being, whereby it is at this time leased out to Jesus College, and as it has been communicated to me by the Rector of Exeter.

· All that their piece of ground, scituate lying and being in the parish of St. Michael's in the city of Oxford, containing in length from North to South 72 feet, and in breadth from East to West 30 feet, on which lately stood two tenements, now pulled down by the said Principal and Scholars, by the consent of the said Rector and Scholars, to new build. And also all that piece of ground, being one hundred and five feet in all, at the North end of the said piece of ground next the street, being 30 feet long the whole Breadth of the said Demised Premises only and four feet deep at the East end thereof and three feet at the West end, which was lately granted or agreed to be granted to the late Principal and Scholars from the City of Oxford (with other Grounds), on which ground against Exeter College Lane the said Principal and Scholars of Jesus College intend to build and lay to the ground belonging to Exeter College ; together with all Buildings thereon erecting and all ways and passages thereunto belonging or used or enjoyed therewith, with their and every of their Appurtenances, which said first mentioned Premises were lately granted to the said Principal and Scholars by the name of all that their messuage heretofore a stable, &c.'

This is the description of the Estate proposed to be sold. In order to obtain further Information concerning it, I had once thoughts of sending a Commission of Enquiry by way of Request to seven or eight Gentlemen at Oxford, but because I am willing to give trouble to as few persons as possible, and because the opinions of a friend or two will give me Full and Entire Satisfaction in this matter, I chose to desire the Favour of Yourself and Mr. Prolocutor (to whom you will be so kind as to give my Service) to let me know your sentiments in Answer to the Two Enquiries Annexed to this Letter. If Mr. Dean of Exeter be now in Oxford, he also, I dare say, will very readily let me have his Sentiments about this affair. Should he be absent, I shall entirely acquiesce in whatever shall be Mr. Prolocutor's Judgment and Yours.

I do not find by Mr. Rector's Letters to me that the Affair is Pressing. I shall be obliged to you if you will let me have your Sentiments at your Leisure. I am, Good Mr. Dean

Your very loving brother and humble servant

N. Exon.

Queen's Square near the Park,
　　Westminster, Oct. 28, 1742.

The Enquiries you will find in the next Leaf.

Qu. 1. Will the selling the Estate above Described be anyway Prejudicial to Exeter College?

Qu. 2. What will be a Reasonable Price (All Circumstances considered) for Exeter College to Demand for the said Estate?

[Whitehall or Leadenhall was sold to Jesus 1821 for £400, Reg. 9 May 1821, and 1845, Wood's *Fasti* 61, Wood's *City*, i. 68, Jesus Statutes 81.]

The Wiclifite movement largely influenced Exeter; its history has been written by John Lewis, a member of the College. In 1382 an assembly of divines censured Wiclif's doctrines, and strong measures were taken by the Archbishop and the bishops against the Wiclifites at Oxford. William Serche the chaplain of the College was removed in 1384 (the year of Wiclif's death) by the Archbishop, who appointed William Talkarn in his place 8 Dec. 1384: Serche however was presented by Richard II to the rectory of West Tilbury in Essex [1] 22 Aug. 1392 and held it till 1408. Did this arise from the favour shown in the royal household to the new views; or had Serche, like so many others, altered his views? One of the Archbishop's commissaries in Serche's case was John de Landreyn, once fellow of Exeter and then of Oriel, who had joined in condemning the Wiclifite doctrines, in 1381. Another, Robert de Tresilian [2] was one of King Richard's strongest supporters and was executed when the king lost power. His fate is the first legend in William Baldwin's *Mirror for Magistrates*, 1559 (*Athenae* i. 341). Thomas Turke, who became fellow this same year 1384, abjured for heresy later on. William de Polmorva had been named fellow of Queen's by the founder of that College [3], and several fellows of Exeter became fellows of Queen's afterwards, viz. Henry Whitefield the provost, Robert Blakedon, William Middleworthy, John Trevisa, William Franke, Robert Lydeford; and these were expelled in 1379 by the Archbishop of York the Visitor. Thomas Swyndon another fellow of Exeter was one of the Commissioners appointed in 1380 to enquire into the troubles at

---

[1] Newcourt ii. 598: the name Serche is very rare.

[2] Rymer iv. 39 (1378), Rogers ii. 616, 34 D. K. Rec. p. 20 (petition of W. Brydport), Warton's *Literature* ed. Hazlitt iv. 165.

[3] Queen's College Statutes, p. 7. For the expelled fellows see Rymer vii. p. 125.

Queen's, and Richard Browne was at Queen's 1386–9. Others became fellows of Merton, such as (not to mention William Read, afterwards bishop of Chichester) Thomas de Brightwell who was professor of divinity there and suffered much from Archbishop Courtenay (Lewis' *Wiclif* 126); Richard Pester who was of three societies successively, Exeter, University and Merton[1]; and Robert Rygge who was repeatedly Chancellor of the University, but was removed in May 1388 when Thomas de Brightwell succeeded, and so again in 1391 when Ralph Redruth[2] succeeded, both of these being also fellows of Exeter. The second and fourth Principals of Hart Hall were fellows of Merton and, as well as the third, became Wardens of New College. Rygge however joined in condemning the Wyclifite doctrines, and it is possible that he belonged to the party which was rather concerned to uphold the independence of the University against the Archbishop's claim to the right of Visitation[3] than to maintain Wiclifism in its entirety; Benedict Brente opposed the Visitation in 1411 and was imprisoned in the Tower (Gutch i. 547–50, iii. App. p. 39, Anstey 250–1). Bishop Brantingham in 1382 sent out the following mandate[4] against Laurence Stevine or Bedeman, who had been preaching in Cornwall[5].

[1] Gutch iii, *Fasti* p. 30; Hist. Comm. v. 477; Huber i. 157, 159. Men passed somewhat freely from one college to another. Thus Exeter contributed three fellows to Oriel, Henry Kaylle 1421, Walter Libert 1425 and John Halse 1427, who became Provosts of Oriel and the last two bishops.

[2] Wilkins' *Concilia* iii. 160, 168 Bedeman or Stephyn, 190 N. Braybroke, 159 Brightwell, 190 Cheyne, 227 Hendyman, 170 Lawndryne, 164 J. Lydeford, 159–60, 166, 168, 171 Rygge, 164 J. Shillingford, 172 R. Snetisham: Richard Snetisham (not Suetisham, see John Snetisham in Brodrick 230), chancellor of Exeter 12 Ap. 1410, d. Dec. 1415. Computus winter 1416 '6½d offered by the fellows on the day of the obit of M. Richard Snetysham once chancellor of Exeter': Tanner 680, *Eccl. Ant.* ii. 143. Lewis' *Wiclif* 370, Wilkins' *Concilia* ii. 172. Grandisson's Reg. writes the name with an *n*, and there is a place Snetisham. In a list of Inquisitors of heresies temp. Henry IV he is spelt Snedisham. See F. D. Mathews' *English Works of Wyclif* pp. iii, xiv Wyclif lodged at Black Hall, xxviii Rigge, xxix Bedeman (traffic in indulgences), xxxix pluralism, xlviii friars, xlix taxes and tallies.

[3] Stubbs' *Constitutional History* iii. 63, 66; Gutch i. 422, 492, 503, 530, 582, iii. *Fasti* pp. 31–3. Thomas Hendeman, when Chancellor, protested against the action of the Archbishop and a Provincial Synod Feb. 1397: Wilkins' *Concilia* iii. 229, cited in Lyte c. xi, Nat. Biog. v. Richard Courtenay p. 341.

[4] The Latin was printed in ed. i. p. 270: see Oliver's *Bishops* 89, Hist. Comm. ii. 129.

[5] John Ball in his confession named John Aston, Nicolas Hereford and Laurence Bedeman as the leaders of Wiclif's party, Nat. Biog. ii. 210.

f

'Thomas &c. to his beloved sons the religious men the Priors of Launceston and Bodmin and to friar Benedict Lugans, S. T. P., Provost of our church of the blessed Thomas the Martyr of Glasney and to the official of our peculiar jurisdiction in Cornwall and to the Perpetual Vicar of S. Probus greeting. Whereas the Reverend father in Christ, William by the grace of God Archbishop of Canterbury Primate of all England and Legate of the Apostolic See in England, and certain of his suffragan bishops, of which number we were, in fit and congruous place assembled, with unanimous consent had providently ordained ..., that the several suffragans of the Province of Canterbury in their dioceses should inquire and cause to be inquired with due solicitude concerning heretic depravity; and it has lately come to our ears that a certain Laurence Bedeman, who goeth in sheep's clothing, having entered our fold secretly with fraud and stealthily under the feigned image of holiness, with foxlike craft endeavours in his public and private discourses to turn aside our sheep and to lead them into various heresies and serious errors, therefore being desirous to chase away such fox from our fold lest he worry our sheep, we commission and firmly enjoin you that you under our authority carefully inquire where and what things the aforesaid Laurence, whether in churches or in other places in Cornwall, and on what feast times or days the aforesaid Laurence may have preached, propounded, said or proffered to our sons and subjects; and also generally of all and singular within the parts of Cornwall anywhere dwelling, of whatever condition or state or honour they may be, who think of the Catholic faith and of its articles otherwise than they should; and what by your inquiry you shall find you shall certify to us by the feast of S. Michael the Archangel, wheresoever we may be in our diocese, by your letters patent containing the series of these things, and also what things and what sort of things the aforesaid false prophet Laurence or any other may have preached against the Catholic faith and the articles thereof; and stating clearly the names also and surnames of all and singular who may have fallen into heresies of this kind, or errors, and their sayings or statements: citing moreover the said Laurence to appear before us at our manor of Clyst on Thursday next after the Feast of the Exaltation of holy Cross, to make a personal statement on these matters and objections to be made to him about them, for due correction of his soul, and to swear for the future . . .' But Stevine afterwards conformed and became Rector of Lifton.

There was a close connection between Exeter and Merton during the Wiclifite period. Walter de Merton had established a college of secular students, who were to be deprived if they took any monastic vows. Hence they sympathised with Wiclif the great enemy of the monks and friars. Lincoln, on the other hand, was founded 1427 in order to supply a perpetual succession of enemies to Wiclif's doctrines, for Richard Fleming bishop of Lincoln had once been a follower of the reformer and now hated him and his memory and his associates[1].

A friendly relation was kept up between Exeter College and Canterbury hall even after Wiclif's time, for in Lent 1448 we have '7d for oblations on the day of the burial of the Warden of the College of Canterbury.' This however may have been only an ordinary act of friendship between Colleges, for in autumn 1471 there occurs '2d offered at Merton at the mass for the Warden[2].' Among the receipts for Lent 1556 occurs '10d for the oblations of those of Magdalen, 12d for the oblations of the fellows of Balliol College commonly called Baylie College.' Exeter used to offer in return at Balliol[3]: 1392 '7d to the fellows offering at Balliol hall on S. Katherine's day,' 1393 '4d to the fellows to offer at Merton at S. John Baptist's feast, 6d for the fellows offering at New College.'

Oxford took a deep interest in the healing of the Forty Years' Schism. Henry Whitefield[4] had managed some college business at Avignon in the winter of 1363, and Thomas White had been sent to the Roman Court in 1376 'pro nostre domus perpetuacione' (see computus of winter 1377), just when that court was returning from Avignon to Rome. In 139⅜ a meeting was held at Oxford about

---

[1] Winter 1408 'vis viiid a M. Ricardo Flymyng in finalem solucionem pencionis scolarum ubi scannum, pro anno ultimo elapso'; Lent 1431 'iiid oblatis pro episcopo Linc.'; Lent 1434 'vd oblatis in die obitus Rectoris Collegii Lincoln.'

[2] Sever: summer 1425 'xs a M. H. Sever pro scolis suis.'

[3] Balliol Statutes p. 14; Balliofergus p. 19; *Early Balliol* by Mrs. de Paravicini 293; on S. Catherine's chapel in Balliol, see Peshall 224.

[4] For an interesting account of a journey to Avignon by John de Middelton in 1331, see Rogers i. 135, ii. 631. The journey from Calais to Avignon took exactly a month. The currency was changed thrice on the road, and the payments at the Curia Romana were made in gold.

the General Council, Gutch i. 534, 544. In the winter of 1408 we
hear of '17d to the ambassadors elected for Union in the Church of
God[1].' Robert Hallam, bishop of Salisbury, who died at the Council
of Constance, had been several times at the College, perhaps on this
errand. In 1399 an entry occurs '3s 4d for bread cheese and wine
for M. Robert Halome,' and again in summer 1402 '5s 8d about
M. Robert Halum.' The visits of Cardinals[2] to England are
mentioned several times: autumn 1357 'for Cardinals' procurations[3]
8s 4d and for the seal of acquittance and labour in the reception 8d';
Lent 1358 '36s 10½d to M. William Stikelyng when he went to
Sarum to get a relaxation of the sentence issued on account of
non-payment of Cardinals' procurations, for the expenses of John Hall
when he was away from the city for two days to consult M. de
Stykeling on this business and for horse hire the same time 22d';
summer 1363 '25s for Cardinals' procurations for three years for the
parish church of West Wittenham, 25s for contumacy in paying the
procurations too slowly, 12s for the expenses of the Rector and one
servant and one horse when the Rector was at Schereborn with the
bishop on this business, 2s for a horse hired on this business, 3d for
mending the servant's shoes (socularum)'; Lent 1375 '18d for
Cardinal's subsidy'; summer 1375 '6d for Cardinal's subsidy'; winter
1375 '12d to the Cardinal of England for the indulgence *a pena et
a culpa*'; Lent 1370 '11s to the lord Pope for tenths'; winter 1377
'4s 5½d for an instrument to excuse us as regards the collector of
the lord Pope, and parchment, and the seal of the Dean of Christianity'
(at Exeter?); summer 1378 '18d to the Pope for each mark, 6d for
three acquittances'; autumn 1398 '21½d for the expenses of a Legate
of the lord Pope[4].'

[1] Rogers iii. 675-6 the clergy paid 4d in the pound to their ambassador at the
Curia Romana, pro Unione &c. in 1407; Peterhouse paid 7d to cost of General
Council, and clergy 2d in the pound, a clerk in Convocation received ¾d in the
pound.

[2] Rogers i. 162; Stubbs' *Constitutional History* iii. 300, and the index p. 648
list of taxes.

[3] Procurations (or proxies), the Case of, by J. Colbatch, Cambridge 1741.
Synodals were a sort of acknowledgement of holding a benefice of the See;
procurations for the expense of visitations, and originally meant provisions,
a meal's meat, a night's lodging, &c., being paid in kind, Nat. Biog. xii. 346.

[4] Taxes to the King occur about the same time: Lent 1374 '16s 8d for the
tenths granted the King and for an acquittance 2d,' so again in summer 1374 and

Henry IV was displeased with the University in 1411, and Prince
Henry defended its liberties. Benedict Brente, fellow of Exeter, was
one of the proctors who were compelled to resign on this occasion,
and committed to the Tower. As soon however as the University
could assert its liberty they were re-elected.

Several members of the College were connected with the House of
Lancaster. William Palmer was physician to Margaret of Anjou,
Walter Lihert her confessor, and promoted by Margaret Beaufort;
John Arundel was physician to Henry VI, John Stanbury his con-
fessor. Thomas Wallebene and Robert Gilbert were with Henry V in
France. Michael Tregury was chaplain to Henry V, and was made by

Lent 1375; summer 1380 '22s 2½d for the subsidy granted the King by the clergy,
and for the portion of the prior of Longa Villa 10s'; summer 1381 '6s 1d to the
abbot of Radyngs collector of the King's subsidy in the archdeaconries of Berks
and Wyltes, granted at Norhamton, for the acquittance 2d'; autumn 1383 ' 16s 3d
for the second half of a tenth granted the King, and for the portion of the Prior of
Longa Villa...'; winter 1385 '16s 2d to the abbot of Malmysbure for the tenths
of the King from Wyttenham'; Lent 1386 '16s 3d to the King for half a tenth from
our church of Wyttenham, and for the acquittance, 4s 5d for expenses to a proctor
in Parlyament'; summer 1387 '16s 1¼d to the abbot of Radyngs for the tenths
granted the King in the last Parliament, 2d for an acquittance,' summer 1388
'16s 4d to Robert de Abyndon for (half) a tenth granted the King in the last
Parlyament,' summer 1389 '16s 3d for tenths granted the King in the last Parlyament, 2d for an acquittance.' A tenth on Wittenham was 32s 2d, winter 1416, and
we hear of a tenth and a half in Lent 1417; in Lent 1378 4l [? 3l] 4s 10½d is
charged for two tenths. The King's tenths are first mentioned Lent 1357 '1½d for
Cleter's breakfast when he came from Malmesbury with an acquittance for the
King's tenths.' In summer 1459 there is a mention of Queen's gold, '12d to
M. John Wynterborn public notary for his labour in framing two *literas procura-*
torias for the College; for carrying the two letters committed to M. Gosse
to London twice for making an enquiry about a sum in the King's exchequer for
Queen's gold...; 26s 8d to John Croke receiver for Margaret Queen of England on
account of a fine of twenty marks long ago made with the King for the purchase of
lands &c. as is shewn in our letters patent; to John Wylyam our manciple for his
expenses going to Coventry on college business and returning 20s.' At this time
the Court was at Coventry preparing for the civil war, and Margaret must have
been making every effort to procure money. Queen's gold * meant a mark
of gold paid to the Queen for every hundred marks of silver paid to the King
in the way of fine or other feudal incident, and, even if not recognisable in Domesday, is probably as old as the reign of Henry I. The proportion of gold to silver
was one to ten † in the early times, and possibly this proportion was maintained
in calculating Queen's gold. A general payment is mentioned Lent 1405 '4s 2d
to the King for the rateable proportion of our rents as other Collegers paid.'

* Stubbs' *Constitutional History* i. 342, ii. 218, Coxe No. cvi.
† Rogers i. 172, 173, 177.

Henry VI Rector of the University of Caen 1431 (he had taught there in 1418) during the English rule in Normandy, when Paris remonstrated with Oxford on the unkindness of setting up a rival University against the mother University of Europe (Lyte c. 12). It may have been this connection with the royal family that induced Henry V's executors (one of whom was Edmund Lacy bishop of Exeter) to give the College 50s 8d in winter 1424, and Cardinal Beaufort's executors a larger sum[1]. The interest in the French war is shown by such entries as winter 1428 '6d oblation for the Earl of Salisbury,' killed at the siege of Orleans. The pressure of the war is seen in such entries as winter 1433 '16s 8d for 19 bushels of corn taken for the king'; sometimes it was necessary to conciliate the king's officers, summer 1438 '20d gift to the officer who takes corn for the king.' John Hancock was Warden of the College at Ottery when Henry VI visited it in 1452. Sir John Fortescue of Exeter College accompanied Queen Margaret in her exile and wrote his book *De Laudibus Legum Angliae* for prince Edward. In Lent 1447 'iiiid oblatis in die obitus domini Ducis Glowcestre.' When Peter Courtenay, bishop of Exeter, returned from exile with Henry VII, the College presented him (winter 1485) with 5 yards of *Crymosen de grano*, which cost £3 6s 8d (Oliver's *Bishops* 111, W. Antiq. i. 144). William Weye was connected with Henry VI's foundation at Eton, and had special leave from the King to make pilgrimages to Compostella and Jerusalem; and his 'Itineraries' contain curious matter; some of the notices are naive enough, such as that where we say

[1] Winter 1447 'viiid Pencaer pro literis et bull. conceptis et directis certis dominis pro bonis quibusdam habendis domini Cardinalis (Beaufort) nuper Winton. Episcopi'; Lent 1448 'xls de bonis Cardinalis per viam mutui'; 'xd pro vino dato Priori domus Cartusie uni executorum bonorum domini Cardinalis nuper defuncti'; 'xvd pro cirothecis datis M. Stephano Wilton [archdeacon of Winchester, see Cassan's *Bishops of Winchester* 258] uni executorum domini Cardinalis'; 'xvis id ob pro expensis Rectoris in adquisicione quinquaginta marcarum de dono executorum domini Cardinalis'; 'pro conductione equorum ab Oxon. Londoniam iiis iiiid'; 'vs iiiid pro conductione equorum a Lond. ad Oxon.'; summer 1448 'xxs de bonis domini Cardinalis'; 'viiilib xiiis iiiid de bonis domini Cardinalis defuncti'; Lent 1450 'xls de bonis domini Cardinalis per viam mutui'; summer 1450 'xls comuni ciste ad satisfaciendum eidem de tanta summa extracta de bonis domini Cardinalis ad usum domus'; Lent 1451 'xilib vs de bonis domini Cardinalis per viam mutui'; summer 1451 'xls de bonis domini Cardinalis per viam mutui'; autumn 1451 'xiilib xvs comuni ciste ad satisfaciendum eidem de tanta summa extracta de bonis domini Cardinalis ad usum domus.'

Good Day the Greeks say Kally Merry; is it possible that Weye did not know the classical Greek words?

But now the study of the Classics had begun to replace that of the Scholastic Logic, a change which formed the basis of the modern system of education, and which gave tone and form to European literature[1]. The Grammar Schools, i.e. Schools of Latin, had much influence in developing a classical English prose. The degrees had long been a fiction—no one had been rejected at Paris from 1395 to 1500. Gascoigne p. 3 complains of degrees being given at Oxford to ignorant and vicious persons through the frequent dispensations from statutes granted for money by the Regent Masters and Proctors. Both Universities had declined under Edward IV. Sir Thomas Elyot was not at either (*Life* ed. Croft p. xxxvii). In 1535 the students were ordered to attend the new classical lectures at Merton[2]. Only Latin had been required from the clergy, or in fact from any one. Amoretto, in the *Return from Parnassus* pp. 25, 43, has been at Cambridge, but knows no Greek.

Englishmen had been attracted to Italy by the spell of that new knowledge, which was also the old. There alone were Greek manuscripts and Greek teachers to be found. There each fresh manuscript was a sacred possession, for what treasures of wisdom might it not

---

[1] Revue des Deux Mondes Dec. 1882; Palgrave in *Nineteenth Century* Nov. 1890; Earle's *English Prose* c. 12; two books of Euclid were read at Oxford in the 15th century, Churton's *Life of Smyth* 151; Hallam *Lit. of Europe* ed. 3, i. 114.

[2] After 1491, Wood's *Athenae* i. 30, 260, Tanner 345, *Collectanea* (O.H.S.) ii. 340, Gutch i. 639, ii. 75, iii. 430, *Oxoniana* iv. 13, Gairdner's *Richard III* p. 143, Gutch's *Collectanea* i. 187, Brodrick 44. Winter 1537 '2s 4d pro stipendio D. Smyth'; autumn 1538 '2s 4d pro lectura doctoris Smyth'; summer 1543 'iiis iiiid doctori Cots pro lectione sua debitis in festo Pasche ultimo'; autumn 1543 'iis iiiid doctori Brode pro lectione sua'; winter 1548 'iis iiiid M. Warde pro lectura philosophica'; winter 1551 'viiid Marbecke pro pulsanda campana ad lecturam theologicam'; Ridley was paid 6s 8d for Greek lectures at Cambridge 1536 from Annunciacion to S. John the Baptist, and again 14s; Rogers iii. 682–3. Lent 1491 'vid pro meremio ad defendendum aquam a muro inter M. Brew et Grosyn'; winter 1491 'xiis a M. Groysine pro 3^bus terminis camere sue'; summer 1492 'xvis a M. Grosyne pro annali reditu camere sue nobis debitis in festo Michaelis proximo futuro'; winter 1492 'iiiis a M. Grosune pro camera sua pro isto termino'; autumn 1493 'viiis a M. Grosun pro duobus terminis cubiculi sui nobis debitis in festo Johannis ultimo'; summer 1519 'xxiiid pro vino dato Doctori Colett 2^bus vicibus (Colet d. 16 Sep. 1519, *Athenae* i. 26). W. B. Gilbert's *All Saints, Maidstone* 51–5. Hallam *Lit. of Europe* ed. 3, i. 231.

contain. There the chains fell off their limbs, and they felt themselves freed once and for ever from that barbarous scholastic system, which claimed authority over all knowledge :

> ' Once remotest nations came
> To adore that sacred flame,
> When it lit not many a hearth
> On this cold and gloomy earth.'

These men returned to make their discoveries known to their country-men, to their fellow-students in the Universities.

Exeter College is favourably known in connection with these men. William Grocyn taught Greek in the College Hall, and Richard Croke sojourned in the College for some time. We find the College twice entertaining Grocyn's friend Dean Colet. The Cornelius mentioned several times in the Computi was probably Cornelius Vitelli [1], a learned Italian who taught Greek in the University, Lent 1491 '6d for a new lock for the door of the fuel-house of Cornelius, and 3d for a key to his study, 5d for mending the books Pantelon' [p. xxxvii]; summer 1491 '3s 6d to a mason for work on the chambers of M. Brew and Cornelius'; autumn 1491 '2s to one working at the chimney of Cornelius for three days, and one day at our inn'; Lent 1492 '20s received from Cornelius for his chamber for a year and a term'; summer 1492 '4s from Cornelius for his chamber last term and 6d for his log-house for last term . . . 16s from M. Grosyne for a year's rent of his chamber due next Michaelmas.' John Skewys [2], Wolsey's trusted agent, was probably a member of the College, and Richard Duck one of the fellows was Wolsey's chaplain in 1517 and proctor for Salisbury in the memorable Convocation of 1529. Philip Bale,

---

[1] Gutch i. 208, 645, Tanner 378, Mullinger 370.

[2] Autumn 1525 'xiid pro indenturis factis inter nos et Universitatem pro quadam portiuncula terre iuxta Aulam Cervinam'; winter 1525 'viiid pro vino dato M. Skewys, vis Collegio Cardinalicio pro annali redditu' (but Lent 1538 '6s Porrett pro superiori reddita debito Collegio Regio Henrici 8ᵗ'); summer 1526 'xiiiid pro cerotecis datis M. Scuys et uxori eius'; Lent 1528 'xviiid pro cirothecis pellitis datis M. doctori Smyth et M. Skewys, xiiid pro vino et ceteris rebus datis M. Lubkyns, M. Wylson, et M. Wylliams Collegii Cardinalis supervisoribus'; winter 1531 'xd pro pare cerotecarum pro M. Skewse' [p. xxiv] ; H. R. 10 Eliz. rotulo cvi (Statutes 3, App. p. 99) 'Rectore et scholaribus tenentibus unius gardini in Cat Street, nuper in tenura Roberti Wryghte, nuper collegio vocato King Henry Theights Colledge dudum spectantis, de fidelitate proinde Reginae nunc facienda exonerandis.'

another fellow, bequeathed to the college 'the works of S. Augustyn, S. Ambrose, Origyn, S. Jerom, and certain books of Bede, and works of S. Gregorye, with other such books as my overseer shall think meyt.' This shows the revival of study. John Dotyn was a 'medicus ac astrologus insignis.' Thomas Harding of New College, afterwards famous as Bishop Jewel's opponent, had a pupil in the College.

The Customs of the College as written down 20 Dec. 1539 illustrate the state of things ; they are as follows [1] :—

Old customs, handed down by men now eighty years old, from still older times. Some of the older ones have a hand drawn against them in the margin (9 and 10).

1. The Statutes order the fellows to wear black boots or of some colour akin to it; and priestly dress, i.e. plain shirts, not parted down to the navel, nor with lappets hanging down like promontories, nor plaits round the neck like courtiers.

2. Bachelors and scholars (*scholastici*) coming to the House of God should avoid all noise, stories, bad manners; let them give themselves to prayer, not to books of profane literature, and uncover their heads during service, and stand up to sing *Magnificat, Nunc dimittis, Te Deum, Benedictus,* but kneel at the *Kyrieleson.*

3. The two junior fellows should alternately guide the singing of the psalms, and the junior should open and arrange the books and, after service, close them and put them back ; and, with the bible clerk, deck the altars with a richer covering on solemn feasts, and take it off towards evening; and read the Epistle at masses for the dead.

4. Now, since most Masters are in holy orders and prevented by various causes, besides the consecration of the Lord's Body, from being in the choir at the beginning of matins and vespers, we exhort the bachelors to come early and be present when the bell stops, lest waiting for them should prevent the chaplain from celebrating mass and cause others not to celebrate or to go away.

5. Bachelors should frequent the public musaeum or library and, after the octaves of S. Dennis, stay there every night from 6 to 8, studying good books, especially of logic and philosophy, unless the Rector thinks good to intermit it owing to excessive cold, or relax it

[1] The Latin is printed in ed. i. p. 182.

to refresh their minds; and they shall observe this rule to Sexagesima, and this shall hold also of the longer disputations.

6. Bachelors should accustom themselves to public lectures and sophisms, either at Harthall, or any other place they may prefer.

7. All fellows leading the life of scholars, that they may the sooner acquire learning, according to Walter Stapeldon's statutes, should attend public lectures at Harthall; and, since logic lectures profit little unless there is constant practice in disputations, they should attend the Sophisms and Variations kept up there with such care, and if they do not, the Principal or his deputy shall punish them, and report defaulters to the Rector for severer chastisement. The same holds of the battellars.

8. Bachelors should not be too familiar with Masters and should respect their higher degree. If any bachelor shares the Rector's dish at dinner or supper, let him eat with his head uncovered.

9. The Rector and fellows feed those in the prison once a week at an expense of $4d$, on such food as will feed many of them.

10. Old fellows are entertained thrice at the College expense by the Rector or his deputy.

11. No one is to rise from dinner till the Rector has said Grace, except for good cause, approved by the Rector.

12. No one is to enter the buttery or take anything, without the presence and leave of the Bookkeeper, Bible-clerk or Manciple.

13. Scholars are to walk about with uncovered heads within the Academy, until they are bachelors and have determined in Lent.

14. Every fellow is to wear the dress of his degree at sermons in S. Mary's and at theological disputations.

15. Bachelors should have gowns reaching down to the knees, till they take their Master's degree.

The College as a whole sided with the opposition to Henry VIII's measures, as did the West of England, from which so many of its members came. John Moreman in particular, Vicar of Menheniot, was an opponent of Queen Catherine's divorce, and was imprisoned in Edward VI's reign. One demand of the Cornish insurgents in 1549 runs thus, 'We will have Dr. Moreman and Dr. Crispin, which hold our opinions, to be safely sent unto us, and to them we require the King's Majesty to give some certain livings to preach among us our Catholic faith.' Moreman was distinguished in the Convocation of 1553. He was also famous in the west as a schoolmaster. John Hooker of Exeter, the antiquary, was brought up under him and praises the goodness of his disposition. At his living of Menheniot he taught the Creed, Lord's Prayer, and Commandments in English, the people hitherto using only the Cornish language. This was probably in obedience to Cromwell's Injunctions of 1536 'to cause their people to learn the Creed, the Lord's Prayer and the Ten Commandments in the vulgar tongue, and to give them plain instructions upon these,' and the similar Injunctions of 1538 and 1547[1]. Cornish plays were still acted in regular amphitheatres, of which there are even now some remains at S. Just near the Land's End and at Perranzabulo. These plays[2] were probably written by ecclesiastics, and the names of places mentioned in them seem to point to the monastery of Glasney near Penryn (founded by Walter Bronescombe bishop of Exeter 1264–7 for thirteen canons and thirteen vicars) as the place where most of the writers resided. John de Landreyn fellow of Exeter was canon of Glasney 1376, William Noe canon 1413; Walter Trengoff was Provost of Glasney 1427–36, and Michael Trewynard and John Evelyn Provosts later on in the century. These University men may have had something to do with the composition of these dramas, in which more art is used in continuing the series of events than we find in the Townley, Chester, and Coventry Mysteries, the contemporary English collections. Norden, writing about 1584, says that 'of late the Cornishe men have much conformed themselves to the use of the Englishe tongue; from Truro Eastwarde it is in manner wholy Englishe.' But as late as 1640 the aged inhabitants of S. Feock, a church attached to Glasney, required the sacrament to be administered to them in the Cornish tongue, and the formula used for this purpose has been preserved[3]. One of the Cornish dramas written by William Jordan was translated into English 'by Mr. John Keigwin of Mousehole of the Lower House at the request of the right reverend father in God

---

[1] Foxe's *Monuments* a. 1554. Jas. Parker's *Introduction to Prayerbook* p. xxi.

[2] *The Ancient Cornish Drama*, by Edwin Norris, Oxford, 1859; *The Life of Saint Meriasek, a Cornish Drama*, ed. Whitley Stokes, 1872; Bibl. Corn. 280, 281, 629. For plays at Ottery see Oliver's *Monasticon* 261.

[3] Hals in Lake's *Cornwall* ii. p. 3.

Jonathan Lord Bishop of Exon 1697.' Two of the Provosts, John Nans and Alexander Penkyll were successively Rectors of Camborne, and one of the plays is on the subject of S. Meriadoc the patron saint of that parish, where the Saint's Well is still known; the MS. of the play was written in 1504 by 'dominus Hadton' while Nans was Rector and the former Rector Penkyll was Provost.

The Valor Ecclesiasticus of 1535-6 gives the revenues of the College as only £83 2s, out of which the Rector and Chaplain have each £4 4d, thirteen Fellows £3 10s 4d each[1]. In 1522 a forced

---

[1] The receipts were, 'from Menheniot £20, Gwinear £26 13s 4d, Long Wittenham £26 (but 14s are deducted), house in S. Peter le Baily 13s 4d, in S. Martin's 6s, from Hart Hall 40s, in S. Mary's 20s, from schools 10s, in S. Michael's 4d, in S. Giles £3 8s, in S. Mary Magdalen 20s (but 12s paid to Godstow, 4d to Osney, 6s to Christchurch, to the City 2s, to John Browne 20d, to S. Peter le Baily 12d, are deducted, 23s in all), Rowland Barratt at Bensington 31s. The total is £83 2s. The payments are, to the chaplain 26s 8d, and 52s for his commons; for the exequies of M. Moore 17s, of Fulk Bowcher and Elizabeth his wife 5s, of William Palmer 5s, of Robert Lidford 5s, of Henry Webber 5s, of Roger Keys 5s, of Nicholas Gosse 13s 4d, of Thomas Carewe 5s, of John Polyng 7s 6d, of Cardinal Beaufort 5s 2d, of the Founder 6s, of Bishop Stafford and Richard Graynfield 5s 2d, of John Kyrkham 15s; for daily mass, &c., 52s, to a parish clerk 3s 2d, to the crier for the dead 2s. The total £11 15s, with the previous deductions of 14s and 23s, makes £13 12s. Deducting this from £83 2s we have £69 10s, part of which is thus distributed :—The Rector and Chaplain have each £4 4d, thirteen Fellows £3 10s 4d each—total £53 15s. The Rector and Fellows petition that the present allowances may be continued, viz.: to the barber 10s, laundress 13s 4d, cook 13s 4d, manciple £3 6s 8d, three servientes £5 4s, manciple 34s 8d; in oblations 2s 8d, to the friars 2s 4d, in chapel expenses £3, in cloths and cups &c. 40s, to the Rector 20s, to the Fellows £6 10s—and 50s for visiting their friends; to seneschal and bailiffs, &c. £3 : the total being £30 7s.' Part of these payments came from room rents, &c.

MS. Survey of Exeter College in the time of Henry VIII, Augmentation Books 441 (Record Office : 'Denariis annuatim solutis versus victum i Rectoris et xiiii Sociorum juxta ratam xiid hebdomadatim ex statuto collegii xxxixli; expensis Rectoris et Sociorum super comunas suas, viz. v principalibus festis vocatis *Gawdye dayes* juxta ratam vid Rectori et cuilibet Sociorum xxxviis vid; denariis in emendatione comunarum suarum ex antiqua estimatione vocatis *contributions* per annum lxxs; mensa v famulorum viz. mancipii promi lectoris bibliae coci et subcoci, cuilibet xd septimanatim; decrementum annuatim ratione panis et aliarum rerum caritate accidentium communibus annis per annum vili; stipendia Rectoris xxs, xiii Sociorum cuilibet xs, et xiiiiº Socio vocato *the chapleyn* xxvis viiid; exhibitiones factae Rectori et Sociis in exequiis pro fundatoribus et benefactoribus cviis iiiid; pro missa quotidie celebranda juxta ratam xiid septimanatim; stipendia famulorum mancipio xxvis viiid, coquo xiiis iiiid, barbetonsori xs, lotrici xxs (? xiiis iiiid).'

There was sometimes trouble with the manciple. Reg. 1557 'Hoc anno Gulielmus Paw (Turner 154, 190, nuper economu seu mancipium huius collegii

loan of £40 was levied by Royal Commissioners on the College. Balliol and Queen's paid the same amount; the highest sums were paid by Magdalen and New College, State Papers Henry VIII, iii. No. 24831. In 1536 Exeter paid 4s 8d for tithes and first fruits, Balliol and University 4s 1d each; and so on up to Frideswide 40s 10d, and Magdalen £3 22d (Bodl. MS. F. F. p. 130). In 1524 Nicholas the cook, rated at 20s, paid 4d subsidy to the King, O. H. S. xvi. 69, see Mullinger i. 551.

That the proclamations of 1534 and 1539 about the names of the Pope and of S. Thomas of Canterbury were obeyed is proved by the erasures in the College copy of the *Sarum Breviary*[1] printed by Chevallon and Regnault in 1531 at Paris, one of the six surviving copies.

The College also possesses nine other Sarum books of various kinds. Other Service Books are occasionally mentioned, a Legenda, a Collectarium in the computus of winter 1457 'iiiis pro ligatura de novo et tectura cuiusdam libri Capellae Collectarium comuniter vocati quem librum habuimus a venerabili domino Edmundo Stafford, iiiid More stacionario pro labore suo duobus diebus appreciando

Exon. exhibuit primo coram aliis venerabilibus viris, deinde coram doctore Raynold huius alme Academiae Oxon. Commissario quosdam articulos contra rectorem et socios collegii predicti; In quibus iniustissime petebat precipue hec quatuor. Imprimis iure officii sui deberi sibi panis potus ceterorumque cibariorum emolumenta. Item collegium teneri ad solvendum debita seu batillos sociorum si qui illorum discederent, non solutis debitis. Item collegium teneri ad solvendum communas, decrementa et batillos suggenariorum si qui ipsorum discederent non solutis debitis. Item collegium teneri ad solvendum debita ac battillos batillariorum, si qui ipsorum discederent non solutis debitis. Que omnia ac singula fuisse iniustissima ac falsissima probatum erat coram commissario predicto non solum testimoniis ex hac parte scriptis infranominatorum gravissimorum virorum vz M. Holwell, M. Bale, M. Smith, M. Dotynne, M. Carter, M. Yendall, M. More et M. Vyvian quondam sociorum predicti collegii; verum etiam sententiis ac calculis quorundam juris peritissimorum qui palam idque sepius affirmabant contra omne Jus et equitatem esse; primo ut servus prescriberet dominis suis quid et quantum stipendii ac emolumenti sibi daretur; dein ut universitas aliqua seu collegium teneretur ad solvendum aliorum aut alia debita quam que prescriberentur a fundatore eiusdem collegii et cetera. Nam sic facile ruina ac subversio omnium collegiorum sequeretur. Atque post hanc litem consopitam de hac re, Collegium obtinuit a dicto G. Paw coram Commissario predicto generalem acquietanciam eius Gul. Paw sigillo sigillatam et propria manu subscriptam que in cista communi reponitur.'

[1] *Breviarii Sarum* fasciculus ii. ed. Procter and Wordsworth, Cambridge, 1879, p. vii.

libros collegii qui traduntur in eleccionibus sociorum': an old Porti-
forium of the Use of Hereford, sold in winter 1449 for vi*s* viii*d*:
a. 1466 a Liber Sermonum factus de tempore per circulum anni. The
destruction of Service Books at the time of the Reformation was perhaps not so extensive as is usually supposed. A far more complete
destruction fell on the Protestant Service Books and Bibles in Mary's
reign. The Library has only two copies of Tyndale's New Testament, No. 3 and No. 5 in Mr. Fry's list[1], and of the latter only two
other copies are known.

The notices in the Computi about the changes made in the services
are very curious and interesting : 1547 ' 20*d* for a book of homilies
and the Royal Injunctions, 13*s* 4*d* for the Old and New Testament in
English,' 1548 ' 4*d* for two books of the Administration of the Communion of the Lord's Body and Blood, 5*s* 8*d* for Erasmus' Paraphrases
in English for Long Wytnam,' 1549 ' 13*s* to M. Whetcomb for replac-
ing in the library a book of the Old and New Testament in Latin, 10*s*
for two books of public Prayers issued by the King's order, 3*s* 4*d* to
dominus Capell for twice writing out the King's Injunctions and some
other things for the use of the College, 10*d* for a New Testament for
the use of the Hall (*received* £16 7*s* 1*d* for a cross and pix and other
ornaments used in the Chapel), 4*s* for two books for singing the
psalms in English,' 1550 '(*received* 10*s* from M. Grylls for the old
Chapel Books,) 8*d* for a book of the ordination of bishops, priests and
deacons,' 1551 ' (*received* £5 6*s* 8*d* for the sale of Chapel ornaments,)'
1552 ' 4*s* 6*d* for a book of public Prayers, 20*d* for a book of psalms in
English,' 1553 ' (*received* 5*s* for the sale of organ pipes,)' 1556 ' 30*s* to
M. Thomas Williams for new books for the use of the Chapel, 6*d*
for the consecration of a Superaltar,' 1559 ' 5*s* for a book of public
Prayers, 10*s* for four Psalters, 6*s* 8*d* for a Communion Table,' 1561
' 16*d* for the Ten Commandments and a new Calendar,' 1565 ' 4*s* for
two Psalters for singing in the Chapel,' 1566 ' 5*s* 9*d* for three Psalters.'
In 1550 the Library had been 'purged' of obnoxious books and some
were burnt in the Market place (Gutch ii. 167 ; Hist. Com. ii. 127,
Dixon iii. 109). On 6 Ap. 1560 Elizabeth authorized the Colleges
to use the Latin prayers, which she had directed her printer Wolf to

[1] *Bibliographical Description of the editions of Tyndale's Version* 1878,
pp. 44, 61.

publish[1]. A copy of Nicholas Grimald's *Archiprophela* (printed Cologne 1548), said to be in his own handwriting, small 4to, pp. 42, bought by George II in 1757, in Brit. Mus., Bibl. Reg. 12 A. xlvi, is dated from Exeter College; *N. and Q.* 7. xii. 285, 10 Oct. 1891.

In 1547 a Devonshire fellowship was given to Maurice Ley an Irishman, for Dr. Cox the chief of the Royal Visitors[2] was pressing every College to take one Irish fellow for the benefit of Ireland and to strengthen the English Church there, but Ley soon vacated and the plan seems not to have been further carried out. The annual election of Rectors now came to an end. William More was continued in office by Edward VI's Visitors, but his term of office ceased abruptly at Mary's accession[3], when the Queen's Visitors put a medical fellow, William Corindon, in his place. Some other fellows vacated this same year, such as Richard Tremayne, well known as a preacher, who fled to Germany. In 1554 the Doctors met at Exeter before disputing with Cranmer and Ridley[4]. Men had not yet taken their sides definitely in the great religious strife, and most adhered to the National

---

[1] Clay's *Elizabethan Services*, Parker Soc. 299–434: *Swainson on Advertisements of* 1566 (1880) p. 23.

[2] Lent 1546 'iis pro duobus caponibus datis doctori Coxe, iiis iiiid dono dato scribis seu clericis eiusdem magistri doctoris Coxe, viiid pro vino dato M. doctori Coxe, iid M. Commissario pro exaratione literarum domino Regi et aliis pro portione nostra, iid pro papiro, xxvs pro portione nostra doctori Cole receptori ut detur Regis officiariis, ob confirmacionem Collegii nostri'; summer 1548 'iis vid hiis qui Regia potestate visitatum venerunt'; winter 1548 'vs pro expensis M. Vivian proficiscentis ad doctorem Cox in collegii negotio'; summer 1549 'xd pauperculis mundantibus curiam et bibliothecam in adventu legatorum Regis; xxixs iiiid pro vino, sacaro, confectis, marmaladye, et succade datis Regis legatis nomine Collegii; vis viiid pro impensis quæ fiebant convivandis famulis legatorum, xxxs pro impensis legatorum Regiæ maiestatis pro toto quo hic manserunt tempore, vis viiid scribæ legatorum'; autumn 1549 'xvid pro publicis Academie statutis bis scribendis; xxvis Rectori et sociis pro stipendiis auctis per Regiæ maiestatis legatos'; summer 1550 'iiili xiiiis vid sociis, debitis illis vice exequiarum'; autumn 1550 'liis Rectori et sociis, olim debitis celebrantibus'; autumn 1559 'ixs pro ostensione 3 procurationum coram Regiis legatis, iiis viiid pro vino cerevisia et *birra* datis Visitatoribus, iiid pro placentis, xvid pro saccoro, xviiis viiid ad sublevandum sumptus Visitatorum': see Gutch ii. 96, 101; Burrows' *All Souls*, p. 72. Compare the question of admitting Scots at Cambridge, State Papers 17 Jan. 1611.

[3] The Computus of autumn 1553 is in another hand, while the Computus for the next year, Oct. 1553—Oct. 1554, is wanting. The other hand may have been that of the maniple, as he writes *farma* for *firma*, &c.

[4] Gutch ii. 125.

Church, hoping that some moderate compromise would be ultimately possible. The Register says, 28 July 1556, 'John Nele and Thomas Pynche were excused from visiting their friends as probationers were wont to do, because Cardinal Pole the Visitor prohibited any one being absent at the time of his Visitation[1]; they were however to carry out the usual custom next year.' John Fessarde one of the fellows was probably a leading man, as he was appointed by Mary to preach through the diocese of Salisbury during the vacancy of the see. We also hear of William Cholwell 'who (*Fasti* a. 1555), being learned and a zealous man for the Roman Catholic cause, was designed by certain of the Queen's Commissioners, 24 Ap. 1554, to preach concerning various matters which were controverted in Queen Mary's reign.' He was perhaps the 'honest and religious teacher who virtuously trained up many of the best gentlemen's sons of Devon and Cornwall at Thomasine Percival's free school of Week S. Mary (Carew's *Cornwall*, ed. 1810, p. 282). But in Elizabeth's time the state of things altered, the Council of Trent made compromise impossible. John Neale, the first perpetual Rector was deprived by the Queen's Visitors for refusing to appear at service in the Chapel. In 1570 William Wyot was imprisoned in the Castle, and in Bokardo from 10 Jan. to Good Friday, for refusing to declare what Papists he knew to be in the College[2]. Romanism was still strong in Devon and Cornwall, whence so many of the members of the College came. In 1579 Strype[3] reports that at the Visitation of 1578–9 'in Exeter College of eighty were found but four obedient subjects, all the rest secret or open Roman affectionaries, and particularly one Savage of that house, a most earnest defender of the Pope's bull and excommunication of the Queen. These were chiefly such as came out of the western parts, where popery greatly prevailed and the gentry bred up in that religion.' Thomas Percy, afterwards one of the conspirators in the Gunpowder plot, was sojourning in the College 5 June 1579, 'not then of lawful age to take an oath.' Robert Yendall, Vicar of the College living of Menheniot, was one of those who abandoned their livings in 1559. He 'fled from the river of Exemouth to Morlaix in Brittany. Smart,

---

[1] Some results of the Visitation are given in the Computus of autumn 1556; the Computus of Oct. 1556—Oct. 1557 is missing, as well as those of 1559-60, 1562 3.
[2] Gutch ii. 169.   [3] *Annals* II. 2. p. 196.

a prebendary of Exeter, went with him.'   Edward Risdon[1] too was
' very instrumental in the foundation of Douay College in 1568.'   In
the list of matriculations 1575, there are some well-known names,
such as that of William Baldwin the Jesuit; Edward Habington,
executed 1586, and possibly William Habington the poet lover of
Castara.

When things became more settled under Elizabeth, there was a
revival of activity in the University, some new colleges were founded,
some old ones improved.   Trinity had already been founded by Sir
Thomas Pope in 1554 and S. John's by Sir Thomas White the next
year.   Elizabeth founded Jesus in 1571, and Nicholas Wadham
was preparing to found Wadham, though the design was not fully
carried out till after his death by his widow Dorothy daughter of Sir
William Petre.   Petre had led the way by what was almost equivalent
to refounding Exeter College in 1564, when an entry occurs in the
accounts, ' 14d for wine and sugar at the reception of M. Wodward[2]
with whom we talked over the plan and design of Sir William Petre'
(domini doctoris Peter).   Sir William[3] was educated at Exeter College,
became a fellow of All Souls in 1523, and was Principal of Peck-
water's Inn or Vine Hall.   He resided long in France and owed
something to his training abroad; when a document was to be translated into foreign languages, he and Wotton were looked on as the
proper persons to do it[4].   He had been seven times ambassador in
foreign countries.   Long afterwards we find him commissioning

---

[1] State Papers, Foreign, 1 Aug. 1559 p. 433, 2 Aug. p. 437, 15 Aug. p. 478,
5 Oct. 1559 p. 66.

[2] John Woodward of Merton, B.A. 1546, R. of Ingatestone, Essex, uncle
of Ralph Sherwine, fellow 1568 ; Newcourt ii. 267, Hist. Comm. v. 473, All Souls
Archives 20, 161, 297, 304, 322.

[3] Oliver's *Collections* 197 ; Pole's *Devon*, Burrows' *All Souls* 81, 116, 315, 390 ;
Catalogue of Ashmole MSS. 1137, 142 ; Burgon's *Gresham* i. 36, 228, index ;
J. Morris' *Troubles of our Catholic Forefathers* ii. 292, and index to i and ii ; *Fasti*
i. 73, 74, 93, 158 ; Newcourt ii. 347 ; Heywood 424, Dixon ii. 25, 115, 147.   There
were portraits of him in the Tudor Exhibition 1890, *N. and Q.* 7. ix. 334.   See
his life in Chalmers' ' *Colleges and Halls.*'   His arms were in a window of
the Crown Inn, Wood's *City* i. 597, Madan's *Materials* 17, Fuller's *Church
Hist.* ed. Oxon ii. 265.   His many-gabled house at Ingatestone is still nearly
perfect.   See C. R. B. Barrett's *Highways, Byeways, and Waterways*, second
series.

[4] State Papers, Foreign, 8 June 1563, No. 862 ; Privy Council N.S. i. 211, ii.
432, and indexes.

Wotton to get him books from abroad[1]. Wotton writes in 1553 from La Ferté Milon that he sends him some books, and had it not been that the prevalence of the plague in that city prevented his going to Paris he would have sent some more, but he trusts to a future occasion. If he has not the Lord Winchester's book called *Marcus Anthonius Constantinus* (Gardiner's *Confutatio Cavillationum*, i. e. reply to Cranmer's answer to the *Explication and Assent of the true Catholic Faith*), it shall be sent to him ; and again from Paris, in 1554, that he has purchased for Petre the new old Pandects of Florence and shall bring them home with him; should he wish for any other book let him mention it in his next and he will do the best he can to procure it. Petre wished Wotton to succeed him as Secretary of State, and Wotton writes in 1556 that as for Petre's office, knowing the weakness of his body and the pains and travail he has sustained therein already, he cannot but think he does well to leave it. And because this office is so easy and pleasant and Wotton so meet a man for it, Petre may be assured that he must needs thank him as much as the thing deserves, that would wish him to it. 'I am now so broken through age since my coming hither that you shall not know me when you see me.   And therefore it is time for me to get me into a corner and take me to my beads and to remember that we have not here *permanentem civitatem* and therefore to begin to put on my boots and prepare myself to go to the other place where we look for rest.' Petre was Secretary of State during the reigns of the four Tudor sovereigns. He was already a prominent man under Henry VIII, at first 1538 as Clerk in Chancery[2] and then as Secretary of State, in which capacity he was one of the special council assigned to help Queen Katherine (Parr) in 1544, when Henry left her Regent during his absence in France. He was one of the Ten Visitors of the University in 1549. On one occasion he presided in Convocation on behalf of the Royal Vicegerent Cromwell, who had in fact first brought him forward[3]. He was one of the twelve councillors of Edward VI named by Henry VIII; and fought for Mary against the party which

---

[1] State Papers, Foreign, 26 Oct. 1553, 17 April 1554, 8 Oct. 1556, 6 May 1557, 5 Mch 1564, No. 220.

[2] Rymer, ed. Hague 1741, vi. part iii. pp. 15, 20, 114, part iv. pp. 128, 148.

[3] Dixon i. 403, 498, Pocock's Burnet vii. 90, Nat. Biog. ii. 155 (his help to Ascham), *N. and Gleanings* v. 134.

was trying to upset Henry VIII's Act of Succession passed in favor of Mary and Elizabeth. Wotton applies to him to intercede for some of his relations who had joined the rebels [1]. It was Petre who advised Mary to forbid the legate entering England, who was sent by the Pope to remove Cardinal Pole. He was an excellent diplomatist and, though he said little during an interview, was an attentive observer of his sovereign's interest. Ah (said Chatillon at Boulogne), we had gained the last two hundred thousand crowns without hostages, had it not been for that man who said nothing. This was Sir William Petre. He ceased to be Secretary in 1557, but a state document written by him occurs as late as 24 Feb. 156$\frac{5}{8}$, and he was Chancellor of the order of the Garter from that year to his death 13 Jan. 157$\frac{2}{3}$. Latterly he suffered much from illness. Peter Vannes writes to him from Venice 10 Oct. 1556 that he is sorry to hear that Petre is somewhat troubled with a spice of the strangolione (quinsey), that he does not know the peculiarities of it, but intending to go to Padua within three days will consult with his friends as to the kind of remedy most propice for him. On 19 July 1560 Petre writes to Cecil that the Queen is minded to begin a progress toward Portsmouth: he wishes much that Cecil would come before her remove, for that he is unable to follow except in a litter, and that not without danger and pain. Petre held some of the Abbey lands, about which Sir Edward Carne writes from Rome 28 July 1555 'Petre's matter is in the hands of the Datary, who has promised favour in all Carne's suits. Had delivered the book to one of experience here to draw a minute thereof. Stands in doubt whether he had all again or no; for if the beginning of the book be "Manerium de Ging ad Petram alias Ging Abbatisse alias dictum Ingatstone in comitatu predicto" with the word "Essex" in the margin, thinks he has all; if that be not the beginning of Petre's book he does lack. Has in all 12 manors, one farm called Salmons and Barowse, and three parsonages, so that he has but 16 pieces in all if that be the whole. If that be the whole he has enough; if it be not, requests Petre will send it him in a little bill.' The endowment of Exeter College however came from some lands which Petre purchased of the Queen for the purpose [2], viz.: the Rectory and Vicarage of

[1] State Papers, Foreign, 23 Feb. 1554.
[2] Sir Walter Mildmay to Sir W. Cecil, with Sir W. Petre's account of lands he had of the Queen for Exeter College, 11 May 1568, Lansdowne MS. 614. x 67*.

Kidlington, the Rectory and advowson of Merton, and of South Newington, and the Rectory of Ardington (Yarnton), some lands in Little Tewe once belonging to Osney Abbey, and some land in Garsington (all in Oxfordshire), together with land at Tintinhull in Somerset. The Vicarage of Kidlington had belonged to Osney, and was now transferred to the College together with the Rectory, by an exception to the usual rule about vicarages. It was annexed to the Rectorship of Exeter College, the Rector holding it without institution[1]. This arrangement is expressly noticed in the statute 12 Charles II cap. 17, sect. 23. Petre settled £79 12s 2d per annum on the College to found seven fellowships, and for the eighth £5 2s and an annual income to the House fund of £11 8s 1¼d, in all £96 1s 3¼d (the revenues of the old foundation were valued in 26 Henry VIII at £83 2s, besides the valuable ground on which the College stood); he left the College £40 by will, and his wife Anne left the same amount. His son John Lord Petre, besides a legacy of £20, gave from himself, his mother, and some friends £15 6s 8d to augment the old fellowships and make them all equal; this annual rent was bought at Mich. 1572 of M. Phylpotte by the College. The Petrean foundation in all was reckoned to be worth £111 7s 11¼d. Sir William reserved to himself and his son the nomination of the Petrean fellows. Afterwards the College was to elect from the counties in which his family held property. These counties were originally Devon, Somerset, Dorset, Oxford and Essex, but before the alteration in 1854 there had been added to them *Yorkshire*, *Lancashire*, Norfolk, *Suffolk*, *Cambridge* (*including the Isle of Ely*), Kent, Middlesex, Hampshire, Northants, Cheshire, Cornwall, Surrey; though the counties italicised had lost their claim by Lord Petre ceasing to hold land in them[2].

---

[1] In 1785 a question arose about the Curacy, the curate being Thomas Bovet. It appeared that the Vicarage is a lay fee, subject to a payment of £10 a year to a curate, and the Rector on vacating the Headship of the College cannot retain the Vicarage. The Rector should grant title to a curate not as Vicar but as Impropriator of the Vicarage, if he is distinctly so from the rest of the College ; but should the Vicarage be given in the grant to the Rector and Fellows, the title should be under the College Seal (letter from Bishop's secretary, Reg. 16 May and 30 Oct. 1785, June 1786, 3 June 1790). See p. lxxxvii.

[2] As to Lancashire men being eligible see case of Rev. Daniel Mathias of Brasenose in Reg. 1792; in 1824 counsel's opinion was taken about the Petrean

Queen Elizabeth's grant of Kidlington[1], &c., ran thus: Elizabeth &c., Whereas our brother Edward 6 by letters patent dated 4 Jan. 1 Edw. 6 [1548] to-farm-let to Richard Taverner the Rectory and *mansion* of Cudlington upon the Greene with buildings tithes &c. (after the end of the estate of Robert Saunders), for 21 years at a rent of £20; and whereas we by letters patent dated 19 Feb. 7 Eliz. [1565] have to farm let to Thomas Frauncis the reversion of the said Rectory &c. (after Taverner's lease), for 30 years at a rent of £20; and whereas we by letters patent dated 24 Nov. 7 Eliz. [1564] to farm let to John Chamberlin 2 messuages and 4 virgates of land in Thorpe, (Thrup, then occupied by Humphry Wells), for 21 years from the previous Michaelmas at a rent of 53s 4d; and whereas our brother Edward by letters patent dated 21 Dec. 5 Edw. 6 [1551] to-farm-let to George Owen Esq. the Rectory of Ardington &c. (then occupied by Richard Andrewes, previously belonging to the monastery of Ensham), reserving the timber, for 21 years from the following Michaelmas at a rent of £7: Know ye that we, for a sum of £1376 11s 4½d from Sir William Petre, grant the said Sir W. Petre the reversion of the Rectory of Cudlington and the rent of £20; and the reversion of the 2 messuages with 4 virgates &c. and the rent of 53s 4d; and the reversion of the Rectory of Ardington &c. and the

qualifications. As to Hampshire and Middlesex see Reg. 1827, p. 116. Old List a. 1724 'Pitt and Scott, both of Dorset, were elected to Petrean fellowships. I doubt whether ever any Dorset men have been elected as of the old diocese of Sarum since the Renovation under Elizabeth's Charter, or whether they are at all eligible since Sir W. Petre's new code and giving a participation of his 8 fellowships to Dorset, which was then and long before in the diocese of Bristol.' Joseph Rosdew in 1827 presented Ashfield ₍3 a. 2 r. 3 p.) in Tangley near Andover to Lord Petre, as a qualification for Hants, and Lord Petre gave the College a lease of it for 100 years on receiving annually a copy of the University Calendar. In 1834 Richard Martin procured the admission of Kent, by buying 4 acres of land in the village of Dunkirk near Faversham and conveying them to Lord Petre, who leased the land to the College on an annual payment of an Oxford Almanac. In 1839 W. Falconer admitted Cheshire by conveying to Lord Petre a small incorporeal hereditament, a rent charge of 10s on an estate called Leighton Hall in Nantwich. In 1847 J. P. Lightfoot admitted Northants by conveying to Lord Petre some ground in the village of Wootton lying across the road on the west side of the parsonage. The same year, 1847, some land was given by a committee of Cornish gentlemen, through the Rev. David Jenkins, to qualify natives of Cornwall. In 1848 Mr. Robert Hichens similarly qualified natives of Surrey.

[1] Partly printed in *Hist. of Kidlington* ₍O. H. S.) 45; for Yarnton see 216.

rent of £7 ; and we grant him all the Rectory of Cudlington with the mansion and tithes &c., and the Vicarage of Cudlington with the buildings &c., and the 2 messuages with 4 virgates in Thorpe &c. (lately belonging to Godstow) ; and the Rectory of Merton with the tithes &c. (lately occupied by Richard Gunter[1]) ; and the Rectory of Ardington with the tithes &c. ; and our messuages &c. in Little Tewe rented at £8 13s 3d (lately occupied by William Raunesford), previously belonging to Osney ; and the Rectory of South Newenton with the tithes &c. rented at £8 (lately occupied by George Gyfford) . . . all without reserving any rent &c., except the £10 issuing from the Vicarage of Cudlington for the Curate's stipend, and the 6s 8d from the same vicarage to the Bishop of Oxford, and the 13s 11¾d to the Archdeacon of Oxford, and the £9 10s 11¾d from the Rectory of Merton to divers persons.

Sir W. Petre's general deed of gift is as follows :

Sciant &c. that I William Petre &c. have given (after obtaining the Queen's licence) to the Rector and Scholars of Exeter College, the Rectory of Cudlington upon the Greene, Oxon, and the mansion house of the Rectory together with the buildings tithes oblations &c., all which lately belonged to Christ Church &c., and was occupied by Richard Taverner ; also the Vicarage of Cudlington wth the buildings tithes oblations &c. lately occupied by Lawrence Atkinson ; the Rectory of Meryton with the tithes oblations &c. lately occupied by Richard Gunter ; the Rectory of Ardington with the tithes &c. lately occupied by George Owen Esq. (Meryton and Ardington were once granted to Cardinal Reginald Pole) ; also my messuages lands &c. in Little Tewe, Oxon lately occupied by William Rainsford ; the Rectory of South Neweton, Oxon with the lands tithes oblations &c. lately occupied by George Gifford (previously belonging to Christ Church &c. and then to Cardinal Pole).   All which rectories &c. Queen Elizabeth gave me by Letters Patent dated Westminster 18 May 7 Eliz. [1565]. I have also given them my messuage &c. in Garsington[2] lately occupied by Thomas Burges alias Smith and Agnes his wife, previously belonging

---

[1] Peshall 269–70.

[2] See 47 D. K. Rec. 229 (6 Edw. I) ; State Papers 3 Ap. 1623 Ralph Kettle [president of Trinity] and Dr. J. Prideaux to the Archbishop, 'G. Melsom distresses the poor by enclosing and ploughing pasture in Gasington Field, which were used by the poor for feeding their cattle.'

to Awdeley's Chantrye in Salisbury Cathedral, which I purchased from Robert Hichcock Esq. of Caverfeild in Bucks and John Gifford of Northall in Middlesex gentleman by deed dated 11 July 5 Eliz. [1563], Hichcock and Gifford having received it by Letters Patent dated 10 July 5 Eliz.   I have also given them my annual rent of £5 from the lands &c. of William Babington [1] Esq. in Nether Cuddington or Kiddington, Oxon and in Over Kiddington, Nether Kiddington, Asterley and Glimpton.   I have also given them my messuage in Tyntenhull and burgage in Mountague, Somerset, both which I purchased of John Hayter and Agnes his wife daughter and heir of Robert Stacy of Tintenhull by deed dated 30 Nov. 4 and 5 Philip and Mary [1557].   And I have given all these [full account repeated in varied language] for the following purposes viz.: the carrying out my Statutes &c. and certain Indentures made between me and the College &c.   And I have made Philip Huckle and John Hourd my attorneys to give seisin of all these to the Rector and Scholars. Dated at Ging Petre [Ingatestone, Essex] 8 Nov. 8 Eliz. 1566.

The following clause occurs in Sir W. Petre's Indented Articles [2] with the College 8 Nov. 8 Eliz.: 'Item that the Vicarage of Cudlington on the Grene, parcel of the premises granted unto the said Rector and Scholars, and their successors, shall be unto John Neale, now Rector of the said College, during only the time he shall continue Rector, and to his successors, Rectors of the said College for the time being; he the said John Neale, and his successors, Rectors there, allowing and paying yearly unto the said College, to the uses set forth in these presents, the sum of £7 6s o¼d [3] at the feasts of S. Michael and the Annunciation by equal portions; and seeing the Cure of the said parish to be served at his the said Rector's and his successors' costs and charges; and seeing the people of the said parish to be well instructed and taught, and keeping all manner of reparations of the Vicarage house, and all other houses thereto belonging, at the cost and charge of the same Rector for the time being; and suffering the scholars of the said College, in time of

---

[1] Computus summer 1566; there is a copy in the muniment room of a recognition by W. Babington to Rector J. Neale 21 Nov. 1566.

[2] The Latin is printed in full in ed. i. pp. liv–vii.

[3] This was afterwards reduced to £4, ed. i. p. lvii.

sickness in Oxford, freely to have the use of the said Vicarage house during the time of the said sickness.' This was by no means a useless permission when Oxford suffered from outbreaks of plague and sickness of all kinds. There were at least 12 such outbreaks in Henry VIII's reign, and a great mortality, especially in the sweating sickness of 1528. Oxford suffered much from plagues all through the middle ages. A number of deaths are mentioned in the Computus of autumn 1407. Autumn 1518 'xxis vid pro comunis Rectoris, Moreman, Waryn, Wyllugby, Chappell Existencium in patria, tempore pestilencie urgente.' The sweating sickness was very fatal in 1485–6, 1489, 1493, 1499–1500, 1503[1]. In 1563 the plague prevented the election of a Rector and the audit of the accounts, and we hear several times of the University being dispersed and one or two fellows only being left in charge of the College.

For the Black Assize of 1577 see Wood's *City* i. 269, Boase's *Oxford* 130; Reg. 21 July 1577, 'morbi πανδημου, et contagione sua inficientis, natura et vi consideratis, Rectoris et maioris partis eorum qui domi erant consensu, facta omnibus tum Rectori tum Scholaribus potestas est rus proficiscendi et ab Academia discedendi ad vigiliam Omnium Sanctorum inclusive excepto Edmundo Lewkenor subrectore, Petro Randall et Jo . . Cornelis, quibus Collegii cura et custodia demandata est (intra quod tempus illi dies minime continentur quos nobis singulis statuta nostra concedunt); . . . . decretum ut tribus illis custodibus, singulis, nullis communis expectatis, 4or solidi singulis hebdomadis numerarentur'; on 23 July however Cornelius left and Stratford took his place; Edmund under cook and Lite vice promus were to receive 2s 6d a week. The plague had been severe in 1575 when Westlake, Sympson, and Carpenter were left in charge of the College; in 1582 it raged 'in duabus aedibus pro foribus Collegii.' In the plague of 1570–1 the Fellows had removed to Abingdon, Computus 'M. Pudsey pro reditu domus quam Abindoniæ conduximus tempore pestis iiili vis viiid; M. Simson et M. Westlake pro eorum industria in conservatione Collegii regnante peste viiili xiis; pro expensis cuiusdam qui illis famulabatur, quem et ipsa pestis infecerit, iiili iis; pro conductis

---

[1] Gutch i. 642, 646, 650, 659, 661 : Autumn 1551 'iiili xs . . . sex septimanas Sudoris periculum eos ab Academia exulare fecerit; xis viiid   . . agebant probationis' (parchment mutilated).

vehiculis ad res nostras Abindoniæ transferendas xxxi*s* vi*d*; pro purgando Collegio et omnibus eiusdem Collegii cubiculis xvii*s* viii*d*.' See *Antiquary* Feb. 1886, *Academy* 23 Jan. 1886 p. 58.

Elizabeth's Charter of Incorporation is dated 22 Mch 1566[1]. She empowered William Alley bishop of Exeter to draw up new Statutes[2] for the College with the advice and consent of Sir William Petre. Under these statutes the Rector was to be at least a Master of Arts and thirty years of age, but not a bishop[3]; and no one was to be elected a Fellow who had more than ten marks of inheritance or life interest. The day of election was 30 June, the morrow of S. Peter and S. Paul. The Subrector was to preside at the disputations in theology, the Dean to preside at the classical and philosophical disputations of the bachelors twice a week, to lecture on logic to the students (*scholastici*) and hear them dispute in logic daily, and require logic repetitions from them thrice a week—but the Dean might pay a bachelor to do his work. He was himself paid by the fees which he received on presenting men for the degree of B.A. or M.A., and by payments of eightpence a quarter from the *commensales* and *battellarii* who attended his logic lecture. He might punish a bachelor by setting him a literary task, or making him dine apart on short commons. Great stress is laid on the public disputations in Hall, on subjects of logic, natural philosophy, metaphysics, or moral philosophy. The discussions lasted for two hours on the written questions that had been proposed, but on feast days or for special reasons the Dean might limit them to one hour. The fellows who were studying theology were to dispute in the chapel on theology once a week in full term, except in Lent. There is a special arrangement for times of pestilence. Logic lectures[4] were given from 6 to 7 in the morning, logical disputations held from 10 to 11 and from 6 to 7 in the evening, repetitions from 3 to 4 on Monday, Wednesday and Friday. The time was reckoned by a waterclock. The usual hour for supper was then at 5 o'clock; dinner had been moved on from

[1] Statutes 3, App. p. 68 ; see p. 86 two mills at Cudlyngton.
[2] They were partly taken from those of Trinity. Stephen Marks and Robert Newton fellows of Exeter were the first fellows of Trinity named in the Charter ; Roger Crispin was another.
[3] Mullinger i. 373. He was not necessarily in Orders. See Brodrick 253.
[4] Compare Mullinger i. 460.

10 to 11 or 12 in the Tudor age[1]. Even in 1760 some people still dined at half-past 12.

Fellows elected before taking their B.A. degree were not to take it till 3 years after their election; a rule not altered until 1854. Masters of Arts, after completing their necessary Regency were to study theology and take their B.D. in ten years from their Regency, and D.D. within eight years afterwards—but this last rule might be dispensed with by the Rector and majority of Fellows. Any one who did not take these degrees within four months after the periods named was to be deprived within the next month. When at a much later period the University decreed that no one who was not in Orders should take the B.D., this rule had the effect of forcing the Fellows to take Orders within ten years and four months from their Regency[2]. A fellowship was vacated at once by marriage[3] or entry into an employment incompatible with residence; and vacated within a year by accession to an inheritance, canonry, or life-income of ten marks a year: if a Fellow took a living worth £8 in the King's Books he vacated within a year unless he resigned the living within that year.

---

[1] Winter 1475 'id pro clipsidris emptis'; Lent 1551 'xiid Westborne pro annua pensione ad custodiendam clepsydram nostram'; autumn 1556 'xiid pro corio pro opere servientis clepsydram'; Lent 1558 'iiiid subcustodi Collegii Marton consumtis in hiis rebus que pertinebant ad machinam horariam.'

[2] Gutch ii. 260, iii. 422, Ayliffe i. 468, ii. 129, Laud's Chancellorship 24, 28, 29, Burrows 352-3. In Colleges which wished to enforce Orders, this was added to the rules about B.D. and D.D., S. John's Statutes pp. 59, 61. In 1594 an order was made that a B.D. must study two years before his grace was propounded: see under 1778. Laud's Statutes of 1634 required disputations and a Latin sermon, the preacher to be in deacon's orders at least. But by custom the Vice-chancellor dispensed with those exercises once a year, and also in favour of the proctors, relieving one of them from the disputations, the other from the sermon. The requirement of a sermon before D.D. is very ancient. In the middle ages some of the greatest theologians were not ordained; and many friars preached who were not in orders; ordination was not made an absolute requisite for preaching till after the Reformation. The Latin sermons at S. Mary's were treated as a divinity exercise of the present day is, only the Vice-chancellor proctors and bedels attending, and there was no public notice. The hour was 9 in the morning. In May 1833 they were abolished, but the candidate was required to show that he was in deacon's orders. A statute of the next month, June 1833, required priest's orders. I owe great part of this note to Dr. Griffiths. Holwell took his B.D. 1790 though not in Orders.

[3] Si quis uxorem duxerit aut matrimonium vel sponsalia contraxerit; this seems to make a marriage engagement vacate the fellowship, but it was not so interpreted in practice. See S. John's Statutes p. 69.

The Rector might hold one living, but only on condition of continued residence in College—and an Ordinance of John Lord Petre allowed him to hold two livings on the same condition, of whatever value they might be, so far as the laws of the land would allow. As the value of money altered these conditions were relaxed. In 1744 Edward Morshead, who was 'seised of a real estate of £10 or £11 per annum,' took a fellowship on the ground that, owing to the altered value of money, this was much below the 10 marks mentioned in the statutes. On 15 Sep. 1758 the Visitor permitted a living worth £80 to be held with a fellowship: and 5 Dec. 1793 other property amounting to £40: on 13 Mch 1804 he increased the limit of £80 to £120 clear value, and on 4 Jan. 1810 that of other property to £100 (i. e. 15 times the value of the old 10 marks; Burrows' *All Souls* 27, Letters from Bodleian i. 150; Wordsworth 569 'in 1718 £20 or £30 a year with a fellowship made a pretty easy subsistence'). Any living might be held, if in Oxford. The case of the altered value of money is well stated in Bishop Fleetwood's *Chronicon Preciosum* 1706 and 8º 1747 with reference to fellowships at All Souls, where the limit was £5. He notices that even the cost of taking a degree had increased fivefold since the middle of the fifteenth century. Another Visitor's decree decides that when three or four Fellows demand a College meeting, the Rector is bound to summon one, and to propose any question which two or more Fellows demand to have put to the vote, and the meeting is not to dissolve till a decision has been come to. All residents were allowed, besides *decrements*, twelve-pence a week for commons[1], which was to be made up to eighteen-pence on five festival weeks. The Rector's stipend was to be 20s, that of the Chaplain 26s 8d, of the Fellows 10s each. There are regulations about dress[2] and about not entering the Buttery without

---

[1] Some curious arrangements about commons occur in 1562-3. See Mullinger i. 460. The reduction of the coinage caused difficulties; winter 1551 'xviiid pro imminutione 3ᵘᵐ solidorum quos habuit in custodia sua M. Randall' (reduction of the coinage); Lent 1552 'xiid pro folio pergameni' (6d had been the highest price before).

[2] A college rule of 1554 shows that the men went bareheaded usually; 11 Oct. 1554 'Et si multis transactis annis consuetudo fuerit prescripta scolaribus ut non velato nec in collegio nec in oppido incederent capite, tamen diversis de causis nobis visum est ipsis concedere ut in oppido pileis uti possint, hac lege ut in collegio veteri non sint liberi consuetudine.' Bloxam i. p. iv.

HISTORY OF EXETER COLLEGE.

leave, and all gaming is forbidden—except that at the usual festival times, All Saints day, Christmas and Candlemas, the fellows might play *pictis cartis vulgo cards* in hall at proper hours and for a moderate sum. Latimer's famous 'Sermons on the Card' delivered on the Sunday before Christmas had a special relevancy to the approaching season[1]. Shooting inside the College is forbidden, and no one may keep hunting dogs, ferrets, rabbits, hares or hawks within the precincts[2]. The Bible was to be read during meals[3] in Hall, and no one was to talk while the appointed portion of Scripture was being read; afterwards they might talk in Latin or Greek but not in English—except on great feasts or unless strangers were present or there was some other reasonable cause such as College business. The battellars were to talk Latin and Greek always while in College unless they were excused for lawful reasons[4]. Nowadays any one who quotes Latin in a College Hall at dinner-time is liable to be sconced. The Fellows sat in messes, four to a dish, and only Masters of Arts might sit at their table unless the Rector and five seniors gave permission to some one else. Lever, the Master of S. John's at Cambridge, in 1550 describes[5] his scholars as going to dinner at ten o'clock, content with a penny piece of beef [about 2 lbs.] among four, having a little *porage* made of the broth of the same beef, with salt and oatmeal, and nothing else. 'After dinner they be either teaching or learning until five of the clock in the evening, when as they have a supper not much better than their dinner. Immediately after the which, they go either to reasoning in problems or unto some other study, until it be nine or ten of the clock, and then being without fire are fain to walk or run up and down, to get a heat in their feet when they go to bed.' Lady Mildred Burleigh 'gave a some of money to the Master of S. John's, to procure to have fyres in the hall upon all sondays and hollydays between the fest of All Sayntes and Candlemas, *whan ther war no ordinary fyres of the charge of the colledg.*' Every one was to pay what he owed to the College within

---

[1] Mullinger i. 609.   [2] See Mullinger i. 373.
[3] In 1549 tenpence was given for a New Testament for the use of the Hall.
[4] On the Latin required for the degree, see Ayliffe ii. 141. Greek is quite a modern requirement, Wordsworth 116.
[5] Mullinger i. 369–70.

three weeks from the end of Term[1]. There were to be three copies of the statutes kept, one by the Rector, one in the Common Chest, and one chained up in the Library, and the statutes were to be read aloud twice a year in Chapel at 8 o'clock in the morning, and any fellow not attending lost a fortnight's commons. This custom of reading the statutes lasted down to our own time. The gates were to be locked at a quarter past nine in the evening and not opened again till five in the morning without leave of the Rector, to whose bedroom the keys were carried; and there are heavy penalties against sleeping out or scaling the College walls. The Domains of the College may be leased out, but not complete manors; and there are to be no reversionary leases at all, and no leases of any kind for more than 20 years; tithes or rectories are only to be let for 10 years, and no Fellow is to take a lease of the College. We see the reason for this in the leases for 41, 50, or 63 years mentioned below as given

[1] MS. IN THE BISHOP'S REGISTRY AT EXETER.

1587, Sep. 25 'hoc anno factum est a domino Joanne Petraeo statutum de annua in perpetuum Bursariorum electione ad summam Collegii scholariumque omnium utilitatem.'

1588, June 30 'hoc anno electi sunt primi hujus Collegii Bursarii, Tho Pawly et Gul. Huishe.'

1590, Sep. 'hoc anno extructa est cella in promptuario ad perpetuum et summum Collegii beneficium scholariumque utilitatem, et reparata est aula, atque elevata eiusdem area; et extructum etiam sphaeristerium.'

Officers were now more regularly elected, and discipline became more strict.

Reg. 30 June 1589 'electi sunt in annum sequentem M. Guil. Orforde concionator, M. Martinus Reade catechista, dominus Elias Cocke moderator philosophiae in capella, custodes clavium cistae de Germin dominus Bosisto, Helme, Eveleighe, auditores M. Eveleighe, M. Sandie.' See p. xxxv.

15 Sep. 1592 'constitutus est M. Croslye pro circuitu et progressu cum Rectore per terras et hereditamenta nostra infra 40ta milliaria.'

Reg. 3 Sep. 1594 'decretum ut quicunque inter prandendum vel caenandum aliquem, absentem, publico huius regni iure non convictum, detrectaverit, a mensa statim ipso facto (vel cum ignominia) removeatur'; 30 Oct. 'quod omnes scholares suscepturi gradum bachalauriatus solvant decano, vel ei saltem plenarie satisfaciant, priusquam presententur, sin vero decanus propter nimiam suam incuriam et negligentiam tunc non acceperit, nihilominus eam pecuniam Collegio solvere tenetur'; 2 Nov. 'ut quicunque commensalis aut batelarius rus esset profecturus illud Rectori vel Subrectori vel Bursariis indicet, ut communarum ratio habeatur'; ' ut unusquisque commensalis vel batelarius ad gradum bachalauriatus vel magisterii promotus, vel eundem quem habuit, vel alterum fideiussorem producat e sociis, ut ratio etiam communarum habeatur'; 29 Nov. 'quod tam battalarii quam socii et commensales habeant in unoquoque ferculo tempore caenae (exceptis diebus pisculentis) cibum qui constat sex denariis.' See p. 349.

to Fellows in 1549 and 1559[1]. Reasonable fines might be taken, and the system of fines went on to our own days. A progress was to be made every three years to visit the College estates, situated not more than 40 miles from Oxford, by the Rector and one Fellow. The statutes end with a description of the duties of the Visitor, and the mode of removing the Rector or any Fellow.

By a later Ordinance[2] a Fellow was to be allowed, if Lord Petre approved, to travel for four years to study medicine or civil law, and this valuable rule was often acted on, the earliest instance being that of Thomas Fortescue in 1566. Sometimes permission of absence was given to Fellows engaged in the service of the Crown abroad (compare Pembroke Statutes p. 20; so at Wadham, Jackson's *Wadham* 63). The influx of new Fellows seems to have incited those of the old foundation to draw up a list of the Fellows from the beginning; and such a list, though very imperfect, was compiled by Robert Newton the Rector and William Wiott the Subrector in 1574. Seven Petrean Fellows were named by Sir William Petre soon after Whitsuntide 1566 and admitted on the 30 June (except Spicer, who was admitted 2 July), and an eighth was appointed by Petre in 1568 after his new gift of three tenements to the College. One of the new Fellows had been a Fellow of S. John's, another was incorporated at Oxford for the purpose of taking the Fellowship, the first named had been a Fellow of the College previously. It shows the unsettled state of men's minds that several of the early Petrean Fellows left the country and became Roman missionaries in England or abroad. John Howlett laboured in Transylvania and at Wilna, Ralph Sherwine was hanged by the side of Campian 20 Nov. 1581, John Cornelius was hanged at Dorchester 4 July 1594; Richard Bristowe became President of Douay, and was the chief of the translators who put forth the Douay Bible. 'These thine unnaturall sons,' says G. Hakewill in his address to Oxford, 'who

---

[1] See too the Act 13 Eliz. c. 10, Hallam *Const. Hist.* ed. 6. i. 224, Ashley *Econ.* 44.

[2] Sir William Petre and his successors are to have the right of nominating two fellows, one of the old foundation and one of the Petrean, 'who are to have full power to absent themselves from College without loss or detriment, and to travel into foreign parts, there to remain for four years so that during that time they resort to some University and therein apply themselves to the study of Physic or Civil Law.' These were to have an allowance of £6 13s 4d *viatici causa*, but not commons. See ed. i. p. lvi.

of late dayes forsooke thee and fledde to thine enemies' campe, Harding Stapleton Saunders Reynolds Martyn Bristow Campian Parsons, even in their fighting against thee, showed the fruitfulnesse of thy wombe, and the efficacie of that milke which they drew from thy breasts.' The Government interfered to secure a safer state of things, and Thomas Glasier of Christ Church was elected Petrean Fellow 4 Oct. 1578, on pressing letters from Sir John Petre, and Rector on the 21st. The Royal Commissioners had held a Visitation of the College on the previous 2 August 'in sacello horam circiter octavam,' and this was the result of their inquiry. On 30 Aug. they removed Carter and Cliffe for a time (Bellott and Dun being elected Sub-rector and Dean in their place), and expelled Cornelius 'for his demerits.' Rector Newton resigned in Oct. 1578, and Glasier was elected in his stead. Thomas Holland was similarly brought in as Rector in 1592 on Glasier's death[1], on Sir John Petre's and Queen

[1] The accounts of Thomas Evely M.A., Glasier's administrator, 27 Oct. 1592 contain some interesting particulars; paid unto Harris the draper for clothe for mourninge coats for his children and servants iiili, given unto the poore people in breade and money xls, Mistris Ellis for rosa Solis xviiid, Doctor Lilly in gloves for his paines in preachinge at the buriall vs, Dr. Case for his paynes taken with Mr. Doctor Glasyer in his sicknes a little table valued and praysed at vs, for coveringe of Mr. D. Glasier's grave in Christchurche xviiid, Mr. Crosse the apothecary for ware had there in the tyme of his sicknes xlvs, Mr. Williams the apothecary xviis xid, John Day his man for his wages due from Michaelmas to our Lady day in Lente xxs, Mr. Clarke for the teachinge of Jane Glasyer on the virginall for halfe a yeare xxs, a messenger which was sent into Sussex touchinge Richard Glasier iiis iiiid, the bordinge of Jane Glasier from the xth of Marche to the xi[th] of August beinge xxi weeks after iis aweeke xliiiis, the bordinge of Richard Glasier from the xth of Marche to the xxix[th] of September beinge xxix weeks after iis the weeke lviiis, for his teachinge or scholinge duringe this tyme and for three books bought of Mr. Joseph for him viiis vid, a new coate made for Richard Glasier ixs iiiid, a hat a paire of stockings and two paire of shoes and a girdell viiis vid, John Jennings for ware and phisicke had in Jane Glasier's sicknes and for her funerall xxxixs. The expenses of the administration came to vili xs vd, the payments from which the above are extracts came to xxiiiili xxiid. The debts due were, to the Bursars for battels lxxiiili iis vid, an arrerage of the yeares rente of the Vicarige of Kidlington viili vis, an arrerage of the Rector's chamber next the gate due for five yeares rente vili xiiis iiiid, halfe yeares rente of litle Tewe iiiili vis viiid, part of an arrerage of Tyntinhull received by D. Glasier of Mr. Peter iiiili xvs, arrerage of the halfe yeares rente of Maynhennet receaved by doctor Kennall and answered Doctor Glasier xli, quarters rente of Coggan's brewhouse xviis, quarters rente of Clifton ferry xs, quarters rente receaved of Jennings the baker viiis iiid, halfe yeares rente of the Vicarige of Kidlington iiili xiiis, halfe yeares rente of three chambers due at the Annunciation

Elizabeth's recommendation : he was one of the translators of the Bible appointed by James I. These able rulers soon worked a great change, and Exeter became remarkable for its discipline and learning, tinged by Puritan views. The state of education had not been good in Oxford for some time ; see Pocock's Burnet vi. 405 (letter of Jewel), 410, 434. William Turner's *Herbal*, Cologne 1561, in the dedication to Elizabeth mentions the low ebb to which the study of botany had sunk in the Universities and in England generally. We now find many donations of books to the Library.

Leicester as Chancellor enforced subscription to the Thirty-nine Articles in 1581 to exclude Romanists or Romanisers; James I in 1616–7 to the 3 articles of the 36th Canon of 1603 to exclude Puritans. By the 33rd Canon it was a title for Orders if a man was a Fellow, or an M.A. of 5 years' standing 'that liveth of his own charge in either of the Universities.'

In 1592, when Elizabeth came to see the amendment in learning and manners, the old rents of the Colleges were taxed, to entertain the Queen, at one per cent. Exeter was rated at a total of £200, the Rectorship was worth £70, the whole annual income £600, there were 30 commoners [1]. There were feasts at degrees and at elections [2]. The constant mention of poverty at this time may be partly due to the fact that the value of silver fell during Elizabeth's reign.

In 1572 we find a list of the members of the College, but without their Christian names. Besides the Rector and 20 fellows, 91 other names occur, including 3 masters, bachelors, undergraduates, servitors and servants. Some can be identified in the matriculation lists (printed ed. i. p. 185 *in the order of the MS.*), since Davells, Banfilde, Evelighe, Strete, Barret, Merser, Zewarde, Coode, Bawden, Davie, West, Foxwell, Sandwithe, Turner, Crandon occur in both lists nearly in this order. See Clark i. 389–91, ii. 32, 63. The list runs thus :—
Mr Newton rector, Wyot subrector, Smale, Paynter, Bearblocke, Westlake, Lewkenar, Carter, Randall, Symson, Batshyll, Leache, Brystowe, Raynolds, Batte, Sherwin, Carpenter, Cliffe, Hole, Donne,

xxxiiis iiiid. The Inventory of goods and chattels amounts to £184 5s 2d. A few of the administrator's payments were not allowed.

[1] Gutch's *Collectanea* i. 190–1, 195, Rogers vi. 661, 709, Boase's *Oxford* 132.

[2] Reg. 30 June 1615 ' probationarii vice convivii quod pro more solebant parare omnibus sociis 4or libras intra duos menses post admissionem Collegio solverent.'

Cogan: Mʳ Whydden, Palmer, German: Sʳ Blake, Conyngsbye, Currie, Cowlye, Carewe, Bucland, German: Fitzherbert, Philpot, Habinton, Vernye, Billit, Brunynge, Bonde, Paschall, Fearne, Roscharocke sen., Roscharocke jun., Davells, Drurie capellanus, Baker, Banfelde, Cophed, Pawlet, Pettyte, Fulforde, Bedlowe; Sʳ Scutte, Harryson, Cooke, Yerworthe; Conyngsbye sen., Conyngsbye jun., Paynter, Ambrose, Turnar, Clyffe, Habyngton, Throgkmorton, Maxfelde, Kyrrye, Eveleghe, Wryghte, Halle, Best, Mortemer, Heliare, Williams, Collamore, Marke, Hyll, Brunynge, Carpenter, Paschall, Younge, Strete, Bamforde, Barret, Merser, Zewarde, Coode, Conacke, Baker, Bawden, Davie, Nutcombe, West, Foxwell: Orton, Smale, Bickell, Paynter, Broughton, Pryckett, Morishe [7 servitors]; Lynell famulus rectoris; Williams; Austine Pryckett plebeii filius Oxoniensis annos natus 15, Cooper, Sandwithe, Tourner, Brunlye, Thorne, Smale, Cheyvenye, Browne, Cramdon, Warde, Robenson [12 poor scholars]. Very few of these men went on to the degree of B.A. Originally the fellows were the only members of the College. But as the College grew in size and the number of rooms increased, it was natural to let them out to other members of the University, or to wealthy clergymen and abbots who preferred living in University society to residing on their livings. This system of non-residence was very prevalent from the Middle Ages down to the present century, notwithstanding Acts of Parliament, the protests of the Puritans, and the efforts of Laud and others to check it. Gradually ordinary undergraduates were admitted as well. These *sojourners*, or *commoners*, either had a table of their own, or dined with the fellows at the High Table, the latter being called in later times fellow-commoners; they were all called *commensales*, and all had the regular commons or weekly allowance. Besides this each of the fellows was allowed to introduce a poor scholar, or servitor, who waited on him, and had his food and education gratis or nearly so. Intermediate ranks occur. Thus the battellars were below the commoners but above the servitors, and did not have the full commons, but smaller allowances for which they paid a special battels, i.e. account. It is a mere guess that the word battels means 'little bats,' i.e. the tallies or notched sticks on which the accounts were kept. One of these tallies still exists in a chest of the muniment room. The

h

distinction between these classes is marked by the different amount of Caution money they paid. Thus a fellow-commoner paid in 1629 £6, an ordinary commoner or sojourner £5, a battellar £4, a poor scholar £2. In the second Caution book 1686 poor scholars are raised to £3, and the figures 6, 5, 4, 3 altered, in a later hand, to 8, 7, 6, 4; but £3 occurs as late as 1726. A few were excused paying Caution altogether, and their names do not appear in the Caution books at all. A poor scholar paid 8d a term for his *cubicle*, while the rent of the better rooms was 2s 8d, while a Prior of Bodmin would pay 5s, and a few rooms were even more expensive. A year's rent for one of the College schools was 6s 8d. A paper of uncertain date gives the Juramentum Commensalium, Battellariorum, et pauperum Scholarium thus :—

You shall swear to maintain and defend the honesty and good fame of this College, as much as in you lyeth.

You shall swear to be faithfull and true to this College in putting on or causing to be put on: whatsoever you shall take for the relief of your self or of any other; and that you shall not by any means or ways seek the hurt or detriment of this College.

You shall swear to observe and keep the ordinary exercise of this house appointed for you, or to endure and sustain the usual and ordinary punishments inflicted for your defaults; neither shall you shew your self any ways untractable or unconformable to the good orders and discipline of this College.

James I sometimes sent mandates for the election of men to Fellowships, as in 1604 and 1607: and he did the same in most colleges. Thus at Magdalen (State Papers 10 June 1604) 'he wishes, should Caple be rejected, to see the return of the votes, that he may proceed as he shall see cause,' and only desisted on a strong remonstrance.

The plague was grievous in 1579, in Sep. 1603, in 1609, and in 1625 when three Fellows died, Maynard, Lane, and H. Hide[1].

---

[1] Gutch ii. 279, 356 : Reg. 27 Aug. 1609 'ingruente peste Subrector et Scholares dimissionem collegii a 28° die eiusdem mensis usque ad 25ᵘᵐ diem Septembris decreverunt; remanentibus ibidem interea Mr. Chambers; Mr. Flemmynge; Mr. Whetcombe; Mr. Vivyan: quibus separatim singulis concessi sunt, qualibet septimana decem solidi, ad uberiorem vitae sustentationem, reliquis vero nempe Mr. Rectori; Mr. Subrectori; Mr. Standard; Mr. Prowse; Mr. Warmstrye; Mr.

Some improvements were now made in the garden. Lent 1566 'xs sociis Collegii Ballioli pro indentura quadam pro horto eius Collegii.' A house near Balliol was given them 6 Oct. 1572 in exchange for their garden (near the School of Theology), adjoining the Exeter garden; the wall between the two gardens was pulled down, and £5 spent on a new wall (finished 21 June 1573, Reg. 24 June) for the garden thus made square. Savage's Balliofergus 34-5, 79 'there is a deed to Exeter College for exchange of our land adjoining to that House for a house and garden lying near to ours, which house and garden must be upon part of the ground where Hammond's lodgings now stand, for it is set lying on the north part of the way leading from Balliol to Magdalene church, on the West part of the wall of Balliol, and therefore it extendeth itself further that way than now it does, viz. quite to the low wall end without; and on the east part of certain tenements belonging to Balliol. Exeter did covenant to pay a yearly rent of 2s 6d for ever to be issuing out of a tenement of Exeter in Magdalene parish, indenture dated 6 Oct. 14 Eliz.[1]'

Among the eminent members of the College at this time was Arthur Chichester, afterwards Lord Chichester of Belfast, so famous in Irish history. Prideaux says in the dedication (to Dr. Hakewill) of his sermon preached at the consecration of the Chapel 5 Oct. 1624 'It was the

Hele; Do. Collyer; Do. Battishill; Do. Polwheele; Do. Peeter; Chaffyn, qui huic decreto interfuerunt, concessum est iisdem frui collegii commodis ac si domi residissent; stipendio promi solidum et sex denarios, subcoqui duos solidos et sex denarios adiicere singulis septimanis placuit.' See a previous entry 6 Sep. 1603.

'Decretum est a nobis 4ᵒʳ Mr. Chambers; Mr. Flemmynge; Mr. Whetcombe; Mr. Vivyan; quibus (eodem tempore) designata est potestas per maiorem partem Scholarium; ut stipendio Townsend adiiciatur tribus septimanis solidum et collegii lotrici Clarke duo solidi et sex denarii.'

In 1637 Convocation was put off from 3 July to October on account of the plague; but Inceptors were to be taken as having completed what was necessary for the M.A., &c., a M.A. paying 10 shillings, a Doctor £10, absentees paying double; Wood's MS. E. 29.

In 1643 there was such a plague of Morbus Campestris [Wood's joke on the deaths in the War] that there were few determiners for B.A.; Peshall 69.

[1] Clark i. p. 159, 27 Jan. 157⅞ 'applicatum ut angiportum inter Coll. Exon. ex una parte et Coll. Linc. et Æn. Nas. ex altera medium ferens intercludi publicis Universitatis sumptibus liceat. Causa est partim quod sterquiliniis eo undique conjectis publico aspectui deformitas fiat, partim quod a nocturnis grassatoribus nec fenestrae tutae nec studentes securi esse possint. Concessa est, modo praefata collegia Exon. Linc. et Æn. Nas. ostia suis sumptibus fieri procurent.'

h 2

honour of my immediate predecessor Dr. Holland [see note in Fuller's *Church Hist.* ed. Oxon ii. 266], his Majesty's Professor of Divinity and father of so many famous bishops and doctors, to be Rector here when Dr. Chetwynd and Dr. Daniel Price now Deans of Bristol and Hereford, Dr. Carpenter, Dr. Fleminge, Dr. Winniffe, Dr. Whitcomb, Dr. Standard and Dr. Sampson Price (besides Drs. Vilvaine and Baskerville known to be worthy physicians) laid those grounds which have since attained that height which now the world takes notice of.' He then mentions 'Dr. William Helme his faithful and industrious Tutor, and those two religious and constant preachers Mr. W. Orford and Mr. Isaiah Farringdon who forgot us not when they left us, but so wrought on the pious dispositions of those excellent men Sir J. Acland and John Peryam Esq. that Exeter College by their bounty got a new Hall and lodgings of more charge and worth than all the former buildings.' A number of foreigners were trained under Prideaux himself, such as John Sigismund Cluverius, son of the geographer, and James and Frederick D'Orville, from Heidelberg (Clark i. 278, ii. 346, iii. 351); besides men like James Casaubon, Secretary Spottiswood, the Duke of Hamilton, &c. Sixtinus Amama the Dutch scholar, who taught Hebrew for 12 years in Oxford, speaks in high terms of Prideaux' management [1] in the preface to his edition of Drusius de Sectis Judaicis, Arnhemiae 1619.

Prideaux was a thorough representative of his University and of his time. On failing to become parish clerk of Ugborough in Devon, he came to College as a poor scholar and served 4 years as *subpromus*, before he was chosen Fellow. In a Latin letter [2] addressed 6 May 1600 'to his assured frind Mr Reaullme Carter at the right Wor. Sr John Petre his house in Aldersgate-streat in London,' he says that Lapthorne has taken a parish and a wife, and asks Carter to speak favorably on his behalf to Sir John Petre, on whose lands in South Brent his family had long lived. He says his mother, a widow, with ten children, could not help him. He was chosen 1600, was Rector 1612, Regius Professor of Divinity 1615–42, and became the leading theologian of the school at Oxford which upheld the doctrine of the Reformers as against the new school represented by Laud. The doctrine of pre-

---

[1] Printed in ed. i. p. xxv; see Clark i. 277, Hearne 5 Sep. 1710.
[2] *N. and Gleanings* v. 134.

destination gave way to that of free will in the Protestant and Roman Catholic churches about the same time, for of the two chief leaders of the new party, Arminius died at Leyden 1609, and Molina at Madrid 1601. Prideaux was shocked when some of the new school maintained that the Pope was not Antichrist. In 1576 [1] the questions discussed, *An sit purgatorium, An sit orandum pro defunctis, An Spiritus Sanctus hominem peccantem, electum tamen, prorsus et omnino deserat tempore peccati* are decided in the negative, and in 1605 it is affirmed that the Pope is Antichrist. But in 1608 Laud answers affirmatively to such questions as *An episcopus tantum possit ordines conferre.* Selden (who was at *Hart Hall* 24 Oct. 1600 age 15), as representing the view of the school to which Falkland, Chillingworth, and Hales belonged, has some strong remarks in his Table Talk [2] about Predestination and Prideaux's view, 'it is a point inaccessible, out of our reach; we can make no notion of it, 'tis so full of intricacy, so full of contradiction'; his remarks are even stronger against Laud's view of the divine right of bishops.

Prideaux's lectures on theology were much admired. John Houghton (who matriculated Leyden 2 July 1632) writes to John Walker 20 July 1635 as a member of Exeter College [3], 'victum meum publica ibidem in aula cum aliis capiendo'; he goes to the Bodleian; Prideaux 'Oxonii gloria, ecclesie lumen maximum, veritatis Anglicanae propugnator summus' at the last comitia most learnedly refuted the errors of Socinus and others about the satisfaction of Christ. Prideaux was popular among the undergraduates, as we see by Shaftesbury's story given below. There were naturally many stories afloat about Prideaux and his Fellows, as about later eminent heads of Colleges. On a blank page in an Oxford statute book of 1638 in the Church library at Crediton is the following, 'Dr. Prideaux is saying, the second Munday in July is Act-Munday duly.' One of the Fellows in Prideaux's time (Wood's *Life* ii. 399) 'sent his servitour after nine of the clock at night with a larg bottle, to fetch some ale from the alehouse. When he came home with it under his gowne, the proctor met him and ask'd him what he made out so late and what he had under his gowne. He answered that his master had sent him to the stationer's to borrow Bellarmine, and that it was Bellarmine that he had under his arme;

[1] Clark i. 194.   [2] Ed. Reynolds 1892, p. 149.   [3] Hist. Comm. xii. 9, 125.

and so went home. Wherupon in following times, a bottle with a great belly was called a Bellarmine, as it is to this day, 1677.'

Two letters to Usher from Hakewill and Prideaux [1] may be given here :—

My very good Lord ;

Your Lordship's favourable interpretation and acceptance of my poor Endeavours, beyond their desert, hath obliged me to improve them to the utmost in your good Lordship's service; and more especially in the good education of that young gentleman (Ja. Dillon [2]) whom you were pleased to commend as a Jewel of price to my care and trust; praising God that your Lordship hath been made his Instrument to reclaim him from the superstitions of the Romish Church, and wishing we had some more frequent Examples in that kind, in these cold and dangerous Times. For his tuition, I have placed him in Exeter Colledg, with Mr. Bodley, a Batchelor of Divinity, and nephew to the great Sir Thomas Bodley, of whose sobriety, gravity, piety, and every way sufficiency, I have had a long trial; and (were he not so near me in Blood) I could easily afford him a larger Testimony. He assures me, that he finds his scholar tractable and studious; so that such a Disposition, having met with such a Tutor to direct and instruct it, I make no doubt but it will produce an effect answerable to our expectation and desire: And during mine abode in the University, my self shall not be wanting to help it forward the best I may. Your Lordship shall do well to take order with his Friends, that he may have credit for the taking up of monies in London, for the defraying his Expenses; for that to expect it from Ireland, will be troublesome and tedious. I wish I could write your Lordship any good news touching the present state of Affairs in this Kingdom; but in truth, except it please God to put to his extraordinary helping hand, we have more reason to fear an utter downfal, than to hope for a rising. Thus heartily praying for your Lordship's Health and Happiness, I rest

Your Lordship's

Exeter Colledg in Oxford,   unfeignedly to command
     July 16, 1628.   GEO. HAKEWILL.

---

[1] *Life of Usher*, by Richard Parr, 1686, p. 398.
[2] See a letter from Dillon to Usher, 16 July 1628, in Elrington's *Usher* xvi. 470.

Most Reverend Father in God;

Your letters were the more welcome unto me, in that they brought news of the publishing of your Ecclesiastical Antiquities, so much desired. In which the History of *Pelagius* and *Faustus'* foysting, being fully and impartially set, will put a period (I trust) to the troublesome Fancies which of late have been set on foot. The sight of such a Work would more revive my Simplicity than the tender of many Preferments so much sought after. Of your purpose of printing *Ignatius* here, I never heard. It had been little civility in me, not to have answered so gracious an Invitation. I am loth to speak, but the truth is, our *Oxford* Presses are not for pieces of that Coin. We can print here *Smiglecius* the Jesuits Metaphysical Logick, and old John *Buridane's* Ploddings upon the Ethicks. But matters that entrench nearer upon true Divinity, must be more strictly overseen. I conceive it a high favour, that it pleased you to make use of my meanness for the placing of your Kinsman. I shall strain my best endeavours to make good your Undertakings to his Friends. Young Tutors oftentimes fail their Pupils, for want of Experience and Authority, (to say nothing of Negligence and Ignorance). I have resolved therefore to make your Kinsman one of my peculiar, and tutor him wholly myself; which I have ever continued to some especial Friends, ever since I have been Rector and Doctor. He billets in my Lodgings; hath (three) fellow Pupils, which are Sons to Earls, together with his Country-man, the son of my Lord Caulfield[1]; all very civil, studious, and fit to go together. I trust, that God will so bless our joint Endeavours, that his worthy Friends shall receive content, and have cause to thank your Grace. Whose   Faithful Servant I remain,

Aug. 27. 1628.   Jo. PRIDEAUX.

Anthony Lapthorne was chaplain to James I and, the king being a profane swearer, Lapthorne reproved the Archbishop of Canterbury, who was present, for not taking notice of the king's swearing on the bowling green. This made the king afterwards tell swearers that Lapthorne was coming. His Puritanism however brought him into trouble with the High Commission. The charge brought against

---

[1] See Laud's Works v. part i. p. 265.

him in Laud's time was that he seldom read the Liturgy except in
Lent, and when he reached the psalms or the lessons would go up
at once into the pulpit, omitting the rest of the service. In his
sermon he frequently reviled some of his congregation in the presence
of strangers whom he had invited to hear him and whom he asked to
assist him in praying out the devils with which his own parishioners
were possessed. He spoke of the clergy generally in disrespectful
terms, and those of his own neighbourhood, Tretire in Herefordshire,
he called idol shepherds, dumb dogs, and soul murderers. These
charges were probably exaggerated, for though he was 9 Oct.
1634 deprived of his benefice and suspended from his ministry for
a time, yet before 19 May 1636 he received permission to continue
his ministry anywhere but in the cure held by him at the time of
his deprivation. John Reynolds left books to Ex. Coll. (Fowler's
Corpus 165). John Flemmyng was chaplain to James I and became
the first warden of Wadham. Thomas Winniffe chaplain to Prince
Charles lost favour for speaking against Gondomar and Spinola when
the Spaniards were overrunning the Palatinate, and was sent to the
Tower[1]. He and Prideaux however were two of the divines of the old
school who were made Bishops by Charles when he was endeavouring
to conciliate the country gentlemen who had opposed Laud's and
Strafford's revolutionary schemes. Prideaux had been reprimanded
by Charles for speaking against the new Arminian doctrines in favour
with Laud[2]; but he, Winniffe, and others of the same school were
unhesitatingly loyal to the king in his troubles, and suffered much
in the Civil War[3]. George Hakewill also was imprisoned for opposing

[1] Camden a. 1622 'Winnif a sacris principi Carolo ejus gratiam excedit, quia in
eleganti declamatione assimulaverit Fredericum regem Bohemie agno, et Spinoloum
lupo sanguinolenti, quod regem male habuit.' Clarendon iv. 423 ed. 1819, State
Papers 13 Ap. 1622, 17 and 28 Sep. and 7 Nov. 1624, S. R. Gardiner's *Hist.* iv.
305. See F. Rous' 'Speech against making Dr Jo. Prideaux, Dr Th. Winniff,
Dr H. Holdsworth, and Dr Hen. King bishops till a settled government in
religion be established' 1642.
[2] Laud's Chancellorship pp. 25, 31, 32, 36, 48, 49, 53, 56, 57, 62, 64, 87, 89, 91,
161, 165, 254, 298.
[3] Clarendon i. § 191 (Laud, entertained too much prejudice to some persons, as
if they were enemies to the discipline of the church, because they concurred with
Calvin in some doctrinal points, when they abhorred his discipline, and reverenced
the government of the church, and prayed for the peace of it with as much zeal
and fervency as any in the kingdom; as they made manifest in their lives, and in

the ill-omened Spanish match. He was an author of some note, especially for his 'Apologie or Declaration of the Power and Providence of God in the Government of the World, consisting in an Examination and Censure of the Common Errour touching Natures perpetuall and Universall Decay,' which has been praised by Dugald Stewart. The Apologie had the honour of being used by Milton in his *Naturam non pati senium* 1628, the year after its appearance. The second edition in 1630 is a fine book. Digory Wheare became the first Camden Professor of History, and was tutor to John Pym. His *Method of reading histories* was still in use at Cambridge in 1700[1]; Nathanael Carpenter's *Philosophia Libera* was an attack on the Aristotelian philosophy and passed through several editions. His *Achitophel* is dedicated to Archbishop Usher, who took him to Armagh. Another eminent fellow was George Hall, afterwards Bishop of Chester. Usher was on friendly terms with the leading members of Exeter College and sojourned a considerable time there during the troubles. Matthew Sutcliffe dean of Exeter named Prideaux, Styles, Norrington and Carpenter members of his College at Chelsea, the fellows of which were to be employed in writing the annals of their times and in combating the doctrines of the Romanists and Pelagians, but the establishment did not succeed, and became at last an asylum for invalid soldiers. Thomas Chafyn was chaplain to William Herbert Earl of Pembroke, famous in connection with the questions about Shakspere's Sonnets; Philip Massinger, who was in his service, was at Alban Hall 1602. Pembroke College was named after him, and he gave the University a large collection of manuscripts. Chafyn preached his funeral sermon at Baynard's Castle in 1630[2]. Wood

---

their sufferings with it, and for it; vi. § 93 Very many persons of quality, both of the clergy and laity, who had suffered under the imputation of Puritanism, and did very much dislike the proceedings of the Court, and opposed them upon all occasions, were yet so much scandalized at the very approaches to rebellion, that they renounced all their old friends, and applied themselves with great resolution, courage and constancy to the King's service, and continued in it to the end, with all the disadvantages it was liable to.

[1] Wordsworth 25.

[2] The Just Man's Memorial . . . as it was delivered in a sermon at Baynard's Castle before the interment of the body, London, printed by Elizabeth Allde for Nathaniel Butter 1630; 4° pp. viii, 39. The Epistle dedicatory 'to the right honorable and most noble, Philip Earle of Pembroke and Montgomery, Lord

ii. 485 tells the following curious story about the Earl. 'A short story may not be unfitly inserted, it being very frequently mentioned by a person of known integrity, whose character is here undertaken to be set down, and who at that time being on his way to London, met at Maidenhead some persons of quality, of relation or dependence upon the Earl of Pembroke (Sir Charles Morgan, commonly called General Morgan, who had commanded an army in Germany and defended Stoad, Dr. Field the bishop of S. Davids, and Dr. Chafin the Earl's then chaplain in his house and much in his favour). At supper one of them drank an health to the Lord Steward; upon which another of them said "that he believed his lord was at that time very merry, for he had now outlived the day which his tutor Sandford had prognosticated upon his nativity he would not outlive; but he had done it now, for that was his birthday which had compleated his age to fifty years." The next morning by the time they came to Colebrook, they met with the news of his death.' Several Fellows were members of the Assembly of Divines at Westminster[1], such as Matthias Styles and John Conant. Nathaniel Norrington was conspicuous in the controversy with the Remonstrants (Arminians); his epitaph in the Chapel ran thus: 'Ubi? hic, Quis? Remonstrantium malleus Norringtonus; proh dolor! sat est.' His tombstone is said to have become the hearthstone in the College kitchen. Another fellow, William Hodges, had to make his submission in Convocation 1631 for preaching against Arminianism in a sermon on Numbers xiv. 4 'Let us make us a captain, and let us return into Egypt.' George Kendal was the author of *Sancti Sancti* (in answer to John Goodwin, the Independent writer), and other learned works

Chamberlaine of his Maiesties Household' is signed T. C. He says 'My very good Lord, Tis the usuall fashion and custome among us that be Preachers (and 'tis as commendable as common) to commit our thoughts to the safe custody of paper that they may not die ; and upon occasion, from the paper, to award them to the Presse, that the dead may live. This fashion have I followed, and yet tis my first aduenture this way; and as my aduenture, so my mishap; that with Croesus sonne, I should stand dumbe all my life long, till now that I have seene my gracious Master strucke dead before mine eyes, and with Elisha forst to cry out after him ; My Master, my Master, the Chariots of Israel and the Horsemen thereof ... none of these things move me ... that I might be held seruicable to the bleeding memory of my deare, deare Master.' In this dedication T. C. deals very faithfully with Lord Philip. The sermon is on ' Esay 57, 1.'

[1] See the list of names in Masson's *Milton*.

on the Presbyterian side [1] (Dredge's *Sheaves* p. 35). Baldwin Acland was tutor of Thomas Clifford, the Lord Clifford of the Cabal ministry. The College was now training men like Sir John Eliot, William Strode, William Noye and Sir John Maynard [2]—the contemporaries

[1] The 'Justa Funebria' in 1613 on Sir Thomas Bodley included poems by Rector Prideaux, Nathaniel Carpenter, Arthur Harris, Robert Oxenbregge Eq. fil. nat. max., Thomas Browne, Peter Prideaux, J. B., J. Shermarius Germanus, John Berry, Bas. Cole, Bernard Greynvile, Matthias Stile.

The 'Threni Exoniensium' in 1613 on Lord Petre contained poems by Bevil Granville, Bernard Granville, Peter Speccott, Paul Speccott, Roger Edgcomb, Samuel Moyle, George Harris, Ralph Michel, Michael Vivian, Richard Amye, Alexander Harry, Richard Collier, John Vivian, John Polwhele.

The 'Academiae Justa Funebria' of 1619 a poem by Roger Jope M.A.

The 'Epithalamia' of 1625 poems by Prideaux, Robert Dormer baron of Wing, John Robarts only son of Lord Truro, Daniel Gotzaeus Palat. Exon. Coll. SS. Theol. Stud., John Hoffmann Germaniâ Archipalatinus e Col. Exon. A.B., Mark Zigler Archipal. e Coll. Exon. S.T. Stud., William Prideaux Doctoris fil. e Coll. Exon., William Hodges, Samuel Austin, William Browne M.A.

The 'Musarum Oxoniensium pro Rege suo soteria' 1633 poems by George Kendal.

[2] He founded two lectureships. The Reg. contains the following letter from Sir John Maynard to the Rector :—

I heretofore received a request from you in the behalf of Exon College which was since seconded by importunity of my brother. And yet I gave not him any assurance of what would be done and especially was unwilling to give you a verball awnswere till that I might do it with confidence and certainty of performance. And of late, having setled a controversy that strooke at the whole estate, desire to make one of our first works to beginne with your howse. We propose to assure fourty pounds per annum or neere thereabout on your howse. We hold yt convenient that the imployment be for a divinity lecture and a lecture for the oriental languages. Twenty pounds or thereabout for the first, twelve pound or thereabout for the second, the residue to the increase of some fellowship of the howse, but not meerly as a fellow but rather to go with some office such as is now least rewarded and best deserves. We desire to settle these things so as the exercises may be without faile performed, and merritt and abilityes respected in the men who shall be preferred, wherein we desire to advise with your selfe and the fellows. And intreat you to write your opinion herein as also how long yt is fitt each lecturer to have his place and what course to take in the preferment of them. We incline to an election in the same manner as the fellows of the howse are chosen. When we shal be informed herein we may the more easily resolve what to doe and how. In which particulars I desire your speedy awnsware if yt stand with your approbation and likinge. And, sir, you see that, though I have not performed your request in specie touching the buildings of the howse, that I have endeavored my best for the more essentiall part of the colledge, to which I shall (as I am bound) always acknowledge my selfe a dettor. And thus with the tender of my service and best respects to your selfe and your wife remaine,

Your lovinge kinsman in all affectionate offices,

London, June 23, 1637. JOHN MAYNARD.

of Hampden and Pym. Eliot matriculated 4 Dec. 1607 age 15. Pym at Broadgate hall, under Digory Wheare's tuition, 18 May 1599 age 15, and Charles Fitz-Geoffrey, also of Broadgate hall, speaks highly of Pym—he afterwards preached the funeral sermon of Pym's mother, Bibl. Corn. 148. Hampden was at Magdalen 30 Mch 1610 age 15.

In 1612 the number of members at the College was 206; including, besides the Rector and Fellows, 134 commoners, 37 poor scholars, and 12 servitors. Exeter then stood fifth in point of numbers: Christ Church had 240, Magdalen 246, Brasenose 227, Queen's 267. The number in the whole University was 2920[1]. The payments in 1619 were £6 7s to the Rector, £3 3s 6d to each fellow[2].

William Noye retained such regard for the care bestowed on him that when the second Lord Petre tried to nominate to the Petrean fellowships—though Sir William Petre had limited this right to himself and his son—and a lawsuit followed in which the College maintained its right to elect under the Statutes, Noye successfully and gratuitously supported the case of the College in the Court of Common Pleas. There is a portrait of him in the Hall. Edward Hyde, the famous Lord Clarendon, stood for one of the Sarum fellowships but unsuccessfully. In an election to a Sarum fellowship 1631 Thomas son of Humphry Hyde forged a certificate of birth in the diocese of Winchester which imposed on Rector Prideaux, and he expelled ten fellows who voted for the rival candidate Goddard. On appeal to the Visitor the forgery was detected, the Fellows restored, and the Rector reprimanded[3]. Another good friend Sir John Acland built the new Hall, with help from Sir John Peryam and others; and Peryam built the rooms which are now the Common-Room staircase. Acland gave £800 towards the Hall, to which the College added £200: Peryam gave £560[4]. The first stone of the new Chapel was laid 11 Mch

[1] Gutch's *Collectanea* i. 196 : Huber i. 450 gives a different account.

[2] Reg. 7 Dec. 1642 'decretum erat ut Rector quadraginta solidos et scholares singuli, sive presentes sive absentes, viginti solidos annuatim accipiant pro augmentis Rectoriarum Southnewington et Meriton conjunctim, sicut solent pro Guinear.'

[3] Burns' *Starchamber* 117, State Papers 1660 p. 91, 219, *Athenae* iv. 834, Colmer's *Vindication* 1691.

[4] Gutch iii. 110, 112, Prince p. 4, *N. and Gleanings* ii. 137, Letters from Dr. Prideaux and Isaiah Farrington to Mayor and Chamber of Exeter, asking them for contributions, State Papers 1631 p. 508.

162⅔, and it was consecrated 5 Oct. 1624: Dr. Hakewill, a nephew
of Peryam and related to Sir Thomas Bodley, gave £1200 towards
it[1]. The first person buried in it was a child of Rector Prideaux,
and there are still several small brasses of the Prideaux family let into
the floor (Hist. Comm. iv. 598). In 1624 a letter of thanks was sent
to R. Sandye alias Napyer for £20 received through Ralph Rudle
towards building a new kitchen. Robert Vilvaine, W. Orford,
W. Helme also each gave £20 to the new library and kitchen:
Ashmole MS. 1730 fol. 148–9 (in fol. i are many names of Western
men).

Many of the Puritans were steady loyalists, and the king had no
firmer supporters than some of those he had most strongly discoun-
tenanced. There were also some royalists of a more pronounced
type. Henry Tozer was at the head of those who stood out against
the Parliamentary Visitors; he heads the 1641–2 list. He was distinguished as Bursar and Subrector. There occurs in Reg. 8 June
1627 an apology made to him by George Mountjoy B.A. on his
bended knees in the new chapel, in the presence of the Rector, Subrector and other Fellows after evening prayers. 'I George Mountioy
doe here ingenuousely confesse and acknowledge before this whole
assembly, that in my late falling out with Mr. Henry Tozer (one of the
fellowes of this House) I behaved myselfe too unscholarly and incivilly;
trespassing thereby against morality, the good discipline of this
Colledge, and my bounden esteeme of the society thereof, for all
which I am hartily and truely sorrowfull as well for the fact itselfe
as for the evill of example committed therein. But I disclaime it for
my own act: it was extremity of passion that then transported me
beyond myselfe. Wherefore I humbly crave pardon thereof first
from the Reverend Rector, next of the Society and in particular of
Mr. Tozer: promising withall to performe hereafter not only all
lawfull respect and obedience to each member of the Society (according
to their distinct places and offices) but also to persuade as many as
I doe or shall knowe to be of a contrary mind unto their duty and
conformity in this and every kind that may concerne the quiet, peace
and established discipline of this Colledge. And this submission
I doe make most willingly, hartily and penitently.'

[1] Gutch iii. 115, 117, Prince 452, Hist. Comm. iv. 598.

Anthony Ashley Cooper Earl of Shaftesbury was a member of Exeter College in 1637. His account of his college career is a curious contribution to the knowledge of University life in the seventeenth century[1]. 'I kept both horses and servants in Oxford, and was allowed what expense or recreation I desired, which liberty I never much abused; but it gave me the opportunity of obliging by entertainments the better sort, and supporting divers of the activest of the lower rank with giving them leave to eat, when in distress, upon my expense, it being no small honour among those sort of men that my name in the buttery book willingly bore twice the expense of any in the University[2]. This expense, my quality, proficiency in learning, and natural affability easily not only obtained the good will of the wiser and elder sort but made me the leader even of all the rough young men of that college, and did then maintain in the schools coursing against Christ Church, the largest and most numerous college in the University[3].

'This coursing[4] was in older times, I believe, intended for a fair

---

[1] Autobiography quoted in Christie's *Life of Shaftesbury*.

[2] I doubt if this is literally the fact. In the Buttery Book for 2 June 1637 (twelfth week of fourth term) 'Barronet Cooper' pays 13s 7d, which is about twice the usual amount, but Champernowney pays 13s 10d, and Bryan 15s 8d: the next week Cooper pays 13s 8d, but Champernowney 17s 3d and Bryan a pound. University Reg. 24 Mch 163$\frac{4}{7}$ 'Anto^n Ashley Cooper, Dorcester. de St Ægid. Wimbourne in Comitatu predicto baronettus annos natus 15.' He was admitted to the Fellows' table 4 Mch 163$\frac{4}{7}$ on paying £6 caution, and his name continued on the books until 12 July 1638; his brother George matric. 1 Ap. 1642 age 17. Philip Champernowne son of Henry, of Modbury, Devon, matric. 21 Nov. 1634 age 16; he was admitted to the Fellows' table 18 Aug. 1634, and his name remained on until 8 Aug. 1637. Henry Bryen son of Sir Barnabas Bryen of Billing, Northants, matric. 19 Aug. 1636 age 15; he was admitted to the Fellows' table 11 Aug. 1636, and his name remained on till 28 Nov. 1637. Cooper's aunt, Martha, married Edward Tooker of Maddington in Wilts (Hutchins iii. 594). John Toker had his name on the books from 31 Oct. 1635 to 20 July 1638 when he was a bachelor (B.A. 24 Oct. 1637), but he belonged to a Cornish family. Giles Tooker son of Edward Tooker of Salisbury, Shaftesbury's cousin, matric. 1 Ap. 1642 age 17.

[3] Gutch ii. 416 'In the second week in Lent (163$\frac{7}{8}$), about the 20 Feb. the students of Christ Church and those of Exeter College grew so unruly (the Masters interposing and wrangling in, and the Undergraduates fighting out of the schools) that the Vicechancellor was forced to command an absolute cessation of all manner of Disputations between the said two Houses.' Laud's Chancellorship 191, Evelyn's Diary ed. 2, p. 7.

[4] Wood's *Life* i. 174, 297, 300, 353, ii. 75, 83, 129.

trial of learning and skill in logic, metaphysics and school divinity, but for some ages that had been the least part of it, the dispute quickly ending in affronts, confusion, and very often blows, when they went most gravely to work. They forbore striking, but making a great noise with their feet, they hissed, and shoved with their shoulders, and the stronger in that disorderly order drove the other out before them; and, if the schools were above stairs, with all violence hurrying the contrary party down, the proctors were forced either to give way to their violence or suffer in the throng. Nay the Vice Chancellor, though it seldom has begun when he was present, yet being begun, he has sometimes unfortunately been so near as to be called in, and has been overcome in their fury once up, in those adventures. I was often one of the disputants, and gave the sign and order for their beginning; but being not strong of body was always guarded from violence by two or three of the sturdiest youths, as their chief, and one who always relieved them when in prison and procured their release, and very often was forced to pay the neighbouring farmers, when they of our party that wanted money were taken in the fact, for more geese turkies and poultry than either they had stole or he had lost; it being very fair dealing if he made the scholar, when taken, pay no more than he had lost since his last reimbursement. Two things I had also a principal hand in when I was at the College, the one, I caused that ill custom of tucking freshmen to be left off; the other, when the senior fellows designed to alter the beer of the college, which was stronger than other colleges, I hindered their design. This had put all the younger sort into a mutiny; they resorting to me, I advised all those were intended by their friends to get their livelihood by their studies, to rest quiet and not appear, and that myself and all the others that were elder brothers or unconcerned in their angers, should go in a body and strike our names off the buttery book, which was accordingly done, and had the effect that the senior fellows, seeing their pupils going that yielded them most profit, presently struck sail and articled with us never to alter the size of our beer, which remains so to this day.

'The first was a harder work, it having been a foolish custom of great antiquity, that one of the seniors in the evening called the freshmen (which are such as came since that time twelvemonth) to the fire, and made them hold out their chin, and they with the nail of their right thumb, left long for that purpose, grate off all the skin from the lip to the chin, and then cause them to drink a beer glass of water and salt. The time approaching when I should be thus used, I considered that it had happened in that year more and lustier young gentlemen had come to the college than had done in several years before, so that the freshmen were a very strong body. Upon this I consulted my two cousin-germans, the Tookers, my aunt's sons (Martha 3 d. of John Cooper m. E. Tooker of Maddington, Wilts), both freshmen, both stout and very strong, and several others, and at last the whole party were cheerfully engaged to stand stoutly to defence of their chins. We all appeared at the fires in the hall, and my lord of Pembroke's son calling me first, as we knew by custom it would begin with me, I, according to agreement, gave the signal, striking him a box on the ear, and immediately the freshmen fell on, and we easily cleared the buttery and the hall; but bachelors and young masters coming in to assist the seniors, we were compelled to retreat to a ground chamber in the quadrangle. They pressing at the door, some of the stoutest and strongest of our freshmen, giant-like boys, opened the doors, let in as many as they pleased, and shut the door by main strength against the rest; those let in they fell upon, and had beaten very severely, but that my authority with them stopped them, some of them being considerable enough to make terms for us, which they did; for Dr. Prideaux being called out to suppress the mutiny, the old Doctor always favourable to youth offending out of courage, wishing with the fears of those we had within, gave us articles of pardon for what had passed, and an utter abolition in that college of that foolish custom [1].'

The discipline [2] of the University needed keeping up. In 1634,

[1] Wood (*Life* i. 134) describes this practice of 'tucking' as existing in Merton when he entered in 1647.

[2] Oxford specially needed discipline owing to the number of alehouses. Laud (Chancellorship ed. 1853 p. 245, and see 179, 202, 237, 258, 261, Burrows 285) says there were 300 alehouses in the place: recusants frequented the Mitre (269 : 215 [? Bennet] Weale of Exeter College was one of those who Romanised). See State Papers Addenda 23 Nov. 1556 for Wine taverns, Ayliffe ii. 242, Cunningham ii. 169.

while the Vice-chancellor was witnessing a tragedy acted by the scholars of S. John's, there was a disturbance in which John Gage (? Gaye) and William Betenson, commoners of Exeter, among others took part. They were forced to ask forgiveness 'on their bended knees in the north chapel of S. Mary's, promising with weeping tears that they would never do anything hereafter against the peace of the academy[1].' The colleges were fond of getting up plays. William Gager, of Christ Church (Tanner 303, State Papers Addenda July 1575 p. 487, Nat. Biog.) had a controversy with John Rainolds president of Corpus in defence of the lawfulness of plays. In Lent 1548 we find that ' 6s 8d was paid for the expenses of acting a comedy in public'; Lent 1551 '5s 3d was paid to Dolye who painted what was needed for acting comedies, and 18s 7d for repairs in Lord's house and the expenses in acting comedies.' In 1637 the College presented a comedy to the University (*Reminiscences of Oxford*, O. H. S., p. 20). The College contributed to our great group of dramatists one eminent name, John Ford, whom Charles Lamb praises so highly.

In 1623 the Vice-Chancellor Dr. Piers directed certain orders to the College (Univ. Archives box P, fascic. 5, no. 7).

The Romanist controversy caused some bitterness at this time. In John Gee's *Foot out of the Snare* 1624, among 'the names of Romish priests and Jesuites now resident about the City of London 26 Mch 1624' occur 'Father Bastin, sometime butler of Exon Colledge in Oxon. He was turned out of his place for cutting twenty pounds off from a brewer's score and coozening the Colledge contrarie to his oath; Father Edwards, sometime of Exon Colledge in Oxon. He went thence with a wench in man's apparell, but belike since a sanctified man.'

In 1634 the College leased ground to the University on which the west part of the Bodleian was built[2].

On 24 Feb. 164½ a Protestation in favour of Liberty and Religion,

---

[1] Nichols' *Topog. and Geneal.* i. 211, Gutch ii. 397. For comedies at Magdalen, see Rogers iii. 663, 685.

[2] Univ. Archives box F, no. 6 draught of lease, no. 7 arbitrement of the ground 5 Ap. 1634, no. 8 acquittance from the College 4 Aug. 1634 for £264 13s 4d. In 1821 leave was given to the University to erect a furnace to warm the Bodleian, at the upper end of the garden next the Rector's lodgings, at an annual quit rent of 10s.

made pursuant to an order of the House of Commons of 30 July 1641, was signed by the members of the Colleges[1].

In 1636 Charles I visited Oxford, when William Herbert of Exeter College made a speech. The College paid £32 6s 8d towards the expenses of the royal visit (Evelyn's Diary i. 662). The king had for some time planned the foundation of fellowships for the benefit of the Channel Islands, to be held at Exeter, Jesus, and Pembroke, and the fellowships were first filled up in this year[2].

When the Civil War approached, Prideaux the Vice-chancellor abruptly left the University about 24 June 1642 without properly resigning office, and Convocation made Dr. Robert Pink of New College Pro-Vicechancellor (Wood's *Life* i. 52). Oxford became the king's head-quarters, many students joined the army, and the work of education was suspended. The College plate offered the king a ready resource for the war. Lord Say had let the Colleges keep their plate on condition that it should not be employed against the Parliament (Wood's *Life* i. 64). The Colleges, considering themselves as trustees of the plate, at first hoped to buy themselves off with ready money; thus Exeter presented the king with £310, of which £138 had to be borrowed, but the king's needs were too pressing and he took the plate as well, on a promise of repayment: it was valued at £750, the pound weight of silver plate being reckoned as worth £3, and of gilt plate somewhat more. This of course allowed nothing

---

[1] Hist. Comm. v. 131.

[2] Laud's Chancellorship 140, Wilkins' *Concilia* iv. 534, State Papers 15 June 1660, Madan's *Materials* 78, 124. See Reg. 4 Aug. 1636. About the Bishop of Winchester's scholarships for the same purpose see Charles II's letter of 11 Dec. 1678 in the Reg., and Reg. 30 June 1680 (Hook's *Archbishops* xi. 302). A royal letter sent in 1680 allowed fellows to be henceforth elected from either Jersey or Guernsey if there was no candidate from the other in its turn. Reg. 1735. On 14 years of the previous lease of property in Lad Lane, London, expiring 25 Mch 1732, a fine of £82 was paid for renewal. Of the Exeter third a quarter, £6 16s 8d was due to the Treasury of the College; the rest, £20 10s was divided, the Rector receiving £1 14s 2d, 22 fellows 17s 1d each. See Rawlinson MSS. class C, no. 421, fol. 62, and Univ. Archives box K. 1. fol. 188, letter 27 Aug. 1680 from C. le Conteur to the Archbishop on the little advantage of the fellowships to the Church. Sir Philip de Carteret (Nat. Biog. ix. 215), according to Prynne, was the only man that procured scholarships and fellowships at Oxford for the islanders of Jersey. Royal letter (Reg. p. 80), 28 June 1680. Charles' Letters Patent are dated 7 June 1636: copy of letters patent in Tanner MSS. 338 fol. 54, see 177, 188 (Evelyn's Diary i. 662): Huber i. 223.

for the workmanship. The College however still possesses an old saltcellar and an egg set in gold[1]. Several of the fellows became officers in the army, such as Matthias Prideaux son of the Rector, and Digory Polwhele. Polwhele was one of the last of those who held out for the king in Pendennis Castle under Sir John Arundel, another member of the College. The College had also contributed an eminent officer to the royal cause in the person of Sir Bevil Grenville[2], one of the leaders of the Cornish force which won victory

[1] The king's letter is dated 6 Jan. 164⅖; 24 Jan. the College petitions that it is against statute, 28 Jan. the king sends a peremptory order, 29 Jan. the College asks that the £138 borrowed may be deducted from the proceeds of the plate, 30 Jan. this was refused; the plate given up 2 Feb. consisted of white plate 208 ℔. 4 oz. 18 p.w. worth £625 4s 6d, gilt plate 38 ℔. 3 p.w. worth £125 8s 9d. A catalogue of the donors of the plate and of their arms was kept; see Hist. Comm. ii. 127, iv. 467, and Gutch ii. 439. The Reg. 28 Mch 1622 shows that the amount of plate was large : see also Reg. pp. 30–4. The College also paid some of the king's foot-soldiers for a month at four shillings a week each (the king's letter of request is dated 27 June 1643). See Hearne's Diary 19 Sep. 1707. For S. John's, see *Life of Wood* i. 94.

Inventory of Reproductions in metal, &c. (South Kensington) p. 112.

Cup and Cover, gold, given by George Hall, bishop of Chester. It has two handles, and is decorated in repoussé with lozenge-shaped gadroons, and engraved with flowers and an inscription. English work, 16th century, height 6 inches, diameter 5 inches.

Cup and Cover, an ostrich egg, mounted in silver-gilt repoussé. The base is engraved with ostriches, and scrolls with inscriptions. The egg rests on the stem of three ostrich legs, and is supported by hinged bands engraved with shields of arms and mottoes. The cover has three plumes, dolphin brackets, and at the top an ostrich. English work 1610, height 21 inches, diameter 5¼ inches.

Cup and Cover, a cocoanut mounted in silver-gilt. The stem is formed by thin bars, resting on leaves ; the cover has a crested rim, and a ball enclosed in leaves of open-work tracery. English work 16th century, height 10 inches, diameter 4 inches.

[2] He was Collector Juniorum in Lent 1614: Reg. p. 223 ' 1613 (1614) in Festo Ovorum electi fuerunt duo Collectores ex hoc Collegio Dominus Bevillus Greene-feild per suffragia et Dominus Henricus Carey ut Collector Honorarius ambo filii equitum auratorum natu maximi : formula creationis Henrici Carey per procura-tores usurpata hic subsequitur : Insuper cum Academiae plurimum intersit ut illustris generis et spectatae doctrinae Juvenes omni modo pro meritis suis honoren-tur, Hinc est quod nos procuratores plurimis gravissimis causis nos eò impellentibus cum consensu Vicecancellarii et sententiis Doctorum creamus et nominamus Hen-ricum Carey artium bacchalaureum e Collegio Exoniensi Honorarium Collectorem una cum nominatis pronunciamus atque hoc summopere gratum designatis.' Bibl. Corn. 190.

For Collectors see p. xxxi, Laud's Chancellorship 257, Terrae Filius no. 42, State Papers 22 Ap. 1656 p. 289 (in Puritan times). Heylin (Bloxam v. 51) says that in his canvass for the Collectorship 7 Feb. 161¼ he was betrayed by Exeter College, and that next year Magdalen voted against Sir Dod of Exeter in revenge.

after victory for the king till Grenville fell at the battle of Lansdown near Bath, and with him the Western army lost its onward impulse. The rhyme ran:

'Grenville, Godolphin, Trevanion, Slanning slain,
The four wheels of Charles' wain.'

Other royalist officers were John Trevanion, Sydney Godolphin the poet who was slain at Chagford 1643, Robert Dormer Earl of Carnarvon killed at Newbury 20 Sep. 1643, Philip Stanhope who fell in defending Shelford House 27 Oct. 1645, Arthur Champernon and Col. H. Champernon in Devon, Lord Charlemont treacherously murdered by the O'Neils 1642, Falkland's son Lorenzo Cary killed in Ireland 1642, Lionell Cary killed at Marston Moor 2 July 1644, Nicholas Kendal at Bristol July 1643 (Clar. vii. 132), F. Glanvill at Bridgwater, Hatton Farmor slain at Culham bridge 11 Jan. 164$\frac{4}{5}$, Thomas Fulford at siege of Exeter 1643, William Helyar of Somerset, John lord Powlet, James Praed of Cornwall, Sir Robert Spottiswoode executed by the Covenanters at S. Andrews 20 Jan. 1646[1].

Some however joined the Parliament, such as Robert Bennett governor of S. Michael's Mount and of S. Mawes, John Billingsley who left for S. John's Cambridge and came back as fellow of Corpus 1648, John Blackmore said to have been knighted by Cromwell,—one of the regicides. Even of those who remained in Oxford about half conformed to the Parliamentary system in 1648, about the same proportion as in the University at large[2].

Thomas Chafyn was among the royalists who suffered loss after the war. Chafyn was one of the royalist fellows who suffered as delinquents (Walker i. 55, ii. 66, Rushworth iv. 202, Nalson i. 734, 782): Commons Journals ii. 72, Die Sab. 23 Jan. 1640-1 'ordered that Dr. Chaffin be forthwith sent for as a Delinquent by the Serjeant at Arms attending on this House, for words by him delivered against the Parliament, in a sermon preached by him in the Cathedral of Salisbury the 22nd of May 1634, the which words were here in the House witnessed by one witness and attested by the subscriptions of several other witnesses': ii. 84, 13 Feb. Die Sab. 1640-1 'Doctor Chaffin who was formerly sent for as a Delinquent by the Sergeant at Arms

---

[1] Fuller, *Church History*, Oxon. ii. 265-6, remarks on the literary ability of the Devon and Cornish men of the College.
[2] Burrows 470.

attending on this House, upon an information delivered against him Jan. 23, was now called into the Bar; where, after he had awhile kneeled, he was bid rise; and the said information against him was read; to which he was suffered presently to make his answer; which when he had done he was commanded to withdraw. The House fell into a debate and consideration of the whole matter: but before they came to any resolution, the Committee that retired into the Court of Wards returned and' [the Chaffin business dropped that Sitting]: ii. 94 Die Lunae i Martii 1640–1 'Whereas Dr. Chaffin was by order of this House formerly sent for as a Delinquent by the Sergeant at Arms attending on this House, for speaking indiscreet words in a sermon preached by him in the Cathedral Church at Salisbury, at a Metropolitical Visitation held there; the which words admit of such an interpretation as reflects, in an ill and scandalous sense, upon Parliaments; the question being now put whether for these words Dr. Chaffin should be committed a prisoner to the Tower; the House was divided, Tellers for the Noe were appointed Sir Jo. Wray Mr. Moore, Tellers for the Yea Lord Compton Sir Neville Poole. With the Noe were 190, with the Yea 189. It was then resolved, upon the Question, that Doctor Chaffin shall be called in to the Bar and, kneeling there, receive a sharp reprehension and admonition, and be enjoined to make a publick explanation of his words, in a sermon, at the Cathedral Church of Salisbury on some Lord's Day within convenient time. He was called in accordingly and Mr. Speaker pronounced this sentence against him, to which he yielded a willing submission; and on his submission of a great deal of sorrow for what was past, is discharged, paying his fees': 20 Oct. 1642 post mer. ii. 817 'Resolved, upon the Question, that Doctor Chaffin be sent for as a Delinquent, for publishing in his parish church the Declaration under the hand of the Marquis Hertford and others his adherents, in justification of their rebellion.' Hist. Comm. vi. 161, 1 Mch 164⁹⁄₇ Draft ordinance to clear the following persons of their delinquency (Lords Journals ix. 44–8 in extenso) George Trevilian . . . Thomas Chafin.

The Parliamentary Visitors in 1648 expelled 10 fellows, and 18 others; Henry Tozer, John Bidgood, William Standard, John Hitchins, John Barbon (scholar), Francis Chichester, Thomas Clifford, Richard

Langworthy, Thomas Browne, John Cutcliffe, William Morris, John Proctor, Thomas Carew, Erisey Porter, Francis Munday, Thomas Finch, Daniel Cudmore (servitor), Henry Bull, George Bull, William Manning, George Berd, John Berry (or Bury) B.A. probationer, Robert Teigh (or Teige, servitor), John Vicary, Baldwyn Acland, William Webber, Bernard Gealard, William Harding (cook). Besides these 28 persons expelled, Polwhele, Matthews and Braine are mentioned in the Visitors' Register in connection with Tozer. Those who submitted were John Martin, John Conant, Antony Clifford, Robert Hancock, Thomas Ince, Richard Guntion, John Francis, Charles Sambe, Thomas Voysey, John Maudit, Edward Searle, John Bartin. The persons put in by the Visitors were Samuel Conant, Peter Fyatt, Francis Howell, Edward Searle, Edmund Davis, Lewis Bradford, Jonathan Wills, William Chidley, Thomas Masters, John Slad, Eaton B.A., [Robert Collins chaplain fellow 1654, William Oliver B.A. fellow (his vacancy 1654 to be filled by a chaplain), E. Anderson B.A. to be fellow 1654,] Michael Dolling, Nathaniel Adams scholar, Samuel Turner scholar, Dollingson to have next vacancy 1648, Antony Jett cook *vice* Harding, Abraham Batten 1648. These arrangements do not quite correspond to what actually took place. Thus William Standard must have afterwards submitted. It is doubtful whether Gealard vacated or was expelled. Anderson did not become a fellow. A new subrector, bursar, and dean were of course appointed. Even the cook was removed. Henry Tozer, who had been a leader among the fellows, retired to Rotterdam and died there as chaplain.

Articles put by way of Question to Mr. Tozer, subrector of Exeter College, 21 Mch 164⅞.

1. What leases have been let by you the subrector and other fellows of Exeter Colledge since the surrender of Oxon.

2. Whoe and how many have been admitted Scholars or Fellows of Exeter Coll. since the beginning of this Visitacion.

3. Whether you have not set up the Common Prayer-booke in Exeter Coll. since the use of it was prohibited, and you yourselfe had for a while layd it aside.

4. Whether you did not check and revile Mr Jo. Mathewes of Exeter Coll. for not comeing to Common Prayr.

5. Why you permit M[r] Polewheele, a scandalous person and a man of blood, to enjoy the profits of his place at Exeter Coll.

6. Why doe you connive at the notorious miscarriages of Teige, your servitor.

7. Why Tho. Voisey, commoner, was expelled your House.

8. Why you did not censure M[r] Bury, Fellow of your House, for a scandalous and daingerous Libell delivered by way of oracion in your hearing[1].

9. Why you discouraged Braine, an ingenious youth of a tender conscience, when he expressed his zeale against supersticion[2].

10. Why you did not punish Bidgood and others for drinkeing of healths to the confusion of Reformers[3].

11. Why you contemned the Order of the Visitors for prorouging of the terme, and permitted ingenious youthes to be sconced for observeing the Order aforesayd.

12. What summ of monies, for what, and by whome, there hath been at any time expended by order of the delegates since June 1647.

Wood adds, 'All which questions being proposed by one of the Visitors (which they framed from the uncharitable information of John Martin, Robert Hancock, and others of Exeter College, that were Delegates appointed by the Visitors), M[r] Tozer desired time to give in his answer; on 27 Mch M[r] Tozer answered, Those queries that have been proposed to me concern the discipline and government of this College, and I have formerly given in an answer in the name of the College, that they could not without perjury submit to any other Visitors than such as their Statutes had appointed. This being taken as a frivolous answer, and not at all pertinent to the Queries, M[r] Tozer was condemned as guilty of high contempt. On 17 Ap. the Commissioners required M[r] Tozer to admit one Peter Fiot a Jersey man into the fellowship of M[r] John Poingdexter, pretended to be void by his long absence from the College. But he refusing to do it, the Commissioners sent their mandatary for the Buttery Book, into which afterwards Sir Nathaniel Brent, with the

---

[1] Wood says, 'this was a Declamation spoken in the public Hall, containing many reflections on the Visitors and Rebels, &c.'

[2] Wood says, 'he refused to come to Common Prayer, and spoke against Surplices.'

[3] Wood says, 'the health was a Cup of Devils to the Confusion of Reformers.'

consent of the Commissioners, expunged the name of Poingdexter, and entred Fiot, commanding the Subrector to give him possession of a chamber and all emoluments belonging to his place : but he refused so to do. On 29 June they sent for Mr Tozer and forbad him to meddle with any Election of Scholars (which by Statute was to be the next day) and to disenable him in that and other matters, turned him out of his fellowship and then sent him to prison because he would not deliver up to them the College Books and Keys, which without perjury he could not do, nor had they any title to pretend to them, no new Head being put in there. Concerning this matter I find a farther account, the Subrector refusing to deliver up the Keys and the Books was imprisoned by the Governour, who sent a guard of musqueteers to his chamber door, where they continued to prevent the fetching out of any of the said Books, &c. And another guard was set at the Chappel door, where they continued till the Election day was past, to prevent the Election, in which time they took out of the Chappel all the Common Prayer Books which were there, and cut the Common Prayer out of such Bibles and Testaments as they found there. But two days after Mr Tozer was released from prison, conditionally that the Keys and Books which he had refused to give up, should not be conveyed out of the College.'

By an order of 21 Mch 164$\frac{8}{9}$ the College debts were to be paid by not filling up the fellowships of Willett and Gealard, and by suspending four more fellowships as they should fall vacant, till the debts were satisfied. The newly-appointed fellows were to take seniority according to the date of their degrees. There is an indignant account of the Visitation, from the royalist point of view, in Thomas Barlow's 'Pegasus, or the Flying Horse from Oxford. Being the proceedings of the Visitors and other Bedlamites there, by command of the Earle of Mongomery. Printed at Mongomery, heretofore called Oxford.' Its tone may be guessed from the opening sentences. 'Tuesday Aprill the eleventh, the long-legged peece of impertinency which they miscall Chancellor was to be brought with state into Oxon; to this end, these few inconsiderable and ill fac'd saints hired all the hackneyes in towne (which were basely bad, yet good enough for them). Out they went and met the *Hoghen Moghen* I told you of; what courtship passed between them at meeting, how hee swore at them, and they said grace at him; how many zealous faces and ill leggs they made, and at what distance, I know not; a long time they were about it.' Wood gives a full account of the Visitation.

The Colleges were much impoverished. On 3 Mch 1649 John Maudit subrector of Exeter College petitions, 'that the College is greatley distressed for want of the arrears due from some of the tenants, and especially Simmons of Hamborough and Dr Parsons principal of Hart Hall; and God having provided a redress by Parliament order, by application to this Committee, they beg a summons to Simmons and Parsons, to show cause for not paying their rents[1].'

On 19 Jan. 164$\frac{9}{2}$ there is a petition about the Channel Island fellowships at Exeter, Jesus, and Pembroke, stating that the Committee for the King's Revenues had stopped the payments due from the London tenants, as taking them for part of the King's Revenues. As this was a mistake, and contrary to the Articles of the Surrender of Oxford, the Committee order the tenants to pay.

Dr. Hakewill was so much respected that no Rector was elected till he died, then John Conant was chosen by the new fellows[2]. Conant was a good scholar and such a master of Greek that he many times disputed publicly in the schools in that language. Prideaux once said of him *Conanti nihil difficile*. He was also a good oriental scholar, knowing Chaldee, Syriac, and Arabic as well as Hebrew. He quitted the College in 1642 but, hoping peace might be made, left his books behind him and they were all stolen. Books were by no means safe at Oxford during the Civil War. When Sir Thomas Fairfax recovered Oxford he took much pains in restoring the Bodleian Library, which had suffered during the Cavalier regime. Conant served a cure sometime at Lymington in Somerset and then at S. Botolph's Aldersgate, afterwards he lived several years as chaplain to Lord Chandos at Harefield near Uxbridge in Middlesex at a salary of fourscore pounds, most of which he gave away. He resigned his fellowship in 1647 from conscientious scruples about the Visitation of Oxford by the Parliamentary Commissioners. But the fellows having suffered from

---

[1] Burrows 218, 224 (suppression of fellowships to pay debts).

[2] Life, by his son John, published 1823 by Rev. William Stanton M.A., and dedicated to John Edward Conant, the Rector's descendant.

the non-residence of the Rector pressed Conant to take the Rectorship, knowing that he would reside. The headship was valued by
the Commissioners at £45 in 1649. Conant was a leader of
the Presbyterian as opposed to the Independent party in the
University[1]. He soon restored the system for which the College
had been famous under Holland and Prideaux and the numbers
increased to two hundred and upwards[2]. 'Once a week he had
a Catechetical lecture in the chapel in which he went over Piscator's
Aphorisms and Woollebius' Compendium Theologiae Christianae
(Basle 1638); and by the way fairly propounded the principal
objections made by the Papists, Socinians, and others against
the orthodox doctrine, in terms suited to the understanding and
capacity of the younger scholars. He took care likewise that the
inferior servants of the College should be instructed in the principles
of the Christian religion and would sometimes catechise them in
his own lodgings. He looked strictly himself to the keeping up
all exercises and would often slip into the hall in the midst of their
lectures and disputations. He would always oblige both opponents
and respondents to come well prepared and perform their respective
parts agreeably to the strict law of disputation. Here he would often
interpose, either adding new force to the arguments of the opponent
or more fulness to the answers of the respondent, and supplying
where anything seemed defective or clearing where anything was
obscure in what the moderator subjoined. He would often go into
the chambers and studies of the young scholars, observe what books
they were reading, and reprove them if he found them turning
over any modern authors, and sent them to Tully, that great master of
Roman eloquence, to learn the true and genuine propriety of that
language. His care in the election of fellows was very singular.

[1] Francis Howell was one of the Independents, Wood's *Life* i. 147–8 : for other
notices of this time, and especially of Conant, see i. 221 opponent to Henry Hickman, 257 forbidding books, 290 hats kept on in church, 298 entertainments, 302
Anabaptists, 317 maypoles, 359 University dress, 360 and 445 silenced at All
Saints ; 268, 312 refused to let Wood see the Registers ; 369, 489.

[2] Few names occur resembling those supposed to be peculiar to the Puritans.
There is nothing strange in such names as Theophilus, Samuel, Malachi. Most of
the Puritan nicknames were invented by their opponents as a joke after the
Restoration. A few occur such as Bezaleel Burt, Cananiel Bernard, Elias son
of Abdias Birch.

A true love of learning and a good share of it in a person of untainted morals and low circumstances[1] were sure of his patronage and encouragement. He would constantly look over the observator's roll and buttery book himself, and whoever had been absent from the chapel prayers or extravagant in his expenses or otherwise faulty was sure he must atone for his fault by some such exercise as the Rector should think fit to set him, for he was no friend to pecuniary mulcts, which too often punish the father instead of the son. The students were many more than could be lodged within the walls, they crowded in here from all parts of the nation and some from beyond the sea. On his receiving the insignia of the office of Vice-chancellor there was such a universal shout of a very full convocation as has hardly ever been known. The first Lent he made a surprising reform in their public disputations which for some years had been managed with such vehemency and disorder as had created several unhappy divisions in the University. The antipathy of his predecessor Dr. Owen to caps and hoods and his attempt for taking them away as Popish relics will not soon be forgotten. But he could never effect it, being opposed by many of the University, and among others by Dr. Conant, who could never discern any shadow of hurt in these decent habits, or any more of Popery in these distinctions of degrees than in the degrees themselves. He opposed Cromwell's plan of giving the College at Durham the privileges of a University, setting forth the advantages of large Universities and the dangers which threaten religion and learning by multiplying small and petty academies. He was instrumental in moving Mr. Selden's executors to bestow his prodigious collection of books, more than 8000 volumes, on the University.' In this period of Puritan ascendancy the disputations in the schools for M.A. were often in Greek. Conant was one of

---

[1] The poverty of some of the candidates for fellowships at this time may be seen from the case of Peter Fiott (Hist. Comm. vi. 150), ' Petition of Peter Fiott, a distressed young scholar of the isle of Jersey to the Earl of Manchester. Petitioner, who had formerly a desire of advancing himself in the study of good letters, is now capable of entering the University, but his mother's means are insufficient to enable him to go there by reason of her exile from her native country, her adherence to Parliament, and her having received no help, though long since ordered. Petitioner therefore prays the Earl to further his journey to Oxford, to enter his name there by liberal contribution, that so his endeavour may not be frustrated by want of means.'

those who advocated the Restoration, and was appointed one of the Committee which met at the Savoy to revise the Book of Common Prayer. But when no alteration in the ceremonies was allowed he felt it his conscientious duty to give up the Rectorship. Yet he refused to lead a party in the separation, and in fact had so little real objection to the Prayer Book that he soon after conformed, and was even reordained priest 20 Sep. 1670 (though he had been previously ordained at Salisbury 28 Oct. 1652), and was instituted Vicar of All Saints in Northampton 15 Feb. 167⁰⁄₁ on the presentation of the Corporation. When most of Northampton perished in the disastrous fire of 20 Sep. 1673 the neighbouring gentry paid him his salary of £100 for that year which his parishioners were not able to raise. John Robartes Earl of Radnor, who had been his contemporary at College, asked a prebend of Worcester for him of Charles II with the words ' Sir, I come to beg a preferment of you for a very deserving man, who did never beg anything for himself.' In his declining age he could scarce be prevailed upon by his physician to drink now and then a little wine. He slept very little, having been an assiduous and indefatigable student for above threescore years together. Whilst his strength would bear it, he often sat up in his study till late at night, and thither he returned very early in the morning. An eminent and early instance of Dr. Conant's contempt of the world was his passing over to his younger and only brother then living (who married young, had many children, and was not so well provided for) his interest in an estate left him by his father, when he had but little more to live upon himself than his fellowship. He was highly esteemed by Bishop Bull and Archbishop Tillotson [1].

'Exeter College flourished much under his government. In his time it afforded a Vice-chancellor, a Proctor, a Doctor of the Chair in Divinity, a Moral Philosophy and Rhetoric Reader to the University, a President of S. John's, a Principal to Jesus, and a Divinity Professor to Magdalen College; not to mention such as were transplanted thence to scholarships and fellowships in other colleges, many of whom were men of eminency afterwards.' Some of these names are those of Francis Howell, Thomas Brancker the mathematician, and

---

[1] Abbey and Overton, *The English Church in the Eighteenth Century* i. 124.

Narcissus Marsh afterwards Archbishop of Dublin, who gave ten thousand volumes to the Library of Trinity College, Dublin.

Exeter sent preachers twice a month to the Tuesday lectures at S. Mary's (Wood's *Life* i. 159).

In 1657 it was proposed that Edmond Prideaux, Attorney General, and his successors, should be visitors of the College instead of the Bishop of Exeter, but this Act did not pass[1].

On 18 Feb. 166½ the great storm 'blowed down a chimney at the corner of Exeter next Lincoln, and if the schollers in the cottle-loft had not perchance rose had bin sorely bruised; both the crosses at the west end of their chappell also downe' (Wood's *Life* i. 432).

In 1662 Conant and six of the fellows were deprived[2], and Lord Petre tried to nominate to the vacant Petrean fellowships (but in vain) Christopher Harris, and John Prince the author of 'The Worthies of Devon[3].' The ejection on 24 Aug., S. Bartholomew's Day, deprived Oxford and the Church of some of their best men, and was quite contrary to the spirit of the union of the two great parties which had brought about the Restoration. Through the stringent nature of the new Act of Uniformity, she lost the services of some of the most devoted of her Puritan sons, men whose views were no way distinguishable from those which had been held without rebuke by some of the most honoured bishops of Elizabeth's time. An attempt was made by John Walker, a fellow of Exeter College, in his book called 'The Sufferings of the Clergy in the Great Rebellion,' to justify the ejection by showing how many royalist clergy had been ejected previously, so that the Act of 1662 might be considered a sort of legitimate revenge. But the episcopalians did not return in 1660 after a victory. They returned by virtue of a union between the two great parties analogous to that which had closed the Wars of the Roses, and by the military predominance of Monk's presbyterian army; and, though the Declaration of Breda reserved the whole of the religious question for the consideration of Parliament, yet that Declaration was certainly not carried out

---

[1] Gutch ii. 680, *Conant's Life* 29, State Papers 1660 p. 301, Heywood 481.

[2] Wood's *Life* i. 453. On 1 Sep. 1662 Rector Conant was deprived; on 4 Sep. Whitway, S. Conant, Brancker and Inglett of Devon, Sainthill and Hearne Petrean fellows—but Hearne was re-elected 30 June 1663.

[3] *Worthies* 633, Petre's letter in Reg. 14 July 1663.

fairly when the bishops used their influence in Parliament to prevent any toleration. The king himself complained of their conduct. The result of their action was disastrous, and Ken, grieving at the orgies of the Restoration, sadly anticipated some new visitation of God's wrath[1]. The new Rector Joseph Maynard, brother of Sir John Maynard, held office less than four years; Wood says of him (*Life* i. 455, ii. 56), 'Exeter College is now (1665) much debauched by a drunken governor; whereas before in Dr Conant's time it was accounted a civil house, it is now rude and incivil; not respecting the magistracy of the University but soe bold as to clap him on the back and cry for new parks when Exeter and Queen's fought Feb. 15 or 16, 166⅘. The quarrell was between Exeter and Queen's, viz. North and West [possibly arising out of a football match[2]]. The rector is goodnatured, generous, and a good scholar; but he has forgot the way of a college life, and the decorum of a scholar. He is given much to bibbing; and, when there is a music-meeting in one of the fellows' chambers, he will sit there, smoke, and drink till he is drunk, and has to be led to his lodgings by the junior fellows[3].' Maynard wrote in favour of his native place Tavistock (Mrs. Bray's *Borders of the Tamar and Tavy*, 1879, ii. 240),

> 'Go to our Oxford University,
> Ask who is best skilled in divinity,
> Who hath the fathers or the schoolmen read,
> They 'll single out a man at Tav'stock bred.'

[1] Wood's *Life* i. 230, 231, 233, 326, ii. 95; Clark's *Colleges* 49.

[2] Penalty for playing football in 1666 inflicted on William Breton of Queen's Coll., John Hortop of Exeter Coll., and William Trevethick, B.A. of Exeter Coll. Probably the football had ended in a free fight (Wood's *Life* ii. 97).

[3] On 19 Aug. 1665 Joseph Maynard rector, John Hearne sub-rector, William Painter dean, of Exeter College, signed the permission for Wood to peruse the muniments and records of that college. 'On 24 Aug. he began to peruse the evidences. These are well ordered, and methodically digested, and are reposed in a lower rome neare to the gatehouse looking northwards. They were taken out of the said roome and carried to the lodgings of the rector of that college called Dr. Joseph Maynard, and in his dining roome A. W. perused them in 4 or 5 dayes; in which time the said doctor was exceeding civil to him. This Dr. was an old standard, had much of a true English temper in him, was void of dissimulation and sneaking politicks, and at leisure times he would entertaine A. W. with old stories relating to the universitie and the learned men of his time. He also then perused some of the registers. On Aug. 29 he began to peruse the catalogue of fellowes of Exeter Coll. which is reposed in the library there, and soon after transcribed it all for his owne use.' Wood's *Life* ii. 44: Wood's excerpts are in his MS. D. 2, pp. 71-106.

Ayliffe ii. 243 quotes two cases of attempts to check the claims of
privilege during this century.   In 1628 Fryer v. Dews (in the King's
Bench), 'Dews, being sued, prayed his privilege, because at the time
of the suit commenced he was a commoner in Exeter College in
Oxford, and brought letters under the seal of the Chancellor certifying
their privilege : and he certified that Dews was a commoner of Exeter
College, as appeared by the certificate of Dr. Prideaux, Rector of the
College ; whereas he ought to have certified, that he was upon
his own knowledge a commoner of the said college, and not upon the
certificate of another : and afterwards a certificate was made of his
own knowledge, and then it was allowed to be good.'   Was this
Thomas Dewe, pleb. of Oxford, who matriculated 13 Dec. 1615
age 16?

Again in 1674, 'Prat being plaintiff exhibited a bill in Chancery
against the defendant Taylour, to have an account of several sums
of money, which the defendant, a fellow of Exeter College, and
a tutor to the plaintiff's son, received towards the necessary occasions
of his son.   The Chancellor by an instrument in writing set forth the
privilege of the University granted by Charters and confirmed by Act
of Parliament: and the defendant was a scholar and resident in
the University, and that they had a Court of Equity, and thereupon
prayed that Taylour might be dismissed.   But the Lord Keeper
did not allow the claim, for that cognizance of pleas in Equity could
not be granted, tho' precedents were shewn of the same claim
allowed in Queen Elizabeth's time.   He asked whether any could
be shewn in my Lord Ellesmere's or my Lord Coventry's time; but
none could be shewn; and thereupon he disallowed the claim and
said that it must be put in by way of Plea : but withal declared that
it should not be on oath, but it should be sufficient to aver the
defendant to be a scholar resident within the University.'   Was
this Isaac Tayler B.A. 19 June 1666, M.A. 27 Ap. 1669?; he was
not a fellow.

A rather curious notice occurs Reg. 19 Dec. 1668 'decretum
est ne dies sabbati deinceps pisculentus sit.   Ut autem damnum
eis inde emergens resarciatur, pecuniae ad finem cujuslibet termini
coquo stipendii nomine solvi solitae pars quinta subrectori, partes
quatuor bursario solvantur.   Ut autem Collegio pro decrementis

plenius quam hucusque factum est satisfiat, socio-commensales denarios tres, suggenarii et batellarii duos addant. Liberentur autem
battellarii onere suas sibi quadras pecunia propria coemendi.' Decrements at first meant deductions from a scholar's endowment, for fuel,
candles, salt &c., and then any one's payment for these. For fish
days see Hallam's *Const.* i. 398, ed. 6.

Wood (*Life* i. 274) notices that music flourished at this time,
and mentions, among other musicians, Narcissus Marsh of Exeter
College, who 'would come somtimes among them, but seldome
play'd, because he had a weekly meeting in his chamber in the said
Coll. where masters of musick would come, and some of the company
before mention'd. When he became principal of S. Alban's hall,
he translated the meeting thither, and there it continued when that
meeting in Mr. Ellis's house was given over, and so it continued
till he went into Ireland and became Mr. of Trin. Coll. at Dublin.'
Wood's *Life* iii. 52, on 21 May 1683 the Duke of York visited
Exeter, among other colleges, ' they went on foot into Exeter College
back-gate which joyns on the west side to the [Ashmole's] musaeum,
where, in the quadrangle, they were received with an English speech
by Dr. Bury the rector, with his fellowes and the rest of the societie in
their formalities by him ; afterwards seing their chappell, where
the duke complained that the communion table stood contrary to the
canon (viz. east and west).' Bury was not a successful ruler. He was
a strong royalist, and was recommended for the Rectorship by Archbishop Sheldon and the Bishop of Exeter, and by a letter from Charles
II requesting his election 'notwithstanding any statute or custom
thereof to the contrary, with which we are graciously pleased to
dispense in this behalf.' The Visitor in the Visitation of 1675 found
serious fault with Bury's management of the College property and
general laxity[1]. In the election of 1669, when there was a dispute
about the number of fellows on each foundation, Bury suspended five

[1] The following curious entries occur, Wood's *Life* ii. 18 ' 25 July 1664 about
11 o'clock at night one Richard Kastlecke [i. e. Carslake] of Exeter Coll., bible
clerk, was killed over against Wilcokses the barber by the Star, by [? John] Turner
commoner of Wadham son of Sir Will. Turner, civilian. He held up his hand
at the next assizes and downe upon his knees for his life. By means of his father
Sir William Turner, Dr., his life was saved. Richard Karslak, pauper scholaris,
came to Exeter Coll. 6 Ap. 1661 ' [son of Richard, of Sidbury, Devon, matric.
6 Ap. 1661 age 18].

of the fellows and by this means gave the candidate he favored a majority. The Vice-chancellor Dr. Fell declared the suspension unjust and invalid, and the next Vice-chancellor Dr. Mews ordered Burgh the other candidate to be admitted fellow. Bury gave way, Burgh was admitted into Hawkey's place who had just resigned, and both the candidates became fellows under a Royal Letter of 30 June 1670, which dispensed with any clause in the statutes that might interfere with this settlement[1].

On 10 Oct. 1689 Bury[2] expelled James Colmer one of the fellows

[1] Some fellows had protested 28 June 1668 against there being 5 Cornish fellows, and on account of Burgh's election 1669 Bury suspended 3 Cornish fellows, Polwhele as elected when there were already 4 Cornish fellows, Paynter for having succeeded to a Devon fellowship, Verman for succeeding to predecessors of an uncertain county: and he further suspended Gooddall and Hawkey. Burrington had 10 votes, Burgh 8 besides the 3 suspended, on which Bury pronounced Burrington elected.

[2] Bp. Trelawney sent an inhibition 14 Nov. 1689, and directed an account of the proceedings to be sent him, and that Mr. Cleaveland and Mr. Maundrel should come to him at London. Bury refused to obey, and the Visitor by a parchment notice fixed to the Chapel door 18 Mch 16$\frac{89}{90}$ cited the Rector and Verman, Lethbridge, Huchinge, Archer, Cleaveland, Adams, Thorn to appear before him on 21 Mch when the Rector and three others entered a protest (but Hutchins and Cleaveland did not agree in it) against the Visitation, and so again on the 25 when the Visitor's Commissary Edward Master LL.D. restored Colmer's name to the Buttery Book. The Rector brought a new charge against Colmer and again crossed his name from the Books, Colmer again appealed and the Visitor summoned all to appear before him on 16 June, when the great gate was shut against him, but he entered another way, and on the Rector presenting a fresh protest snatched it from him and trod it under foot. The Visitor appealed to the Privy Council against the College for contempt of his jurisdiction. At the election of 30 June 1690 the Rector, Subrector, Hearn, Lethbridge, Archer, Adams, Thorn, Crabb, Vivian, Bonamy, and Kingston elected John Vivian in Colmer's place; Hutchins and Ratcliff voted for him conditionally 'if his place were vacant'; Cleaveland, Read, Harris, Bagwell, Maundrel, Webber, and Levet denied that there was any vacancy. The Visitor came again 24 July and another attempt was made to shut the gate against him. On the 25th he suspended 11 Fellows for three months for contumacy, and afterwards excommunicated Kingston. On the 26th he expelled the Rector and ordered him to give up the management to the Senior Fellow on pain of the greater excommunication. The non-suspended Fellows elected William Paynter Rector 15 Aug. 1690, who took the oath in December. The case then came before the King's Bench, which on 13 Jan. 1691 ordered the management of the College to be left with Dr. Bury till the case was settled, but Vivian's title to the fellowship was held over and he was not to vote. There were double elections to several fellowships by the rival Rectors and the Fellows who adhered to them. For the case in the King's Bench and the House of Lords see Skinner's Reports pp. 447–516, Trin. term 6 William and Mary, tit. Philips and Bury, Lansdown MS. 614. i; Heywood on Univ.

on a charge of incontinence, but the evidence was so worthless that the Vice-chancellor disallowed it, and the Visitor Jonathan Trelawney bishop of Exeter ordered Colmer to be restored. The Rector again crossed Colmer's name out of the books, and on this the bishop held a formal Visitation of the College, when the Rector tried to shut the gates against him. At last the Visitor expelled Bury and the fellows who joined him in opposing the Visitation, and William Paynter was elected Rector in his stead, but it was four years before the case was finally settled on appeal to the House of Lords. Other charges were brought against Bury in the Visitation.

Reform 1853 p. 415; E. Stillingfleet's Ecclesiastical Cases part 2 1704 pp. 411–36; D. K. R. 13 App. vi. p. 36; and Ranke's *England* vi. 257 translation. The Register p. 88 contains the following summary, ' In lite contra Visitatorem nomine magistri Painter; termino S. Michaelis pro Rectore argumentum habuit D. Tho. Trevor regiae majestatis solicitator generalis; proximo termino nil actum, impedito per negotia Parliamentaria et Regia domino Jo. Somers regio tum attornato postea magni sigilli custode. Illo ita promoto argumentum pro Collegio habuit M. Wallop; D. Justiciario primario de sensu statuti dubitante, cum absurdum videatur Rectorem sine consensu suo amoveri non posse ut litera statuti de Visitatione significare videtur, de interpretatione statuti causam nostram egit D. Blencow serviens ad legem: D. Guilelmo Gregory uno e Justiciariis defuncto, et D. Sam. Ayres in ejus locum succenturiato ut novus judex de tota lite certior fieret argumentum aliud a D. Webbe habitum. Tandem termino S. Trinitatis 1694 sententia a Judicibus lata, tribus pro Rectore, D. autem Justiciario primario pro Visitatore censentibus. Dixit enim D. Justiciarius Visitatores Collegiorum Fundatorum munere fungi, Collegiorum autem praefectos et socios pro elemosynariis habendos ad arbitrium Fundatoris amovendos, nec quicquam id mereri magis quam contumaciam; verba autem statuti nequaquam ita interpretanda ut Rector sine consensu suo amoveri non possit, nec necessarium esse aliorum consensum licet Scholaris sine consensu Rectoris et trium scholarium e maxime senioribus expelli non possit. Post latam a Judicibus in Banco Regis sententiam, causa per appellationem sive scriptum errois in superiorem Parliamenti domum a reverendo Visitatore transfertur. Ibi, auditis hinc inde jurisconsultis, a longe majore Baronum parte decernitur ut judicium in Banco Regis datum reversetur [10 Dec. 1694]. Quo judicio a Justiciariis rescisso, iterum jussere Barones ut dicti Justiciarii dirigerent Vicecomiti Oxoniensi scriptum possessionis quo M. Gulielmum Paynter in aedes Rectoratus mitteret. Quod per officiarium suum fecit Feb. 11° 1694 (169$\frac{4}{5}$). Vivian, Preston, Martin, and Pinbay were consequently removed 19 Feb. 169$\frac{4}{5}$ as illegally elected. The Visitor restored Lethbridge and S. Adams on their submission 7 Mch 169$\frac{4}{5}$, and Kingston 20 Ap. 1695; Verman submitted 19 Oct. 1700 and was restored at the Visitor's request to his privileges, and to his arrears ' at the request of my very good friend Mr. Smith Chancellor of the Exchequer' (28 Nov. 1700). John Meddens M.A. of Wadham was 'moderator' at Ex. Coll. about 1690, ' the Fellows being at variance among themselves,' Hutchins i. 236; *Athenae* iv. 394, 484–5. The Bishop's Articles of Enquiry 1690 are in the muniment room.

He had sold the place of cook to Robert Harding for £150, and received £50 from Hedges the next cook that Harding might resign in his favour. He had also sold the place of butler to William New for £170. The Rector's answer denies most of the statements [1], and there is so much cross-swearing among the witnesses that it is difficult to make out the real state of the case about Colmer, but Bury's conduct had been very arbitrary. The main circumstance in Colmer's favour is that he was supported by two of the fellows Ezra Cleaveland and Henry Maundrell, who were men of high character. Colmer states that Thomas Kingston the chaplain who supported Bury 'is registered in Mr. Dangerfield's Diary as one of his singular friends and companions.' But probably what told most against Bury was his having published in 1690 *The Naked Gospel*, for which he was ultimately charged with Socinianism [2], and the book itself was ordered by the University, 19 Aug. 1690, to be burnt. Bury published a new edition with alterations and explanations, but could not get a hearing. He anticipated the view of Locke, that the fundamental points of religion were few and simple, and that the main part of the existing theology was an accretion from the time of the Middle Ages : if we returned to the primitive doctrine, there would be more hope of union among Christians : he appealed to such texts as Acts xx. 20, 'I kept back nothing that was profitable unto you, but have shewed you, and have taught you publickly and from house to house, testifying both to the Jews and also to the Greeks, Repentance towards God, and Faith towards our Lord Jesus Christ.' Bury's case was thought one of some hardship and there was a debate on it in the House of Lords, but ultimately Paynter was confirmed in the place of Rector. Bury was Rector during James II's reign, when—perhaps as part of the king's plan of giving University appointments to Roman Catholics—Lord Petre sent a letter naming a Petrean fellow [3]. On the College refusing

---

[1] See list of pamphlets in Bibl. Corn. 772-3, and Wood's Collection no. 631.

[2] See *The answer to an heretical book called the Naked Gospel*, by William Nicholls fellow of Merton, London 1691 : compare Abbey and Overton i. 488.

[3] On 23 June 1685, on the death of John Bury, Lord Petre sent a letter naming Fitzwilliam Southcott in his place; Reg. Dec. 2 1686 'Dec. 2 1686, petitionem suam supremis regiis de rebus ecclesiasticis Commissariis exhibuit dominus Thomas Petreus; Dec. 11, literae citatoriae a dominis Commissariis missae ad

to accept the nomination as being against the statutes which gave the
election to the Rector and Fellows, Lord Petre brought an action

*nos allatae jubentes ut responsum quamprimum exhiberemus; Jan. 13, contra-
petitio e consilio domini Johannis Maynard ad legem servientis regii, egregii
benefactoris nostri, per dominum Newton LL.D. exhibita, a Commissariis cum
indignatione rejecta tanquam curiae contemtrix, mandatumque ut responsum per
syndicos communis sigilli authoritate communitos proxima curiae sessione
exhiberemus; Jan. 20, syndici facti dominus Rector, M. Hearne, M. Paynter et
M. Burrington S.T.B., responsum a se subscriptum exhiberunt, Diploma regium,
Articulos inter dominum Gulielmum Petreum et Collegium reciprocos, Collegii
tum vetera tum Petreana Statuta, determinationem Gulielmi olim episcopi
Exoniensis Visitatoris super eadem lite, Duodecim virorum in curia communium
placitorum in aula Westmonasteriensi veredictum, 73 demum annorum interruptam
hujus juris possessionem allegantes; Responsum in curia Commissariorum lectum;
datum domino Petreo 14 dierum spatium, jussumque ut utraque pars alteri
munimenta sua communicaret. Petiit dominus Petrens Diploma Articulos
Feoffamentum statutorum librum, et obtinuit omnium vel aspectum vel exemplar;
petierunt Syndici nostri jactatam in petitione Submissionem Collegii 7mo Eliz.
domino Gulielmo Petreo factam communi sigillo firmatam: respondit procurator
vestigia quidem ejus habere se, scriptum autem ipsum non habere; Feb. 2,
appropinquante jam die liti dirimendae destinata procurator Petreanus dilationem
vafre obtinuit, Commissariorum registrarium et procuratorem nostrum decipiens;
Feb. 17, die tandem critico petitio domini Petrei et Collegii Responsum in curia
de novo perlecta coram domino Petreo, cui dominus Cancellarius palam declaravit
plene a Collegio responsum, et nisi de rebus factis vel fallerent vel errarent causa
cadere non posse; respondet dominus Petre advocatos suos statim adfore causam
suam acturos; curia interim exire jussi omnes; post dimidii circiter horae moram
adsunt illi, nos intromissi; ex parte domini Petrei steterunt dominus Ricardus
Allibon eques et Guilielmus Williams quondam domus Parlamenti inferioris
prolocutor; tempora praeterita causatus D. Allibon tanquam Petreanae religioni
ac inde familiae iniqua, nihil jam inde diuturnam Collegii possessionem causae
suae obfuturam sperare se professus, mox diplomate munitum D. Guilielmum
Petreum statuta pro libitu condidisse eandemque potestatem haeredibus suis
dedisse cumque istiusmodi potestati nihil detrahere posset Articulis tamen
confirmatam esse ut ex ultimo patet quem [ye controleing article] appellitavit,
haec et similia D. Allibon; ad eundem sensum locutus est alter causidicus
Williams, addito perquam modestum et rationabile esse ut liceat fundatoribus eos
nominare qui munificentia sua gaudeant. Dominus Jefferys totius Angliae
Cancellarius, supremus hujus curiae Commissarius respondit; De Statutis Collegii,
modo pro statutis admissa fuerint, statuere penes Visitatores esse; hoc autem
statutum nunquam a Collegio admissum sed perpetuo repudiatum, nec jam de
dubio agniti statuti sensu, sed de factis inter benefactorem et Collegium reciproce
sigillatis agi, nec proinde ad hanc curiam litem istam spectare; adjecit ejusmodi
statutum condendi potestatem dominum Petreum omnino nullam habuisse nec
magis quam John a Stiles &c. Dominus Herbert banci regii Archijusticiarius et
Commissarius alter addidit, non novum Collegium fundasse D. Guilielmum Petreum
sed veteri novos scholares addidisse, quod cum sine consensu priorum scholarium
facere non posset, mutuo per articulos conventum quid utrinque faciendum esset,
ejusmodi proinde pactis de statutis judicandum, de pactis autem judicare penes hanc
curiam non esse. Quum itaque litem hanc tanquam non ecclesiasticam sed civilem*

before the High Commission Court, which he lost. The College thought it unbecoming to demand the £60 expenses from the descendant of their second founder, and the relations between Lord Petre's family and the College have generally been of a friendly character, Sir John Maynard and Sir George Treby pleaded for the College, and Chancellor Jeffries said in his familiar way that a pretended statute appealed to by Lord Petre's counsel was nothing to the point, and that Sir William Petre had no more power of making such a statute than John a Stiles.

Wood's *Life* iii. 385—'30 Mch 1692 Oxford thieves found out, examined, and discovered at the Georg Inn. The keeper of it had received some goods that were taken from Mr. Lethbridge of Exeter College ... Ap. 11 or 12, news came that White the Oxford thief was taken and committed to Stafford jayle. So 'tis hoped that company of thieves that rob'd so often last winter is broke. But he denied it at the gallowes ... 11 July, Act Munday (if there had been an Act), was executed by hanging early in the morn, in the Castle-yard, one Robert White, somtimes a servitour of Ch. Ch., son of Almond White a barber living neare the Miter Inn in Oxon, for stealing a clock from a certaine person of Ch. Ch., a plate from All Souls College, another from C.C.C., and books and cloths from Mr. Lethbridge of Exeter College. Evidence came in against him

ad hanc curiam non spectare dicerent Commissarii, rogavit D. Ri. Allibon quo ergo domino Petreo confugiendum ut jus suum sibi vindicaret. Respondit dominus Cancellarius, Hoccine a nobis? Sedemus nos litium dirimendarum et criminum puniendorum judices, non litigantium consiliarii. Rogavit demum D. Cancellarius causidicos nostros ecquid haberent quod curiae proponerent. Gratias agentibus illis et satis jam ab ipso dictum respondentibus missi facti sumus. Itaque jam secundo tacentibus nostris lite ista liberati sumus; ut enim jam a D. Cancellario ita olim a D. Archijusticiario in communibus placitis causa nostra tanquam ab advocatis acta est; plane ut praescribere posse videamur non tantum de ipso jure sed de modo jus defendendi. Plurimum debet Collegium D. Johanni Maynard et D. Georgio Treby equitibus qui egregiam pro nobis operam navantes mercedem recusarunt, quo etiam nomine D. Colding causidico, licet inferioris ordinis jam tamen industrio, devincti sumus. His adjecimus D. Ward celeberrimum et in cancellaria et in aliis curiis causidicum, Doctorem Newton et Doctorem Hedges in lege civili insignes advocatos. Regii autem Commissarii erant D. Jeffery supremus Angliae Cancellarius, D. Herbert Archijusticiarius, Comes Mulgrave supremus camerarius, comes Sunderland concilii regii praeses idemque secretarius, Comes Huntington, episcopi Dunelmensis et Roffensis. Collegii circiter librarum sexaginta damnum accessit, quum impensorum resarcitionem a tanti benefactoris haerede petere incongruum videretur.' Documents in a box.

about the clock and cloths, but none concerning the plate. He was
accused for being one of the knot of robbers who committed several
robberies in the night time last winter in Oxon; but he several times
denied it to the vicechancellor in prison and at the gallowes; otherwise,
as 'tis thought, if he would or could have confessed the knot he would
have been saved. He was a handsome yong man and therefore
when he was to be executed the maides of the towne had dres'd up an
ordinary body to beg him to be her husband, and shee appeared at the
gallowes and desir'd him; but [this was] denied unless he would
confess the knott.'

The list of Nonjurors in Kettlewell's *Life*, App. p. xii, shows few
names at Oxford, only about a couple of dozen, for most of the
Jacobites took the oath to the new king and then conspired against
him. Thomas Polwhele, fellow in 1664 and V. of Newlyn, was
one of the two nonjuring incumbents in Cornwall: the other was also
an Exeter Coll. man, James Beauford of Lanteglos by Camelford. At
the election in 1719 Betty, Bartlett and Eastway had equal votes with
Philip Hicks, George Snell and William Hume, and Dr. Robert
Shippen the Vice-chancellor, a well-known Jacobite, selected the three
former; but Bartlett and Eastway were rejected 6 July 1720, at the
end of their year of probation, for disaffection and drinking the
Pretender's health [1].

Since the Restoration discipline had been bad [2]. The state of the
College (and of the University) had altered much for the worse since
the time of Rectors Prideaux and Conant. Cicero's words became

[1] See p. cxxxviii. For a similar case in 1748 see Wordsworth 62.
[2] Wood's *Life* ii. 83 (1666), 'One Drinkwater, an undergraduat of Exeter
College with a red face was taken at the taverne by Dr. John Fell vice-chancellor.
He asked him his name. *Drinkwater*, answered he. Is this a place for *you*, saith
the vice-chancellor, who is your tutor? Mr. Goodall (*quasi* good-ale) replyed he.
Excellent and verie ridiculous; get you home for this time.' Wood's *Life* iii. 3,
S. John's and New College in 1682; 139, '18 Ap. 1685 Sat. at night, a bastard laid
neare the dore of Mr. William Paynter at Exeter Coll. and laid to his charge, but
knowne to be a tric of malice by a pupill of his that he caused to be expell'd;
6 May, John Jago of S. Marie hall, sometimes pupill to Mr. Painter of Exeter
Coll., expell'd by a programma stuck up in publick places for defaming Mr.
Painter his tutor by laying a bastard at his dore in Exeter Coll., Jago was forc'd
out of Exeter Coll. some time before for debauchery, by his tutor Painter'; and
355 (in 1691). As late as 1775 Campbell says in his visit to England, 'The Fellows
of All Souls did nothing but clean their teeth all the morning, and pick them all
the evening . . . almost all the gownsmen we saw were tipsy.'

applicable to many a man (Cluent. § 72) *Ea vitia quae a natura habe-bat, etiam studio atque artificio quodam malitiae condivisset.* Dean Prideaux[1] speaks of Exeter College as worse than Christ Church, 'nothing but drinking and duncery,' 'Exeter College is totally spoiled and so is Christ Church.' The Solitary in *Tom Jones* who relates his history to the hero describes himself as having been at Exeter, but perhaps only as being a western man : the story however is not a flattering one. The humorous notices of Oxford in the *Spectator* all point the same way. We have the evidence of Swift, Defoe, Gray, Gibbon, Johnson, John Wesley, Lord Chesterfield and Lord Eldon all agreeing in this point, that both the great Universities were neglectful and inefficient in the performance of their proper work[2] : Lord Eldon and Vicesimus Knox agree in stating that the examinations had long been a fiction, and this may have led to Adam Smith's view of the uselessness of endowments for promoting real knowledge. Chesterfield says of Carteret lord Granville ' he degraded himself by the vice of drinking which, together with a great stock of Greek and Latin, he brought away with him from Oxford '; his devotion to Greek and Latin was his own. Clarendon makes one of the speakers in his *Discourse concerning Education* complain of the great schools for sending up ' lubberly fellows, after they are 19 or 20 years of age, who bring their debauchery with them.'

It was during this time that the Library was burnt down 2 Dec. 1709. Hearne says in his diary (ii. 318, 320, 330), ' This morning, very early, began a fire in the scrape-trencher's (quadrae sculptricis) room of Exeter College. This room being adjoyning to their Library, all the innerpart of the library was quite destroyed, and only one stall of books, or thereabouts, secured. The wind being low, and there being good assistance, it was extinguished by eight o'clock, otherwise it might have burnt the public library, which is not many yards distant from it, on the east side. This library was formerly the college chapel, which so continued till the year 1625. The wind at this time was west. Though the writer of these memorials be not at all given to superstition, and does not very easily give credit to the great number of instances that are given in miscellaneous discourses of

---

[1] *Letters* ed. 1875 p. 13, Hist. Comm. v. 374, 376.
[2] Abbey and Overton ii. 44.

dreams, yet he cannot but here observe two considerable accidents that happened to himself. The night in which the fire broke out at Exeter College he had little sleep, being strangely disturbed with the apprehensions of fire, which seemed to him to be so near as to come to the hall (Edmund hall) and to catch the upper part of it. This apprehension continued violent, and he had only a sort of an inter- rupted broken sleep, till such time as he was called up to go to look after the library.' As the wind was west, it may have blown the smoke to Edmund Hall, and if Hearne's window was open and the smoke reached his nostrils during his sleep, it might account for his dream. The library was soon after refurnished. But in 1778 it was taken down and rebuilt, the College having received[1] in 1774 a large accession of MSS. and printed books by the benefactions of Edward Richards Esqre and Joseph Sanford B.D., sometime members of this House, and the latter afterwards fellow of Balliol (Reliquiae Hearnianae 16 Mch 172$\frac{4}{9}$, see Coxe).

A considerable improvement was effected in the College by John Conybeare and some newly elected Fellows. Conybeare, elected in 1710, was tutor to Archbishop Secker and to Chancellor Talbot's sons. In 1732 he published an answer to Matthew Tindal's *Christianity as old as the Creation* (Matthew Tindal and his nephew Nicholas were both at Exeter College). Conybeare's answer was highly appreciated by his contemporaries, and Lechler the German historian of English Deism expresses his admiration of it[2]. In 1735 he published 'Calumny refuted, an answer to the personal slander of Dr. Richard Newton.' Newton had become Principal of Hart Hall in 1710 and had procured an act of parliament for converting it into Hertford College[3]. He now maintained that Hart Hall had always been really independent of Exeter College; and Dr. Hole the Rector of Exeter, who was a weak man[4], gave him free access to the muniment room

[1] Gutch iii. 115.

[2] Abbey and Overton i. 198, 230; Leslie Stephen's *English Thought in XVIII Century* c. 2 § 11, c. 3 §§ 58-60, 63, c. 9 § 9.

[3] Gutch iii. 641, 647: he was B.A. of Christ Church 12 May 1698; and died 21 Ap. 1753 aged 77 years 4 months, *Terrae Filius* ii. 129-81. In 1733 he published 'Letter on expense of University Education to A. B. fellow of E. C.' In 1833 the College bought 2 old seals that had belonged to Hart Hall.

[4] The *Terrae Filius* of 1733 said that Exeter was governed by old women, Wordsworth 305. But this referred to a past state of things.

to consult the old documents. Conybeare thought that Newton on this occasion removed the early documents about Hart Hall, which are now missing. Newton was more honourably distinguished by his effort to diminish the expenses of a University career (Brodrick 135), for which he was made the subject of many jokes by the *Terrae Filius*, Nicholas Amhurst, afterwards so well known as editor of Bolingbroke's journal 'The Craftsman.' When poor Newton said that 'he supped in the Refectory and neither varied the meat nor exceeded the proportion set before the lowest commoner,' Amhurst notes 'This part is liable to dispute. I will only put you in mind of the late instance of PEASE and BACON. You remember what you said, upon that occasion, viz. Is such diet as this to descend to the populace.'

Conybeare became Rector of Exeter 1730, after Hole's death, and his exertions in the restoration of discipline and learning recommended him to the Crown, which appointed him Dean of Christ Church 1733, 'to cleanse out that Augean stable.' In 1735 West writes to Gray from Christ Church 'a country flowing with syllogisms and ale, where Horace and Virgil are equally unknown[1].' At Exeter Conybeare put a stop to the habit of selling the servants' places[2], and restored the long neglected lectures. An account of his reforms is printed from the College Register below a. 1733, and later regulations a. 1739. Hearne however, who always means a Jacobite when he speaks of 'an honest man,' speaks disparagingly of Conybeare, who was by no means a Jacobite. Sir John Saint Aubyn, a leading Jacobite in the Commons, was of Exeter College. Walpole said of him, 'All these men have their price except the little Cornish baronet,' and on Walpole's disgrace Sir John was a member of the committee

---

[1] Mason's *Gray* 1820 p. 10 (17 Gray's opinion of Cambridge).

[2] On 2 May 1746 Alexander Shilfox the cook died, and the office was continued to his wife for three years for the benefit of his orphan children; and 16 Sep. 1748 given to the eldest son Alexander, who was removed for misbehaviour 8 Nov. 1754, and Robert Curtis appointed by the Rector and seven Senior Fellows. On 14 Ap. 1761 'were appointed by the Rector and seven Seniors, Charles Curtis and Ann Horner widow jointly to the office of *Promus*, Charles Curtis appointed by the Rector Surveyor of the buildings, Ann Horner *Tonsor*'; for the intervention of the seven Seniors in appointing servants, see a. 1733. Charles Curtis proved dishonest, and on 9 June 1786 William Brickland was made Book-keeper (Promus) and William Taylor Storekeeper (Subpromus), and Robert Smith Overseer of Buildings; Brickland was dismissed for drunkenness 26 Mch 1790.

appointed to inquire into his conduct. Faction was still strong in Oxford. In 1719 there was a disputed election in the College and three Jacobite candidates had an equal number of votes with three others. Dr. Robert Shippen the Vicechancellor a well-known Jacobite selected the three candidates of his own party. Two of them however, William Bartlett and Richard Eastway, were dismissed the next year for disaffection and drinking the Pretender's health. We have a rather pathetic *Complaint* in 1754 by rector Bray against the members of Trinity, then a Jacobite College, for grossly insulting him, breaking the College windows several times, and behaving in a very ungentlemanly way. The authorities of S. John's in a similar case had made reparation, but the president of Trinity, George Huddesford, although Vice-chancellor, had refused to listen to what he called 'personal complaints.' The high character of Ken and a few others has shed a lustre over the Nonjurors and Jacobites, but Johnson had a low opinion of the Nonjurors, and the Jacobite chiefs in Oxford had not only notoriously perjured themselves, by taking the oath to the new dynasty, but had largely contributed to injure the morality and discipline of the place. Their ablest man, William King, principal of S. Mary Hall, wrote obscene poems, notorious even in that unscrupulous age. Perhaps the last occasion on which the Jacobite feeling was strongly displayed was in 1755 when the County election was held in Broad street. The Tory and Jacobite party guarded the approaches to the polling booths and prevented the Whigs from coming to vote. Some 'Queries' published on the occasion ask, 'Did not the Old Interest mob, on the morning of the first day of the Poll, seize every access to the front of the booths, and guard it almost twenty men deep? Was not the same done, early, every succeeding day of the Poll?' The Whig voters however passed through Exeter, and got to the booths. On this Vice-chancellor Huddesford made some remarks in Convocation on 'the infamous behaviour of one College,' which led to a series of Pamphlets. Wadham, Merton, Exeter and Christchurch were the four Whig Colleges[1]. The accession of George III however ended Jacobitism. They changed the idol, says Burke, but preserved the idolatry.

A revival of interest in Academical studies is shown by some new

---

[1] Wordsworth 612, 615.

foundations. In 1710 Meriel Symes of Somerset founded an exhibition for a poor scholar. There was some trouble afterwards about the claims of founder's kin, for families not really connected with Meriel Symes put in claims[1]. It was the number of forged claims at All Souls that caused the publication of the valuable *Stemmata Chichleana*. In 1715 Dr. Hugh Shortridge acting for Dame Elizabeth Shiers founded two new fellowships for Herts and Surrey, though it was not until S. Stephen's day 1744 that they were actually created. Shortridge also gave the College the best part of the funds of the Library, and a fund for buying advowsons[2]. Dr. John Reynolds founded the

[1] See p. 201.

[2] Dr. Hugh Shortridge was of Witheridge in Chulmleigh, Devon, to the poor of which parish he gave a legacy of £100, and where he had relations both of his own name and others, some in humble condition. Several of his family had been members of Exeter College, and he returned to the College in 1679 with his pupil Sir George Shiers, only child of Robert and Lady Elizabeth Shiers and heir to Slyfield in Surrey. Sir George died 1685 at the age of 25 and Lady Elizabeth 14 Aug. 1700 of cancer at the age of 66, and was buried at Fitcham, her husband had d. 1669 age 56. She left Dr. Shortridge her executor to arrange her benefaction to Exeter College. Her epitaph at Great Bookham, Surrey, runs thus :—S. M. Elizabethæ, Roberti Shiers de Slyfield House, Armigeri, uxoris pientissimæ, ex quo sex suscepit liberos, quemque per 32 annos vidua deflevit. Per quod tempus animam Deo ardentissimâ pietate, rem familiarem pauperum necessitatibus levandis consecravit. Quibus tamen ægris vulneratisve medicas adhibuit manus, adjunctaque pharmacis pietate, felicissimo successu clarissimos Æsculapii filios exæquavit. Utroque parente illustris, multo virtutibus illustrior, tandem cancri viscerum acerbissimos dolores per biennium passa, quæ naturam quidem debellavit, nec tamen patientiam Christianam labefactavit, cælo maturam efflavit animam Aug. 14: 1700: Ætat: 66.

Hugo Shortridge Rector de Fetcham, quem ex asse Hæredem reliquit, hæc monumento hoc inscribi curavit, quod ipsa adhuc vivens condidit.

By indenture dated 25 July 1715 (see Reg. 19 Nov. 1787: trust deed to Sir F. Vincent bart. 25 June 1715, in our box) he vested the estates in trustees for the benefit of his relations for three years, and after that time to pay £100 a year to the bursar of Ex. Coll. to augment the commons of the Rector and Fellows ; and £100 a year to be paid to the Rector of Exeter, Rector of Lincoln and Principal of Jesus for 20 years to accumulate for the purpose of buying four advowsons for Ex. Coll., two in Hertford and two in Surrey, or near those counties, which the Rector and Fellows were to take by seniority. After the 20 years the £100 to be paid to Ex. Coll. on condition that two new Fellows be elected on S. Stephen's day (Dr. Shortridge's birthday), one from Herts. and one from Surrey—one of them to be a senior B.A. and to take deacon's orders at 23 and assist the Chaplain, the other to be of at least two years' standing in the University and take deacon's orders at 23 and assist the Chaplain if the first assistant shall be minded to resign or shall die. One third of the £100 is to go to the College Treasury, the rest to the general dividends. Shortridge gave £20 a year to William Sheppard, or

Reynolds exhibitions in 1756, three from Eton and three from Exeter; Eton has appropriated her three, it is not clear by what right. St. John Eliot founded two Eliot exhibitions from Truro school.

Some of the Fellows of this period redeemed the fame of the College. Joseph Atwell, George Stinton and Francis Milman (a learned physician) were fellows of the Royal Society. John Upton was known for his edition of Arrian's Epictetus and of Spenser's Faerie Queen, and for his Observations on Shakspere; James Edgcombe wrote in answer to Chubb the Deist; Benjamin Kennicott was the leading Hebrew scholar of his day and collated the Hebrew

Shepheard, for life, and then to Sheppard's mother, and sister Elizabeth for their lives (Elizabeth d. 26 July 1780), and then to be paid to the Rector of Ex. Coll. to be given thus, £5 apiece to the two chaplains, £4 to the Subdean, £2 to the *Moderator*, £3 for a dinner at the Fellows' table on S. Stephen's day, £1 to the senior of the Battelers' table for a dinner there on the same day. No timber was to be felled on the estates for 40 years except for repairs, then the proceeds of felling timber to be paid to Ex. Coll. Library; see Reg. 19 May 1744; the first two Fellows on the new Shiers foundation were elected 26 Dec. 1744, S. Stephen's day; Manning and Bray's *Surrey* ii. 692; Clutterbuck's *Hertfordshire* i. 340. On 29 Dec. 1781 the Visitor determined that the Rector might take one of Dr. Shortridge's livings; but Rector Bray who d. 1785 left a bequest of £500 to augment the Rectorship (Reg. 5 June 1786), as long as the Rector shall not take a Shortridge living (otherwise to go to Domus); and 1794 £100 a year was added by the College to the Rector's income as long as the Rectors refrain from taking a Shortridge living—the question arising about Bushey in Herts; this was confirmed 10 Mch 1798 when it was further resolved that the whole payment to the Rector should be made up to £500 a year, the overplus to be repaid to the College if it should be more than previous deficiencies, this money payment to include receipts from dividends, Bursars, clear income of Kidlington, interest on Dr. Bray's £500, the £100 voted in 1794, room rent, receipts from allowance of commons, future donations or bequests (£800 was voted 16 June 1798 for improving the Rector's lodgings); on the improvement of the Rector's income see 3 Nov. 1825 and the Report on Domus at the end of the third Register. The Reg. 27 Jan. 1803 contains an account of the Shortridge Fund for buying advowsons. When the timber on the Shortridge estates came to be cut in 1813, the Vicars of Leatherhead &c., who had the right to the underwood only, claimed all, but after a friendly Chancery suit the College right was allowed (Reg. 12 Mch 1813, 19 June 1817, 27 May 1818, 4 Feb. 1822). On 22 Aug. 1822 the Rectories of Rype and Waldron near Lewes in Sussex were bought out of the Shortridge and Richards living funds (see particulars in the Register). On 7 Feb. 1840 the R. of Shillingstone near Blandford in Dorset was bought for £3350 out of the Shortridge Fund. See further 24 Feb. 1824 on Bushey, in 1835 the College gave £100 towards the erection of a Chapel of Ease, and a Communion Service for its use (Reg. p. 49).

MSS. of the Bible; John Stackhouse's edition of Theophrastus 'de historia plantarum,' Critical remarks on Ælian and other authors, and works on British plants and algae had some reputation; Stephen Weston was known for his Oriental studies, and some of his Chinese studies were remarkable: William Holwell Carr made a fine collection of Italian paintings which he bequeathed to the National Gallery; Demainbray was Royal Astronomer at Richmond; Stephen Peter Rigaud was Savilian professor of Astronomy, and printed Bradley's Works and Harriot's Papers and the Arenarius of Archimedes, and Notices concerning Newton's Principia; he further selected the contents of 'Correspondence of Scientific men of the 18th century.' Among those who were not fellows Jonathan Toup held a leading place as a critical scholar, and had some influence on Porson.

A letter from Walter Kerrick to Edward Weston, dated Uxbridge, 8 June 1767 (Hist. Comm. 1885, p. 406) gives an interesting picture of a pupil being introduced to his tutor. 'I take the first opportunity of informing you that I have settled my friend Stephen Weston at Exeter College. His name was put into the Books on Monday night. Dr. Kennicott was at his villa about 7 miles from Oxford, but he returned to College on Tuesday, and we had the honor of drinking tea with him and Mr. Stinton Mr. Weston's tutor. He is reckoned a very sagacious good tutor, and I conclude from the fullness of the College that the character I heard of him is a just one. They found a difficulty in accommodating Mr. Weston with a room. The income to it was only 4 Pound, and I think a little papering and a few more chairs will make it very neat and commodious. The young man seemed to like his destination very well and, from my knowledge of him and his conversation, I must promise myself everything that is good from him. It would be injustice to him not to acquaint you with what Mr. Stinton told me; He said, after overhawling him, that he found him an admirable scholar. If the little I have done in conducting my cousin to Oxford is agreable to Dear Mr. Weston, it will be the highest pleasure to him who has the honor' &c.

The question about rooms was always a difficult one. On 30 June 1761 'it was decreed that whoever is permitted to take a chamber shall continue to be tenant of that chamber and pay the rent, unless he obtains leave to move into another chamber that may become

vacant and untenanted; and tho' he should be permitted to retire into
the country in vacation times, yet he shall not be permitted to throw
up his room under colour of renting a garret, but shall go on paying
his quarterly rent for the room he had taken, in the same manner as
if he were personally resident in College.'

Matriculation Examinations only began in 1827, and at Oriel and
Balliol only. The Final Examinations in the last century were a
farce; Lord Eldon humorously describes the two questions asked
him viz. What is the meaning of Golgotha? and Who founded
University College? Scholars were looked down on, and hardly
regarded as gentlemen by the regular commoners [1].

John Wesley's father Samuel had been at Exeter College; and one
of the fellows, Thomas Broughton, had already come under Wesley's
influence in 1732, before his election, and was in 1743 secretary of the
Society for promoting Christian Knowledge. George Thomson V. of
S. Gennys is referred to in Doddridge's *Life of Colonel Gardiner*, as
the second remarkable instance of conversion: and Samuel Walker of
Truro was a name known far and wide in Evangelical circles. Some of
the later fellows also belonged to the evangelical school, such as John
David Macbride.

It has been remarked that the revival of religious feeling in the 18th
and 19th followed the same course as in the 16th and 17th centuries.
First came the renewed sense of personal relation to God, among the
Reformers; then the idea of church authority among the Caroline
divines, then the Latitudinarian movement. Similarly the Evangelical
revival of the last century led to the High Church and Broad Church
phases of thought. But there is a danger in drawing sharp lines, and
when it is said that the Evangelical party declined and the High
Church took their place, it is not really meant that spiritual and
personal religion declined, but that its activity took another form [2];
the young men who in the previous generation would have followed
the lead of Simeon, now followed the lead of Keble and Newman.
The essential feelings co-existed in all three periods, but in different
proportions and relations. Such constituent elements of religion tend

[1] Pattison's *Memoirs* 125.
[2] Burgon's *Twelve Good Men*; Overton, *The English Church in the nineteenth century* 93 (1894).

to clear themselves gradually of the accretions that have grown up under the influence of successive schools of thought. And, again, the movement of 1833 was not a sudden revolution. The way had been prepared by the steady efforts of the Evangelical, High Church and Liberal parties in the church, to restore religious feeling; efforts that already showed a marked success, which those who write about the new movement are apt to suppress or minimise. When that movement[1] gave a new direction to the activity of the English church, Exeter contributed several men of mark to its ranks, such as J. B. Morris, Upton Richards, J. D. Dalgairns, W. Lockhart (whose secession caused Newman such trouble at Littlemore[2]); but of these the ablest man was William Sewell[3]. He did much to raise the intellectual tone of the College, was a many-sided man, and the earliest advocate of University Extension[4]. His pamphlet *Suggestions for the Extension of University Teaching* 1850 states his object as 'the diminution of the expenses of education, its extension in the best form—that form which the Universities alone are capable of supplying—its expansion to its utmost limits, so that it may embrace the whole kingdom, not even excluding the most distant colonies. Though it may be impossible to bring the masses requiring education to the University, may it not be possible to carry the University to them? The University possesses a large amount of available resources and machinery, consisting partly of pecuniary means, partly and principally of men of high talents and endowments. These may be made instrumental in establishing professorships, lectureships, and examinations in the most important places in the kingdom. The institution of these professorships and lectures would be strictly analogous to the original foundation of the Universities themselves. The authorities of the places would no doubt gladly provide the requisite accommodation for the delivery of lectures, holding examinations, &c. Cambridge would take its due

[1] For outside views of the movement, see Lecky, *History of Rationalism* i. 172–3, 287; *Fortnightly Review* Oct. 1893 p. 452.

[2] Pattison's *Memoirs* 193, 210.

[3] See T. Mozley's *Reminiscences* c. 73; Newman's *Letters* ii. 261, 315, 320, 323, 341, 345; Pusey's *Life* i. 293, 302–4, 379, ii. 42, 65, 67, 70, 204, 209, 269, 287; Pattison's *Memoirs* 24, 246, F. D. Maurice's *Life* i. 210, 280, 293 and 301 (on Carlyle), 387.

[4] See an appreciative notice in Wells' *Oxford and Oxford Life* c. ix; *Oxf. Univ. Extension Gazette* Jan. 1894, p. 45 (with picture from photo).

share of the work. The cycle of instruction would embrace the various subjects comprehended in the University examinations. By originating such a comprehensive scheme, the Universities would become the great centres and springs of education throughout the country and would command the sympathy and affection of the nation at large, without sacrificing or compromising any principle which they are bound to maintain.' It should be added that all this was, of course, to be in the interest of the Church, for one of his main principles was 'that the Catholic Church only has the power or the right to educate.'

He was the first person I heard dilate on the theory of Folklore, and explain the permanence of detail in early stories by showing how conservative nurses and children are in always repeating a thing in the same form of words. A child will correct you if you happen to vary the wording. He used to say that Herodotus was largely in-debted to the Arabian Nights, meaning of course that common fund of Eastern stories, which the Arabian Nights have preserved in their latest and fullest literary form. He was a great conversationalist, and what Johnson called a clubbable man.

He at first warmly supported the new movement; but when Newman began to move away from the influence of Keble, and fell under the influence of De Maistre and Lamennais[1] (he had begun to lose his hold on Anglican church views as early as 1839), and his younger supporters, such as J. B. Morris, Ward, and others claimed to hold all Roman doctrine in the English church[2], and especially after the appearance of Tract 90 in 1841, Sewell like Hook, W. Palmer of Worcester, and other steady churchmen, recoiled and made a stand; they saw at last that Whately had been right in issuing his warning note *Tendimus in Latium*. Mozley speaks of Ward's *monstrous cobwebs*, and it was a common saying that it was hard to have to face a new dissolving view once a month. Sewell's article in the *Quarterly*[3] of March 1842 marked the turn of the tide. In form it was quite innocent, it made no allusion to existing controversies. It was *only* an account of the Caroline Divines, showing how they did not speak

[1] Mozley ii. 209, Newman's *Letters* i. 444, ii. 238, 305.
[2] Mozley ii. 225.
[3] He wrote 15 articles for the *Quarterly* between 1837 and 1845.

evil of the Reformation or the Reformers, did not reject the name of Protestant (Laud said on the scaffold, 'I have always lived in the Protestant religion established in England, and in that I come now to die'), did not spend their time in pointing out the defects of the Church of England, while glossing over those of Rome, and palliating what they could not praise; on the contrary, Andrewes, Laud, and others carried on a strong polemic against Rome. But all these things were just what the younger men of the movement were doing, and the article naturally irritated them. Morris said, 'Is he not rightly called *Suillus*, for he will never go the whole hog'; but the pun was perhaps borrowed from Whately.

Most leading men, from Newman to Darwin, have been great novel-readers. The chiefs of the movement, from Newman down to Gresley and Paget, *wrote* novels[1] to illustrate their views, often with a large element of caricature in them; in one, the puritan, Melchizedek Howl, is made to say, 'Behold I will build unto myself a pue.' Sewell's novel *Hawkstone* was of a very sensational character. The low-church parson is let off easily, he is only taken by Irish conspirators into an underground cave and has to take an oath, with his lips set to a cup of blood, that he will not tell. But of the two chief villains (Jesuits) one fled away shrieking into a secret passage, where he was eaten by rats, who had evidently begun at the extremities, and the walls were convulsively scrabbled over with gory fingers; the other fell on his hands and knees, during a fire, into the melting lead of a reservoir. This was not quite original, for Tony Foster had fled into a secret passage at Cumnor, and Chowles in Old St. Paul's had gone down in the molten lead. All these caricatures have perished, but the religious idea took a gentler form in his sister Miss Sewell's *Amy Herbert*, and other tales; while Miss Yonge's stories have been the delight of two generations of readers. Miss Yonge notes the change in the general view, when she makes Lucilla Sandbrook say, 'The last generation was that of mediaevalism, ecclesiology, symbolism, whatever you may call it. Married women have worked out of it. It is the middle-aged maids that monopolize it.' Sewell wrote many books, of which his *Christian Morals* and *Christian Politics* were perhaps the chief, but they were

---

[1] Newman's *Letters* ii. 117.

l

very paradoxical. When he wrote of Tract 90 as leading men to receiving *paradoxes and therefore errors*, Church notes 'good, *vide Christian Ethics*[1].' He was perhaps thinking of such passages as that which Lecky notices[2], 'I believe that a geologist deeply impressed with the mystery of baptism—that mystery by which a new creature is formed by means of water and fire—would never have fallen into the absurdities of accounting for the formation of the globe solely by water or solely by fire. He would not have maintained a Vulcanian or a Neptunian theory. He would have suspected that the truth lay in the union of both.' There is a curious smatter of scientific talk in these books. Some were shocked at the comparison, in the *Christian Politics*, of the three parts of the British Constitution to the three Persons of the Trinity.

When A. P. Stanley came up to Balliol in 1834, Moberly at Balliol, Johnson at Queen's, and Sewell at Exeter were spoken of as the three best college tutors in Oxford. Sewell's lectures were very interesting, partly because he wove in whatever he was thinking about, with little regard to the subject of the lecture. Once, when we ought to have been construing the Georgics, he spent nearly the whole hour in discussing Newman's Theory of Development. 'There are little machines,' he said, 'which will develop a small portrait into a large one, preserving the proportions. But if the machine so enlarged the nose and dwarfed the rest, that you could see little else but nose, it could hardly be called a legitimate development. Yet that is Mr. Newman's idea of development. He has really taken his idea simply from the actual growth of the Roman church, and almost ignores the existence of the Greek church, merely saying it is a case of arrested development like China.' It is curious to note that R. H. Froude[3] wrote as early as Aug. 1835, 'You lug in the Apostles' Creed and talk about *expansions*. What is the end of expansions? Will not the Romanists say that their whole system is an expansion of the Holy Catholic Church and the Communion of Saints?' Sewell adhered to Keble's rule *Quod primum, verum*. He was fond of saying

---

[1] Newman's *Letters* ii. 333.

[2] *History of Rationalism* i. 290 ; see ii. 236.

[3] Newman's *Letters* ii. 127 ; see 241 Newman himself on 'developing in new ways.'

that the same end might be arrived at by a variety of means, sometimes quite opposite means.   Thus the Baptist's ascetic life, and our
Lord's presence at feasts were both means to the same end.   So
again S. Paul recommends celibacy as good in a time of mission
work and persecution, but in a settled church it is better that the
clergy should be married, and the parson's wife and daughters are
often his best curates.   Miss Mozley was gratified by finding Newman[1]
once (though in a bantering tone) say, 'Parsons' wives are useful in
a parish, and that in a way in which no man can rival them.'   But
Newman spoke satirically of the married clergy in *Loss and Gain*.
Ward's sudden marriage, after his fierce denunciations of that state,
was a great shock to the party.

Sewell said, 'They call a miracle a suspension of the Laws of Nature.
Why, we are always suspending those laws.   Iron naturally sinks in
water, but we bend it into shape, and use the law of displacement of
fluids, and the iron ship floats.   But properly speaking no law is
suspended, we do but fight one law of nature by another.   And this
is what most of our improvements come to.'   When some spoke
slightingly of the 'Evidences,' Sewell said, We need all the help we
can get.   The men in S. Paul's ship did not ride at one anchor only;
no, they *cast four anchors out of the stern, and wished for the day*.   He
upheld the divine right of kings, but with a reservation.   Kingship
arose, he said, often from force or fraud, but long possession sanctified
it.   Three generations are enough for this.   Even if the Jacobites
might rise against George I or George II, yet George III had the
divine right.   If Cromwell had made himself king, and his son Richard
had succeeded, and then Richard's son, that son would have had the
divine right.   This did not please some of our Stuart devotees who
held that the divine right lasted for ever in one family.   But, subject
to this reservation, he upheld the theory of Passive Obedience.

What the men most complained of was his forcing them into the
schools before their sixteenth term; which, as they then came into
residence only in the fourth[2] (sometimes fifth) term after matriculation,
gave them too little time; and this, when other colleges such as
Balliol fixed no such limit.   One man went to Alban Hall rather than

[1] Newman's *Letters* ii. 211; see Wordsworth 344.
[2] Newman's *Letters* i. 27.

submit to the rule, and got his first class from thence. The College rule was not really so strict, but Sewell so applied it.

But he was sometimes as fanciful in his lectures as in his books. C. H. Pearson was shocked at his dictum that the highest class of animals, the vertebrate, was constructed as a type of the Cross. Marcus Southwell was once so annoyed that he said, ' Why does he call it lectures on Plato, on Butler and so on, when it is all lectures on Sewell.' His etymologies were more than pre-scientific. Once he derived *periwig* from the Greek περιοικος, 'a house round the head,' ' the *w* is the Greek digamma, represented as usual by omicron.' Every one was taken aback, and only one man ventured to say, with hesitation, 'I—I thought that *periwig* was another form of the French *perruque*.' Sewell laughed and said, 'Of course you are right.' Another time, after some similar derivation, Mackenzie Walcott, who had little regard for his brother Wykehamist, said, respectfully, ' Might we not, Sir, on these principles, derive *teapot* from *tepeo*.'

It was at one of these lectures that Sewell burnt a book which he thought obnoxious, in 1849, the last time a book has been publicly burnt in a College hall. The scene is thus described by the owner of the book, Arthur Blomfield[1], now R. of Beverston and R.D. of Dursley, Glouc.:—'I had just bought the "Nemesis of Faith," or as it was called, "Faith with a Vengeance," when on Tuesday morning, Feb. 27, 1849, I, an undergraduate of Exeter College, attended a lecture in hall. The Rev. William Sewell, Sub-Rector of Exeter College (not "Dean of the Chapel") was lecturer. He declaimed loudly against Froude's "Nemesis of Faith." Hearing, on my own confession, that I possessed it, he requested me to bring "that book" to him. No sooner had I complied with his request (Sewell was my college tutor) than he snatched the book from my hands and thrust it into the blazing fire of the college hall (not "quadrangle"). I see him now, with hall poker in hand, in delightful indignation, poking at this, to him, obnoxious book. In a few hours this " burning of the book" was known all over Oxford. As your article justly remarks, "the burning only served as an advertisement."'

It was a sight to see Sewell lecturing, or rather talking, in the hall.

[1] Letter in *Daily News* 2 May 1892.

He used to stand with his back to the great hall fire, and his gown gathered up in his left hand. His gown and surplice were usually nearly as ragged as those of Pusey and Burgon, which were said to be a grief of mind to their lady friends. But let us be just to them. They were thinking of other things, it is doubtful whether they ever thought about their dress. Sewell used to tell a story about himself, which illustrates the communistic system that prevails on a College staircase. Often you do not get your own glasses, teacups, spoons, forks, &c., but those that happen to be ready to the servant's hand, no matter whose they are. But this does not often extend so far as in Sewell's case. One Saturday his laundress said to him with a curtsy, Please, Sir, you want some new shirts. Why, Mary, he answered, looking down at his wrists with justifiable pride, this seems a very good shirt. Yes, Sir, she replied, with another curtsy, but, for some time you have been *living on the staircase* (i. e. wearing other people's shirts). This communism had its objectionable side. A man on the staircase, who was fond of natural history, kept a hedgehog, unknown to Sewell, and the creature sometimes strayed. One night, Sewell, hearing something scuttling about the room, jumped out of bed to see what it was, and came with his bare foot down on the hedgehog : naturally, for some little time, he did not walk quite easily.

Sewell objected to University Commissions [1]. He said the Colleges could and should reform themselves. All old laws tend to become obsolete, and much is gradually dropped or adapted to new require-ments. Let the Colleges make the necessary changes, throw open the close fellowships and scholarships, at least in part, and public opinion would support them. Unfortunately there were two objections to this view— plausible as he always made his views ; first that the favoured districts would not give up the close endowments without an Act of Parliament, and secondly that a large part of the Oxford fellows opposed an obstinate *non possumus* to every change, and appealed to the intentions of the founders, which few of them carried out either as to residence or study. The only resource to compel the performance of the trust, or to carry out the changes made necessary by the lapse of time, was to call in the intervention of the

[1] Pattison's *Memoirs* 75, 244, 255, 304, Newman's *Letters* ii. 238, 296 abuses in Colleges, Stanley's *Life* i. 418, 433-4, founders' wishes.

sovereign power, the State, which was done at last in 1854. Even
then only 3 Colleges, Exeter, Lincoln, and Corpus, availed themselves of the privilege allowed them of drawing up their own
statutes. The remaining Colleges left it to the Commissioners to
draw up 'Ordinances' for them. Sewell wrote a squib called *The
University Commission or Lord John Russell's Postbag* (an idea taken
from Thomas Moore), issued anonymously at Oxford in 1850 in
4 parts, and J. T. B. Landon wrote, anonymously, two supplements
to it, called *Eureka*, 1850 and 1853.

Sewell did a considerable thing in founding the Colleges of
S. Columba near Dublin and Radley near Oxford. His books are
forgotten, but his memory will survive as the founder of Radley. A sad
disregard of economy in carrying out his ideas loaded him with debts,
which marred the happiness of his later years, and severed his
connection with Radley College over which he presided; but the
work was taken up by other hands, and continues to flourish.

J. B. Morris, a fair scholar and theologian, was one of the most
curious men of that excited time. In 1842 he gained the prize
for an 'Essay towards the Conversion of Learned and Philosophical
Hindus.' Newman says of him[1], 'he is a most simple-minded,
conscientious fellow, but as little possessed of tact or common sense
as he is great in other departments. He had to take my church in
my absence. I had cautioned him against extravagances in S. Mary's
pulpit, as he had given some specimens in that line once before.
What does he do on S. Michael's day but preach a sermon, not
simply on angels, but on his one subject, for which he has a mono-
mania, of fasting; nay, and say that it was a good thing, whereas
angels feasted on festivals, to make the brute creation fast on fast
days, so I am told. May he (*salvis ossibus suis*) have a fasting horse
the next time he goes steeple-chasing. Well, this was not all. You
may conceive how the Heads of Houses, Cardwell, Gilbert, &c.,
fretted under this; but the next Sunday he gave them a more
extended exhibition, *si quid possit*. He preached to them, *totidem
verbis*, the Roman doctrine of the Mass; and, not content with that,
added in energetic terms, that every one was an unbeliever, carnal,

---

[1] Newman's *Letters* ii. 291, 4 Nov. 1839. See Mozley ii. 305, Pattison's
Memoirs 184, 222.

and so forth, who did not hold it. To this he added other specula-
tions of his own still more objectionable. This was too much for any
Vice-Chancellor. In consequence he was had up before him; his
sermon officially examined; and he formally admonished; and the
Bishop written to. The Bishop is to read his sermon, and I have
been obliged to give my judgment on it, which is not favourable, nor
can be. I don't suppose much more will be done, but it is very
unpleasant. The worst part is that the Vice-Chancellor [Gilbert] has
not said a single word to me, good or bad, and has taken away his
family from S. Mary's. I cannot but hope that he will have the good
sense to see that this is a mistake.'

Morris and some others led a very ascetic life. All through Lent
Morris took no food till sundown, and then only two handfuls of peas
which he immersed in a little saucepan till they were soft enough for
mastication. Dalgairns nearly lost his life at the close of the Lent of
1840; for 36 hours before Good Friday he had abstained from food
altogether; late on the evening of Holy Thursday his scout found him
lying on the floor, and he would not have recovered from his swoon
but for prompt help. Froude (*Remains* i. 49–50, 212) remarks
that fasting incapacitated him for work or thinking.

Morris' conversation consisted largely in turning the English Church
into ridicule. He passed his time in rooms in the front Tower, reading
the Fathers, and cutting jokes upon our stepmother, the Church of
England. Just before his secession the Bursar named him University
preacher, to show that his brother fellows did not mistrust his loyalty
to the Church. He accepted the nomination quite cordially, and
went over almost immediately. The College naturally thought this
an ungenerous return for their confidence. But Morris found
that his convictions were no longer such as were consistent with
the obligations incumbent on a fellow of the College at that day,
and he resigned his fellowship. Morris lived in London during
the latter part of his life, in very poor circumstances. Old friends
would make him come and dine, but after two or three times, when
he found his attempts at converting them a failure, he would refuse
to see them again. His special devotion was to the Virgin, and he
wrote a book called *Taleetha Koomee*, to show how Christ's words
'Damsel, I say unto thee, Arise' were a type and prophecy of the

Assumption of the Virgin. Once when walking with a friend by a fine new church, his friend said, 'Who will be worshipped there, Morris, in fifty years' time?' and he answered, 'Either Mary, or Mary Anne!' Other persons have shared Morris' belief that posterity will run into one of two opposite extremes, and that either Romanism or Socialism will be the dominant power in the future. But the dilemma is a very unsafe argument.

He was the last believer in the Phœnix[1], and his letter about it is a good illustration of the fanciful reasoning of that time. 'If an animal existed which served a particular prophetical function when the reality had been in one Person, there might be no more need of it, and so it might become extinct, if it is extinct . . . All dispensations of Providence contain anomalies, and so the anomalousness of the Phœnix seems to be almost positive evidence to induce one to believe it.' The reader who consults the writings of that troubled time may smile or sigh over them. Morris was a very likeable man. T. Mozley[2] says, 'My sufferings at the hands of " Jack Morris " I have already described. But people love those most they have taken most pains with. What would I give to have a day with him now, and hear his searchings and ramblings into the region of the supernatural! not but that all nature was supernatural in his eyes.'

But in the turmoil of the Tractarian movement the proper work of the University and of the Colleges had not been wholly neglected. There were other men who were carrying on the regular teaching of the College with very different aims and interests; and Frederick Denison Maurice refers with deep gratitude to the kindness and generosity shown him by Jacobson (afterwards Bishop of Chester) and J. L. Richards (afterwards Rector[3]). Jacobson, a friend of Sterling, had arranged that Maurice should enter at Exeter, and be allowed to count his Cambridge terms. Jacobson writes, 'As to your talk, about not keeping next term—were you not just beginning, before the long vacation, to do something like an ordinary mortal? Is there a chance of your doing half as much at home? Would anybody but a feelosofer the likes of you have set to work

---

[1] *Notes and Queries* 7. vi. 481 (1888).
[2] *Reminiscences* ii. 10, 229.
[3] Their letters in Maurice's *Life* i. 111–2 ; and see 99, 131, 179, Nat. Biog.

to write a new three-volume novel [Eustace Conway]. As to money I have no doubt that I shall be able to help you. Indeed I know that I shall without any inconvenience; so don't go and borrow dishonestly, neither stay away rusticating and psychologizing, but come here and mind your books like a good boy. I see every reason for your coming, and so did Sterling.' Richards writes, 'I hope you will allow me to do for you what I have done before now for other pupils, which is, advance any money you require for your immediate use, and that you will come up and keep the term. I recommend you to get the examination over as soon as possible. It might be more for your interest to aim a little lower than your merits might justly entitle you to aspire to, than to encounter the anxiety and expense which a lengthened time of preparation must entail.' The confidence and friendly tone between Maurice and the tutors shows how the Tutorial system acted when properly worked. Maurice soon betook himself to the real work of his life, a prolonged effort to reach the mind of the working man, and help him to improve his condition. He thought that the Church of England, as an institution, ought to grapple with contemporary forms of social evil, so as to exhibit Christianity as the true source of every effective social amelioration. If the movement had affected him, he soon took his own line, and after 1848 many others did the same. 'Experience like a tide soaks all absorbing in,' and the present leaders of the movement have their minds opened to the claims of Criticism[1], and still more to the position of Labour and the need of a higher organization of work. When Canon Scott-Holland refers to Maurice's *Kingdom of Christ* as authoritative; when Mr. Gore presides over a meeting in Exeter College hall, held in 1893 to consider the claims of labour, and Mr. Tom Mann is one of the chief speakers, it is clear that the old views have changed. The early leaders took no interest in the efforts of Maurice and Kingsley to improve the condition of the working classes in London and elsewhere[2].

The interest in the controversy between the Churches of England and of Rome began to flag. The secession of 1845 cleared the air,

[1] Stanley said to Pattison, 'How different the fortunes of the Church of England might have been if Newman had been able to read German.' Newman confesses the failure of the movement in his *Anglican Difficulties*; see Stanley's *Life*, i. 370.

[2] Newman's imagination was attracted (*Letters* ii. 285) by the account of the Capuchin in *I Promessi Sposi*.

and the political events of 1848 turned men's minds into other channels. They no longer discussed such questions as, whether the Church of England was bound by the four first or six first General Councils, whether England was in a state of schism or no, whether our position was one of continuous appeal to a General Council, &c. The question too of University Reform and the relation of the Professoriate to the Collegiate or Tutorial system attracted general attention.

Here we may put together some notices about the more material aspects of the College. There have been considerable changes in the buildings during the last hundred years. In 1778 the Library was rebuilt after a design by the Rev. William Crowe. On 8 May 1788 it was resolved to remodel the front and windows of the College. On 10 June 1820 a new porch for the Hall, surmounted by a clock, was completed: the porch cost £103 11s 3d, the clock £125 12s 3d; a water tank also was constructed in the Library Court, for £88 17s 3d, containing 350 gallons. In 1821 a servants' hall was constructed for the use of the Common Room[1] and Bursary in the adjoining cellar, with a passage under the Bursary, at a cost of £309 3s. As far back as 10 Nov. 1740 it was ordered that a lamp should be put up to light the quadrangle (Wordsworth 688). Gas lights (Wordsworth 408, 410) appear in 1820, perhaps to give way in turn to the electric light in 1894. The new buildings east of the gate in Broad Street were commenced 1833, and completed May 1834, they cost £3574 11s 3d. In 1833-4 also the buildings from the Hall round to the Chapel were new faced towards the Turl with Bath stone, oriel windows inserted, and the tower considerably altered; the upper part of the tower was found to be so weak that the face of it was made to recede somewhat, and four turrets added to carry off the awkward appearance occasioned by the projection of the quoins; the garrets on this side were raised considerably; the inner face of the tower towards the quadrangle was also refaced. In 1836 the interior of the Chapel was repaired and coloured and the glass cleaned.

In 1854 New Buildings were begun with a tower facing Broad

---

[1] The 'Common Parlor' was used earlier at Cambridge than at Oxford. Our first Common Rooms were at Merton and S. John's just after the Restoration. See Clarke-Willis i. 225, Rogers v. 688, Oxford Architect. Soc. 1887. p. 115, Qu. Rev. 1887, p. 432, Boase's Oxford 168, Wordsworth 148, 663.

Street; they contained 18 sets of rooms in addition to a large room over the gateway in the Tower, and the first contract was for £3976. Next year the foundation of the New Library was laid, the first contract being for £2988, exclusive of the foundations. (The commissioners allowed first £4500, and then £1200 more, of the Library funds to be thus used, see Reg. 1854, and 8 May 1858.) In 1856 a new Rectory House was built, together with eight sets of rooms between the Rectory and the Old Broad St. Buildings; the first contract was for £5000. In 1856 the Chapel was begun, the first estimate being for £7045, with £500 for a turret, and £405 for doors, floor, &c. but all these estimates were much exceeded. The architect was Sir Gilbert Scott, who had reported that the North wall of the Chapel was in a very dangerous state, but there was great difficulty in pulling it down. The first stone of the Chapel was laid by the Bishop of Rupert's Land (David Anderson, an old scholar of the College) 29 Nov. 1856. It was consecrated on S. Luke's day 18 Oct. 1859 (Cox 426) by the Bishop of Oxford in the presence of the Visitor, Bp. Phillpotts. The money for these buildings had been accumulating for some years, the late Rector J. L. Richards gave £1000 and many persons then or previously Fellows of the College gave £100 each (which was nearly the value of a year's fellowship at that time), some of the Fellows also each giving a couple of the marble or serpentine pillars, and great liberality was shown by old members of the College; the screen and organ were given by the undergraduates. The organ has been twice reconstructed since that time. The new Chapel occupies the site of the former Rector's house at the east end of the old Chapel, in addition to the ground on which the old Chapel stood. As part of an old City Ditch ran close to the north side, very deep foundations were required, and many cartloads of stone besides all the stone work of the old Chapel were used in these foundations. The new Rector's house was built on the site of the old S. Helen's Quadrangle, which included 22 sets of rooms, so that there are only 14 sets of rooms gained in addition to the previously existing accommodation.

Many portraits were placed in the Hall during this period. In 1780 William Peters painted a picture of Walter de Stapeldon (said to be copied from a portrait of Bossuet), and it was placed at the east

end of the Hall[1]. In 1785 William Holwell painted a picture of
Sir William Petre and gave it to the College. In 1832 a portrait of
Bishop Prideaux was placed in the Hall. It is a copy from an
original picture at Laycock Abbey in Wilts, made by an artist called
Smith, who made another copy for Dr. Burton, the Regius Professor
of Divinity. Smith also copied the picture of the first Earl of
Shaftesbury at the Charterhouse in 1834. The portrait of Rector
Jones was painted by Phillipps 1833, but the engraving by Cousins,
who introduced some alterations, is a better resemblance. The
portrait of J. T. Coleridge was painted by Pickersgill in 1835, but
it is not so good a likeness as the engraving from Mrs. Carpenter's
portrait of the Judge. The portrait of Sir Charles Lyell is a good
copy. That of Rector Cole by John Opie the Cornish artist is an
original and good.

In 1833 sermons were delivered in the Chapel every Sunday
evening for the first time, the duty being undertaken by Richards the
subrector, and Sewell. In 1871 the Visitor ratified a shortening of
the week day service in the Chapel. A musical service has been
added on Sundays, Saints' Days, and Eves, and the Organist Scholarships have brought forward several men of mark.

There have been disputes at different times about the respective
rights of the Colleges and the City of Oxford. In 1843 the City
of Oxford endeavoured to rate the Colleges to the Poor Rate and
tried the case with Exeter College. A parishioner of S. Michael's
was found to object to the rate, on the ground that Exeter College
was not rated. The rate was referred to the Recorder to be
amended, and he placed the College on the Rate Book. A distress
was levied and some College plate taken. The College brought an
action of trespass, and the issue was tried at the Summer Assizes, but
a verdict was given for the College on three points, (1) That the
Recorder had no jurisdiction under the Local Act which regulated the
Poor Rate in Oxford; (2) That the Rector's lodgings should have
been rated separately from the College; (3) That the old foundation
of Exeter College is not in the parish of S. Michael's (see Jackson's
Oxford Journal 20 July 1844). The city was therefore nonsuited;

[1] Gutch iii. 113. There are few Colleges, except Christ Church, that possess
many original portraits. See list of our portraits p. 274.

but the University felt that the exemption from the Poor Rate was unfair, and a friendly arrangement was come to on the question.

In 1846 the College settled a suit with the City about some ground lying on the south side of the old City wall and extending from the Turl to the wall that divides the College from the Theatre court, about 18 poles in length, and running from north to south about 3 poles from the City wall to the ancient part of the College (except a bit of ground called 'The Mount with the two studies,' a part of the freehold conveyed by the City to the College about 1780 and known as Mr. Alderman Wright's house in Prideaux buildings; this excepted piece may have been that on which two rooms stood, one above and one below, which adjoined the north side of the Rector's lodgings and the south side of Prideaux buildings, uniting the two). The buildings on that site at this time were a considerable portion of the Rector's lodgings, nearly the whole of the north aisle of the Chapel and about nine sets of rooms west of the Chapel. The City stated that the ground in question was leased to the College for 99 years from 1622; that this lease was surrendered 1682 and a fresh lease taken of 99 years from that date, and the City contended that from 1781 the College were tenants at will at a quit rent of £1, as it was doubtful if there was any subsequent transaction. The College now agreed to pay £2000 to the City for a conveyance in fee of the property, the £1 quit rent and any other acknowledgment to cease; the City was further to grant a new lease for the strip out of the street extending along the whole of the west and part of the south front of the College and held under the City for 1000 years from 1698–9. The fine and fees in 1682 were paid by Mr. Alderman Wright, and this may account for the absence of such a charge from the Rector's Computus of that year; it is explained in some degree by the fact that Alderman Wright obtained at this time a new lease of Rector Prideaux' house of North Hall by some arrangement with the College, for which the payment of the fine and fees may have been a consideration. The lease of 1682 and that for the 1000 years were however not to be found in the College archives (see Reg. 1741 [1]), and there was great difficulty

---

[1] Reg. 6 June 1741 new lease from Mayor and Bailiff of Oxford (see Reg. 1843), 28 June fine of £12 from them: 10 May 1832 arrangement about the ground on the Broad Street frontage (see 1839).

about the whole matter.   See Reg. pp. 99, 137.   In 1849 the College bought of the City the fee of the site and buildings in Broad Street, heretofore held under lease, for £2100.

In 1848 the servants were all urged by the Rector to insure their lives and distinctly informed that, if they neglected to do so, no provision would be made by the College for them or their families.   Nearly all insured their lives in sums varying from £200 to £500 (Reg. p. 149).

We may here put together a number of detached occurrences.   On 9 July 1745 the Rector was allowed to invest £800, taken from the Common Chest, 'collybo vel trapezitis vel alicui alii mensae publicae nummariae,' so long had the old custom lasted of keeping money unemployed.   At the same time it was proposed, and carried 8 Nov. (Bray dissenting) to sell part of the garden near the Radcliffe Library to the University.   Few parts of Oxford have been more altered in their appearance than those which now form the Radcliffe Square. In 1821 Leadenhall was sold to Jesus College for £400.

On 2 Dec. 1788 a sum of five guineas annually was voted to Dr. Holmes for collating manuscripts of the Septuagint.

In 1793, 16 Colleges employed Bolton of Witney as brewer, as the Oxford brewers had raised the price per barrel from 30s to 32s by a combination: only three Colleges brewed for themselves, Merton, Queen's, and S. John's.

In 1794 the College gave £50 towards the Home Defence of the country.   The Funds were so low that in 1797 the College bought £1000 consols at 50¼ per cent., thus giving only £503 15s, including commission of £1 5s.

On 11 Ap. 1818 £100 was voted to the Public Fund for building churches and chapels.

But who will give us a history of the social changes during this century[1], and tell us how *constitutionals* came in, just before Arnold's time, and have since been largely superseded by athletics; how the change of the dinner hour from 5 to 7 made afternoon teas a necessity and, more generally, how the habit of rising later and going to bed later has altered so many things in our daily life.   This change

[1] Wordsworth 170 constitutionals, 180 and 365 bowls, 177 football, 408 and 172 reading-parties, 548 lecture-rooms, 510 (and Burgon 4) gutters (see Boswell's *Johnson* ed. 1887 v. 22, 268, Clark i. 157, Boase's *Oxford* 59, 193).

brought in Sunday evening services[1], though the clergy at first opposed them as Methodistical. But the Evangelicals, as usual, led the way in this movement. Bowls used to be played in the College gardens after dinner, from 7 to 9 in the summer evenings; but, when the dinner hour moved on to 7, it was too late to play, as it got dark and the dew began to fall. For the same reason the custom of taking a walk in the summer evening has ceased. All games have altered. Football, which in Laud's time was played in the streets, and was therefore forbidden, has now reached a dignity which assimilates it to the tournaments of the Middle Ages. And Golf has conquered England as well as Scotland, and become a fanaticism. Cricket was always played, but was not such an institution or such a show as at present. The poet says truly :—

> Then cricket rules the noontide hours,
> And maidens in and out of teens
> Peruse each other's lace and flowers,
> And wonder what on earth it means.

But the maidens now know all about cricket, and Miss K. Gent reports[2] that it is sometimes played at the Ladies' Halls. The benighted Londoner who thinks these Halls are frequented by long rows of pale heavy-eyed girls bending over books on a lovely summer afternoon, would be astonished to see the energy and animation which they devote to all sorts of games on the lawn.

The way in which men dressed in Keble's and Arnold's time now seems strange to us[3].

The order of gentlemen-commoners[4] has disappeared. They dined at High Table with the fellows, and only attended such lectures as they liked. For these privileges they paid somewhat higher fees; and often bequeathed their silver tankards when they left to the College, or requested that their caution-money might be laid out in tankards for the use of the Hall; and some tankards still preserve their names. They at last objected to the fees, and were abolished. But the system suited some men who came up at a more advanced age, and wished to reside for a time at the University.

---

[1] Overton, *The English Church in the Nineteenth Century* 141.
[2] Wells, *Oxford and Oxford Life* 160.
[3] Burgon's *Twelve Good Men* 200.
[4] Wordsworth 646, 680.

With the coming in of the Examination system, reading ceased to be contemptible, the Scholars of a College were no longer looked down on by the Commoners, and the greater facility of travel made reading-parties common, commoner at one time than they are now. In olden days tutors taught their classes in their own rooms, now every College has lecture-rooms. Of course, as soon as the system of inter-collegiate lecturing came in, more space was required. And now there are not a few lady-students. The men's rooms too now boast sometimes of sofas and easy chairs, comforts unknown to the primitive age. The Indoor has grown with the growth of the Outdoor life. The sanded floors and spittoons of the common rooms gave way to carpets in the early part of this century. Dr. Lightfoot told us that, when it was first proposed to have a carpet, the then senior Fellow put his back against the door and said, ' Gentlemen, if you will introduce such a monstrous luxury, I will never enter this room again.' And he never did. One great modern improvement is the abundance of artificial light for reading in the evenings. Men once had not the genial inspiration of good candle-light or lamplight. The quite modern institution of tubbing in the mornings made it necessary to lay water on every floor of every staircase. The paving and lighting of the streets has been a great benefit. In 1770 there was no pavement in the High except before S. Mary's. The streets were paved with small pebbles, a depressed gutter ran down the middle of each street to collect the rain, and it was difficult to avoid being splashed with the filthy mud. Johnson used to stand astride over these kennels wrapt in meditation. It was the Commissioners' Act of 1771 that enabled some active-minded men in the University and City to effect valuable changes.

It is difficult to collect information about College Clubs. There was a Debating Society at Exeter in 1793 (Wordsworth 587). Sewell founded a Moral Philosophy Society that had some vogue. About 1839-41 there was a good Essay Club in Exeter, of which Powles, King, Morton, Langhorne, Northcote, Cowburn, Crosse, and Ewart were members. Powles published an Essay on Greek Banquets, and R. J. King two Essays, ' On the Supernatural Beings of the Middle Ages,' and ' On the origin of the Romance Literature of the xii and xiii centuries, chiefly with a reference to its Mythology.' Ernest

Hawkins was connected with the Oxford Club of the *Ramblers*, which was kept up in London at his rooms in Vernon Place under the title of the *Vernon* (C. H. O. Daniel, *Our Memories*, 89).

Most Colleges have their debating club, Exeter has its Stapeldon Club, which also acts as a committee of the Junior Common Room. Not to speak of Shakespeare clubs and chess clubs, the Musical Society is of repute, even beyond our College walls, as are also the Dialectical Society and Theological *Seminar*. These Societies and Seminars take the place of the mediaeval *Disputationes in Aula*. Not that they are descended from them, but that similar needs produce similar institutions. For there is something in the collision of intellects, in the living sparks struck out in conversation and discussion, that supplies a stimulus not given by merely reading books; and the recluse student misses a good deal by not mingling with his equals, and hearing their objections and opposing views. Almost more than anything else, this tends to clear up a man's mind and, even if he does not succeed in convincing his opponents, he often succeeds in gaining some access to fresh vistas of thought.

But Oxford has a social as well as an intellectual side, and athletics take a very leading place [1]. Mark Pattison once said, as he was walking round the Parks, that the main business of the University consisted in cricket and croquet, varied, occasionally, by a little reading and writing. Exeter College was the first to start an athletic gathering; some even ventured to say, the first in the world, since the Olympic Games. The following is an authentic account [2]. 'The year was 1850. It was the evening after the College Steeplechase (vulgarly called the *College Grind*). Some four or five congenial spirits were sipping their wine in the rooms of R. F. Bowles (brother to John Bowles, the well-known coursing squire, of Milton Hill). Besides the host there were James Aitken, George Russell (now Sir George Russell, of Swallowfield), Marcus Southwell, and Halifax Wyatt. The topic was the event of the day, and the unsatisfactory process of *negotiating* a country on Oxford hacks. "Sooner than ride such a brute again," said Wyatt,

---

[1] See the amusing article in the Revue des Deux Mondes Feb. 1894, p. 882, *L'Éducation en Angleterre.—Éducation Physique et Morale*.

[2] Shearman's *Athletics and Football* (Badminton Library 1887), p. 41; see the first programme, p. 45; and short memoirs of the leading men, pp. 43-6.

whose horse had landed into a road on his head instead of his legs,
" I 'd run across two miles of country on foot." " Well, why not?" said
the others, "let's have a College foot grind;" and so it was agreed.
Bowles, who always had a sneaking love for racing—born and bred
as he was near the training grounds on the Berkshire Downs—
suggested a race or two on the flat as well. Again the party agreed.
The conditions were drawn up, stakes named, officials appointed, and
the first meeting for *Athletic Sports* inaugurated. On the first afternoon
there was to be a *chase*, two miles across country, twenty-four jumps,
£1 entry, 10s forfeit; and on a subsequent afternoon, a quarter of
a mile on the flat, 300 yards, 100 yards, 140 yards over ten flights of
hurdles 10 yards apart, one mile, and some other stakes for " beaten
horses," open to members of Exeter College only. Notice of the
meeting, with a list of the stakes, was posted in the usual place—
a black board in the porter's lodge. Plenty of entries were made, in
no stake less than ten; for the steeplechase there were twenty-four
who started.

   ' The course chosen was on a flat marshy farm at Binsey, near the
Seven Bridge Road; it was very wet, some fields swimming in water,
the brooks bank high, and a soft take-off, which meant certain
immersion for most, if not all, the competitors. Twenty-four went
to the post, not twenty-four hard-conditioned athletes in running
toggery, but twenty-four strong active youngsters in cricket shoes and
flannels, some in fair condition, some very much the reverse, but all
determined to do or die. Plenty of folk on horse and foot came to
see this novelty, for in modern as in ancient Athens men were always
on the look out for some new thing; and in this instance, judging
from the excitement and the encouragement given to the competitors,
the novelty was much appreciated.

   ' As about half of the twenty-four starters left the post as if they were
only going to run a few hundred yards, they were necessarily soon
done with. Aitken, gradually coming through all these, had the best
of the race until one field from home, where Wyatt and J. Scott, who
had been gradually creeping up, ran level. They jumped the last
fence together. Wyatt, who landed on firmer ground, was quickest
on his legs, and ran in a comparatively easy winner. There was
a tremendous struggle for the second place, which was just obtained

by Aitken. The time, according to the present notion of running, must no doubt have been slow, but the ground was deep, the fences big, and all the competitors were heavily handicapped by wet flannels bedraggling their legs.

'Of the flat races, which were held in Port Meadow, on unlevelled turf, no authentic record has been preserved of all the events. The hurdle-race was won by E. Knight, R. F. Bowles being second. The 100 yards by Wyatt, and he also won one or two of the other shorter races; but for the mile he had to carry some pounds of shot in an old-fashioned shot-belt round his loins, and was second to Aitken, who won. Listen to this, ye handicappers of the present day !

'In 1851 Exeter followed up the autumn meeting of 1850 with a summer meeting on Bullingdon, and we think that both a high and broad jump were introduced in the programme. Lincoln was the next to take up the idea, then a college in Cambridge in 1855. Balliol, Wadham, Pembroke and Worcester followed the example in 1856, Oriel 1857, Merton 1858, Christ Church 1859, and in 1861 separate college meetings had become general. At the close of 1860 the Oxford University Sports, open to all undergraduates, owed their foundation to the exertions of the Rev. Edwin Arkwright of Merton. After this, the thing went like wildfire, spreading simultaneously on every side; but after colleges and schools, we believe that the *Civil Service* was the first association formed for the promotion of Athletic Sports, in 1864.'

Exeter was the third club to have a cricket ground of its own. Brasenose and the Bullingdon club had grounds in 1835, and Exeter in 1844.

It may be interesting also to give a brief summary of the boat races, for the latter part of which I am indebted to Falconer Madan Esq.

In 1824 Exeter was at the head of the river in the famous White Boat, of which there is a picture. The boats at that time were crowded into Iffley Lock and got away in regular order, thus allowing each in turn a considerable start. There were only three boats on the river that year, Christ Church, Brasenose and Exeter. Exeter bumped Brasenose the first night, and then Christ Church took off. The crew were J. T. Wareing, W. D. Dick, S. Parr, Douglas (? Thomas Douglass), J. C. Clutterbuck (fellow 1822), J. G. Cole (fellow 1825),

Roger Pocklington, stroke H. B. Bulteel (fellow 1823). The coxswain was Joe Pocklington (who took the name of Senhouse). Outriggers were not yet invented, and the men rowed in tall hats[1]. The stroke's son and coxswain's son were both afterwards strokes of the University Eight. The original stroke was Henry Moresby, but he was displaced. He came from Plymouth and persuaded them to let him get a boat built there. It was brought round by sea to Southampton, and old Davis at Oxford arranged for bringing it up on a carriage, supposed to be the first time a boat travelled by land. When that genial old geologist, so well known in Torquay, Edward Vivian, was up at a Gaudy some years ago, and went in to see the junior Common Room, he looked up at the picture of the White Boat and said, 'Ah! that was the year I matriculated.' The men crowded round him as if he was a survival from prehistoric times, and he had to tell the whole story. He told them too that when he and William Pengelly explored Kent's Cavern, the Torquay book club expelled him, geology being then looked on as heretical[2].

Beginning with 1837, Exeter has been at the head of the river thirty-seven days, viz.: during all 1838 (6 times), all 1857 (8), all 1858 (8), 1859 (1), 1882 (2), all 1883 (6), all 1884 (6), keeping her place once during three years, and again during two. In the Torpids, beginning with 1852, she was at the head fifty-nine days, viz.: 1854 (2), all 1855 (6), all 1856 (6), all 1857 (6), 1858 (4), 1859 (4), all 1860 (6), 1863 (2), all 1864 (6), all 1865 (6), 1866 (5), all 1868 (6). In number of days (59) she is second only to Brasenose (103), but who can match Brasenose? There is a tradition that whenever the great chesnut tree in Exeter garden stretches out its boughs so as to touch Brasenose, Brasenose is fated that year to lose her place on the river; this happened in 1892, but usually her oarsmen have 'gained the weathergage of fate.' The Exeter colours are: Jersey, white trimmed with magenta; Jacket, magenta trimmed with black; Hat, black straw with magenta ribbon.

The 5th of November seldom troubles the present authorities, but it was not so in 1843. Some of the men who had bought explosives which they could not let off on the regular day stored them up until

[1] Wordsworth 174, 176.
[2] Vivian d. 30 Mch 1893, Pengelly d. 17 Mch 1894.

the 12th, when they exploded two small barrels of them in the quad at 2 in the morning, causing some damage and a noise that was heard far over Oxford. The 'dons' failed to discover the culprits. One of the conspirators, George Seton, now a Scotch advocate, famed for heraldic and genealogical lore, published (in London) 'The College Lark' in three cantos, now a very rare work. Another of the conspirators was E. H. Kittoe, V. of Boldmere, Birmingham (just dead, 22 Feb. 1894).

The Library contains about 40,000 printed books, and 184 manuscripts. Among the latter are two parchment Latin Psalters, finely gilded and illuminated. One is unique, in that it was the family bible of the Lancastrian and Tudor Houses[1]. From the joint occurrence of the Royal arms and those of Bohun, and the words *Domine salvum fac Hunfridum servum tuum* in a collect at the end, it was probably written for Humphrey de Bohun, Earl of Hereford, grandson of Edward I, who died 1361; and its probable date is about the time of the battle of Crecy, 1346. It may have passed to the royal family through his grandniece Mary, who married Henry IV in 1380 and died 1394. Her sister Eleanor married Edward III's son, Thomas of Woodstock, after 1374. It seems specially to have belonged to the Queens, for on the first leaf we have *This boke ys myn Elysabeth ye qwene*; and below *This boke is myn Katherine the qwene*, i. e. Elizabeth of York and Catherine of Aragon: and it may have been the book from which the royal children learnt their Latin.

In the Calendar are births, deaths and marriages of the royal family up to the time of Henry VIII, and no doubt it passed to Elizabeth, who gave it to Sir William Petre, and he gave it to the College which he had refounded. It is the sole source for the date of the birth of Henry VII, i.e. 28 Jan. 145$\frac{9}{7}$, 'the noble king Harry the vii was borne festo Agnetis secundo[2] A. D. 1456, and wedded queen Elisabeth festo Sancte Prisce virginis [i.e. 18 Jan.] A.D. 1485, after the compteng of England.' The initial letters give the Biblical History of Genesis and Exodus, and at the end many figures of Saints. Folio 34 is

---

[1] Coxe, no. 47, p. 17; F. Madan, *Books in Manuscript*, 1893, p. 110.
[2] It is true that Bernard André (*Vita Henrici VII*, Rolls Series) meant to give this date, but the MS. is so confused that the editor could not make it out.

a beautifully coloured double page, with two large and several small
medallion pictures, and in the left hand margin musical instruments[1],
dulcimer, rebeck, recorder, &c.   At the end of the book is a metrical
version of the Commandments—

i Love God aboven alle thing	ii Swere nat fals nor in vayn bi hym.
iii Kepe the holy dayes devoutely	iiii Obeye thy fadirs reverently.
v Slee noo man bi worde nor dede	vi Bere noo false witnesse I the reed.
vii Steel nat but paye thi detts truely	viii Doe thou never noo lychery.
ix Thyn neyboures spouse or goods worldly desire nat in hert consentengly.	

The other Psalter[2], written more towards the end of the 14th century,
has a series of very fine Initial Letters, of English work (the Calendar
too contains English Saints, e. g. S. Swithin), and several large
illuminations. One of them represents David dancing before the
Ark, while Michal is pointing her finger at him in scorn from the
balcony of a fortress, just by the portcullis. Another shows Absalom
caught in a tree, and Joab in the garb of a medieval knight is running
him through with a lance. On Joab's golden shield is a black lion
rampant. Below, David, seated on an uncomfortable looking gate, is
tearing his hair as the messenger brings him the news. The first
verse in the Calendar is 'Prima dies mensis et septima truncat ut ensis.'
The Illuminator of those days took special delight in his Initial
Letters—

> Finished down to the leaf and the snail,
> Down to the eyes on the peacock's tail;
> There now is a swallow in her nest,
> I can just catch a glimpse of her head and breast,
> And will sketch her thus in her quiet nook,
> For the margin of my Gospel Book;

and in the luxuriant leafage, which starting from the Initial creeps
round and clasps the whole page.

Among the invocations of Saints is Sancte Lodowice. At the end
are twenty-seven Latin lines on the kings of England, from Alfred to
Richard II (regnat), with the years of their reigns and their burial

---

[1] England was once a great musical nation, and her Universities are the only
ones in Europe that confer musical degrees. See Mr. Southgate's remarks in the
Roll of Union of Graduates in Music 1893–4, p. 74. The Tudor family were
all musical. Henry VIII composed anthems which used to be played at Christ
Church and Magdalen, and some of which have been lately published in London.
[2] Coxe, no. 46, p. 17.

places; perhaps written by a schoolboy in Richard's reign.   There may have been a pedigree on an opposite page, for he says ' Henricus filius Imperatricis de linea Aluredi, *ut in sinistra parte patet.*'

Among the printed books given by Sir W. Petre in May 1567 was John Benedict's Latin *Concordantiae utriusque Testamenti*, Paris, Guillard and Warencore 1562 ; and bound with it F. Hectoris Pinti Lusitani *in Esaiam Commentaria*, Lyons, Pagan 1561 ; so that Petre had the latest books from Paris and Lyons.

The Library also possesses the two rare books printed at Tavistock—

(1) Boetius de Consolatione Philosophiae.   The title shows a seated King (Christ, or the Father) with the emblems of the four Evangelists in the corners, and under it

> The Boke of comfort called in laten
> Boetius de Consolatione philosophie
> Translated in to englesse tonge.

At the end is

CObꓘNOMEN TRANSLATORIS.

> Wyth al my hert to do yow reuerence
> And seruyse / such as of me may be wrought
> Lawly under youre obedyence
> To plesen yow yf I suffysed ought
> Wyth al my hert / as euer I haue besoght
> No thyng coueyt I of youre excellence
> Eternally but that I may be brought
> My souereyn lady in to your presence

> > Here endeth the boke of comfort called
> > in latyn Boecius de consolatione Phil.
> > Enprented in the exempt monastery of
> > Tauestok in Denshyre. By me Dan
> > Thomas Rychard monke of the sayd
> > Monastery / To the instant desyre of
> > the ryght worshypful Esquyer Mayster
> > Robert Langdon. Anno d. MD xxv.
> > > Deo Gracias.

(arms of Langdon, a chevron between three animal heads).

ROBERTUS LANGDON.

The Anagram contains the translator's name Waltwnem, i.e. John Walton abbot of Osney (Gutch i. 638, Oxoniana ii. 4, Tanner 753, Bibl. Corn. 305, Wood's *City* ii. 216), who made this translation in 1410 at the request of Elizabeth Berkeley   A MS of it exists at

Balliol (Warton *Hist. Eng. Poetry*). Robert Langdon was of Keverell in S. Martín's by Looe, Cornwall, and died 2 Nov. 1548 (Visit. Corn. 275).

A former owner has written his name on the title, Liber Guilielmi Lodouici 1550.

(2) The Tinners' Charter. The title has, under the arms of England?

> Here foloyth the confirmation of the Charter
> perteynynge to all the tynners wytbyn the
> coūtey of deuonshyre / wyth there statutes also ma-
> de at crockeryntorre by the hole assēt and cōsēt of
> al the sayd tynners. yn the yere of the reygne of our
> souerayne Lord kynge Henry ỹ VIIJ. the secūd yere

At the end is

> Here endyth the statutes of the stannary
> Imprented yn Tauystoke ỹ / xx day of August
> the yere of the reygne off our soueryne Lord
> kynge Henry ỹ. VIIJ the XXVJ. yere.

God saue the kyng.

Opposite is Christ on the Cross, and at the back the same picture of the seated king at p. clxvii. Some one has written 'Figura Dei Patris huic similis reperitur in missali Herford in Bibl. Bodl.'

The book contains 26 leaves.

On the death of the lamented Alfred Edersheim in 1889, his widow most generously presented his library to the College. It consisted largely of Hebrew and Talmudic and early Christian literature, and had been selected with a special view to illustrating the history of the centuries immediately preceding and following the Birth of Christ. She only made one condition, that the books should be lent freely to all members of the University who were working on the subject. This was exactly what we should have wished, for the Library has been freely opened to members of the University, an intercollegiate courtesy now generally practised.

The Library has the advantage of looking out on one of the pleasantest gardens in Oxford, an advantage shared by the reading room of the Bodleian. They say that gem-engravers, when their eyes are tired, look on a green emerald for a little rest and refreshment; perhaps the green turf and the trees of a garden may have the same effect. There is a tradition that the winding path in the garden was planned by Hogarth, to illustrate his idea of the line of beauty— but it is not easy to give any authority for such traditions, except what they say to you in Italy, *ci si dicea.*

This sketch of the history of the College in its relation to the history of the University may fitly be brought to a close with the first half of the present century[1]. The old order has passed away, and a new state of things has been created by the action of the University Commissions of 1854 and 1877, and by the Universities Tests Act of 1871. The executive Commission of 1854, following the Commission of inquiry which reported in 1852, made some additions to the Professoriate, but its chief work was the removal of local restrictions on endowments. At the great mass of the Colleges the Scholarships had been confined to the natives of certain localities, and the Fellowships were bound by the same restrictions, which were to a large extent removed in 1854. In that year, before the new statutes came into operation, there were about 130 Scholarships in the University which were open, or might be thrown open in default of fit candidates from the favoured localities. At the present time there are not less than 420 such Scholarships besides the Close Scholarships and Exhibitions still retained, and a large number of Open Exhibitions of recent foundation. At Exeter College the Fellowships, with the exception of the Chaplain Fellowship to which the Dean and Chapter of Exeter still nominated, were thrown open in 1854, and were reduced in number to fifteen, the revenues of the suppressed Fellowships being applied to the foundation of Open Scholarships. The clerical restriction on the Fellowships (except the Chaplain Fellowship) was partly removed, as a Fellowship under the new statutes was not vacated through failure to take Orders until the end of fifteen years from election, and any one who had served the College for ten years as Tutor or Lecturer was allowed to retain his Fellowship for life, if he remained unmarried and did not hold a benefice or possess property of more than a certain value. The Commission of 1854

[1] I am indebted for this part of the text to the kindness of the Rector.

on the other hand, in the case of the Rectorship, made the obligation of Holy Orders more binding than before, as this obligation had previously arisen only from the attachment of the Vicarage of Kidlington to the office (without any institution), and there had been some doubt whether the Rector might not still be a layman, and perform the duties of the Vicarage by deputy. All the Fellowships and Scholarships were still restricted to members of the Church of England.

The Universities Tests Act removed this restriction, except from the Chaplain Fellowship, but the Fellowships were still vacated at the end of fifteen years unless the holder were in Orders, or had earned his exemption from this obligation by service to the College. The Rectorship was still confined to persons in Orders.

The University Commission of 1877 carried still further the changes which had been introduced in 1854, and in 1871. The conception of the University as an institution distinct from the Colleges had been already revived, and had found expression in the statute for the admission of Non-Collegiate Students in 1868. The Commission of 1877 developed this conception, and endowed the University at the expense of the Colleges, giving at the same time a further extension to the Professoriate. The Commission also to a great extent released Fellows in the various Colleges from the restrictions of celibacy, while it made all Fellowships terminable, some absolutely, others concurrently with the College office to which they were attached. It sanctioned the establishment of a pension scheme for College officers, and it removed the obligation to take Holy Orders from all Fellowships, except a few which were still retained as endowments for persons discharging clerical duties in the Colleges, and from almost all the Headships including the Rectorship of Exeter College. This state of things, so far as the clerical restriction is concerned, is not unlike that contemplated by Stapeldon, as the Founder originally required only one Fellow, the Chaplain, to be in Holy Orders. In dealing with the Scholarships of this College the Commission did not alter the statutes of the former Commission, but it paid more regard to the wants of poor men[1], as it gave the

---

[1] Eton, Winchester, and nearly all the old schools and colleges were founded expressly for poor men. For whose benefit do they exist now? In this matter of education the rich have divided the goods of the poor. It has been propo.ed

College power to found Exhibitions, while it limited all Exhibitions both in the present, and in the future, to persons who are in need of assistance at the University. An audit by authorised accountants is now required.

The changes which have taken place at Exeter College since 1854 are very similar to those which have been experienced throughout Oxford. There has been an irresistible movement drawing the English Universities into the current of national life in England[1]. What has seemed to be a revolution has been to a large extent a return to the original conception of the relation of the Universities to the nation, with such alterations as have been made necessary by the course of time. The members of Exeter College welcomed the inevitable change. Exeter was one of three Colleges[2], which alone among the Colleges of the University co-operated with the Commission of 1854, and drew up its own statutes with the sanction of the Commission[3]. It therefore enjoyed the privilege of altering them after the expiry of the Commission with the consent of its Visitor, the Bishop of Exeter. In 1877 a new body of statutes had been prepared by the College for the acceptance of the Visitor. These statutes contained most of the provisions which were afterwards approved by the Commissioners. The changes which have been introduced in the last forty years have no doubt had some injurious effects; but, like most changes which have become inevitable, they have done more good than harm, and have had many compensating advantages. When there was a number of Fellowships restricted to natives of Devon and Cornwall, many of the ablest men born in those counties held Fellowships in the College for a time, and reflected credit on it by their distinction in after life,

that rich men's sons should be elected, as now, to Open Scholarships, but mainly as an honour, while Scholarships of the full value should be reserved for poorer men. This is one of the ideas now being brought forward on the subject. *See* Boase's *Oxford* 118, Burgon 186, 221, 233.

[1] See J. Wells, *Oxford and Oxford Life* 1892; Boase's *Oxford* ch. 7; Brodrick's *History of the University of Oxford* ch. 19; Goldwin Smith, *Oxford Revisited* in *Fortn. Rev.* Feb. 1894, p. 149.

[2] Fowler's *Corpus* 324.

[3] The old offices mentioned on p. 353 naturally ceased or rather were merged in the offices of the tutors or lecturers, appointed by the Rector (subject to the approbation of the College), whose duties are assigned them at the Educational meetings of the Fellows.

such as the late Sir John Coleridge, the present Lord Chief Justice of
England, Mr. Froude, Mr. Justice Kekewich, and Mr. H. F. Tozer[1].
But the freedom now accorded to the College, by which' it is
permitted to offer a Fellowship to any rising scholar or man of
science, to some extent atones for the loss it has sustained. Even
before 1854 the Petrean Fellowships had been accessible to the
natives of several English counties, and had added many distinguished
members to the College. Among these we may be allowed to
mention Josiah Forshall, the editor of Wiclif's Bible, Professors
Rawlinson, Ince, and Palgrave, the late Bishops Jacobson of Chester,
and Mackarness of Oxford, Mr. Justice Chitty, the Bishop of Southwell, the late Canon George Butler, and Canon G. H. Curteis. Since
1854 while Professors Holland, Bywater, Ray Lankester, and Pelham,
and Sir C. A. Turner (formerly Chief Justice of Madras) became Fellows
by open competition, the late Professor Moseley, and Professor Sanday
have been nominated to Fellowships in recent years; and Professor
W. M. Ramsay, now of Aberdeen and formerly Professor of Classical
Archaeology at Oxford, was enabled by the timely offer of a Fellowship
to prosecute those researches in Phrygia which have added so much to
the reputation of English scholarship[2]. The Chaplain Fellowship is no
longer in the gift of the Dean and Chapter of Exeter; but the Stapeldon
Scholars, who in some respects more nearly than the modern Fellows
answer to Stapeldon's idea of a Fellow of a College, still maintain the
local connexion of Devon and Cornwall with Exeter College; and
the old attachment between those counties and the College has by
no means died out. The removal of the celibate restriction has no
doubt materially affected the social life within the Colleges. But
it was impossible any longer to maintain the old system. In
former times, when laxer notions were prevalent, it had not conduced

[1] Among the old Devon exhibitioners still living is Mr. R. D. Blackmore, the
author of *Lorna Doone* and other well-known tales.
[2] An unusually large number of Professorships has been held in recent years by
present or former members of the College. To the names of Fellows or Ex-Fellows
mentioned in the text may be added those of two former Scholars of the College,
Professor Napier, and Mr. W. Baldwin Spencer, formerly Fellow of Lincoln, and
now Professor of Biology in the University of Melbourne. Professor Butler of
S. Andrews, son of Canon George Butler, was a commoner. Nor should we omit
to mention here the names of Sir Gardner Wilkinson and Sir Charles Lyell, who
early in this century were also commoners of the College.

to morality in the University. Dr. Macbride, who was elected to a Fellowship in 1800, when pressed to write the reminiscences of his early days, declined to do so on the ground of the scandals which he would have to record. There were not a few concealed marriages (Wordsworth 569)[1]. The religious movement in Oxford, and the general improvement in social morality had raised the standard of practice, and wiped away these reproaches; but when the majority of Fellows of Colleges no longer took Holy Orders, or had any other profession than that of College Tutor, it was impossible to retain the ablest men in Oxford without removing the obligation of celibacy. Its removal has been attended with a great increase of literary and scientific activity. It has necessarily been supplemented by a pension scheme which will enable the Colleges to provide for the retirement of men who have rendered them service, before they become incapacitated for their work. The life of the undergraduates in Colleges has been far less affected by legislative changes than might have been antici-pated. Fashions vary from generation to generation. The University examinations are constantly undergoing changes, and are generally increasing in range and thoroughness. But the general character of College life has been little altered. Many of those who lamented the abolition of tests, and of clerical restrictions on Fellowships, foreboded a lapse into irreligion, or at least into indifferentism. It is true that compulsory attendance at Chapel has been abolished; but there never was a time within living memory when there were so many voluntary religious associations, or when there was so much genuine and intelligent interest in religious questions among the under-graduates. In fact the Universities reflect the state of feeling and opinion outside. The most prominent characteristic of University history in the present century is the action on the Universities of the various movements of thought on speculative, religious, political and social questions, and the counter-action of the Universities on these. Some people may regret that the University has ceased to be, if indeed it ever was, the home of lost causes; but an institution that

---

[1] One of these *cryptogams*, who had taken a country living, when asked how he could hold a Fellowship and yet be married, replied, with a dark look, A man who can hold his tongue can hold anything. But this story has been told of others. Many Oxford stories are like blank cheques which you can fill up with any name and any date.

was only the home of lost causes might perhaps in these days be somewhat peremptorily called to account. Yet, although the Universities have participated deeply in all the changes that have affected the life of the nation, their influence must continue to be in some respects essentially conservative. The best knowledge, which it is their special province to acquire and to transmit, is independent of the fashion of the day. The Universities have also exhibited a type of life which with many slight variations has maintained a strong identity. Hence both for University men and for the world at large the history of the Universities has had a peculiar attraction; and so long as it maintains its continuity, a sketch of the varying fortunes of one of the older Colleges of Oxford will not be without its interest both for the general reader and for the members of that College for whom it was originally designed.

The main authorities used are as follows:—

Computi Rectoris, from the year 1324[1]. From about 1396 the Computi often omit the Christian names of the Fellows, and hence some difficulty arises. References such as 'autumn 1407' belong to the Computi. The last parchment Computus is that for autumn 1566: in the previous one there occurs 'vid pro cartaceo quodam libello in quo inscribenda sunt singula quoquo tempore a Rectore recepta et recipienda.' This paper book, marked H, runs from autumn 1566 to autumn 1639. A similar book, marked B, runs on to 1734. More modern books follow. There are also Bursars' Books from the Stuart times, and Quarterly Books, and Kitchen Books, and Promus' Books (which are duplicates of the Bursars' Books), but some in each series are missing. There is one Quarterly book 1596–8, but the series begins with 1603, though with a gap between 1637 and 1651. There are Kitchen (Buttery) books of 1593, 1596, 1602, 1603, and then 1624. The Promus' books begin at Lady-day 1762, but have been preserved only when the Bursars' books are missing. There are also some 'Cate books' from 1670. All these books contain curious information, e. g. 'the size of bread: a penney white is 10 oz. 14 p.w, a penney wheaten 16·6, a penney household 21·13; Feb. 12 174⅝ a penney white 9·12, wheaten 14·10, household 19·8.'

Caution books, due to Henry Tozer, who remodelled the mode of keeping the accounts. The first book begins 30 May 1629 (transcribed 1639 from an older book), but the place of birth or abode is not entered until Feb. 166⅘, when John Hearne began the practice, perhaps owing to the disputes which led to the contested election of Burrington and Burgh. The second book runs from 17 July 1686 to 28 Jan. 174¾, the third from 3 Feb. 174¾ to May 1823. The first index extends from 1629 to 1776, the second from 1776 to 1843.

Matriculation books, beginning 16 May 1768.

The College Register begins 25 Oct. 1539, but the binder has put 1541–2 first by mistake. The second Register runs from 30 June 1619 to 1737; the third from 1737 to 1824 and has an index. The first has this entry, 'Hunc librum emebat Johannes French Rector huius Collegii A.D. 1541.' Francis Webber entered the birthplaces of the Fellows chosen during his Rectorship in a small catalogue, and many testimonials for Orders, of Fellows and others, in the Register. Rector Stinton made a volume of Excerpts from the Registers.

Book of Evidences, i.e. transcripts of College charters and documents.

Book of College Leases, transcribed by John Eveleigh, Fellow 1578.

Benefactors' Book, illustrated; began to be compiled when W. Paynter was Rector 1703.

Old List of Fellows, made by W. Wyatt, Fellow 1562.

There are no contemporary lists of Fellows prior to the commencement of the College Register on 25 Oct. 1539. The previous names are given as they stand in the Computus Rectoris of each term, and as a Fellow is only named there when his commons are diminished by his going out of residence for a time, the lists are anything but complete, especially as some of the Rectors' Accounts are missing. Not a few men must have been Fellows for some time before their names appear. It is also difficult to assign the Fellows to their respective counties. The Chaplain is sometimes known by the larger yearly payment he receives. Some of the names belong to well known Devonshire or Cornish families, or the Fellows are ascertained from other sources to have been born in one of those counties. The dates when one Fellow vacated and another was elected in his place are sometimes given in the computi, but the records are too imperfect to

offer much help of this kind. Help is sometimes gained from other
sources. Thus William Franke is given as Fellow in 1370; but, as
a document of 26 Oct. 1371 calls him Senior Fellow, he must have
been Fellow at least as early as 1362. The same document shows
that John Skylling, who occurs as Fellow in 1385, must have been
Fellow as early as 1371. See also the case of W. de Heghes 1337.
It is not till 1372 that a complete list of 15 Fellows can be made out.
To quote the names under one year from the Old list will show its
imperfection : '1423 Edmund Fitchet A.M. and Rector, Benet, Treinges,
J. Brente, J. Beawcombe A.M., Stone, Zeate, W. David A.M.'; here
Treinges is a misreading for Walter Trengoff, Zeate a misreading for
Yeate, and four have no Christian names assigned them. By com-
paring the names as given in the text it will be seen how little help
was to be got from the Old list, and how necessary it was to reconstruct
the whole account from the computi and other documents. Nevertheless
some names have been inserted, for which the Old list is the only
authority, as documents now missing may have been used in its
compilation. After the Register begins the names are given more
correctly, and after some time a few particulars are added to some
names, but rarely more than a line or two, and it cost much labour to
find out what became of the Fellows, what preferment they held, and
so on.

It should be noted that the first edition of this work still retains
a value of its own, owing to the Latin documents given in it, not
reprinted here, and to a, in some respects, fuller text and index.

A volume published by me this year, *The Commoners of Exeter
College*, completes the list of members, and gives fuller accounts of
many names incidentally mentioned here.

Mr. H. Hurst has kindly taken in charge the illustrations and the
accompanying tables. He found it very difficult to make sure of the
exact situation of the old Halls, most of which perished early; but
had the benefit of working on a previous plan kindly supplied by
Mr. F. P. Morrell, who had it from his father. One main difficulty
occurs at the SW. corner of the College, which is not described as
occupied by any Hall, and where we are not quite certain about the
position of the lane and of S. Mildred's church. Wood (*City* i. 115)
only says of Castell Hall '*about* the corner at the W. end of S. Mildred's

Lane.' An Osney rental of 1259 (Wood D. 2. p. 458 S. Mildred's) says 'domus in *occidentali* parte ecclesiae quae fuit Johannis de S. Johanne,' &c., next to which is 'domus super terram Wyger ex opposito eiusdem ecclesiae,' &c. There is also some doubt about the two towers on the N. side of the College. The summary at the end of Prideaux' Survey says '2 Towres which were formerly in the Rector's backyard and garden, now all demolished.' The eastern of these, south of the centre of the Ashmolean, seems from an old map (B) in the Rector's possession to have been *Almond's* (p. 313) and may be part of the land sold to the University (Wood's *Life* iii. 78, Comp. Vice-Canc. 1678–9 'to Dr Bury for ground bought of Exeter College for Ashmole's Repository 80 *li.*'). About the other there is no doubt, as the foundation has been seen by many people.

Some apology is due for reproducing a copy only of Agas' view of the College. The original is rather small for easy comparison with Bereblock; and it is so torn, blotted and stained, that it is doubtful if a tolerable negative can be obtained from it; it is also defective towards the bottom. Whittlesey's copy of it contains a few departures from the original. Mr. Hurst has therefore worked out an enlarged copy of the Agas, and supplied the defective parts from Whittlesey. A dotted line in the lower part of the view shows how far Agas and his copyist have been taken as authorities. The Clarendon Press has shown its usual skill in taking the negatives.

The Author is much indebted to the Rector and Bursar, to Professor Bywater, Falconer Madan, Esq., Sub-Librarian of the Bodleian, W. B. Gamlen, Esq., of Exeter College, Secretary to the University Chest, and other friends; but, above all, to his brothers G. C. Boase and F. Boase, who have devoted much time to reading the proofs, and have contributed much additional information; and to Prebendary Hingeston-Randolph, and to J. Ingle Dredge, Vicar of Buckland Brewer, who have done him a similar kind office, the former supplying details from his unrivalled knowledge of the Epis-copal Registers, the latter by the use of his Collections amassed from the parish registers of Devon and through an unwearied cor-respondence with the Western clergy. For special family history he has not seldom consulted Winslow Jones Esq. Any one working on these subjects must acknowledge his obligations to Clark's *University*

n

Register (O. H. S.), and to Foster's monumental work, the *Alumni Oxonienses*; as well as to Crockford's *Clerical Directory*, with its ever-increasing fullness of information.   Nor must he omit his obligations to Horace Hart, Esq., Controller of the Clarendon Press, for giving him the benefit of his experience, and it would be ungrateful not to thank the Compositors and the Pressmen for their care.

The author will be grateful for any further additions and corrections.   A few lines of facts and dates (as all engaged on such tasks are aware) often represent the work of hours; *Facilia putant omnes quae iam facta.*

LIST OF AUTHORITIES.

——————

Anstey, H., *Munimenta Academica* (Rolls Series). 2 vols. 1868.

Army List, Nov. 1814–93; Hart's *New Army List* (quarterly) 1839–93; Hart's *New Annual Army List* 1840–93; *Official Army List* (quarterly) 1880–93; *List of General and Field Officers* 1754–1868.

Athenae Oxonienses, by A. Wood, ed. P. Bliss. 5 vols. 1813–20. 5 contains Fasti.

Ayliffe, *Ancient and Present State of the University of Oxford*. 2 vols. 1714.

Balliofergus, by H. Savage, Master of Balliol. 1668.

Bibliotheca Cornubiensis, by G. C. Boase and W. P. Courtney. 3 vols. 1874–82. Paged throughout.

Biography, *see* Bibliotheca, Gillow, Modern, National, Tanner.

Blomfield, Jas. C., *Deanery of Bicester*, 7 parts. 1882–93.

Bloxam, J. R., *Register of Magdalen College*. 8 vols. 1853–85.

Boase, C. W., *Oxford* (Historic Towns). 1887.

Bodleian Charters, ed. W. H. Turner. 1878.

Brighton College Register 1847–63, by H. J. Matthews. 8vo. Brighton. 1886.

Brodrick, G. C., *Memorials of Merton College* (O. H. S.). 1885.

Bruton Register 1826–90, by Rev. T. Augustus Strong. 1892.

Burrows, Montagu, *Register of the Visitors of the University of Oxford*. 1647–50 (Camden Soc. 1881).

Calamy, Edm., *Nonconformists' Memorial*, by S. Palmer, ed. 1802 (abridgement of Calamy's *Account and Continuation*).

Calendars of Oxford University, beginning 1810. That for 1856 contains the first Register of *Congregation*.

Cambridge, *see* Cooper, Mullinger.

Carthusians, List of, 1800–79, by W. D. Parish. 1879.

Catalogue of Oxford Graduates 10 Oct. 1659–31—*Dec.* 1850. Ed. 1851.

Church of England, *see* Wilkins.

Clark, A., *see* Oxford, and University Register.

Clergy Lists, first printed 1841. Crockford's *Clerical Directory* began 1858 ; R. Gilbert's *Clerical Guide*, 4 vols., 1817–22–29–36. *See* too Foster, Le Neve, Newcourt, Walker.

Collectanea Cornubiensia, ed. G. C. Boase 1890.

Conant Family, A History and Genealogy of the, by Frederick Odell Conant of Portland, Maine, U.S.A. 1887 : *see* too W. Boys' *History of Sandwich* 274.

Cooper, C. H. and T., *Athenae Cantabrigienses* 1500–1609. 2 vols. 1858–61 (all published).

Cornwall, see Bibliotheca, Collectanea, Lake, Royal, Vivian.

Cotton, H., *Fasti Ecclesiae Hibernicae.* 4 vols. 1845–50.

Cox, G. V., *Recollections of Oxford.* 1868.

Coxe, H. O., *Catalogus Codicum MSS. Coll. Exon.* 1852.

Deputy Keeper of Records, Reports of, 1840–93.

Devon, see Drake, Dredge, Ecclesiastical, Lysons, Notes, Pole, Vivian, Western.

Dorset, see Hutchins.

Drake, Sir W. R., *Devon Notes.* 1889.

Dredge, Rev. J. Ingle, *A Few Sheaves of Devon Bibliography.* 4 parts. Plymouth, 1889–93; *Devon Booksellers and Printers* 1885–87–91 ; *George Downame* 1881 ; *Robert Mossom* 1882 ; *Abednego Seller* 1886 ; *Rectors of Parkham* 1888 ; *Samuel Bolton* 1889 ; *Richard Bernard* 1890 ; *Marwood Briefs* 1893 ; *Frithelstock Priory* 1894.

Ecclesiastical Antiquities in Devon, by G. Oliver. 3 vols. 1839–42.

Eton School Lists, 1791–1877, ed. H. E. C. Stapylton. 3 parts. 1874–84.

Exeter, see Monasticon, Oliver, Registers, Vivian.

Exeter College, see Coxe.

Fasti, see Athenae.

Fortescue Family, History of the, by Thomas Erskine Lord Clermont, of Exeter College. 1869.

Foss, E., *Biographia Juridica* (1066–1870). 8vo. 1870.

Foster, Joseph, *Alumni Oxonienses* (1715–1886). 4 vols. 1887–8 ; (1500–1714) 4 vols. 1891–2 ; two final volumes, *Oxford Men and their Colleges* (1880–92). 1893.

Foster, Joseph, *Index Ecclesiasticus* 1800–40. Ed. 1890.

Foster, Joseph, *Men at the Bar.* 1885.

Gardiner, R. B., *S. Paul's School Admission Register* (1748–1876). 1884.

Gardiner, R. B., *The Registers of Wadham* (1613–1719). i. 1889.

Gascoigne, T., *Loci e Libro Veritatum.* Ed. Thorold Rogers. 1881.

Gillow, Joseph, *Dictionary of English Catholics.* 3 vols. 1885–7 (all published).

Griffiths, J., *Index to Wills proved in the Court of the University.* 1862.

Gutch, J., *Wood's History of Antiquities of University and Colleges.* 3 vols. 1786–96.

Gutch, J., *Collectanea Curiosa.* 2 vols. 1781.

Hearne, Diary (O. H. S.). 3 vols. Ed. C. E. Doble : the later parts are quoted from Bliss' *Reliquiae Hearnianae.* 2 vols. 1857.

Heywood, Jas., *Recommendations of the Oxford University Commission.* 1853.

Historical Manuscripts, Reports of Commission on, begun 1870.

Honours Register of the University of Oxford to 1883. Two previous editions were called *The Oxford Ten Year Book,* the ed. of 1888 is called *Historical Register.*

Huber, Victor Aime, *The English Universities,* transl. by F. W. Newman. 3 vols. 1843.

Hutchins, *The History and Antiquities of Dorset,* new ed. 4 vols. 1861–73.

Ireland, see Cotton.

Jackson, T. G., *Wadham College, Oxf.* 1893.

Kidlington, Yarnton and Begbroke, History of O. H. S.), by Mrs. Bryan Stapleton. 1893.

Lake, *Parochial History of Cornwall,* ed. Joseph Polsue. 4 vols. 1867–72.

Laud's *Chancellorship,* in Laud's Works. 1853.

Law List 1775–1893 ; *see* too Foss, Foster.

Le Neve, *Fasti Ecclesiae Anglicanae,* ed. Hardy. 3 vols. 1854.

Literary Anecdotes, see Nichols.

Lysons, D. and S., *Magna Britannia.* Devon, 1822.

Lyte, H. C. Maxwell, *History of University of Oxford to* 1530. 8vo. 1886.

Maclean, Sir J., *The History of Trigg Minor in Cornwall.* 3 vols. 1867–79.

Madan, F., *Manuscript Materials for History of Oxford.* 1887.

Magdalen Muniments, by W. D. Macray. 1882.

Manchester School, Admission Register 1730–1837, by J. F. Smith. 4 vols. 1866–74.

Marlborough College Register 1843–69.

Medical Directories 1845–93. *See too* Munk.

Merchant Taylors School, Register of the Scholars of, by C. J. Robinson. 2 vols. 1887.

Modern English Biography from 1851, by Frederic Boase. vol. i ᴬ–H). 1892. Vol. ii in progress.

Monasticon dioecesis Exoniensis, by G. Oliver. 1846. Supplement 1854.

Mozley, T., *Reminiscences,* chiefly of Oriel College. 2 vols. 1882.

Mullinger, Jas. Bass, *History of University of Cambridge to* 1625. 2 vols. 1873–84.

Munk, W., *Roll of College of Physicians,* ed. 2. 3 vols. 1882.

National Biography, Dictionary of, begun 1885. 37 vols. published.

Navy List 1815-93 ; *Royal Navy List* 1878–93, by F. Lean.

Newcourt, R., *Repertorium Ecclesiasticum Londinense.* 2 vols. 1708-10.

Nichols, J., *Literary Anecdotes and Illustrations of the 18th century.* 9 vols 1812–15 ; 8 vols. (continuation) 1817–56.

Notes and Gleanings, Exeter. 16 Jan. 1888–1893.

Notes and Queries. 1849-94.

Oliver, G., *Bishops of Exeter.* 1861.

Oliver, G., *City of Exeter.* 1861.

Oxford, see Anstey, Athenae, Ayliffe, Boase, Bodleian, Calendar, Catalogue, Cox, Foster, Griffiths, Gutch, Hearne, Heywood, Honours, Huber, Laud, Lyte, Madan, Pycroft, Rowing, University, Visitations, Wood, Wordsworth.

O. H. S., Oxford Historical Society's publications, began 1885.

Oxford Colleges, ed. A. Clark. 1892.

Oxford University Gazette, began 28 Jan. 1870.

Oxoniana (anon.), by Dr. J. Walker of New College. 4 vols. 1810.

Phillipps, Sir T., *Institutiones clericorum in comitatu Wiltoniae* 1279–1810. 2 vols. 1825.

Pole, Sir W., *Collections towards a description of Devon.* 1791.

Pycroft, Jas., *Oxford Memorials.* 2 vols. 1886.

Registers of Bishops of Exeter, ed. F. C. Hingeston-Randolph, 3 vols., viz. Bronescombe 1257–80, Quivil 1280–91, and Bitton 1293–1307 (1889), Stapeldon 1307–25 (1891), Stafford 1395–1419 (1886).

Royal Institution of Cornwall, Journal of, begins 1864 (Reports 1838–62); quoted as R. I. C.

Rogers, J. E. T., *History of Agriculture and Prices* 1259–1793. 6 vols. 1866–87.

Rowing Almanack. 1891.

Rugby School Register 1675–1887. 3 vols. 1881–91.

Rymer's *Foedera*, referred to by date; 10 vols. 1745; new ed. 4 vols. 1816–69, not finished.

St. Paul's School, see Gardiner.

Shadwell, L., *Registrum Orielense.* i. (1500–1700). 1893.

Smith, W., *The Annals of University College.* 1728.

Stapeldon's *Register*, ed. Hingeston-Randolph 1892, *see* Registers.

Statutes of the Colleges, ed. University Commission. 3 vols. 1853; Appendix to iii is Calendar of Public Records, and p. 107 Valor 'Liber Universitatis Oxon.'

Tanner, T., *Bibliotheca Britannico-Hibernica.* 1748.

Thomson, W., *An Open College best for all.* 1854.

Tonbridge School Register 1820–86, by W. O. Hughes. New ed. 1893.

Turner, W. H., *Records of City of Oxford* 1509–83. 1880.

University Boat Races 1829–83, *Record of*, by G. G. T. Treherne and J. H. D. Goldie. 1884.

University Oars 1829–69, by J. E. Morgan. 1873.

University Register (O. H. S.). i. (1449–63, 1505–71) ed. C. W. Boase, and ii. 1–4 (1571–1622) ed. A. Clark. I follow Wood in giving the licence for M.A. as the date of that degree; but sometimes only the *supplicat* for the degree occurs, or the date of the *inception* i. e. actual commencement of lecturing. The Registers begin to give the father's name from 11 Oct. 1622, and again from 14 Dec. 1660.

Uppingham School Roll. 1824–84.

Visitation, Oxon Heraldic, ed. W. H. Turner (Harleian Soc. 1871).

Visitations of Cornwall, The, ed. Col. J. L. Vivian, Exeter, 1887.

Visitations of Devon, The, ed. Col. Vivian, began 1888 (I sometimes refer to the *Harleian* editions).

Visitations of Oxford, ed. W. H. Turner 1871 (Harleian Soc.).

Vivian, Col., *Marriage Licences of Diocese of Exeter,* 1323–1631. 3 parts published.

Walker, J., *Sufferings of the Clergy.* 1714.

Warton, T., *Life of Sir T. Pope.* ed. 2.

Wells, J., *Oxford and Oxford Life,* 1892.

Western Antiquary, ed. W. H. K. Wright. Plymouth, 1882–93.

Westminster School past and present, by F. H. Forshall, 1884; *Register* 1764–1883, by G. F. R. Barker and A. H. Stenning, 1892.

Wilkins, David, *Concilia Magnae Britanniae et Hiberniae.* 4 vols. 1737.

Wilts, *see* Phillipps.

Winchester; List of Wardens, Fellows and Scholars, by T. F. Kirby, 1888; *Register of Commoners* 1836–90, by C. W. Holgate, 1891.

Wood's *City of Oxford,* ed. Clark. 2 vols. 1889–90; for the part not yet published I refer to the edition by Peshall 1773.

Wood's *Life and Times* (O. H. S.), ed. A. Clark. 3 vols. 1891–4; vol. 4 is not yet published.

Wordsworth, Chr., *Social Life at the English Universities in the eighteenth century.* 1874.

ABBREVIATIONS.

a.—anno.

adm.—admitted.

admin.—administration of will or property.

b.—born.

bap.—baptized.

C.—Curate.

D. K. Rec., *see* Deputy (above).

d.—died.

d. or dau.—daughter.

disp.—dispensed.

Eccl. Ant., *see* Ecclesiastical (above).

ed.—educated.

el.—elected.

G. C.—gentleman commoner.

instit.—instituted.

lic.—licensed.

m.—married.

M.—matriculated.

O. H. S.—Oxford Historical Society.

pres.—presented.

R.—Rector.

R. I. C., *see* Royal (above).

res.—resigned.

sup.—supplicated.

vac.—vacated.

V.—Vicar.

v.—voce.

REGISTER OF EXETER COLLEGE.

THE College was founded in 1314 by Walter de Stapeldon, bishop of Exeter, under the name of Stapeldon Hall. Deeds of 1314 and 1315 mention the Rector and Scholars, i. e. Fellows, but no names occur until 1318. The contractions Corn., Chapl., Dev., Guer., Jer., Petr., Sar., Shi. denote the Cornish, Chaplain, Devon, Guernsey, Jersey, Petrean, Sarum, and Shiers foundations; small letters show that the attribution is doubtful.

John **Parys, Dev. 1318**; M.A., Rector Oct. 1318—Oct. 1319, when probably not in full orders. Stapeldon's Reg. 28 Ap. 1321 'apud Lamhethe optinuit M. Johannes dictus Paris clericus ad minores quos nondum etc., et omnes sacros ordines, literas dimissorias in quibus non erat facta mencio de titulo in huiusmodi sacris ordinibus exhibendo' (was his fellowship his title?); ordained acolite in the Bishop's chapel at London 7 June 1321; subdeacon at Bishop's Waltham 13 June 1321 by Rigaud de Asserio, bishop of Winchester (with Philip de Chalvedone); 19 Sep. 1321 Master John Paris deacon received V. of Laundeghe, i.e. Kea in Cornwall, *de gracia domini*. He covenants in a deed dated 9 July 1319 that the Chapel shall not prejudice S. Mildred's Church, witnesses Masters Richard Noreys, Henry Bloyou, Stephen Pyppcote, John de Sevenasche; for Noreys see Stapeldon's Reg. **295** :—a Richard Noreis, R. of Inwardleigh 21 July 1317, *acolite*, had leave of absence to *study* 2 Oct. 1317, 11 Feb. 131$\frac{7}{8}$ (with letters dimissory), 27 Sep. 1319, 9 Sep. 1320, 22 Aug. 1322, 22 Sep. 1324; Henry Bloyou, R. of Ruan-Lanihorne 10 June 1320, ordained subdeacon 20 Sep. 1320, had letters dimissory for deacon's and priest's orders 3 Feb. 132$\frac{0}{1}$. Were all these Fellows?

Philip de **Chalvedone** (? from Chalvedon, now Chaldon, Dorset);

B

ordained acolite at Totnes 18 Sep. 1316; had letters dimissory for
taking any orders 19 Feb. 132⁰⁄₁ at London, as *M.A. of Stapeldonehalle*;
deacon at Bishop's Waltham 13 June 1321 by Rigaud de Asserio,
bishop of Winchester, as *Master Philip de Clauedone*; priest at Exeter
19 Sep. 1321 on a title given by Ralph Vautort.

Stephen de **Pippecote** (Pippacot in Braunton), **Dev. 1322**; M.A.;
acolite 18 Dec. 1311, witness to a Chapel deed 9 July 1319, Rector
1322–25; his Computus 13 Oct. 1324—19 Oct. 1325, the first extant,
says he was Rector the previous year, and a Ledeneporche deed
10 May 1323 calls him Rector, so that he was Rector 1322–25.

John de **Nymeton** (Nympton in Devon), **Chapl. 1324.**

John de **Sevenaysshe** (a place Sevenashe, see Pole 406), **Dev.
1324**; M.A.; tonsured at Totnes 6 Mch 131⁰⁄₁, witness to a Chapel deed
9 July 1319, Rector 1325–26; and his name occurs in Winter 1329;
Wood D 2 p. 88; his Computus for Lent 1326 mentions Richard
Pyn, and Masters Richard de Bynescote [? Wynescote, R. of Iddesleigh
and Preb. of Crediton, subdeacon at Axminster 20 Sep. 1320, also
called de Honemanacote]; and Walter de Lappeflod [R. of Bridford
21 Sep. 1318, had letters dimissory 23 Sep. 1318, subdeacon at East
Horseley, Surrey 7 Ap. 1319; deacon 20 Sep. 1320, with Wynescote;
had letters dimissory 20 Oct. 1322]. Bishop Grandisson wrote to
Master Richard de Ratforde from Chudleigh 5 Dec. 1329: 'Regracia-
mur vobis quod Librum Sermonum Beati Augustini pro nobis, prout
Magister Ricardus filius Radulphi, ex parte nostra, vos rogavit, retinu-
istis, nobisque et condiciones ejusdem significastis et precium. Et,
quia ipsum Librum habere volumus, lx solidos sterlingorum Magistro
Johanni de Sovenaisshe, Magistro Scolarum nostre Civitatis Exoniensis,
pro ipso Libro tradi fecimus, ut nobis eundem, quamcicius nuncii
securitas affuerit, transmittatis. Libros, eciam, Theologicos Originales,
veteres saltem et raros, ac Sermones antiquos, eciam sine Divisionibus
Thematum, pro nostris usibus exploretis; scribentes nobis condiciones
et precium eorundem. Et parati erimus pro vobis facere prout con-
venit locis et temporibus.'

Henry de **Tiverton** (Tuuerton), **Dev. 1324**; M.A., Rector 1333–34.
His Computus is the first that gives the expenses for each week.

John de **Kelly, Dev. 1326**; M.A., Rector 1326–27. He is
mentioned in the winter term of 1329; perhaps R. of Kelly, Devon.

William de **Ponte, Chapl. 1326.** Two of the name occur, as
acolites 21 Dec. 1308 and 13 June 1310, subdeacons 6 Mch 131⁰⁄₁ and
11 Mch 131½, priests 22 Dec. 1313 and 21 Dec. 1314 (a monk at

Tywardreath, Cornwall).   The chaplain must be distinguished from
the monk.   The name Pontey still survives in Devon.   A Chapel deed
25 Ap. 1326 calls him chaplain ;   the witnesses are Robert Kary,
Henry Wall, Henry de Tiverton, Robert de Middellond, *scholars of
the University*.   Kary and Middellond were Fellows of Merton 1322
and 1330.   Middellond was also Treasurer of Exeter Cathedral, and
d. 1367.   Several Fellows of Exeter became Fellows of Merton.

Richard de **Pyn, Dev. 1326**; M.A., occurs Lent 1326, Rector 1327–
30; R. of Wittenham 1333 ; d. before 1355, when Roger Cristemasse
is called his executor.   His first Computus is for a whole year, 15 Oct.
1328—14 Oct. 1329.

William de **Polmorva, Corn. 1333** ; Polmorva is in S. Breock ; the
form 'Palmorna' arises from *u*, i. e. *v*, being misread as *n* ; called
dominus in 1333, M.A., Rector 1336–37, perhaps Fellow till 1340 ;
Fellow of Univ. Coll. 1341 (Smith 98) ; of Queen's 1341–48, one of the
Fellows named by the founder ; subdean of Exeter 9 June 1349—
29 Dec. 1355; Chancellor of the University 1350–51, adm. by the
Archbishop of Canterbury, after the Bishop of Lincoln had refused to
confirm his election, Canon of Windsor 1352–62, Archdeacon of
Middlesex 21 Sep. 1361, d. 1362, his bequest of £5 to the College
was paid in Lent Term 1363 ; Bodleian Charters 3, Wilkins' Concilia iii. 3–8 ; Patent 36 Edw. III part 2 memb. 27, Le Neve i. 389,
ii. 328, iii. 378, Anstey 168–72, Hist. Comm. ii. 139, Gutch i. 451,
481, iii. 139 ; Rolls of Parl. i. 16 ; Lyte 169 ; Bibl. Corn. 505, Coll.
Corn. 744–5 ; Wood D 2 p. 462.

William de **Brokelond, Dev. 1333** ; received the first tonsure as
a boy 23 Sep. 1319, M.A., Fellow till 1337 ; V. of Dawlish 26 Jan.
13$\frac{39}{40}$–1341, Eccl. Ant. ii. 143, 169 ; a John de Broclonde was Preb.
of Exeter 1260 (Bronescombe 480).

William **Dobbe, dev. 1333** ; two of the name received the first
tonsure 21 Dec. 1308 and 23 Sep. 1319 ; M.A., Rector 1334–35,
in 1334 he taught in one of the College 'schools.'   In 1333 he gave
two schools in Scolestrete to Stapeldonhalle ; he is referred to in the
Computus of 1337.

John de **Hemeleston** (? Helmeston in Bishop's Tawton, or Broad-
Hempston), **dev. 1333–7** ; 'capellanus,' took the service for the regular
chaplain 'dominus Stephanus' at the end of 1333.

Walter de **Blachesworth, dev. 1333–7** ; called *dominus* in 1334.
There is a manor named 'Blackworthy' in Stoodleigh near Tiverton ;
a Walter de Blaccheworthy was bailiff of Bampton, Oxon, 1326

(? father of the Fellow).   Stapeldon's Reg. 7 Aug. 1323, Osney,
Walter de Blaccheworthe acolite obtained letters dimissory.

Stephanus, Chapl. 1333; 1334 '*dominus* Stephanus capellanus,'
1337 '*magister* Stephanus.'

Thomas **Trener, corn.** 1334 ; M.A., occurs in Lent 1334.   See
Phillipps a. 1337.

John **Casse, corn.** 1334-7.

William de **Heghes, Dev. 1337** ; called M.A. and M.D. in a University petition of 1348 to Clement VI.   Sir William atte Heghen collated
to R. of Clist Fomison [now Sowton], Devon 10 Ap. 1322, exch. for
Nans Founteyn, i. e. St. Petrock Minor, near Padstow, 19 May 1337,
but instit. the same day to V. of Halberton, which he exch. with
Master William de Brokelond for V. of Dawlish 14 Aug. 1341 ; exch.
with Sir Goceline de Snetesham for R. of S. Mary Steps, Exeter
14 May 1344 ; R. of Stythians 1361 ; Eccl. Ant. ii. 43, 143, R. I. C.
vi. 246.   If we read aright in the Computus of 1336–37 *completurus
annos suos*, he may have been elected thirteen years previously.

William **Capell (de Capella), Dev.** Lent **1337,** in place of Heghes ;
Bronescombe's Reg. 43.

Walter **Polmorpha, Corn. 1337** ; probably related to William de
Polmorva.   In Old List.

Walter **Molle, dev. 1337,** M.A.   In Old List.   A Sir William le
Mol d. R. of Alverdiscott 23 June 1320.

Walter **Cotte, dev. 1337.**   In Old List.   The name occurs at
Dartmouth, Hist. Comm. v. 601, 603.

Thomas **Trotter, 1337.**   In Old List.

John **Tresulian, dev. 1337** ; called ' M.A. universitatis *procuratori
seu rectori'* in the petition of 1348 to Clement VI ; R. of Duloe, Cornwall 21 Sep. 1349, d. Avignon 4 July 1361.   In Old List.

John de **Blankeswille, dev. 1344** ; M.A., Rector 1344.   The deed
transferring Sheld Hall to Ex. Coll. 2 Aug. 1344 mentions John de
Blatcheswall, Rector ; John de Landreyn, John Estcolme, and Robert
Fromonde, Fellows.

John de **Landreyn** (one Landreyn is in Northill, another in
Ladock), **Corn. 1344** ; called M.A., M.B., scholar in theology six years,
in a University petition of 1362 to Urban V ; D.D. ; Fellow of Oriel
1360, one of the two Senior Fellows there 1386, and had joined in
condemning the Wyclifite doctrines 1381 (Fasc. Zizaniorum 112, 288).
Gutch i. 499 ; Wood's City i. 147 ; Statutes iii. App. pp. 31, 39 ; Le
Neve iii. 548 ; Clark's Oxford Colleges 98 ; John Landyran was

Canon of Windsor 1 Jan. 137$\frac{5}{8}$, but exchanged with Richard de Brokelby for a preb. of Glasney near Penryn 11 Jan. 137$\frac{3}{8}$ (Newcourt i. 750); summer 137$\frac{5}{8}$ 'iiii*d* pro vino dato magistris Johanni Landreyn et W. Stykelyngh quando tractaverunt de negociis Roberti de Trethewy.' See Coxe no. xxviii. Lambeth Reg., Langham, fol. 29, 18 Oct. 1366, William de Daventre, provost of Oriel, as proctor for Master John Landreyn, returns him as resident in Lincoln diocese, and as holding the church of St. Mawgan in Kerrier, Exon diocese, worth £10 a year, and as expecting a prebend at S. Asaph by provision of Pope Urban V, being M.A. and D.D. and M.D. He d. 1409 (Martin Lercedekne was R. of Mawgan 1410). In Oriel Treasurer's Accounts 14$\frac{99}{10}$ occurs 'pro vino dato presbiteris pro exequiis M. Johannis Landreyn iiii*s*,' and next year ' in septimana Ascensionis pro vino pro Landreyn.'

John **Estcolme, Dev.** 1344.

Robert **Fromonde, Dev. 1344**; (a Robert Fromond was preb. of Exeter 1293, of Chulmleigh 1310); Proctor 1350; Grandisson's Reg. I. 161^b letter of dispensation (under a permission from Clement VI, given 19 Jan. 134$\frac{4}{5}$ at Avignon, to dispense in the case of 7 fit persons begotten ' de presbiteris aut in adulterio ex uno parente vel utroque') to Robert Fromond clerk to take orders though son of a priest and an unmarried woman; notary M. Richard de Todeworthe clerk, at Chudleigh 23 July 1349, in presence of M. Benedict de Pastone canon of S. Probus in Cornwall, Richard de Campo Arnulphi [Champernon] 'domicello Exoniensi,' Besanc' de Nauntre of the diocese of Besançon. Similarly Reg. I. 162^b 'Dominus, virtute quarundam literarum apostolicarum sibi concessarum, quarum tenor superius in proximo folio de verbo ad verbum inseritur, dispensavit cum magistro Godefrido Fromonde [? Robert's brother], clerico, Exoniensis diocesis, de presbitero genito et soluta, quod, defectu hujusmodi non obstante, ad aliud beneficium migrare posset etc., juxta vim formam et effectum literarum apostolicarum predictarum, presentibus tunc in hujusmodi dispensacione Magistris Benedicto de Pastone Sancti Probi, Ricardo Noreys Exoniensis, ecclesiarum canonicis, R. Chambernon, J. Clifforde, et magistro David Aliam [Stapeldon's Reg. 503, 523], ac N. Braibroke clerico, qui eodem die creatus fuit in notarium, ut supra, et habuit inde literam sub data supradicta et sigillo Domini.'

Robert de **Trethewy, Corn.** 1353; one Trethewy is in Ruan Lanihorne, another in S. Levan; M.A., *in jure canonico Scolari, Exon.*

dioc., petition to Urban V 1362; Rector 1354—June 1357, still Fellow 1358. He and John Cergeaux obtained a grant of Culverd Hall from John Martyn and his wife Alice Pulteneye 28 Oct. 1353.

John **Cergeaux** (Serjeaux), **Corn. 1353**; M.A., ? preb. of Endellion 26 May 1391; Stafford's Reg. 53, 54, Maclean i. 500: a William Serjeaux is mentioned in 1356; Coll. Corn. 886.

Robert de **Tresulian, corn. 1354**; M.P. Cornwall 1368, advocate at Cornish Assizes 1369, Justice of King's Bench 6 May 1378; a Commissioner to repress disorders in the University 1380, Gutch i. 497; Chief Justice 22 June 1381. He was consulted by the College on law matters: Computus winter 1354 '1*d* pro potu ad Tresulian, Byrnely, et ad magistrum Galfridum, qui venerunt ad tractandum de convencione inter nos et Johannem Davyntru': autumn 1357 'xiiii*d* pro expensis R. Tresulian et J. Hall quando transierunt apud Wittenham et convenerunt cum Thoma Broun de fructibus': summer 1358 'iiii*d* pro vino dato M. Willelmo Stykelyng et aliis magistris cum Roberto Tresulian quando tractaverunt de emcione domus J. Daventre [i.e. Hambury Hall]: iii*s* iiii*d* traditis Roberto de Tresulian quos ad (se?) vendicabat pro labore quem habuit in negociis domus.' Pole 88, 347, 380 claims him for Devon, but the Manor of Tresilian is in Cornwall, where he also held Tremodret, Binnamy, Stratton, and Scilly: Ancient Deeds (D. K. Rec. 1890) i. 558; executed at Tyburn 19 Feb. 138⁷⁄₉ (Foss iv. 102: Bibl. Corn. 786–7, Coll. Corn. 1268, Stafford's Reg. 273, 299; his son John indicted in Parliament on Monday after Holy Cross, 21 Richard II). Maclean ii. 23 44; Eccl. Ant. ii. 202. He held some Halls in Oxford which, with the patronage of a chapel in All Saints, were, on his attainder, sold by the Crown to William of Wykeham for 240 marks; one was the Cross Inn in the Corn Market, Wood's City i. index, ii. 110, Oxf. Arch. Soc. 1880–82 p. 17, iii. 146. Reg. of Bishop Buckingham of Lincoln 13 Ap. 1388 'Ricardus Resingdon presbiter presentatus per . . . Ricardum etc., racione terrarum et tenementorum, que fuerunt Roberti Tresulian chivalier, in manu sua per judicium in Parliamento redditum existencium, ad cantariam in ecclesia Omnium Sanctorum Oxon per Johannem Stodley nuper fundatam, vacantem.' There is a curious entry in Rogers ii. 616 '1384 Oxford, expenses paid at Robert the Tiler's funeral by Tresilian, Chivaler: lintheamen 10*d.*, beir 3*d.*, wax 4*d.*, pulsatio campane 2*d.*' He m. Emeline d. of Richard Hiwyshe, of Stowford, Devon by Alice d. of Ralph Blanchminster. She m. (2) 30 Nov. 1388, at S. John the Evangelist,

Friday Street, London, Sir John Colshull, and d. 1413. Colshull got a grant of Tremodret 1391. The lands in Tresilian and Padstow were bought by John Hawley of Dartmouth (49 D. K. Rec. 207), who m. Tresulian's d. Emelin (their d. Elizabeth m. John Coplestone). 20 June 1388 Robert Tresilian was enfeoffed, with Emma now his widow, by Guy Blankmoster, Parson of Lanalwes, of the manors of Bename, Stratton, and the Isle of Scilly: 9 Feb. 1389 Rob. Tresilian was convicted in Parliament, the morrow of Purification anno 11; Emma his wife, widow of Richard Renti, died in the minority of Elizabeth, d. of said Richard and Emma, and wife of John Tynteyne, who came of age anno 1, order for livery to said John and Elizabeth, Close Roll 12 Richard II.

John **Wiseburg**, Dev. winter 1354—autumn 1361; M.A., Rector May—Oct. 1359 in place of John Halle; see a. 1356.

William **Fatte** (Vatte), **Dev.** 16 Oct. 1354 to Lent 1358; senior fellow after Rob. Trethewy in 1357.

John **Flemyng, Corn.** winter 1354—winter 1356.

John **Excestre**, Dev. winter 1354 to Lent 1357; see Computus winter 1360; preb. of Exeter, preb. of Hereford 1396, d. 1400; Monast. Exon. 300, Suppl. 26. Stafford's Reg. (94, 180) 15 June 1398 complaint of *dominus* John Excestre, R. of Ipplepen [15 Sep. 1396–1400], against some who broke into the Rectory and took away the Church muniments.

Robert de **Clyste** (Clest), **Dev.** 1354; B.D., Rector 1359–65; Canon of Exeter 1365; a bequest from him occurs Lent 1396 'xiii*s* iiii*d* de executoribus M. Roberti Clyst per manus M. Roberti Rugge'; perhaps Chaplain 1355–56; mentioned in a petition to Urban V in 1362 as M.A. Exon. dioc.

Henry **Whitefield, Dev. 1355**; (? Whitfield in Marwood, Devon; Drake 121), M.A.: called 'Exon. M.A., B.D.' in petition to the Pope: managed some College business (as well as for Queen's) at Avignon in winter 1363 (another instance occurs in 1376), for which £3 was paid him: Fellow of Queen's 1353, Provost 1363; Archdeacon of Barnstaple 1374–84; gave Exeter College two books in autumn 1383, d. autumn 1387, and bequeathed some money and books on medicine to the College (Coxe no. xxviii, xxxv); summer 1389 'centum solidos de bonis M. Henrici Wytfeld pro libris philosophie emendis'; with this money, apparently, 'Burley super Libros Ethicos' was bought (cost 14*d* to bind), and 'Burley super Topicis Aristotelis' (cost 13*d* to bind); summer 1391 'iiii*s* pro Burle super Logicam, ultra pecunias magistri Henrici Whitefeld.' The Provost of Queen's, and William Franke, Robert Lydeford, John Trevisa, fellows (all formerly fellows of Exeter) were expelled by the Archbishop of York, the Visitor, 1379 : Gutch i. 496, iii. 146, Balliofergus 63, Rogers i. 136, Hist. Comm. iv. 443, Fasc. Zizaniorum 514–15, Ayliffe ii. 142, Hist. Comm. ii. 139, 140, 551, Computus of Lent 1386, and of 1387, W. Thomson *An Open College* 26, 30, 32, Clutterbuck's *Hertfordshire* i. 189, Clark's Oxford Colleges 135, 143, 147.

Peter **Trevet, Dev. 1355**; perhaps Fellow till 1366; Pole 165.

Walter **Bery** (Bury), **Dev.**, occurs summer **1355**; M.A.   A Walter Bury was R. of Norygge and then of Chilcomb and then of Hardington 1398–99; Hutchins ii. 740.

John **Halle, Dev.** autumn **1356**; M.A., Rector 1357–59; died in spring 1359.

Richard **Colshulle** (Coleshill, Colleshele), **Dev.** autumn **1356**— Lent 1359; M.A.

Thomas de **Kelly, Dev.** autumn **1356**; M.A., Rector 1368–69. Summer 1375 'xi*d* cum obolo pro vino pro Thoma Weston iudice inter domum nostram et Thomam Kelly pro quodam libro domus nostre inpignorato nomine Kelly'; winter 1380 'xiii*s* iiii*d* in partem solucionis arreragiorum magistri Thome Kelly quondam Rectoris domus predicte.'

William **Aleyn, dev.** autumn **1356**; vac. autumn 1361.   Was he afterwards at Balliol?   Hist. Comm. iv. 447.

John **Restaurok** (Rescowroc), **Corn. 1356**; vac. 1366; John Roscarrock was V. of S. Kew, Cornwall 1383, R. of S. Mabyn 14 Sep. 1383 (Restaurek), res. 1415 (Maclean ii. 98, 461), Penitentiary 15 Jan. 14⁰⁸/₁₀: but these may be different family names; the letters c and t are constantly confused, Stafford's Reg. 305.   Roscourek occurs in Bronescombe's Reg. 231.   See Visit. Corn. 3, 99.   A name Restarick still occurs at Bideford.

Thomas de **Hanneye** (just north of Wantage), **Sar.** occurs autumn **1356**; Pits 482, Tanner 376.

Walter **Estcolme**, (Fellow of Merton 1349), **Chapl.** autumn **1357**; vac. autumn 1358, V. of Gwennap, Cornwall before 1381, R. of Stoke Damerel and Preb. of Glasney; d. 1410.   Stafford's Reg. 94, 114, 174, 210, Brodrick 205.

John **Loderm, dev. 1358.**   In Old List.   John Lovedrem occurs in Oliver's Eccl. Ant. ii. 89.   One of the latter name was R. of Landewednack, Cornwall 1320, Stapeldon's Reg. 228.

William **Stykelyng, 1358**; M.A.; Fellow of Merton 1350.

William **Reade, dev. 1358**; called 'Exon. clerico, sac. pagine prof.' in petition to Pope; M.A. and Fellow of Merton 1344. Brodrick 211, Grandisson's Reg. 17 Aug. 1354, 'M. Willelmus Red, socius domus scolarium de Mertone' as acolite had letters dimissory 'ad titulum dicte Domus'; Provost of Wingham, Kent to 1369; Bishop of Chichester 1369, d. 18 Aug. 1385. Gutch i. 488, iii. 5, 17, 98, 109, 114; Stephens' Chichester 119. An indenture dated the Sunday after S. Luke 48 Edward III, i.e. 22 Oct. 1374, shows that he delivered to M. T. Worthe, *Consocius* and Rector of the scholars, £20 for the repairs of the library, and 25 MSS.: another indenture between J. Jakys, Rector, and J. Bampton archdeacon of Lewes, and M. Richard Pestour kinsman of the Bishop, 8 Aug. 1 Henry IV, 1400, says that he had given books to Merton to be kept and used as at Exeter (Wood D 2, p. 74, and list of his books p. 106); he also gave books to Balliol and New College, i.e. to all the Colleges then existing; Bodleian MS., Digby 176, fol. 2ᵃ 'Liber scolarium de genere venerandi patris domini Willelmi Reed episcopi Cicestrensis, Oxonie successive studentium. Ex dono venerandi patris predicti per Custodem et Rectorem domorum de Merton et Stapelton in Oxonia vel per eorum librarios eisdem scolaribus iuxta facultates et merita ipsorum cuiusque ad tempus sub cautione iuratoria prouide liberandus,' see Cat. Digby MSS. p. 60, 187; summer 1401 'xxxiiiid seratori pro tribus seris pro cista librorum Rede et clavibus eorundem'; summer 1419 'xxxiiis iiiid pro uno portiforio ex legacione Rede vendito'; summer 1432 'pro ligacione unius libri de electione Reed xd'. Hist. Comm. ii. 135: Phillipps i. 54, 84, 135; N. and Q. 26 May 1877 p. 405; Coxe no. xxxii; Pits 857, Tanner 547, 618, Godwin in 1615 'Reade built the library of Merton to which he left his portrait and many tables and astronomical instruments which exist to this time'; Fasc. Zizaniorum 516, Grey Friars (O. H. Soc.) 236.

Walter **Ramesbury, Sar.** summer 1358—Lent 1360; M.A., Fellow of Merton 1364, Brodrick 212; Preb. of Hereford 1368, Precentor 1381, d. 1406. Summer 1359 'pro journellis Walteri Remunsburi qui recessit in die sabbati id ob, et Walteri venientis in die lune viid'; Lent 1409 'iiili vis viiid de executoribus M. Nicholai Rammysbury'; R. of Donheved S. Andrew 1361–1399, Phillipps i. 53, Hutchins iii. 686, 722, iv. 232. One of the name 18 Feb. 132⁹⁄₇ (Pat. Rolls Edw. III i. 15, 70; see Le Neve i. 486, 531) may have been his father.

Hugh **Wyche**, dev. 1358; Fellow till summer 1361.

William **Aston**, 1358; Le Neve i. 601, 615, ii. 69. In Old List. Was he related to John Aston, Nat. Biog. ii. 210?

Robert de **Bossorn, Corn.** 1358; ? born at Bosorn in S. Just in Penwith, the name occurs as Boshorn 131¾, Stapeldon's Reg. 498; B.A. 1364: Wood, D. 2, 98 identifies him with Robert Boson, Chancellor of Exeter, who d. 1399. That office was held successively by Boson, Rugge, Snetisham, and Hendeman, 3 at least Fellows of Ex. Coll.; see a. 1372 (Archdeacon); Stafford 32.

William **Pyneton** (Penyton), **Chapl.** Lent—autumn 1359, probably b. in Devon, and mentioned also in 1360.

William **Hille,** dev. winter 1359; vac. Lent 1360.

Gregory de **Bottelegh, sar.** autumn 1359; vac. 1362; R. of Shepton Mallet, Som. 1378; Weaver's *Som. Incumbents.*

John **Crabbe, Corn.** autumn 1359—winter 1361.

John **Capelle, Dev.** Lent 1360.

John de **Brendon, Dev.** 1360; 'presbyter of the diocese of Exeter and over 26 years of age in 1361'; pres. 7 Mch 136⁹⁄₁ to Wittenham; a legacy from him to the College is mentioned in autumn 1361.

Roger **Dounhed,** or Donhayfd, **sar.** winter 1360, to autumn 1361; ? from a place so named in Wilts. Dunheved was also the old name of Launceston.

Robert **Cary,** dev. 1360, to autumn 1365. See a. 1324, and Computus of autumn 1355.

John **Drakes,** dev. 1360. In Old List; ? V. of S. Stephen's by Saltash 13 Dec. 1390.

Robert **Blakedon,** or Blackdon (a place in Paignton), **Dev.** winter 1361; M.A., Rector 1365-66, his Computus is beautifully written; ordained at Exeter, summer 1364; Fellow of Queen's 1372-75; Fasc. Zizaniorum 515, Hist. Comm. ii. 140.

William **Middelworthy, Sar.** winter 1361 to winter 1365; M.A., Fellow of Merton 1365, Brodrick 211. Perhaps the 'Middelworthe of the Diocese of Sarum,' Fellow of Canterbury Hall, who was turned out with Wiclif by the Pope's commissary just before 1369; at Queen's 1369-82, in 1385 he paid 13s 4d for his chamber there, i.e. he had ceased to be Fellow; Fasc. Zizaniorum 515, 519, Church Qu. Oct. 1877 p. 124, 126-7, 133; Wood's City i. 174, ii. 283; gave £17 to Exeter College in 1406, the date of his death; Lent 1407 'vli ex dono venerabilis viri M. Willelmi Mydelworde'; 'xiiiid distributis inter socios in die obitus M. W. Midelworde'; Gutch i.

483, 497; Rymer iv. 65 (1379), Hist. Comm. ii. 140; Patent 1 Richard II (Statutes iii. App. p. 33), order to arrest Richard de Thorp clerk, William Frank clerk, and William Middelworthe clerk, who were commanded to come before the King in Chancery, bringing with them the seal of the College called Quenehalle Oxford, but treated the order with contempt, and detained the seal, charters, deeds, writings, keys, books, and other goods belonging to the College. William Frank delivered them up the day before S. Dunstan 1 Rich. II.; the indenture gives the names of 26 books.

Robert **Rygge**, or Rugge, **Dev.** Lent **1362**; vac. autumn 1372; M.A., D.D., secular priest, perhaps related to Thomas de Bitton bishop of Exeter; Chancellor of the University 1381–82, 1384, 5 Mch 138$\frac{4}{5}$, and 1391 (Rogers i. 122, ii. 643, 667, Lewis' Wiclif 361, Adam de Usk p. 7, Knighton Col. 2705, Twyne iv. fol. 573); Canon of Exeter, Archdeacon of Barnstaple 16 Feb. 139$\frac{4}{5}$–1400; Chancellor of Exeter 30 Jan. $\frac{1388}{1400}$, dead before 1410 (Stafford's Reg. ix. 114, 144, 311); founded a 'Chest' for loans to poor scholars. (Lent 1393 'iii*s* iiii*d* de quaternis venditis de cista magistri Roberti Rygge.') He was one of the Wiclifite fellows of Merton, and suffered much from Archbishop Courtenay (Brodrick 212, 223), but apparently joined in condemning the Wiclifite doctrine in 1381; Fasc. Zizaniorum 113 288, Church Qu. Oct. 1877 p. 126, 140, Chronicon Angliæ (Rolls Series) p. 341, 344–45, 350; Wood's City i. 380, Wood's MS. F. 3. p. 9 letter from Richard II 27 Nov. 1385; Gutch i. 499, 506, 510, 516, 519, 534; Statutes iii. App. pp. 36, 39, 40.   Summer 1410 'iii*li* de manibus M. Thome Come pro legato Collegio nostro per M. Robertum Rygge'; 'ix*d* pro cariagio unius libri dati nobis per M. Robertum Rygge'; 'iiii*s* cursori pro portacione librorum nobis legatorum per M. Robertum Rygge'; autumn 1410 'xxiii*d* o*b*. pro tribus cathenis ad cathenandum libros nobis legatos per M. Robertum Rygge et M. Johannem Lydeforde, xv*s* x*d* Roberto Bokbynder pro ligatura octo librorum et pro reparacione aliorum librorum universorum, et pro pargameno iiii*d*.'   Acad. May 1882 p. 360, and June p. 397, Eng. Hist. Rev. v. 329.

John **Trevisa, Corn.** Lent **1362** to winter 1365; from Crocadon in S. Mellion near Saltash, b. about 1342, Fellow of Queen's 1369–74, expelled 1379 by the Visitor the Archbishop of York, but as late as 1396 he was paying xiii*s* iiii*d* for a chamber at Queen's; chaplain to Thomas Baron Berkeley (said to have been a pupil of Wiclif) V. of Berkeley, canon of Westbury near Bristol; d. about 1412.   He translated Higden's *Polychronicon*, Bartholomew Glanville's *De Proprietatibus Rerum*, Vegetius *De Re Militari*, Occam's *De Potestate Ecclesiastica et Saeculari*, Archbishop Fitzralph's *Sermon against the Mendicant Friars*, and other works; Babington's ed. of Higden i. p. liii, iii. p. xxviii; Hist. Comm. i. 60, ii. 128–29, 140–1, iii. 424, iv. 417, 421, 598, vi. 234; Gutch i. 496; Statutes iii. App. p. 34; Pits 567, Tanner 720, Fuller's Worthies i. 217; Demaus' *Tyndale* 12; Carew's Cornwall ed. 1811 p. 269; Sat. Rev. 5 Ap. 1879 p. 428, William Thomson's *An Open College* 31, 32, Lyte 311–12; Blades' Caxton 255; Bibl. Corn. 795–8, Church Qu. Oct. 1877 p. 127, Trans. Bristol and Glouc. Archaeol. Soc. 1877. Lent 1362 'pro dietis Johannis Trevyse qui venit ad comunas die dominica viii*d ob.*'; autumn 1362 'xl*d* J. Trewysa ad visitandum amicos'; autumn 1363 'xii*d* pro conductione duorum equorum quando Rector et Johannes Trewyse fuerunt apud West Wyttenham ad componendum cum firmariis pro horreo faciendo'; autumn 1364 (pensiones sociorum) 'viis v*d ob. q.* Johanni Trevisa.'

Thomas **Swyndon, sar.** Lent **1362** to autumn **1365**; a Commissioner in 1380 to enquire into the troubles at Queen's; Rymer iv. 27 (1378); Gutch i. 496, Statutes iii. App. p. 34. A Thomas Swyndon was Preb. of Alton Australis, Sarum 1388, Hutchins iv. 461.

John **Foxleye** (Voxlegh), **sar. 1362**; V. of Somerford Keynes, Wilts, d. 1384; Phillipps i. 69; Foss' *Biographia Juridica*, Bodleian Charters pp. 132, 549. John de Foxleye (? Baron of the Exchequer 1309) was Commissioner at Oxford 1314, Gutch i. 385.

Thomas **Southdon, Dev.** summer **1362** to 1363; Eccl. Ant. ii. 77.

John **Williams**, autumn **1362** to summer **1372**.

John **Otery, Dev.** autumn **1362**; M.A., ? Rector 1367; V. of Ashburton, exch. 7 May 1397 for S. Mary Church, Devon. Stafford's Reg. 142, Eccl. Ant. i. 187.

John **Trevet, Dev.** autumn **1362**. A family of Trivet lived in Sidbury, Devon.

William **Capell, Chapl.** autumn **1362** to 1364.

John **Kendal, Corn.** summer **1363** to summer 1364.

Adam, Chapl. autumn **1363** to autumn 1365; but the succession of Chaplains is not clear.

Thomas de **Brightwell**, or Brytwylle, **sar.** Lent **1364** to winter 1365; (? from Brightwell near Wallingford;) Fellow and Professor of Divinity at Merton 1368 (Brodrick 202); D.D., suffered for his Wiclifite views from Archbishop Courtenay; R. of Tarent Hinton,

Dorset, exch. for deanery of Leicester coll. 1381; Preb. of S. Paul's
4 Nov. 1386; Dean of Newark, Preb. of Lincoln; Chancellor of the
University May 1388–1389 in place of Robert Rygge; d. 1390.
Gutch i. 493, 504, 506, 519, App. 33; Foxe ed. Townsend iii. 27;
Hutchins i. 318; Fasc. Zizaniorum 288, 304, 308; Lewis' *Wiclif*
126; Church Qu. Oct. 1877 pp. 126, 132, 140; Nat. Biog. vii. 167.

John **Parke**, dev. autumn **1364**; M.A.; rented a school of the
College in summer 1374; Parke (or Parch) canon of Exeter is mentioned autumn 1407, 1410.

Robert de **Lydeford, Dev**. autumn **1365** (perhaps 1362) to autumn
1375; M.A.; Rector 1373–74; Brantingham's Reg. 33ª, 11 May
1373 'Londoniis, Robertus Lydeford clericus habuit literas dimissorias
ad ordines minores et ad sacros omnes ordines ut in forma'; Fellow
of Queen's 24 Oct. 1375; expelled by Archbishop of York 1379;
R. of Lockyng, Berks 1399–1400, pres. by monastery of Abingdon;
d. Oct. 1412, Gutch i. 496, calendar at end of Statutes iii. p. 34,
Computus Lent 1400; summer 1401 'xl*s* collatis a M. Roberto
Lideforde rectore de Lochynge pro erectione nove camere; vi*s* viii*d*
collatis ab Agnete uxore Chydeley ad eandem edificacionem, xx*s* a
Roberto Boterwyk ad eundem usum'; Lent 1407 'vi*d* in gantaculo
M. Roberti Lydeford quando primo venit in vigilia S. Thome, et in
drageto pro eodem magistro xi*d*, et in cibis equorum suorum quando
fuit nobiscum secundo tempore x*d*, et in bona cervisia in camera
Rectoris in crastino S. Thome vi*d*'; summer 1407 'vi*d* pro aqua
medicinali pro oculis M. Roberti Lydefford et pro expensis factis
circa famulum eiusdem, xviii*d* in expensis M. Nicholai Wymboll
quando visitavit predictum in nomine Collegii cum Rectore, et pro
equis xii*d*'; Lent 1409 'viii*d* Radulpho Morwyll pro expensis suis
et unius presbiteri qui missi fuerant ad M. Robertum Lydeford, iiii*d*
uni puero pro portacione vestimentorum Radulphi Morwyll et unius
presbiteri ad rectoriam M. Roberti Lydeford, iiii*d* pro vino dato
memorato presbitero qui fuerat cum M. Roberto Lydeford tempore
Natalis, et pro labore Radulphi Morwill xii*d*'; winter 1409 'vii*d* pro
pabulo equi M. Roberti Lydeford quando visitavit nos tempore nundi-
narum [perhaps on S. Frideswide's day, Oct. 19], xx*d* circa eundem
M. Robertum quando iantatus fuit nobiscum et pro diversis potacio-
nibus suis in villa et in nundinis, xix*d* pro cirothecis et cena datis
eidem, vii*d* pro cultellis datis famulo suo, vi*d* pro coopertoriis ciphorum
eidem M. Roberto eciam datis'; 'iiii*d* circa M. Johannem Metforde
quando rogavi ipsum ad citandum duos homines de Stevynton ad

instanciam M. Roberti Lideford'; summer 1411 'viii*d ob.* pro vino misso ad M. R. Lydeforde, et pro electuario eidem misso xvi*d*'; winter 1412 'iiii*d* pro proclamatione [i.e. by a bedeman, see a. 1404; Murray's Eng. Dict.] facta tempore mortis Lydeford, viii*d* pro conductione unius equi pro cariagio vestimentorum versus Lokynge, iiii*d* pro cariagio unius olle enee [a copper pot hung over the kitchen fire; Stapeldon's Reg. 568, Rogers iv. 616] versus Collegium nostrum per M. R. Lydeford nobis date'; summer 1413 'lx*s* a Johanne Kyngysmyll in festo Natalis S. Johannis Baptiste in partem solucionis xviii marcarum nobis per M. Robertum Lydeford legatarum.' John Lydford, archdeacon of Totnes, d. 1407, Computus autumn 1398, autumn 1410.

Thomas **Carey, dev. 1365**; R. of Kilkhampton, Cornwall 8 Sep. 1382; his bequest of one mark was received summer 1393, and another sum winter 1393, when he is called 'Canon of Exeter'; d. before 1395.

John **Tremayne, corn.**, occurs winter 1365; Monast. Exon. 308.

Robert **Scharschille**, or Scharishill, **sar.**, occurs winter 1365.

John **Giffard, dev.** in winter 1365.

John **Fisstorne** (? Fisserton in Bishop's Tawton), **dev. 1366**. In Old List.

Luke **Helland, corn. 1366**; a John Helond is mentioned in 1364.

John **Swyndon, sar. 1367**, ? already fellow in autumn 1365; Fellow of Merton 1368, Brodrick 214.

William **Franke, Sar. 1370**, vac. 27 Mch 1372; M.A., Rector 1370–71, senior fellow by 26 Oct. 1371 (? therefore fellow before 1362); Fellow of Queen's 1371, expelled 1379 by the Archbishop of York; Gutch i. 496, iii. 146; Statutes iii. App. pp. 33, 34; ? R. of Broughton, Wilts 1400, res. 1407. Phillipps i. 87, 95, Hutchins i. 585–6, 594, W. Antiq. i. 136.

John **More, Dev. 1370** to autumn 1376; M.A., Rector 1374–75; R. of S. Petrock's, Exeter; his will is mentioned winter 1386; gave £20 towards building the Library. Another John More was presented by the College to Wittenham, and is mentioned in the Computi autumn 1381 to 1398. Lent 1374 'xx*s* Johanni More pro expensis suis quando fuit in negociis domus tempore Willelmi Frank et pro pensione sua que fuit a retro tempore Johannis Dagenet.' Brodrick 210, Stafford's Reg. 259.

John **Dagenet, dev. 1371**; M.A., Rector 1371–72.

Martin **Archdeacon** or Ercedekne or L'erchdeken, **Corn.** summer
1372 to 1374; (7 s. of Sir John and Cecily, R. I. C. ix. 430, 435;)
M.A., rented a school of the College 1379–81, mentioned summer
1391.   Brantingham's Reg. 15 July 1379 'Londoniis, magister
Martinus Lercedeakne rector de Lanyhorne habuit licenciam de
studendo, iuxta capitulum *Cum ex eo*, per biennium'; R. of Radipole,
Dorset, res. 1422; Hutchins ii. 483; Stafford's Reg. 2 June 1410
leave of absence to Martin Lercedekne M.A. R. of Mawgan in
Keyryer, 'in decretis licenciatus,' for a year, to reside as Canon at
Exeter; and a licence to preach in Latin or English; Roger Martin
was adm. to Mawgan 5 May 1433, vac. by death of Martin Lercedekne,
pres. by Thomas (? Whalesborough); Maclean iii. 257, 259, 275;
R. of Georgeham 15 July 1422, patron for this turn Sir Henry
Talbot; Canon of Glasney, Bosham, and Crediton, Stafford's Reg.
240.   In his will (Chichele's Reg. at Lambeth i. fol. 435), made
Monday in Pentecost week 1430 in his 'hospicio' at Exeter, he
mentions his brother *dominus* Michael, sister Isabel, and Richard
Alet; and leaves 20s to the Scholars of Stapyldon Hall to pray for
his soul and that of Robert Boson, and 20s to the Scholars of Oriel
Hall: to his nephew Michael 'Repertorium meum super Sextum
et Clement.' (Coxe no. xvii, xxii, xxxi): to his church of S. Mawgan
(Stafford 240, 319, instit. 1410), Cornwall a priest's vestment of red
cloth powdered with golden birds, his *Legenda Temporalium et Sanctorum ad usum episcopi J. de Grandisson*, £10 for repairs, and 6s 8d
to the poor: 6s 8d to the poor of his former church S. Rumon
(Ruanlanihorne): his furred robe to Walter Davy M.A.: to his
church of S. George de Hamme a part of the cross on which the
Lord Jesus was suspended, contained in a precious golden circlet;
his Concordances to the church of St. Thomas of Glaseney: 13s 4d
to the Prior and Convent of Launceston: executors his nephew
Michael treasurer of Exeter [23 Ap. 1418], M. William Fylham
archdeacon of Cornwall, M. Richard Marke R. of S. Martin within the
close of S. Peter, Exeter.   In Oriel Treasurer's Accounts 1411–12,
among the contributions for parishioners of S. Mary's for work on
the stalls, occurs an entry 'de magistro Martino Archedeken xxs.'
Michael Archdeacon was promoted when very young, and in minor
orders,? to Gwinear, Cornwall 1384–85, to Haccombe (patron a
Lercedekne) 30 July 1400 and again 18 Dec. 1409 (patron
a Courtenay), res. 18 Mch 141⅔ (Eccl. Ant. i. 160, Maclean iii. 257,
259, 275), Canon of Crediton 1419, R. of Chagford 30 Sep. 1434–1440

(Stafford's Reg. ix, 161); d. 4 Ap. 1443 ; D. K. Rec. 44 p. 614, 48 p. 221 letters of attorney to William abbot of Torre and Michael Lercedekne clerk, going abroad 27 Nov. 1422; Hewett's Cath. of Exeter, App. p. 26 ; Stafford's Reg. 27 Feb. 139$\frac{5}{8}$ at Battys ynne, Oxon, dispensation to Michael Leardecrune clerk Exon. dioc. to take orders although son of an unmarried man and woman ; 29 May 1401 licence to Michael Lercedekne archpriest or rector of Haccombe, sub-deacon, to study at Oxford for seven years; 6 May 1402 letters dimissory to Michael Lercedekne.   Summer 1421 'iis viiid circa M. Rogerum Bolter, Michael Lercedekne, et Johannem Schute quando fuerunt nobiscum.'   In his will dated 5 Jan. 144$\frac{1}{2}$, proved 28 Feb. 144$\frac{6}{7}$, he left 'ad fabricam Turris sive Campanilis seu ad Campanas ecclesie S. Wynneri in Cornubia xls' viz. 20s from the goods of Martin Lercedekne and 20s from his own : and 16s 8d to Thomas Come.

Thomas **Filly, dev.** summer and autumn **1372.**

John **Henry** or Herry or Harry, **corn.** summer **1372**—winter 1379 ; M.A., Vice-Rector 1377–78 ; V. of Gwennap 22 Sep. 1381, R. of Endellion 1394, exch. for V. of Gwinear 19 Mch 140$\frac{4}{5}$, res. 1438, all in Cornwall.   Stafford's Reg. (117, 123, 141) 10 Oct. 1411 licence to John Harry, V. of Wynner to celebrate in a chapel of S. Wynner.

Richard **Rowlond, dev.** autumn **1372**—autumn 1376 ; ? Fellow previously ; M.A. in 1366 ; a family name at Exeter.

Henry **Beamond, Dev. 1372**, vac. 1 Nov. 1382, d. autumn 1415 ; of Exon. dioc., M.A.; Computus Lent 1374 a payment due to him in the time of Dagenet's Rectorship, i. e. 1371–72 ; summer 1411 'xiid ob. M. H. Beamond, quando fuerat nobiscum'; winter 1411 'iiiid pro vino dato procuratoribus M. Henrici Bewmond'; Lent 1413 'liiis iiiid procuratori M. Henrici Beaumond in finalem solucionem decem marcarum sibi debitarum'; autumn 1415 'iiid ob. oblatis in die funeralium Beaumond'.

Richard **Browne, Dev.** autumn **1372**—autumn 1379 ; M.A., Vice-Rector 1378, Rector 1378–79, Canon of Exeter; at Queen's 1379–89, W. Thomson's *An Open College* 32 ; Queen's Coll. Computus 1387 'Expens. M. Ric. Broun usque partes suas, circa Exon, pro libris quos legavit M. Hen. Witfeld xiis iiiid, pro cariagio librorum xxd.' Ex. Coll. Computus summer 1414 'iiiid pro vino dato executoribus M. Ricardi Brown'; 'iiiid pro emendacione duorum librorum quos habuimus ex dono M. Ricardi Brown.' The Old List gives R. Browne as a Fellow in 1409 ; but, if so, it may have been another R. Browne.

John **Hennok** (Henokes, Ennok; this family, in Hennock parish, was connected with the family of Clist), **Dev.** autumn **1372**; chamber-fellow with Dagenet in rooms *ad ostium.*

John **Dedemor, Chapl.** 18 Sept. **1372** to Lent 1374; M.A., mentioned in winter 1377; ? R. of North Benfleet, Essex, 12 Dec. 1386; d. 1392; Newcourt ii. 46.

Richard **Pester, Dev.**, occurs summer and autumn **1372**: mentioned autumn 1400; R. of Widworthy, Devon, in 1388 (Ancient Deeds, D. K. R. i. p. 449), a kinsman of Bishop Reade (see 1357, Hist. Comm. v. 477, Brodrick 224). A Richard Pestour (? his father) was R. of Widworthy 12 Dec. 1349; N. and Gleanings iv. 35, 59, 173, 189.

John **Coly**, or Colie, **dev. 1372**; M.A., vac. 31 Oct. 1379.

Thomas **Worth, corn. 1372**; M.A., Rector 1375–77; ? vac. 17 Oct. 1379; a leader in the dispute against the Civilians 1376; Gutch i. 489.

Laurence **Stevine, corn. 1372**; M.A., Rector 1379—Mch 1380; vac. 16 Ap. 1380. Brantingham's Reg. 20 Sep. 1379 'Londoniis, dominus contulit Laurencio Stevyn Exon diocesis primam tonsuram habenti literas dimissorias ad omnes ordines tam minores quam sacros a quocunque episcopo etc., et presbiteratus ordines a quocunque episcopo etc.'; but the bishop in 1382 ordered the Priors of Launceston and Bodmin, and friar Benedict Lugans, S.T.P., provost of Glasney, and the Official of the bishop's peculiar jurisdiction in Cornwall, and the vicar of Probus (? William Noe), to examine into Bedeman's preaching in Cornwall. L. Stephyn *alias* Bedeman, of Ex. Coll., renounced Wiclifism 18 Oct. 1382, when the Archbishop restored him to his academical rights, Gutch i. 492, 506, 509, English Works of Wyclif, p. xxix. Stafford's Reg. 22 Nov. 1397 leave of absence for a year to M. Laurence Stevyn *alias* Bedeman, R. of Lifton; 15 Jan. 140⁸⁄₁₀ named Penitenciary; 11 June 1410 Laurence Bedeman, B.D., R. of Lifton, lic. to preach in Latin or English. Stafford's Reg. 18, 241, 256, 338 and *v.* heresy. Fasc. Zizaniorum 274, 310, Foxe's Monuments ed. Townsend iii. 805, 809. Nat. Biog. ii. 210, iv. 108.

John **Skyllinge, Sar.**, already fellow 18 Sep. **1372**; a commissioner 14 Feb. 140⅔ to inquire about the property of Queen's College; Statutes iii. App. p. 50.

Reginald **Povy, Sar.** Dec. **1372** to winter 1377; autumn 1391 '1*d* pro potu ad M. Reynaldum Povy'; a 'dominus Riginaldus' is mentioned summer 1397, Lent 1398, summer 1400. Reginald Povy was Patron and Rector of Colerne, Wilts 1401; R. of Upwey, Dorset 1410 (Poney, *u* and *n* confused): Phillipps i. 69, 87, Hutchins ii. 847.

William **Wedemore, dev. 1374**. In Old List. A William Wedmore was abbot of Dunkeswell, Devon 1353–82.

William **Noe** (? Noy), **corn. 1374**; a previous William Noe was V. of Probus 1349; V. of Probus, appointed Penitenciary 15 Jan 14$\frac{99}{10}$; 27 Mch 1413 William Noe, chaplain, and canon of Glasney, licensed to preach in Latin or English. Stafford's Reg. 114, 204, 263. In Old List.

Phillip **Stone, dev.** Lent **1374** to autumn 1376.

John **Uggeborwe** (Huggeburgh), from Ugborough in Devon, **Chapl.** Lent **1374** to autumn 1376. A patron of Mamhead 9 Ap. 1400, of Stoke Fleming 1 Mch 140$\frac{0}{1}$: Stafford's Reg. 186, 210.

John **Horton, Dev.**, el. 18 June 1374; d. 29 Nov. 1374.

Henry **Parker**, 1374. In Old List.

Martin **Lydeford, Dev.** 1374; Rector 1374.

Walter **Ufcote** or Offecote, **Dev.** 3 Dec. **1374**, in place of Horton, to autumn 1375; rented a school of the College 1379—Lent 1381.

Ralph **Redruth** (Redruffe, Ruderhith), **Corn. 1374**; D.D., one of the two Senior Fellows of Oriel before July 1373, and in 1386; Chancellor of the University 1392: of Ex. Coll. 1392, lately of Oriel; Gutch i. 525, 528, iii. App. p. 3, Rogers ii. 646 (Feb. 1395), Statutes iii. App. pp. 39, 46, Smith 264, Bokenham's Reg. (Lincoln) fol. 359, Le Neve iii. 548, Clark's Oxford Colleges 98: R. of Grittleton dioc. Sarum, when instit. to R. of Creed in Cornwall 18 Nov. 1395 in the person of his proxy Nicholas Herry, M.A., patron Richard II, in exchange with John Grey; 22 Dec. 1395 collated Canon of Glasney on resignation of John Grey, Michael Cergeaux his proxy, and Nicholas Harry, Sacristan of Glasney, proxy for Grey; exch. Creed for Saint Columb Major 6 July 1399, d. 1404: 24 Mch and 1 Ap. 1396 'licence to M. Ralph Redruth *sacre pagine professori*, R. of S. Crida in Cornwall, to hear confessions &c.'; 15 Sep. 1400 leave to Ralph Rudruth R. of S. Columb Major, to celebrate in oratories &c. Stafford's Reg. 54, 114, 162, 200, 280, 310.

William **Talkarn** or Talcaryn, **Corn.** summer **1375**; M.A., Rector Mch—Oct. 1380; **Chaplain** 1384–94; William Serche was removed by the Archbishop, who appointed Talkarn in his place; the order 8 Dec. 1384 is drawn up by his Commissaries, Robert Rygge Chan-

cellor of Oxford, John Landreyn D.D., and Thomas Chylyndon
Doctor of Decrees.   Autumn 1393 'viiis a M. Willelmo Talkarn in
plenam solucionem unius basse scole.'   He was V. of S. Erth, Cornwall 17 Dec. 1395–1431, Dean of Crantock 11 May 1418, d. 1431 :
Monast. Exon. 55; Rogers ii. 646 (Feb. 1395).   Stafford's Reg. 313,
16 Nov. 1400 commission (renewed ten times subsequently) to
William V. of S. Ercus to hear confessions; 15 Feb. 140¾ leave to
M. William Talkarn V. of S. Ercus to celebrate once a year, on
Easter Monday, in a chapel of S. Ercus near Trefussa; 9 Oct. 1411
preaching licence to William Talkarn senior, V. of S. Ercus, *in Artibus
magistro et scolari in theologia*, and Reg. 159 (senior and junior).

William **Slade, Dev.** autumn **1375** to 1384; M.A., Vice-Rector
1378, Rector 1380–84; V. of Cotleigh 1385, of Axmouth 1393–
1397, Eccl. Ant. ii. 84; Warden of Ottery 1397, d. 1399; Monast.
Exon. 261, 371 'born in Devon, brought up at the school in Exon,
thence sent to Oxford, where he became very well learned, especially
in Aristotle, whose works he did read openly in the schools, to his
great commendation; when made Abbot of Buckfast he furnished the
house with fair buildings, and adorned the Commonwealth with his
learning, leaving behind him xiii books of his own penning.'   These
included De Anima, Super 4 libros sententiarum, Flores Moralium,
Grostest super Decem Precepta (Leland Coll. iii. 152, Pits 530,
Rowe's Cistercians 95–100).   Stafford's Reg. 13 Dec. 1396 letter
from Official of Court of Canterbury, dated 9 Dec., on complaint of
M. William Slade V. of Axmouth against Sampson Trigal prior of
Lodres, dioc. Sarum (Hutchins ii. 308–9); Reg. 11, 143, 157, 192,
330.   His Computus gives the expense of building a Library.

John **Russell, dev.** Lent **1376** to 1387; M.A., rented a school of
Ex. Coll. 1380, ? V. of Dean Prior, Devon 24 Nov. 1407; Stafford's
Reg. 163.

William **Dyer** or Deyer, **sar.** Lent **1376** to autumn 1387; M.A.;
a William Dyer, V. of Bray, Berks, d. 31 Jan. 144⁰⁄₁; Ashmole's
Berkshire iii. 8.   A William Dyare chaplain V. of Great Fontmel
17 Mch 1406 exch. 1442 with John Hunt, Hutchins iii. 561.

John **Mattecotte** (Mathecok, Lyson's Devon 437 Maddacott),
dev. autumn **1376** to winter 1386, M.A.

Thomas **White** (Wite, Wit), Rector **1378**, but his work was done
by a succession of Vice-Rectors, John Henry, Richard Browne,
William Slade, Henry Beamond.   See Lewis' *Wiclif* 280.

John **Gardiner, Dev.** summer **1378** to 6 Ap. 1381; Fellow of

Merton 1382 and 1388 (Carole Hall deed No. 29); mentioned autumn 1399: R. of Exminster 8 Jan. 139⅘, d. 1400, Eccl. Ant. ii. 24. Stafford's Reg. 172, 29 Jan. 139⁴⁄₇ leave of absence for a year to M. John Gardiner, R. of Exminster; 380, 20 May 1400 will of John Gardyner R. of Exminster, leaves his sister Johanna 13s. 4d., and legacies to Richard Drake clerk *si velit scolas excercere*, and to Roger Jurdan *clerico meo*; executors his brother Henry Gardiner and Richard Skinner chaplains and Roger Jurdan clerk; will proved 31 May 1400 by Richard Hals canon of Exeter, Chancellor of the Bishop; succeeded at Exminster 8 June 1400 by Henry Gardyner, also a fellow of Ex. Coll., who exch. 9 Jan. 140⅚ for Yate, Glouc., Eccl. Ant. ii. 24. Stafford's Reg. 18 Dec. 1396 dispensation to M. Henry Gardiner R. of Meavy, acolite, to *study* at Oxford for three years, and letters dimissory for orders; 4 Oct. 1399 Henry Gardyner chaplain sent as agent to Rome; 12 Ap. 1402 leave of absence for two years to Henry Gardyner R. of Exemynster, *in obsequiis Guydonis episcopi Meneviensis*; winter 1463 'xxs a M. Henrico Gardiner via doni quia quondam hic erat socius'; if this was the same man, he was very old. Reg. 110.

John **Were, Chapl.** autumn 1378 to summer 1381.

Robert **Ivon** or Yvon, **dev.** autumn 1378 to autumn 1381.

Richard **Wodeford, Dev.** 1378 to autumn 1383: Prior of S. John's Hosp. Exeter 1384, d. 6 Aug. 1428; Monast. Exon. 301. Summer 1379 'xs Ricardo Wodeford pro pensione sibi debita anno preterito.' A Richard de Wodeford was R. of Widworthy 21 Mch. 133⅔, a Sir John de Wodeford 21 May 1348; N. and Gleanings iv. 135, 137.

Thomas **Dyre, dev.** summer 1379; M.A., Rector 1385–89. Chaplain 1390–93, V. of Bampton, Oxon 1399.

William **Serche,** ? **Chaplain 1381,** removed 1384 by the Archbishop for Wiclifism; Computus winter 1386 and Lent 1387.

John **Nude** or Nuda, **dev.** 4 Nov. 1382—31 Oct. 1388; ? succeeded Beamond; M.A.; Eccl. Ant. ii. 63.

John **Jaycok, dev.,** occurs autumn 1383. A John Jaycock was witness to a deed about the cemetery of Kingsbridge 23 Ap. 1410.

John **Bydelwille** or Bydewill, **Dev.** 1383 to winter 1385; ? lived afterwards at Henley, and died before autumn 1409, when we have 'xxd cuidam presbitero de Henley qui portavit nobis octo quaternos legatos per Johannem Bydewill quondam consocium Collegii nostri'; Stafford's Reg. 14, 193, 287.

Thomas **Lange, Corn.** autumn 1383 to 1396, Chaplain winter

1393, afterwards lived at Exeter, mentioned in summer 1398;
22 Ap. 1407 leave to M. Thomas Lange R. of Yenstowe (Instow),
subdeacon, to *study* at Oxford for one year; 22 Jan. 141⁰⁄₁ Thomas
Lange R. of Yenstowe admonished to reside; Stafford's Reg. 221,
234.

Thomas **Browne, sar.** autumn 1383 to Nov. 1389; Gutch i. 595.

Thomas **Hendyman** or Hyndeman, **corn. 1383**; D.D., Rector
16 Oct. 1389—2 Ap. 1390, Chancellor 1395-97, 1399-1400; Dean
of Crantock, Cornwall 8 Dec. 1390, exch. for Wardenship of Cemetery
at S. Austell 25 Feb. 14⁰⁸⁄₁₀, res. 1411, instit. to Clare portion, Tiverton
11 Dec. 1398, to Sampford Courtenay 12 Mch 140¾, to Widecombe
in the Moor 27 Aug. 1412, exch. for Farway 26 Oct. 1412, to preb.
of Heyes in Exeter Castle 3 Sep. 1413, V. of S. Winnow 2 Jan. 141½,
res. 1412, archdeacon of Exeter 28 Feb. 14⁰⁸⁄₁₀, R. of S. Mabyn 13 Ap.
1415, Chancellor of Exeter 19 Jan. 141⁸⁄₉—1428, R. of South Perrot,
Dorset 12 June 1428, res. almost at once; R. of the first portion of
Crewkerne; d. before 1445; Hutchins ii. 169; Gutch i. 526, 532,
Maclean ii. 461; Statutes iii. App. p. 48; Rogers ii. 643, 646; paid
the College 10s. in 1385 for rent of School 'ubi scamnum situatur in
medio,' and in autumn 1397: autumn 1414 'iiis viiid cursori pro
cariagio vii librarum quas recepit de M. Thoma Hendeman.'
Stafford's Reg. 18, 62, 67, 127, 159, 167, 177, 199, 225; Lyte 292.

Richard **Mark** or Marks, **Corn.** autumn 1384; M.A., Rector
2 Ap. 1390–1391, vac. before 1396; summer 1404 'xd latori qui
portavit nobis casulam nigram cum pertinenciis quam habuimus ex
dono M. Ricardi Mark.' Stafford's Reg. 5 Jan. 14⁰⁸⁄₁₀ preaching
licence to Richard Mark, M.A., R. of S. Martin in Exeter, to which he
had been instit. 12 Ap. 1407.

Roger **Wilberte, sar.** autumn 1384 to Lent 1386.

Robert **Marschel, dev.** autumn 1384, vac. before 1396; M.A.,
Rector 11 Oct. 1393–1394; R. of Musbery, exch. 15 May 1403 for
Harberton, 13 Oct. 1405 for Widecombe, 11 Nov. 1410 for S. Mary
Steps, Exeter, 31 Mch 1412 for Greinton, Som.; Stafford's Reg. 171,
176, 189, 220, 252.

John **Sawyer** or Sayere, **dev.** autumn 1384 to 1391. Stafford's
Reg. 16 July 1398 indulgence to those who contribute for John
Sayer 'Cantuar. in obsequiis Regum Anglie per plures annos,' his
house having been burnt &c.; 22 June 1411 letters dimissory to John
Sayer who already has the first tonsure.

Thomas **Plymiswood, Dev.** autumn 1384 to 1396. V. of

Heavitree, Exeter 9 Sep. 1396, exch. with John Wydelonde for
Bampton, Oxon 28 Oct. 1401; **Chaplain** for a short time from
13 Nov. 1395; d. 1418; Stafford's Reg. ii. 295^b ordinance 28 Mch
1401 for V. of Heavitree, and 5 June 1411 to Thomas Plymmeswode,
V. of Bampton, Oxon, M.A., leave to preach in Latin or English;
summer 1417 'viii*d* famulo M. Thome Plymmyswode quando portavit nobis ii libros nobis datos per magistrum suum, xvi*d* pro aqua
vite et zuccara missis M. Thome Plymmyswode'; winter 1417 'xi*d*
ob. circa M. Thomam Plymyswode quando detulit nobis ii libros';
autumn 1418 'xii*d* famulo M. Thome Plymyswode quando portavit
nobis libros legatos'; autumn 1418, 'iiii*s* iii*d* circa vicarium de Wittenham, dominum Walterum, et alterum de Bampton, executores M.
Thome Plymyswode, quando fuerunt nobiscum in prandio'; winter
1418 'ix*d* pro cathenacione librorum remanentibus post distribu-
cionem factam sociis de summa legata eisdem per M. Thomam
Plymmyswode'; winter 1418 'xxiii*d* circa dominum Walterum Abraham et pro cena et i pari cerotecarum dato sibi et Waltero Fysher
quando M. Johannes Saunder et ipsi assignabant nobis Dominicam
Lincoln cum Sermonibus et Mandatis eiusdem [Robert Grostete,
bishop of Lincoln], pro anima M. Thome Plymmyswode.'   Giles'
Bampton xxxvi. 57; Coxe no. xxi, xxiii, xliii.; Stafford's Reg. 12, 126,
177, 294, Gascoigne 43, 170.

Thomas **Turke, Sar.** autumn 1384; named **Chaplain** by Dean
and Chapter of Exeter 30 Ap. 1393 (Reynolds' *Abstract of Chapter
Acts* p. 12, and 13 Nov. 1395 'on the res. of the Venerable Thomas
Turke, Chaplain of Exeter College, we appoint Thomas Plymeswode
M.A. in his place'). Turke was V. of Bere Regis, Dorset 1411
and abjured for heresy, Hutchins i. 155. Principal of Hart Hall
1399–1400; Vice-Custos of Winchester sch. 1400 (Kirby's Winchester p. x, 3 'M.A., from Swindon, adm. 22 Ap. 1400, res. as beneficed 1401': p. 41 John Turke 1415, ? R. of Chaldon Herring,
Dorset 1443). Computi winter 1399, winter 1401, summer 1410;
winter 1397 'vi*s* viii*d* de M. Thoma Turk, ad edificacionem novi
cameni'; summer 1398 'iii*s* viii*d* de Johanne Bouryngh de pecunia
data ad novos camenos'; Gutch i. 488.

Thomas **Cole, dev.** autumn 1384 to 1394. Stafford's Reg. 17
Mch $\frac{1399}{1400}$ letters dimissory to Thomas Stephyn alias Cole (? the
same); 14 May 1410 letters dimissory to Thomas Cole deacon.
Thomas Stephyn chaplain collated to canonry of Exeter 24 Mch
141$\frac{5}{6}$, Stafford's Reg. 169.

Peter **Gilbert, corn.** autumn **1384** to summer **1392**; M.A.; acted for Bennyngs in Cornwall.

Helias **Stoke** (Stocks), **corn.** autumn **1384** to summer **1397**; M.A., Rector 14 Oct. 1391–1393; ? succeeded Talkarn; R. of Greinton, Som., exch. 31 Mch 1412 for R. of S. Mary Steps, Exeter; collated 31 Jan. 141⅚ to canonry in Crantock; summer 1436 'xis iiiid ex legato M. Elie Stoke.' Stafford's Reg. 160, 338; Catalogue of All Souls' MSS. no. lxxix.

John **Bennyngs, Corn.** 1385, d. 8 May 1387; 'Procurator' for the College in Cornwall, and died owing 20s, which was repaid in 1390 and 1392.

Henry **Mage, dev.** Lent 1386, d. 3 Mch 138⁶⁄₇.

John **Honta, sar.** Lent 1386; see a. 1376.

Peter **Gybbe(s), Dev.** Lent 1387 to 1391; M.A., ? 'magister Peter' mentioned 1392; rented a school of the College autumn 1390.

Robert **Symond,** Lent 1387; Stafford's Reg. 345.

John **Hatter, sar.** winter 1388 to summer 1389.

John **Tatyn, sar.** 1389, vac. before 1396.

John **Dowrish, Dev.** Lent 1390 to 1391; Prior of St. John's, Exeter 31 Aug. 1428, d. 2 May 1451; Monast. Exon. 301, Stafford's Reg. 431.

Jordan **Langston, Dev.** summer 1390 to summer 1394.

John **Gynne, corn.** summer 1390 to winter 1405; M.A., Rector 1395–99; John Gynne or Junne, V. of Brent 11 Feb. 140⁶⁄₇, first tonsure 9 June 1408, named Penitenciary for deanery of Totnes 15 Jan. 14⁹⁹⁄₁₀ and on 8 subsequent occasions. Stafford's Reg. 22 Sep. 1413 disp. to John Gynne clerk to take orders and any benefice, though son of an unmarried man and woman, and p. 37, 433 (another J. G. p. 120).

Richard **Penwyne** (Pyngwyne), **Corn.** 15 Ap. 1390 to summer 1402; M.A., Rector 1400–1; winter 1396 'extra villam infirmus'; Stafford's Reg. 210, 448, 456, 464 Eccl. Ant. i. 211.

Geoffrey **Prentys, Dev.** Lent 1392 to winter 1404, ? in place of Dowrish; M.A., Rector 1401–2. Stafford's Reg. 22 Oct. 1403 to Geoffry Prenteys of Exon dioc. M.A. the first tonsure, 22 Dec. ordained acolite, 23 Feb. 140⅔ subdeacon on title from Rewley abbey, Oxford, 15 Mch deacon on same title, 19 Mch priest. Canon of Windsor, Ashmole's *Berkshire* iii. 247.

Thomas **Robyn, sar.** 1392, ? in place of Sawyer; vac. before 1396.

John **Boswellec** (Bosvelhec), **Corn.** 1392 to winter 1399 ; M.A. ;
Boswellick is in S. Allen, Cornwall.   Stafford's Reg. 15 June 1397 to
John Bosvelec the first tonsure and letters dimissory.

John **Pendestock** (? Pondestock, Poundstock), 1392.   In Old List.
For A. W. Poundstock, see Stafford's Reg. 13, 22, 146, 298.

John **Forde, sar.** summer 1393 ; Hutchins ii. 387, Brodrick 220.

John **Bowring, Dev.** summer 1394 to Lent 1401 ; M.A. ;
Stafford's Reg. 33, 65, 190, 398; 6 May 1397 letters dimissory for
orders to John Bowryng clerk, 10 Aug. 1411 John Bowryng R. of
chantry at Slapton penitenciary for deanery of Woodleigh, 9 Nov.
1411 Rev. Thomas Taylor and John Bowryng executors to will of
John Comb R. of North Hywysch.   He left a medical MS. to New
College, Coxe MSS. N. Coll. no. clxix 'Magister Johannes Bouring
quondam socius collegii Exoniensis, compos mentis sue, legavit
istum librum catenandum in libraria collegii Wyntoniensis, in quo
continentur diversi tractatus medicinarum compositarum.'

John **Jakys, Dev.** summer 1394 to winter 1401 ; determined as
B.A. 1398, M.A., Rector 11 Oct. 1399 to 1400 ; his Computus is
beautifully written.   Stafford's Reg. 211, 223 (note 3) 21 July 1410
leave of absence up to Michaelmas for *dominus* John Jakys R. of
Stoke-Rivers near Barnstaple.   Sir John Jakes was priest vicar
Exeter Cathedral 25 Oct. 1328.   J. Jakys held the chantry of S.
Nicholas in S. Edmund's, Sarum 1419, Phillipps i. 109, Newcourt i.
691.   John Jakys, Fellow of New College, B.A. 18 Ap. 1513, was
V. of Madron, Cornwall 1534.

Alexander **Cortays, Dev.** Lent 1396 to winter 1405 ; M.A., R. of
Instow 19 Sep. 1412.   As only 'Alexander' is mentioned up to
winter 1402 and, after that, 'Alexander Cortays,' it is possible,
though not probable, that they were two different persons.   Stafford's
Reg. 72, 180, 222, 3 Oct. 1412 preaching licence to Alexander
Courteys M.A., R. of Yenstow, and so again 22 June 1414.

Thomas **Noreys, sar.** Lent 1396 to winter 1406 ; M.A., Vice-
Rector and then Rector 1405-6, in orders.   Stafford's Reg. 264.
The name also occurs in Devon.

John **Ladde, dev.** Lent 1396 to winter 1403 ; M.A.   The name
occurs in Devon, Hist. Comm. v. 204.

John **Schute** (so he spells his name ; elsewhere Shute, Suete,
Swethe ; from Shute near Colyton), **Dev.** 1396 ; M.A., B.D., Rector
1404-5 ; Stafford's Reg. 161, 187, 193, 326, 18 Dec. 1396 leave
to John Shute R. of Meavy to *study* at Oxford for three years,

leave prolonged for 3 years 22 Ap. 1401, renewed for 1 year 27 Mch 1405 ('subdeacon'), and 19 Sep. 1406 ; V. of Bishop's Nympton 27 Aug. 1406, Chaplain to the Bishop, R. of Meavy 1400–7 collated to Paignton 22 Feb. 140⁹⁄₄, R. of S. Breoke, Canon of Ottery and of Exeter ; 21 Jan. 141²⁄₃ leave to preach in Latin and English ; archdeacon of Exeter 21 Sep. 1417, d. 1426, will made 2 May 1425, Lacy's Reg. iii. 499ᵇ 'lego ad tenendum anniversarium diem cum exequiis precedentibus in collegio sive aula de Stapyldon x*li*, ita quod quolibet anno distribuantur inter socios in die obitus mei x*s*' ; winter 1421 'x*ixd* pro vino dato M. Johanni Schute quando fuit apud Bampton'; a Walter Schute, R. of Tedburn S. Mary 1413 (William Schute was R. 1399), occurs Lent 1421, Lent 1424. Foxe's Monuments ed. Townsend iii. 96, Eccl. Ant. i. 176, N. and Gleanings i. 12, iv. 139.

John **Cowling, Corn.** Lent 1397 to summer 1407 ; M.A., Rector 1402–4 ; V. of S. Minver 7 Ap. 1407, d. 1434 ; Maclean iii. 19. Stafford's Reg. 73, 29 Jan. 139⁸⁄₉ disp. to John Cowlyng *scholar* to take orders, though son of an unmarried man and woman (disp. from Rome dated 'vi nonas Maii Bonifacii Pape viii anno nono'), per John Brode clerk notary public, 'data et acta sunt hec in quadam camera magna a retro Aula Maiori [University College] infra prioratum S. Fritheswide municipii Oxoniensis Ord. S. Augustini Linc. dioc., presentibus M. Ricardo Hals ipsius domini episcopi cancellario, M. Johanne Orum, Johanne Jakys, Willelmo Penbegil' &c.

Robert **Roberts, corn.** Lent 1397 to summer 1401.

John **Brode, Chapl.** 24 Feb. 139⁶⁄₇ to autumn 1400. Stafford's Reg. 39, 402 twice.

William **Swyndon, Sar.** Lent 1397 to summer 1398 ; Fellow of Winchester 1400–1, res. as beneficed 1412, Kirby's Winchester 3. Autumn 1409 'de Willelmo Swyndon et domino Elia x*ld* ad usum nove fenestre in Aula nostra'; and in the expenses 'x*lis* vi*d* pro nova fenestra facta in Aula nostra'; Phillipps i. 110 *bis* (1420).

— **Hugh** (Hugo), **dev.** autumn 1397 to Lent 1403, M.A. : winter 1428 'iii*s* iiii*d* de M. Hugone pro quodam libro sibi vendito.'

Richard **Wodeman, dev.** autumn 1399 ; d. 30 Oct. 1404.

William **Penbegyll, corn.** 30 Oct. 1399 to 14 Oct. 1409, in place of Boswellec (but Pits 890 says 'Devoniensis, civitate Isca,' see Tanner 588) ; M.A., Rector 1406–7. Stafford's Reg. 290, 31 Dec. 1407 leave to William Penbigell clerk to take orders, though son of a married man and unmarried woman, present Richard Penwyn

chaplain; 10 May 1408 letters dimissory to William Penbegyll,
M.A. to take the first tonsure.   William Penbukull paid 10s. for rent
of rooms in Oriel in each of the years 1412, 1413.

— **Calystoke** (? from Calstock in Cornwall), **Chapl.** autumn **1399**
to winter 1403, in place of Brode.

Thomas **Wallebere, sar.** summer **1401** to Lent 1404 ; Fellow of
Merton 1404, in France with Henry V in 1417, Brodrick 38, 221,
228: preb. of S. Paul's 4 June 1416, res. 1445, Newcourt i. 217,
ii. 292.   Stafford's Reg. 24 Sep. 1408 disp. to Thomas Wallebeare
clerk to take orders, though son of an unmarried man and woman,
present John Schute V. of Paignton, and Robert Olyver.

William **Grene, dev.** autumn **1401** to summer 1413 ; Stafford's
Reg. 5 May 1405 leave of absence to William Grene R. of Clyst
S. Mary for a year, 24 Nov. 1407 letters dimissory to William Grene
already tonsured and Reg. 295; M.A., Rector 1409-11; Anstey
677 : John Grene, Principal of Hart Hall 1408-10, is mentioned in
the Computus of Lent 1409, see Newcourt i. 592, ii. 386.   Autumn
1413 ' xiiis iiiid a M. Willelmo Grene per manus M. Willelmi Fylham
in partem solucionis Missalis antiqui sibi venditi'; winter 1413 ' vis
viiid de magistro W. Trengoff in finalem solucionem cuiusdam
Missalis quod habuit Grene.'

Walter **Pyry, dev.** winter **1402**, d. Lent 1409; Lent. 1409 ' iiiid
octo sociis ad offerendum in die sepulture M. Walteri Pyry.'

Robert **Gilbert, corn. 1402,** M.A.; Warden of Merton 1417, and
in France with Henry V that year, Bishop of London 1436, d. 1458 ;
Gutch i. 555, iii. 6, Brodrick 38, 159, 221, Wilkins' Concilia iii. 172,
Newcourt i. 22, 254.

Benedict **Brente, dev.** summer **1403** to Lent 1415, ? in place of
Hugh; Stafford's Reg. 468, 10 Sep. 1409 letters dimissory to Benedict
Brenta, M.A., subdeacon ; Proctor 1411, res. Sep. 1411 (Lyte c. xi),
Rector 1413-14; licensed to preach in church of Brent 3 Ap. 1416,
in deaneries of Woodleigh and Plympton 27 Jan. 141⅜.   Stafford's
Reg. 37, W. Antiq. vii. 212.

Walter **Trengoff, Corn.** autumn **1403** to winter 1417; Stafford's
Reg. 357, 443, 450, 466, 473, 23 July 1411 disp. for Walter Treyngoff
clerk and tonsured, to take orders, though son of a *priest* and an unmarried woman, and letters dimissory ; 11 June 1412 Walter Treyngoff
V. of S. Neot has been preaching without a licence ; a John Trengoff
was V. of St. Neot 17 Dec. 1369 (? Walter's *father*); M.A., D.D.,
Rector 1411-13, Chancellor 1418-19, Provost of Glasney, Cornwall

19 Sep. 1427, res. Oct. 1436, Archpriest of oratory of the Trinity at Burton, Whippingham, I. of Wight, res. to Bishop of Winchester 1440; Archdeacon of Cornwall 2 Oct. 1436 to 144⅘ when he died; Anstey 271, 274, 276-7; Monast. Exon. 49; Sir R. Worsley's Hist. of Isle of Wight 180; Lent 1414 'xvis iiiid M. Waltero Trengoff pro labore suo quem sustinuit pro pecuniis nostris adquirendis in Cornubia'; Lent 1417 'iid datis Wygan ad portandum unam cedulam M. Waltero Trengof'; Lent 1444 'xiiiid pro cirothecis missis M. Trengoffe'; Bibl. Corn. 784, N. and Gleanings v. 48.

Thomas **Pyryton, Chapl.**, ? only Lent **1404.**

Thomas **Combe** or Come, **Dev.** summer **1404,** d. summer **1418,** M.A.; summer 1418 'iiid datis Radulpho *bedeman* pro proclamacione fienda in die funeralium M. Thome Come'; autumn 1418 'iis iiid homini qui portavit nobis libros legatos per M. Thomam Come.'

William **Payn, dev.** summer **1404** to **1415:** M.A., Principal of Hart Hall **1414.** Summer 1414 'xiiis iiiid de M. Willelmo Payn in partem solucionis pensionis Aule Cervine pro anno presenti.' See a. 1407 (Morewyll). A Peter Payne was a strong Wiclifite, Gutch i. 543, Tanner 582, Lewis' *Wiclif.*

William **Andrew, Corn.** autumn **1404** to Lent **1422;** M.A., Principal of Hart Hall **1411,** Proctor **1416;** Principal of Checker Hall **1411-15;** winter 1411 'xs de Willelmo Androw in partem solucionis Aule Scakkarii pencionis pro anno presenti'; ? R. of S. Dionis Backchurch, London 1422-30, Newcourt i. 330. Stafford's Reg. 428.

William **Fylham,** (? from Filham in Ugborough), **Dev. 1404;** Rector **1407-8** and **1415;** Stafford's Reg. 10 Sep. 1409 letters dimissory to William Fylham M.A. who already has the first tonsure; 20 Sep. 1414 licence to William Fylham M.A. and scholar in theology to preach in Latin or English in the deaneries of Plympton, Woodleigh and Totnes; dean of Crediton 20 Sep. 1417, licensed to preach in the Cathedral and all churches in Devon 2 Dec. 1417; R. of Stoke-in-Teignhead 1 Feb. 141⅚; Archdeacon of Cornwall 29 May 1419-1436, Chancellor of Exeter to his death in 1439; bur. in Cathedral; Oliver's Bishops 281, 288 he settled a dispute at Glasney 1427, R. I. C. vi. 223. His will in Lacy's Reg. iii. 506a 'ego Willielmus Fylham, sacre pagine professor licet indignus, et canonicus ecclesie cathedralis Exon, compos mentis, viiio die mensis Octobris A. D. millesimo CCCCmo XXXVto in hospicio meo Exon condo testamentum meum in hunc modum   lego scolaribus collegii Exon in Oxonia cs ad tenendum anniversarium obitum meum per x annos post mortem meam, ita quod quolibet anno de illis cs distribuantur equaliter inter scolares predictos xs.' Autumn 1409 'iiiid ob. circa M. Johannem Dymmok qui fecit procuracionem pro M. Willelmo Fylham, Come et aliis ad faciendum finem cum Johanne Cararthyn pro fructibus ecclesie nostre in Cornubia,' winter 1413 'xxs de M. Willelmo Fylham pro uno calice emendo' (and 'xxxiiiis iid pro uno calice ad usum capelle'; and Lent 1414 'iiid pro sanctificacione calicis et tuelle,' see Acad. Dec. 1886 p. 396); Lent 1417 'iiid a M. Willelmo Fylham pro focalibus sibi venditis'; winter 1424 'xxd pro vino misso M. Willelmo Fyllam quando erat Bamptonie'; and see summer 1425; Lent 1441 'xiid de excrescenciis obitus M. Willelmi Fylham'; autumn 1441 'xls de bonis M. Willelmi Fylham per manus M. Johannis Hankkok executoris eiusdem'; Lent 1442 'iis remanentibus de obitu M. Willelmi Fylham'; Lent 1444 'iis de pecuniis residuis ultra administrata sociis in obitu Fylham'; and Lent 1446; Stafford's Reg. 109, N. and Gleanings iv. 188.

(Robert) **Benet**, sar. Lent to winter **1405**; a Robert Benet was Principal of Salesbury Hall 1458, Anstey 620, 676, 741, 745; summer 1429 'iiis iiiid pro cameris Benet et Pyper'; summer 1431 'pro camera Benet vd.'

John **Beaufitz, dev**. winter **1406** to 1413; M.A.; Brodrick 218; Stafford's Reg. 22 Dec. 1403 letters dimissory to John Beaufysz acolite Exon. dioc. for taking orders. Stafford's Reg. 389.

— **Bernard, dev**. winter **1406** to summer 1411; Stafford's Reg. 20 429; 171 Roger Bernard R. of S. Paul's, Exeter, d. 1411.

— **Helias** (Helys, Elyes), winter **1406** to summer 1407; 'Elias' occurs Lent 1409 to autumn 1413, who may not be the same; we have in autumn 1409 'de Willelmo Swyndon et *domino* Elia xld ad usum nove fenestre in Aula nostra, *Magistro* Elya iiis iiiid ad eundem usum.' Stafford's Reg. 164 Thomas Helys R. of Dodbroke 6 Nov. 1409, d. 1410; and 196 Thomas Elys; Brodrick 228.

Robert **Kingsford, dev**. Lent **1407** to winter 1412, determined as B.A. 1409.

Ralph **Morewyll, Dev**. Lent **1407** to autumn 1425, M.A., Rector 1419–22; perhaps studied law; summer 1415 'vd pro i clave et emendacione sere in scolis M. Radulphi Morewyll'; autumn 1415 'pro emendacione studii M. Radulphi Morewyll ixd'; autumn 1418 'iiiid Morwylle pro scriptura indenturarum'; Lent 1445 'iiiid Pencaer pro litera attornatoria pro M. Radulpho Morewell'; V. of Sutton, i.e.

S. Andrew's, Plymouth 7 Sep. 1433, canon of Exeter, d. 146$\frac{4}{8}$. Will
in Nevill's Reg. 141^a, 3 July 1464, proved 8 Ap. 1465, 'lego librum
vocatum Sententia super primam Sententiarum, 2º folio *Procedit ista*,
collegio Exon in Oxon, lego eidem collegio librum continentem
sermones Leonis (?) pape, item xl*s* reponendos in cista communi ad
orandum pro anima mea, lego cuilibet socio eiusdem collegii existenti
in *Placebo*, commendacionibus, et in missa pro [? defunctis, in die]
obitus mei xii*d*, lego ciste de Gilleford in Oxon x*s* reponendos ad
orandum pro anima mea.' Stafford's Reg. 231, 24 May 1412 commission to Ralph Morwyll and William Payn clerks, and William
Andrew on the part of Ralph Kyngisford deacon, Exon. dioc.

John **Sawnder** or Sander, **Chapl.** summer **1407** to autumn 1419;
M.A.; autumn 1419 'iii*s* iiii*d* de Johanne Sawnder pro scolis suis';
and so in autumn 1414; collated dean of Crediton 24 Feb. 141$\frac{8}{9}$,
Stafford's Reg. 160; 21 Nov. 1409 letters dimissory to John Saunder,
already tonsured; 16 Feb. 14$\frac{09}{10}$ to John Saunder subdeacon.

Henry **Kaylle** (Kayel, Kael), **Corn.** occurs in summer **1407**, ? in
place of Cowling; Provost of Oriel 1421, and ordained subdeacon
21 Dec. 1421 on his title as Provost, d. 1422; Gutch iii. 126; summer
1422 'ii*d* oblatis in die obitus M. Henrici Kayl.' He gave evidence
Sep. 1411, age 21, at the inquiry by the Archbishop's Commissary
into the conduct of members of Oriel.

John **Alwarde, sar.** winter **1408** to autumn 1419; M.A., Rector
1416–17 and 1418–19, Proctor 1417, R. of Stokebruerne, Northants
(see account of a MS. given by him to the College in Coxe no. xvi),
dead in 1458; autumn 1414 'x*s* a M. Johanne Alward pro pensione
scolarum suarum pro anno'; summer 1431 'a M. Johanne Alward ex
dono de debito M. Johannis Brent iii*s* iiii*d*'; winter 1453 'x*d* pro
cerothecis datis M. Johanni Alward et *capellano suo*' (? does this show
he was a man of rank; the Aylwards were from Hampshire, W. Antiq.
vii. 212, Stafford's Reg. 429).

Robert **Fitz Hugh** (3 s. Henry Lord Fitz Hugh), **dev. 1409–10**;
M.A.; archdeacon of Northampton 10 July 1419, preb. of Lincoln
1417, and 4 Aug. 1419–1431, and of Lichfield to 1428, Bishop of
London 16 Sep. 1431, d. 15 Jan. 143$\frac{5}{6}$; Balliol Statutes pref. p. iii,
xx: see, however, Gutch iii. 54; first mentioned winter 1399 'i*d* pro
bona cervisia in camera Fyzhugh quando fecit fenestram suam,' last
in summer 1410 'xvi*d* de dono M. Roberti Fytzhu.' Newcourt i. 22,
391, 496.

— **Erlestoke** (? from Erlestoke in Wilts), **Sar.** autumn **1409** to autumn 1413. A Thomas Erlestoke of Broughton near Bampton, Oxon, occurs 1405, Bodleian Charters p. 321.

Henry **Whitehead, Corn.** 16 Oct. **1409** to autumn 1420, in place of Penbegyll; M.A., Rector 1417–18. Stafford's Reg. 19 Feb. 141$\frac{3}{4}$ letters dimissory to Henry Whythede, and 30 May 1414.

Walter **Colys, corn. 1409**; M.A. In Old List. See a. 1418.

(? John) **Hele, dev.** winter **1411** to summer 1420; M.A.; Lent 1418 'xiid puero Hele [i.e. of Hele] quando portavit nobis ferinam in die S. Thome'; John Hele mentioned in autumn 1438 may be the same. Stafford's Reg. 126.

(? John) **Yeate**, or Yate (a family at Lyford in W. Hanney, Berks, Warton's Life of Sir T. Pope p. 2; at Wittenham, St. John's Statutes p. 85, 132); **sar.** Lent. **1413** to Lent 1418; Lent 1413 'id pro expensis Yate versus Walyngfordiam in negociis nostris'; Lent 1415 'iiid pro emendacione sere in camera Hele et Yate.' A John Yate was V. of Monkton-Farleigh 1424, of Inglesham 1451, Phillipps i. 115, 142, Newcourt i. 744.

John **Brente**, perhaps brother of Benedict Brent, **Dev.** autumn **1413** to winter 1430, M.A. by 1420.

Walter **Davyd** or Davy, **corn.** winter **1413** to 1430; M.A.; autumn 1426 'iis a M. Waltero Davyd quod non erat presens in eleccione Rectoris.' Stafford's Reg. 431.

John **Taylor, dev.** summer **1414** to summer 1417: Stafford's Reg. 347, 25 Aug. 1414 disp. to John Taylor clerk to take orders, though son of an unmarried man and woman.

John **Beaucomb, Dev.** autumn **1415** to autumn 1416; M.A.; ? Vice-Rector 1423; autumn 1420 'xxxs M. Johanni Beaucomb in partem solucionis quinque marcarum pro colleccione et cariagio garbarum apud Wyttynham'; a John Bawcomb was R. of Lympston, Devon 25 Oct. 1448, d. 1451; Eccl. Ant. iii. 92. Stafford's Reg. 16, 8 Aug. 1411 disp. to take orders for John Baucomb clerk, though son of an unmarried man and woman.

(? John) **Stone, dev.** autumn **1415** to Lent 1420: a John Stone had been Principal of Hart Hall 1403 and 1407; summer 1432 'pro cirothecis domino J. Stone iid ob.' Hutchins iii. 560, Le Neve i. 628, ii. 57, 102. A John Stone was secretary to Henry IV, archdeacon of Northampton 1413, preb. of Lincoln 1429; a William Stone occurs 20 Henry VI with a John Certeyn (a William Certeine occurs below); W. Antiq. vii. 212. A family of Stone occurs at Trevigo, Cornwall; Visit. Corn. 446.

Edmund **Fitchet, Dev.** autumn **1417** (? before) to autumn 1425, B.A. by 1420, M.A.; Rector 1422–24; V. of Brent, Devon, will dated 12 Sep. 1427, Lacy's Reg. iii. 500[b] 'lego M. Willielmo Fillam unum librum vocatum *Flecto genua*, item collegio Exon in Oxon *Flores Parisienses*'; his brother John was Abbot of Buckfast 16 Oct. 1440–1447, Monast. Exon. 371; summer 1425 'iiis *id* pro conductione equorum versus Londonias pro Edmundo Fychet'; Maclean ii. 43.

William **Certeine, Dev.** Lent **1418** to autumn 1422; M.A. by 1420; autumn 1418 'iiis iiii*d* a Willelmo Certeyn pro scolis in quibus determinavit anno preterito.' Stafford's Reg. 430 twice.

Robert **Atwelle** (Welle), **dev.** Lent **1418** to Lent 1420; ? of Wellhouse, Dodbrooke, Devon. Stafford's Reg. 423.

William **Collys** (Coll), **corn.** winter **1418** to autumn 1427; B.A. by 1420: precentor of Exeter 4 Ap. 1437; will 1 Nov. 1452, proved 14 June 1453; winter 1418 'iii*d* pro emendacione superpellicii Willelmi Coll'; was John Coll, autumn 1411, John Collys M.A., V. of Kidlington 1407?; Walter Collys occurs winter 1430 and summer 1431. William Colle, tonsured Clyst 16 Feb. 141¾, acolite 22 Sep., subdeacon 22 Dec., had letters dimissory 23 Dec. His brother, Walter Colle, acolite Clyst 23 Sep. 1413, deacon 21 Sep. 1415, priest 13 June 1416; instit. 6 May 1413 to Milton Damerel, 27 Sep. 1415 R. of Pitt portion at Tiverton, had licence 16 Oct. 1413 of non-residence for 3 years to *study* at Oxford, again 31 Oct. 1415, 3 Oct. 1416, and 21 Ap. to 1 Nov. 1418; occurs 146⅝ as *Sir* Walter Coll, chaplain of S. Mary Magdalene, Launceston, W. Antiq. x. 157. Were these the same as our William Coll or Collys 1418, and Walter Colys 1409?; but our Walter was M.A.; Stafford's Reg. 64, 257.

John **Colyforde, Dev.** summer **1419** to autumn 1427, B.A. by 1420, M.A., Rector 1425; John Colyford, deacon, had letters dimissory 13 June 1413 'ad titulum monasterii de Newnham,' Stafford's Reg. 468; he may be the 'dompnus' or 'dominus' Johannes mentioned in the Computi of summer and autumn 1429, summer 1430, summer 1431, autumn 1432, winter 1433, winter 1434; Prior of S. John's Exeter 1451–68, d. spring 1468; Monast. Exon. 301; Lent 1440 'vis viii*d* acquisitis per instanciam M. Johannis Colygford pro ligatura unius libri'; summer 1450 'quinque libris ex dono M. Johannis Colyfford ad orandum pro animabus Elisabethe Cheseldon et Margarete Heedon' (Heydon); autumn 1451 'v libris ex dono M. Johannis Colyfford ad orandum pro animabus domini Thome Karew militis et domine Elisabet uxoris eiusdem,' Visit. Dev. 134, Stafford's Reg. 51.

Robert **Stonard** (Harl. Visit. Corn. 290), **Chapl.** autumn **1419** to autumn 1421, pres. by Dean and Chapter 27 Feb. 141$\frac{3}{9}$; autumn 1421 'ii*d* oblatis in die funeralium Capellani'; a (Sir) Robert Stonard, R. of Trevalga, Cornwall 1421–49, of Helland 1444, res. 23 Dec. 1465: Maclean ii. 11, iii. 287; Newcourt ii. 138, 643; Brodrick 225.

Walter **Lihert** (Le Hart, Lyard), son of a miller at Lanteglos by Fowey; **Corn.** summer **1420** to autumn **1425**, not B.A. in 1420, M.A., B.D., D.D.; R. of Lamarsh, Essex 1427 (patron Margaret Beaufort), of Tillingham 1428 (patron the King); Principal of S. Martin's Hall in S. John's parish 1444, rebuilt chancel of S. Mary's, Oxford 1462, Wood's City i. 595, ii. 19; R. of Hyam, Som., of Nettleton, Wilts 1434–41 (patron the Abbot of Glastonbury, Phillipps i. 125, 132), Fellow of Oriel 15 July 1425 as B.A., Provost 1 June 1435 (Reg. of Bishop Grey of Lincoln 4 June 1435), res. 28 Feb. 144$\frac{5}{8}$, Bishop of Norwich 24 Jan. 144$\frac{5}{8}$, Confessor to the Queen, ambassador to Savoy 1449; d. Hoxne 17 May 1472; his 'Body Stone' is still in the Cathedral, the sculptured roof of which was built by him; E. M. Goulburn *The ancient sculptures in the roof of Norwich Cathedral* 1876; Blomefield's Norfolk i. 131, ii. 380–82, 488, iii. 535; William of Worcester 113, 307; Gutch i. 605–8, iii. 127, 131, 287; Peshall 57, 66; Burrows' All Souls 25; Gascoigne p. xviii, lxvii–viii. 28, 40, 42, 215: Westcote's Devon 603; Wallis' Cornw. Reg. 374; Political Poems and Songs, ed. Wright (Rolls series) ii. p. lvii, 233; Statutes of Oriel p. 26 : Newcourt ii. 74, 361, 598, All Souls' Archives 154, 159, 289, Bodleian Charters 224, 358; Clark's Oxford Colleges 104–5, 123, Ramsay's *Lancaster and York* ii. 129, Oxf. Archit. Soc. N. S. i. 174, iv. 325; Hist. Comm. v. 485; Wood D. 2 p. 469, Nat. Biog. i. 344; Bibl. Corn. 211, 1219, Coll. Corn. 325; summer 1444 'xx*li* a M. Waltero Lyhert per viam mutui super unam obligacionem comuni sigillo sigillatam'; autumn 1447 'iiii*d* Pencaer pro una litera concepta domino Norevic. episcopo.'

John **Burwick**, or Borwyk, **Dev.** Nov. **1420** to autumn 1430; M.A.; he became a sort of pensioner on the College. The name still occurs in South Devon.

John **Arundel**, **Corn.** Nov. **1420** (when not yet B.A.) to autumn 1430; Wood's City i. 596; M.A., M.B., Principal of Aula Nigra; Proctor 1426 (Anstey 280, 728), Chaplain and Physician to Henry VI (Rymer 6 Ap. 1454); held stalls at Wells, Lichfield, Lincoln, Hereford, York, S. Paul's, Windsor 1448; R. of Trowbridge, Wilts 1455–58, archdeacon of Richmond 1457, Bishop of Chichester 1458–77, d. 18 Oct. 1477; Athenæ ii. 693; Strickland's Queens of England ed. 4, ii. 215; Phillipps i. 147–48 ; Stephens' Chichester 166. There was more than one John Arundel about this time. Autumn 1422 'xxs Arundell et sociis suis pro colleccione garbarum apud Wyttynham'; autumn 1429 'vis de magistro Johanne Arundel pro pencione camere Abbatis de Notelegh'; winter 1456 'pro scriptura unius litere misse M. Johanni Arundell et copie unius bulle Regie xiid'; winter 1479 'xls a magistro Arundell per manus Doctoris Stevennys'; Bibl. Corn. 1038, Tanner 50, Nat. Biog. ii. 146, v. 387, C. S. Gilbert's Cornwall ii. 665.

Thomas **Gourde, dev.** Nov. **1420** to autumn 1427; see Bishop Lacy's Commission 1420; winter 1423 'vid Thome Goorde pro ligacione duorum librorum.' Stafford's Reg. 432.

William **Palmer** (? s. John, M.P. Launceston), b. Bradstone, **dev.** Lent **1421** to autumn 1434; B.A. by 1420, M.A., Rector 1425–32, Precentor of Crediton; instit. R. of Ringmore 2 Oct. 1434, pres. by Robert Kirkham, res. 1465; visited the College on behalf of the Visitor 1439 and 1453, Lacy's Reg. 2 Oct. 1439, 16 Ap. 1453; Winter 1439 'xxviiis iiiid allocatis M. Willelmo Palmer visitanti Collegium ex mandato domini Exon., pro expensis suis in via; ixs vid pro expensis suis Oxon.; notario in causa visitacionis iis'; the results of the visitation are seen in payments by certain Fellows autumn 1440, autumn 1441, autumn 1442, Lent and autumn 1443; autumn 1446 'viiid pro vectura duorum vestimentorum ex dono M. Willelmi Palmer.' An indenture between the College and W. Palmer 25 July 1460 provides for the celebration of his obit; Johnes' *History of Bradstone.* Wood D. 2 p. 106.

Michael de **Tregury, Corn.** summer **1422** to autumn 1427 ; M.A., paid Univ. Coll. 13s 4d in 7 and in 9 Henry VI for Hampton Hall, Wood D. 2 p. 27, 473; Proctor 1434, archdeacon of Barnstaple 16 June 1445–1449, Chaplain to Henry V, Dean of S. Michael of Pencryche Herefs., Archbishop of Dublin 1449–71. On the Taking of Constantinople he proclaimed a 3 days' fast and 100 years' indulgence to all who observed it. There exists a bull of excommunication against certain persons for laying violent hands on him. He d. 21 Dec. 1471; bur. in S. Patrick's near the altar of S. Stephen, tomb was discovered **1730** by Dean Swift (Ware's Irish Prelates and Harris' Continuation). In his will he directs William Wise (? Weye) to make a pilgrimage in his stead to S. Michael's Mount in Cornwall; Gutch

i. 563, iii. App. p. 45 ; Anstey 324, 508 ; Pits 662, Tanner 721, D. K.
Rec. 48 p. 380, 2 Ap. 1449 grant to Michael Tregorre, Queen's
Chaplain, of tithes of S. Peter de Bovyng, Guisnes, as held by the late
rector W. Tregorre, and p. 421 ; Bekyngton's Correspondence i. p. cix ;
Davies Gilbert's Cornwall iv. 141–51 ; Bibl. Corn. 760 ; Lent 1424
'xiii*s* iiii*d* a Mychaele Tregorre Principali Aule Scaccarii in partem
solucionis pro anno presenti.'

Thomas **Fry, Chapl.** autumn **1422** (and perhaps previously) to
Lent 1427 ; M.A., mentioned summer 1429, winter 1446 ; instit. to
R. of Sutton Walrond, Dorset 9 Nov. 1441, res. 1445 ; Hutchins iv.
109.

John **Halse** (2 s. John, Justice of King's Bench, Visit. Devon 439),
Dev. adm. 12 Oct. **1423**, vac. autumn 1427 ; M.A., B.D., Proctor 1432,
Anstey 298–9 ; Provost of Oriel 23 Mch 144$\frac{5}{6}$, to which College he
gave lands, res. 4 Mch 144$\frac{8}{9}$, Dean of Exeter 1457–9, archdeacon of
Norfolk 14 Feb. 1448–1459, sup. D.D. 16 Mch 14$\frac{4.8}{6.0}$, Bishop of Lichfield 25 Nov. 1459, d. 1490, bur. in Cathedral.   The Justiciary who
d. 1434 was a benefactor to the College; autumn 1424 'vis viii*d* ex
dono venerabilis domini, domini Johannis Hals justiciarii Regis';
winter 1429 'pro vino dato Hals justiciario viii*d*'; autumn 1434
'xxviii*s* de bonis Johannis Hals pro reparacionibus'; winter 1434
'xl*s* ex bonis Johannis Hals quondam justiciarii per manus Johannis
Udy executoris dicti Johannis'; Lent 1436 'x marcis de bonis
Johannis Hals assignatis pro edificacione tenementi de Peke'; autumn
1436 'xl*s* de bonis Johannis Hals per manus M. Willelmi Fylham,
xl*s* de eisdem bonis per manus M. Johannis Udy'; a Richard Hals
occurs winter 1435 ; Eccl. Ant. i. **17** ; Stafford's Reg. **121, 417**,
Clark's *Oxford Colleges* **104**, Ffoulkes' *S. Mary's* **205**.

John **Rowe** (Raw), **corn.** Lent **1426** to Lent 1441 ; M.A., Rector
1433–40, Sub-dean of Exeter 28 Aug. 1441, R. of Exminster 31 Jan.
144$\frac{7}{8}$; autumn 1430 'v*s* de J. Rawe pro quodam libro perdito,
2° folio *Totum quod est*'; Lent 1442 'ii*s* viii*d* pro uno fixorio vendito
et dato Collegio a M. Johanne Row'; summer 1450 'quinque libris
a M. Johanne Row canonico ecclesie cathedralis Exon. de bonis
Willelmi Wynard, ad usum reparacionis Aule Cervine'; winter 1458
'x*d* pro una lagena vini data M. Johanni Row et domino Martino
Dyer canonicis ecclesie cathedralis Exon.'; [Nevill's Reg. 6 Sep. 1464
Martin Dyer leaves money for finding scholars at Oxford to pray
especially for his most gracious master; N. and Gleanings iv. **189**;]
Lent 1464 'x*s* iiii*d* M. Gotysford pro expensis suis in adquirendo

pecuniam nobis legatam a M. Johanne Row cum certis libris in manus (*sic*) suis remanentibus ad terminum vite sue'; his will 8 Sep. 1462, proved 24 Dec. 1463 (Eccl. Ant. ii. 25) 'volo ut quilibet socius collegii Exon. in Oxon. presens in exequiis meis inibi celebrandis habeat xx*d*, do ad reparacionem tenementorum dicti collegii situatorum in Balliolo Oxon. xxv*s*, volo ut dictum collegium habeat illam parvam Bibliam 2° folio *Vitam respicias*, cum omnibus aliis libris dicto collegio intitulatis, volo ut dicto collegio de residuo bonorum meorum, debitis meis persolutis, provideatur juxta discrecionem executorum meorum.' A John Rowe subdeacon had letters dimissory 12 Sep. 1416, Stafford's Reg. 472.   M. John Rawe of Exeter diocese was ordained subdeacon 19 Sep. 1433 on a title from the Convent of S. Frideswide in Oxon. A John Rawe of Exeter diocese was ordained deacon 20 Dec. 1432 by Bishop Lacy on a title from the Convent of Tavistock for all holy orders, priest 11 Ap. 1433.   N. and Gleanings ii. 94 our J. R. gave a toft and close on S. David's Hill to S. Petrock's, Exeter; iii. 152.

Thomas **Freeman, Dev.** adm. 12 May **1426**, Chaplain from Lent 1427; M.A., d. 8 Dec. 1439; ? V. of Braunton, Devon, Stafford's Reg. 106.

John **Hancock, corn.** summer **1426** to autumn 1432; M.A., Warden of Ottery 31 Aug. 1446 (in whose time Henry VI visited Ottery College; Monast. Exon. 261); autumn 1459 'vi*s* viii*d* ex dono M. Hancok ad orandum pro anima M. Willelmi Fylham.'

Robert **Peper, sar.** summer **1426** to autumn 1434, still held rooms 1464; M.A.; William Peper was Principal of S. Mildred's Hall 1438, Anstey 521, 'R. *alias* W.' Wood's City i. 595, Wood D. 2 p. 418; a Thomas Pepyr (Pipre) occurs as a lawyer in summer 1355, autumn and winter 1357; winter 1443 'a M. Roberto Peper xii*s* pro camera bassa sub Libraria'; Robert Pepyr, V. of Moreton, Dorset, d. 148$\frac{4}{5}$, Hutchins i. 405.

John **Hunt, dev.** autumn **1426** to autumn 1436; M.A.; a John Hunt was R. of S. James', Shaftesbury 1440, Hutchins iii. 58.

John **Rygge, Dev.**, adm. 20 Ap. **1427**, perhaps when Freeman succeeded to the Chaplaincy, vac. autumn 1442; M.A., Rector 1440–41, ? Principal of Pury Hall 1438, Anstey 521; R. of Honiton 23 Mch 145$\frac{8}{9}$, Treasurer of Crediton, d. 1459, Eccl. Ant. ii. 78; summer 1446 'vi*s* viii*d* ex dono M. Johannis Rigge.'

Richard **Bele, corn.** Lent **1429** to autumn 1438, M.A. before 1439; Hutchins i. 105, iii. 372.

Thomas **Clerk,** Lent **1429**, d. 22 Sep. 1436: his will, 21 Sep.,

proved 29 Sep. 1436 in Oriel before the Commissary, Thomas
Grevely, Univ. Reg. Aaa fol. 9; Ffoulkes' *S. Mary's* 97; his body to
be buried in S. Michael's Churchyard at North Gate, to the high
altar *pro decimis oblitis* 2s, to repair of the church 20*d*; Griffiths 13.

John **Bulsey, sar.** summer **1429** to Oct. 1445, M.A. before 1439,
Senior Fellow autumn 1442 and Vice-Rector. Stafford's Reg. 430.

Michael **Trewynard,** b. S. Ives; **Corn.** autumn **1429** to autumn
1438; M.A., sup. D.D. 18 Jan. 145¾, lic. 1454; Principal of Hart
Hall 1436-8 and 1441-4, Provost of Glasney in Cornwall, d. 11 Ap.
1471; William of Worcester 122, 128; Monast. Exon. 49; Lent 1434
'xx*d* datis per M. Michaelem Trewynard ad fabricam quandam in
Aula Cervina'; summer 1455 'pro clavis emptis et circa hostium
M. Mychaelis Trewynard occupatis 1*d.*'

William **Weye, Dev.** autumn **1430** to autumn 1442; M.A., B.D.,
Fellow of Eton 1453-146⅔, then a monk at Edyngdon, Wilts,
d. 30 Nov. 1476; he was in his 55th year 146⅔, i.e. born 1408;
his *Itineraries* (ed. G. Williams 1857 for the Roxburghe Club, the
map publ. 1867) describe three Pilgrimages, to Compostella in 1456,
to Jerusalem in 1458 and 1462, Henry VI having given him official
leave to make them; he celebrated mass at Jerusalem *cum cantu
organico*; Warton's Hist. of Poetry ed. W. C. Hazlitt iii. 338; Tanner
759; Gutch ii. 25; Lent 1440 'pro cariagio unius pelvis ex dono
M. Willelmi Wey iiii*d*'; Lent 1451 'x*d ob.* pro 3ᵇᵘˢ virgatis de *rebyn*
pro pannis pro altaribus datis a M. Willelmo Way, viii*d* pro viridi
bokcram pro eisdem pannis, viii*s* pro factura eorundem'; summer 1457
'uni adducenti duo volumina Collegio a M. Willelmo Wey missa
iii*s* iiii*d*'; an earlier William Waye occurs in Stafford's Reg. 397,
474.

— **Toker** (Tucker, from the weaving trade, then flourishing in the
west, *Quarter Sessions under James I.* p. 93), **corn.,** ? only one term,
Lent **1431**; ? Henry Toker, R. of Littleham, Devon 1455, d. 1477.

— **James,** Lent **1431** to autumn 1438, still *dominus* summer 1435.
Richard **Lane, corn.** summer **1431** to autumn 1435.

John **Westlake, Corn.** winter **1433** (or before) to summer 1444,
M.A. before 1439, Senior Fellow winter 1442, Rector 1442-3; Prin-
cipal of Hart Hall 1438-41, Wood's City i. 596; added to the College
Chapel in 1488; Gutch iii. 116; Anstey 520; autumn 1442 'xii*d* a
Magistris Johanne Westlak et Thoma Copylston pro camera sub alta
camera Aule Scaccarii'; autumn 1488 'iiii*li* ex dono M. Johannis
Westlake, ad sustentacionem edificii nostri'; summer 1480 'xii*d* a

M. Westlake ad reparandum tabulam pone supremum altare in capella nostra'; winter 1482 'vis viiid a M. Willelmo Merefild quos contulit M. Westlake ad emendam novem crucem'; ? V. of Pinhoe 12 Feb. 149⅚, d. 1500; Eccl. Ant. ii. 127.

(? Thomas) **Cowling, Corn.** winter 1433 (or before) to autumn 1438; M.A. Stafford's Reg. 200.

John **Lyndon, Dev.** autumn 1434 to autumn 1442; Rector 1441-2; autumn 1445 'xd pro vectura xxii librarum de cera ex dono M. Johannis Lyndon'; Lent 1452 'viid pro vectura xiiii librarum de cera data Collegio a M. Johanne Lyndon decano Criditonie' [Monast. Exon. 76]; so winter 1460: winter 1469 'iis pro caleptra data M. Johanni Lyndon'; Lent 1487 'vli vis viiid a M. Johanne Philip decano Criditonie ex legacione M. Johannis Lyndon pro eius obitu futuros per xvi annos in Collegio inter socios observando'; winter 1443 'iid pro cathenacione doctoris de Lira super Evangelia, dati per decanum Criditonie' (the College already had Lira, winter 1437 'coopertura Lire in iiii voluminibus et cathenis'); Anstey 270, Gutch i. 406, Tanner 495.

John **Hamelyn, dev.** only autumn 1434: a James Hamlin, Canon of Exeter, died in or before 1478 (mentioned in a Menheniot deed of that date); Newcourt ii. 304; John Hamelyn occurs in Thomas Clerk's will 1436.

John **Holdich, Dev.** 19 Oct. 1434 to winter 1437; winter 1429 'pro camera Holdeche xxd'; M.A., V. of Maker (Devon, but in archdeaconry of) Cornwall 19 Nov. 1437.

John **Godeswayne, corn.** 25 Mch 1436, res. 27 June 1445; M.A. before 1439; Anstey 739, 740 John Hosborn B.A. punished for an offence against him; Gutch i. 56; summer 1442 'xviiis iiid datis M. Johanni Goodswayn pro reparacione camere in Aula Scaccarii'; Lent 1443 'xd Penkeyer pro litteris conceptis Fundatori [i. e. Bishop Lacy] et M. Henrico Webber, et una littera procuratoria deliberata M. Johanni Goodswayn ex parte Collegii'; summer 1443 'in expensis M. Johannis Godeswayn abhinc equitantis in Cornubiam in negociis Collegii et istuc revertentis in Collegii negociis ixs'; winter 1443 'iiis viiid pro expensis M. J. Gutsuayn in Cornubia.'

— **Caundel, sar.** 1436, d. Lent 1437; places of the name occur in Dorset, Hutchins iii. 664, 725, iv. 136, 141, 143; and see ii. 492, Wood's City i. 590.

— **Markewyke,** or Marwyk (a family name in Suffolk), ? Chapl.; adm. 25 Dec. 1436, vac. autumn 1441. See autumn 1444.

William **Sende, sar.** winter **1437** to Lent 1445; B.A. 1439, M.A., Principal of Hart Hall 1444.

William **Baleham, dev.** autumn **1438** to Lent 1444; B.A. before 1439, M.A.; Lent 1444 'xvi*d* magistro W. Balam ad visitandum amicos, et quia non fuit presens in electione Rectoris perdidit ii*s*.'

John **Evelyn, Dev.** autumn **1438** to summer 1451; B.A. by June 1439, M.A., B.D. 6 July 1449; Rector 1443–47 (till 1449); Commissioner for building the New Schools, Anstey 569, 736; V. of Ipplepen, Devon 24 (28) June 1469–1483 and perhaps longer; Provost of Glasney, Cornwall 1471, exch. for canonry in Exeter Cathedral 1477; Monast. Exon. 49, Suppl. 26; autumn 1443 'vi*s* viii*d* a M. Johanne Evelyn pro defectu variacionis quam fecisset apud Augustinenses ex iniunctione sibi facta per Visitatorem'; paid caution for Peter Hall 1444, and for Peter Hall in the name of William Raffe inceptor in Arts 1449, and for Black Hall in the name of William Thomas B.A. 1449, Wood's City i. 596, 598.

Richard **French** (? from N. Tamerton), **corn.** winter **1439** (and perhaps before) to winter 1455, determined as B.A. Lent 1442, M.A., B.D. 23 June 1454; Rector 1449–53; Principal of Laurence Hall 1445, Wood's City i. 594; V. of Barnstaple 1 Aug. 1462; but still in College rooms winter 1468; Eccl. Ant. iii. 20.

John **Andrew, Corn.** June **1439** to autumn 1448; B.A. before 1439, M.A., Principal of Hart Hall 1445; R. of Dunchideock 16 July 1447, res. 1449, of Roseash 18 Sep. 1465, res. 1468; Lent 1444 'v*d* pro i vecte pro scola M. Johannis Andryw et pro i circulo ferreo pro ostio gardini'; Hutchins iii. 366, 372, 575, Eccl. Ant. ii. 11.

John **Codie** (Codde), **Chapl.** autumn **1440** to winter 1446; M.A.; ? the J. Gody who was a Principal 1446, Wood's City i. 594; R. of Ilfracombe 15 Dec. 1459, d. 1470, Eccl. Ant. ii. 136; autumn 1465 'iii*s* iiii*d* a M. Johanne Codi pro bassa camera ubi ponit vocalia (focalia) sua'; autumn 1470 'iii*s* iiii*d* pro bassa camera M. Johannis Cody, cuius anime propicietur Deus.'

Richard **Bokeler, sar.** autumn **1440** to autumn 1448; B.A. 1441, M.A., B. Can. L., sup. D. Can. L. 4 Feb. 145$\frac{5}{6}$; William Bokeler founded a *bursa* (winter 1457, Lent 1458); Dr. Bokelere is mentioned 1457, Anstey 750; autumn 1454 'ix*s* a M. Ricardo Bokeler pro pencione camere magne in Checkerhall pro duobus terminis.' Hutchins iv. 436 Walter Bokeler.

William **Raffe** (? s. W., V. of Stithians 1413, Wendron 1417), **Corn.** 7 July **1442** to winter 1455; M.A. 1449, ? Princ. of Aristotle's Hall

1438, of Pery Hall as well in 1451, of Laurence Hall 1452, Anstey
520, 620; winter 1453 'pro equo conducto pro M. Willelmo Raff
versus Sarum xx*d*'; autumn 1444 '*xli* xiiii*s* v*d* a domino Jacobo
Raffe, vicario S. Hillarii in Cornubia [19 May 1430, Maclean i. 282];
pro fructibus ecclesie S. Wynnery pro A.D. MCCCCXLIII⁰ in partem
solucionis eorundem'; summer 1446.

Thomas **Reynold, sar.** 21 or 22 Oct. **1442**; B.A. by 1446, M.A.
1449, Principal of Laurence Hall 1446 and 1451, Anstey 604, 618;
Wood's City i. 594; Proctor 1452, mortally wounded in May when
mediating between the scholars of the 'Hospicium Pekwadir' and
those of S. Edward's Hall, Anstey 734 expenses for his wound
10 June 1452, Gutch iii. App. p. 54. Oriel accounts 12 July 1452
'in oblationibus in ecclesia S. Michaelis in obitu Magistri Thome
Reynolds procuratoris viii*d*; in oblationibus in collegio Exon. pro
anima M. T. Reynolds vii*d*.'

Thomas **Hawkins**, or Haukyn, **sar.** 21 or 22 Oct. **1442** to summer
1448; M.A. 21 June 1449; Principal of Peter Hall, Wood's City i.
598; treasurer of Oriel 1451–3, Provost Nov. 1475; Precentor of
Salisbury 6 June 1471, Archdeacon of Stafford 1459, of Worcester
12 Nov. 1467 (Oriel Statutes p. 31); Preb. of Lichfield 147⁰₁; d.
Salisbury Feb. 147⁷₈, bur. in Cathedral; autumn 1480 'iiii*li* vi*s* viii*d* ab
executoribus M. Haukyns'; Lent 1482 'xl*s* ab executoribus M. Thome
Haukyns per manus M. Laury'; summer 1482 'xl*s* a doctoribus Jane
et Seggdeen [? John Segden, Wood's City i. 599] executoribus M.
Thome Haukynys per manus M. Willelmi Mundi.' Coll. Top. and
Gen. i. 240.

Robert **Takyll** (? of Honiton, Eccl. Ant. ii. 75), **Dev.** adm. 20 Dec.
1442, vac. autumn 1448; M.A.; Lent 1450 'iiii*s* viii*d* a M. Roberto
Takell per manus M. Willelmi Wode pro quodam equo empto a M.
Johanne Evelyng'; he occurs also winter 1452; Principal of Mildred
Hall 1454, Wood's City i. 596, 606.

William **Wode, dev.,** adm. 20 Dec. **1442**, vac. Lent 1450; determined as B.A. autumn 1445; Principal of Laurence Hall 27 Oct.
1448, Wood's City i. 594; Lent 1464 'iii*d* pro vectura vestimentorum
nobis collectorum a M. Willelmo Wode.' John Wode is mentioned
Lent 1446 as *attornatus noster*.

Walter **Windsor, Dev.** 24 Mch. **144**³₄; afterwards Chaplain, vac.
autumn 1458; M.A. 1449, Rector 1453–7, Proctor 1455, Principal of
Hart Hall 1448–51, Anstey 619; see a. 1464; Sub-Dean of Exeter
1480–82, R. of Shillingford to 1491; Oliver's Bishops 295, Eccl. Ant.

ii. 59; summer 1458 'xv*d* Johanni Godyssone stacionario pro labore suo in ponendo cathenas super vj volumina, quorum tria sunt ex dono M. Rogeri Keys, et duo ex dono domini Johannis Frensch quondam capellani de Etona, et sextum volumen fuit extractum a Libraria in tempore M. Walteri Wyndesore.'

William **Mogys** or Mogas, summer **1445** to autumn 1459, M.A. 3 Mch 14$\frac{48}{50}$; Proctor 1452 in place of Reynold, one of the 4 *Magistri Stantes* 29 Jan. 145$\frac{5}{8}$, Rector 1457–9; still held rooms in 1470; collated to archd. of Stafford 1468 by John Halse, Bishop of Lichfield, once Fellow of Ex. Coll.; R. of Hartlebury, Worcs. 12 Oct. 1472–1501.

Robert **Wylkyn, dev.** Lent **1446** to summer 1460, Chaplain 1458–59 in place of Thomas Baron; M.A.; autumn 1447 'vi*s* viii*d* a M. Roberto Wylkenys pro scola sua pro anno futuro.'

William **Thomas, Corn.**, adm. 24 Mch 144$\frac{5}{6}$, vac. autumn 1460; B.A. 1449, M.A. 15 Feb. 145$\frac{1}{2}$, Rector 1459–60, Principal of Black Hall 1449, of Laurence Hall 1452, 1458, Anstey 676, 747, Wood's City i. 594, 596; studied law or medicine; autumn 1451 'pro expensis Willelmi Thomas versus Cornubiam in ponendo beneficium S. Wynneri ad firmam xiii*s* iiii*d*,' also autumn 1456, and summer 1458; perhaps dead in 1476, Lent 1476 'ii*s* Johanni Harrys et stacionario pro appreciacione bonorum magistri Willelmi Thomas'; summer 1476 'xxiii*s* iiii*d* pro libro magistri W. Thomas vendito qui vocatur *Codex*.' See 1470. Univ. Reg. 10, 19, 24, 26.

John **Fraunceys, dev.**, adm. 23 June **1446**; adm. at Merton 3 Nov. 1447; B.A. 1 July 1449, M.A. 11 Feb. 14$\frac{49}{50}$; summer 1453 'v*d* oblatis in die obitus M. Frauncis socii Collegii Mertonis'; Brodrick 236.

Thomas **Baron** (Baron senior), **Chapl. 1447**, vac. autumn 1458; M.A. 1449; autumn 1446 'iiii*s* a domino Thoma Baron pro scola sua.' Newcourt ii. 320: Principal of Mildred Hall 1446, Wood's City i. 595; gave MS. no. iii to the College, Coxe p. 2.

John **Chepman, Dev.** summer **1448** to Lent 1452; Principal of Mildred Hall 1450, Wood's City i. 595; adm. to compurgation 10 Feb. 145$\frac{1}{2}$ on a charge of incontinence, M. Baron being one of the Compurgators, Anstey 625; autumn 1450 'viii*d* pro lecto empto pro Chepman.' The will of John Chepman of Honiton was proved 13 Aug. 1406, and his son John was one of the executors; was this son father of the Fellow?, Stafford's Reg. 386.

John **Baker, sar.** autumn **1448** to summer 1454; B.A. 30 June 1449, M.A.; V. of Wittenham 1462, d. 1487.

John **Tregansowan, Corn.** Dec. **1449** to summer 1454; M.A.
3 Mch 14$\frac{4.9}{50}$; Curator of Robury Chest 1450, Supervisor of wine
1455; Principal of Hart Hall 8 Oct. 1451–1463, Anstey 678, 688;
V. of Damerham, Wilts 1453–9 (as Tregunson); exch. for Morwenstow, Cornwall with William Colyn or Colyns, but res. on a life
annuity of ten pounds, in favour of John Tedy 27 Mch 1478.

Thomas **Wodeward, dev.** summer **1450** to autumn 1452; B.A.
30 June 1449; Oriel accounts 1452 'in vigilia S. Bartholomei
[=23 Aug.] in oblacionibus in collegio Exon. in missa Thome
Wodeward bachallarii iii*d*.' The will of Thomas Wydewere was
proved in the Chancellor's Court 17 Oct. 1452.

Thomas **Stephens** or Stevyn, **dev.** summer **1450** to autumn 1457;
M.A. 15 Feb. 145$\frac{1}{2}$, D.D.; Principal of a Hall 1450, Wood's City i.
594; Fellow of Eton 1466–80, Commissary (Vice-Chancellor) of the
University several times 1466–80; Warden of Ottery to 1489; Gutch
iii. App. 60–63: Anstey 618, 720; Monast. Exon. 261, 278.

— **Lysewille, dev.** summer to winter **1450.**

Thomas **Gotysford** (Cottisford), **Dev.** summer **1452** to summer
1466; determined as B.A. in 1456, M.A.; became Chaplain about
1460; resident autumn 1467; Principal of Laurence Hall **1461,**
Wood's City i. 594, 598, Anstey 688.

John **Julyan, dev.** winter **1452** to autumn 1467; B.A. 1454, M.A.
1457, Senior Fellow winter 1461–62 and Vice-Rector (probably
owing to Gotysford becoming Chaplain, and so losing seniority);
Principal of S. Peter's Hall, attached to the College, 1458, Wood's
City i. 598; acting as Deputy Judge for the University; pres. 30 Aug.
1466 by Convent of S. Frideswide to S. Clement's; Anstey 678, 750;
summer 1466 'ii*s* pro renovacione unius libri domus positi in Cista
Wyntonie in nomine M. Johannis Julyan; xvi*s* pro redemcione
Spalterii [*sic*] glosati positi in quadam cista per M. Charde'; autumn
1471 'vii*s* a M. Holcumbe pro obitu M. Johannis Julyan, cuius
anime propicietur Deus.'

Henry **Bryan, dev.** Dec. **1452** to winter 1454; Fellow of Merton
1455, Brodrick 237; Anstey 749 Henry Bryan one of 'bachillarii
collatores apud fratres Augustinenses disputationum'; Newcourt ii.
592.

Nicholas **Stanbury, dev.** Dec. **1452** to autumn 1467; B.A. 1454,
M.A. 1457, Principal of S. Peter's Hall Dec. 1462, Anstey 688;
summer 1479 'iiii*d* Stanbury pro factura unius litere attornatorie
vel procuratorie'; winter 1479 'viii*d* M. Stanbury pro fabrica unius

litere attornatorie pro M. Brew'; so winter 1481; Newcourt ii. 592;
Visit. Corn. 443.

William **Baron** (Baron junior), **dev.** Lent **1453** to winter 1464;
B.A. 1455, M.A.; Principal of a Hall 1457, Wood's City i. 594;
Rector 1460–64; still resident 1479; V. of Menheniot, Cornwall
1479, d. 1501; Anstey 676; Oliver's Bishops 110.

John **Mitchell** (Mychall), **sar.** summer **1454** to autumn 1461, B.A.
1459; Hutchins ii. 640.

Richard **Lowe, sar.** winter **1454** to Lent 1457; determined as
B.A. 1455; a Richard Lawe or Lowe was R. of Honiton 22 May
1442, d. 1451, Eccl. Ant. ii. 78.

Richard **Aschendon** (Aysshendon: Ashendon is in Bucks), **sar.**
Lent **1456** to autumn 1459; B.A. 7 Nov. 1457.

Ralph **Helmer** (perhaps from Kingston), **Dev.** Lent **1456** to
autumn 1457; B.A. 1454, determined 16 Feb. 145$\frac{4}{5}$.

Walter **Kingdon, Corn.** autumn **1456** to winter 1468; B.A. 1459,
M.A., disp. 14 June 1463: preb. of S. Patrick's, Dublin 1468;
'Master Walter Kingdon' witnesses a deed 1477, Allen's Liskeard
39; Lent 1474 'iiii*d* pro posicione iiii graduum ante cameram
M. Kyngdon, xvi*d* pro uno novo lecto in nova camera et imposicione
unius postis in pede graduum ante hostium M. Kyngdon'; R. of
S. Martin's by Looe, Cornwall 1490: mentioned in Computus of
1493 as in orders, and in Clifton Ferry deed 1493; Cotton ii. 136.

Walter **Halse, Dev.** adm. 20 Dec. **1457,** vac. after autumn 1459;
determined as B.A. summer 1459; winter 1458 'xiiii*d* pro expensis
Rectoris, Willelmi Baron et Walteri Halse in eundo apud Sutton ad
respondendum Officiali Barkeschyrie in negociis Collegii.'

John **Phylypp, Dev.,** adm. 1 July **1458,** vac. winter 1470; B.A.
1455, M.A., Rector 1464–70; resident in College 1474, mentioned
in Clifton Ferry deed 1493; (a John Phelypp was R. of S. Olave's,
Exeter 8 Sep. 1467, res. 1501, Eccl. Ant. i. 129;) Dean of Crediton;
gave 3 books to the College in summer 1508: gave £3 6s. 8d. about
1483 to build the kitchen; subscribed to the new hall of the College,
Gutch iii. 112; Macray's Annals of Bodleian 316 he gave two of
the College MSS. to the Bodleian in 1468, now 'Bodl. 42,' and
'Digby 57 'olim liber M. Jolyffe,' Cat. MSS. Bodl. ix. 59; Lent
1476 'iiii*d* pro vectura panni linei dati Collegio per M. Johannem
Phylyp'; so winter 1478; Waters' *Geneal. of Chesters* i. 7.

John **Tillie, dev.,** adm. 1 July **1458,** vac. after autumn 1459;
determined as B.A. in Lent 1458.

John **Leche, sar.**, adm. 1 July **1458**, vac. after autumn 1459; B.A. 1462; Hutchins iii. 428.

Herveus **Charde, Dev.**, adm. 13 Mch 145$\frac{2}{3}$, vac. in or after autumn 1462; B.A. 1456, M.A.; winter 1466 'iis pro renovacione unius libri positi in Cista Cecestrie per manus M. Chard'; Lent 1470 'iiiis pro renovacione cuiusdam libri positi in Cista de Selton per manus M. Hervei Charde'; autumn 1470 'ixs iiiid pro redemcione cuiusdam libri positi in quadam Cista Universitatis per M. Charde, iiiis pro renovacione Avicenne positi in quadam Cista Universitatis per predictum magistrum'; summer 1472 'iiiis pro renovacione caucionis M. Chard'; winter 1473 'iiiis pro renovacione unius libri in Cista de Rober impositi per manus M. Charde.'

William **Atwille, dev.** winter **1460** (or before) to summer 1466. The will of William Atwyll, R. of Bondleigh, Devon (bur. S. Michael's, Oxford, 1465, Wood D. 2 p. 100) was proved 24 Aug. 1465, Griffiths 3.

Richard **Payne, Dev.** winter **1460** (or before) to autumn 1474 (or later), B.A. 1462, M.A.; Anstey 688 'procurator Australis pro quodam horto juxta Aulam Laurencii, nomine Ricardi Payne (1462).' Wood's City i. 599; Campbell's Henry VII, ii. 190 (Rolls Series).

William **Major, corn.** winter **1460** (or before) to autumn 1474 (or later); M.A., Proctor 1472; Rector 1471–74; Chaplain at Ottery; present at making of William Holcomb's will 1499: Monast. Exon. 278.

William **Demett, Sar.** winter **1460** (or before) to summer 1464 'dominus.' Wood's City i. 599 Dymett.

— **Andrew, corn.** adm. 5 Ap. 1461, vac. autumn 1469; M.A.; autumn 1480 'xxd a M. Andrv, pro scola ubi scannum, pro parte unius termini': a William Androw was R. of Forrabury, Cornwall 2 July 1489; Maclean i. 589.

Richard **Bradleghe, Dev.** adm. 23 June **1461**, vac. autumn 1478; disp. 9 June 1463, B.A. 1466, M.A.; Proctor 1474; Rector 1475 to 14 Mch 147$\frac{7}{8}$; gave 20s towards the Chapel Cross autumn 1498; Ffoulkes' *S. Mary's* 206; a Richard Bradley was V. of Calwodeleigh (now Calverleigh) 25 Ap. 1460, Eccl. Ant. i. 100; Hutchins i. 582.

William **Brewe, Corn.** autumn **1462** to autumn 1494 (or later); M.A., in orders, Proctor 1470; Principal of Laurence Hall 1467, Wood's City i. 594, 598, Anstey 723; held rooms in College 1492; autumn 1461 'vis viiid a Willelmo Brew pro expensis suis circa beneficium nostrum S. Wynneri in Cornubia'; summer 1480 'viiili xvis viid a M. Willelmo Brewe pro prima parte solucionis xvii*li* xiii*s* iiii*d* pro fructibus nostri beneficii S. Wynnery in Cornubia pro A. D. MCCCCLXXIX°.' See Clifton Ferry deed 1493. His exequies were still celebrated in autumn 1556.

John **More, dev.** Lent **1464** to autumn 1466; B.A. 1466; resident 1470.

John **Harrowe, dev.** Lent **1464** to autumn 1478, Chaplain 1466; disp. as B.A. 27 Mch 1462, M.A., Proctor 1468, Principal of Hart Hall 1472; gave 6*s* 8*d* in 1483; a Chapel deed dated 25 Nov. 1477 says that Rector Bradle refused to receive his resignation of the Chaplaincy from his proctor Walter Wyndesor.

John **Orelle** or Oryal, **sar.**, adm. 23 Mch 146$\frac{4}{5}$, vac. winter 1481; determined as B.A. autumn 1467, M.A., Senior Fellow autumn 1478, Rector 4 July 1478–79; winter 1481 'xxii*d* pro ostio fabricato in camera M. Orell, et pro fabrica unius formule in Aula nostra.'

John **Tharssher** (? from Wilts), **sar.**, adm. 6 July **1465**, Fellow only one term; Principal of Sykyll Hall 1462, Anstey 688, Wood's City i. 599.

William **Luky, corn.** adm. 14 Dec. **1465**; determined as B.A. Lent 1466, M.A.; Newcourt i. 346.

William **Holcomb, Dev.** adm. 7 June **1466**, vac. Lent 1476; determined as B.A. autumn 1468; M.A., resident 1482; 'Lector in S. Laurence's Hall in S. Michael's parish'; V. of E. Morden, Dorset 16 Sep. 1475, res. 1478, Hutchins iii. 514; Precentor of Ottery, V. of Ashburton and of Ipplepen; by his will 1499 (Monast. Exon. 278, Suppl. 26) he bequeathed to Ex. Coll. 'librum sermonum factum de tempore per circulum anni [Tanner 503], ad orandum pro anima M. Willelmi Maior quondam Rectoris dicti Collegii Exon.' and perhaps other books; winter 1472 'iiii*li* vi*s* viii*d* a M. Holcombe pro anima M. Johannis Pittis' [N. and Gleanings i. 12].

William **Juner, Dev.** adm. 5 July **1466**, vac. autumn 1478; determined as B.A. autumn 1468, M.A.; two of this family occur as Rectors of Loxbeare, Devon, Eccl. Ant. i. 141.

William **Mylplaysh, Sar.** adm. 5 July **1466**, d. 14 July 1478 (there was a plague 1477–79); determined as B.A. autumn 1468, M.A., Rector 14 Mch—14 July 1478; see a. 1470 (William Jane). Melplash is in Netherbury, Dorset, Hutchins ii. 115.

(John) **Yonge, dev.** adm. 2 July **1468**, vac. winter 1469; M.A.

John **Gubbe, sar.** adm. 2 July **1468**, vac. autumn 1479; M.A., R. of Puryton and V. of Kemell, Wilts 1478; Phillipps i. 166.

Richard **Mayow** (Maiowe, Mayhow), ? b. Bray; **Corn**. adm. 22 June **1469**, vac. winter 1469; M.A., Principal of Hart Hall 1468–76, sup. B. Can. L. 4 Feb. 145⅚, Canon of Exeter, d. 1499; Gutch iii. 645, Athenæ ii. 709; C. S. Gilbert's Cornwall i. 145 'at his decease he made Thomas Harrys, archdeacon of Cornwall, his executor.'

— **Warburton**, adm. 1 Feb. 14⁷⁰⁄₇₁, vac. autumn 1471.

John **Anger, corn**. adm. 30 June **1470**, vac. autumn 1477; determined as B.A. autumn 1471, M.A.; winter 1476 ' iiiis viiid a M. Anger pro aliquibus bonis M. Thomas sibi venditis'; ' iiid a M. Anger pro uno libro sciencie medicinalis M. Thomas.' William of Worcester 123 'dominus Johannes Anger fuit vicarius Magistri Michaelis Trewynnard' (provost of Glasney). Was the name Auger?

William **Jane** (Jaan), **dev**. adm. 30 June **1470**, vac. autumn 1479; M.A.; resident 1482; executor for Rector Mylplaysh 1478, and ? for Thomas Hawkins 1482; R. of Exminster, d. 1500; gave the College £3 6s. 8d. in summer 1500; Eccl. Ant. ii. 25.

Roger **Page, dev**. adm. 21 Dec. **1471**, vac. autumn 1474.

Walter **Coose** or Couse, **dev**. adm. 27 June **1472**, vac. Lent 1488; Chaplain autumn 1478; M.A., Principal of Hart Hall 1478, 1486; see Clifton Ferry deed 1493.

John **Rowe, dev**. winter **1475** to Lent 1490; still B.A. in Oct. 1479; M.A., in orders.

Thomas **Symon** (Symon senior), **dev**. winter **1475** to summer 1483; determined as B.A. autumn 1477, M.A., in orders: a Thomas Symons was V. of Bishop's Tawton, Devon 9 Dec. 1489, d. 1518; Eccl. Ant. iii. 19.

John **Smythe, sar**., adm. 18 Nov. **1475**, vac. Lent 1490; M.A., D.D., Rector 1485–87; Canon of St. Paul's 13 Feb. 148½.

William **Merifeld, corn**., adm. 18 Nov. **1475**, vac. winter 1482; determined as B.A. summer 1474; M.A. 6 Oct. 1479, Rector 1479–80; V. of Bodmin 1489, d. 1494; winter 1479 ' M. Babb celebranti pro M. Myryfyld iiid.' See Clifton Ferry deed 1493.

James **Babbe, Dev**. adm. 30 Jan. 147⅚, M.A. by Oct. 1479; in orders; Principal of Hart Hall 1482; Proctor 1483; Rector 1482–84; (?) d. winter 1485 of the sweating sickness.

Note.—Bodl. MS. 42 once belonged to Exeter College. It contains a MS. of beginning of 14, and one of beginning of 15 century. 'Liber Magistri J. Collis emptus a domino W. Palett, A.D. 1472, precium viis . . . . haec est caucio M. Babbe, M. Merefeld, et Johannis Mane, excepta in Cista Germeyne in v die mensis Octobris A.D. mccc7ix (*sic*), et est liber cum diversis contentis, 2° folio

Ecclesie et habet 2 supplementa, primum e byblia 2° folio *Edisserunt*, 2ᵐ supplementum est liber Januensis 2° folio *Nec ligaturam*, et iacet pro xlviii*s* viii*d* . . . .
Item lego collegio Exon. librum in pergameno scriptum continentem tabulam
Nicholai de Lira super bibliam et cum ceteris, et volo quod transeat in communi
electione librorum. Teste Ricardo Smyth. . . . . Ex legacione M. Jacobi Babbe.
. . . . volo quod restituatur . . . . de electione Smale.' It contains an Alphabetum Graecum Numerale, folios 281-2 are written *plumbeo stilo.*

Thomas **Lawry**, **Corn.** adm. 16 Nov. **1476**, vac. autumn 1484;
determined as B.A. Lent 1476, M.A. 1479, in orders; a Thomas
Lawry was R. of Washfield, Devon 8 Oct. 1460, Eccl. Ant. i. 138.
See Clifton Ferry deed 1493.

John **Mayne** (Maan), **dev.** autumn **1477**, vac. Lent 1489; a John
Mane was R. of S. Tudy before 1498, and V. of S. Kew 21 Oct. 1500,
both in Cornwall; d. 1523; Maclean ii. 98, iii. 314; summer 1480
'xv*d* a Johanne Mane datis ad fabricam cerii Paschalis' (it cost 18
pence); Coll. Corn. 547.

Richard **Palmer**, **dev.**, adm. 30 May **1478**, then transferred to
the Chaplaincy, vac. autumn 1491; determined as B.A. summer
1478, M.A.

Thomas **Ruer** (Rewer), **sar.**, adm. 4 Mch 147 8/9, vac. autumn 1491;
determined as B.A. Lent 1478, M.A.; Rector 1487–88; in orders, so
stated in a deed concerning Peyntour *alias* Culver Hall 28 Jan. 148 7/8.

John **Frendship**, **dev.**, adm. 4 Mch 147 8/9, vac. Lent 1487; held
a Chantry at Windsor, d. before Oct. 1509, F. F. (Bodl.) p. 2 *b*; Gutch
i. 514. See Clifton Ferry deed 1493.

— **Saunders**, **corn.**, adm. 19 June **1479**, vac. Lent 1486.

Richard **Symon** (Symon junior), **dev.**, adm. 20 Nov. **1479**, vac.
summer 1483; a Richard Symon determined as B.A. summer 1469.

Richard **Panter**, **corn.**, adm. 20 Nov. **1479**, vac. winter 1494;
M.A., Rector 1488—20 Dec. 1494; Principal of Hart Hall 1488;
V. of Menheniot, Cornwall, dead in 1513; Coll. Top. et Gen. i. 241.

Richard **Roberd**, or Roberts (often called Robyns), **Corn.**, adm.
22 June **1482**, vac. autumn 1498; Rector Lent—autumn 1495; sup.
B.C.L. 24 Jan. 150 6/7; Eccl. Ant. ii. 29.

Peter **Carsley** (Casely, Caslay), **Dev.**, adm. 5 July **1483**, vac. Lent
1487; M.A., D.D., Proctor 1488; canon of Exeter, V. of Menheniot
before 1513; V. of Broad Clyst, Devon, d. 1536, Eccl. Ant. i. 126;
executor to William Holcomb 1499; Monast. Exon. 48, 278; State
Papers 1531 p. 6. Acts of Congregation 15 Mch 150 5/8 'supplicat
Petrus Caseley sacre theologie professor quatenus secum gratiose
dispensetur pro generalibus processionibus, deposicionibus, et convoca-

tionibus nisi nominatim vocetur. Hoc est conlatum conditionate quod solvat xl*d* ad fabricam domus Congregacionis'; 28 Mch 1511 'decretum est quod M. Doctor Carseley reciperet excrescencias caucionis sue vendite ex Cista de Langton, quia repertum est in registro Ciste de renovacione illius caucionis et vendicionis eiusdem.'

(? William) **Edwards** or Edwardys, **sar.**, adm. 19 Dec. **1483**, vac. Lent 1486; M.A., in orders, mentioned winter 1489 : a William Edwardys, M.A., sup. B.D. 26 May 1506; a W. E., R. of Owre Moyne, Dorset 15 June 1515, res. 1521, Hutchins i. 460.

William **Forde, dev.**, adm. 31 Jan. **148⅘**, vac. autumn 1498; M.A., V. of Yeovil 1519; Lent 1529 'xxii*s* vi*d* a M. Stockton ex legacione vicarii de Yevyll quondam socii huius Collegii' : summer 1529 'xvii*s* vi*d* de executoribus vicarii de Evyl, quondam huius loci socii quos nobis per testamentum dedit'; autumn 1529 'iiii*d* in expensis super M. Stockden.' A William Forde was V. of S. Clement's, Cornwall 1503.

John **Atwell, dev.**, adm. 17 Mch **148⅝**, vac. winter 1500; M.A., Rector 1495–99; 4 marks were received from his executors in winter 1503.

— **Fletcher**, adm. 3 June **1486**, vac. summer 1487.

John **Jolliffe, corn.**, adm. 16 Dec. **1486**, vac. autumn 1499; M.A., Proctor 1493; in orders. Lent 1522 'xiii*d* pro vino dato M. Jolyff quondam huius collegii socio.' Hutchins iii. 374, 633.

John **Hicks, Dev.**, adm. 16 Dec. **1486**, vac. Lent 1499; M.A., in orders, resident 1506; one of the name was R. of Exminster 2 Sep. 1500 and d. 1527; another, V. of Newton S. Cyres 27 Sep. 1513, d. 1523, Eccl. Ant. ii. 25, 69. Acts of Congregation 21 May 1505 'supplicat M. Joannes Hyckes M.A., quatenus non teneatur interesse generalibus processionibus, causa est quia habet quandam egritudinem. Hec est concessa simpliciter'; 26 June 1505 'supplicat M. Johannes Hyckes M.A., quatenus cum eo graciose dispensetur pro omnibus exequiis cum quibus potest congregacio dispensare, et pro omnibus convocacionibus cancellarii et procuratorum nisi fuerit nominatim vocatus. Hec est concessa simpliciter.'

Walter **Dudman, Dev.** Lent **1488** to winter 1500; M.A., Warden of Ottery, Devon 16 Oct. 1518, d. 1525; Monast. Exon. 261.

Peter **Druett** or Dreweyt, **Dev.** Lent **1488** to autumn 1498; V. of S. Thomas' near Exeter 2 Aug. 1506, res. 151½, Eccl. Ant. i. 57; rented College rooms 1517–22. Hist. Comm. v. 603.

— **Grede**, or Greyde, **Dev.**, adm. 29 Mch **1488**, vac. autumn 1501;

M.A., in orders; summer 1510 'vis viii*d* a dono M. Grede per manus M. Doctoris Mychell.'

John **Trotte, Chapl.**, adm. 29 Mch **1488**, d. autumn 1512; M.A., Principal of Hart Hall 1495; B.D. 13 Dec. 1506; autumn 1489 'memorandum quod a quadam bursa in Cista ablate fuerunt per Rectorem iiii*li* date a domino Johanne Trott, expendende in beneficium nostrum de Wytenham Comitis ex consensu sociorum pro reparacione orii [=horrei] in dicto beneficio, circa quam reparacionem expenduntur, prout patet ex speciali compotu coram sociis inde facto iii*li* ii*d ob.*, remanent in dicta bursa xix*s* ix*d ob.*'

— **Brendon, Dev.**, adm. 30 Oct. **1489**, vac. winter 1490; in orders; winter 1494 'iiii*s* pro comunis domini Brendon in tempore vacacionis ex decreto sociorum.'

John **Goldyng, corn.** autumn **1490** to autumn 1501; M.A., in orders; autumn 1527 'iiii*d* pro vino dato M. Goldyng in Londino, iiii*d* pro vectura vestium sacerdotalium ex dono M. Goldyn in Cornubia'; mentioned autumn 1531, and winter 1543. Newcourt ii. 275. He gave the College £20 in 1524.

William **Glover, dev.**, adm. 5 Nov. **1490**, vac. autumn 1501; M.A., in orders; Principal of Hart Hall 1496; one of those who received Henry VII's injunctions 1499 against scholars hunting in forests of Shotover, Stow, &c., Gutch i. 658; a William Glovier was V. of Colyton, Devon 14 Oct. 1508, Eccl. Ant. ii. 7.

Thomas **Tremayne, dev.**, adm. 25 June **1491**, vac. autumn 1504; ? s. Nicholas, by Joan d. and h. of Sir John Dodscomb, Visit. Corn. 616; M.A., Rector 1502–3; V. of Witheridge, Devon 15 Feb. 1517, d. 1521, Eccl. Ant. i. 191.

Thomas **Michell, Corn.**, adm. 16 June **1492** 'dominus,' vac. autumn 1501; Rector 1499–1501; D.D. 13 Dec. 1506, Commissary (Vice-Chancellor) 1509–10; canon of Exeter and of Wells, warden of Ottery 27 July 1513, V. of Ipplepen 24 June 1513–1533, R. of Kenne 21 Dec. 1517, d. 1533; Wood's Fasti i. 19, 26, 28; Monast. Exon. 261 and Suppl. 26, Eccl. Ant. i. 39; Lent 1534 'vis viii*d* pro exequiis doctoris Mychyll'; Hutchins i. p. lxv.

— **Chubbe** or Chubbys, **dev.**, adm. 20 Oct. **1492**, vac. autumn 1498; in orders; a William Chubbe res. the R. of S. Leonard's, Exeter 1503; Eccl. Ant. i. 166.

William **Toker** (Tucker), **dev.**, adm. 27 Nov. **1495**, vac. winter 1499; B.D. 10 Feb. 151½, disp. 21 Oct. 1527 because lame; Lent 1496 'xiiii*d* pro asseribus, clavis, et opere unius carpentarii facientis lectum et panniplicium in camera domini Willelmi Toker,' &c.; admin. of his goods 16 Jan. 1529, Griffiths 62, Monast. Exon. 278.

William **Ewen** or Ewyng (Yewan), **sar.**, adm. winter **1497**; M.A., Principal of Hart Hall 25 Oct. 1503-1506; killed in a riot between Northern and Southern scholars in front of S. Mary's 8 Aug. 1506. Archbishop Warham had difficulty in saving the University from losing its privileges on this account; Gutch i. 664; Hutchins ii. 633-4.

John **Rugge** or Rigge, **Dev.**, adm. 30 June **1498**, vac. winter 1503; M.A., Rector 1501-2; Principal of Hart Hall 1501-3 and then in orders; see a. 1505.

James **Michell, Corn.**, adm. 30 June **1498**, vac. autumn 1511; M.A.

William **Bery** or Bury, **Dev.**, adm. 10 Nov. **1498**, vac. winter 1508; M.A., in orders, Rector 1506-8.

John **Elys, dev.**, adm. 8 June **1499**, vac. autumn 1501; probably a law student; autumn 1501 'remanent in manibus domini Johannis Elys nuper socii de bonis Collegii xxxvs iiid ob.'; summer 1503 'xiid M. Elys pro consilio circa composicionem de Mayhenett.'

Gerens (Gerendus) **Raffe, Corn.**, adm. 29 June **1499**, vac. autumn 1511; Rector 1503-4; Acta Congregationis 13 Dec. 1506 'supplicat M. Gerendus Rafe M.A. et scolaris sacre theologie quatenus studium 12 annorum in logicis philosophicis et theologicis una cum responsione in novis scolis sibi sufficiat ut admittatur ad lecturam libri Sententiarum. Hec est concessa conditionate quod bis opponat ante gradum et semel predicet post gradum preter formam'; B.D. 30 Jan. 150⁸⁄₇; R. of Alphington, Devon 12 May (? Mch) 151¾, d. Ap. 1529; Eccl. Ant. i. 75. A full pardon was granted to Gerard Rauff or Rafe, Rector, and the Scholars of the College, for all possible crimes committed before 23 Ap. 1 Henry VIII (1509): it is on two large skins, the Great Seal is lost.

John **Parkhouse, Dev.**, adm. (? 24) Jan. **1500**, vac. winter 1519; Principal of Hart Hall 1506-10; Custos of Audley Chest, July 1510; B.A. 3 July 1506, M.A. 7 June 1510 (Parkehuste); canon of Exeter, R. of Manston, Dorset 18 July 1531-1547, Hutchins iii. 76, Wood's Fasti i. 15. William Parkhouse (State papers 11 Mch 1536 p. 238) lic. to exchange Combe in Tynhead, Sampford Courtenay, Clare portion in Tiverton, and V. of Sidbury, which he held by certain dispensations, for other incompatible benefices; d. 1541, Harding's Tiverton iv. 38; Acta Congregationis 6 Feb. 150⅔ 'supplicat

M. Guilelmus Parkhouse M.A. et scolaris in medicinis quatenus studium decem annorum in logicis philosophicis et medicinis cum lectura publica libri Prognosticorum Hipocratis et carminum Egidii de Urinis sibi sufficiat ut admittatur ad lecturam alicuius libri eiusdem facultatis, qua admissione habita possit admitti ad incipiendum in eadem facultate.   Hec est concessa conditionate quod procedat ante festum S. Johannis Baptiste proximum.   Alia quod legat librum Regiminis Acutorum ante gradum susceptum.'   Summer 1541 'xls pro asportatione legatorum Willelmi Parkhows'; Computus 1544 'memorandum quod solvebam pro obitu M. Parkouse 3° anno 15 sociis duobus sacerdotibus vs iid'; 1545 'quarto anno 14 sociis 3 sacerdotibus iiiis xid.' Oriel Reg. 1 June 1519 Mr. William Parkhouse allowed to be 'communarius apud nos et sedere in mensa communi nobiscum pro tempore quo nunc est permansurus in Universitate.'

(? Christopher) **Barons**, adm. 17 Dec. 1500, vac. autumn 1509; in orders; probably the Christopher Barons M.A. 8 Mch 150$\frac{7}{8}$.

John **Holwell, dev.**, adm. 22 Jan. 150$\frac{9}{1}$, vac. autumn 1508; M.A., B.D. 1500, Principal of Black Hall near Hart Hall 1505, Wood's City i. 596; res. V. of Bodmin 1516; Canon of Exeter, V. of Okehampton 1536, Preb. of Crediton 1536, living 1557; a John Holwell was V. of Tedburn, Devon, and of Stoke Gabriel, Devon 26 Ap. 1528, but res. 1528, Monast. Exon. 85, 86: State Papers 1532 p. 733; Wood's Fasti i. 4; Eccl. Ant. i. 212, ii. 157, 161, 166, 174, 181; Maclean i. 147; W. Antiq. xi. 100.   Winter 1557 'xxd a M. Holwell (? the same) pro sumptibus Letherne (?), olim *scolaris* huius Collegii, ante œconomo nostro Paw, nunc nobis ex compositione quadam [made in 1557] debitis; iis a M. Martyn pro expensis Drew *scolaris* huius Collegii ex eadem compositione nobis debitis.'

Richard **Duck**, or Doke (? Duke, Visit. Devon 311), **Dev.**, adm. 12 June 1501, vac. summer 1515; M.A., Proctor 1509; adm. B.D. 19 June 1515, D.D. 1516; Vice-Chancellor 1517–19; rented College rooms 1518–20, Chaplain to Wolsey, Canon of Exeter, Archdeacon of Salisbury 1536, Preb. of Wells 1537; present at opening of Henry VIII's Divorce case; Proctor for Salisbury in Convocation of 1529, d. before 2 Aug. 1539; Wood's Fasti a. 1509, 1516, 1517; Gutch ii. 10; Wilkins' Concilia iii. 737, Pocock's Burnet iv. 288; Univ. Reg. p. 297 on 10 July 1510 he offered caution for Laurence Hall, with John King and George Taylar as securities, Wood's City i. 594; State Papers 31 May 1529 and iv. p. 2699; summer 1528 'iid tabellario ad tradendum literas M. doctori Doke, ixd pro cirpis pro camera M. Doctoris Doke'; autumn 1539 'xi*d* pro concathenatione libri quem domini Dook et Pollerd dedere bibliothece nostre.' Turner p. 11.

— **Way, corn.,** adm. 30 June **1501,** vac. Lent 1505; M.A.; a John Way was R. of Trevalga, Cornwall 1538, and married 5 Jan. 15$\frac{9}{50}$; Thomas Waye and Nicholas Andrew were monks at Glastonbury, Dugdale's Monast. i. 9; and Glastonbury often occurs in the Computi; Univ. Reg. i. 289, 293 — Way, M.A. 1505.

— **Andrew, corn.,** autumn **1501** to autumn 1506; a John Andrew was V. of Gluvias, Cornwall 1536; another John Andrew V. of Bideford 16 Ap. 1524, d. 1547, Eccl. Ant. iii. 41; a William Andrew R. of Powderham d. 151$\frac{2}{3}$, Eccl. Ant. i. 28, see ii. 172, 190; a Thomas Andrew V. of Barnstaple 25 Sep. 1526, d. 1528, Eccl. Ant. iii. 30. Thomas Androw or Andrews was adm. B.C.L. 4 July 1513, ? the Fellow.

Richard **Northcot, dev.,** adm. 25 Feb. 150$\frac{1}{2}$, vac. autumn 1511; M.A. 10 June 1506; V. of Wittenham 1511; winter 1521 'iiii*li* xiii*s* iiii*d* accomodatis M. Norcot ex consensu maioris partis sociorum.' Acta Congregationis 10 Feb. 150$\frac{5}{8}$ 'supplicat dominus Ricardus Northcott B.A. quatenus studium trium annorum in eadem facultate cum novem responsionibus, 2^{abus} apud fratres Augustinenses, 3^{bus} in quodlibetis, 2^{abus} in formalibus disputationibus, cum duabus in duabus quadragesimis sibi sufficiat ad incipiendum in eadem. Hec est concessa conditionate quod bis disputet preter formam post gradum susceptum.'

Symon **Todde, sar.,** summer **1502** to autumn 1514; M.A. 7 Nov. 1508, in orders; Rector (perhaps 12 Ap. 1511, and) 1512 to summer 1514; Custos of 'Exeter Chest' in the University July 1510; Lent 1527 'viii*d* pro jantaculo dato M. Tode in aula.'

Thomas **Mede,** adm. 17 Dec. **1503,** vac. summer 1518; B.A. 3 July 1506, M.A. 8 May 1509. Acta Congregationis 18 May 1505 (Univ. Reg. 290) 'supplicat Thomas Meede scolaris artium quatenus tres anni in ordinariis, cum una magna vacatione, cum responsione unius bacallarii in quadragesima sibi sufficiant etc. Hoc est conlatum conditionate quod determinet proxima quadragesima et bis intret preter formam.' Principal of Hart Hall 1510–14, Guardian of Queen's Chest July 1510; Senior (southern) Proctor 1513; Rector 1514–15 and 1516–18; V. of Menheniot; dead in 1529.

James **James** or Jamys, **dev.,** only occurs autumn **1504**; M.A.

William **Kingdon, Corn.,** adm. 20 Oct. **1504,** vac. winter 1514.

Acta Congregationis 25 June 1506 'supplicat Willelmus Kyngdon scolaris artium quatenus studium 4ᵒʳ annorum, cum tribus magnis vacationibus, sibi sufficiat etc.   Hec est concessa conditionate quod determinet proxima quadragesima'; B.A. 3 July 1506, M.A. 8 May 1509, in orders; auditor of Rothbury Chest and Guardian of Queen's Chest summer 1513; R. of Endellion, Cornwall 19 May 1533, res. 1534; Maclean i. 492.

John **Rugge** or Rigge, **Dev.**, summer **1505** to autumn 1519. Acta Congregationis 24 May 1506 'supplicat Joannes Rigge scolaris artium quatenus studium trium annorum in hac universitate, cum responsione uni bacallario ultima quadragesima sibi sufficiat ut admittatur ad lecturam etc.   Hec est concessa conditionate quod bis intret preter formam proxima quadragesima'; B.A. 3 July 1506, M.A. 8 May 1509, sup. B.D. 11 July 1519; auditor of Dunkam Chest 1515; Rector 1515–16; ? V. of S. Thomas, Exeter 26 Ap. 1528, and treasurer of Crediton, d. 1537, Executor John Bery, fellow 1526; Eccl. Ant. i. 54, 57, ii. 78, 160, 168.   See a. 1498.

John **James** or Jamys, **dev.**, adm. 26 May **1506**, vac. Lent 1520; B.A. 12 Feb. 150⁸⁄₉, M.A. 10 Oct. 1511, in orders; auditor of Queen's Chest summer 1513; autumn 1520 ' iii*s* vi*i*i*d* a M. Johanne Jamys et Henrico Tregassy pro 2ᵒᵇᵘˢ coclearibus promptuarii deperditis.' A previous John James, Canon, was residing in autumn 1504.

Thomas **Davy** or Davyd, **Corn.**, summer **1507** to winter 1513; M.A., in orders, probably the Thomas Davyd who had leave to incept 8 May 1509 with Mede, Kingdon, and Rugge; summer 1509 'pro factura studii in camera M. Davyth xx*d*.'

Nicholas **Smale, corn.**, summer **1508** to Lent 1516; B.A. 12 Feb. 150⁸⁄₉, M.A. 10 Oct. 1512; auditor of Fen (Vienna) Chest 1513; collated to R. of Thenford, Northants 1524, but renounced, R. of Wappenham 1525, Canon of Lincoln 1526; R. of Clyst S. George, Devon 1536, d. 1553, Eccl. Ant. i. 154.

Thomas **Irish, dev.**, adm. 18 Nov **1509**, vac. summer 1516; B.A. 2 July 1509, M.A. 10 Oct. 1512, in orders; auditor of Shelten and Warwyke Chests summer 1513; Principal of Hart Hall 26 Nov. 1514–1522, Proctor 1517.

John **Moreman, Dev.**, adm. 29 June **1510**, res. 6 Nov. 1522 (Simon Atkins was candidate for the fellowship; and Hugh Oldham, Bishop of Exeter, irritated at his not being elected, founded two fellowships for the diocese of Exeter at Corpus 1517 instead of at Exeter, Gutch iii. 393, Fowler's *Corpus* 382); b. Southhole near

Hartland, B.A. 29 Jan. 150⅖, M.A. 10 Oct. 1512, sup. B.D. 2 Aug. 1524; D.D. 16 Dec. 1529; auditor of Dunkam Chest 1513, Guardian of Nele and Cycester Chests 1519; Principal of Hart Hall 1522–27; V. of Midsomer Norton, Som. 1516; R. of Holy Trinity, Exeter 25 Sep. 1528–1529, V of Menheniot 25 Feb. 1529 (valued at £21 15s. 5d. in 1536, Eccl. Ant. ii. 184: 188 Preb. of Glasney, valued at £1 6s.); Canon of Exeter 19 June 1544 (and said to have been Dean), V. of Colebrooke, Devon 25 Oct. 1546. He disputed against the Protestants in Convocation Oct. 1553 (Foxe v. 178, Froude ed. 1860 vi. 115, Dixon iv. 78, 80, 90, 91): Acts of Privy Council N. S. iv. 63 letters to dean and chapter of Excester to restore and allowe to Doctour Morman and Crispin, prisoners in the Tower, theyr porcyon of theyr dividentes of theyr prebendes within the churche of Excester, so as they may therewith pay theyr dietes and fees in the Tower, 29 May 1552; again iv. 243; living on 20 May 1554 (South Petherwin deed at Ex. Coll.), but d. before Aug. 1554, N. and Gleanings v. 16, 55; State Papers 1531 p. 6, 2 Mch 153⅘; Pocock's Burnet v. 374, 601; Athenæ ii. 82–83, Bibl. Corn. 369–70, 1288, Nat. Biog. Computus of winter 1515 'viii*d* a M. Moremane pro *scolari* suo Baron pro stipendio camere sue pro uno termino'; summer 1527 'xl*s* a M. Moreman pro Aula Cervina, vi*s* pro Aula Nigra'; winter 1547 'xx*s* a M. Moreman ex legatis M. Trehaux' (the Trehawks lived at Menheniot, Visit. Corn. 574), 'iiii*d* pro asportatione xx*s* a M. Trehaux'; summer 1548 'xx*s* sociis ex legatione M. Trehaux in Cornubia'; College Reg. 24 Oct. 1554 'recepi omnia Augustini opera ex dono magistri et doctoris Moorman.'

William **Smythe, Sar.**, adm. 26 June **1511**, vac. winter 1521; sup. B.A. 8 Ap. 1511; M.A. 5 Nov. 1515; sup. B.D. 30 Nov. 1526; Rector 1519–21, priest of S. Thomas' in Salisbury, State Papers 11 Nov. 1533; living 1557; Warton 9; winter 1543 'iiii*d* pro vino et piris datis M. Smythe.'

John **Waryn**, or Warren, **corn.**, adm. 26 June **1511**, vac. summer 1520; B.A. 31 Jan. 151⅘, M.A. 5 Nov. 1515, in orders; bursar 1520; R. of Lifton, Devon, and R. of Roche and V. of Altarnon, Cornwall 1536, Eccl. Ant. ii. 180, 183, 186; a John Waryn was V. of S. Issey, Cornwall 3 Sep. 1517; a John Waryn had been R. of Menheniot 1411, and Canon of Exeter 23 June 1419, Stafford's Reg. 169, R. I. C. 1879 p. 223, N. and Gleanings i. 12; autumn 1517 'xvi*d* ex M. Warryn pro *scolaribus* suis pro ultimo termino'; summer 1520 'v*s* iiii*d* a M. Waryn pro camera domini Shelston *scolaris* sui pro 2ᵒᵇᵘˢ terminis, xvi*d* a M. Waryn pro camera domini Ashely pro dimidio anni.'

Thomas **Vyvyan, Corn.**, autumn **1511** to autumn **1520**; sup. B.A. 20 June 1511; M.A. 5 Nov. 1515, Guardian of Cycester Chest 1519, in orders; Rector 27 Mch 1518—8 Oct. 1519; ? that younger brother of Thomas Vyvyan, prior of Bodmin 1507, also called Thomas who was V. of Bodmin 27 Nov. 1516, Maclean i. 133, 147; if so, four fellows of Exeter were Vicars in succession, William Merifield, John Holwell, Thomas Vyvyan, Sir John Dagle; autumn 1515 'x*s* de Priore de Bodimonia pro cubiculo suo pro duobus terminis'; autumn 1517 'iii*s* iiii*d* ex M. Vyvyon pro una de scolis nostris pro dimidio anno, viii*d* ex eodem M. Vyvyon pro cubiculo in quo iacebat *scolaris* suus Tankerd pro uno termino' [Sir Thomas dictus Tankarde d. 15 Mch 132$\frac{0}{1}$, Stapeldon's Reg. 184; Stafford 437, 443, 450]; summer 1522 'xxv*s* iiii*d* a M. Vyvyan pro cambera sua nobis debitis in festo annunciacionis dominice ultimo preterito'; Lent 1527 'xi*li* a M. Vyvyan firmario nostro de Gwynner.' Another Thomas Vyvyan was fellow 1539. A Thomas Vyvian was preb. of Glasney 1535–48, then aged 70, R. I. C. vi. 261; Eccl. Ant. ii. 188, 190–1.

Richard **Browne, Chapl.**, adm. 9 Mch 151$\frac{2}{3}$, vac. Lent 1517; B.A. 10 Mch 151$\frac{5}{8}$; M.A. 4 May 1520 as chaplain; Eccl. Ant. iii. 41.

Thomas **Allyn**, or Allynge, **corn.**, winter **1513** to autumn 1520; B.A. 3 July 1514, M.A. 16 Dec. 1516.

William **Poskyns, sar.**, adm. 3 Nov. **1514**, vac. autumn 1515; B.A. 31 Jan. 151$\frac{2}{3}$, resident winter 1517. A William Poskyn, B.A., was R. of Corscombe, Dorset 39 Mch 1522, Hutchins ii. 96 (iii. 681 John Poskyn 1541; a John Poskyns was B.A. 19 June 1507, M.A. 1510).

William **Reskemer, Corn.**, adm. 15 Dec. **1514**, vac. autumn 1520 (? 2 s. John, by Catherine Tretherffe); sup. B.A. 25 Mch 1511; M.A. 5 Nov. 1515, Auditor of Queen's chest 1516, resident 1527; R. of Ladock, Cornwall 15 Jan. 15$\frac{18}{46}$–1558, V. of Constantine 1536, d. 1558, Eccl. Ant. ii. 186, 189; autumn 1517 'vi*s* viii*d* a M. Reskemer pro una de nostris 4^{or} scolis pro toto anno'; summer 1536 'iiii*s* vii*d* *ob.* pro domino Paw pro debitis M. Reskemer'; Visit. Corn. 396.

Philip **Bale, Dev.**, adm. 5 July **1515**, vac. Lent 1530; sup. B.A. 30 June 1516; M.A. 5 June 1521; sup. B.D. 29 Jan. 153$\frac{2}{3}$ after 12 years' study; Proctor 1524; Rector 14 Dec. 1521—6 Oct. 1526; Vice Rector (Senior Fellow) autumn 1529; R. of Honiton 3 Jan. 15$\frac{32}{40}$, of Combe Raleigh 1555, d. 1559, Eccl. Ant. ii. 78; by will

6 May, proved 14 June, 1659 left the College 'the works of S. Augustyn, S. Ambrose, Origyn, S. Jerom, and certeyn books of Byde (Bede), and works of S. Gregorye, with other such books as my overseer shall think meyt'; the Latin of his Computi is strange, and he writes Odstocke for Woodstock, howde hosse for wood house; autumn 1529 'iis viii*d* Bale, Pekyns, Biblie lectore euntibus ad Clyfton Ferye' (see Lent 1403 'ii*d* pro expensis Clerici Biblie quando ivit Abendon ad loquendum cum firmariis nostris').

John **Willoughby** (Willobi, Wyllugby), **sar.**, adm. 8 or 15 Dec. **1515**, vac. autumn 1520; sup. B.A. 4 Nov. 1513; M.A. 16 Dec. 1516; ? R. of Baverstock, Wilts 1521 pres. by abbess of Wilton, called John *Major* at his death in 1527; a John Willoughby was R. of Haccombe, Devon in 1536, Eccl. Ant. i. 161, ii. 161; autumn 1497 Edward Willugby, Dean of Exeter, is mentioned; winter 1515 'xxviii*s* v*d* o*b*. pro expensis Rectoris et eius servientis apud Londinum pro elapsu electionis domini Johannis Willobi et Hugonis Gylett in loco domini Willelmi Poskyns versus archipresulem [ecclesie] Cantuariensis tunc Universitatis Oxonie cancellarium' [i.e. Warham]; Hutchins iv. 103, Visit. Corn. 556.

Edmund **Fletcher, corn.**, adm. 8 May **1516**, vac. summer 1529; B.A. 2 July 1515; sup. M.A. 8 Nov. 1518, incepted 28 Feb. 151$\frac{8}{9}$; sup. B.D. 28 July 1530; Rector 1526–29, chaplain of the University, i.e. librarian; Lent 1520 'vi*d* carpentario pro fabricacione unius parvi tecti supra hostia camerarum M. Warynge et M. Fletcher, xiii*d* pro quibusdam asseribus ad fabricam predictam necessariis'; autumn 1541 'vi*li* pro legatis M. Flacher'; winter 1542 'iiii*s* viii*d* pro exequiis Edmundi Flatcher.'

Thomas **Lake, dev.**, adm. 18 June **1516**, vac. summer 1529; B.A. 3 July 1514, disp. for M.A. 2 Feb. 151$\frac{3}{4}$ as about to take orders at home.

John **Morcomb, Corn.**, adm. 6 May **1517**, vac. Lent 1518; M.A., in orders: a John Morcom was B.A. 3 July 1506, sup. M.A. 13 May 1510, Principal of Black Hall 1511, Wood's City i. 596; Auditor of Hussey Chest winter 1512; pres. to R. of Winterborne Houghton, Dorset, by Sir John Arundel, 30 Aug. 1519, R. of Slapton collegiate church 1535 (surrendered 17 Nov. 1545), of Okeford-Fitzpaine, Dorset 1546, Hutchins i. 330, iv. 334; ? R. of S. Ervan, and of Mawgan in Pyder 1536, Eccl. Ant. ii. 178, 191.

John **Nicolls, Chapl.**, summer **1518** to winter 1523; B.A. June 1518 'secular chaplain'; R. of Landewednack, Cornwall 1536–49, Eccl. Ant. ii. 189.

Richard **Chapell, corn.**, autumn **1518** to Lent 1520; B.A. 28 Feb. 151⅜.

William **Slade, Dev.**, adm. 23 Oct. **1519**, vac. winter 1526; B.A. 19 Jan. 151⅚, M.A. 5 June 1521; chantry priest of Bromham S. Nicholas, Wilts 1521, d. 1537; Hutchins iv. 424.

John **Moxhay, Dev.**, adm. 20 Jan. 15¹⁹⁄₂₀, vac. Lent 1528; M.A. 5 June 1521; V. of Pinhoe 17 June 1527, Eccl. Ant. ii. 127; admin. bond 4 Ap. 1528, Griffiths 43.

Bartholomew **Michell, Corn.**, adm. 3 Ap. **1520**, vac. Lent 1527; determined as B.A. Mch 151⅜, M.A. 26 Oct. 1521; allowed 26 July 1523 to sell his dress of Regent Master; fellow of Eton 11 Jan. 152⅚, sup. B.D. 10 Oct. 1533; R. of Ludgvan, Cornwall 1536.

John **White, Corn.**, adm. 3 Ap. **1520**, res. autumn 1533; B.A. 18 July 1519, M.A. 6 July 1523, in orders; Principal of Hart Hall 11 July 1527–1531; winter 1529 'vis viii*d* a M. Whyte bursario pro scolis magistrorum Lacy et Burley'; winter 1532 'iiii*d* M. White propter pecuniam allatam de Gwynner'; winter 1542 'xii*d* Johanni coquo equitanti Bamptoniam pro M. White, jussu doctoris Wright.'

Richard **Martin, Sar.**, adm. 23 June **1520**, vac. winter 1523; in orders; B.A. 14 Mch 152¾; became M.B. with John Tooker 13 July 1538; summer 1522 'x*d* M. Martyn pro capicio ad componendum capam in nostro sacello'; winter 1523 'xii*d* M. Marten equitanti versus Bensynton'; pres. to Winfrith Newburgh, Dorset 28 June 1524, d. 1540; Hutchins i. 446.

John **Bere, Corn.**, winter **1521** to autumn 1531; sup. B.A. 20 June 1517, sup. M.A. 12 July 1520, in priest's orders by winter 1521, Rector 1529–31; R. of Endellion 23 May 1534, of Camborne 1542, d. 1563; Maclean i. 492.

John **Toker** (Tucker), **corn.**, adm. 16 Nov. **1521**, vac. Lent 1526; sup. B.A. 15 Jan. 152⁰⁄₁; M.A. 6 July 1523, judge for inquiring into the peace between East Gate and S. Martin's Church in July 1523; adm. to practise in medicine 14 May 1530, disp. 28 June 1530 to take the place of a M.D. next Act, and the preceding Vesperies, because Humfrey Bluet of Merton wants to incept, and there is only one other Doctor of that faculty; M.B. and D. 13 July 1538; Proctor 1525; Canon of Cardinal College 1529; Wood's Fasti a. 1525, 1538; Gutch iii. 422; Eccl. Ant. i. 169, 204, ii. 160, 201; Lent 1529 'xxii*d* circa fratrem magistri Toker in camera Rectoris.'

John **Collyns, dev.**, winter **1521** to summer 1529; B.A. 5 Nov. 1520, M.A. 6 July 1523, in orders; ? R. of Sutton Mandeville, Wilts

1531-7, of Rushall 1537-8, executed with the Pole family 1538 for treason; Phillipps 201, 206, 208.

Eurin **Cocks** (Cokkys), **sar.**, winter 1521 to winter 1529; B.A. 30 June 1523, M.A. 9 Nov. 1526, he was to read the book *de longitudine et brevitate vite* before his degree, and the two books *de generatione* in his own house 'fixis scedulis'; Guardian of Burnel Chest 1527.

Thomas **Forde, dev.**, adm. 25 Mch 1522, vac. Lent 1526; B.A. 30 June 1523, in orders.

Stephen **Carslegh** (Caslegh), **Dev.**, adm. 20 Dec. 1522, vac. winter 1532; B.A. 25 Feb. 152½, M.A. 19 Feb. 152⅘, sup. M.B. Jan. 154⁰/₁ after studying 12 years.

John **Conner** or Cunner (? from Gwithian, Cornwall; Conner Downs are in Gwinear), ? chorister of Magdalen 1501, demy 1508 as Cannar (Bloxam i. 6); B.A. 28 Oct. 1510, M.A. 29 Jan. 151¾; adm. **Chapl.** 15 Dec. 1523 in place of Nicolls, vac. Lent 1549; sup. B.D. 27 Oct. 1524; winter 1514 'iiis iiiid de M. Cunner pro scola sua pro duobus terminis'; V. of S. Peter's in the East, Oxford; V. of Wittenham about 1540; d. 1569, inventory of his goods 3 Dec. 1569, Griffiths 16.

John **Pekyns, Sar.**, autumn 1524 to autumn 1534; B.A. 27 July 1523; M.A. 9 Nov. 1526, sup. B.D. 26 Mch 1534; Bursar 1530, Rector 1531-34, Proctor 1533; canon of Westminster 3 May 1543; instit. R. of Bradwell juxta Mare, Essex 5 Mch 154½ on present. of Queen Katherine Howard [beheaded 13 Feb. 154½], deprived before 1 May 1554; Wood's Fasti a. 1526, 1533; Athenæ ii. 750; Newcourt ii. 85, 169; Turner 117; a note to the Computus of autumn 1533 charges him with cheating the College of £12 1s. 5½d. in his accounts; autumn 1545 'viili viiis id a M. Pawe pro allocatione panis quem Johannes Juner subministravit Collegio nostro in partem solutionis debitorum M. Pekens, deducto scilicet emolumento obsonatoris ex octo libris et xviiid quam alioqui summam putaretur predictus Johannes solvisse Collegio in pane'; winter 1547 'xiis Juner pistori pro M. Peckens,' Lent 1548 'vis viiid Juner pistori pro debitis antiquis ex mandato Vicecancellarii.'

James **Bayly**, **sar.**, adm. 31 May 1526, res. 1 Dec. 1539; B.A. 2 July 1526, M.A. 5 July 1529, Vice-rector 1535; ? V. of Preshute, Wilts 1533, res. 1544, of Burnham, Som. 1538, of W. Harptree 1543; see a. 1549, Phillipps i. 203; ? Fellow of Eton 1554; winter 1531 'id fabro lapidario emendanti focum M. Jacobi Bayly.' Lent 1548 'ixs pro semianno cubiculi M. Bayli': Hutchins i. 108, ii. 655, iii. 465.

John **Bery** or Bury, Dev., adm. 7 July **1526**, vac. autumn 1536;
B.A. 30 June 1523, M.A. 9 Nov. 1526, B.D. 14 June 1543; Rector
1534–36; resident 1539–43; V. of Axmouth 26 Ap. 1536, d. 1558,
Eccl. Ant. ii. 85, 162; ? R. of S. Columb Major, Cornwall; winter
1531 'viid Johanni Osburne pro quadam tabula et studdys que
habuit M. Bery ad amplicionem sui musei'; ? Rector of S. Mary
College 20 July 1548, when John Man, Principal of White Hall in
S. Michael's, complained of Bury receiving Thomas Wysse from White
Hall without his leave, R. Newton's *University Education* 38; Univ.
Reg. i. 175, Clark i. 283, Tanner 505, Wood's City i. 587, ii. 232, 242.

William **Cholwell**, Dev., adm. 15 Feb. 152⁹⁄₇, vac. autumn 1536;
B.A. 27 Feb. 152⁹⁄₇, M.A. 5 July 1529, sup. B.D. 30 Mch 1555; lic. to
preach 1547, under Edward VI, Dixon's Church Hist. ii. 486; V. of
Colaton Raleigh, Devon 1548, deprived 1556, Eccl. Ant. iii. 96; R. of
Southhill, Cornwall 1551.

Edward **Lee** or Ley or Lye, dev., adm. 9 Mch 152⁹⁄₇, vac. summer
1530 ('Lye recessit in die Jovis *in annos*,' i.e. on 9 June); B.A. 30
June 1523, M.A. 10 Feb. 152⁷⁄₈; R. of Sowton, Devon 23 Mch 15²⁸⁄₃₀,
V. of Brampford Speke 21 May 1529, d. 1540; Eccl. Ant. ii. 44, 113
(his will), 167, 168.

John **Dotyn**, Dev., adm. 20 June **1528**, res. 27 Oct. 1539; b. Har-
bertonford, Totnes; B.A. 1 Aug. 1524, M.A. 5 July 1529, sup. M.B.
1534, adm. to practise 16 July 1542, sup. M.D. 1 June 1559; Rector
1537–39; V. of Bampton, Oxon 1534, res. 155⁸⁄₉, Giles' Bampton
xxxvii; Canon of Exeter, pres. by Sir John Arundel of Lanherne to
R. of Whitstone, Cornwall 1537, res. 1554 (R. Dottyn R. of Whitstone 25 Sep. 1554), V. of S. Issey, Cornwall 1543, R. of Aveton
Gifford, Devon 1554, of Kingsdon, Som. 1558; d. Kingsdon 7 Nov.
1561, his epitaph says 'Hic jacet magister Johannes Dotin, medicus
ac *astrologus* [i.e. astronomer] insignis, quondam hujus ecclesie pastor,
necnon Collegii Exonien. Oxon. Rector, qui obiit 7° Novembris A°
Dni. 1561, cui gloriosam concedat Dominus resurrectionem';
Collinson's Somerset iii. 195. He gave the College a house and land
in Bampton 1557, and his medical books, including the Galen of 1521
and 1533; Wood's Life ii. 20, Fasti a. 1534, 1559; Gutch iii. 114;
winter 1531 'vid pro quadam sponda ad usum cubiculi M. Dottyns.'
The Recovery of the land at Bampton by J. Dotyne plaintiff against
John Hastings def., wherein is exemplified the pleading in Mich. Term,
dated 30 Oct. 2 and 3 Philip and Mary (1555) has a fine impression
of the handsome seal 'pro brevibus.'

Robert **Marshall, Dev.**, adm. 19 June **1529**, vac. 1529; B.A.
7 Feb. 15$\frac{2}{3}\frac{9}{0}$; ? R. of Nymet Tracey 1536, Eccl. Ant. ii. 169.

William **Saunders, sar.**, adm. 27 Nov. or 4 Dec. **1529**, vac. Lent
1535; B.A. 7 Feb. 15$\frac{2}{3}\frac{9}{0}$, M.A. 29 Nov. 1532 : R. of Stock-Gaylard
15 Jan. 1538, of Hazelbury Bryan **1544**, both in Dorset; Hutchins i.
280, iii. 690.

Thomas **Edgcombe** or Eggecome, **Dev.**, adm. 4 or 11 Dec. **1529**,
vac. Lent 1536; B.A. 12 Nov. 1527, M.A. 19 June 1531, in orders;
fellow of Eton 1536, Viceprovost, d. **1545**; Gent. Mag. Library,
Bucks p. 289; Visit. Devon 324. A John Edgcombe, of S. Aldate's,
Oxford, about 1500, left money for prayers for the souls of Thomas
Eggecombe D. CAN. L., Sir Richard Eggecombe, Alice Eggecombe,
Richard Eggecombe, and Thomasina Eggecombe; Gutch i. 473,
Bodleian Charters 293, 348.

James **Carter, corn.**, adm. 22 Jan. 15$\frac{2}{3}\frac{9}{0}$, res. 24 Ap. 1538; B.A.
19 June 1531, M.A. 22 Nov. 1533, living 1557.

Henry **Laurence, dev.**, adm. 9 Ap. **1530**, res. 9 Oct. 1543, having
completed his full time; B.A. 7 Feb. 15$\frac{2}{3}\frac{9}{0}$, M.A. 29 Nov. 1532, V. of
Kidlington; Rector 17 Oct. 1541—9 Oct. 1543, d. 24 June 1545,
will 5 June 1545, his body to be buried in Kidlington church,
within the chancel of our Blessed Lady; to the stone of Jesus
3s. 4d.; to the bellringers at my burial 8d.; to the College my books,
and 40s. which Philip Bale parson of Honiton owes me, witness
Augustine Cross priest; Gutch iii. 114, Hist. of Kidlington (O. H.
Soc.) 44.

— **Jamys**; autumn **1530** 'vs Jamys pro pensione sua; xiiis iiiid
Sawnders, Eggecombe, Laurence, et Jamys ad visitandum amicos';
but Jamys does not occur again.

Richard **Martyn, dev.**, adm. 10 Oct. **1530**, res. 18 Mch 153$\frac{7}{8}$;
B.A. 19 June 1531, M.A. 22 Nov. 1533; ? V. of Colebrook, Devon
14 Aug. 1554 in succession to John Moreman (N. and Gleanings v.
16), and ? R. of Oare, Som. 1554.

John **French, Dev.**, adm. 3 Dec. **1530**, vac. 16 Jan. 154$\frac{3}{4}$, having
taken a living 16 July 1543; B.A. 13 July 1530, M.A. 22 Nov. 1533,
B.D. 26 May 1543; Principal of Hart Hall 22 Nov. 1535–1541;
Rector 25 Oct. 1539–1542, ? resident 1557; chaplain of Eton; gave
the College Rufinus' translation of Josephus (Coxe no. xxv). He
held Rowlin's Chantry, Barnstaple, 1553, see Chanter's *Barnstaple*
128.

William **Lawse, Corn.**, adm. 25 Nov. **1531**, res. 15 Oct. 1537;

sup. B.A. June 1532; M.A. 14 Nov. 1535; *supervisor vicorum* July 1536; V. of S. Gennys, Cornwall 1548.

NOTE.—Winter 1531 'Debita Collegio anno predicto: for maister Vyllerys chamber iii quarters xiiis vi*d*, of Master Medys executors x*li*, of Gwynner xx marks, of Bynsynton xxxi*s*, of Catstrete x*s*, of the Mancyple vii*li* ix*s* i*d*, of John Carpenter iii*s*, of John Nyxon for maister Peverys st. . . . viii*s* viii*d*, of John Nyxon for maister Flacher x*s*, of master doctor Moreman at Mychaell laste x*li*.'

Augustine **Crosse, Dev.**, adm. 14 Dec. **1532**, vac. 9 Oct. 1546; B.A. 29 Nov. 1532, M.A. 14 Nov. 1535; judge for inquiring into the peace outside the E. gate July 1536; Rector 17 Oct. 1543–1546; Fellow of Eton 1547, Wood's Fasti a. 1535; V. of Modbury, Devon 1552, of Dorney, Bucks 1553, R. of Sturminster Marshal, Dorset 28 Aug. 1559, d. 1563, Hutchins iii. 366. Crosse and Nanconan are the first *two* Bursars mentioned in the *Register*. Acta Curiae Cancellarii 11 Nov. 1545 'Tresham Commissario. Comparuit coram nobis M. Augustinus Crosse et requisivit nomine Johannis Preuit a Johanne Gylney viis vi*d* in presentia predicti Gylney confitentis se tantum debere dicto Crosse, super quo decrevimus ex consensu partium ut Gylney solvat dicto Crosse iii*s* ix*d* in festo Purificationis prox., pro cuius solutionis securitate induxit cautionem viz; togam remanentem in manibus Thome Hodgson; et decrevimus alios iii*s* ix*d* solvendos dicto Crosse in festo Annunciationis beate Marie prox., et pro hac solutione facienda per ipsum Gelney fidejussit M. Thomas Yonge in legibus baccalaurius.'

Martin **Collyns** (Collins senior), **Corn.**, adm. 22 Nov. **1533**, res. 5 Nov. 1541; sup. B.A. 9 Dec. 1531; M.A. 14 Nov. 1535, R. of Horsmonden, Kent 1542, of Midley 1545, Canon of Rochester 1556 and 1561; summer 1540 'viii*d* M. Collyns pro parva campana.'

William **Payne, Corn.**, summer **1535**, res. 31 Mch 1540 'per manus magistri Collyns'; sup. B.A. June 1532 ; M.A. 20 Ap. 1537; winter 1537 'xiiii*d* M. Payn pro exequiis tempore sue egrotationis'; autumn 1539 '10*s* M. Payn pro asportatione pecuniæ e firmariis S. Wynneri'; ? R. of Rowberrow, Som. before 1547.

John **Lillyngton** (a parish so called lies south of Sherborne, Hutchins iv. 194), **Sar.**, adm. 1 May **1535**; B.A. 5 Feb. 153⅘, incepted as M.A. 7 July 1539, d. 20 Ap. 1540 of consumption. Wood D. 2 p. 102.

— **Howell** (Hoylle), **dev.**, adm. 13 Ap. **1536**; occurs also next term, but the Computus of Oct. 1536—Oct. 1537 is lost, and several

previous Compuli are in a bad state; ? William Howell who was
B.A. Magdalen 12 July 1536.

William **More**, **Dev.**, adm. 15 Oct. **1537**, vac. after Oct. 1553;
B.A. 13 Feb. 153$\frac{7}{9}$, M.A. 6 Dec. 1541, B.D.; Rector 17 Oct. 1546–
1553, being continued in office by Edward VI's Visitors (Dr. Cox's
letter in the Reg. is dated Windsor 16 Oct. 1548, Gutch ii. 87);
Principal of Hart Hall 25 Dec. 1544—5 Jan. 154$\frac{5}{6}$, R. of Stoke
Rivers, Devon 1551, living 1557; a William More was R. of
Mamhead, Devon 2 Jan. 154$\frac{7}{8}$, res. 1581, Eccl. Ant. iii. 67; autumn
1543 'xx$d$ a M. More pro scola M. (John) Lutley'; winter 1544
'xxii$s$ vi$d$ M. More et M. Nonconon ad solvendum pro exequiis
Johannis More, quam scilicet summam oportet illos resolvere Rectori
posteaquam acceperint redditus a Rawlyns et Langley.' Lent 1556
'vi$d$ tabellario pro portatione casei missi a M. More.' Reg. 17 Oct.
1549.

NOTE.—Reg. 17 Oct. 1549 'non licuit ut electio novi Rectoris iuxta consuetum
collegii morem celebraretur. Regiæ majestatis authoritas obstabat quominus id
fieret, nam aestate proxime antea praeterlapsa a Regis legatis sive (ut loquuntur)
visitatoribus constitutum est, ut Guilielmus Morus, qui tunc temporis Rector erat,
postea non annuum et arbitrarium gereret magistratum sed perpetuum, ita ut vitae
suae et rectoratus idem esset finis, nisi regendi munus ipse ultro a se ablegare vellet,
statutumque etiam ab eisdem est ut hac in parte simile ius perpetue foret illis qui
in eius locum postea succederent.' Compare the visitors' regulations in All Souls'
Statutes p. 85.

John **Tremayne**, **Dev.**, adm. 16 Oct. **1537**, res. 12 Mch 154$\frac{0}{1}$;
(? brother of Richard, fellow 1553;) B.A. 13 Feb. 153$\frac{7}{3}$; in autumn
1538 Tremayne, Yendall and Nanconan are readmitted, but the cause
is not stated.

John **Peter**, **sar.**, Lent **1538** (probably before), res. 6 Mch 154$\frac{1}{2}$;
B.A. 20 Ap. 1537.

John **Holman**, **dev.**, Lent **1538**, vac. autumn 1539; summer 1539
'5s D. Holman pro asportatione pecunie de Gwynner.'

Robert **Yendall** (Endall), **corn.**, adm. 6 Ap. **1538**; res. 16 Oct.
1543; B.A. 23 Feb. 153$\frac{7}{9}$, M.A. 6 Dec. 1541; V. of Menheniot
27 Oct. 1554; Monast. Exon. 206, Wilkins' Concilia iv. 140; State
Papers (Foreign) 2 Aug. 1559 p. 436–7, 5 Oct. p. 16–17, Coll. Corn.
237, N. and Gleanings v. 55.

Thomas **Nanconan**, **Corn.**, adm. 21 May **1538**, vac. Lent 1546;
B.A. 13 May 1538, M.A. 6 Dec. 1541; autumn 1538 '5s a domino
Nanconan ex dono domini Udi Pengwyne presbiteri commorantis in
ecclesia S. Columbe Cornub.' The name occurs in S. Columb Reg.

Thomas **Vyvyan** or Vivion, **Corn.**, ? adm. June **1539**, vac. autumn 1549; B.A. 6 Dec. 1541, M.A. 9 Oct. 1544, B.D. 18 July 1552, D.D. May 1558; Principal of Hart Hall 5 Jan. 154⁴⁄₈–1548 (his fidejussores were Wi. Pawle and T. Williams); V. of S. Just in Penwith 15 Feb. 154⁷⁄₉, 'Thomas Vyvyan junior presented by Thomas Vivyan clerk and John Vivyan junior'; R. of Philleigh, Cornwall 1552; Polwhele's Cornwall v. 154, Clark i. 283.

Roger **Harwarde** or Harode, **dev.**, el. before 25 Oct. **1539**, adm. 5 Dec., vac. 1558; B.A. 18 Feb. 153⁸⁄₉, M.A. 11 Oct. 1543; V. of Poundstock, Cornwall 1549.

John **Pruett** or Pruyt, Prewett, **Sar.**, el. 2 Dec. **1539**, adm. 17 Jan. 15³⁸⁄₄₀, res. 10 Dec. 1543; B.A. 18 Feb. 153⁸⁄₉, M.A. 11 Oct. 1543; re-elected 17 Oct. 1544 in place of Fessarde (*see* 1543), for whose re-election there was an equal number of votes, but the Vice-Chancellor Richard Smythe appointed Pruett on 23 Oct.; he vac. again before 4 Dec. 1544, where see Reg.

NOTE.—The Register begins thus on p. 30 (earlier pages out of place) :—

25° die mensis Octobris anni Christi 1539 electus erat Johannes French, principalis aulae Cervinae, rector Collegii Exon. pro anno futuro.

Nomina sociorum Johannes French rector, M. Jacobus Baylye, M. Johannes Cunner capellanus, M. Henricus Laurens, M. Augustinus Crosse, M. Martinus Collyns, M. Wilhelmus Payne, M. Johannes Lyllyngton, dominus Petrus, Wilhelmus More, Johannes Tremayne, Robertus Yendall, Thomas Nonconon, d. Robertus Harwarde, Thomas Vivyan scolaris.

Suggenarii magister Bury, M. Richardus Hals, dominus Johannes Yong unus e bonis hominibus de Astrihge in com. Buckyngham, dominus Wilhelmus Downam, M. Copston; M. Wilhelmus Hyberdyne sacre theologie bachalaurius, M. Collyar, M. Johannes Shere; Jacobus Bayly.

In 1540 sojourners M. Bury, M. Baly, dominus Downam, M. Collyar, M. Weston, M. Waterhouse. In 1541 sojourners M. Bury, M. Hals, M. Weston, M. Waterhouse, M. Copstone, M. Varnan, dominus Downam, et M. Mayo. On 16 Nov. admitted to commons M. Vernon and John Blunt suggenarii. 4 Mch 154½ M. Whyting adm. sojourner, on 14 May 1542 dominus Downam adm. to commons. On 17 Oct. sojourners MM. Bury, Hals, Weston, Waterhouse, Varnan, Copstone, Blunt, Mayo, Whyting, and on 3rd Nov. M. Mayo.

In 1543 sojourners M. J. Burye, M. N. Weston, M. Th. Waterhouse, M. R. Vernan, M. N. Mayo, M. S. Whyting.

17 Oct. 1562 nomina commensalium M. Rolfe (quanquam in triennium absens), M. Arscot, M. Geare, M. Whiddon, M. Amerson, M. Dotin, M. Stocker, M. Gylford, M. Tufton, M. Arscot alteri consobrinus, M. Grevell, suggenarii plerique generosi nonnulli vero presbiteri. Adde etiam alium generosum M. Bygge, Farrant et Nelande.

Richard **Harris**, **Corn.**, el. 1 Ap. **1540**, adm. 22 May; d. 4 July 1541: Misc. Gen. i. 241–43 (monthly series).

John **Collyns** (Collyns junior), **dev.**, el. 28 Ap. **1540**, adm. 23 June; sup. B.A. Feb. 15$\frac{39}{40}$; M.A. 11 Oct. 1543, adm. M.B. and to practise 18 Mch 155$\frac{8}{9}$, sup. M.D. May 1566; ? R. of S. Just, Cornwall 1543, ? R. of Parkham 6 May 1545, of Holbeton 1554, R. of Huish 1563, of Doddiscombleigh 18 Nov. 1566; d. 4 Jan. 1577; brother-in-law of John Wether, R. of Littleham, who left 5s. to him, and 40s. to each of his 3 daughters; Clark iii. 24.

William **Grylls, dev.**, el. 13 Mch 154$\frac{0}{1}$, adm. 16 Ap., full Fellow 16 Ap. 1542, vac. autumn 1551; B.A. 6 Dec. 1541, M.A. 9 Oct 1544. See a. 1553; autumn 1544 'vi*d ob. q.* pro comunis Grylls pro 3^{bus} diebus ruri tempore pestis.'

John **Dagle** or Dagull (one of the name was canon of Bodmin priory, pensioned 1538 on £5 6s. 8d. a year), **Corn.**, 17 Oct. **1541**, adm. 27 Nov., full Fellow 5 Nov. 1542, res. 9 May 1543: B.A. 7 Ap. 1544, portioner of Bampton, Oxon 1549; V. of Morval, Cornwall 1549, of Bodmin 21 Nov. 1550, of Stoke Gabriel, Devon 1554, bur. 15 Dec. 1564; Maclean i. 138, 148; autumn 1541 'iis viii*d* a domino Dagle pro cubiculo suo uno termino.' See Univ. Reg. i. 108.

William **Duck** (Dooke), **Dev.**, 6 Nov. **1541**, adm. 3 Dec.; B.A. 17 Feb. 153$\frac{3}{9}$, M.A. 9 Oct. 1544, one of the 'Theologi' at Christ Church 1547 'of Devon, age 30,' ? R. of Thornton-le-Moor, Cheshire 1553.

NOTE.—In 1541 there were only four Masters of Arts, French, Conner, Crosse, (Martin) Collins.

John **Whetcombe, Dev.**, 7 Mch 154$\frac{1}{2}$, adm. 8 Ap.; B.A. 17 Feb. 153$\frac{8}{9}$, M.A. 11 Oct. 1543, R. of Stockleigh English, Devon 1549 (as Whitcombe); was John Whetcombe, fellow of Merton 1565, his son? John Whetcombe, Fellow 1602, may have been the grandson; autumn 1544 'iis viii*d* M. Whetcum pro communis 2^{arum} hebdomadarum sibi concessis agenti ruri superiori termino ob pestem evitandum.' Hutchins ii. 79, 133, iv. 195.

Robert **Talkarn** (Tolcaron), **Corn.**, 19 May **1543**, adm. 1 Oct., vac. 1551; B.A. 24 July 1545, M.A. 4 Feb. 154$\frac{7}{8}$. Reg. 1544 'Robertus Talcaryne, etsi per voces non fuerit confirmatus in societate nostra, hoc ipso tamen ratificatus est quod juxta statuti prescriptionem in sodalitio commemoratus est absque calumpnia et contradictione duarum partium'; Autumn 1550 'iiii*li* M. Tolkarne ex communi consensu omnium sociorum.' Acta Curie Cancellarii p. 6 *b.*, 27 Feb. 154$\frac{5}{6}$ 'Comparuerunt M. Clemens Perrott et dominus Robertus Talcarun, et sese obligaverunt in summa decem librarum

ad usum domini Regis solvendarum, quod quidam Johannes Fitz
collegii Exon. *scolaris* comparebit et juri stabit in causa perturbationis
pacis inter ipsum et Richardum Flaxon [Turner 66] coram nobis
audienda et terminanda, quocunque tempore intra annum proximum
sequentem fuerit, vel alter eorum fuerit legitime submotus et restitutus,
sed et dictus Johannes Fitz similiter est obligatus in aliis decem libris
sterlingorum.' [Signed] Clement Parott, Robert Talcarn, John Fytz.

Nicholas **Gaye**, **Dev.**, el. 16 Oct. **1543**, adm. 23 Oct.; full Fellow
26 Oct. 1544; B.A. 17 Jan. 154¾, M.A. 4 Feb. 154⁷₉.

William **Corindon**, Corydon, Corndon (2 s. Henry), demy of
Magdalen 1540; **Corn.**, 16 Oct. **1543**, adm. 23 Oct., res. 26 July 1556;
B.A. 24 July 1545, M.A. 4 Feb. 154⁷₉, sup. B.D. 25 Jan. 155⅝;
appointed Rector 1553 in place of William More by Mary's Visitors;
Reg. 7 May 1551 'a Rectore et majore parte sociorum constitutum
est ut M. Corndon liber foret a studio sacrarum litterarum et operam
suam maxime daret rei medicae; cujus deinceps se sectatorem fore
sponte est coram Rectore et sociis professus; juxta injunctiones Regia
potestate nobis traditas'; Wood E. 29 says 'in medicorum scholam
commigravit 15 June 1551 cum consensu vice-cancellarii'; autumn
1543 'vis a M. [Hugh] Weston pro cubiculo, viii*d* ab eodem pro
cubiculo *scholastici* sui Cornedon.' R. of Lifton. Bloxam iv. 85,
Visit. Devon 236.

John **Fessarde** (Fezard), **Sar.**, el. 11 Dec. **1543**, adm. 12 Jan. 154¾,
vac. 1544 by being absent more than five months; B.A. 17 Jan.
154¾, resident 1551; M.A. 13 July 1554, State Papers 30 May 1558;
chantry priest of Mere 1543, V. of Tisbury 1544–65, both in Wilts,
R. of Donhead S. Mary 1555, deprived 1565, R. of Holy Trinity,
Shaftesbury 1556, V. of Great Fontmell 1559, both in Dorset;
Phillipps i. 210, 218, 222, 223; summer 1553 'iiis iiii*d* M. Pawe
pro M. Fezarde debitis illi olim cum esset socius.'

Philip **Randell** (s. Thomas, of Lamerton, Devon); **Dev.**, 23 Jan.
154¾, full Fellow 9 Mch 154⁵₆, res. 17 Oct. 1557; B.A. 24 July 1545,
M.A. 4 Feb. 154⁷₉, M.B., Rector 17 Oct. 1556—17 Oct. 1557,
Principal of Hart Hall 9 Mch 15⁴⁸₅₀–159⅞, bur. 11 Mch 159⅞ in
S. Peter's in the East, in his 85th year; the brass plate, still in the
Vestry in 1820, is quoted in Peshall 84, 88, and App. p. 12 it says
he *died* on 11 Mch; Athenæ i. 480. William Randall, of Milton
Abbott, Devon, was his heir, Wood's City i. 304. Turner 403 speaks
of Richard (? mistake for Philip) Randell, M.A., Principal of Hart
Hall, and Alice his wife, formerly wife of William Forest (he d. 1579).

In 1579 Hart Hall had 54 commoners on the butler's book, the 'lector catechismi' was Anthony Corano, a Spaniard (Clark i. 153, 156, Nat. Biog. xii. 253), and LL.D. of a foreign University, who sup. D.D. 2 Ap. 1576. The Chancellor called him before him 17 May 1582 to hear any charges as to his life and doctrine, 'having with me some of the French Church and others.' He was at Christ Church 1 Oct. 1586. The Hall (including Black Hall and gardens) was *taxed* 17 Sep. 1551 by M. Thomas Vivian and M. Maurice Bullocke, and by two burgesses, William Thomas and James Dodwell, at 33*s.* 4*d.*; securities Thomas Williams and James Colynson. Gillow iii. 367: Notes relating to Family of Randall, Rendell, and Rundell, by W. W. Rundell 1892.

Robert **Taynter, Sar.** 4 Dec. **1544**, in place of Pruett, after Pruett's second election, adm. 3 Jan. 154$\frac{4}{5}$; full Fellow 5 Jan. 154$\frac{5}{6}$, res. 25 July 1546 for a fellowship at Magdalen, when 'there was no one in the University capable of succeeding' (*see* a. 1551); B.A. 13 Nov. 1542, sup. M.A. 1548 and 1549, expelled 20 July 1552 from the Congregation of the University because, though an M.A. of 2 years' standing, he had never taken the oath, but recalled and took it the same day (Univ. Reg. i. 204, Clark i. 89); R. of Fonthill Gifford, Wilts 1550, B.D. 22 Feb. 155$\frac{4}{5}$; V. of Selborne 1555; Phillipps i. 214.

Thomas **Hill, Dev.** 17 Oct. **1546**, full Fellow 8 Nov. 1547, vac. Oct. 1549; sup. B.A. Mich. 1546, determined next Lent.

Robert **Capell** or Capull, **Corn.** 17 Oct. **1546**, vac. 1553; sup. B.A. 1549, ? R. of Willingale-Spain, Essex 1546.

Henry **Reynolds** or Renolds, **Sar.** 8, and adm. 18, Jan. **154$\frac{6}{7}$** in place of Taynter, vac. 1551; sup. B.A. 1549.

Maurice **Ley** or Lye, an Irishman, **Dev.** 16, and adm. 29, Jan. **154$\frac{6}{7}$**, vac. 1548; B.A. 1545 (Marsilius Lee), M.A. 4 Feb. 154$\frac{7}{8}$.

Robert **Newton, Dev.** el. 29 Mch (or 15 Ap.) **1548** in place of Maurice Ley, adm. 13 May, Rector 17 Oct. 1557–1559, Second Perpetual Rector 31 Oct. 1570, res. 4 Oct. 1578; B.A. 1552, M.A. 1 July 1557, B.D. 14 Feb. 157$\frac{5}{6}$ after 20 years' study in theology; R. of Bugbroke, Northants 1560, in Sep. 1575 the Bishop of Peterborough 'called him into residence'; had leave of absence 2 Feb. 157$\frac{7}{8}$ on prospect of a benefice: the second Fellow named in the Charter of Trinity 1555, but did not accept, Wood's Fasti a. 1557, Gutch iii. 107, 518, 520, Warton 316, 318, Clark i. 99.

William **Pascawe, Chapl.**, adm. 13 Feb. **154$\frac{8}{9}$**, ? vac. Lent 1552.

Stephen **Marks, Corn.** 29 Nov. **1549**, res. Oct. 1556; B.A. 1552, M.A. 11 July 1554, sup. B.D. 10 Oct. 1559; Rector 17 Oct. 1555–1556; the first Fellow of Trinity 30 May 1556, but quitted his fellowship 1560; Gutch iii. 518, Warton 316, 318, 321, 390, 394.

John **Collyns, dev.** 24 Dec. **1549**, vac. 1551, re-elected, again vac. 27 Feb. 156½; B.A. in 1552, M.A. 17 July 1553: sup. for licence to preach 8 July 1572 as **M.A.**, after 12 years' study in theology; Reg. Nov. 1560 'domum nostram in Catstreete una cum parva eidem contigua in annos 63 locavimus magistro Baylye medico, aliamque pandoxatoriam in parochia sancti Egidii Mᵒ Collins adhuc socio nostro in annos 50 ex suo ipsius desiderio': Clark iii. 24 he is confused with John Collyns, fellow 1540.

Robert **Venner, Dev.** 14 Mch 15⁴⁹⁄₅₀, adm. 31 July, vac. 1551.

Roger **Crispin,** exhibitioner Oriel 18 May 1547; **Dev.** 10 Ap. **1550**, res. 9 (10) June 1556; B.A. 8 Dec. 1554, M.A. 8 July 1558, M.B. July 1562; Fellow of Trinity 30 May 1556, vac. about All Saints 1562; residing in Exeter College 1560, Warton 400.

William **Peryam** (1 s. John, of Exeter, by Elizabeth d. of Robert Hone of Ottery; her sister Joan m. John, father of Sir Thomas Bodley), b. Exeter 1534; **Dev.** 25 Ap., but res. 7 Oct. **1551**; M.P. Plymouth 1562, barrister M.T. 1565, party to an Oxford suit 2 Mch 158⅝, Clark i. 106; Chief Baron of Exchequer Jan. 1593, and knighted, d. Little Fulford near Crediton 9 Oct. 1604; his 3 wife, Elizabeth d. of Sir Nicholas Bacon, and a benefactress to Balliol, d. 3 May 1621; of his 4 daughters and heiresses, Mary m. 30 July 1583 Sir William Pole the Antiquary, Elizabeth m. Sir Robert Basset, Jane m. Thomas Poyntz of Essex, Anne m. William Williams of Dorset; N. and Gleanings iii. 113, iv. 48, 150; Gutch iii. 79, 110, 113; a William Pirion was at Christ Church 1 Oct. 1551; Wood F. 28 p. 172.

John **Bonetto, Corn.** 25 Ap. **1551**, d. 2 July 1551, 'idoneus scolaris ditionis Cornubiensis non reperiebatur qui in eius locum eligeretur.'

Richard **Reede, dev.** 28 Ap. **1551**, forfeited for absence, but re-elected 17 Ap. 1557, deprived 24 June 1559; B.A. 8 Dec. 1554, B.C.L. 21 Feb. 155⁸⁄₉, ?V. of Coleridge, Devon 1554, ?incorp. as M.A. from Camb. 14 Oct. 1560; Univ. Reg. i. 243.

Edward **James** or Jamys, **dev.** 2 May **1551**, res. 14 June 1557; B.A. 9 Dec. 1553; ?V. of S. Michael Caerhays, Cornwall 1573,

? V. of Bovey Tracey, Devon 13 Aug. 1576–1577; autumn 1556 ' xii*d* M. Jamys primario Aulæ Albæ pro exscriptione libelli exhibiti adversum nos per M. Paule in curia domini Vicecancellarii.'

Thomas **Elston** or Eston, **chapl.** 30 May **1551**, ? vac. 1552.

Hercules **Ameridith** (2 s. Griffith, M.P. Exeter); **Dev.** 12 Oct. **1551**, vac. **1553**; Lent **1553** ' x*s* Herculi Ameridith ex communi sociorum consensu cum in Galliam proficisceretur '; sup. B.C.L. Oct. 1564.

Reginald **Daniell, Dev.**, adm. 23 Dec. **1551**, res. 3 Mch 155$\frac{5}{8}$; V. of Sancreed, Cornwall 1553.

Thomas **Martyn** (Martin major), **dev.** 18 Oct. **1552**; B.A. 9 Dec. 1553; Hutchins iii. **740**, Pits **763** (' Bercheriensis 1563,' ? the same), ? beneficed in Essex.

John **Martyn, Chapl.**, adm. 6 Dec. **1552**; B.A. in 1553; winter 1552 ' xiii*s* iiii*d* sacerdoti obeunti munus sacellani per estatem '; ? V. of Somerton, Som. 1554.

Richard **Tremayne** (s. Thomas, of Collacomb near Tavistock, by Philippa 1 d. of Roger Grenville of Stowe), B.A. Broadg. H. 154$\frac{7}{4}$; **Dev.** 28 Mch **1553**, M.A. 17 July 1553, B. and D.D. 15 Feb. 156$\frac{5}{8}$, vac. by flying to Germany in Mary's first year, re-elected 17 Oct. 1559 in place of Reede; vac. by absence 8 May 1560; of Broadg. H. 20 Feb. 156$\frac{1}{2}$; archdeacon of Chichester 7 Ap. 1559–1560 (Rymer, under Elizabeth p. 85); gave the College Montanus' Bible; R. of Doddiscombleigh, Devon 15 Jan. 156$\frac{0}{1}$, res. 1564; V. of Menheniot 1559–84, R. of Combe-Martin, Devon 1569; proctor in Convocation 1562, signed the document that established the Thirty-nine Articles, Wilkins' Concilia iv. 238, 240; Treasurer of Exeter 10 Feb. 15$\frac{59}{80}$– 1584, bur. Lamerton 30 Nov. 1584, will proved 15 Dec. 1584; m. Johanna d. of Sir Peter Courtenay of Ugbrook 19 Sept. 1569, she d. 1595; Eccl. Ant. iii. **72**; C. S. Gilbert's Cornwall ii. 293; Bibl. Corn. **778**, Visit. Corn. **617**; English Garner ii. 522, Grosart's *Townley MSS, Robert Nowell*, 202–3.

Roger **Evans, Corn.** 28 Mch **1553**, res. 26 May 1556; Fellow of Trinity 30 May 1556 when already B.A., sup. M.A. 8 Ap. 1559, res. 1559, Warton **401**; R. of Bridestowe, Devon 1571.

James **Farrant, Dev.** 14 Oct. **1553**; B.A. 8 Dec. 1554, d. 31 Jan. 155$\frac{6}{7}$.

William **Grylls, dev.** 23 Nov. **1553**, but does not occur again; perhaps the William Grylls, M.A., Fellow in **1541**, was re-elected for a short time.

Henry **Dotyn, dev.**, adm. 24 Mch **$155\frac{3}{4}$**; vac. 1560; sup. B.A. 25 Jan. $155\frac{5}{6}$; M.A. 31 Jan. $15\frac{59}{60}$; V. of Bampton 28 Feb. $155\frac{8}{9}$ 'by the resignation of John Dotyn' (Giles' Bampton xxxvii, Wood's Life, ii. 21) his uncle; resident 1565; ?R. of Stokeinteignhead, Devon 1569. Autumn 1556 'ii*s* ii*d* pro tribus foliis membranæ pro carta ad scribendum inventarium bonorum Collegii ex iussu Visitatorum, iii*s* iiii*d* domino Dotten pro exscriptione statutorum et inventarii bonorum Collegii quæ exhibita erant Visitatoribus.' He left £20 to the College.

Sampson **Spoure, Corn.**, adm. 11 Oct. **1554**, res. Ap. 1557; sup. B.A. 25 Jan. $155\frac{5}{6}$.

William **Woderoffe, Chapl.**, adm. 4 Ap. **1555**, vac. 1559, B.A.; V. of Cullompton, Devon 16 Feb. $155\frac{8}{9}$, R. of Lydeard S. Laurence, Som. 1561–73, d. 1573; Eccl. Ant. i. 114; State Papers Henry VIII iv. p. 2686.

Robert **Elston** (Eston, Eyston), B.A. Brasenose 9 Nov. 1554; **Sar.**, adm. 26 Ap. **1555**, vac. by absence 21 Mch $155\frac{8}{9}$. Winter 1555 'iiii*d* domino Elstone ad respondendum pro Collegio in curia domini Broun militis' [? in the North Hundred].

John **Neale, dev.** 4 Mch **$155\frac{5}{6}$**; B.A. 14 Dec. 1557, M.A. 28 Nov. 1560; Rector 18 Oct. 1560–1565, 'elected while B.A., such was the scarcity of Masters,' Perpetual Rector after Whitsuntide 1566, deprived by Elizabeth's Visitors 12 Oct. 1570 for refusing to appear before them; in 1568 had leave to visit his blind father and orphan nephews; Fellow of S. John's (was he a nephew of Alexander Belser first president of S. John's?); he reached Douay 1 June 1578, was sent to England 1580, imprisoned and banished 1585, Douay Diaries 27, 142–3, 159 (he was then 'old'), 261, 291 'Exoniensis'; Hist. of Kidlington (O. H. Soc.) 285; Bodl. Cat. *v.* Oxonia p. 920 (for Neale and Bereblock); Wood's Fasti a. 1557, Gutch ii. 169, Rot. Orig. 8 Eliz. p. 2, rot. 90. Chardener is called his *poor Scholar* 1564 (Clark i. 287), ? the same as John Chardon, fellow 1565.

Thomas **Pinche, Corn.** 27 May **1556**; B.A. 14 Dec. 1557, M.A. 24 July 1563; adm. Chaplain 13 Ap. 1559 in place of Woderoffe, res. 15 Aug. 1572. Winter 1561 'xxx*s* domino Pintch ex largitione sociorum qui solitis commodis privatur'; winter 1563 'xxx*s* M. Pynche ita uti ad sepius solitum est pro compensatione *Pretende*'; so Lent 1564 'xxviii*s* viii*d* Smale, Fortescue, Babbe, Napper, et Rysdon pro suffragiis et exequiis' (compensation for former profits).

George **Fitz** (? s. John, by Agnes d. of Roger Granville); at Ch. Ch. 24 Dec. 1554 'from Devon, age 17'; **Dev.** 10 June **1556**, but res. same day; no successor was elected till after the Vacation, because the Fellows could not agree; B.A. 9 Dec. 1556, perhaps at Inner Temple 1559 'from London.'

William **Cliffe, Dev.** 10 Oct. **1556**, d. 19 Jan. 155$\frac{7}{9}$.

Richard **Fountayne** (? 3 s. Hugh, Visit. Devon 368), **dev.** 10 Oct. **1556**, res. 17 Jan. 155$\frac{6}{7}$; sup. B.A. May 1556; M.A. 15 Feb. 15$\frac{58}{80}$, resident Lent 156$\frac{2}{3}$ and 1565, V. of Brent 8 May 1561, of Loddeswell 1573, both in Devon, canon of Exeter 1573; Monast. Exon. 372, Visit. Devon 368; Herbert Reynolds' *Odd Ways in Olden Days Down West* 1892 p. 19–20.

Christopher **Smale** (in 1567 and 1573 called an only child, his father living but mother dead, she was ill on 30 Mch 1567, his father d. 1574), **Corn.** 26 Oct. **1556**, vac. by absence in the plague time, re-elected 9 Mch 156$\frac{1}{7}$, res. 1575 rather than take the degree of B.D., Douay Diaries 9, 145, 148, 150, 153; B.A. 3 Mch 155$\frac{6}{9}$, M.A. 24 July 1563, Clerk of the Market 10 Oct. 1569, Reg. p. 99; John Oldacre of Derby, his *serviens*, **M.** 3 Dec. **1575** age 21.

Richard **Spicer, Dev.**, adm. 17 Ap. **1557**, vac. by absence 25 Feb. 156$\frac{0}{1}$; B.A. 1 Feb. 155$\frac{3}{9}$, M.A. 24 July 1563 : re-elected 27 Feb. 156$\frac{1}{3}$, res. 14 Oct. 1562; (probationer fellow Merton 1562, rejected 1563, Brodrick 265;) re-appointed as the first Petrean Fellow 1566, res. 23 June 1567; made Reader 1566, and allowed the same year to teach boys in the country.‑

Thomas **Kempthorne** (o. s. John Ley *alias* Kempthorne, of Tonacombe in Morwenstow, by Thomasin d. and h. of Jordan), **Corn.** 17 Ap. **1557**, vac. by absence 1 May 1560; B.A. 3 Mch 155$\frac{9}{9}$; V. of Morwenstow 1560–94, bur. there 29 Ap. 1594; m. 8 Sep. 1562 Thomasin d. of John Cholwell; Coll. Corn. 447.

Francis **Banger**, or Beanger, **Sar.** 15 June **1557**, vac. by absence 26 June 1559; R. of Winterbourne Abbas, Dorset 1558; Hutchins ii. 198.

Thomas **Fortescue, Dev.** 17 Oct. **1557**, res. 10 Feb. 155$\frac{9}{9}$, (? at Corpus 2 Nov. 1560), re-elected 2 Dec. 1561 in place of Bellew; ? at Middle Temple 1561 as 2 s. Edward; full Fellow 20 Mch 156$\frac{2}{3}$, in charge of the College during the plague of 1564; sup. B.A. 8 Ap. 1559; M.A. 29 Oct. 1562; re-appointed as Petrean Fellow 1566, and permitted to travel in France and elsewhere for four years to study medicine or law, with an allowance of £6 13s. 4d. and the rent of his rooms; res. 1569; Athenæ ii. 342. A Thomas Fortescue wrote *the Foreste* 1571, translated from Pedro Mexia's *Silva de varia* *lecion*; Warton's *Poetry*, Ticknor i. 494, Bullen's *Marlowe* xxiii. Was he Thomas Fortescue of Dartmouth, who d. 1602 and left a bequest to the College?; *Fortescue Family* ii. 26.

John **Farrant, dev.** 27 Jan. **$155\frac{7}{8}$**, vac. by absence 30 Mch 1559.

John **Babbe**, Exhibitioner at Oriel 1551; at S. Mary H. 11 Aug. 1552; **Dev.** 19 Jan. **$155\frac{8}{9}$**, vac. by absence, re-elected 9 Mch $156\frac{4}{5}$; B.A. 14 Dec. 1561, sup. M.A. 10 Mch $156\frac{4}{5}$.

William **Pollard**, **Dev.** 16 Feb. **$155\frac{8}{9}$**, vac. by absence 25 Feb. $156\frac{4}{5}$; B.A. 4 Dec. 1561, at Inner Temple 1563 as of Horwood, Devon; Lysons' Devon cxxv, Visit. Devon 597, Visit. Corn. 372.

Richard **Braye**, **Corn.** 17 Ap. **1559** in place of Pinche (transferred to Chaplaincy); B.A. 4 Dec. 1561, res. 4 Feb. $156\frac{3}{4}$ on being el. and adm. to All Souls 3 Feb.; B.C.L. 19 Aug. 1566, sup. D.C.L. 3 Oct. 1573; Principal of New Inn H. 1570–1. Lent 1566 'xiiii*li* vi*s* viii*d* a vidua Polkynhorne et domino Braye de Collegio Omnium Animarum pro Gwynner debitis nobis hoc pascate iam instante.' Reg. 22 Oct. 1591; Gutch's *Collectanea* ii. 277.

William **Shepereve** (Shepree, Sheperye), Exhibitioner at Oriel 19 Aug. 1556; **Sar.** 17 Oct. **1559**, res. Mch $156\frac{4}{5}$, re-elected 18 Ap. 1566, in place of Napper; re-elected 30 June 1567 into his own vacant place, vac. 1568, Athenæ i. 669; B.A. 4 Dec. 1561. Reg. 1561 'mense Julii locavimus et concessimus tres indenturas, unam (de Long Witnam) domino Shepreve in annos 41: aliam (de Gwynner) Ricardo Neale; terciam (of a house in S. Mary Magdalen parish) Somersbye.' Douay Diaries 6, 25, 104, 274, 342 (letter from him), 360.

Robert **Napper** (3 s. James, of Swyre, Dorset), **Sar.** 17 Oct. **1559**, adm. 6 Jan. $156\frac{0}{1}$, full Fellow 17 Jan. $156\frac{2}{3}$, vac. by absence 11 Ap. 1566; B.A. 29 Oct. 1562, M.P. Dorchester 1586–7, Bridport 1601, Wareham 1604–11; at Middle Temple 1565, Chief Baron of Exchequer in Ireland 1593, knighted 1593, Sheriff of Dorset 1606, bought estate of Middlemarsh, d. 20 Sep. 1615, his wife Magdalen d. 5 Mch $163\frac{5}{6}$; Wood's Fasti a. 1562; Hutchins ii. 185, 370, 770, 772, iii. 125, iv. 483.

Ralph **Gittisham** (Gittsom, Jutsam) singing clerk at Magdalen 1559; **Dev.** 17 Oct. **1559**, vac. by absence in plague time 25 Feb. $156\frac{4}{5}$, re-elected May 1565, allowed to teach boys in the country 10 Aug. 1566, being poor, and so 8 Mch $156\frac{6}{7}$ (so Wylliams 1564, and Carpenter 1575, and H. Paynter 1577), vac. 7 Dec. 1567; his brother was very ill in 1567; B.A. 29 Oct. 1562, M.A. 17 May 1566;

Bloxam ii. 40; winter 1560 'vi*d* domino Jutsam pro exarando presenti compotu'; winter 1561 'xviii*d* Gutsam pro exscribenda compositione de Mahinnet.'

William **Paynter, Corn.** 7 May **1560**, res. 30 June 1575; B.A. 4 Dec. 1561, M.A. 14 Ap. 1565, 'in actu stetit' 18 Feb. 156⅝, B.C.L. 18 Feb. 15⁶⁹⁄₁₀; Reg. a. 1614; Lent 1564 'ii*s* vii*d* pro emendatione vitrei in cubiculo domini Paynter et Bedlow'; R. of Halstowe, Kent 1564, of Swyre, Dorset 1567, ? through James Napper of Swyre, father of Robert Napper fellow 1559. He gave evidence 1614 as remembering the settlement of the Petrean benefaction.

Richard **Southerne** (Sotherne, Sowthorne), b. Exeter, scholar of Trinity 7 June 1558 age 16; **Dev.** 14 June **1560**, vac. by absence 20 Aug. 1562; B.A. 28 May 1560; Warton 421; a Thomas Southern, Treasurer of Exeter Cathedral 1531–57, is mentioned in the Computus of summer 1532.   State Papers 1532 p. 733.

Henry **Chichester, Dev.** 22 Oct. **1560**, res. 3 July 1563.

John **Bellew,** or Bedlow (2 s. William Bellew, of Ash in Brampton, by Anne d. of Sir Hugh Stukley), **Dev. 1561,** res. 1 Dec. 1561; B.A. 10 May 1563, M.A. 4 July 1566, sup. B.C.L. 1570; living 1620 as priest of Bratton Fleming, and bur. 20 Ap. 1622 at Monkleigh. Lysons' Devon cxxxiv, Visit. Devon 69.

Edward **Risdon** (s. Giles, of Bableigh), bap. Parkham 1 June 1541, **Dev.** 4 Mch 156⁰⁄₁, res. 20 Jan. 156¾ 'duplici sacerdotio donatus' (i. e. having taken two livings, viz. R. of Mawgan, Cornwall 1562, of Sutcombe, Devon 1564); B.A. 29 Oct. 1562, 'sojourning in College' 1565, M.A. 17 May 1566; Jesuit priest, one of the founders of Douai College; no one appeared for some time to stand for the fellowships of Chichester and Risdon; Athenæ i. 513, Visit. Devon 649, Dodd's *Church History*, Trans. Devon Assoc. 1886, N. and Gleanings i. 152, 175.

William **Wyatt,** Wyet, Wiott, (s. Philip), bap. Braunton 14 Dec. 1539, **Dev.** 13 Oct. **1562,** adm. 5 Feb. 156¾; B.A. 23 July 1563, M.A. 17 May 1566, B.D. 14 Feb. 157⅝; Sub-rector 1574; had leave of absence 1573 on account of his mother's health; R. of Whitestaunton, Som. 1576, of Tawstock, Devon 4 June 1577, had leave of absence 7 Feb. 157⁷⁄₉ because of a dispute as to this living; d. in college 5 Mch 157⁸⁄₉, and bur. in S. Michael's, Oxford. Visit. Devon 317, Eccl. Ant. ii. 119, Guteh ii. 169.

Peter **Randell, dev.** 15 Oct. **1562,** adm. 1 Ap. 1564, full Fellow 10 Ap. 1565, res. 1583; B.A. 18 Ap. 1567, M.A. 16 Feb. 157½.

NOTE.—Reg. 1562, 'decretum portionem panis quo per singulos dies sumus pasturi (nimirum decimam terciam singulorum panum portionem que lucrum panis vulgo, Anglice the vantage, appellatur) haud ulterius aut in communem aut in economi sed rectoris duntaxat utilitatem transferri adeo ut in posterum semper liceat rectori decimam terciam paitem singulorum panum per universum annum in collegium nostrum adductorum sibi quasi ius suum iustissimum vendicare, recipere et in proprium sui ipsius usum prout sibi soli quoquo tempore videbitur dispensare et collocare, preter stipendium sibi a fundatore concessum in statutis expressum.

Preterea quemvis tam sociorum quam commensalium et battillariorum intra mensem aut aliquanto minus spacium si recte facileque fieri possit quovis termino cuiuslibet anni finito economo statim pro battis omnibus satisfacturum ut is etiam ipse pinsoribus ceterisque quibus debet singulis (quantum ad nostram victus rationem spectat) debita statim persolvat.'

17 Oct. 'Chichester, Wiet, et Randall electi in communarum participationem nondum admittuntur quia hac tempestate (in tanta scilicet charitate rerum prope omnium) magis gravatur collegium quam ut singulos sustinere queat.'

156⅔, 'Sub quadragesimam hoc anno, in tanta nimirum annone, edulii, ceterarumque rerum caritate, preterea cum erarii penitus exhausti tum numeri nostrum omnium quorum victus, ac stipendia vel a statutis concessa approbante vetustate non modo censum nostrum quotannis exhauriunt sed etiam magnopere superant (quod ex annuali computu per multos retro annos constitit) haud modica ratione habita, statuimus cuilibet licitum esse socio per fusius tempus quam statuta liquidis verbis patiantur (quamvis statutorum sensui sive fundatoris sententie tanta iam penuria coacti refragari haud existimemus) rusticari, spaciari seu peragrare nempe ad biennium modo literis vacet et honestis incumbat disciplinis donec debita cuique stipendia, communas et id genus alia largiri consueta nobis commode ministrare collegium suffecerit. Ita tamen quemlibet abesse oportet ultra consuetum et a statuto prescriptum tempus, ut omni alio emolumento pro huius absencie ratione privatus cubiculi sui duntaxat commodo fulciatur unde socius in dies agnoscatur et iuris nostri particeps assidue pro tempore habeatur.'

14 Oct. 'Rector obtulit computum suum coram sociis (ut mos inolevit) reddendum. Sed quod duo duntaxat socii tunc temporis domi adessent, nempe Mr Pinche et dominus Brey, visum est illis et rectori eundem in aliud tempus cum plures socii sufficientes testes domum sese reciperent (consopita nimirum pestilencia que tam Oxonie quam aliis multis in locis ea tempestate ingruebat) differre, et inchoatum (prout suadent statuta) relinquere. Eademque de causa nec rector constituto tempore creatus erat nec computus sub natalem domini (inchoatus) conficiebatur quem tamen vicem gerens uti prius reddere voluit.'

1564, Mch 30, 'decretum ut cui liberet liceret sese absentare ingruente denuo pestilencia usque ad diem veneris sub festum Dionisii salvo cuiusque iure concessaque cuique ita absenti summa xiiiid' (i. e. weekly).

Some of the sojourners behaved badly, 'adeo dulce illis erat nondum ad virilem etatem provectis hominibus in summam licenciam parum pecunie parcentibus vivere; Unde profecto satis superque exploratum habuimus statutorum morumve quantumvis brevem intermissionem boni ordinis esse solutionem magistratuum et rectorum contemptum ac certe ansam et maximam quasi fenestram ad omnem fere nequitiam.'

NOTE.—Winter 1563, 'xls a M. Geare pro reddito nuper acquisito nobis per eas pecunias que nobis ea sola de causa date sunt et tradite a preposito et sociis

Collegii beate Marie [i.e. Oriel] prout auctoramentum seu litera obligatoria plenius testatur.'

NOTE.—Reg. 23 July 1564 'dominus Pinch et dominus Smale inceperunt in artibus ac statim a prandio in viperiis (quod aiunt) una cum magistro Fortescue sodali necnon [Olivero] Whiddon et [Gulielmo] Stocker suggenariis (qui paulo ante inceperunt [8 May 1563]) agitabant et steterunt. Tercio dehinc die una omnes gradum complevere.'

NOTE.—In 1564 Humphrey Farrand was butler, Thomas Smallpage manciple, Clark i. 288.

NOTE.—Summer 1564. . . 'Hic animadvertendum antiquum computandi ordinem ex unanimi nostrum consensu, pestilencia nimirum ingravescente, cessasse ac singulis sociis ab hoc tempore segregatis metuque pestis peragrantibus summam quatuordecem denariorum septimanatim usque ad diem Veneris sub diem Dionisii esse concessam, proinde hoc modo computandum est ut sequitur, "xi*s* viii*d* pro communis 10 sociorum 7 septimana," etc.'; autumn 1564, 'iii*li* iiii*s* ii*d* M. Smale quod sibi custodiam Collegii, quantumvis grassante pestilencia seu alio quovis casu contingente, assumeret.'

NOTE.—Summer 1565 'iiii*d* bedello pro exemplare novorum statutorum Universitatis.'

John **Wylliams, Corn.** 9 Feb. **$156\frac{3}{4}$**, adm. 17 Oct. 1564; B.A. 6 Ap. 1566; M.A. 21 Nov. 1569: a teacher in the country 1569 *necessitate cogente*; removed 12 Aug. 1572 for not taking his M.A. at the proper time; M.A. 12 Oct. 1573; Clark i. 86.

Raymond **Westlake, Dev.** 1 Mch **$156\frac{3}{4}$**, adm. 17 Oct. 1564, vac. by absence in plague time, re-elected 9 Mch $156\frac{4}{5}$, adm. 15 Ap.; full Fellow 27 Oct. 1565, res. 30 June 1580; B.A. 6 Ap. 1566, M.A. 21 Nov. 1569; gave two silver cups to the College in 1580. Douay Diaries 184, 20 Jan. 1582; Clark i. 244, 389 William Hobson, his *serviens*, **M.** 3 Dec. 1575 age 23.

Giles **Crede, dev.** 1 Mch **$156\frac{3}{4}$**, adm. 12 May 1565, vac. by absence 25 Feb. $156\frac{5}{6}$, V. of S. Minver, Cornwall 27 Jan. $157\frac{6}{7}$–1593, bur. 3 Ap. 1593; Maclean iii. 20.

Simon **Trippe**, at Corpus 14 Ap. 1559, Fellow 12 Feb. 1563 'lector humanitatis'; **Dev.** 3 Mch **$156\frac{4}{5}$**, res. 19 May 1565, preferring to remain at Corpus; B.A. 18 Ap. 1564, M.A. 10 July 1568; Fowler's *Corpus* 122, 133–7.

John **Chardon, Dev.** 3 Mch **$156\frac{4}{5}$**, adm. 14 Oct. 1565 (the Reg. 24 Oct. 1566 has a curious entry about him), had leave of absence 18 May 1567 to take a living, res. 6 Ap. 1568; B.A. 18 Ap. 1567, M.A. 27 Mch 1572, B.D. 15 Nov. 1581, D.D. 14 Ap. 1586; V. of Heavitree 9 Aug. 1571–1595, of Colebrooke 16 May 1573, R. of Tedburn S. Mary 1581–95, Canon of Exeter 1581–95; sojourning in College 1572; R. of Cahir 1596, Bishop of Down and Connor

4 May 1596, Warden of the College of Youghall 1598, d. 1601;
Sermon on Funeral of Sir Gawen Carew 22 Ap. 1584 at Exeter,
publ. London 1586; Wood's Fasti a. 1567, 1572, 1581, Athenæ i.
715, ii. 845, Prince 200, Eccl. Ant. i. 48, Cotton's Fasti Hibern. iii.
204, Tanner 165 *v.* Chardon and Charlton, Clark i. 43, 134, N. and
Gleanings v. 16, Nat. Biog.   John Charlton dedicated his translation
from Cornelius Valerius' Ethics, *The Casket of Jewels,* 1571, to Sir
Gervas Clifton as 'your dayly oratour,' and speaks of himself as 'late
fellow of Exeter College,' and then schoolmaster of Worksop in
Notts; he speaks, puritanically, of 'brutish Venus plaies.'

John **Simpson, Sar.** 9 Mch 156⅘, adm. 1 Nov. 1565; B.A. 18 Ap.
1567, M.A. 5 Dec. 1570; left in charge of the College during the
plague of 1570; d. 1577, probate of will 10 Sep. 1577, Griffiths 60.
His *serviens,* Edmund Brindley, of Derby, **M.** 3 Dec. 1575 age 21;
and John Newman is called 1577 his late *poor scholar.*

James **Brooke, Dev.** 1 Nov. 1565, adm. 27 June 1566; M.A., vac.
1567.

Henry **Battishill** (? 3 s. John, of Westwyke; Visit. Devon 52),
Dev. 6 Feb. 156⅝, adm. 27 June 1566; B.A. 29 Nov. 1569, M.A.
26 June 1572; removed 3 Ap. 1573 for holding the benefice of
Lifton over a year (from 1571), worth more than £8 in the King's
Books, and thus requiring residence.

NOTE.—Seven fellows were named by Sir William Petre soon after Whitsun-
tide 1566, and admitted on 30 June, except Spicer, who was admitted 2 July.
Henceforth the day of election is 30 June, unless otherwise noted; but that for the
Shiers fellowship (1744) on Dec. 26.

John **Neale** (Fellow 1556), Rector 1566, deprived 12 Oct. 1570.

Richard **Spicer** (Fellow 1556), **Petr.,** adm. 2 July 1566, res.
23 June 1567 'altero genu egrotaret.'

John **Berblocke** or **Beareblocke,** b. near Rochester, Fellow of
S. John's 1558, B.A. 29 Mch 1561, M.A. 13 Feb. 156⅝; ? named
Petr. on 2 Ap. 1566, adm. 30 June and made Dean; in 1570
Sir W. Petre allowed him leave of absence for 4 years, B.C.L. 1572
in some foreign university; Proctor 1569 (with Thomas Bodley);
author and artist; made views of Colleges, now in the Bodleian, for
Elizabeth's visit in 1566, Gutch ii. 159, iii. 103; Tanner 82, 538,
Nat. Biog.

Edmund **Lewkenor** (? s. Edward, groomporter, d. in the Tower
1566), B.A. S. John's, Camb. 156⅘, from diocese of Chichester
(Cooper ii. 251), Fellow 1563; **Petr. 1566,** incorp. Oxford 1 July,

M.A. 21 Ap. 1567, res. 26 Nov. 1577, d. in Belgium.   J. Morris'
Condition of Catholics under James I pp. xi, cci, ccliv, Douay Diaries
10, 153, 156, 162, 165, 167, 222, 226, 230, Jessopp's *One Generation
of a Norfolk House* 151, 157; ? wrote *The Estate of the English
Fugitives* 1591, printed in Sadler Papers ii. 478.   Rice Powell of
Brecknock was his *serviens* 3 Dec. 1575 age 16.

Kenelm **Carter**, B.A. 18 Feb. 156⅝, **Petr. 1566**, res. 25 Jan. 158⅔;
M.A. 21 Nov. 1569.

John **Howlett**, b. Rutlandshire 1548, B.A. 26 June 1566; **Petr.
1566**; allowed to incept 21 Nov. 1569, but 'non stetit in comitiis';
allowed to travel abroad Mch 1570; a Jesuit at Louvain 1571
aged 24, d. Wilna 17 Dec. 1589.   Parsons, the Jesuit, edited a book
1580 under his name; Nat. Biog.

Walter **Crosse**, not yet B.A., **Petr. 1566**, soon vac. by absence ;
Thomas Fortescue (*see* 1557 and 1567) was appointed in his place,
who res. 1569.

James **Raynolds** (4 s. Richard, and brother of John president
of Corpus; Wood's Life i. 304, Fowler's *Corpus* c. 6), **Petr. 1566**;
B.A. 29 Nov. 1569, M.A. 20 June 1573, College Reader 30 June 1577
'qui nostrae iuventuti praelegeret et eam instrueret vel historiarum
cognitione vel poetarum, vel aliarum disciplinarum preceptis ut leges
nostrae postulant imbueret'; d. 1577, inventory of goods 21 Oct. 1577,
Griffiths 52.

Richard **Bristowe** (b. Worcester about 1538), B.A. Ch. Ch. 17 Ap.
1559, M.A. 26 June 1562; opponent in Nat. Philos. 3 Sep. 1566 at
Elizabeth's visit; **Petr.** 2 July **1567**, vac. 1572; went to Louvain,
Reg. 1570 'trans mare literis incumbit,' D.D. Douay 3 Aug. 1579,
President of Douay and one of the translators of the Bible, d. at
Mr. Bellamy's house, Harrow 14 Oct. 1581 ; Gutch ii. 159, Warton
408, Eadie's Hist. of Bible ii. 116, Lingard vii. 27, Simpson's Campion
11, 46, 93, 94, 204 Apology to W. Fulk, 288–9, 303 his widowed
mother Jane had lost her other son; Hazlitt's *Handbook of English
Literature*; Gillow i. 300, Nat. Biog. i. 316, 321, vi. 356, ix. 204
(censured by W. Fulke, and Oliver Carter).   A MS. in Lord Macclesfield's library at Shirburn castle, Oxon, pressmark North Library 113
c 37 *Lyfr Duwiol* i. e. a Godly book, is a Roman Catholic primer
in Welsh subsequent to the Reformation.   At fol. 70–107 are *y ffyd
Gristnogaid* &c., 'the Christian faith and the mode whereby it is
shewn to the illiterate,' by Mr. Dr. Bristow.

John **Leach** (? s. John, of Crediton), **Dev. 1567** in place of

Fortescue, res. 20 May 1577 (his letter is preserved); B.A. 5 July 1567, M.A. 5 Dec. 1570, B.D. 14 Feb. 157$\frac{5}{8}$; had leave of absence 1573 to tend his aged father, and 20 Oct. 1575 to defend a right of patronage; R. of Washfield 14 Jan. 1574, of Arlington, of Talaton 1576, all in Devon, Eccl. Ant. i. 139; m. Elizabeth d. of Sir Alexander Napper, Visit. Corn. 283, Visit. Devon 526; sup. licence to preach 14 Jan. 157$\frac{9}{7}$; Chancellor and Canon of Exeter 6 Ap. 1583, d. 1613; Wood's Fasti a. 1575.

John **Batt, Dev. 1567**, vac. by absence 1579; B.A. 24 Nov. 1570, M.A. 27 June 1573.

Robert **Carpenter, Sar. 1568**, removed 30 June 1579 for absence in Ireland; B.A. 22 Nov. 1571, M.A. 18 June 1575; 10 Nov. 1575 allowed leave of absence for 4 years to teach in a school or the like, because of his poverty.

Nicholas **Cliffe, Dev. 1568**; res. 1584, when he gave the College the Epistles of Erasmus; B.A. 29 Nov. 1571, M.A. 2 July 1574, B.D. 7 Dec. 1584; his father just dead in July 1581; R. of Rewe, Devon 20 May 1585, res. 1590, Eccl. Ant. ii. 148; R. of Maiden Newton, Dorset 1586; R. of W. Horndon 3 Nov. 1591, patron Thomas Petre; R. of Ingatestone 17 Nov. 1609, patron John Petre; R. of W. Tilbury 21 Dec. 1616, patron James I, all in Essex; d. 1619; Athenæ iii. 122, Newcourt ii. 342, 348, 598.

Thomas **Hole, Dev. 1568**; 16 Dec. 1577 leave of absence for 3 years in Devon for his health's sake; removed 30 June 1579 for absence at the University of Paris; B.A. 22 Nov. 1571, M.A. 2 July 1574; Douay Diaries 122.

Ralph **Sherwine**, of diocese of Lichfield, **Petr.**, full Fellow 10 July **1568**; appointed by Sir William Petre after his new gift of three tenements to Exeter College; vac. 1575, having received leave 4 July from Sir John Petre to study medicine abroad; B.A. 22 Nov. 1571, M.A. 2 July 1574; made a priest at Douay 23 Mch 157$\frac{9}{8}$; hanged 1 Dec. 1581 with Campion; Wood's Fasti a. 1571, 1574, Athenæ i. 478, Howell's State Trials i. 1064, Dodd's Church History; J. Morris' Troubles of our Catholic Forefathers; Douay Diaries 8, 27, 184, Simpson's Life of Campion 108–20, 183, 189, 257, 280–1, 298, 316–18, 322, Pits 778, Tanner 667. His brother's daughter Helen married William Allen, linendraper and citizen of London: Hist. Comm. v. 473 mentions a *Vita et Martyrium Rodolfi Sheruini sacerdotis*, and that his uncle was John Woodward.

Edmund **Cogan, Petr. 1570**, adm. so young that his probation was continued a second year, and Dun considered his senior (letter of John Wodeward 20 Feb. 15$\frac{69}{70}$, and of Sir John Petre 31 May 1572, in Reg.), full Fellow 2 July 1572, B.A. 3 Áp. 1574, had leave of absence 6 Aug. 1576 and 16 Dec. 1577 to look after affairs which *illius et patris capiti imminebant*, expelled 1579 for breach of statutes, when the Commissioners ordered £10 to be paid him : Reg. 24 Jan. 15$\frac{79}{80}$. N. and Q. 29 Sep. 1877 p. 255; Letters of administration for a B.A. of this name Oxford 4 Oct. 1639.

Robert Newton (Fellow 1548), Rector 31 Oct. 1570, res. 4 Oct. 1578.

William **Dun** or **Donne** (y. s. Robert, of London), **Petr. 1570,** Sub-rector 158$\frac{1}{2}$, res. 26 June 1583; B.A. 9 Feb. 15$\frac{69}{70}$, M.A. 20 June 1573, M.B. 27 Feb. 15$\frac{79}{80}$, M.D. 21 Jan. 158$\frac{2}{3}$, Fellow Coll. of Phys. 1592, Lumleian lecturer Dec. 1602 ; Wood's Fasti a. 1581, 1582, Munk i. 102, was practising medicine 1582 ; had leave 15 Ap. 1575 to go abroad for 4 years, and again 23 July 1580 to visit his sister who was dangerously ill.

Vincent **Marston**, exhibitioner Oriel 7 Nov. 1567, his place was filled up 15 Mch 156$\frac{8}{9}$ 'discedentis'; B.A. Alban H. 16 Feb. 157$\frac{0}{1}$; **Chapl.** 12 Oct. **1572,** res. 30 May 1577 ; M.A. 1 July 1573, Canon of Exeter 1577, R. of Lezant 1577, of Lanreath 1583, both in Cornwall; Wood's Fasti a. 1574 (Devonshire men of the name).

Henry **Paynter, Corn. 1573,** res. 1587; B.A. 1 July 1573, M.A. 27 June 1577 ; 28 Oct. 1577 had leave of absence to teach boys, being very poor ; in 1584 gave some Lexicons, and Plato, Plutarch, and Thucydides to the college; V. of Seaton, Devon 1612; Visit. Corn. 353.

John **Cory** or Currye, B.A. 15 Nov. 1570, **Corn. 1573,** M.A. 2 July 1574; 4 July 1575 had leave from Sir John Petre to study medicine abroad, vac. 1578; Visit. Devon 235, Athenæ i. 478, Douay Diaries 8, 276.

Oliver **Whiddon** (3 s. Sir John), B.A. 4 Feb. 156$\frac{9}{1}$, M.A. 8 May 1563, **Petr.** 27 Oct. **1573;** he had been sojourning in the College 1562 and 1565, and been Canon of Exeter 1567 and Archdeacon of Totnes 5 June 1568, and wished the honour of being on the foundation of the College, res. 26 Nov. 1573 ; R. of North Bovey 1562, of Combeinteignhead 1572, of Haccombe 21 May 1575, all in Devon, and of Yoxhall, Staffs.; will proved 10 Dec. 1580; Wood's Fasti a. 1563, Athenæ i. 483, Prince 760; Visit. Devon 355; Oliver's Bishops 292 : Clark ii. 6, 32 ; see the curious dispute about his will in Herbert Reynolds' *Odd Ways in Olden Days Down West* 1892 p. 18.

John **Coningsby** or Connisby (s. Sir Henry, of N. Mims, Herts; Visit. Herts 45), at Ex. Coll. 1572; **Petr. 1574**, vac. by absence 1580; on 26 Feb. 157⅞ the grace of John Cuningsbie was to be refused for a year unless he made full apology and submission in Congregation for his ill mind in religion and calumnies and irreverent behaviour to some members of Congregation, Clark i. 38 : killed at Ostend.

John **Cornelius** or Cornellis, b. of Irish parents at Bodmin, **Corn. 1575**, expelled 3 Aug. 1578 for popery by Royal Commissioners; 'Cornelius *alias* Mohun' was hanged at Dorchester 4 July 1594; J. Morris' Troubles of our Catholic Forefathers ii. 24, 97, 99, 127, 154, 335, 408; Douay Diaries 156, 160, State Papers Addenda Oct. 1593 p. 356, Nat. Biog.

Reginald **Bellott** (1 s. Francis, of Cosham, Wilts, afterwards of Bochym, Cornwall, by Ann d. of Reginald Mohun of Boconnoc), **Corn.' 1575**, res. 30 June 1584; B.A. 3 Mch 157¾, M.A. 27 June 1577 'concionator'; incorp. Camb. 1581; sup. licence to preach 18 May 1582; in 1583 disputed Sir John Petre's *mode* of nominating to the Petrean Fellowships, but John Popham attorney general, and Thomas Egerton solicitor general decided against him, and he was deprived of all rights under the Petrean Statutes, letter of Council 22 July 1583 in Reg.; the Council also ordered Sir W. Petre's arms and some verses on a dial, which had been defaced, to be renewed; V. of Menheniot 1584; in 1581 had leave of absence to read a theological lecture in Exeter Cathedral; gave the College a Hebrew Bible; will proved Exeter 5 June 1600 by his widow Dorothy d. of John Dynham of Wortham (? m. about 1585); State Papers 27 May 1583 Raynold Bellott and the Fellows thank Walsingham for inhibiting the Earls of Bedford and Leicester, and the Rector, from proceeding any further in the extraordinary election of Sir John Petre's scholars, inclosing statement of particulars; Visit. Corn. 26, Visit. Devon 316 : Carew styles 'Billet, Tremayne and Dennis, three well born, well learned, and well beloved incumbents of Menheniot.'

Arthur **Stratford, Petr.** full Fellow **1577**, had leave of absence 28 Oct. 1577 to carry on a suit with a Bristol man, vac. 30 Sep. 1578 by absence; Douay Diaries 167, 263, and index.

NOTE.—There was a Visitation of the College by the Bishop of Exeter 3 and 4 Feb. 157⅞.

Edmund **Leighe, Chapl.**, adm. 30 May **1577**, B.A. 3 Mch 157$\frac{4}{5}$, had leave of absence 22 Jan. 157$\frac{7}{8}$ to cure a bad hand: John Marks did chaplain's duty for him; d. 1579, a year of plague.

Nicholas **Mercer** or Merser, pleb., at the College 1572, **M.** 3 Dec. 1575 age 17 [but Clark ii. 63 note], B.A. 11 Feb. 157$\frac{4}{5}$; **dev. 1577**, res. 30 June 1586; M.A. 14 Mch 157$\frac{8}{9}$; Proctor 1584; sup. licence to preach 1 July 1586; V. of Rousdon, Devon 14 Oct. 1581, Canon of Exeter 1583, V. of Bishopsnympton 1585, R. of Pitt's Portion at Tiverton 1591; d. 1597; Eccl. Ant. ii. 82.

Thomas **Bruning** (arm. f.), b. Wilts, **M.** 20 Dec. 1577 age 23, **sar. 1578**, res. 1584; B.A. 27 Jan. 158$\frac{1}{2}$; lic. to practise in medicine 16 Ap. 1602; 'nomen adhuc inter Romano-Catholicos provincie Bercheriensis bene notum' (18 Nov. 1588); his brother d. 1583.

John **Tooker** or Tucker (a John Tuckar of Cornwall **M.** after 3 Dec. 1575 age 20, ? son of John Tucker of Helland), **Petr. 1578**: on 14 May 1580 had leave of absence to visit his aged parents; vac. by m. 1583 (? Anne d. of Hugh Pollard, Visit. Corn. 521); B.A. 11 July 1581, M.A. 7 July 1584; R. of Helland 1580, of Cardynham 1583, both in Cornwall, d. 1602; Maclean ii. 12.

Thomas **Pawley**, pleb., **M.** 3 Dec. 1575 age 17, Clark ii. 64, 99; **Corn. 1578** (another candidate had equal votes, but the Vice-Chancellor, William Cole, nominated Pawley), res. 30 June 1595: B.A. 13 July 1582, M.A. 10 July 1584.

John **Eveleighe** (2 s. John, of Holcombe in Ottery, Visit. Devon 1564 ed. Colby p. 94, W. Antiq. x. 73), **M.** after 3 Dec. 1575 (? 1577) age 16; **Petr. 1578**, full Fellow 4 Oct. 1578, res. 3 Nov. 1593; B.A. 11 July 1581, M.A. 4 June 1584, incorp. Camb. 1585; Proctor 1590, Principal of Glouc. H. 1599, of Hart. H. 1599–1604 (having been Vice-Principal to Principal Randell from 1593); on 3 Nov. 1593 had a lease of Hart Hall from the College for 21 years, and of Tintinhull, Som. for 20 years; d. of the plague, State Papers 14 Aug. 1604; bur. S. Mary Magdalen church, Oxford 10 Aug. 1604; a copy of his will in College Transcripts fol. 47: 'he left certain lands and tenements to Exeter College, which were refused by the Society.' Clark i. 32, 129, 191, 397–8; m. Prudence d. of Dr. Robert Barnes, fellow of Merton, she was bur. S. Giles 14 Aug. 1652 (?); Wood's Life i. 279.

Thomas **Halle**, B.A. 21 Feb. 157$\frac{6}{7}$ 'Hale,' **Petr. 1578**, res. 16 July 1583; incorp. Camb. 1578, sup. M.A. Oxford 4 May 1579, ? M.A. Camb., incorp. Oxford 11 July 1585; R. of S. Olave's,

Hart St., London 1583, res. 1590, of Beaumont, Essex 1591, res. 1599.

Stephen **Fountayne** (? 2 s. Thomas, by Joan Pole; Visit. Devon 368), pleb., b. Devon, **M**. 20 Dec. 1577 age 19; named **Petr**. 30 June **1578**, full Fellow 4 Oct. 1578, res. 10 July 1588; B.A. 22 Nov. 1581, M.A. 4 June 1584, R. of Petertavy, Devon 1587; married.

Thomas Glasier, B.A. Ch. Ch. 12 Dec. 1561, M.A. 17 Jan. 156⁴⁄₅, B.C.L. 5 Nov. 1569, D.C.L. 29 Nov. 1577, Proctor 1570; el. and adm. **Petr.** full Fellow 4 Oct. **1578**, on pressing letters from Sir John Petre; el. Rector 21 Oct. 1578; gave the College some books 1582; advocate Doctors Commons 13 Oct. 1590 (Coote's *Civilians*); Pro-Vice-Chancellor 1591, d. 9 Mch 159½; administration bond 19 Ap. 1592, Griffiths 24; Wood's Fasti a. 1577; State Papers 1568 p. 324, Gutch ii. 247, Turner 352, Clark i. 41, 157.

John **Heywood**, pleb., of Oxford, **M**. Brasenose 28 Ap. 1576 age 16; probably the same as John Heiwod of Ex. Coll., b. Oxon, **M**. on or after 20 Dec. 1577 age 20, pleb., since these early dates are confused; adm. **Petr.** 1 Mch 157⁸⁄₉, full Fellow 6 July 1579, had leave of absence 6 Aug. 1580 to obtain an exhibition; refused his B.A. 17 Dec. 1583 by the University, Clark i. 227; res. 7 Mch 158¾. Reg. 11 Sep. 1580 'The chamber under the Rector's lodgings now held by John Haywood [it abutted on the Rector's private garden] is to be annexed to the Rector's lodgings, he paying 20s. yearly to the College for its use '; Douay Diaries 13, Pits 753.

Thomas **Duck** (s. Philip, pleb., of Heavitree, Exeter, who d. just before Sep. 1580, by Dionis Pine), **M**. 20 Dec. 1577 age 20, **Chapl**. 24 Ap. **1579**, adm. 1 May, res. 1584; B.A. 23 Mch 158⅔; R. of S. Mabyn, Cornwall 10 Mch 158¾, d. 1629, his wife Elizabeth survived him; Maclean ii. 462, Visit. Devon 309.

Adrian **Whicker**, (s. John, of Gittisham, Devon, R. of Kirtlington, Oxon, d. 1616), **Dev. 1579**, res. 16 June 1589; B.A. 7 Feb. 157⅞, M.A. 19 Feb. 158⅔; Clark iv. 442, Oxf. H. Soc. Collect. ii. 105.

William **Endecotte**, pleb., **M**. 20 Dec. 1577 age 19; **Dev. 1579**, d. 1582.

Gilbert **Coode** (4 s. Walter, of Morval, by Edith d. of Peter Coryton), bap. 28 Aug. 1552, **M** Hart H. 22 Dec. 1573 age 17 (?): **Corn. 1579**, res. 30 June 1588; B.A. 7 Mch 157⁸⁄₉ (Clark i. 54), M.A. 19 Feb. 158⅔; V. of Liskeard 8 May 1589, of S. Wenn 1589, d. 163⅜; Visit. Corn. 95, Lake iv. 316, C. S. Gilbert's Cornwall ii. 73. 641.

William **Huish** or Hewyshe, pleb., **M.** after 3 Dec. 1575 (? 1578) age 19 (his father just dead in Sep. 1580, Clark i. p. xxiv, ii. 64, 99); **Dev. 1579**, B.A. 13 July 1582, M.A. 27 June 1584; res. 30 June 1593, being adm. R. of Kilkhampton in Cornwall 22 Sep. 1592 on pres. by Sir Bernard Grenvyle; canon of Wells 1593, d. 1611.   His terrier is printed in Exeter and Plymouth Gazette 3 Dec. 1879.

Christopher **Pope**, b. Dorset, **M.** Jesus 20 Dec. 1577 age 15; **Sar. 1579**, res. 24 June 1586; B.A. 7 Feb. 158⅔, incepted as M.A. 7 July 1584, R. of Long Bredy, Dorset 1585; gave Plutarch's Moralia to the College 1585.

Richard **Sandye**, pleb., b. Devon, **M.** 20 Dec. 1577 age 18; **Dev. 1580**, res. 30 June 1590; B.A. 21 Jan. 158¾, M.A. 28 June 1586, R. of Great Linford, Bucks 1589; gave Jewel's Apology and Hieroglyphica Pierii to the College; Athenæ ii. 103.

William **Orforde**, B.A. Magd. H. 7 June 1580; **Petr. 1580**, res. 29 June 1614; had leave of absence 15 July 1581 to visit his sick and aged father, M.A. 3 May 1583, B.D. 4 July 1594, lic. to preach 2 May 1595; R. of Clyst Hydon, Devon.

Richard **Mercer**, **Dev. 1582**, res. 30 June 1596; B.A. 14 July 1585, M.A. 11 July 1588, sup. B.C.L. 24 May 1595; Clark iv. 298.

Lewis **Barfield**, pleb., b. London, **M.** Balliol 2 May 1581 age 18; recommended by the Bishop of London, adm. **Petr.** full Fellow 26 June **1583**, res. 6 Nov. 1592; B.A. 6 July 1586, M.A. 28 June 1589; V. of Heston, Middlesex 3 Mch 159½, of Dunmow, Essex 2 Feb. 159¾, d. 1597, Newcourt i. 646, ii. 226.

Alexander **Crosley**, pleb., b. Oxford, **M.** Jesus 1 Dec. 1581 age 18; then at Ex. Coll., B.A. 28 June 1583, adm. **Dev.** full Fellow 29 June **1583**, res. 17 Nov. 1597; M.A. 16 May 1586, sup. B.D. 13 Nov. 1611, R. of Wickham, Hants 1611.

Paul **Leighe**, **Petr. 1583** (Thomas Upham had equal votes, but the Chancellor named Leighe), d. 1587.

Thomas **Upham**, pleb., of Devon, **M.** Magd. H. 25 Feb. 158⁰⁄₁ age 20; **Petr.** 22 July **1583**, res. Nov. 1592; B.A. 10 Nov. 1586, M.A. 30 June 1589; R. of E. Worlington, Devon 1591–1603, V. of S. Andrew's, Plymouth, d. Aug. 1603, bur. there, left a widow Frances, and 5 daughters, Ann, Mary, Judith, Frances, Elizabeth; W. Antiq. xi. 25.

Nicholas **Gill**, pleb., b. Devon, **M.** 17 Nov. 1581 age 17, **Petr.** 29 Mch and full Fellow 10 July **1584**, res. 25 Sep. 1595 to avoid expulsion for grave scandal; B.A. 8 Ap. 1587, M.A. 29 Oct. 1589,

V. of Brent, Devon 1600; gave Erasmi Adagia to the College 1584;
A. H. A. Hamilton's *Quarter Sessions* 1878 p. 84.

Eustace **Marshall**, pleb., b. Devon, **M.** Alban H. 20 Dec. 1577
age 17, B.A. 26 Jan. 158$\frac{9}{1}$, M.A. 2 July 1583; pres. **Chapl.** 13,
and adm. 21, June **1584**, res. 1586; R. of Langtree, Devon 1585.

John **Wills, Dev. 1584**, res. 30 June 1593; B.A. 4 Dec. 1587,
M.A. 13 Ap. 1592, R. of S. Mary Bothaw, London 12 June 1601,
pres. by Dean and Chapter of Canterbury, res. 1606, R. of Bentley-
parva, Essex 1 July 1606 S.T.B.

Thomas **Cole, Sar. 1584**, B.A. 13 Feb. 158$\frac{3}{4}$, M.A. 26 June 1587,
incepted 10 July; res. 1595.

James **Pallawin**, pleb., **M.** 17 Nov. 1581 age 20, **Corn. 1584**, res.
1601; B.A. 7 July 1584, M.A. 26 June 1587, B.D. 7 Dec. 1597,
V. of S. Keverne, Cornwall 1598, of Brailes, Warwicks. 1612.

John **Dotyn** or Dotten, pleb., b. Devon, **M.** 1 Feb. 158$\frac{3}{8}$ age 18,
Dev. 1584, d. 1586.

Thomas **Denys** or Dennis (s. Thomas, of Creed, Cornwall, by
Margaret d. of Thomas Tremayne of Collacombe), b. Devon, **M.**
19 Oct. 1582 age 18, **Dev. 1586**, res. 17 May 1601; B.A. 6 July
1586, M.A. 28 June 1589, B.D. 10 July 1600; pres. to Menheniot
3 May 1600, and held it for 37 years, d. 1637; m. Grace, d. of John
Polwhele; Visit. Corn. 36, 138, Coll. Corn. 203.

Thomas **Mercer**, pleb., **M.** 11 Oct. 1583 age 13, **Dev. 1586**, res.
15 June 1601; B.A. 29 Oct. 1589, M.A. 23 June 1592.

Martin **Reade**, pleb., b. London, ed. S. Paul's sch., **M.** S. John's
1575 age 17; Clark i. 19, 369 being poor he went to Cambridge,
came back 6 Aug. 1577; B.A. 26 Nov. 1577, M.A. 7 June 1581
(incorp. Camb. 1585); adm. **Chapl.** 24 Oct. **1586**, res. 1592; B.D.
14 July 1592. Reg. 13 July 1592 'data est venia M. Reade ut possit
abesse a 13° die Julii usque ad 13um diem anni sequentis; modo sub-
stituat sufficientem deputatum ad celebrandum preces in Collegio
secundum statuta; et conciones habeat sufficientes in parochiis nostris
ecclesiasticis.'

James **Eveleighe** (? 7 s. John, of Holcombe in Ottery; Visit.
Devon 336, and see a. 1578), b. Devon, **M.** 26 Feb. 158$\frac{4}{5}$ age 16,
Petr. 1587, res. 1601; B.A. 9 July 1590, M.A. 10 May 1593,
? knighted. The Rectory of Kidlington was leased to him by the
college 16 July 1601 for 10 years at a fine of £300. Reg. 11 Nov.
1593 'admissi sunt duo commensales, (? Abraham) Smith discipulus
M. Jacobi Eveleigh, et (John) Sparke discipulus domini Georgii

Hockins'; John Sanford, of Bucks, his servant, **M.** 20 Feb. 159$\frac{5}{8}$ age 28.

William **Helme**, pleb., of Wilts, **M.** Alban H. 10 July 1584 age 19; **Sar. 1587**, res. 30 June 1615; B.A. 9 July 1590, M.A. 10 May 1593, B.D. 23 Mch 160$\frac{8}{4}$, B.C.L. 9 July 1613; V. of Evendale, Worcs. 1610, of Bishopston, Wilts 1613–39, had a year's leave of absence 1614 on account of a suit about his living, d. 1639; Prince 49, Athenæ ii. 330, iii. 265, Gutch iii. 112, 116, Phillipps ii. 7, 19.

Ralph **Bosisto** (? s. Ralph, of S. Levan, by Catherine d. of Walter Tregosse, Visit. Corn. 51; his father died before 21 July 1587), **M.** 11 Oct. 1583 age 19, B.A. 21 Feb. 158$\frac{6}{7}$, **Corn. 1587**, res. 30 June 1596; M.A. 29 Oct. 1589; V. of Constantine, Cornwall 1598, bur. 23 Oct. 1601.

George **Hocken** or Hockyns, pleb., **M.** 8 July 1586 age 16, **Corn. 1588**, res. 30 June 1602; B.A. 9 July 1591, M.A. 6 May 1594, B.D. 20 Ap. 1602; Clark i. 203.

Elias **Cocke**, pleb., of Essex, **M.** S. John's 2 July 1585 age 18; B.A. 27 Nov. 1587; adm. **Petr.** 19 July 1588, M.A. 30 June 1591, expelled by Sir John Petre 13 June 1592; his right to expel was very doubtful.

John **Jones** or Johnes, pleb., of Devon, **M.** Queen's 2 July 1582 age 15, B.A. 10 Nov. 1586; **Dev. 1589**, M.A. 23 May 1590; res. 30 June 1593; R. of High Bickington 1592, V. of Holcombe Burnell 30 Mch 1595–1617, both in Devon; Hutchins iii. 603.

Isaiah **Farrington** or Farindon, pleb., b. Devon, **M.** 11 Oct. 1583 age 18, B.A. 21 Feb. 158$\frac{4}{7}$, **Dev. 1590**, M.A. 18 May 1591, B.D. 6 May 1602, res. 27 June 1604; R. of Lympstone 21 May 1603, ? V. of Otterton 1621, d. summer 1630.

Thomas Holland (2 s. William, of Burwarton, Salop), b. Ludlow, exhibitioner Oriel 23 Sep. 1569 to 1573, ? at Middle Temple 1571 (? at Gray's Inn 16$\frac{09}{10}$); Chaplain Fellow of Balliol 13 Jan. 157$\frac{2}{3}$, Rhetoric Reader at Balliol 1575–7, B.A. 9 Dec. 1570, M.A. 21 June 1575, B.D. 13 July 1582, D.D. 15 July 1584, Canon of Salisbury 1590, R. of Rotherfield Grays, Oxon 1591, Reg. Prof. Div. 1589; responded before the Queen, when she was at Oxford 22–28 Sep. 1592, and before James I in 1605, Nichols' *Royal Progresses*; Chaplain to Leicester in the Netherlands; adm. **Petr.** full Fellow 29 Mch **1592** in place of Glasier; Rector soon after in place of Glasier on Sir John Petre's and Queen Elizabeth's recommendation; but the Headship was disputed and Holland was not elected till

24 Ap., after N. Mercer, who was really elected, resigned his claim
at Lambeth, before Archbishop Whitgift, the Bishop of Oxford, and
Lord Buckhurst Chancellor of the University 1 Ap. 1592; d. 17 Mch
161½, bur. 26 Mch in S. Mary's Chancel, Richard Kilbye preached
his funeral sermon, Pattison's Casaubon 412; his will proved 20 Ap.
1612, Griffiths p. 31.   His widow Susanna sold Holland's stable to
Prideaux, who made a kitchen of it.   Gutch ii. 244, 282, iii. 107;
Reliquiae Bodleianae 158, 192 (building at Ex. Coll.), 251, 291 (door
towards Ex. Coll.); Peshall 69; Westcote's Hist. of the Bible 148;
Yorkshire Diaries (Surtees Soc. 1875) p. 410; Wood's Life i. 426,
State Papers 22 Oct. 1617, 11 Aug. 1618, Birch's James I i. 164,
Nat. Biog.   There is a picture of Holland in the Hope Collection,
Oxford.   His servant Robert Todmorton M. 20 Feb. 160⁴⁄₅ age 60
(did not sign, but made his mark, Clark i. 230 twice, iv. 235).

Thomas **Came**, pleb., b. Devon, M. 15 June 1588 age 18, **Petr.**
17 June **1592**, res. June 1606; B.A. 3 Feb. 159½, M.A. 12 Nov. 1594;
Athenæ ii. 445.

Edward **Toose** or Towse, of Suffolk, M. Lincoln 28 Nov. 1581
age 18, B.A. 10 July 1585, M.A. Exeter 23 May 1590; **Petr.** full
Fellow 25 Nov. **1592**, res. 20 June 1600; B.C.L. 27 Oct. 1595, Clark
i. 114; he gave the College a silver saltcellar.

Nathaniel **Aylmer** or Elmer (s. John, bishop of London), b. Leics.,
M. 28 Ap. 1592 age 16, **Petr.** full Fellow 25 Nov. **1592**, d. 3 Mch 159⁴⁄₅.

Narcissus **Hele**, pleb., b. Devon, M. 13 Dec. 1583 age 16, B.A.
21 Feb. 158⁶⁄₇, M.A. 4 Feb. 159⁰⁄₁; **Chapl.** adm. 3 Mch 159⅔, res. 1597;
B.D. 10 July 1600; V. of S. Keverne, Cornwall 1598, R. of Bishop's
Teignton 30 Mch 1604, res. 1 Dec. 1610, of South Pool 1605, of
Ideford 1 Dec. 1610 (patron Sampson Hele of Gnaton for this turn,
Visit. Devon 462), all three in Devon; Eccl. Ant. i. 65, 121, iii. 4;
his widow Alice administered to his effects 10 June 1613; Lysons'
Devon p. cxxiv.

Anthony **Lapthorne**, b. 1572, B.A. Balliol 19 June 1593; **Dev.**
1593, vac. by marriage 25 Ap. 1600; M.A. 8 July 1596; chaplain to
James I, R. of Lanrake, Cornwall 1600, of Minchin Hampton, Glouc.
7 May 1611, of Tretire, Herefs. till deprived 9 Oct. 1634; named R.
of Sedgefield, Durham May 1647, by the Westminster Assembly, but
opposed by James Innes, Hist. Comm. vi. 147; Gardiner's Personal
Government of Charles I ii. 211, 352.   Hearne 11 Oct. 1712, State
Papers 1611 p. 29, 1640 Ap. p. 93, 1 Nov., 3 and 11 Dec. 1656,
7 Ap. 1657.

Simon **Baskerville** (s. Thomas, apothecary, of Exeter), b. Exeter 1573, bap. S. Mary Major 27 Oct. 1574, **M.** 17 Mch 159½ age 18, **Dev. 1593**; in 1608 had leave to travel for two years; res. in France ' 1 June 1609, Roman style' (? at Blois); B.A. 8 July 1596, M.A. 24 Ap. 1599, M.B. and D. 20 June 1611, Proctor 1606, at Lincoln's Inn 1625, physician in Fleet St., London, Fellow of Coll. of Phys. 1615, physician to James I and Charles I, knighted at Oxford 30 Aug. 1636 by Charles I, d. 5 July 1641 age 68, bur. in a north aisle of S. Paul's, London; Clark i. 129, 192, Hearne 2 Mch 172⁰⁄₁, Rawlinson MSS. class C. No. 402 fol. 13 ; Nat. Biog.

Christopher **Gover**, pleb., **M.** 17 Mch 159½ age 18; **Dev. 1593**; B.A. 8 July 1596, d. 1599.

John **Bonner** (s. William, scrivener, London), **M.** Balliol 10 Oct. 1589 age 12; **Petr.** 20 Nov. 1593, full Fellow 5 July 1594, B.A. 4 Dec. 1596, d. 5 Mch 159⅞.

Everard **Chambers**, under-butler, adm. **Petr.** full Fellow 13 June **1595**, res. 1623; B.A. 12 July 1598, M.A. 17 May 1601, B.D. 14 Nov. 1611; Clerk of the Market 1615-6 (O. H. Soc. Coll. ii. 106); Gutch iii. 111; Reg. 2 Sep. 1605, 21 Feb. 160⅚, 13 Mch 160½ 'concessae sunt mutuo de pecuniis Collegii sex librae M. Baskervile decano et totidem M. Chambers aedificaturis nova musea supra duas illas cameras superiores quae sunt iuxta Collegium Jesu : ea conditione uti illi ipsi aut quicumque alii, qui tribus annis proxime sequuturis easdem sunt possessuri, annuatim solvant Collegio quatuor libras, donec nimirum duodecim librae mutuo datae resolvantur : eodem tempore illis concessi sunt duo arborum trunci, quibus solidius edificia conficiant'; 2 Sep. 1605 'concessa est potestas M. Chambers supra portam posticam Collegii nostri, quae sita est iuxta Collegium Jesu, aedificia construendi eademque constructa ad suum commodum quiete possidere per annos quadraginta, solvendo annuatim Collegio pro reditu quatuor denarios'; 21 Feb. 160⅚ 'empta sunt nova aedificia impensis constructa Magistri Chambers supra portam posticam precio ducentarum viginti sex librarum sex solidorum et octo denariorum, tribus vicibus solvendorum'; 17 July 1610 'usus cubiculi M. Baskervile ei concessus est usque ad diem octavum Decembris proxime sequentem, modo concedat interea eius successori musæum et locum in eo commodum commorandi; usus cubiculi M. Winniff ei concessus est usque ad 8ᵘᵐ diem Decembris, modo nihil postulet pro musaeis ab ipso constructis in eodem et musæum locumque commodum concedat eius successori ibidem interea commorandi ; usus cubiculi M. Spicer ei similiter concessus est, modo interea musæum locumque commorandi commodum eius successori concedat et proventum musæorum pro ultima anni quarta parte ad cubiculi illius reparationem'; 9 Sep. 1612 'decretum erat ut qui musæa possiderent in Turri occidentali annuos reditus in cautionem M. subrectori præsolvant, quam si qui forent qui solutionem recusarent aut subterfugerent, eo ipso ab omni iure quod prius occuparant sunt amovendi, et in eorum vices praedictaque musæa alii arrogandi'; 18 June 1613 'conclusum fuit inter M. Chambers et M. Amy decanum, secundum statutum de dissentionibus sedandis pag. 30, ut predictus M. Amy solveret M. Bursario Juniori ad insequens festum Michaelis £5 1s. 1d., et predicto M. Chambers £2 10s. ad festum proxime sequens nativitatis Christi pro tertiis cubiculi superioris Januae posticae attigui, quod predictus M. Chambers suis sumptibus auxerat.' Chambers' receipt is at beginning of Computus Book H.

John **Flemmyng** (s. Nicolas, of Landithy in Madron, by Elizabeth d. of Jenkin Keigwin of Mousehole), **M.** 22 Feb. 159$\frac{2}{4}$ age 18, Reg. 20 Feb. 1593 'admissi duo *commensales* Alford discipulus M. Henrici Paynter et Flemming discipulus domini Hocken'; **Corn. 1595**, res. 27 June 1613; B.A. 12 July 1598, M.A. 17 May 1601, B.D. 14 Nov. 1611, D.D. 9 Nov. 1613: Proctor 1609; R. of Camborne, Cornwall 1612-17, Chaplain to James I, First Warden of Wadham 2 Sep. 1613, d. 17 Mch 161$\frac{6}{7}$, bur. in Wadham Chapel, admin. 12 May 1617; Gutch iii. 595, Clark i. 210, 403, Hist. Comm. v. 479; Gardiner's Wadham 20, Jackson's Wadham 76, 82.

Thomas **Winniffe** (s. John, pleb., d. 1630, bur. Lambourn), b. Sherborne, bap. 1576, **M.** 22 Feb. 159$\frac{2}{4}$ age 18; **Sar. 1595**, res. 30 June 1609 as holding livings above the statutable value (adm. to Willingale Doe, Essex in May, to Lambourn 15 June 1608, and held both till 1642); B.A. 12 July 1598, M.A. 17 May 1601, B.D. 27 Mch 1610, D.D. 5 July 1619, incorp. Camb. 1628; chaplain to Prince Henry and Prince Charles, and to Charles when king; Dean of Gloucester 10 Nov. 1624-1631, of S. Paul's 8 Ap. 1631-1654, Bishop of Lincoln 5 Jan. 164$\frac{1}{2}$, d. Lambourn 19, and bur. 26 Sep. 1654; left the living of Lambourn by will to his nephew Peter Mews; Hooker i. p. 101 ed. 1845, Gauden's *Suspiria Ecclesiae Anglicanae* 614; Athenæ iii. 434, iv. 813; Milman's *S. Paul's* 330; Newcourt; Hutchins iv. 211, 262; State Papers 13 Ap. 1622, 17 and 28 Sep. and 7 Nov. 1624, S. R. Gardiner iv. 305, Clarendon ed. 1819 iv. 423.

Richard **Carpenter**, pleb., b. 1575, **M.** 28 May 1592 age 15, B.A.

19 Feb. 159⅝; **Corn. 1596**, res. 30 June 1606; M.A. 7 Nov. 1598, B.D. 25 June 1611, D.D. 10 Feb. 161⅝; ? V. of Cullompton 12 Feb. 1601, res. 1626, Eccl. Ant. i. 114; R. of Sherwill 1605, Georgeham 1606, Loxhore 1611, d. Loxhore 18 Dec. 1627 age 52; m. Susanna d. of John Trevelyan of Nettlecombe, Som.; Trevelyan Papers (Camden Soc.) iii. p. xxv. (battels at that time); Drake 246; Reg. 16 July 1602 'dimidia pars pecuniarum mutuo concessa est M. Carpenter, quas expensurus esset in novis extruendis musaeis supra cameram suam, quae inferiori parti sacelli ex adverso opponitur; eadem prorsus conditione et lege qua antea 13° die Martii pecuniae mutuo datae sunt magistris Baskervile et Chambers aedificaturis'; Clark i. 213, Nat. Biog.

George **Hakewill** (3 s. John, of Exeter, by Thomasin d. of John Peryam), bap. S. Mary Arches, Exeter 25 Jan. 157⅚, **M**. Alban H. 15 May 1595; **Dev. 1596**; allowed to travel for four years in 1604; was at Heidelberg one winter, with Abraham Scultetus and David Parrey, *Answer to Dr. Carrier* 1616 p. 29; 11 July 1609 allowed 8 terms towards his B.D. as absent over sea; res. 30 June 1611; B.A. 6 July 1599, M.A. 29 Ap. 1602, B.D. 27 Mch 1610, D.D. 2 July 1611 (Clark i. 208), at Lincoln's Inn 1614; Archdeacon of Surrey 7 Feb. 161⅝, Chaplain to Prince Charles, but imprisoned with his brother William in Aug. 1621 for opposing the Spanish match; State Papers 2 Dec. 1612, 29 July 1619, 28 July and 25 Aug. 1621, 4 Jan. 1622, 30 Dec. 1661; Rector of Exeter College 1642; d. 2, and bur. 5, Ap. 1649 at Heanton Punchardon, Devon, of which he was Rector since 1611, will proved 2 May; m. Mary Ayres widow, of Barnstaple, 4 July 1615 (mar. lic. 23 June, Exeter); she was bur. Barnstaple 5 May 1618; Westcote 545, Fuller's Church Hist. ed. Oxon ii. 265, Anne Halkett's Memoirs p. iii, Arber's *Stationers' Register* iii. pp. 211, 237, 271 (Answer to Camden), 298*b*, iv. 16; Chanter's *Barnstaple* 104, Dredge's *Sheaves* 70. A letter of his occurs in Parr's Life of Usher p. 398: Reliquiae Bodleianae 67, 352: Laud's *Chancellorship* 254, Nat. Biog. xiii. 150; Reg. 15 May 1602 'admissi sunt commensales Johannes et Georgius Williams fratres germani et *scholares* inceptoris Georgii Hakewill'; 8 Sep. 1665 'M. Crediford a Rectore et scholarium tunc in sacello presentium maxima parte nominatus est ad concionandum in sacello Octobris die 5°, juxta pacta inter Collegium et Rev. virum doctorem Hakewill, cui nominationi ipse ibidem expresse consensit' (i.e. to celebrate the consecration of the Chapel, see 1623). Coxe's Cat. of Corpus MSS. no. cccvii. Richard

Goring dedicated his *Theophilus* to Hakewill, ed. i. 1610, ii. 1612. There is a portrait of him in the College Hall, and an engraving.

Alexander **Spicer**, son of a minister, b. Somerset, **M.** 8 July 1591 age 16; **Petr.** 27 July **1596**, res. 1600; B.A. 28 Feb. 159$\frac{4}{5}$, M.A. 5 Nov. 1597, incorp. Camb. 1608; Dean of Killaloe 26 Mch 1628– 1637, promoted by Sir Arthur Chichester, Lord Belfast; he was Chichester's chaplain, and wrote an elegy on his death 1625; Arber's *Stationers' Register* iii. 281*b* (Sermon at Coleraine), iv. 98; Athenæ ii. 408; Visit. Devon 273. Prince says he was born at Exeter.

Francis **Hore**, pleb., b. Bucks, **M.** 3 Feb. 159$\frac{7}{8}$ age 18; at All Souls; **Petr.** 20 May **1597**; in 1608 allowed to travel for 4 years, further leave given 21 Mch 161$\frac{1}{2}$, res. 18 Ap. 1612; B.A. 2 June 1600, M.A. 11 May 1603.

Richard **Pyle**, pleb., b. Devon, **M.** 20 Feb. 159$\frac{5}{6}$ age 18; adm. **Chapl.** 14 June **1597**, d. 1598.

Robert **Edgerley** (s. Francis, of Milton, Oxon), bap. Milton 5 May 1577, **M.** 24 Oct. 1595 age 17 (with his brother Francis age 16) adm. **Petr.** 25 Nov. **1597**; B.A., res. 1602; Visit. Oxon.

Richard **Raynolds**, pleb., b. Devon, **M.** 20 Feb. 159$\frac{5}{6}$ age 17, adm. **Chapl.** 13 Ap. **1598**, res. 22 Aug. 1608; B.A. 8 May 1601, M.A. 30 June 1603; V. of Wittenham 1607, sequestered 1647; V. of Egloshayle, Cornwall 21 Mch 16$\frac{09}{10}$–1614; R. of Stoke Fleming 1614, of Woodleigh 1615, both in Devon; Maclean i. 414.

Robert **Vilvaine** (s. Peter, pleb., Steward of Exeter, d. 5 Sep. 1602, his widow Ann d. 24 Sep. 1616, both bur. Allhallows, Exeter), b. Exeter, **M.** 22 Feb. 159$\frac{3}{4}$ age 18, **Dev. 1599**, res. 30 June 1611; B.A. 9 May 1597, M.A. 11 July 1600 (incorp. Camb. 1608), M.B. and D. 20 June 1611; physician at Exeter; founded Library in Lady Chapel of the Cathedral; published 1654 *Theoremata Theologica, Compendium of Chronography, Epitome of Essays* ('a fardel of 76 fragments' Wood); presented the 2 former to the Library, with an address printed opposite the title. He rescued Allhallows, Exeter, from demolition 1658, being a parishioner, by buying it from the Corporation for £50; d. 21 Feb. 166$\frac{2}{3}$ age 87, bur. in the choir of the Cathedral, Polwhele's Devonshire ii. 17, 32; m. Ellenor d. of Thomas Hinson of Tavistock (Visit. Glouc. 83), she was bur. Allhallows 7 Dec. 1622; Athenæ iii. 631, Gutch iii. 112, 115, 116; J. E. Bailey's *Fuller* 349; Izacke's Reg. 142, 156–9; W. Antiq. v. 3, viii. 185; N. and Gleanings i. 187, ii. 166, iii. 6; Clark i. 129, 192; Cotton's *Records of Exeter* 178–9; State Papers 17 Ap., 10 June,

23 Sep. *bis*, 4 and 29 Oct., 4 Nov. 1662.   Richard Isack, chamber-layne of Exeter, gave Vilvaine's *Enchiridion Epigrammatum*, Lond. 1654, to .Wood 1680, Wood's Life ii. 485.

John **Standard** (s. Edward, by Elizabeth Holloway of Water Eaton), b. Oxon 1581, **Petr. 1600**, res. 30 June 1614 on m. Bridget d. of Sir John Lenthal of Cutslow : B.A. 30 June 1603, M.A. 25 May 1606, B. and D.D. 10 Feb. 161$\frac{9}{7}$; J.P. for Oxfordshire, lord of Whithill in Tackley, Oxon, R. of Tackley, d. there 16 Dec. 1647; see 1644; Visit. Oxon 252 ; Hist. of Kidlington (O. H. Soc.) 47, 51, 152–3, 156.

William **Prouse** (? 2 s. Richard, mayor of Exeter, Visit. Devon 628), b. Devon, **M.** 15 Ap. 1597 age 16, **Petr. 1601**, res. 30 June 1610; B.A. 22 Oct. 1600, M.A. 30 June 1603 ; V. of Culham, Oxon 1614–45, of Wittenham, Berks 1617, d. 164$\frac{4}{5}$.   Reg. 16 Feb. 16$\frac{99}{10}$ 'concessa est proxima præsentatio vicariæ de Longwitnam magistro Prouse post resignationem magistri Raynolds sive cessionem sive amotionem quamcunque'; 12 Dec. 1611 'concessa est M. Prowse quondam socio proxima praesentatio vicariae nostrae de Longwittnam, ad spatium tantum sex annorum, quæ tunc denuo reddenda est in manus Rectoris et Scholarium; ad quod præstandum obligavit se, et alium stipulatorem adiunxit'; 6 Oct. 1617 'concessa fuit advocatio rectoriæ nostræ de Longwitnam M. Guilielmo Prowse sub con-ditionibus in obligatione quadam expressis gerente datum 9 October 1617.'

Christopher **Collyer**, pleb., **M.** 22 Feb. 159$\frac{3}{4}$ age 16, B.A. 28 Feb. 159$\frac{7}{8}$, M.A. 17 May 1601; **Corn. 1601**, res. 27 June 1604 ; V. of Lanlivery 1604, of Egloshayle 26 Nov. 1614, bur. 5 Feb. 163$\frac{2}{3}$; Maclean i. 415.

John **Trelawny**, pleb., **M.** 22 Feb. 159$\frac{3}{4}$ age 16, B.A. 8 June 1597, M.A. 11 July 1600 ; **Dev. 1601**, res. 30 June 1606; C. of S. Tudy, Cornwall 1606, bur. there 13 Jan. 161$\frac{4}{5}$; Maclean iii. 314.

John **Prideaux** (4 s. John, pleb., and kinsman of Edmund Prideaux attorney-general ; Maclean ii. 208), b. Stowford, Ivybridge 17 Sep. 1578, **M.** 14 Oct. 1596, *subpromus* of the College (his letters in N. and Gleanings v. 134 about the chance of obtaining a fellowship), **Dev. 1601**, vac. 1612; B.A. 31 Jan. $\frac{1599}{1600}$, M.A. 11 May 1603, B.D. 6 May 1611, D.D. 30 June 1612 ; Rector 4 Ap. 1612 ; m. (1) Mary granddaughter of Dr. Taylor, (2) Mary d. of Sir Thomas Reynell, widow of William Goodwin, dean of Christ Church; his sons John and Matthew were bur. at S. Michael's, Oxford 1 Sep. 1622, Robert

14 May 1624, Peshall 27, 149, app. p. 2 ; his son Col. William fell at
Marston Moor, Stukeley's Mem. i. 3–4 ; Matthias was Fellow 1644.
Wood's Fasti i. 299, 362, ii. 5; Prince 654, 661, 696. He says in
his dedication of *Euchologia* to his daughters Sarah Hodges and
Elizabeth Sutton, 'you being the only survivors of the nine children
that God had blest me with by your long since deceased mother . . .
that famous martyr Dr. Rowland Taylor . . . because by your mother
you are lineally descended from him . . . the chain of pearl he only
left your great grandmother, his dear wife, was no other but the Book
of Common Prayer.' Athenæ i. 265–273, ii. 103, iii. 265, iv. 807,
index (Dean Fell made unjustifiable alterations in Wood's account of
Prideaux), Wood's Life i. 76, 84, 85, 154, 426, ii. 51, 103, 174
(borrowing books from Cotton Library), iii. 154, Bibl. Corn. 1286,
Letters from Bodleian iii. 616; Gutch i. 54, ii. 324, 328, 377, 382,
392, 424, 438, 440–1, iii. 107; Arber's *Stationers' Register* iii. 306
a.b., iv. 18, Parr's *Life of Usher* 399, Masson's Milton ii. 225, 325,
513, Perry's *Church of England* 384. On a brass in Harford church,
Ivybridge 'Here rest the bodies of John Prideaux of Stowford, and
Agnes his only wife, the parents of 7 sonnes and 5 daughters. To
whom John Prideaux their 4th sonne Doctor of Divinity and the King
Majesties Professor thereof in the University of Oxford, Rector of
Exeter Colledge and Chaplain to Prince Henry, King James the First
and King Charles the First, hath left this filial remembrance July 20
1639.' Clark i. 138–9, 209 twice, 291–4, 405, Hist. of Kidlington
(O. H. Soc.) index, N. and Gleanings ii. 46, 175, Nat. Biog.
vii. 301.

Walter **Dotyn** or Dotten, son of a merchant, **M.** 17 Oct. 1600
age 16, **Dev. 1601**, d. 20 Feb. 160$\frac{3}{4}$ (the plague was raging this year)
in his 20th year, bur. S. Michael's, Oxford; for his Latin epitaph see
Peshall, app. p. 1.

John **Whetcombe** (connected with Sir W. Petre, Visit. Essex 521),
b. Dorset, **M.** Oriel 14 Oct. 1597 age 17, B.A. 11 July 1599; **Petr.**
3 June 1602, res. 12 May 1610; M.A. 17 Dec. 1602, B.D. 27 Mch
1610 (incorp. Camb. 1610), D.D. 30 June 1612 ; R. of Frome Vau-
church 1620–35, V. of Maiden Newton 1622–38, both in Dorset,
bur. 30 May 1640 age 60; his wife Ann d. of Thomas Holland
(Rector of Exeter) survived him ; Hutchins ii. 688–90, iii. 713, 718,
iv. 195, 198, Clark i. 209.

Digory **Wheare**, pleb., b. Berry Court, Jacobstow, Cornwall 1573;
M. Broadg. H. 6 July 1593 age 19, B.A. 5 Feb. 159$\frac{7}{8}$, M.A. 16 June

1600; **Corn.** 1602, res. 30 Ap. 1608; travelled abroad with his patron, Lord Chandos; first Camden Professor of History 16 Oct. 1622–1647, appointed by Camden through Lord Chandos' influence with Thomas Allen; Principal of Glouc. H. 4 Ap. 1626–1647, d. 1 Aug. 1647, bur. 3 Aug. in the College Chapel under the eagle; Wood's Fasti i. 272, Life ii. 398, Athenæ iii. 216; Gutch ii. 359, 513, iii. 120, Suppl. 207; Dean Prideaux's Letters (Camden Soc.) p. 63; Hist. Comm. ii. 143. His s. Francis was at school with Sir William Davenant under Charles Sylvester at Oxford, Letters from Bodleian ii. 303; Bibl. Corn. 864–66, Laud's *Chancellorship* 193, 298, Clark i. 255, 291, 406, Nat. Biog. i. 313.

Richard **Amye, M.** 23 Mch 159$\frac{8}{9}$ age 16; subscribed 14 July 1602, B.A. 17 July 1602; **Dev.** 1604, adm. to Bodleian 1605, M.A. 17 Dec. 1605, B.D. 17 Dec. 1618; lic. to preach 7 July 1618, Clark i. 265; R. of Carfax 12 Aug. 1617, City Lecturer at Carfax 15 Oct. 1618, d. about Christmas 1618: inventory of goods 25 Jan. 16$\frac{18}{20}$, Griffiths 3; Reg. 19 Nov. 1610 'decretum est M. Amy, M. Collyer, dominum Carpenter, et dominum Petrum in communas recipiendos esse, ea conditione ut solvant bursariis ea debita singula quæ ab illis debentur in hoc tempore, sive pro ipsis sive pro ipsorum *scholaribus*, secundum decreta Collegii, intra festum Annunciationis proxime sequentis, et interea permittant bursariis recipere omnes pecunias sibi debitas a Collegio, sive stipendii sive finis sive reditus frumentarii ratione, in partem dictæ solutionis, donec ipsi plenarie satisfaciant'; 30 June 1614 'impetravit absentiæ veniam M. Amye ad placitum per totum annum ut liberius curæ pastorali vacaret.'

Solomon **Hext**, pleb. (? of the Hext family of Kingston in Colaton Raleigh), **M.** 24 Oct. 1600 age 15, B.A. 20 June 1604; **Dev.** 1604, on the recommendation of James I, who also recommended Amye and Christopher Palmer, but the latter was not elected, State Papers 10 and 26 June 1604; d. 23 Nov. 1606 in his 22nd year, monu. erected by his brother Thomas in S. Michael's Church, Oxford, Peshall app. p. 1.

Richard **Collyer, M.** 9 Dec. 1603 age 19, **Corn.** 1604 in place of his brother Christopher, res. 29 June 1614; B.A. 15 July 1607, M.A. 23 June 1610; R. of Ideford, Devon 8 Ap. 1614, d. 1628: Eccl. Ant. i. 65, Bibl. Corn. 1128.

John **Warmestry** (? related to Thomas Warmestry, dean of Worcester), b. Worcs., **M.** 31 Oct. 1600 age 19; **Petr.** full Fellow 1606, res. 30 June 1615; B.A. 5 Feb. 160$\frac{3}{4}$, M.A. 31 Oct. 1606 (incorp. Camb. 1612); had leave of absence 1614 for a year, having taken R. of Ipsley, Warwicks.; State Papers 1660 p. 16, 106–7, 558.

John **Vivian** or Vyvyan (3 s. Hanniball, of Trelowarren, by Philippa Tremayne), **M.** 4 Feb. 159$\frac{9}{10}$ age 15, B.A. 22 Oct. 1600, M.A. 30 June 1603, **Corn. 1606**, res. 25 June 1629 (Reg. 1621); B.D. 6 June 1614 (incorp. Camb. 1620), lic. to preach 1 July 1617, V. of Banwell, Som. 1628; perhaps gave the Eagle in the Chapel 1637, Gutch iii. 117; will 3 May 1636, proved 10 Nov. 1638. Reg. 23 July 1621 'concessum est M. Vivian S.S. Theologiæ bacchalaureo 1 ut differre posset doctoratus gradum per integrum adhuc decennium. 2 ut abesset a Collegio usque ad festum Nativitatis Christi proxime sequentis. 3 ut peteret pecuniam ab hæredibus domini Caroli Crooke, nempe centum libras, quas ex testamento nobis legavit. 4 ut colligeret pecuniam Collegii nomine, sibi quod esset Bursarius a Cornubiensibus vel Devoniensibus debitam'; Bibl. Corn. 831, Visit. Corn. 529.

William **Battishill, M.** 23 Mch 160$\frac{3}{4}$ age 15, **Dev. 1606**, res. 23 June 1618; B.A. 14 July 1609, adm. to Bodleian 1610, M.A. 4 May 1612 (the grace of the College in Reg. 29 Ap., see 7 July); V. of Shebbear 1620, bur. 30 Nov. 1666, Walker ii. 193; m. 28 Ap. 1623 Catherine d. of Roger Dene of Newton S. Petrock by Elizabeth d. of John Wood of Lew Trenchard, she was bap. 10 Oct. 1589, bur. 28 Aug. 1627, arms, a cross crosslet in saltire between 4 owls, impaling a lion rampant i.e. Dene; he m. 2 Susanna, bur. 16 June 1671, and had by her William, Elizabeth, Peter, Katherine; and Jonathan bap. 29 Mch 1636, servitor Ch. Ch. 10 Mch 165$\frac{9}{10}$, bur. 3 Oct. 1713, m. Mary d. of Francis Strood R. of Ideford, she was bur. 27 July 1697; Foster i. 88.

Nathanael **Carpenter** (s. John, Cornish by birth, R. of Northleigh, Devon 1587, who d. 1621, for on 4 Ap. 1621 Bishop Cotton admitted Joseph Hull B.A. on the presentation of Thomas Hull yeoman of Crewkeherne, to whom Sir John Petre had assigned the presentation, Bibl. Corn. 63, 1115), b. Northleigh 7 Feb. 158$\frac{8}{9}$, **M.** Edmund H. 7 June 1605; **Dev. 1607** on James I's letter of recommendation; Michael Jermyn had equal votes, but the Vice-Chancellor Henry Airay decided in favour of Carpenter; B.A. 5 July 1610, adm. to Bodleian 1610, M.A. 28 Ap. 1613, B.D. 11 May 1620; one of his pupils was Sir W. Morice, Secretary of State 1660. His *Geography*, with woodcut diagrams, 4° was published Oxford 1625. He was

chaplain to Archbishop Usher, and d. Dublin 1628, his funeral
sermon by Robert, Usher's brother, who had induced him to live
at Armagh; a biography of him in Corpus MS. cccviii fol. 66*b*, and
in Rawlinson MSS. class C. No. 146 folio 346 by Hearne; he was
schoolmaster of the King's wards in Dublin, i. e. minors whose parents
were Romanists. Athenæ ii. 287, 322, 421; Dredge's *Sheaves* 33;
W. C. Hazlitt's *Collections* 62; C. S. Gilbert's Cornwall ii. 49;
R. J. King's Sketches and Studies 307; State Papers Addenda
15 Nov. 1606, Clark i. 322: Hist. MSS. iv. 590, N. and Gleanings
v. 26, Nat. Biog.

John **Polwhele** (2 s. Degory, of Treworgan in S. Erme, by
Catherine Trencreek), **M.** 31 Oct. 1600 age 14 (with his brother
Thomas, age 15), B.A. 21 Oct. 1607, **Corn. 1608**, res. 1622; M.A.
23 June 1610 (incorp. Camb. 1612), B.D. 25 Ap. 1621, V. of
Whitchurch, Devon 1622, see Marriage Licenses 9 June 1623; will
15 May, proved 13 June, 1648; Visit. Corn. 377.

William **Hele** or Heale, pleb., b. Devon, **M.** 14 Mch $\frac{1599}{1600}$ age 18,
B.A. Broadg. H. 13 Dec. 1603, M.A. 3 July 1606; adm. **Chapl.**
22 Aug. **1608**, expelled 7 May 1610 for absence; V. of Bishop's
Teignton 1 Dec. 1610, of Rattery 1620, both in Devon, d. 1627;
wrote *Apologie for Women*, 4° Oxon 1609, in answer to Dr. William
Gager, who at the Act of 1608 maintained that it was lawful for
husbands to beat their wives; Gutch ii. 256, Warton's English Poetry
iii. 306, Nat. Biog.

George **Petre** or Peter ('s. George, of Bristowe' [Bristol]), b.
Devon, **M.** 8 Mch 160$\frac{4}{5}$ age 16, **Petr.** full Fellow **1609**, res. 30 June
1619, £5 was paid him 14 Aug. 1621; B.A. 26 Oct. 1608, adm. to
Bodleian 28 Jan. 161$\frac{0}{1}$, M.A. 4 June 1611.

Thomas **Chafyn,** of Wilts, **M.** Alban H. 19 Oct. 1599 age 18;
Sar. 1609, res. 30 June 1621; B.A. 9 July 1612, M.A. 27 Ap. 1615,
B. and D.D. 9 July 1628, d. 1646; preacher at the Temple Church;
R. of North Newton (with preb. annexed) 1627, of Fofunt 1628,
of Mere 1630, all in Wilts, Phillips ii. 14; preb. of Salisbury; preb.
of Llandaff 30 July 1630; Arber's *Stationers' Register* iv. 203;
Hutchins iii. 565, 690; State Papers 4 July 1628. Wilts Visit.
51, 57.

John **Collins,** pleb., **M.** 29 Nov. 1605 age 17, **Dev. 1609**; B.A.
9 July 1612, d. 1613.

Alexander **Jermyn** (s. Alexander, pleb., of Exeter), b. Devon, **M.**
10 Dec. 1602 age 18 (with his brother Philip, age 14), B.A. 28 June

1606, adm. to Bodleian (as *German*) 20 Mch 160$\frac{3}{6}$, M.A. 21 June 1609, adm. **Chapl.** 7 May **1610**, d. 1614.   Clark i. 267.

Edward **Cotton** (2 s. William, bishop of Exeter), b. Middlesex, **M. Ch. Ch.** 20 Mch 160$\frac{4}{9}$ age 18; at Middle Temple 1606; B.A. 14 Oct. 1609, **Petr.** full Fellow 17 May **1610**, res. 1612; M.A. 2 July 1612; R. of Duloe, Cornwall 15 Jan. 161$\frac{0}{1}$ (sequestered 1 May 1647), of Petertavy 1611, canon of Exeter 1611, Chancellor 1613, R. of Bridestowe 1614–47, of Shobrooke 3 July 1615, Archdeacon of Totnes 10 Feb. 162$\frac{1}{2}$, d. 8 Oct. 1647; his wife Margaret, dau. of William Bruton, d. 10 Aug. 1643; Wood's Fasti i. 334, 347, Oliver's Bishops 292, Eccl. Ant. iii. 59; Visit. Devon 241; Maclean i. 653.   N. and Gleanings iv. 161, State Papers 1660 p. 83, 215, Cases in Starchamber (Camden Soc.) 1886 p. 153, Hist. Comm. vii. 9, Lords' Journals x. 43.

Matthias **Styles**, of Alphington, Devon, b. Devon, **M.** 27 June 1606 age 15, at Inner Temple 1608, B.A. 27 Jan. 16$\frac{08}{10}$, adm. to Bodleian 1610; **Petr. 1610**, res. at Venice 30 Sep. 1628; M.A. 26 Oct. 1612, Proctor 1621, B.D. 18 July 1623, D.D. 6 July 1638; Chaplain to Sir Isaac Wake the Ambassador at Venice 1624, 'profecturus 22 Ap. 1624,' and married there 1628 (but ? married at S. George's); candidate for chaplaincy of Levant Company 1626, on nomination of Sir Francis Stewart, but not elected (J. B. Pearson's *Chaplains to the Levant* 39, 48); State Papers 11 Nov. 1627; R. of S. George's, Botolph Lane, Eastcheap, 18 June 1630, sequestered 1643, and of St. Gregory near S. Paul's; canon of Lincoln 1631, R. of Orsett, Essex 5 Jan. 164$\frac{0}{1}$, in the Assembly of Divines at Westminster 1643; d. 1660; Wood's Fasti a. 1638, Reg. a. 1623 at end. Reg. 17 Aug. 1618 'decretum est ut camera in Turre Chamberiana maxima, quam antea occupabat M. Robertus Sims, cum duobus museis cubiculo annexis et tribus museis superioribus versus Collegium Jesu spectantibus, inter cameras ad socios spectantes annumeraretur et prima hac vice subesset usui magistri Stile qui præcedentem suam cameram sublatis aulæ veteris fundamentis quibus eniteretur amiserat'; Newcourt i. 354, ii. 454, Masson's Milton ii. 522, Rev. W. Palin's *More about Stifford* 1872 p. 78, Clark i. 322.

Theophilus **Gale**, arm. f., **M.** 11 Oct. 1605 age 17, B.A. 5 May 1609, **Dev. 1611**, vac. his fellowship 1621 by m. Mary Ryder widow, of King's Teignton, 8 Dec. 1620: he m. (2) Bridgett Waldron of Seaton 11 Feb. 162$\frac{2}{3}$, Vivian's Marriage Licenses p. 70, 80; M.A. 29 Jan. 161$\frac{1}{2}$, B.D. 19 June 1619 (incorp. Camb. 1619), D.D. 7 May

1624; preb. of Exeter 30 Oct. 1620, V. of King's Teignton, Devon 1620, res. 30 June 1621, d. May 1639; father of Theophilus Gale, who wrote *The Court of the Gentiles*; Eccl. Ant. i. 182, Lysons' Devon 495, Clark i. 268.

John **Conant** (s. Richard, pleb., of E. Budleigh, Devon, by Agnes d. of John Clarke, m. 4 Feb. 157$\frac{8}{9}$), bap. E. Budleigh 18 Mch 158$\frac{4}{5}$, **M.** 15 Nov. 1605 age 18, B.A. 5 May 1609, **Dev. 1611**, res. 30 June 1620; M.A. 29 Jan. 161$\frac{1}{2}$, B.D. 2 Dec. 1619 (incorp. Camb. 1620); C. of S. Botolph, Aldersgate, R. of Lymington, Som. 1619, then of S. Thomas at Salisbury; in the Assembly of Divines 1643, d. Sarum 13 Ap. 1653, Masson's Milton ii. 517; publ. *Two Sermons* 1643; his nephew John was R. of Ex. Coll. 1649 (see his life 2, 6, 10), but the Rectory was first offered to the uncle; Wood's Fasti i. 393; Prince 234, *Conant Family* 58–67, 89–91.

John **Prideaux** (Fellow 1601), el. Rector 4 Ap. 1612, res. 3 Aug. 1642; Vice-Chancellor 1619, 1620, 1624, 1625, 1641; Reg. Prof. of Divinity 8 Dec. 1615–1642, canon of Christ Church and R. of Ewelme, Oxon; V. of Bampton 17 July 1614, res. 1634, V. of Chalgrave 1620, R. of Bladon 1625 both in Oxon, canon of Sarum 1620; el. Bishop of Worcester 22 Nov. 1641, through his pupil James, Marquis of Hamilton, consecr. 19 Dec. The Puritan confiscation forced him to sell his library (Continuation of Godwin, Nash's Worcester), he was allowed 4s. 6d. a week, d. at house of his son-in-law, Dr. Sutton, Bredon, Worcs. 20 July 1650, bur. 16 Aug.; Bloxam v. 59, 62, Brodrick index; Bull's Life p. 11; State Papers 8 Dec. 1615, 22 Oct. 1617, 11 Aug. 1618, 27 Sep. 1622, 3 Ap. 1623, 19 Nov. 1624, 17 Jan. 1642 and 30 Sep. p. 397, Dec. 1643 p. 511; Hist. Comm. i. 27, 100, iii. 234, iv. 464, v. 372–3, Rawlinson MSS. ii. index, All Souls' Archives 316.

John **Bayly** (s. Lewis, bishop of Bangor), b. Herefs., at Ex. Coll. **1611** age 16, subscribed 16 Ap. 1613; **Petr.** full Fellow 27 Ap. **1612**, res. 30 June 1619; 'M. 21 Ap. 1615, son of a Dr., age 19' Clark ii. 329, 336 (the University Register carelessly kept); B.A. 4 May 1615, adm. to Bodleian 1615, M.A. 25 June 1617, B. and D.D. 7 Dec. 1630, preb. of Bangor 2 Oct. 1617, and Precentor 1620, Guardian of Christ's Hospital in Ruthyn 1621; R. of Llanddyfnan in Anglesey 1619, sinecure R. of Llandrillo in Rhos, Denbighs. 1619, V. of Llantrissant, Anglesey 1620, R. of Llanfwrog, Denbighs. 1621, of Llanbadr-dyffryn-Clwyd 1623, sinecure R. of Llanynio 1631; State Papers 6 Nov. 1619, Chaplain to Charles I, d. summer 1633; Athenæ

ii. 499; Laud's *Chancellorship* 26, 27, 31, Thomas' *St. Asaph* 420, Foster i. 91, Nat. Biog. iii. 448.

Samuel **Cosens**, B.A. 28 June 1606, M.A. 4 June 1611, **Petr.** adm. 14 May **1612**, full Fellow 15 Dec. 1612, res. 30 June 1624; B.D. 16 Feb. 162½, V. of Farnham 1622, of Dorking 1623, both in Surrey; Clark i. 267.

John **Balcanquall** (related to Walter Balcanquall, Dean of Durham 1639-45), M.A. Edinb. 27 July 1611 *minister verbi*; **Petr.** 13 Jan. 161⅔ by James I's request to Sir John Petre, though it was against the statutes, incorp. 14 Jan., adm. to Bodleian 4 Feb. 161⅔, full Fellow 7 May 1613, res. 30 June 1618; B.D. 2 Dec. 1619, R. of Tatenhill, Staffs. 1618, canon of Rochester 1628, V. of Boxley, Kent 1639, d. 1646; Wood's Fasti i. 351, Athenæ iii. 270, Clark i. 275, 374.

Nathaniel **Norrington** (s. Simon, R. of Uplyme, Devon 1560), b. Uplyme, his mother a widow with several children, as stated by John Drake, Esq. of Ash, and eight of the parishioners: **M.** 18 Mch 160⅞ age 17, B.A. 4 June 1611, adm. to Bodleian 1611, **Dev. 1613**, M.A. 5 July 1614, B.D. 3 July 1624; lived some years in an academy in Holland (Reg. 23 July 1621), and disputed against the Remonstrants; d. Senior Fellow 11 Jan. 163 0/1, bur. 13 Jan. in the Chapel; Wood's Fasti i. 415; Gutch iii. 117-8, 120, Carpenter's *Geography* 247, Clark i. 271.

Alexander **Harry** (a minister's son, kinsman of William Hicks of Paul in Cornwall), **M.** 23 Nov. 1604 age 16, B.A. 26 Oct. 1608, adm. to Bodleian 1610, M.A. 4 June 1611, **Corn. 1613**, res. 30 June 1628; Lecturer at Carfax 20 Dec. 1620; B.D. 25 Ap. 1621; wrote *Revelation Revealed*, d. before 1661; Wood's Fasti i. 398, Athenæ iii. 490 and *v*. W. Hickes; Bibl. Corn. 208, 238.

Arthur **Harris** (4 s. Arthur, of Hayne in Devon, and Kenegie in Cornwall; Lysons' Devon cxxix), **Petr. 1614** (Reg. p. 253, 263, 279); expelled 30 June 1621 for absence; B.A. 7 July 1617, M.A. 5 May 1620; the first Petrean Fellow elected without nomination; Lord Petre d. 1613, his son tried to nominate Philip Francklyn of Univ. Coll., and a law-suit followed, in which the College maintained its right to elect by statute; Reg. p. 253-68, on p. 258 is a letter to Sir John Doderidge about it; Davies Gilbert's Cornwall iii. 155; see a. 1662, 1685.

Anthony **Standard**, pleb. (perhaps brother of John and Robert), b. Oxon, **M.** 16 June 1615 age 19, **Petr. 1614**, vac. by marriage 1628, B.A. 7 July 1617, M.A. 5 May 1620.

George **Beard** (son of a minister), **M**. 16 June 1615 age 18, **Corn.** **1614**; B.A. 7 July 1617, M.A. 5 May 1620, B.D. 22 Mch 163$\frac{0}{1}$ (as Bird), lic. to preach 1633, d. Sub-rector 20 Oct. 1638, bur. in the Chapel, administration bond of will 7 Nov. 1638, Griffiths 5; Gutch iii. 120. Reg. 6 July 1621 'indulta erat venia M. Georgio Beard lectori ut abesset a Collegio usque ad festum Michaelis proxime sequentis, ea lege ut alium magistrum idoneum substitueret qui vices ejus in lectione Rhetorica et Mathematica fideliter obiret'; Clark i. 194.

Lawrence **Bodley** (nephew of Sir Thomas, ? s. Laurence D.D., R. of Shobrooke, Devon, d. 19 Ap. 1615, Eccl. Ant. iii. 58), **M**. Merton, adm. to Bodleian 20 May 1613, B.A. 19 Oct. 1614, adm. **Chapl.** 5 Nov. **1614**, vac. 1632 by taking a living, M.A. 25 June 1617 (incorp. Camb. 1618), B.D. 14 Dec. 1626, D.D.; Tutor of James Dillon, Lord Roscommon, who entered Ex. Coll. 1628; R. of Clyst Hydon, Preb. of Exeter 7 Oct. 1633–1634, d. 1634, funeral sermon by Richard Peck (? V. of Cullompton); Prince 101; Wood's Fasti i. 416, 453, ii. 390; Gutch ii. 314; Reliquiæ Bodleianæ 173, 272, 382, Clark i. 17, 275, N. and Gleanings ii. 187, iv. 181 (Bodley family); Laud's *Chancellorship* 53, Conant's *Life* 3.

William **Hyde** (s. Sir Lawrence, of Salisbury), bap. Salisbury 17 Jan. 1596, subscribed 1 July 1613, **Sar. 1615**, B.A. 16 July 1618, M.A. 27 June 1621, bur. in Cath. Salisbury 24 Nov. 1630; Scrutator at the first election of Proctors under a new system 1628; but, this failing, the Scrutators acted as Proctors. This led to the Laudian Cycle of Proctors 1629; Gutch ii. 361; Bloxam v. 45; State Papers Addenda 13 June 1604 (pedigree), Sep. 1628 p. 341, 22 Dec. 1628; Clark iii. 366.

Thomas **Woodyates**, b. Devon, B.A. 23 May 1609, adm. to Bodleian 1613, M.A. New Coll. 28 June 1615; **Petr. 1615**, res. 30 June 1618; preb. of Lytton at Wells 22 Oct. 1617, V. of Stowey 1619, R. of Corton Dinham 1620, both in Som.; a letter dated 1616 from Nicholas Fuller, addressed 'to my very goode fryeind Mr. Thomas Woodyates fellowe of Excester Colledge in Oxford at his chamber there,' is printed in J. E. Bailey's *Life of Thomas Fuller* 764–5. A Thomas Woodyates (? his father) was preb. of Combe at Wells 24 Jan. 160$\frac{9}{10}$. There is a place called Woodyates in Dorset, Hutchins iii. 441, 607; Clark i. 73, 276: State Papers 4 May 1624.

Denys **Prideaux** (s. Sir Thomas, of Nutwell), **M**. 2 Dec. 1614 (with Thomas Prideaux), B.A. 28 Feb. 161$\frac{8}{9}$, **Dev. 1618**, res. 1630;

M.A. 26 June 1619, Proctor 1626, Bloxam v. 53 ; R. of Lympstone
1630, of Bishop's Morchard 163⅜, both in Devon, preb. of Exeter
163¾, bur. 12 Nov. 1640; Eccl. Ant. iii. 93 ; Maclean ii. 235.

John **Dodd** or Dods, b. Middlesex, **M.** 4 Nov. 1614, **Petr. 1618** ;
B.A. 22 Ap. 1618, M.A. 22 Jan. 162⁰₁, B.D. 7 Dec. 1630, d. Sub-rector
1631 ; the College, as his affairs were embarrassed, took out letters
of administration from the Bishop of London, and at Oxford 3 Dec.
1631, Griffiths 18 ; Arber's *Stationers' Register* iv. 267, Bloxam v. 52.

John **Hunt**, pleb., b. Devon, **M.** 22 May 1612 age 17, B.A. 8 Feb.
161⅝, **Petr. 1618**, res. 30 June 1621 ; M.A. 19 Oct. 1618, sup. B.D.
25 Nov. 1626, B.D. 31 Jan. 164²₃, R. of Loxhore, Devon 1628, of
Exford, Som. 1629.

Rees (Rhesus) **Allanson**, b. London 29 Mch 1601, ed. Merchant
Taylors, **M.** 20 June 1617 age 17, **Petr. 1619**, B.A. 18 July 1622,
res. 24 June 1626 before a Proctor of the Court of Arches in London ;
? Robinson i. 83.

Richard **Cottle** or Cottell (? 1 s. Mark, of N. Tawton, Visit. Devon
1564 ed. Colby p. 70), pleb., **M.** 13 Dec. 1615 age 19, B.A. 21 Jan.
161⅞, **Dev. 1619** ; M.A. 17 Oct. 1620, administration bond and
inventory 2 Nov. 1622, Griffiths 15. William Cottell of Larkbear,
Exeter (d. 1632), had a son Richard, who is said to have died *sine
prole.*

John **Lane** (s. Valentine, pleb., V. of Dodford, Northants), bap.
Dodford 24 July 1603, **M.** 24 Oct. 1617, **Petr. 1619** ; B.A. 6 July
1622, d. 1625.

Robert **Mercer**, **M.** 17 Dec. 1619 age 17, **Dev. 1620**, d. 1623.

William **Scobble**, pleb., **M.** 16 June 1615 age 17, B.A. 19 Oct.
1618, M.A. 12 June 1621, **Dev. 1621**, res. 1626.

Freeman **Page** (1 s. Freeman, by Judith 1 d. of W. Cotton bishop
of Exeter), b. Finchley 26 Feb. 160¾, **M.** 3 May 1621, **Petr. 1621** ;
B.A. 25 Oct. 1624, M.A. 2 June 1627, Proctor 1633, d. 2 Nov. 1634,
bur. Shobrooke, Devon, administration bond Oxford 29 Nov. 1634,
Griffiths 46 ; Eccl. Ant. iii. 60 ; Laud's *Chancellorship* 82, Maclean i.
652.

Henry **Hyde**, arm. f. 1, b. Wilts, **M.** 23 Ap. 1619 age 17, B.A.
17 Feb. 16¹⁹₂₀, **Sar. 1621**, M.A. 6 July 1622, d. 1625. Athenæ iii.
1018 (Hyde family). Was Henry elder brother of Clarendon (Edward
Hyde)? Clarendon's Life ed. 1857, i. 5 ; Hutchins iii. 135, State
Papers 1649 p. xxxv, 198 ; 1660, p. 218 ; Laud's *Chancellorship* 53,
57, 58, 65, 69.

Richard **Bowyer** or Boyer (5 s. Sir John, of Knipersley, Staffs.), **M**. 13 Jan. 162⁰⁄₁ age 18 (with his brother James, age 20), B.A. 31 Jan. 162⁰⁄₁, **Petr. 1621**; d. 1622.

John **Maynard**, arm. f. 1, **M**. 26 Ap. 1621 [wrong date] age 17, adm. to Bodleian 13 Ap. 1621, B.A. 25 Ap. 1621, **Petr. 1622**; d. 1625; Clark iv. 7.

Jonathan **Polwhele** (7 s. Degory), **M**. 15 Oct. 1619 age 19, B.A. 27 June 1622, **Corn. 1622**, res. 30 June 1635; M.A. 4 May 1625; R. of Windlesham 1635, V. of Bagshot, both in Surrey.

Philip **King** (s. John, Dean of Christ Church and Bishop of London), b. London, **M**. Ch. Ch. 19 Ap. 1616 age 13, student 1616, B.A. 3 Dec. 1618 (with his brother William), M.A. 7 July 1621, **Petr. 1623**, res. 1629; B.D., recommended by the King for D.D. 31 Jan. 164⅔, D.D. 17 Dec. 1645; public orator 28 July 1625–1629; R. of S. Botolph, Billingsgate 1636, sequestered 1642; took refuge in Oxford, m. Mary d. of Lyonell Day of Warwicks.; Treasurer of Chichester 12 July 1660, Archdeacon of Lewes 19 Dec. 1660–1667, canon of S. Paul's 1660–6, R. of Felpham and of Selsey 1660, of Slinfold 1662, all in Sussex; of Hitcham, Bucks Sep. 1666 to Mch 1667; d. childless 4 Mch 166⁶⁄₇; Walcott's *Fasti Cicestrenses* 16; Wood's Fasti ii. 89, Athenæ i. 761, ii. 435, iii. 841, Hearne iii. 237, *Brief Martyrology* in Mercurius Rusticus ed. 1685; Poems of Bishop Henry King ed. Hannah 1843 p. xcv–viii.

Henry **Tozer**, pleb., b. North Tawton, 1602, **M**. 3 May 1621 age 20, B.A. 18 June 1623, **Dev. 1623**; M.A. 28 Ap. 1626, Lecturer at Carfax 21 Oct. 1632; B.D. 28 July 1636, V. of Yarnton 1644, but probably served it from Oxford, Hist. of Kidlington (O. H. Soc.) 222; 'Tozer, Procter, and Acland were allowed the degree of D.D. 6 June 1646, but did not take it,' Wood's Fasti ii. 100; called before the Visitors 21 Mch 164⁷⁄₈, expelled 26 May (he had been on the Delegacy to answer the Visitors in 1647), and imprisoned in *Bokardo*, Masson's Milton ii. 522; d. 11 Sep. 1650 chaplain at Rotterdam. Athenæ iii. 239, 273; Oxoniana iv. 203, Prince 787, Lysons' Devon 482, Hist. Comm. ii. 127, Journal of House of Commons ii. 541, State Papers 17 May 1630, Burrows 501. Laud's *Chancellorship* 19, 254, Conant's Life.

John **Procter**, pleb., b. Devon, subscribed 22 Oct. 1619, **M**. 17 Dec. 1619 age 18 (Clark ii. 378, 380; Nathanael Brocke 378–9 is a similar case), B.A. 27 June 1622, **Petr. 1623** (James Bampfield had equal votes); expelled 1648, restored 1660, d. 23 Feb. 167⁰⁄₁, bur.

in the College chapel; M.A. 4 May 1625 (incorp. Camb. 1635), B.D. 16 July 1636; on the Delegacy for the defence of Oxford 1642, Burrows ix; inventory of goods 2 Mch 167$\frac{0}{1}$, Griffiths 50; Prince 7; Gutch ii. 447, 597; Wood's Life ii. 96, 217, Milton ed. Hawkins iv. p. 13; Wood's MS. F. 35 p. 245.

Henry **Willett** (s. Henry, woollen draper), b. Exeter, **M.** 18 Mch 162$\frac{4}{5}$ age 17, **Petr. 1624**, vac. 1652, Burrows 198, 501; B.A. 21 Feb. 162$\frac{7}{9}$, M.A. 28 Ap. 1632, cr. B.D. 31 Jan. 164$\frac{2}{3}$, adm. B.D. 10 Oct. 1643; Visit. Devon 137; was he R. of Horwood in Devon 1650, 'value £50, a preaching minister, patron Eliz. Futts,' Lansdown MS. 459?

Joseph **Maynard** (2 s. Alexander, of Tavistock, and brother of Sir John), **M.** 13 Dec. 1622 age 15, B.A. 21 June 1625, **Petr. 1625**, vac. 1653; M.A. 13 May 1628, B.D. 28 July 1636, R. of Loddington, Northants 1640, Proctor 1662, el. Rector 18 Sep. and adm. 25 Oct. 1662 in place of Dr. Conant; D.D. 2 July 1663, res. 30 Ap. 1666 at Gunners Bury, Middlesex, the house of Sir John; Preb. of Exeter 25 Aug. 1666 by exchange with Dr. Bury, his successor in the Rectorship; V. of Bampton, Oxon 23 Dec. 1662; pres. by the King to V. of Menheniot 24 Dec. 1667, D. K. Rec. 46 p. 83; d. 1670, his will is in the Prerogative Office (Duke 24); Bishop Conybeare's Letter to Dr. Webber 1753; Reg. 19 Feb. 166$\frac{2}{3}$; Athenæ ii. 87: Wood's Life i. 455, ii. 44; Gutch iii. 108; Visit. Devon 140; Hearne ii. 322; was he V. of Milton Abbot 1646, Hist. Comm. vi. 129?

Edward **Carpenter**, b. Middlesex, **M.** 4 May 1621, B.A. 18 June 1623, **Petr. 1625**, res. 23 Feb. 164$\frac{0}{1}$; M.A. 28 Ap. 1626, B.D. 16 July 1636 (incorp. Camb. 1640), D.D. 19 Ap. 1662; V. of Melksham, Wilts 1639, of Clevedon 1660.

Nathaniel **Terry**, cler. f., of Wilts, **M.** 9 May 1617 age 17, B.A. 21 June 1620, M.A. 7 May 1623 (incorp. Camb. 1626), **Sar. 1625**, B.D. 7 Dec. 1630, res. 13 Oct. 1640; R. of Thornbury 1641, V. of Paignton, both in Devon, d. 1668; Eccl. Ant. i. 177.

Thomas **Collins**, **M.** 4 May 1621, B.A. 10 June 1624, **Dev. 1626**, M.A. 13 May 1628, res. 1634; ? preb. of Exeter 1633, R. of Sampford Peverell 1633, V. of Colyton 31 Aug. 1636, bur. 30 Ap. 1665; Eccl. Ant. ii. 8; Clark iii. 430. A T. C. was B.A. 21 June 1625.

Baldwin **Acland** (3 s. John, by Elizabeth d. of Nicholas Duck, recorder of Exeter 1617–28), bap. S. Olave's, Exeter 13 Ap. 1607, **Petr. 1626**; vac. by m. 1652 Mary sister of his pupil Thomas Lord Clifford of Chudleigh; **M.** 3 July 1629 age 20, B.A. 9 July 1629,

M.A. 28 Ap. 1632, Proctor 1641, B.D. 22 Nov. 1642, nominated D.D. (then of Univ. Coll.) 1 June 1646, but refused to be created; R. of N. Cadbury, Som. 1 Dec. 1643, declined to take the *Engagement* 1650, R. of Tedburn S. Mary 1651–72, preb. of Lincoln 12 Sep. 1660–7, preb. and treasurer of Exeter 10 June 1667, d. 27 Aug. 1672, bur. Tedburn; Prince (who m. his sister's daughter, Gertrude Salter) 7; Oliver's Bishops 284; Visit. Devon 7; Le Neve ii. 108; Bishop Bull's Life 1827 p. 9, 14; Burrows 130.

William **Hodges** (1 s. Thomas, of Slapton, Foster says, 's. of William, pleb., of Hampton'), **M.** 16 July 1625 age 20, B.A. Hart H. 27 Jan. $162\frac{6}{7}$; **Dev. 1628**, res. 30 June 1634, m. Sarah d. of Dr. Prideaux (Visit. Worcs. 59); M.A. 17 June 1629, B.D. 21 Feb. $16\frac{39}{40}$, D.D. 28 Nov. 1661; V. of Bampton, Oxon 5 July 1634 by res. of J. Prideaux (Giles' Bampton xxxix), R. of Ripple, Worcs. 1643, Archdeacon of Worcester 1645, d. 3 Sep. 1676, four days after his son Thomas (M.A. of Balliol, V. of Bampton); Wood's Fasti ii. 260, Athenæ iii. 268; Gutch ii. 375, 377, 583, 739, iii. 377; Calamy ii. 27; Laud's *Chancellorship* 56, 58, 60–62, 66, 70, Ranke iii. 408; Hist. Comm. vii. 106; Rawlinson MSS. Class C. No. 182, fol. 124 petition to the Lords from William Hodges, ejected Vicar of the first portion of Bampton, Oxon, with an order thereon 23 June 1660.

Henry **Hole** (s. Christopher, pleb., of Totnes), **M.** 13 Dec. 1622 age 17, B.A. 27 Jan. $162\frac{6}{7}$, **Petr. 1628**, res. 30 June 1634; M.A. 17 June 1629 (incorp. Camb. 1635); V. of Egloshayle, Cornwall 4 Oct. 1633, bur. 20 Mch. $16\frac{59}{60}$; Maclean i. 415.

Joseph **Squier** (s. Roger, V. of Helland), **M.** 28 May 1623 age 20, B.A. 22 June 1626, **Corn. 1628**, vac. 1647 by having taken R. of Lifton, Devon 1646, Hist. Comm. vi. 135; M.A. 30 Ap. 1629 (incorp. Camb. 1635), B.D. 17 July 1640; for John Squier see Coxe's Cat. no. x.

John **Watts** (s. Nicholas, pleb., of Tavistock), **M.** 18 Feb. $162\frac{6}{7}$ age 20, B.A. 17 June 1629, **Dev. 1629**; M.A. 28 Ap. 1632, d. 1634, administration bond 5 Mch $163\frac{4}{5}$, Griffiths 65.

Thomas **Denys** (1 s. Thomas, Fellow 1586), bap. 15 July 1604, **M.** 13 Dec. 1622, B.A. 22 June 1626, M.A. Glouc. H. 30 Ap. 1629; incepted Ex. Coll. 1629, **Corn. 1629**, vac. by marriage 1643; B.D. 21 Feb. $16\frac{39}{40}$; Visit. Corn. 138.

William **Cotton** (? 1 s. William, Precentor of Exeter and son of Bishop Cotton; N. and Gleanings iii. 65; if so, he d. 25 Dec. 1673, not in orders), b. Devon, **Petr. 1629**, res. 30 June 1639; B.A. 7 July

1632, M.A. 30 Ap. 1635; Visit. Devon 241, Maclean i. 652. One of the name d. R. of Nether Broughton, Leics. 1646.

NOTE.—The Caution Book begins 30 May 1629.

George **Kendal** (1 s. George, by Anne Cooke of Exeter), b. Cofton, Dawlish 1610, **M.** 18 Feb. 162⁴⁄₉ age 16, B.A. 3 June 1630, **Dev. 1630**; M.A. 9 May 1633 (incorp. Camb. 1634), B.D. Jan. 164½; recommended for Rector by Charles I in place of Prideaux 1642, vac. 1647 by having taken R. of Kenton, Devon 1646; D.D. 4 July 1654; R. of Blisland, Cornwall on Charles I's presentation 26 Nov. 1643, deprived 1655, Preb. of Exeter 164⁵⁄₆, deprived of Kenton 1662 for nonconformity, R. of S. Bennet, Gracechurch St., London 1656 (?), moderator of first general assembly of ministers of Devon 1655; m. Anne dau. of Periam Pole; d. Cofton 19 Aug. 1663, monu. there. He was at Hemel Hempstead in 1642; Lords' Journals vi. 433, 446, 470, 480, 501, 509, 558–9. Wood's Fasti ii. 162, Gutch iii. 107; Eccl. Ant. ii. 142; Visit. Devon 514, Nat. Biog.

Francis **Goddard** (s. Edward, of Woodhay, Hants), b. Wilts, **M.** 2 Dec. 1631 age 20, **Sar.** 7 Oct. 1631, res. 30 June 1642; B.A. 4 Nov. 1634, allowed to incept 10 June 1637, M.A. 1641, sup. M.B. 8 July 1636, M.B. 18 July 1640, M.D. 19 July 1641; F.R.S., Weld's *Royal Society* p. 35.

George **Hall** (3 s. Joseph, bishop of Exeter and Norwich), bap. Waltham Abbey, Essex 24 Aug. 1613, entered Ex. Coll. 1628 age 16, **M.** 9 May 1631 age 19, B.A. 30 Ap. 1631, **Petr. 1632**, res. 30 June 1638; M.A. 17 Jan. 163¾ (incorp. Camb. 1635), D.D. 2 Aug. 1660, inducted to Menheniot 8 Oct. 1637 (witness his brother Joseph Hall, notary public, Bibl. Corn. 203, 968, 1214), sequestered 1645, and also from V. of Wickhambrook, Suffolk, V. of Willingdon, Sussex 1647, preacher of S. Bartholomew's Exchange, preb. Exeter 23 Dec. 1639–166⁰⁄₁, Archdeacon of Cornwall 7 Oct. 1641–1660, canon of Windsor 28 July 1660, Chaplain to Charles II, V. of S. Botolph, Aldersgate 1655, Archdeacon of Canterbury 14 Aug. 1660–8, consecr. Bishop of Chester 11 May 1662; d. Wigan 23 Aug. 1668 age 55; gave the College, after the death of his wife Gertrude, d. of Edward Meredith of Maristow (m. Mullion, Cornwall 28 June 1641, bur. Wigan 13 Mch 166⁸⁄₉), his golden cup (Life of Joseph Hall, by G. Lewis p. 432, see 426 pedigree), and his estate in Trethewin near S. German's in Cornwall, worth £40 a year; Collier ii App. No. 83 p. 94; see Reg. 167⁴⁄₅; Hist. Comm. vii. 106, Bridgeman's *Hist. of*

Wigan ii., Nat. Biog. His portrait is in the College Hall, another is in Emmanuel, Cambridge, a third in possession of Mr. Rodd of Exeter. Under his charge his brothers John and Edward (Fellow 1638), the Bishop's 5 and 6 sons, **M.** from Essex 13 May 1635 ages 16 and 14.

John **Conant** (1 son Robert, pleb., by Elizabeth Morris), b. Yattington, Bicton 18 Oct. 1608, sent by his uncle John to Free School at Ilchester, then under Thomas Branker, **M.** 18 Feb. 162$\frac{4}{7}$, B.A. 26 May 1631, **Dev. 1632**, res. 27 Sep. 1647; R. of Whimple, Devon 1645, V. of Abergele 1657, M.A. 12 June 1634, sequestered to church of S. Thomas, New Sarum 1645, D.D. 31 May 1654, Regius Professor of Divinity 1654–60; Rector 1649; Hutchins iii. 334 gives some extracts from his letters (see 514). Conant Family p. 74–86; Masson's Milton ii. 517; Rawlinson MSS. class C. No. 945, 986 fol. 3 *b*; Nat. Biog. iv. 387, xi. 465. His uncle Roger, bap. 9 Ap. 1592, went to America 1623, and founded the Conant family there, d. 19 Nov. 1679; English Garner ed. Arber ii. 464–5, 560, 618.

Robert **Snowe** (s. Thomas, pleb., of Exeter), **M.** Wadham 19 June 1629 age 18; battellar Ex. Coll. 5 Feb. 16$\frac{29}{30}$ to 1631; B.A. 17 Oct. 1631, **Chapl. 1632**, the letter of the Dean and Chapter dated 17 Nov. 1632 is transcribed in Prideaux' copy of the Statutes; res. 19 Mch 164$\frac{1}{2}$, having been adm. R. of Morchard Bishop, Devon 21 Mch 164$\frac{0}{1}$, res. 1662; M.A. 3 July 1634; Eccl. Ant. iii. 51, Calamy ii. 52. See cancelled entry of his election in 1631 in the Register.

John **Hakewill** or Hackwell (s. George, R. of Ex. Coll.), bap. Barnstaple 12 May 1616; commoner 24 Ap. 1632 to 13 Oct. 1634, **M.** 16 Nov. 1632 age 17 (with another John Hakewill, 1 son of John of Exeter), B.A. 12 June 1634, **Dev. 1634**; M.A. 29 Ap. 1637, adm. (with his brother William, Clark i. 237) to the Bodleian 30 Ap. 1635, R. of Heanton Punchardon, bur. there 2 Mch 165$\frac{4}{5}$.

Samuel **Hall** (4 s. Bishop Joseph), bap. Waltham Abbey 28 Oct. 1614, **M.** 9 Dec. 1631 age 16, B.A. 22 Ap. 1634, **Petr. 1634**, vac. 1639 on m. Elizabeth d. of Thomas Rolle, of Lewknor, Oxon, she was bur. Stoke Canon 19 Mch 168$\frac{3}{4}$; his 1 d. Elizabeth m. Stokein-teignhead 21 Ap. 1664 Bampfylde Rodd; the y. d. Mary m. Stokein-teignhead 27 Oct. 1664 (Sir) Thomas Walker, merchant, of Exeter. M.A. 19 Jan. 163$\frac{6}{7}$, R. of Petertavy, Devon 18 Oct. 1637, Subdean of Exeter 22 Sept. 1641, removed from Petertavy 164$\frac{8}{9}$, R. of Stoke-inteignhead, Devon 1652, d. 15 Mch 167$\frac{4}{5}$ age 63, bur. Stoke Canon; Athenæ iii. 31; Walker ii. 27^a.

Thomas **Fortescue** (3 s. of John, of Fallapit in E. Allington, by

Sara d. of Sir Edmund Prideaux), bap. 7 July 1615, **M**. 9 Sep. 1634, **Dev. 1634**; expelled 1648 by the Visitors; B.A. 6 July 1637, M.A. 18 Ap. 1640.   Fortescue Family ii. 27, 40, Visit. Devon 365, Wood's Life iii. 425.

Richard **Prideaux** (s. George, pleb., of Sutcombe), b. Devon, **M**. 2 Dec. 1631 age 18, B.A. 9 June 1635, **Petr. 1635**, res. 9 Dec. 1643; M.A. 7 Ap. 1638; V. of Easton Neston, Northants 1643, sequestered to R. of Greens Norton, Northants 1645 by the Westminster Assembly; lived at Newcastle on Tyne, d. 1663; Maclean ii. 225.

Richard **Newte** (3 s. Henry, of Tiverton), bap. 24 Feb. 161$\frac{2}{3}$, poor scholar 22 Mch 16$\frac{29}{30}$ to 3 July 1635, **M**. 3 Feb. 163$\frac{1}{2}$ age 18, B.A. 25 June 1633, **Dev. 1635**, res. 1642; M.A. 5 May 1636; R. of Clare and Tidcomb portions at Tiverton 27 Oct. 1641, had licence from the King 10 Feb. 1644 to remain abroad 3 years, N. and Gleanings v. 87; R. of Heanton Punchardon 1656, chaplain to Charles II; d. 10 Aug. 1678; Athenæ iv. 485; Prince 609; Harding's Tiverton iii. 108, iv. 41, 44; Hist. Comm. vii. 107, Drake 6.

Degory **Polwhele** (spells himself *Polewheile*; 4 s. Thomas, of S. Erme, by Dionis d. of Judge John Glanville of Tavistock), commoner 24 June 1634 to 30 July 1635, **M**. 9 Sep. 1634 age 17, **Corn. 1635**; B.A. 30 Oct. 1638, M.A. 25 June 1641, had leave to take M.B. 24 Jan. 164$\frac{7}{8}$, admitted to practise 1 Feb. 164$\frac{7}{8}$, expelled 1648, about 1650 practised physic in Cornwall, M.D. 7 Aug. 1660; the Chancellor's letter for Polwhele's M.D. mentioned his services at Pendennis &c., and that he followed the King to Holland: restored to his Fellowship 1660, vac. by m. Margaret 1663; will 25 Sep. 1672, proved 17 Feb. 1673; Wood's Fasti ii. 234, Gutch ii. 352, Burrows 500, Bibl. Corn. 506, Visit. Corn. 377.

John **Poindexter** (so he spells his name; 2 s. Edward, by Pauline Ahier), b. S. Saviour's, Jersey Ap. 1609, ? B.A. Pemb., Camb. 16$\frac{29}{30}$, M.A. 1633; G. C. Ex. Coll., as M.A., 9 Oct. 1635 to 3 Nov. 1636, **Jer. 4 Dec. 1635**, adm. 4 Aug. 1636, expelled 1648, in Secretary of State's Office under Lord Digby, Lieut. Bailly of Jersey 1669–76, m. 1659 Anne d. and coh. of Laurence Hamptonne, viscount of Jersey, d. 2 Sep. 1691 age 83, monu. S. Saviour's; Wood's Life i. 440; Falle's book on Jersey was based on Poindexter's materials. Poindexter's own book *Caesarea* was not publ. till 1889 (see Falle's Jersey ed. Durell 1837 p. 280).   Poindexter wrote two law treatises still in use, *Commentaires sur les lois de Jersey*, and *Commentaires sur la Costume reformée de Normandie.*

Edward **Hall** (6 s. Bishop Joseph), bap. Waltham Abbey 23 July 1620, **M.** 13 May 1635 age 14 (with his brother John age 16), B.A. 9 Nov. 1637, **Petr. 1638**; M.A. 11 June 1640, d. 24 Dec. 1642, bur. Norwich Cathedral; Athenæ iii. 31.

William **Jesse** (s. Richard, pleb., of Exeter), poor scholar 9 Oct. 1632 to 4 July 1639, **M.** 21 June 1633 age 17, 'pensionarius Aclandianus,' B.A. 25 June 1636, M.A. 13 June 1639; **Petr. 1639**, res. 30 June 1642; V. of Torbrian 1663, and of Broad Hempston, both in Devon, canon of Exeter 1675, d. before 1680, D. K. Rec. 46 p. 104.

Erisey **Porter** (4 s. Richard, of Trematon in S. Stephen's by Saltash), bap. S. Stephen's 5 Jan. 161$\frac{5}{6}$, poor scholar 6 Oct. 1635 to 3 July 1639, **M.** 11 Dec. 1635, B.A. 26 Ap. 1639, **Corn. 1639**, expelled 1648; M.A. 7 Mch 164$\frac{1}{2}$; R. of Butterleigh, Devon 17 Dec. 1644; C. S. Gilbert's Cornwall ii. 241; Visit. Corn. 385, 641; Burrows 500.

Pollard **Northcote** (8 s. John, of Yewton, Crediton), bap. Newton S. Cyres 15 Sep. 1618, commoner 9 Ap. 1638 to 3 July 1639 (payment by Ames Northcote M.A.), **M.** 9 Mch. 163$\frac{7}{8}$ age 16, **Petr. 1639**, d. Hayne in Newton 1641.

Matthias **Prideaux** (2 s. Rector Prideaux), b. Oxford, Aug. 1622, **M.** 3 July 1640 age 15, el. 30 June 1641; B.A. 2 Nov. 1644, M.A. 3 Dec. 1645, in the chancellor's letter to convocation, to have his exercises remitted, he is styled Captaine Mathias Pridiaux of Ex. College; d. London 1646 of small pox; Prince 660; Athenæ iii. 199. His *Easy and compendious Introduction for reading Histories* was published 1648 by his father.

Antony **Clifford** (3 s. Simon, of Westminster), b. Wilts, **M.** Glouc. H. 27 June 1634 age 18; B.A. 24 Oct. 1637, M.A. 25 June 1640, **Sar. 1641**, delegate of the Parliamentary Visitors 1647, B.D. 2 Feb. 165$\frac{2}{3}$, R. of South Moreton, Berks 1659; vac. 1662 by having taken the R. of Newton Ferrers, Devon 1661; R. of Aveton Gifford 1674; d. 1685; State Papers 1660 p. 135, 507, Burrows 141, 339, 499, Visit. Devon 195; Visit. Wilts 66; Robinson i. 24.

Richard **Parr** (s. Richard, W. Antiq. ix. 110, Barker's *Parriana* i. 187, of Devon and Ireland, perhaps d. 1643, Bishop of Man), b. Fermoy 1617, **M.** 6 Nov. 1635 age 18, adm. **Chapl.** 7. Ap. **1642**, res. 1649; B.A. 13 June 1639, M.A. 23 Ap. 1642; D.D.; chaplain and biographer (1686) of Archbishop Usher, who lived some time in Exeter College, he was with Usher the last 13 years of his life; canon of Armagh (refused the deanery of Armagh, and an Irish

bishopric), V. of Reigate 1647, patron Sir Roger James; V. of
Camberwell 18 Dec. 1653, R. of Bermondsey 1654; lic. 10 Ap. 1649
to m. Elizabeth d. of Sir Roger James and relict of Henry Royse of
Reigate, bur. 13 Nov. 1688; he d. Camberwell 2 Nov. 1691;
Evelyn's Diary Feb. 1672, 20 Feb. and 2 Oct. 1681, 18 Ap. 1686;
Wood's Life i. 76, 77; Athenæ iii. 344, iv. 341, 808; Cotton's Fasti
Hibern. iii. 57; Blanch's *Parish of Camberwell* 1875 p. 279 and
index; Hist. Comm. vi. 157, State Papers July 1660 p. 148, 'The
Judges Charge, at S. Mary Overies in Southwark Martii 22, 1658, by
Rich. Parr M.A., Pastor of Camerwel.'

John **Mauduit** or Maudit (s. Isaac, of Exeter; N. and Gleanings
iv. 79), poor scholar 8 Oct. 1635 to 14 July 1642, **M.** 30 Oct. 1635
age 15, **Dev. 1642**, vac. 1652; B.A. 12 Oct. 1639, M.A. 6 July 1642;
Chaplain in Parliamentary army; Proctor 1649, Wood's Life i. 155;
preached before Cromwell at S. Mary's Oxford 20 May 1649, Burrows
500, Ffoulkes' *S. Mary's* 286; made student of Ch. Ch. 1650, by the
Parl. Visitors; left his benefice in Devon 1662 and Penshurst in Kent
(Dr. Hammond's living) for nonconformity, d. 6 Mch 1674 at Ottery;
published 'Sermons' 1649; Wood's Fasti ii. 9; Calamy ii. 2; Walker
ii. 116; Gutch iii. App. 135; Bodl. Cat. v. Maudit J.; Misc. Gen.
1881 p. 22.

Francis **Soorten** (s. Elisha, of N. Buckland), ed. Plymouth Free
Sch., poor scholar 14 Aug. 1637 to 14 July 1642, **M.** 12 May 1637
age 15, B.A. 13 May 1641, **Petr. 1642**, M.A. 24 Feb. 164¾; vac. by
becoming R. of Honiton 1648, vac. for noncomformity 1662, d.
8 Aug. 1689, Calamy ii. 41, and *Continuation* 275; m. Amy, aunt
of Sir William Courtenay, who was patron of Honiton; Eccl.
Ant. ii. 79.

John **Martin** (s. John, of Cockington, Devon), commoner 23 Feb.
163⅞ to 17 July 1640, again 30 May 1642 to 11 Nov. 1647 as
bachelor and battellar; **M.** 9 Mch. 163⅞ age 18, B.A. Magd. H.
18 Nov. 1641, at Lincoln's Inn 1641, **Sar. 1642**, delegate of Parl.
Visitors 1647, M.A. 14 Ap. 1648; res. 1657, Gutch ii. 553; one of
the name was V. of Compton Chamberlaine, Wilts 1645; Phillipps ii.
22, and see 32, 35; Athenæ iv. 388. Burrows 102, 207, 500.

John **Bidgood** (s. Humphry), b. Exeter 13 Mch 162¾, **Petr. 1642**,
expelled 1648, restored 1660, res. 1662; M.A. 24 Mch 164⅘, M.B.
24 Jan. 164⅞, adm. to practise 1 Feb. 164⅞, M.D. of Padua, incorp.
Ex. Coll. 20 Sep. 1660, hon. Fellow of College of Physicians 1664,
Fellow 1686, d. Exeter 13 Jan. 169⁰⁄₁, bur. in the Cathedral; Wood's

Fasti ii. 105, 226 ; Wood's Life ii. 186, iii. 353, 375 ; Gutch ii. 553, 594 ; Polwhele's *Devonshire* ii. 21, 41 ; Nat. Biog. ; he left his money to a distant relative, having disinherited his natural son, J. Sommers of Trinity.

George Hakewill (Fellow 1596), el. Rector 23 Aug. and adm. 19 Nov. 1642 in place of Prideaux, though the King had recommended George Kendal by a letter dated York 25 June 1642; on the breaking out of the Civil War he retired to his R. of Heanton Punchardon, Devon (given him 1615 by Sir Robert Basset of Heanton Court), where he died 2 Ap. 1649 ; his picture is in Ex. Coll. Hall, and there is an engraving of it. His monu. was so much broken that the College put up a marble slab on the wall of the Chancel at Heanton 1891, with his arms and motto (*Cor meum ad Te domine*), and a copy of the inscription on his tomb (plate of it in W. Antiq. Mch 1891, contributed by Rev. J. Ingle Dredge).

Arthur Bury or Bery (they called him *blackberry* because he was a little black man; Wood's Life ii. 195; s. John, V. of Heavitree, N. and Gleanings iv. 65), battellar 30 Mch 1639 to 11 Nov. 1647, **M.** 5 Ap. 1639 age 15, B.A. 29 Nov. 1642, **Petr.** 1643, full Fellow 6 May 1645, ejected 1648, when he went to Devon and married [he m.(2)1669 Mary Southcott of Exeter, widow of William Guise late fellow of All Souls] ; R. of Duloe, Cornwall 1648, of Packington, Som. 1649 ; restored 1662 ; M.A. 7 June 1645, B. and D.D. 27 June 1666 ; el. Rector 27 May 1666 in place of Maynard, he was 'a presbyterian, double-married,' says Wood, Life ii. 78 ; expelled 26 July 1690 by Bishop Trelawney the Visitor. He gave over £700 for College buildings, especially for an addition to the Rector's lodgings. He was V. of one third of Bampton, Oxon 28 June 1671, res. 1707 ; preb. of Exeter 166$\frac{2}{4}$–66, Chaplain to the King ; his book *The Naked Gospel*, part i. *Of Faith*, was publ. 4°, 1690 ; d. at his house in South Petherton, Som. 3 May, and bur. 6 May 1713 (Postboy of 16 May cited in Atterbury's Misc. Works i. 479); W. Antiq. vi. 180, 224; Ayliffe ii. 83, 85, 86, 88 ; Burrows 13 ; Wood's Life i. 41, ii. 488, 491, iii. 68, 328, 330, 332, 334, 425 (20 June 1693), 337–41. 345, 352, 360, 364, 435, 452, 474, 479, Athenæ i. 4, iii. 377, iv. 482 ; Prince 152–4 ; Catalogue of Wood's MSS. No. 79; Gutch ii. 553, iii. 108, 110, and App. 247 ; Bibl. Corn. *v.* Trelawny (Bishop Jonathan) 772–3 ; Philos. Trans. 8 Mch 1708 (vol. 26); Hearne's Diary 17 Aug. 1689, 20 Feb. 1706, 21 Ap., 8 May, 3 Nov., and p. 376 ; Gough's *British Topography* ii. 147 ; Hist. Comm. v. 376, 380, xii. 7. 194 (the *Terræ Filii* 1684);

N. and Q. Dec. 1869 p. 552; Eccl. Ant. ii. 149; Nat. Biog. His
son Arthur, of King's Coll. Camb., M.B. 1696, M.D. 1718 (Potes'
Registrum Regale 1847), physician at Exeter, bur. S. Mary Major
6 May 1725, presented Communion plate to South Petherton.

Barnard **Gealard** or Gailard, poor scholar 25 May 1638 to 17 July
1648, **M.** 2 Nov. 1638 age 15, B.A. 27 Ap. 1642, **Corn. 1644**, vac.
1648; M.A. 21 Jan. 164⅘; R. of Bridford 14 June 1661, of Poltimore
22 Ap. 1663, canon of Exeter 1671, Sub-dean 1675, d. Poltimore
20 Nov. 1693; Oliver's Bishops 296, Eccl. Ant. ii. 131, iii. 79,
Burrows 500.

William **Standard** (s. John, Fellow 1600, of Whitehill, Oxon),
battellar 9 Dec. 1641 to 11 Nov. 1642, **M.** 16 Dec. 1641 age 15,
Petr. 1644; B.A. 12 July 1647, M.A. 28 May 1650 (incorp. Camb.
1653), B.D. 15 Dec. 1660, vac. by m. 1665 in Devon; el. *Prælector
linguæ Hebraicæ* 1 July 1650; Burrows 60.

Nathanael **Haydon** (s. John, pleb., of Crediton), poor scholar
16 Aug. 1637 to 14 Jan. 164½, **M.** 13 Oct. 1637 age 17, B.A. 25 June
1641, **Dev. 1645**, vac. 1647; R. of Alwington near Bideford 1655,
d. 3 June 1668; Lysons' Devon cxcix; Polwhele's Devon iii. 423,
Charities of Devon ii. 291.

John **Sweete** (s. Andrew, ? Adrian), b. Modbury, Devon, **M.**
24 May 1639 age 15, Scholar of Corpus 26 Nov. 1641 age 18; B.A.
11 Feb. 164⅔, M.A. 13 Oct. 1646; **Petr. 1647**; ? R. of Ilchester
1690, and bur. 17 Aug. 1713: a John Swete was C. of Bradninch,
Devon 1663; a John Swete, V. of S. Keverne, Cornwall, d. 1695.

John **Bury** or Bery (s. John, of Bury), b. 1624; **M.** 17 May 1639
age 16; B.A. 1 Feb. 164⅔, at Middle Temple 1646, **Dev. 1647**,
expelled 1648; Walker ii. 116; Harding's Tiverton iv. 88; Gutch ii.
595; another John Bury occurs in Wood's Fasti ii. 70; *see* Foster i.
116 no. 30, and 219 no. 30.

Thirteen Fellows were put in by the Visitors in 1648, who made
Clifford sub-rector, Martin bursar, and Hancock dean. There were
13 vacancies, 10 of them owing to royalist Fellows being expelled,
viz.: *Cornish*, Polwhele, Porter, Squire (vac. 1647); *Devon*, Tozer,
John Conant (res. 1647), Fortescue, Procter, Kendall (vac. 1647);
Petrean, Soorten, Bidgood, Bury, Sweete; *Jersey*, Poindexter. Subscription to the oath of allegiance ceased, and the succession is
continued wholly from the Register till 24 Aug. 1662, the day fixed
for nonconformists quitting their fellowships; Gutch ii. 583, 597.

Robert **Hancock** (s. Robert, of S. Germans'), battellar 20 Nov.

1640 to 17 Aug. 1642, **M.** 27 Nov. 1640 age 17, M.A. 14 Ap. 1648 (incorp. Camb. 1653), appointed **Corn.** Fellow and Dean 5 July 1648, vac. 1657; pres. by the University to S. Martin's by Looe 8 Mch 165⅔; D. K. Rec. 46 p. 60; Wood's Life i. 157, 163; Gutch ii. 553, 596, 632, Burrows 500.

Edward **Searle**, battellar 18 Mch 16³⁸⁄₁₀, B.A. 21 Nov. 1643, appointed **Petr.** Fellow and Moderator in the Chapel 24 Ap. 1648, M.A. 6 July 1648, Delegate of Visitors 1649, vac. by marriage 16⁴⁸⁄₅₆; Burrows 501.

Francis **Howell** (s. Thomas, pleb., of Gwinear), **M.** 24 July 1642 age 17, cr. M.A. 14 Ap. 1648, appointed **Corn.** Fellow and Greek Reader 10 Aug. 1648, Proctor 1652, Whyte Professor of Moral Philosophy 25 Mch 1654: one of the Visitors of the University in 1655 (with Dr. Conant); res. his fellowship 1658, Principal of Jesus College 24 Oct. 1657–1660, Cassan's Bishops of Salisbury iii. 59; d. an Independent at Bethnal Green, Middlesex 10 Mch 1679, bur. in Bunhill Fields. He is said to have come to London after the Restoration as assistant to Mr. John Collins, minister of the church founded by Dr. Thomas Goodwin; but d. before him: Wood's Fasti ii. 111, 186; Athenæ iv. 99, 248; J. B. Marsh's *Memorials of the City Temple* 272–3; Nat. Biog. For a previous Dr. Howell at Jesus *see* Wordsworth 284.

Thomas **Masters**, B.A. Magd. H. 15 Ap. 1648, **Dev.** 11 Oct. 1648, vac. 165⅞; M.A. 29 Jan. 165⁰⁄₁; ? R. of Congerston, Leics. 1661, Hist. Comm. vii. 107; Burrows 502.

Abraham **Batten**, B.A. New Inn H. 4 July 1648; **dev.** 11 Oct. 1648; M.A. 22 Ap. 1651; Burrows 381, 425. 'There ought to be 4 Cornish fellows, but Mr. Battin was put into one of their places, hence a Cornish fellow was elected 30 June 1657 instead of for Battin's county.'

Samuel **Conant** (s. John, Fellow 1611), adm. Emmanuel, Camb. 15 Jan. 164⅝; **dev.** 20 July 1648, ejected 1662; B.A. 26 May 1649, M.A. 29 Ap. 1652, B.D., Proctor 1657, Cassan's Bishops of Salisbury iii. 149; presented by the University to the R. of Brown Candover, Hants 1658; chaplain to Dr. Reynolds bishop of Norwich, R. of Felthorpe, Norfolk 1662–5, of Lytchet Matravers 1662, of Child Ockford 1673, both in Dorset, of Holy Trinity, Dorchester 1704 or 1705, res. 1706; d. Lytchet Matravers 18 Nov. 1719 in his 92 year; Wood's Life ii. 508, iii. 477, Athenæ iv. 397; Hutchins iii. 333–4, iv. 84. He was elected Rector 1695 by the five Seniors expelled for

adhering to Dr. Bury, but never got possession. He left some books
to the College. For books of his at Wimborne see *The Library* i. 413.

Peter **Fiott, M.** New Inn H. 13 Feb. 164⅜; **Jer.** 24 Ap. **1648**;
B.A. 31 May 1649, M.B. 9 July 1652, M.D. 18 June 1657, removed
1660 for not proceeding M.A., ? living as a doctor in London 1669;
Evelyn's Diary 10 July 1654; Gutch ii. 575, Burrows 502, 568;
Hist. Comm. vi. 150, vii. 9, 17 Feb. 164⅞ payment of £100 to
Mrs. Mary Fiott (Lords' Journals x. 47).

Edmund **Davy** or Davis (2 s. Robert Davie of Canonteign in
Christow, Devon), commoner 13 Mch 164⁹⁄₀ to 23 Jan. 16⁴⁸⁄₅₀ (Davies),
M. 9 Ap. 1647 age 16, **Petr.** 10 Aug. **1648**, res. 1664; B.A. 15 June
1650 (as Edward Davys), M.A. 25 Ap. 1653; M.B. and D. 28 June
1665, Physician at Exeter 1667–93, d. there 22 Jan. 169⅔, bur. in
Lady Chapel of Cathedral; Prince 281–84; Visit. Devon 269, N. and
Gleanings 106, Burrows 502.

Lewis **Bradford** (s. John, pleb., of Harford, Devon), poor scholar
4 Feb. 164⁹⁄₁ to 23 Jan. 165⁰⁄₁, **M.** 9 Ap. 1647 age 19, **Petr.** 10 Aug.
1648, vac. 1657 : B.A. 31 May 1649, M.A. 29 Ap. 1652, presented
by the University to R. of Goodleigh, Devon 23 Ap. 1655, in place of
Thomas Downe, res., under 3 James I c. 5 ; Burrows 501.

John **Sladd** or Slade (s. Bennett, of Filleigh, Devon), b. Devon,
battellar 25 May 1647 to 7 Jan. 16⁴⁸⁄₅₉, **M.** 9 Ap. 1647 age 17 ; **Dev.**
11 Oct. **1648**, res. 23 Sep. 1657 : B.A. 15 June 1650, M.A. 25 Ap.
1653 : presented by the University to R. of Ockham, Surrey 8 Feb.
165⁴⁄₅, Manning and Bray's Surrey, Foster iv. 1363 ; ? R. of Burgh-
clere, Hants 1656 : Burrows 502.

William **Chudley** or Chidley (y. s. Sir George, of Ashton, Devon),
commoner 25 May 1647 to 23 Oct. 1649 (Chudleigh), **M.** 21 May 1647
age 19, **petr.** 10 Aug. **1648**, vac. 1656, Burrows 501 ; B.A. 12 Feb.
164⁴⁸⁄₅₀, M.A. 24 June 1652, Visit. Devon 190, Lysons' Devon cxxiii,
Hist. Comm. vii. 105.

Jonathan **Wills** (1 s. John, V. of Morval, Cornwall, see 1584);
M. 13 Feb. 164⅜ as Willis; **Corn.** 10 Aug. **1648**, when not yet B.A.;
vac. by m. St. Tudy 11 Mch 165½ Amye 6 d. of Humphry Nicoll of
Penvose ; R. of S. Mabyn 1652–55, of Lanteglos *cum* Advent 1655,
ejected 1662 ; living at S. Mabyn 1665, Report of Bishop Ward to
Archbishop Sheldon in Lambeth Library, Tenison MSS. 639 fol.
304, 411 ; d. Helland 1691, bur. S. Mabyn 11 Sep. 1691 ; Maclean
ii. 305; Visit. Corn. 559: Calamy i. 354; Bibl. Corn. 889, Burrows 502.

William **Oliver**, b. 27 Nov. 1627, battellar 3 Dec. 1648 to 22 Ap.

1650, **M.** 3 Dec. 1648, **petr. 1648,** adm. Chaplain by order of Visitors 17 Jan. 165$\frac{0}{1}$, res. Oct. 1653; cr. M.A. 23 Nov. 1655, 'formerly of this and of the other University, now a minister of the Gospel in the remoter parts of this nation'; R. of Launceston and Master of Grammar School, ejected 1662, ? m. Launceston 3 Feb. 164$\frac{7}{8}$ Alice Middleton; d. there 6 July 1681 (tablet in church); Calamy i. 354 (as John), Lake iii. 67, Peter's *Launceston* 320, 330, W. Antiq. x. 169.

John Conant (Fellow 1632), el. Rector 7, and adm. 29, June 1649, on Hakewill's death, by the new Fellows with consent of the Visitors, Burrows xliv, lxxv, 218, 242, 246, 251, 274, 318, 340, 356, 400, 418, 426, 499; Vice-Chancellor 9 Oct. 1657 to Aug. 1660; D. K. Rec. 46 p. 40, Presbyterian commissioner at Savoy Conference, Bull's Life 11; expelled for nonconformity 24 Aug. and his place declared vacant 1 Sep. 1662 ; he afterwards conformed; V. of S. Mary, Aldermanbury, London 1670; V. of All Saints, Northampton 15 Feb. 167$\frac{0}{1}$, Archdeacon of Norwich 8 June 1676 in place of his wife's uncle, John Reynolds; Preb. of Worcester 3 Dec. 1681; m. Aug. 1651 Elizabeth y. d. of Edward Reynolds afterwards Bishop of Norwich, who survived him and by whom he had 6 sons and 6 daughters; in Convocation 1690, Vox Cleri 62 ; d. 12 Mch 169$\frac{3}{4}$ in his 86 year, blind with age; monu. at All Saints, Northampton ; six volumes of his sermons were published; there are thirty MS. volumes of his sermons in the Bodleian, Addit. MSS. ; Wood's Life ii. 348, 557, iii. 21, 49, 154, 225, Gutch ii. 645, 652, 662, 673, 696, iii. 108; State Papers 28 Feb. 1654; Lysons' Devon 446; Burrows' *All Souls* 211. The College possesses a common-place book with 'Conant' written on it. He disgusted Wood by not letting him see the University Registers. For notices of his family see Hist. of Kidlington (O. H. Soc.) index ; for their arms 78, 79, 148. His 1 son John wrote his father's life.

Richard **Harte** or Heart, poor scholar 30 Oct. 1649 to 6 Aug. 1653, **M.** 12 Nov. 1650; **Dev. 1652,** vac. 1655 ; B.A. 22 June 1653.

Robert **Collins,** commoner 18 Sep. 1649 to 3 Aug. 1653, **M.** 21 Oct. 1650, Foster i. 309 ; **Petr. 1652,** transferred by the Visitors to the Chaplain's place 22 July 1654 (the changes in the Chaplain's place at this time are not very clear, see 1654, Burrows 393–4 two chaplains), vac. 1655 ; B.A. 6 July 1553, M.A. 5 July 1655; for a Robert Collins of Talaton, Devon, see Calamy ii. 74.

John **Francis** (s. John, of Tiverton), poor scholar 28 Mch 1648 to 26 Aug. 1651, **M.** 13 Feb. 164$\frac{8}{9}$, B.A. 23 Oct. 1651, **Chapl. 1652,** res. 1655; M.A. Ch. Ch. 26 May 1654, ? V. of Daventry 1667, and bur. there 3 Mch 168$\frac{7}{9}$; Baker's Northants i. 328.

John **Hopping**, battellar 16 Sep. 1650 to 2 Sep. 1653, **M.** 12 Nov. 1650, **Dev. 1652**, B.A. 26 May 1654, M.A. 9 Ap. 1657 (a pastor); after 1662 became pastor at Exeter and d. 4 Mch 1705; lic. 31 Dec. 1663 to m. Gertrude Ford widow, of S. Thomas', Exeter; Calamy ii. 108, Burrows 381, 502.

Samuel **Dell** (? related to William Dell, Nat. Biog. xiv. 324), poor Scholar 18 Sep. 1649 to 27 Dec. 1653, **M.** 12 Nov. 1650, **Corn. 1652**, vac. 1656; B.A. 22 June 1653; R. of Exton, Som. 1658; Wood's Fasti ii. 110, Athenæ index; Gutch ii. 657; Maclean i. 50, 53, Coll. Corn. 201, Lake iv. 125, State Papers 1649 index.

Richard **Inglett** (? y. s. Giles, of Lamerton, and bap. Chudleigh 30 Aug. 1632; Visit. Devon 500), battellar 29 Ap. 1650 to 25 July 1653, **M.** 12 Nov. 1650; **Dev. 1652**, expelled 1663 for nonconformity, practised physic at Plymouth; B.A. 21 Jan. 165$\frac{3}{4}$, M.A. 20 June 1656, extra lic. of Coll. of Phys. 1661; Calamy i. 228, Polwhele's Devon ii. 126–7, Burrows 381, 502.

John **Saunders**, b. Exeter, battellar 31 Oct. 1649 to 20 July 1652, **M.** 12 Nov. 1650, **dev. 1 Ap. 1652** by the Visitors in place of Wills (Wills held a Cornish fellowship); B.A. 13 June 1653, M.A. 19 Ap. 1656 (as Richard); R. of Hampden, Bucks 1657, expelled 1662 and d. within a year; Calamy i. 303; Eccl. Ant. i. 141, ? R. of Loxbeare 6 Feb. 1661, deprived 1662.

Humphry **Sainthill** (s. Humphry, R. of Zeal Monachorum, Visit. Devon 1663, Vivian's Marriage Licences 15 Dec. 1623, 15 Aug. 1625), battellar 15 Oct. 1650 to 13 July 1653, **M.** 12 Nov. 1650, **Petr. 1653**; expelled 1662; B.A. 28 June 1656, M.A. 11 June 1658; V. of Buckfastleigh, Devon 1672; Eccl. Ant. ii. 17, **19**; Trans. Devonshire Assoc. xxi. 383.

Richard **Crossing** (? s. Philip, bap. S. Petrock's, Exeter 31 May 1632, Visit. Devon 255), battellar 8 Nov. 1649 to 5 Ap. 1654, **M.** 12 Nov. 1650, B.A. 13 June 1653, **petr. 1654** in place of Oliver, 'qui locus jam Capellani officio in perpetuum destinatus est,' vac. 1656; M.A. 23 Ap. 1656; V. of Otterton, Devon 5 Dec. 1662, and (?) of Kenton 1662; d. 5 Jan. 168$\frac{4}{9}$; Eccl. Ant. i. 135, Calamy ii. 265.

Richard **Whitway**, pleb. (? s. Rev. William, of Morebath, who m. Agnes Lake, widow, of Morebath, 4 May 1631), b. Devon, battellar (? 19 Ap.) 1652 to 22 Aug. 1654, **M.** 1 June 1652, **Petr. 1654**, B.A. 9 Ap. 1657, M.A. 13 May 1659; when expelled 1662 he became chaplain to Sir John Maynard in Devon, but died of small-pox in a few weeks; Calamy i. 228.

Thomas **Lethbridge**, battellar 13 Mch 165$\frac{0}{1}$ to 11 Aug. 1655 (payment to William Lethbridge), **M.** 13 Mch 165$\frac{0}{1}$, B.A. 12 Oct. 1654, **Petr. 1655**; M.A. 29 May 1657, B.D. 17 Dec. 1667; suspended 1690, restored 1695, d. 1 Sep. 1695, bur. 2 Sep. in the Chapel age 72, admin. bond 14 Oct. 1695, Griffiths 39; Gutch iii. 120, Wood's Life iii. 362, 385, 488.

John **Spicer**, pleb., **M.** Magd. H. 19 Nov. 1650, B.A. 8 Feb. 165$\frac{2}{3}$, M.A. Wadham 28 June 1655; **Chapl.** 7 July 1655, d. 1655.

Thomas **Brancker** (s. Thomas, schoolmaster at Barnstaple), b. Barnstaple Aug. 1636, battellar 8 Nov. 1652 to 19 July 1655, **M.** 27 Nov. 1652 age 17, B.A. 15 June 1655, **Dev. 1655**; M.A. 22 Ap. 1658, expelled 1662; V. of Whitegate, Cheshire, R. of Tilston 1668, Master of the school at Macclesfield; d. 26 Nov. 1676, bur. Macclesfield Church.   He published the *Doctrine of the Sphere* 1662, and an *Introduction to Algebra* 1668; Nat. Biog.

Edmund **Fidoe**, of Shelsley, Worcs., **M.** Wadham 14 Nov. 1650 servitor (as Edward), scholar 1651, B.A. 4 Feb. 165$\frac{2}{3}$, M.A. 22 June 1655; **Chapl. Ex. Coll.** 12 Jan. 165$\frac{5}{6}$.

John **Ford** (? s. Charles, of Fordmore; if so, Roger Ford 1663 was his brother), commoner 17 June 1652 to 10 July 1655, **M.** 20 July 1652; B.A. 30 Jan. 165$\frac{5}{6}$; **Dev. 1656**; M.A. 29 June 1658, res. July 1664; R. of Whitstone, Devon 10 Feb. 165$\frac{7}{3}$, and V. of Totnes 1664–71, d. 22 Mch. 167$\frac{0}{1}$; Eccl. Ant. ii. 31.

John **Parker** (? s. James, of Trengoff in Warleggan), bap. there 1633, battellar 7 Aug. 1652 to 18 Jan. 165$\frac{5}{6}$, B.A. 28 Feb. 165$\frac{5}{6}$, **Corn. 1656**, res. 18 Jan. 165$\frac{7}{8}$; M.A. 6 July 1658; 'he did not declaim, or was examined for his degree, because he had an impediment in his speech, yet he delivered in writing his declamations to the Vice-Chancellor and Proctors,' Wood's Extracts from Univ. Reg.

Stephen **Bloy**, poor scholar 28 Mch 1651 to 9 July 1656, **M.** 13 Mch 165$\frac{0}{1}$; B.A. 17 Dec. 1654, **Petr.** 5 July 1656 in place of Crossing (Chaplain); vac. 1659; M.A. 29 May 1657; V. of Chudleigh, Devon 1665, d. 1673; Eccl. Ant. i. 25.

John **Hearne**, pleb., battellar 9 Aug. 1653 to 26 Aug. 1657, **M.** 21 June 1653; B.A. 6 Feb. 165$\frac{0}{7}$, **Petr. 1657**, expelled 1662, re-elected 1663, Reg. 30 June, 11 and 27 July 1683; M.A. 21 June 1659, B.D. 15 June 1669, D.D. 4 Mch 168$\frac{9}{7}$; Proctor 1664; R. of S. Ann's, Soho 1 Ap. 1686–1704, Dean Prideaux's Letters p. 87;

removed from his place as Fellow 1690 by Bishop Trelawny, for holding that living with his fellowship; Wood's Life ii. 54, 155, 334, 380, iii. 303, 380, Athenæ iii. 128; *see* in Bury and Colmer pamphlets, An Account &c. 33, *The Case of Exeter College* 50, A Defence &c. 39; Hutchins ii. 125.

George **Verman** (? s. John, of Lamorran), battellar 22 May 1655 to 24 July 1657, **M.** 31 May 1655; **Corn. 1657** in place of Hancock (*see* 1669); B.A. 3 May 1660, M.A. 21 Jan. 166⅔ (incorp. Camb. 1664), B.D. 7 July 1674, Proctor 1672 (he praised Wood's Hist. et Antiq. Oxon. in his speech; Wood's Life ii. 261, iii. 440); ? R. of Mells, Som. 1693; d. 29 Mch 1718 age 83, bur. in College chapel; will proved 24 Ap. 1718, Griffiths 63; Gutch iii. 121; Visit. Corn. 526, Hearne 5 Jan. 1706, 25 Nov. 1707.

William **Paynter** (s. William and Jane, of Antron in Sithney), b. Trelissick in S. Erth, bap. S. Erth 7 Dec. 1637; poor scholar 27 Feb. 165⅚ to 3 July 1657, **M.** 29 Mch 1656; **Corn. 1657** in place of Masters, though Masters was a Devon Fellow, *see* 1669; B.A. 3 May 1660, M.A. 21 Jan. 166⅔ (incorp. Camb. 1664), B.D. 7 July 1674, D.D. 27 June 1695; Rector 15 Aug. 1690 (and then, as Rector, removed 1695 from Dr. Bury's fellowship to Colmer's); Athenæ iv. 499, 501 'Paynter *alias* Cambourne' presented to R. of Wootton, Northants 24 July 1686, and so vac. his fellowship Feb. 168⅞; continued to hold Wootton with the Rectorship; Vice-Chancellor 1697; d. Wootton 18 Feb. 171⅝ age 80; adm. bond 2 Ap. 1716, Griffiths 47; Nichols Lit. Anecd. i. 102. He m. (1) Mary d. of Rector Conant, widow of M. Pool, M.D., b. 1657, d. 7 May 1693, monu. at Wootton; (2) Sarah d. of Francis Duncombe of Broughton, Bucks, she was bur. Ilsington, Devon 22 Sep. 1725 in 77 year. Mary (prob. their d.) m. Ex. Cath. 11 July 1723 Philip Nanson, V. of Ilsington; Bibl. Corn. 434; Visit. Corn. 353; Davies Gilbert i. 350, Polwhele v. 173, Wood's Life iii. 15.

George **Credeford**, pleb., battellar 21 Feb. 165⁹ to 26 Aug. 1658, **M.** 10 Mch 165⁹, **Dev. 1658**; B.A. 13 July 1661, M.A. 23 Ap. 1664 (incorp. Camb. 1668), res. 1670, R. of Torbrian, Devon 1669.

George **Gooddall**, poor scholar 12 May 1656, **M.** 23 July 1656, **Corn. 1658**, full Fellow 9 July 1659, res. 27 June 1689; B.A. 13 July 1661, M.A. 23 Ap. 1664 (incorp. Camb. 1668), B.D. 13 Oct. 1674, R. of Padworth, Berks; Wood's Life ii. 83.

Narcissus **Marsh**, pleb., b. Hannington near Highworth, Wilts 20 Dec. 1638, **M.** Magd. H. 25 July 1655; B.A. 12 Feb. 165⅞, **Sar.**

1658, full Fellow 9 July 1659, res. 12 Oct. 1673; M.A. 13 July 1660, B.D. 12 Dec. 1667, D.D. 23 June 1671 (incorp. Camb. 1678), V. of Swindon, Wilts 1662–3, Principal of Alban H. 12 May 1673, V. of Gresford, Denbighs. 1686–90; Chaplain to Seth Ward, Bishop of Salisbury, and to the Earl of Clarendon; Provost of Trinity, Dublin Dec. 1678, Bishop of Leighlin and Ferns 20 Feb. $168\frac{2}{3}$, Archbishop of Cashel Dec. 1690, (preb. St. Asaph 1690–1), of Dublin 1694, of Armagh $170\frac{2}{3}$, d. 2 Nov. 1713, bur. 6 Nov. S. Patrick's churchyard, Dublin; Phillipps ii. 25, 27; Athenæ iv. 498, 892, Wood's Fasti ii. 199; Wood's Life ii. 264, 468, 558 (his love of weekly concerts endeared him to the music-loving antiquary), iii. 77, 435; Gutch iii. 110; Philos. Transactions no. 156; Rawlinson MSS. class C. no. 983 and index. He wrote *Essay on the Doctrine of Sounds*, &c. His MS. diary, beginning 20 Dec. 1690, remains in the Library of ten thousand volumes, which he presented to Trinity, Dublin. Letters from Bodleian i. 76; E. Bernard (Bentley's correspondent, Wordsworth 92, Nat. Biog. iv. 379) went to Holland to buy some of James Golius' MSS. for him, 103–8 his letter on founding a library at Dublin; Hearne ii. 60, 2 Nov. 1705, 21 Aug. 1710. He is said to have spent £20,000 on works of public good. See John D'Alton's *Memoirs of Archbishops of Dublin* 290–98; *Vox Cleri* ed. 2. 1690. His portrait is in Ex. Coll. Hall.

Ozias **Upcott** (? s. William, V. of St. Clement's), battellar 30 Sep. 1656 to 16 July 1659, **M.** 23 July 1656, **Corn. 1659**, res. $166\frac{3}{4}$; B.A. 12 July 1662; R. of Honiton 8 Jan. $166\frac{2}{3}$ to $169\frac{8}{9}$, d. 6 Feb. $169\frac{8}{9}$: Eccl. Ant. ii. 79, Coll. Corn. 1124.

Thomas **Matthewes** (signs himself Mathew), battellar 18 Ap. 1657 to 19 Oct. 1660, **M.** 15 June 1657, **Petr. 1660**, res. 20 Dec. 1670, having taken a living; B.A. 16 July 1663, M.A. 28 Ap. 1666; V. of Merton, Oxon 1668 (Reg. 1 July 1668, 15 Dec. 1670); ? R. of Alwington 1668, of Alphington 22 Feb. $167\frac{6}{7}$, both in Devon, bur. Alphington 15 Aug. 1712; Eccl. Ant. i. 76.

John **Harris** (s. John, pleb., of S. Issey, Cornwall), poor scholar 13 May 1656 to 7 Sep. 1660, **M.** 29 Mch 1656, B.A. 2 June 1659, made **Chaplain** 6 Sep. **1660** by the Royal Commissioners, probably in place of Fidoe, res. 1666; M.A. 11 Ap. 1662; ? V. of S. Issey 25 Aug. 1666, of S. Clether 11 Dec. 1672, both in Cornwall, bur. S. Issey 27 Ap. 1696.

William **Priaulx** (s. Peter, Esq.), sojourner 23 Jan. to 16 July 1661, **M.** 5 May 1661 age 17, **Guer. 1661**, vac. 1662; Hutchins ii. 107.

George **Snell** (s. John, minister, of Thurlestone, Devon), battellar 15 Mch 166⁰/₄ to 16 July 1662, **M.** 12 July 1661 age 17, **Petr. 1662** in place of his kinsman Bidgood; B.A. 14 Oct. 1665, M.A. 28 May 1668; vac. 1671 by having taken the V. of Menheniot; R. of Thurlestone 1679, preb. of Kerswell in Castro Exon. 1679, preb. of Exeter 31 Jan. 168⅙–1700, archdeacon of Totnes 18 May 1694, d. 14 Jan. 170⁰/₁; Prince 75; Oliver's Bishops 292, Gutch's Fasti 246.

Joseph Maynard (Fellow 1625), el. Rector 18 Sep. 1662, res. 30 Ap. 1666.

Philip **Horseman** (s. of a minister), **M.** Magd. H. 28 Mch 1655, B.A. 12 Oct. 1658; **dev. 1663**; M.A. 4 July 1661 (incorp. Camb. 1664), d. 3 May 1668, bur. in the College chapel, Wood's Life ii. 155.

Samuel **Masters** or Master (s. George, of Sarum), **M.** Wadham 13 Nov. 1662 age 16, Gardiner i. 246; **Sar. 1663**, res. July 1681; B.A. 14 July 1666, M.A. 27 Ap. 1669, B.D. 8 May 1680; preacher at Stanton Harcourt and South Ley, Oxon, chaplain to Earl of Radnor and preacher to Hosp. of Bridewell 1677, canon of S. Paul's 1678, preb. of Lichfield 18 May 1680, R. of Shottesbrooke 1685–93, of Dunton May to Sep. 1693, both in Berks, V. of Burton on Trent; d. Bath 12 Sep. 1693, bur. in the Abbey; published *Sermons*; gave some books to the Library; Wood's Fasti ii. 289, Athenæ iv. 385, Hearne ii. 60, 419.

Peter **Carey** (s. Peter, of S. Peter's Passe), **M.** 3 Ap. 1663 age 18; **Guer. 1663** (nomination from Bailiff and Jurats of Guernsey received 23 Mch); B.A. 14 July 1666; vac. by having taken the R. of S. Saviour's, Guernsey 1669, and married 1670.

Ames **Crymes** (Reg. 1671; 5 s. Ellis, of Buckland Monachorum, Devon), **M.** Lincoln 21 Feb. 166½ age 17; commoner Ex. Coll. 13 June to 3 July 1663, **Petr. 1663**, vac. 1683 by promotion; B.A. 14 July 1666, M.A. 15 June 1669, B.D. 8 May 1680; Chaplain at Tangier 1676; R. of Curry Malet, Som. 1681, of Huxham 28 May 1690, of Buckland Monachorum 1 Nov. 1708, both in Devon; bur. 22 May 1709; Wood's Life ii. 304, 498: Gutch iii. App. 246; Eccl. Ant. iii. 82; Jewitt's Plymouth 233, Visit. Devon 259; Reg. 13 Feb. 167⅘ 'M. Crimes et M. Bravel Tangerium profecturis ut ibidem prædicantium munere fungantur venia in quinquennium concessa, cum ea insuper gratia ut omnibus commodis et dividendis aeque ac præsentes fruantur.'

Richard **Hutchins** (s. Richard, pleb., of Carway, Devon), battellar 2 Ap. 1661 to 6 July 1663 (as Huchins), **M.** 3 Ap. 1661 age 16, **Dev.**

1663; B.A. 14 July 1666, M.A. 27 Ap. 1669, B.D. 8 May 1680; d. 2 Ap. 1718, four days after his old friend George Verman, and lies buried beside him in the Chapel, will proved 16 Ap. 1718; benefactor to the College; Griffiths 33, Gutch iii. 120.

Thomas **Hawkey**, arm. f., sojourner 30 Dec. 1658 to 7 July 1663, M. 11 Dec. 1658; B.A. 31 May 1662, **Corn. 1663**, res. 1668; M.A. 8 Ap. 1665; R. of Marhamchurch, Cornwall 19 Aug. 1673–1728.

Matthew **Hole**, poor scholar 19 Mch 165⁷⁄₁ to 3 Dec. 1661, then battellar to 7 July 1663, M. 18 Mch 165⁷⁄₈, B.A. 15 Oct. 1661, **Dev. 1663**; M.A. 14 June 1664, B.D. 13 Oct. 1674, D.D. 1 June 1716; Lecturer at Carfax 18 Dec. 1668, V. of Bishop's Lavington, Wilts 1673–74; vac. Feb. 168⁴⁄₇ by having taken the R. of Stogursey near Stowey, Som. Jan. 168⁷⁄₆; preb. of Wells 1 Mch 168⁷⁄₈; R. of Fiddington, Som. 1708–11; el. Rector 8 Mch 171⁵⁄₈ and readmitted Devonshire Fellow in place of Hutchins; d. 19 July 1730 age 90, bur. in the College chapel, will 4 May 1730, Griffiths 30. A volume in Bishop Conybeare's handwriting contains ' letters and papers relating to the dispute between Dr. Hole and some of the Fellows 1720' (chiefly about Hart Hall, and Dr. Newton), and see Conybeare's ' Calumny Refuted' 99, Terrae Filius nos. xxix, xxx; Wood's Fasti ii. 248, 344; Polwhele v. 170, Hearne ii. 95; wrote 'Practical Discourses on various parts of the Liturgy of the Church of England,' 5 vol. Oxon 1717; Nat. Biog.

Samuel **Norris** (s. John, minister of Alborne or Aubourne, Wilts), battellar 1 July 1661 to 3 July 1663, M. 5 Ap. 1661 age 17, **Petr. 1663**, vac. 1682 by having taken a living; B.A. 14 July 1666, M.A. 27 Ap. 1669, B.D. 3 May 1680; Proctor 1679; R. of Tylehurst 1681, of Englefield 1708, both in Berks; will 3 Mch 173⁸⁄₉.

George **Bruton**, arm. f. (Reg. 1664, 1671 his fellowship regarded as Petrean), M. Balliol 31 July 1658, B.A. 5 May 1662; commoner Ex. Coll. 16 Ap. 1663 to 15 July 1664, **Dev. (Petr.) 1664**; M.A. 18 Jan. 166⁴⁄₅; R. of S. Ewe, Cornwall 1670, d. Ex. Coll. 23 Dec. 1671, bur. 25 Dec. in the Chapel, will propounded June 1672 (no record of probate), Griffiths 10; Gutch iii. 121; left money to the College, Reg. 9 Jan. 167⁴⁄₅, Wood's Life ii. 236.

Sampson **Bastard** (3 s. William, of Gerston, Devon, by Johanna d. of Sampson Hele), bap. W. Alvington 26 Dec. 1643, commoner Ex. Coll. 17 Mch 166½ to 8 July 1664, M. 26 Ap. 1662 age 17, **Petr. 1664**, res. 1670; B.A. 4 July 1667, M.A. 9 July 1670; R. of South Pool, Devon 1668–76, d. 12 Sep. 1676, inscription to his memory in the chancel; *Kingsbridge and Salcombe* 1819 p. 190, Visit. Devon 50.

Thomas **Polwhele** (2 s. John, of Treworgan, and nephew of Degory, Fellow 1635), sojourner 17 Dec. 1662 to 1 July 1664, M. 17 Dec. 1662 age 17, **Corn. 1664**, vac. 1678 by having taken 1677 the V. of Newlyn, deprived 1690 as a Nonjuror; B.A. 4 July 1667, M.A. 23 June 1671; Oliver's Bishops 158; Maclean ii. 306.

John **Gough, M.** Magd. H. 21 Mch 165⅝ servitor, B.A. 16 Nov. 1661, M.A. 28 June 1664; **Petr. 1665**, res. 1672; ? at Lincoln's Inn 1658 as 1 s. Robert, of Verneham Dean, South Hants.

Arthur Bury (Fellow 1643), el. **Rector** 27, adm. 29, May **1666**.

Richard **Beswick**, poor scholar 30 Jan. 16⁵⁸⁄₅₉ to 24 Oct. 1663, then battellar to 5 Jan. 166¾, **M.** 11 Ap. 1660, B.A. 22 Oct. 1663; M.A. New Coll. 15 June 1666; adm. **Chapl.** 8 Nov. **1666**, res. 1671; V. of Westport, Wilts 1670–1705, d. 1705.

Nicholas **Burrington** (y. s. Gilbert, of Jewes Hollicomb, Devon), commoner 25 Mch 1667 to 12 Jan. 16⁶⁸⁄₇₀, **M.** 22 Mch 166⁹⁄₇ age 16, **Dev. 1669**, vac. 1690; B.A. 4 July 1672, M.A. 22 Ap. 1675, B.D. 5 July 1686, R. of Easington, Oxon 1677–86, V. of Exminster 13 Ap. 1689–1717, d. 21 May 1717; Eccl. Ant. ii. 25, Visit. Devon 120.

Edward **Burgh** (s. Edward, pleb., of Preston, Som.), battellar 14 June 1662 (the bursar calls him *Birch*) to 29 Oct. 1666, **M.** 28 June 1662 age 17, **Corn. (Petr.) 1669** in place of Hawkey, res. 1678. In 1671 Burgh's fellowship was made a Petrean one, so that the eight Petrean Fellows now were Hearne, Crymes, Norris, Burgh, Matthewes, Bruton, Gough, Bravell; B.A. 28 Ap. 1666, M.A. New Coll. 21 Jan. 166⅝, canon of Wells 1670, R. of Stoke Gifford 1672, of Monksilver 1675, of Sutton Bingham, Som. 1676, of Melbury Bubb, Dorset 1677.

Richard **Bravell** (s. Dr. Thomas, of Compton Abbot, Dorset, Hutchins iii. 536), **M.** Edmund H. 18 Oct. 1662 age 16, B.A. 16 June 1666, M.A. 27 Ap. 1669; **Petr. 1670**, res. 1682; B.D. 14 June 1680 by diploma when chaplain to the garrison of Tangiers, to which place he went 1676 (Wood's Fasti ii. 377), 'where he hath showed himself so useful to the public that upon his desire of returne the Bishop of London and other eminent persons required his continuance there,' Wood's MS. E. 9: V. of Welton, Yorks. ? 1682.

Elias **Carteret** (1 s. Philip, bailiff of Jersey, by Mary de la Place, and nephew of Sir George Carteret, whose d. Louisa m. Sir Robert Atkins), b. 1652, sojourner 15 May 1669 to 21 July 1670, **M.** 21 May

1669, **Jer. 1670** in place of Carey, res. 1678; B.A. 3 July 1673, M.A.
6 Ap. 1676; m. Mary Hancock of Wilts; pres. 1678 by Sir Robert
Atkins to R. of Cotes, Glouc., R. of Poole, Wilts 1692–1720; ? V. of
Stonehouse, Glouc.; Rawlinson MSS. Class C. 421 fol. 189; d. Cotes
30 Dec. 1720; Phillipps ii. 56, Bigland's *Gloucester* 430.

Charles **Tarleton** (s. Rev. John, of Wembworthy, Devon), **M**.
Wadham 9 July 1666 age 16, B.A. 22 Ap. 1670; adm. **Chapl.** 25 June
1671; M.A. 16 Jan. 167⅔; res. 1677 on taking R. of Bicton, Devon.

Thomas **Hurrell** (s. John, of Hendham, Devon), battellar 25 Mch
1661 to 14 July 1667, **M**. 3 Ap. 1661 age 18, B.A. 15 Oct. 1664,
M.A. 20 June 1667; **Dev. 1671**, res. Dec. 1673; R. of Bere Ferrers,
Devon 1673–1721, d. **1721**.

John **Hodder** (s. Rev. John, of Thorncombe, Devon), b. Whitchurch,
Dorset, **M**. Wadham 1 Mch 166⅝ age 15, B.A. 19 Oct. 1669; **Petr**.
1671; M.A. 7 June 1672; d. 6 Mch 167¾.

John **Searle** (s. Thomas, pleb.,) b. Aveton Gifford, battellar
18 Mch 166⅝, **M**. 26 Mch 1669 age 19; **Dev. 1671**, res. 29 Ap. 1680
on pres. to V. of Broad Hempston, Devon 10 Ap. 1679; B.A. 3 Nov.
1674, M.A. 16 June 1677; D. K. Rec. 46 p. 104.

John **Bury** (s. Arthur, Rector 1666), battellar 13 Mch 166⁴⁄ to
25 Ap. 1670, **M**. 6 Mch 166⅞ age 13, B.A. 30 Oct. 1671, **Dev. 1672**,
the Vice-Chancellor selecting him in preference to John Eveleigh who
had equal votes, and who was elected Fellow 1674; M.A. 21 Oct. 1675,
M.B. 2 May 1681; had leave 1679 from Lord Petre to study four
years in a foreign university, d. 1685; Wood's Life ii. 319.

Balthazar **Vigures** (s. Robert, of Parkham), battellar 14 July 1668 to
16 July 1672, **M**. 9 July 1668 age 18, B.A. 20 Ap. 1672, **Petr. 1672**, rejected 12 July 1673 at end of year of probation; M.A. Alban H. 17 Dec.
1675, Wood's Life ii. 351, 17 July 1676 *bannimus* stuck up on the
Schooles gate to expell Balthazer Vigures, *Terræ filius* on Act Saturday,
for egregiously abusing the Doctors and not submitting; P.C. of Frithelstock, Devon 1681–2, bur. Parkham 9 May 1689; his d. Frances bap.
Parkham 8 Sep. 1681; Mary bap. 23 Mch 168¾, bur. 10 Oct. 1685.

Thomas **Trevethick** (s. Rev. William, of S. Eval, Cornwall, and
Petrockstow, Devon), poor scholar 19 Ap. 1669 to 7 June 1673, **M**.
26 Mch 1669 age 17, B.A. 12 Oct. 1672, **Petr. 1673**, M.A. 28 June
1675, d. 21 Dec. 1676, bur. in the College chapel; Wood's Life ii.
362, Lake i. 373, Bibl. Corn. 800, Coll. Corn. 1090.

Philip **Bennett** (s. Francis, of Smallbrooke near Warminster,
Wilts), b. Devizes, battellar 3 Mch 166⁸ to 22 Sep. 1674, **M**. 5 Mch

$166\frac{8}{9}$ age 19, B.A. 12 Oct. 1672, **Sar. 1674**; vac. by m. June 1688; M.A. 28 June 1675, B.D. by diploma 3 Nov. 1685 when on the King's service in Jamaica; Wood's Fasti ii. 398.

John **Eveleigh** (s. Edward, pleb., of Exeter), battellar 6 Ap. 1668 to 23 Sep. 1674, **M.** 14 Mch $166\frac{7}{8}$ age 17, B.A. 16 Oct. 1671, M.A. 25 June 1674, **Dev. 1674**, res. July 1681; R. of South Sydenham, 1680, V. of Lamerton 1711, both in Devon.

Benjamin **Archer** (s. Edward, pleb., of Cookham), battellar 20 Ap. to 3 July 1674; **M.** Pembroke 17 May 1670 age 15, B.A. 20 Jan. $167\frac{3}{4}$; **Petr. 1674**, suspended 1690, res. Nov. 1692; M.A. 26 Oct. 1676 (incorp. Camb. 1681), B.D. 31 May 1688, ? V. of Easter Alta, Essex 1671, R. of Wexham 1683, V. of Quainton 1692, both in Bucks, d. 1732; Wood's Life iii. 67.

William **Crabb** (s. William, R. of Childe Okeford, Dorset 20 July 1660, D. K. Rec. 46 p. 41), **M.** Wadham 17 July 1669 age 15, B.A. 10 Ap. 1673; **Petr. 1674**, vac. by m. 1687; M.A. 21 Feb. $167\frac{5}{6}$, B.D. 19 Mch $168\frac{6}{7}$; R. of Childe Okeford Inferior 1687, of Hammohun 1709–19, instit. to R. of Bloxworth 17 July 1723, bur. 12 Aug. 1747 age 95; Hutchins iv. 83, 84; D. K. Rec. 46 p. 41.

Samuel **Adams** (s. John, pleb., of Oxon), b. Oxford, battellar 11 Mch $167\frac{2}{3}$ to 5 July 1677, **M.** 14 Mch $167\frac{2}{3}$ age 16, B.A. 17 Oct. 1676, **Petr. 1677**, suspended 1690, restored 1694, res. 1715; M.A. 23 June 1679, B.D. 6 Aug. 1690; R. of Wootton, Northants 1716, d. 3 Ap. 1741; Wood's Life ii. 497, iii. 256, 496, Hearne 7 Dec. 1705.

Lewis **Stephens** (3 s. Lewis and Elizabeth), b. Braunton, Devon 13 Feb., and bap. 21 Mch $165\frac{3}{4}$, scholar Gonville and Caius, Camb. 6 Nov. 1671 age 17, B.A. 1675, incorp. Oxford 26 Feb. $167\frac{7}{8}$, M.A. 29 Oct. 1678 (incorp. Camb. 1680) **Chapl.** 25 Feb. $167\frac{7}{8}$, res. 17 Ap. 1680, replaced his name 21 June to 3 Oct. 1681; V. of Treneglos, Cornwall 14 Feb. 167^{8}–1685, of Menheniot 1685–$172\frac{4}{5}$, d. there 1 Jan. $172\frac{4}{5}$ in his 71 year (monu.); famous as a botanist; m. Rachel d. of Oliver Naylor, canon of Exeter; Moyle's Posthumous Works i. 413–4; Lake iii. 312; Bibl. Corn. 686; Vivian's Marriage Licenses 5 May 1625, Venn's *Admissions to Gonville and Caius, Cambridge* 275.

Nicolas **Kendall** (1 s. Bernard, of Lostwithiel, by Anne Snell), b. 28 Jan. $165\frac{6}{7}$, commoner 9 July 1673 to 11 July 1678, **M.** 9 July 1673, B.A. 10 May 1677, **Corn. 1678**, res. 25 May 1681; M.A. 22 Jan. $16\frac{79}{80}$ (incorp. Camb. 1699); V. of Lanlivery 1681–$17\frac{39}{40}$,

R. of Sheviock 1693–1740, preb. of Exeter 23 Jan. $168\frac{7}{8}$–$17\frac{3}{40}$, Archdeacon of Totnes 28 July 1713–$17\frac{38}{40}$, m. Lanlivery 14 Oct. 1686 Jane d. of Thomas Carew, d. 3 Mch $17,\frac{38}{40}$ bur. 7 Mch in Exeter Cathedral; Lake iii. 23, iv. 146, Polwhele v. 165, C. S. Gilbert ii. 178; Coll. Corn. 449; Visit. Corn. 260.

Robert **Ratcliffe** (s. Richard, pleb., of Broad Clyst, Devon), b. Tawstock, battellar 2 June 1674 to 30 July 1679, **M.** 10 Ap. 1674 age 17, B.A. 16 Oct. 1677, **Petr. 1679** (Thomas Martyn B.A. had equal votes, but the Vice-Chancellor selected Ratcliffe), vac. Aug. 1692 by having taken a living: M.A. 15 June 1680, B.D. 16 July 1691; R. of Colne-Rogers 1694, and V. of Stonehouse, both in Glouc.

NOTE.—Allowances were granted 1679 to the Fellows absent on State service, Crymes, Bravell and Bennett, in consequence of a Royal Letter, for which see the Register 25 Ap. 1679.

Christopher **Furneaux** (1 s. John, of Stoke Damerel, Plymouth), poor scholar 2 Ap. 1674 to 6 July 1680, **M.** 3 Ap. 1674 age 17, B.A. 16 Oct. 1677, **Dev. 1680**, res. June 1688; M.A. 8 July 1680, C. of Great Torrington 1683, V. of Whitchurch (worth £90 a year) near Tavistock 1688 (? 1697); m. Sarah Doidge; see *Pedigree of Furneaux* 1876.

Michael **Guerdain**, (so he spells his name; others spelt it Geurdon, Jourdain; 1 s. Denis M.D., by Mary Herault), battellar 7 May 1677 to 7 July 1680, **M.** 30 Mch 1677 age 16, **Jer. 1680** in place of Carteret (though Carteret was also from Jersey), Tanner MSS. 338 folio 188; B.A. 14 July 1683, d. unm. 1684, bur. Cassington, Oxon; admin. bond 23 May 1690, Griffiths 25.

Gilbert **Geere** (s. John, pleb.), b. Kenn, Devon, battellar 1 July 1670 to 23 Dec. 1674, **M.** 9 Dec. 1670 age 18, B.A. Hart H. 7 July 1674, M.A. 3 May 1677; **Chaplain** 24 Sep. 1680, B.D. 6 Mch $168\frac{7}{8}$; vac. 1689 by having been admitted R. of Kenn 26 Mch 1688, bur. 1 Ap. 1726; Eccl. Ant. i. 42, Lysons' Devon 297.

Jonathan **Hooker** (s. Balsam, of Trelissick in S. Ewe), b. S. Ewe, poor scholar 12 to 25 Ap. 1673, battellar 23 June 1677 to 19 July 1679; **M.** 22 Mch 167^2 age 17, B.A. New Inn H. 17 Oct. 1676; M.A. Ex. Coll. 23 June 1679; **Corn. 1681**, vac. by marriage 1682, R. of Sandy, Beds 1683. C. S. Gilbert under S. Ewe; Bishop J. Moore's *Diaries at Cambridge* 1679 May, 'Mr. John Laurence and Mr. Jonathan Hooker, both recommended by Mr. Prideaux for preferment in Cornwall, very deserving men.'

Ezra **Cleaveland**, b. Honiton, poor scholar 19 Feb. $167\frac{7}{8}$ to

18 July 1682, **M.** 20 Mch 167⅞ age 16, B.A. 17 Oct. 1681, **Petr.
1682**, vac. 1698 by having become R. of Powderham 8 Ap. 1697,
res. Powderham 1700, R. of Honiton 28 July 1699, Eccl. Ant. i. 30,
ii. 79; M.A. 19 June 1684, B.D. 25 June 1695, d. 7 Aug. 1740,
epitaph in Gent. Mag. May 1793; he wrote a History of the Family
of Courtenay (his patrons at Powderham and Honiton), fol. Exon
1735; Gibbon says, ch. LXI, 'the Rector of Honiton has more
gratitude than industry, and more industry than criticism.'

William **Read** (s. William, archdeacon of Barnstaple), b. Drewsteignton, battellar 18 Mch 167⅜ to 8 Aug. 1682, **M.** 1 Ap. 1679
age 16, **Dev. 1682**, vac. Feb. 169½ by having taken the V. of
Ilfracombe 15 Nov. 1690: B.A. 9 July 1685, M.A. 30 Ap. 1688;
R. of S. Breock, Cornwall 1690, ? d. 1703, Eccl. Ant. ii. 139.

Charles **Masters** (s. Rev. Thomas, of Tatenhill near Burton, Staffs.
? the fellow of 1648), battellar 29 Mch 1680 to 14 July 1682, **M.**
1 Ap. 1680 age 17, **Sar. 1682**; B.A. 9 July 1685, d. of small pox
31 Dec. 1685 and bur. next day in the College chapel; Wood's Life
iii. 173.

John **Harris** (1 s. John, of Aveton Gifford and of Stodbury,
Devon), b. Aveton Gifford, Wood's Life 1 July 1685; sojourner
15 Ap. 1678 to 28 Oct. 1679, and 12 Ap. to 26 May 1680, **M.**
16 Ap. 1678 age 17, B.A. 3 May 1679, at Gray's Inn 1679, M.A.
21 Mch 168½, lieut. in company of scholars against Monmouth's
rebellion 1685, **Petr. 1683**, vac. by marriage June 1701; B.D. 6 July
1693, Proctor 1687; ? Dean of Burian, Cornwall 1717, V. of Treneglos
23 Mch 171⅞, R. of Landulph 172⁰⁄₁–1735, ? d. 1742. Hasted's
Canterbury ii. 74; Visit. Devon 450, Wood's Life iii. 217.

Philip **Thorne** (s. John), b. North Molton, Devon, poor scholar
26 Nov. 1679 to 14 July 1683, **M.** 12 Dec. 1679 age 17, B.A. 8 June
1683, **Petr. 1683**, vac. 1694; M.A. 27 Ap. 1686; V. of Burpham
1694–1701, of Arundel 1701–15, of Lymister 1701–15, all in Sussex;
Wood's Life 30 Jan. 169⅔.

James **Colmer** (s. Hugh, R. of Ladock), b. Truro, sojourner
16 May 1681 to 28 Ap. 1682, **M.** 19 May 1681 age 16, scholar of
Corpus 27 Ap. 1682; **Corn. 1683**; B.A. 12 Ap. 1686, M.A. 3 May
1689; M.B. 6 Nov. 1690; expelled by Rector Bury 10 Oct. 1689
on a charge of incontinence, restored by the Visitor Bishop Trelawny,
vac. 1695.

John **Bonamy** (s. Rev. Peter), **M.** Pemb. 16 Feb. 168⅘ age 16;
Guer. 1685, vac. 1694; B.A. 12 Oct. 1688, M.A. 4 Ap. 1694; R. of

S. Peter du Bois, Guernsey 1692, Dean of Guernsey, Sark, Alderney 1717 and as late as 6 Nov. 1732, when he sent the nomination of a Fellow; R. of Bramdean, Hants 1719, of Bleadon, Som. 1719–39, d. 27 Dec. 1739.

John **Bagwell** (s. Francis, pleb.), b. Colyton, battellar 18 Ap. 1681 to 7 July 1686, M. 8 Mch 168$\frac{0}{1}$ age 17, B.A. 14 Oct. 1684, **Dev. 1686**, M.A. 28 May 1687, minister at Merton, Oxon 1690, Proctor 1695; vac. Oct. 1697 by having taken V. of Pelynt 1696 ; V. of Bishop's Nympton, Devon 1695, of S. Eval 1707, R. of S. Ive 20 Feb. 170$\frac{5}{6}$–1725, V. of Colan 1715–17, all in Cornwall, preb. of Exeter 1700, bur. S. Ive 26 Mch 1725; Bibl. Corn. 1045, Lake i. 174, Wood's Life iii. 482.

Henry **Maundrell** (s. Robert, pleb., of Compton, Wilts), b. near Marlborough, battellar 27 Sep. 1682 to 6 July 1686, M. 4 Ap. 1682 age 16, B.A. 15 Oct. 1685, **Sar. 1686**; M.A. 19 June 1688, chaplain at Aleppo 20 Dec. 1695, B.D. by decree 28 June 1697, C. of Bromley, Kent 1689–95 (J. Dunkin's Hist. of Bromley p. 27), Chaplain to Factory at Aleppo (at salary of 400 dollars, with £20 to increase the Library there) and famous for his travels, Hearne ii. 419, 14 Ap. 1718; d. Aleppo before 15 May 1701; St. John in his *Lives of Travellers* says that Maundrell, on his way to the East, stopped at Frankfort, where Job Ludolphus pointed out to him some passages in Scripture which might be elucidated by a visit to certain places in the Holy Land. His travelling companion, Richard Chiswell (Nat. Biog. x. 266), wrote Journals, which are in Brit. Mus. Addit. MSS. 10623. Reg. 27 Jan. 169$\frac{4}{5}$ 'venia concessa est M. Maundrell a Societate Mercatorum in regionibus Turcicis negotiantium in capellanum electo ut abesse possit a Collegio ad spatium quinquennii'; *see* also 15 June 1700. Spence's Anecdotes 276. Maundrell published a sermon on Eccl. vii. 16–17, preached before the hon. company of merchants trading to the Levant Seas Dec. 15, 1695, London 1696, 4º; J. B. Pearson's *Chaplains to the Levant Company* 1883 gives accounts of Barth. Chappell, H. Maundrel, Mathias Stiles. His 'Journey from Aleppo to Jerusalem at Easter A.D. 1697' was publ. Oxford 1703, 8º; at the end of the Travels are two letters to Mr. Daniel Osborn, fellow of Ex. Coll., dated 10 Mch 169$\frac{8}{9}$ and 12 Ap. 1700. Addit. MS. Brit. Mus. 24107, a letter-book of Sir Charles Hedges, judge of Admiralty Court 1694–1702, contains many letters to his nephew 'Maundrell of Aleppo'; Biog. Univ., Nat. Biog.

John **Crabb** (s. Rev. William, of Childe Okeford, Dorset), battellar

27 Mch 1682 to 8 July 1687, **M.** 7 Ap. 1682 age 16, B.A. 15 Oct.
1685, **Petr. 1687**, vac. 1694; M.A. 19 June 1688; Sub-librarian of
Bodleian, Hearne's Life p. 14, Macray's Bodleian Library 131,
Wordsworth p. 5, Letters from Bodleian 1813 i. 174; chaplain to
E. Fowler Bishop of Gloucester; C. of Breamore near Salisbury for
38 years, R. of Tarrant Hinton 1712–48, V. of Tarrant Monkton
1705–49, bur. 24 Mch 174⁸⁄₉; his monu. at Breamore says 'auctor
Georgianae et aliorum carminum celebrium latine et anglice'; he
married four times; lic. 31 Oct. 1693 to m. Dorothy Waller, of
Beaconsfield, Bucks, spinster, age 27, at Wexham, Bucks (Harl. Soc.
24 p. 209); his wife Grace was bur. 25 Oct. 1744, age 53; his
widow Elizabeth 13 Mch 1777 age 67; the arms above the monument are Gules a Chevron Or between in chief two fleurs de lis, and
in base a crab of the second.   Crest a demi-lion rampant Or;
Hutchins i. 274, 318, iii. 576.

Thomas **Vivian** (s. John), b. S. Issey, poor scholar 20 Mch 168⅔
to 20 Dec. 1686, then battellar to 6 July 1688, **M.** 23 Mch 168⅔
age 17, B.A. 26 Oct. 1686, **Corn. 1688**, resigned at Dublin 23 May
1700; M.A. 1 June 1689.

Francis **Webber** (s. Nicolas, of Exeter), sojourner 3 Oct. 1685 to
6 July 1688, **M.** 17 Dec. 1685 age 17, **Dev. 1688**, vac. 1706; B.A.
24 Nov. 1692, M.A. 9 July 1694; P. C. of Clyst Honiton, R. of
Stockley Pomeroy 1709, preb. of Exeter 3 May 1709, d. 1737.

Henry **Levett** (s. William, of Swindon, Coxe no. xxxiv), **M.**
Magd. H. (where a William Levett became Principal 1681, Bloxam
v. 278) 12 June 1686 age 18; demy of Magdalen 1686–7; **Sar. 1688**,
res. 26 Aug. 1700; B.A. 24 Nov. 1692, M.A. 7 July 1694, M.B.
4 June 1695, M.D. 22 Ap. 1699; physician to the Charterhouse, and
to S. Bartholomew's Hosp., London 1707; competed with Edward
Martyn for the Rhetoric prof. in Gresham College 4 Dec. 1696;
d. Charterhouse 2 July 1725, bur. at foot of altar; his widow m.
Andrew Tooke, master at the Charterhouse and author of 'The
Pantheon'; Munk ii. 22, Wood's Life iii. 444, Gutch's Fasti 246,
Bloxam vi. 53, 197.

Thomas **Kingston** (s. Richard, of Elton, Hunts.), battellar 17 Mch
168⅘ to 23 Ap. 1689, **M.** 12 Dec. 1684 age 18, B.A. 13 Dec. 1688,
Chapl. adm. 24 Ap. **1689**; did not subscribe the oaths until some
time after he was full Fellow, being suspended by Bishop Trelawny,
and excommunicated 25 July 1690 for reading prayers in the Chapel
after his suspension, *see* Colmer's *Vindication* 16, *An Account of Pro-*

ceedings &c. 5, 23; M.A. 14 May 1696, d. 1703; admin. bond 26 Nov. 1703, Griffiths 37.

Henry **Northcote** (2 s. Sir Arthur, of King's Nympton, by Elizabeth 1 d. of Sir Francis Godolphin), bap. 31 Mch 1665, sojourner 25 Feb. $168\frac{6}{7}$ to 6 July 1689, **M.** 7 Mch $168\frac{6}{7}$ 'of Hain in Devon,' **Dev. 1689**, vac. 1704; succeeded to the Baronetcy on the death of his brother Sir Francis in July 1709; B.A. 22 July 1693, M.A. 13 Ap. 1695, M.B. 22 Ap. 1697, M.D. 1 July 1701; m. Tawstock 18 July 1703 Penelope y. d. of Edward Lovett of Liscombe in Soulbury, Bucks, and Corfe in Tawstock, by Joan, only child of Jas. Hearde of Corfe; d. 5 Feb. $17\frac{29}{30}$.

Henry **Huthnance** (s. Henry), b. Gwinear, battellar 1 July 1686 to 12 July 1689, **M.** 16 July 1686 age 19, **Corn. 1689**, vac. by m. June 1695; B.A. 8 July 1692, V. of Breage, Cornwall 1697.

John **Snell** (s. John), b. Exeter, sojourner 5 Ap. 1688 to 18 July 1690, **M.** 5 Ap. 1688 age 15, **Dev. 1690** in place of Burrington (one of the *five* Cornish fellows); res. 1698; B.A. 22 July 1693, M.A. 16 Mch 1696, V. of Heavitree 1698, preb. of Exeter 1701, d. 4 Sep. 1728, bur. Heavitree 9 Sep.; Eccl. Ant. i. 49; Polwhele's Devon ii. 25, N. and Gleanings i. 175, 192, iv. 71.

John **Vivian** (s. Richard, R. of S. Ervan, d. 1708), b. S. Ervan, battellar 16 Feb. $168\frac{6}{7}$ to 11 July 1690, **M.** 18 Feb. $168\frac{6}{7}$ age 15, **Corn. 1690** in place of Colmer (unjustly expelled); removed the same year by the Visitor; B.A. 22 July 1693; R. of Otterham 1707–8, of S. Ervan 1709–12, V. of Colan 1712–14, of Manaccan 1714–16, R. of Pitt portion at Tiverton 1716–34, d. 1734.

William Paynter (Fellow 1657), el. **Rector** 15 Aug. **1690**, d. 18 Feb. $171\frac{5}{6}$.

John **Cooke** (s. Francis), b. Exeter, sojourner 7 Feb. $168\frac{7}{8}$ to 23 Oct. 1691, **M.** 10 Feb. $168\frac{7}{8}$ age 15, **Petr. 1691** (by the Fellows who were not suspended) in place of Hearne, full Fellow 9 July 1692, but not really adm. till 19 Feb. $169\frac{4}{5}$, Reg. p. 88; res. 3 Nov. 1705; B.A. 14 July 1694, M.A. 17 Ap. 1697, Proctor 1702, preb. of Exeter 1702, of Winchester 1712, ? Vicar of Bovey Tracey 15 Aug. 1704, res. 1715, of Harberton 1710, R. of Chilbolton, Hants 1715, of Bishop's Waltham 1717; d. 1744; Eccl. Ant. i. 87.

William **Preston** (s. Rev. William), b. Ashton near Exeter, battellar 17 Mch $168\frac{6}{7}$ to 2 July 1692, **M.** 16 Mch $168\frac{6}{7}$ age 16; B.A. 19 Nov. 1690, **Dev. 1692** in place of Reade, removed 1695 with Martin and Pinhay by Dr. Paynter as having been illegally elected by Dr. Bury

during the lawsuit and by Fellows then under suspension by the
Visitor; M.A. 7 July 1694, ? R. of Barwick, Som. 1703.

John **Martin** (s. John, of Sherborne), b. Sherborne, battellar 19 Mch
16⅘⅙ to 2 July 1692, **M.** 9 Ap. 1690 age 17, **Petr. 1692** in place of
Ratcliffe, removed 1695; B.A. 26 Mch 1696; instit. to V. of Long
Burton, Dorset, 5 Oct. 1696, R. of Lillington 1712, of Folke 1713–7,
bur. Folke 26 Sep. 1717; Hutchins iv. 135, 185, 199.

Joseph **Pinhay** (s. Richard of South Pool, Devon), b. Sherford,
Devon, poor scholar 28 Nov. 1689 to 7 July 1693, **M.** 10 Dec. 1689 age
19, **Petr. 1693** in place of Archer, removed 1695; B.A. 21 June 1693.

Thomas **Wise** (s. John, pleb., of Dorchester, Oxon), b. Drayton near
Abingdon, poor scholar 8 Dec. 1687 to 18 July 1691, then battellar
15 Jan. 169½ to 7 Mch 169¾, **M.** 16 Dec. 1687 age 16, B.A. 15 June
1691, **Petr. 1694** in place of Martin (or Crabb, or Ratcliffe; Reg.
p. 88; el. in the same way as John Reade); M.A. 7 July 1694, B.D.
30 Oct. 1705, D.D. 10 July 1708; R. of S. Alphege with Northgate,
Canterbury 1709, and one of the six preachers of the Cathedral, V. of
Beakesbourne, Kent 1711, Chaplain to Princess of Wales 1721 and
to Duke of Ormond; preb. of Lincoln 1720, d. 24 July 1726;
wrote 1706 an abridgment of Cudworth's 'True Intellectual System
of the Universe'; 1711 *The Christian Eucharist rightly stated*, &c.;
Hearne 12 Dec. 1705, 16 May 1708; Wood's Life iii. 471, Athenæ
iv. 503.

Henry **Edwards** (s. Zachariah, pleb.), b. Oxford, poor scholar 11
Nov. 1689 to 11 July 1694 (his father signs), **M.** 10 Dec. 1689, B.A.
21 June 1693, el. 30 June 1694, M.A. 6 May 1696, vac. 13 July
1703 by having taken R. of Wootton Fitzpaine, Devon 1702; V. of
Chard, Som. 1706, canon of Wells 1709.

Edward **Payne** (s. Edward, by Jane 1 d. of Jean Mallet), **M.** Pemb.
8 Dec. 1691 age 15 'son of a poor man'; **Jer. 1694**, res. on promotion 1702; B.A. 17 July 1697; ? R. of S. Ouen, Jersey 1700.

John **Reade** (s. William, archdeacon of Barnstaple), b. Drewsteignton, Devon, battellar 13 Dec. 1686 to 18 July 1691, **M.** 17 Dec.
1686 age 18, B.A. 21 June 1690, M.A. 26 May 1693, **Dev. 1694** in
place of Preston (or W. Reade, Reg. p. 88), not adm. till 19 Feb.
169⅘, vac. 1704; V. of Barnstaple 1703; index to Bodl. MSS. vol. iv.

Daniel **Osborn** (s. Thomas), b. Stoke Gabriel, Devon, poor
scholar 16 June 1685 to 18 July 1690, then battellar 1 May 1693 to
Mch 169¾, **M.** 18 July 1685, B.A. 30 Ap. 1689, M.A. 30 June 1693,
Petr. 1693 in place of Archer (or Pinhay, Reg. p. 89): adm. 6 May

1695, full Fellow 9 July 1695; B.D. 23 Ap. 1703, d. 12 May 1710 of small pox, bur. in the Chapel the evening of the next day, admin. bond 24 May, Griffiths 45; Gutch iii. 120, Hearne 12 May 1710.

Robert **Rous**, Rector Bury's Devonshire Fellow (s. Robert), b. Exeter, battellar 20 Jan. 16$\frac{89}{90}$ to 22 Aug. 1692, **M.** 10 Ap. 1690 age 17, B.A. Pemb. 18 Dec. 1693; **Dev. 1695** in place of Colmer (Colmer's Cornish fellowship was given to Rector Paynter, and Rous el. in place of Rector Bury), vac. 1715; M.A. 16 June 1696, B.D. 8 May 1707, R. of Offwell, near Honiton 1713.

John **Walker** (s. Endymion, mayor of Exeter 1682), bap. S. Kerian's, Exeter 21 Jan. 167$\frac{3}{4}$, battellar 11 Ap. 1692 to 4 July 1695, **M.** 19 Mch 169$\frac{1}{2}$ age 17, **Petr. 1695**, vac. 1700; B.A. 4 July 1698, M.A. 13 Oct. 1699 (? incorp. Camb. 1702), D.D. by diploma 7 Dec. 1714 for his book on the *Sufferings of the Clergy in the Grand Rebellion*; R. of S. Mary Major in Exeter 22 Aug. 1698, vac. by d. of Richard Carpenter; R. of Upton Pyne, Devon 17 Oct. 1720, vac. by d. of James Gay, on pres. of Hugh Stafford of Pyne; preb. of Exeter 1714, bur. 20 June 1747 on N. side of Chancel at Upton Pyne; his widow Martha (Brooking) was bur. 12 Sep. 1747 age 67 (m. in the Cathedral 17 Nov. 1704); Hearne 7 June 1714; Eccl. Ant. ii. 55; Bibl. Corn. 845; W. Antiq. vii. 13; *Devon and Exeter Daily Gazette* 19 Feb. 1887.

Thomas **Acland** (3 s. Sir Hugh), b. Columb John in Broad Clyst, **M.** Wadham 23 Nov. 1693 age 16, sojourner Ex. Coll. 9 Ap. to 7 July 1696, **Dev. 1696**, vac. 1713, m. Sowton 12 Feb. 1712 Catherine Wilcocks; B.A. 6 July 1699, M.A. 13 May 1702, preb. of Cutton in Castro Exon. 1703, of Exeter 13 Aug. 1713, R. of Nympton S. George 1713 and V. of Brent 1716, both in Devon, d. 11 Sep. 1735; C. S. Gilbert i. 562, Visit. Devon 5.

Richard **Vyvyan** (1 s. Charles, of Merthen in Constantine), sojourner 5 June 1694 to 7 July 1696, **M.** 5 June and subscribed 7 July 1694 age 17, at Middle Temple 1694, B.A. 169$\frac{5}{6}$, **Corn. 1696**, vac. 24 Feb. 169$\frac{8}{9}$ by succeeding his uncle Sir Vyell in the Baronetcy; m. S. Eval 9 Nov. 1697 Mary d. and h. of Francis Vyvyan of Coswarth; M.P. S. Michael, Cornwall 1700-2, Cornwall 1702-8, 1712-13, imprisoned in the Tower for Jacobitism 1715, d. 12 Oct. 1724; Visit. Corn. 531; Bibl. Corn. 840.

Thomas **Rennell** (s. Thomas, pleb.), b. Chudleigh, Devon, battellar 21 Feb. 169$\frac{2}{3}$ to 5 July 1698, **M.** 6 Ap. 1693 age 18, B.A. 15 Oct. 1696, **Petr. 1698**, vac. 1713; M.A. 9 June 1699, B.D. 27 Jan. 171$\frac{9}{1}$,

D.D. 9 Feb. 171$\frac{0}{1}$, R. of Drewsteignton 1711–53; tutor to Thomas Rundle bishop of Derry; published sermons 1705.

Edmund **Granger** (s. Rev. Thomas), b. Lamerton, battellar 26 Mch 1694 to 5 July 1698, **M.** 30 Mch 1694 age 17, B.A. 14 Oct. 1697, **Dev. 1698**, vac. 1710; M.A. 14 June 1700, V. of Bramford Speke 24 Aug. 1708, and R. of Cruwys Morchard 1709, bur. there 21 Jan. 173$\frac{7}{8}$.

William **Mervin**, senior (2 s. William, R. of Heanton Punchardon, by Christiana Newte), bap. 6 June 1676, **M.** Ch. Ch. 30 June 1693 age 16, B.A. 30 Ap. 1697, **Dev. 1698**, vac. 1709 by taking the R. of Tawstock, in succession to Oliver Naylor, to hold for Chichester Wrey, a minor (see Bray's case 1731); M.A. 1 Feb. $\frac{1699}{1700}$; m. Letitia d. of Thomas Bouchier, Principal of Alban Hall, she d. 13 May 1730 age 43; R. of Heanton Punchardon 1719–29, d. 20 July 1744; Lysons' Devon 262; Eccl. Ant. ii. 114, 120, Wood's Life ii. 253.

Thomas **Paynter** (s. Francis, of Boskenna in Burian), b. Boskenna, battellar 23 Nov. 1696 to 2 July 1698, **M.** 12 Dec. 1696 age 16, **Corn. 1698**, vac. 7 July 1704 by not proceeding to B.A. (Reg. 1 May 1700, 27 Feb. 170$\frac{0}{1}$); B.A. 9 Dec. 1708; V. of Gwinear 11 Oct. 1711, bur. 26 May 1732.

William **Williams** (s. William; Lake iii. 46), b. Bodinnick in Lanteglos by Fowey, sojourner 30 Sep. 1697 to 12 July 1700, **M.** 26 Nov. 1697 age 16, **Corn. 1700**, vac. 1719; B.A. 16 July 1703; M.A. 16 Ap. 1706, Proctor 1710 (Hearne 11 Ap. 1711), M.B. and D. 18 Ap. 1711, practised physic at Exeter.

John **Haviland** (s. John, pleb.), of Bridgwater, **M.** Balliol 31 May 1698 age 16; battellar Ex. Coll. 5 Feb. to 12 July 1700; **Petr. 1700**, vac. 1724; B.A. 16 July 1703, M.A. 16 Ap. 1706, B.D. 15 July 1716, R. of Portland, Dorset 1717–25, of Wargrave, Oxon 1719–21, V. of South Petherwin, Cornwall 1722 (lessee of the great tithes 1720), R. of Coryton 1723, of Lew Trenchard 1735, both in Devon; d. 1762, *Archæologia* i. 49 (1770).

Robert **Shortridge** or Shortrudge (s. Philip, of Thelbridge, Lysons' Devon 496), b. Witheridge in Chulmleigh, Devon, battellar 3 June 1695 to 18 July 1701, **M.** 7 May 1695 age 17, B.A. 17 Jan. 169$\frac{8}{9}$, **Petr. 1701**, vac. 1719; M.A. 14 Feb. 170$\frac{1}{2}$, B.D. 10 July 1713, R. of Clannaborough near Crediton 1707, of Down S. Mary 1717, both in Devon; Hearne 7 May 1710.

George **Stubbes** (s. John, R. of Little Hinton, Wilts), **M.** Univ. Coll. 21 Mch 169$\frac{7}{8}$ age 15; sojourner Ex. Coll. 5 Ap. to 11 July

1701, **Sar. 1701**, vac. 1725; B.A. 20 July 1704, M.A. 29 Ap. 1707; Chaplain to Paul Methuen ambassador in Spain, and allowed commons and profits of fellowship during his absence by the King's mandamus 7 Ap. 1718 (but this not to be a precedent; Coryton when abroad 1742–46 had no such allowance, nor anything more than an absent Fellow, since his being in the King's service was only an excuse for non-residence); also Chaplain to G. Dodington (afterwards Lord Melcombe) at Madrid; the Vice-Chancellor demanded his sermon 1722 *A constant search after truth* for examination; V. of Wittenham 1722, R. of Pewsey, Berks 1724, chaplain to Duke of Ormond 1724, to Frederick Prince of Wales 1734, R. of Tolleshunt Knights 1734, of S. Lawrence Newland 1737, both in Essex; R. of Tarrant Gunvile in Dorset, where he m. Susanna King 28 Oct. 1736; Hearne ii. 386, Hutchins iii. 460–1, P. Stubbes' *Anatomy of Abuses* ed. Furnivall 1882 part 2, p. xxx.

William **Shadwell** (s. William, pleb., of Salisbury), M. Hart H. 2 Ap. 1696 age 16, B.A. 18 Dec. 1699; **Sar. 1701**, vac. 1713; M.A. 23 June 1702.

Thomas le **Breton** (s. David, pleb., by Mary Dupin), M. Pembroke 22 Oct. 1695 age 15, B.A. 9 June 1699, M.A. 21 Ap. 1702; **Jer. 1702**, res. 1 July 1707; m. Mary d. of Raulin Robin; ancestor of W. Corbet Le Breton; R. of S. Mary's, Jersey 1706–28, Dean of Jersey 1714, d. Oct. 1728.

John **Baron** (s. William), b. Egloskerry, Cornwall, battellar 15 Mch 169$\frac{7}{8}$ to 4 Jan. 170$\frac{3}{4}$, M. 8 Mch 169$\frac{7}{8}$ age 17, B.A. 14 Oct. 1701, **Chapl.**, adm. 30 Dec. **1703**, when in Deacon's Orders; vac. 1713; M.A. 23 June 1704; Coll. Corn. 53.

George **Blake** (s. Thomas, R. of Alwington, Devon), bap. there 29 June 1682, battellar 15 Mch $\frac{1699}{1700}$ to 8 July 1704, M. 13 Mch $\frac{1699}{1700}$ age 16, B.A. 21 Oct. 1703, **Petr. 1704**, vac. 1715; M.A. 10 June 1706, R. of Alwington 1713–63, d. 29 May 1763 in 81st year, the 50th from his institution. There are monuments to father and son.

Samuel **Trelawney** (s. John, of Plymouth), sojourner 25 Feb. 170$\frac{1}{2}$ to 8 July 1704, M. 4 Mch 170$\frac{1}{2}$ age 17 'of Ham, Devon,' **Dev. 1704**, vac. 1711; B.A. 11 July 1707, M.A. 22 Ap. 1710, M.B. 28 Ap. 1711; Hearne 4 July 1711.

George **Saffin** (s. George), b. Exeter, sojourner 13 Mch 170$\frac{1}{2}$ to 8 July 1704, M. 23 Mch 170$\frac{1}{2}$ age 18, **Dev. 1704**, d. 31 Aug. 1707, bur. in the Chapel; Gutch iii. 120.

Richard **Fincher** (s. James, R. of Duloe, Cornwall, and previously of Lanteglos by Fowey; Lake i. 304, iii. 46), sojourner 1 Mch $\frac{1699}{1700}$ to 13 July 1705, **M.** 28 Feb. $\frac{1699}{1700}$ age 18, B.A. 16 Nov. 1703, **Corn.** 1 July **1705** (William Vivian had equal votes, but the Vice-Chancellor chose Fincher), vac. **1707**, m. Mary Carey niece of Thomas Rolle V. of Veryan; M.A. 10 June 1706; V. of Veryan 24 Oct. 1706, d. 1724; Chester's Westminster Reg. p. 19.

Gilbert **Yarde** (s. Gilbert), b. Exeter, battellar 14 June 1700 to 13 July 1706, **M.** 25 June 1700 age 17, at Middle Temple 1700, B.A. 9 May 1704, **Petr. 1706**, vac. by m. 1717; M.A. 20 Jan. 170$\frac{6}{7}$, R. of Bickleigh, Devon 1722–40; Westcote 601.

James **Thorne** (s. John), b. Southmolton, sojourner 10 Mch $\frac{1699}{1700}$ to 7 July 1707, **M.** 28 Feb. $\frac{1699}{1700}$ age 19, at Inner Temple 1700, B.A. 21 Feb. 170$\frac{3}{4}$, **Dev. 1707**, vac. 1727; M.A. 8 July 1707; R. of Harnhill, Glouc. 1715, of Eche or Hethe, Oxon 4 Oct. 1723–1725; R. of S. Ive, Cornwall 1725–40, bur. 9 Mch 1740; m. S. Ive 25 Feb. 1733 Mrs. Elizabeth Iliffe; Coll. Corn. 987.

John **Vyvyan** (3 s. Charles), bap. Constantine 25 Feb. 168$\frac{5}{6}$, sojourner 24 Feb. 170$\frac{4}{5}$ (as of Trelowarren) to 7 July 1707, **M.** 7 Mch 170$\frac{5}{6}$, **Corn. 1707**, vac. 1717; B.A. 8 July 1710, M.A. 20 Ap. 1713, presented by his brother Sir Richard to R. of Pitt Portion, Tiverton 26 July 1716, d. Dec. 1734.

William **Mervin**, junior (s. Rev. Jonas, of Morthoe, Devon), b. Barnstaple 1682, battellar 5 May 1701 to 8 July 1708, **M.** 10 May 1701; B.A. 7 Mch 170$\frac{4}{5}$, **Dev. 1708**, vac. 1719; M.A. 10 July 1708, B.D. 4 July 1719; R. of Beaworthy 28 Dec. 1715, of Clare Portion, Tiverton 13 May 1721 on the death of W. Mervin (R. 15 Feb. 167$\frac{3}{9}$ to 1721), patron Samuel Burridge (Harding's Tiverton iv. 47), of Atherington 1728, of Georgeham 1729, of Heanton Punchardon 1730–44, all in Devon, d. 17 Dec. 1759 (Lysons' Devon 62: see *Kingsbridge and Salcombe* 189); m. Dorothy d. of Gawen Hayman R. of South Pool near Kingsbridge.

Thomas **Seale** (s. Peter, by Mary de Carteret), **M.** Pembroke 2 Dec. 1706 age 16; **Jer. 1708**, res. 5 Sep. 1729; B.A. 14 July 1711, M.A. 2 June 1715; R. of Broad Somerford, Wilts 1728–71, of S. Clement's, Jersey 1734–46, d. 1771; m. Elizabeth Dumaresq.

Richard **Harding** (s. Richard, pleb., of Fremington), b. Combmartin 19 Sep. 1687, battellar 1 Ap. 1707 to 8 July 1709, **M.** 3 Ap. 1707, **Dev. 1709**, vac. 1715; B.A. 9 July 1712, M.A. 1 July 1715, R. of Marwood, Devon 1714–82, d. May 1782 age 95.

Robert **Rogers** (s. Antony, pleb.), b. Henstridge, Som., battellar 7 Feb. 170$\frac{5}{8}$ to 14 July **1710**, M. 30 Oct. 1705 age **17**, B.A. 23 June 1709, **Petr. 1710**, vac. 1718 by instit. to Abbas-Combe, Bath and Wells 8 May 1717; instit. to Rimpton 31 Oct. 1719, d. 1726 (Som. Incumbents 2, 176); M.A. 28 May 1712, Proctor 1718.

John **Conybeare** (s. John, V. of Pinhoe, Exeter 1684–1706), b. Pinhoe 31 Jan. **169½**, ed. Tiverton, battellar 23 Feb. 170$\frac{7}{8}$ to 10 June 1710, M. 22 Mch 170$\frac{7}{8}$, **Petr. 1710**, el. Rector 6 Aug. 1730, res. 29 Jan. 173$\frac{2}{3}$ for the Deanery of Christ Church (patent dated 12 Jan.; Hearne 28 Jan. and 8 Mch 173$\frac{2}{3}$, 2 Nov. 1734; Wordsworth 304, 437), Bishop of Bristol 14 Nov. 1750, d. 13 July 1755; B.A. 9 July 1713, M.A. 16 Ap. 1716, B.D. 11 July 1728, D.D. 24 Jan. 17$\frac{29}{30}$, Proctor 1725, R. of S. Clement's, Oxford 1724–34; his wife Jemima was bur. 1 Nov. 1747 (Misc. Gen. June 1885). In 1727 he wrote a Visitation Sermon on *Subscription*; in 1735 *Calumny refuted, an answer to the personal slander of Dr. Richard Newton;* two volumes of Sermons were published in 1757 after his death, and 4600 copies subscribed for, to make some provision for his family; his portrait is in the Coll. Hall; Nat. Biog.

William **Furneaux** (s. William, pleb., and Mary), of Gerrington, Devon, bap. Churston Ferrers 30 Ap. 1691, battellar 19 Mch 170$\frac{7}{8}$ to 10 July 1710, M. 22 Mch 170$\frac{7}{8}$ age 16, **Dev. 1710**, B.A. 9 July 1713, M.A. 12 July 1716, M.B. and D. 5 July 1721, d. 1722.

Christopher **Furneaux** (1 s. Christopher, Fellow 1680, of Torrington), b. Tavistock, battellar 28 Mch 1710 to 10 July 1712, **M.** 31 Mch 1710 age 17, **Dev. 1712**, removed 2 July 1729 for contempt of statutes; B.A. 9 July 1715, M.A. 24 Ap. 1718, M.B. 8 July 1719, bur. Liskeard 15 Mch. 17$\frac{29}{30}$.

John **Bere** (s. Richard, of Hockworthy, Lysons' Devon cxxxiv, 273), b. Morebath near Tiverton, battellar 9 Ap. to 6 Aug. 1709, 12 Feb. to 18 July 1711, 25 Jan. 171$\frac{1}{2}$ to 16 Jan. 171$\frac{6}{7}$, 11 Feb. 171$\frac{6}{7}$ to 10 July 1717, **M.** 15 Ap. 1709 age 17, B.A. 25 Oct. 1712, **Dev. 1713**, took the oaths at Cullompton 16 Jan. 171$\frac{4}{5}$, res. June 1733; M.A. 6 July 1715, R. of Puddington, Devon 1719, d. 1783.

John **Warren** (s. John, of Plymouth), b. Plymouth, **M.** 18 Dec. **1710** age 18, at Middle Temple 1710, **Petr. 1713**, res. June 1733: Maynard Hebrew Reader for one year from Mich. 1732 (N. and Gleanings iii. 56); B.A. 4 July 1716, M.A. 1 July 1718, R. of Eche or Hethe, Oxon 8 Oct. 1725 to 1732, but curate of Eche to 1756, m. 21 Dec. 1727 Grace Ward of Eche; pres. by the College to R. of

Baverstock, Wilts 1732, d. 1774; Phillipps ii. 64, 87; Rawlinson MSS. Class C no. 167.

James **Marchant** (s. Thomas, pleb., of Tisbury, Wilts), **M.** Hart H. 14 July 1708 age 18, B.A. 3 May 1712; **Sar. 1713**, M.A. 1 July 1715, vac. 1721.

Thomas **Snell** (s. Rev. Thomas, of Bampton, Oxon), at Winchester 1704, **M.** 3 July 1708 age 18, adm. full **Chapl.** Fellow 21 June **1715**, res. 9 Feb. 171$\frac{7}{8}$; B.A. 7 May 1712, M.A. 28 June 1715, V. of Bampton 11 Feb. 171$\frac{4}{5}$ by res. of his father Thomas; d. 1758; Giles' Bampton xlii, 45, 59.

Nicholas **Hickes** (s. Nicholas, R. of Cheriton Fitzpayn), battellar 12 Ap. 1706 to 22 Jan. 171$\frac{4}{5}$, **M.** 30 Ap. 1706 age 17, B.A. 17 Feb. 17$\frac{08}{10}$, M.A. 25 Oct. 1712, **Dev. 1715**, vac. by m. 1720; R. of S. Mary Arches, Exeter 1722, V. of Menheniot 1724, d. in the Vicarage House 1740 'suapte manu jugulo seu gutture præciso.'

Richard **Fowell** (2 s. William), b. North Huish, Devon 5 Oct. 1695, **M.** 1 Ap. 1712, **Petr. 1715**, res. 21 May 1724, m. Anne d. of Jas. Harris of Salisbury, she d. 8 July 1768; B.A. 8 July 1718, R. of Hilperton, Wilts 1723–50, V. of Corsham 1727–50, R. of Ermington, Devon 1747–50, d. Corsham 1750; Visit. Devon 371, Misc. Gen. N. S. iv. 332.

Peter **Sweet** (s. Peter, pleb., of Crediton), b. Torrington, battellar 21 Mch 171$\frac{2}{3}$ to 8 July 1715, **M.** 26 Mch 1713 age 19, **Dev. 1715**, B.A. 16 Mch 171$\frac{8}{9}$, d. 1719, bur. in the Chapel; Gutch iii. 120.

NOTE.—The Succession Act of 1 George I ordered Fellows to take the oaths of allegiance and abjuration, and certificates of their doing so are in the College Register. Seale took them at the Cour Royale of Jersey 3 Nov., Williams before the Court of King's Bench 17 Nov., Warren at Plymouth 5 Dec., W. Mervin R. of Beaworthy at Pilton in Devon 28 Dec.; at the Sessions at Oxford, Verman Thorne and Hickes 16 Dec., Sweet 19 Dec., Haviland 24 Dec., Christopher Furneaux 28 Dec., Hutchins and Adams 31 Dec., Rogers 11 Jan., Conybeare and W. Furneaux 12 Jan., Fowell 16 Jan., Dr. Paynter 19 Jan., George Lacy Symes scholar 21 Jan., Christopher Crouch 18 Jan.; Shortridge at Sampford Courtenay in Devon 9 Jan.

Matthew Hole (Fellow 1663), el. **Rector** 8, and adm. 12, Mch 171$\frac{5}{6}$, d. 19 July 1730.

William **Stephens** (s. Lewis, Fellow 1678), b. Menheniot 26 Dec. 1692, battellar 3 Jan. 170$\frac{7}{8}$ to 1 July 1712, **M.** 22 Mch 170$\frac{7}{8}$ age 15, B.A. 13 Oct. 1711, M.A. 28 June 1715, adm. **Chapl.** 12 Mch 171$\frac{5}{8}$, res. 17 Ap. 1719; one of the Vicars of Bampton, Oxon 17 Ap. 1718, res. 1723; V. of S. Andrew's, Plymouth 4 Oct. 1723, d. 16 Mch 173$\frac{1}{2}$

and bur. 18 Mch in chancel of S. Andrew's, leaving a widow Gertrude with five small children and one unborn; Jewitt's Plymouth 324, 327, Bibl. Corn. 688, Dredge's *Sheaves* 50, W. Antiq. x. 186.

James **Kendall** (4 s. Nicholas, Fellow 1678), b. Pelynt 2 Nov. 1697, at Winchester 1708, **M.** 17 Dec. 1715, **Corn. 1717**, vac. by m. 9 Feb. 17$\frac{2}{3}\frac{9}{0}$ Margaret d. of Thomas Worth; B.A. 8 July 1720, M.A. 8 June 1722, V. of Alternon 28 Feb. 1729, and of Egloshayle 18 June 1731, d. 173²; Maclean i. 415, D. K. Rec. 30 p. 450, Coll. Corn. 448.

John **Torre** (s. John, R. of S. John's, Cornwall), sojourner 12 Mch 171$\frac{5}{8}$ to 10 July 1718, **M.** 15 Mch 171$\frac{5}{8}$ age 17, **Corn. 1718**, vac. 1728; B.A. 20 Mch 172$\frac{1}{2}$, V. of S. Winnow 20 Jan. 172$\frac{3}{4}$, of S. Breward 30 Sep. 1726, bur. S. Winnow 11 Sep. 1728; Maclean i. 369.

George **Boughton** (s. Rev. Nathaniel), b. Launceston, battellar 8 Mch 171$\frac{4}{8}$ to 10 July 1718, **M.** 14 Mch 171$\frac{4}{8}$ age 17, **Corn. 1718**, B.A. 21 Mch 172$\frac{2}{3}$, M.A. 12 July 1725, d. 1726, bur. in the Chapel; N. and Gleanings iii. 96.

Joseph **Atwell** (s. Rev. Matthew, of Buckland Monachorum, Visit. Devon 30), b. Moreton Hampstead, battellar 8 Ap. 1712 to 5 July 1718, **M.** 12 Ap. 1712 age 16 (with his brother Matthew, age 18), B.A. 21 Oct. 1715, M.A. 13 June 1718, **Petr. 1718**, had leave of absence for four years from Lord Petre 1 Mch 172$\frac{3}{4}$ (Reg. a. 1728) to study in foreign universities, he travelled with the son of Lord Chancellor Cowper; B.D. 11 July 1728, D.D. 19 Ap. 1733 (both divinity degrees while a layman), F.R.S. 1730; el. Rector 17 and adm. 22 Feb. 173$\frac{8}{9}$, res. 3 Mch 173$\frac{0}{9}$, d. just before Aug. 1768; took priest's orders 1736, Preb. of Gloucester 173$\frac{8}{9}$–1768, of Southwell 173$\frac{8}{9}$, of York 173$\frac{7}{9}$, of Westminster 1759; V. of Fairford 1738, R. of Oddington 1739, both in Glouc., Chancellor of Norwich; added many notes to Robinson's 'Hesiod,' e. g. on the 'Dog Days,' and on 'The Rising of Sirius'; and published *Conjectures on the nature of Intermitting and Reciprocating Springs*; he was a generous subscriber to Lewis' *Life of Pecock* (Nichols iv. 192–93); Bodl. MS. Add. C. 90 fol. 94 (his early life), W. Antiq. iv. 252, Polwhele's *Reminiscences* i. 64, Spence's Anecdotes 333; Egerton MS. 1955 contains letters of Warburton to Atwell 4 Sep. and 9 Dec 1755 (given imperfectly in Warburton's Works xiv. 257), see F. Kilvert's *Selections from Warburton's Papers* 253, *Letters from a late Prelate to one of his friends* (i. e. Warburton to Hurd) 1809 p. 415, 418, Granger's *Letters* p. 167.

William **Shepheard** (s. Rev. William), b. Ashreigney, Devon, battellar 21 Oct. 1714 to 10 July 1718, **M.** 22 Oct. 1714 age 17,

B.A. 27 June 1718, **Petr. 1718**, vac. 1727; M.A. 3 July 1722, V. of
Lelant, Cornwall 1726, R. of Ashreigney 1727–47. Some of his
sermons were published after his death, by subscription, at Sherborne
1748.

Thomas **Bailey**, so he signs himself (s. Robert, pleb., of Norley,
Devon), b. Norley, **M.** 3 Mch 171$\frac{4}{5}$ age 17, **Petr. 1718**; B.A. 7 Mch
172$\frac{1}{2}$, M.A. 27 July 1723, d. 12 May 1733, bur. in the Chapel, will
proved 13 June 1733, Griffiths 4; Gutch iii. 120; Peshall 218 '*Bail*
fellow of Exeter.'

Augustine **Question** (s. John, pleb., of Withycombe, Som.), b.
Carhampton, battaller 24 Mch. 17$\frac{0.9}{10}$ to 11 Mch 171$\frac{3}{4}$, and 26 June
to 10 July 1718, **M.** 27 Mch 1710 age 19, B.A. 13 Oct. 1713, adm.
Chapl. 5 June **1719**; M.A. 19 May 1720; C. of Merton, Oxon
19 Sep. 1730; res. his fellowship at S. Enoder, Cornwall 18 Nov.
1731, of which he had become Vicar 1730, res. 1734; V. of Veryan,
Cornwall, 14 Nov. 1734–1740, pres. to Menheniot 23 Sep. 1740 (the
form of presentation given in the Reg. was successfully disputed by
the Dean and Chapter of Exeter), d. 3 and bur. 6 June 1753; his
benefaction to Menheniot is given in Lake iii. 313.

Joseph **Betty** (s. John, of Paul), **M.** Hart H. 16 Feb. 171$\frac{3}{4}$ age
16, B.A. 11 Nov. 1717; **Corn. 1719**; M.A. 15 June 1720; poisoned
himself with laudanum 1 Jan. 173$\frac{0}{1}$ to escape his creditors (the date
8 Jan. in the Register and on his monu. in the Chapel was purposely
misstated), admin. bond 29 Jan. 1731, Griffiths 6; Gutch iii. 120,
Bibl. Corn. 22; Sermon before the University 21 Sep. 1729; the
same versified by Jacob Gingle 1729.

William **Bartlett** (s. Elis, Lysons' Devon cxxxiii, 63, W. Antiq. xi.
61), b. Branscombe, Devon, battellar 3 Feb. 171$\frac{4}{5}$ to 17 July 1719,
M. 5 Feb. 171$\frac{4}{5}$ age 19, B.A. 7 Nov. 1718, **Petr. 1719**, rejected
6 July 1720, Lake iii. 112; ?R. of Templeton, Devon 1 July 1725,
d. 1747; Eccl. Ant. i. 107.

Richard **Eastway** (s. Richard, R. of Sutcombe, by Elizabeth
Hooper of S. Martin's, Exeter; m. Clyst S. George 30 Ap. 1689; he
d. 20 May 1726 in 70 year, she d. 24 Jan. 173$\frac{0}{1}$ in 66 year), b.
Sutcombe 16 Mch 169$\frac{6}{7}$, battaller 9 Ap. 1715 to 20 July 1719, **M.**
9 Ap. 1715, B.A. 14 Oct. 1718, **Dev. 1719**; rejected 6 July 1720;
M.A. Lincoln 10 June 1721, R. of Wargrave, Oxon, but lived at
Staunton Harold, Leics., d. Feb. 1777.

Robert **Symons**, b. Exeter; of Clare, Cambridge; incorp. 28 Feb.
172$\frac{0}{1}$ as B.A., **Dev. 1721**, vac. 1727: M.A. 4 July 1723, made V. of

S. Mary Arches at Exeter by Bishop Weston, but was deprived and went to Ireland; was famous for his talent in mimicry. See *The Mimic*, by the Rev. Mr. Pitt, in Dodsley's Collection iii. 74; Gent. Mag. 1780 p. 407.

Francis **Fort**, of Sidney, Camb., B.A. 1720; **Petr. 1721**, incorp. 8 July, M.A. 28 June 1726, vac. 1728; R. of Huntsham, Devon, ? d. 1765.

Joseph **Birchinsha** (s. Rev. David, of Lydford), **M.** Wadham 28 May 1718 age 18; **Dev. 1721**, vac. 1730; B.A. 7 July 1724, M.A. 2 July 1725, promoted by Thomas Rundle bishop of Derry.

Henry **Goldwyer** (s. William, of Salisbury), at Winchester 1712, **M.** Wadham 16 Mch 171⅜ age 18; **Sar. 1721**, B.A. 23 Nov. 1725, M.A. 5 July 1726, d. 23 Oct. 1731.

John **Wilcocks** (s. Rev. John, of Exbourne; a John Wilcocks was R. of Morchard Bishop 1688–1719, Eccl. Ant. iii. 51), **M.** Oriel 8 Mch 17$\frac{18}{20}$ age 17; **Dev. 1722**, vac. 1729; B.A. 17 July 1725, M.A. 5 July 1726, R. of Zeal Monachorum, V. of Cullompton 27 May 1733, d. 1756; Eccl. Ant. i. 115.

William **Reynolds** (s. John), b. S. Laurence, Exeter, 1705, **M.** 24 July 1721 age 16, **Dev. 1723**, res. 4 Ap. 1741; B.A. 5 July 1728, M.A. 10 May 1732; one of the Vicars of Bampton, Oxon; V. of Veryan, Cornwall 5 Jan. 174$\frac{9}{1}$–Sep. 1743, Master of Exeter School 1733-43, d. 28 Jan. 1750.

Robert **Scott** (s. Robert, pleb.), b. Belchalwell, Dorset, battellar 1 Mch 172½ to 14 July 1724, **M.** 13 Mch 172½ age 17, **Petr. 1724**, res. 28 June 1741; B.A. 7 July 1727, M.A. 5 July 1728, B.D. 7 June 1739; C. of Merton, Oxon 29 Sep. 1739, pres. to R. of Wootton, Northants 17 Ap. 1741, d. 16 May 1761; Reg. 30 June 1738.

Henry **Pitt** (s. Christopher, and brother of the translator of Virgil and Vida; Hutchins iv. 91), b. Blandford Forum, Dorset, **M.** 10 Oct. 1722 age 16, **Petr. 1724**; B.A. 7 July 1727, M.A. 22 May 1729, d. 1733.

Benjamin **Langley** (s. Rev. Thomas), b. Compton-Beauchamp, Berks, poor scholar 27 Nov. 1721 to 14 Aug. 1725, **M.** 16 Mch 17$\frac{18}{20}$ age 15, B.A. 10 May 1725, **Sar. 1725**, res. 17 Oct. 1732; M.A. 24 Mch 172⅜; R. of Compton, and of Mursley in Bucks, d. 1777.

John **Cary** (s. Nicholas, bur. S. Winnow 13 May 1747), bap. Liskeard 23 Jan. 170⅚, battellar 16 Mch 172⅔ to 1 July 1727, **M.** 15 Mch 172⅔, **Corn. 1726**, res. 173⅔ on promotion to a living; B.A. 9 July 1729, M.A. 27 Ap. 1730, V. of Culmstock, Devon;

of S. David's Exeter, exch. for S. Winnow, Cornwall before 1754,
d. 6 May 1759.

James **Cosserat** (s. Abraham, pleb., of Bideford; called 'Mourtes
alles Cosseret' in the Bideford Reg., probably a French refugee; by
Hester), bap. Bideford 24 Jan. $\frac{1699}{1700}$ 'John' (if the same as James)
battellar 31 May 1721 to 20 Jan. 172$\frac{5}{6}$, **M.** 25 May 1721 age 19, **Dev.**
1727, B.A. 26 Feb. 172$\frac{4}{5}$, M.A. 22 May 1728, B.D. 7 June 1739, D.D.
8 May 1750, R. of S. Clement's, Oxford 1751, d. 7 Mch 1760 age
61, when senior Fellow, bur. in the Chapel; Gutch iii. 120; Cat. of
Prints and Drawings in Brit. Mus., Polit. Satires 3, part ii. 933–6.

James **Edgcombe** (s. John), b. Tavistock, battellar 21 Dec. 1722
to 15 July 1727, **M.** 17 Dec. 1722 age 17, **Dev. 1727**; B.A. 13 June
1726, M.A. 18 Ap. 1729, B.D. 8 May 1736, D.D. 18 Jan. 173$\frac{39}{40}$,
Proctor 1733, el. Rector 11 Ap. 1737; R. of Barwick in Elmet,
Yorks. 1749, d. 16 May 1750 age 45, bur. in College Chapel; Gutch
iii. 120 and App. 245; Gent. Mag. June 1749; wrote a sermon 1736
on *The Insufficiency of Human Reason* (in answer to Chubb); was he
R. of Ackworth near Pomfret? see his letter 1 July 1749 in the Reg.

Robert **Michell** (s. William, pleb.), b. Maker in Archdeaconry of
Cornwall, poor scholar 9 May 1723 to 8 July 1728, **M.** 17 May 1723
age 17, B.A. 26 Jan. 172$\frac{6}{7}$, **Corn. 1728**, M.A. 14 Oct. 1729, d. 22
Dec. 1730.

Francis **Webber** (s. Francis, Fellow 1688), b. Clyst Honiton,
sojourner 1 Oct. 1725 to 8 July 1728, **M.** 20 Oct. 1725 age 17,
Petr. 1728; B.A. 7 July 1731, M.A. 10 May 1732, B.D. 10 Dec.
1743, D.D. 9 July 1750, Proctor 174$\frac{9}{1}$; el. C. of Merton, Oxon
2 Oct. 1731, R. of S. Clement's, Oxford Nov. 1734, pres. to V. of
Burford by Bishop Secker, and a good deal non-resident from 1747,
though always elected to some College office; wrote *Defence of Exeter
College*, in answer to Dr. Huddersford, 1755, and sermons and
pamphlets; in 1750 preached at consecration of Bishop Conybeare,
who gave him the V. of Newchurch, I. of Wight, May 1751; el.
Rector 5 June 1750 after several scrutinies; instit. to Menheniot
8 Sep. and inducted 6 Oct. 1753; Dean of Hereford 1756, d. 29 Sep.
1771 age 64, bur. in the Chapel; Gutch iii. 120; Reg. 18 July 1741
'electus est in alterum Lectorum ad lecturas adhuc *indotatas* [Gutch
ii. 900, Bloxam vi. p. vi] hujus Universitatis designandorum in biennium proxime secuturum Franciscus Webber A.M.' (See 16 July
1755, 13 Dec. 1763, 8 July 1771, 15 July 1778.) His portrait is in
the Coll. Hall.

John **Upton** (s. Rev. James, of Ilminster, Somerset, who ed. Aristotle de Arte Poetica, &c.; Reliquiæ Hearnianæ 23 Feb. $172\frac{5}{6}$), b. Taunton 1707, **M.** Merton 15 Mch $172\frac{4}{5}$ age 17; **Petr. 1728**, res. 10 Feb. $173\frac{6}{7}$; B.A. 7 July 1730, M.A. 10 May 1732; R. of the sinecure of Llandrillo in Denbigh, and of Great Rissington, Glouc., and of Seavington with Dinnington in Som. 1732–7, preb. of Rochester 19 Jan. $173\frac{6}{7}$, d. 9 Dec. 1760; edited Arrian's Epictetus 1737 and Spenser's Faerie Queen 1758, and wrote *Observations on Shakespere*. See Nichols' Literary Anecdotes on Upton family, Misc. Gen. Nov. 1886 p. 161, Oct. 1887 p. 350, Nov. 1888 p. 167, Feb. 1890 p. 21, Mch p. 45, May p. 73, 75.

William **Hole** (s. Rev. Joshua), b. Southmolton, battellar 18 May 1727 to 11 July 1729, **M.** 18 May 1727 age 17, **Dev. 1729**, res. 2 Aug. 1745; B.A. 6 July 1732, M.A. 26 June 1733, B.D. 20 Ap. 1744, el. C. of Merton, Oxon 28 Oct. 1733 and 4 Sep. 1740, preb. of Exeter 1744, Archdeacon of Barnstaple $174\frac{2}{3}$, V. of Bishop's Nympton 10 Dec. 1763–1782, pres. to Menheniot 3 and instit. 11 Jan. 1782, d. 26 Oct. 1791; Moore's Devon ii. 834; Eccl. Ant. iii. 88; Coll. Corn. 383; wrote *The Ornaments of Churches* 1761 (ed. by Rev. Thomas Wilson), with reference to the decoration of S. Margaret's, Westminster; and a sermon preached at the consecration of Werrington church in Devon 7 Sep. 1743, Oxford 8° 1743. He is said to have put *The Exmoor Scolding* into form (Gent. Mag. Library ii. 329). For his s. Lewis see Mod. Eng. Biog.; N. and Q. 5. ix. 386, Gent. Mag. 1791 lxi. 975.

Walter **Moyle** (s. Walter, of Bake, S. German's, the author), bap. 14 Sep. 1710, G. C. 7 June 1728 to 4 July 1730, **M.** 25 June 1728, **Corn. 1730**, d. 16 Sep. 1732, bur. S. German's.

Charles **Webber**, Webber junior (s. Rev. Francis, Fellow 1688) b. Clyst Honiton, **M.** Queen's 1 Ap. 1728 age 18; sojourner Ex. Coll. Dec. 1728 to 3 July 1730, **Dev. 1730**, res. 29 June 1762, having been presented to the R. of Wootton in Northants 1 July 1761, and given a bond of £500 to resign his fellowship by next S. Peter's Day, according to the terms of the donation, d. 29 Ap. 1764; B.A. 5 July 1733, M.A. 19 June 1734, B.D. 24 Nov. 1744; el. to C. of Merton, Oxon 30 Sep. 1734, 30 Sep. 1741, 4 Oct. 1746, Chaplain at Calcutta.

John **Cocke** (s. William, pleb., of Plymouth), **M.** Corpus 31 Mch 1726 age 13; **Dev. 1730**, res. $175\frac{0}{1}$; B.A. 12 June 1730, M.A. 14 June 1732, B.D. by decree 17 Dec. 1743 (Reg. here, and 30 June and 17 Dec. 1744).

John Conybeare (Fellow 1710), el. **Rector** 6 Aug. **1730**, res. 29 Jan. 173⅔.

William Pease (s. Rev. Francis), b. Clyst St. George, battellar 16 Mch 172⁴⁄₇ to 2 July 1731, **M.** 17 Mch 172⁴⁄₇ aged 16, **Dev. 1731**, vac. by m. June 1747; B.A. 27 Oct. 1730, M.A. 28 June 1733, B.D. 24 Nov. 1744; V. of Great Milton, Oxon 1749 ; Reg. 20 Dec. 1746 'electus est M. Pease a Rectore et Scholaribus qui nominetur ad vicariam de Steeple Morden in agro Cantabrigiensi, et ad eandem a Guardiano et Scholaribus Collegii B. Mariae Winton (vulgo New College) secundum mutuam Collegii Novi et Collegii Exon. hac in parte concordantiam praesentetur.'

Thomas Bray (s. Nicholas, pleb.), b. Stratton 1706, poor scholar 1 Ap. 1726 to 8 July 1731, **M.** 31 Mch 1726, **Corn. 1731**; B.A. 14 Oct. 1729, M.A. 4 July 1732, B.D. 10 Dec. 1743, D.D. 15 Dec. 1758; el. to C. of Merton, Oxon 26 Sep. 1735 and 1 Oct. 1742, instit. to Harnhill and Driffield in Glouc. 5 and 12 Aug. 1748 (see the Visitor's letters in the Reg. 174⁸⁄₉ on his holding these livings for a minor under a resignation bond; W. Mervin, Fellow 1698, had vacated his fellowship in a similar case, and the Rector opposed the practice of resignation bonds, but the Visitor decided otherwise; compare Rodd's case 1802); he ceded them 1776 on being instit. to R. of Dunsfold in Surrey, as he had before been to Bix in Oxon 1774 (Bixbrand and Bixgibwen, near Henley), in 1776 Dean of Raphoe in Ireland, which he exchanged with Dr. James King 20 Sep. 1776 for Dunsfold and a canonry of Windsor; el. Rector 22 Oct. 1771, d. 28 Mch 1785, bur. in the Chapel; Gutch iii. App. 245, 247, Gent. Mag. 1785 lv. 324, Bibl. Corn. 41,1093. He was said to have written *Mr. Boots' apology for the conduct of the late H . . S . . . . ff* 1753.

John Edwards (s. Henry), b. Launceston, sojourner 12 May 1729 to 8 July 1731, **M.** 12 May 1729 age 17, **Corn. 1731**; B.A. 13 July 1734, vac. Sep. 1738 by holding two livings in Cornwall, being R. of Forrabury 5 Sep. 1737–1751, and Minster 6 Sep. 1737–1753; also V. of Lewannick 11 May 1752–1753, d. 1753; Maclean i. 590, 604.

Peter Daniel Tapin (the first time two Christian names occur; s. Daniel, a French Protestant refugee from Barhais, by Mary Seale, sister of Thomas Seale, Fellow 1708), b. S. Helier's Feb. 170⅝, battellar 27 Mch 1725, as Peter Tapin, to 6 Oct. 1726, **M.** 13 Ap. 1725 age 19, B.A. Pemb. 12 Feb. 172⁸⁄₉; **Jer. 1731**, M.A. 10 May

1732, removed 1733 by Bishop Weston (Walpole's Letters i. p. lxi.) as not duly elected, see Weston's two decrees in the Reg.; R. of S. Heliers' 1735, d. Jan. 1761.

William **Walter** (s. George, of S. Anne's, Westminster), **M.** Edmund H. 12 Nov. 1722 age 15, B.A. All Souls 25 Feb. 172$\frac{5}{6}$, M.A. Edmund H. 12 July 1729, chaplain Ch. Ch. 1730; adm. **Chapl.** 15 Jan. 173$\frac{1}{2}$, res. 9 Jan. 173$\frac{5}{6}$ on his instit. to R. of Arlington near Barnstaple 10 Jan. 173$\frac{4}{5}$; Reg. 23 Jan. 173$\frac{4}{5}$ 'decretum est ut communae unius Scholaris cum pertinentibus addantur communis illius Scholaris qui officio Capellani, absente M. Walter, perfuncturus est. Causa est quod M. Walter, ad ecclesiasticum beneficium ab Universitate Oxon. promotus, expensas graves et molestias jura Universitatis defendendo sustinuit [it was in the gift of a Roman Catholic]. Eidem ecclesiae ipsiusque curae personaliter incumbere tenetur, nec intra annum ab adeptione dicti beneficii sodalitium suum tenetur relinquere'; so in the case of Thomas Granger 1736.

John **Stephens** (s. Rev. George, of Christian Malford), b. Shrivenham, Berks, sojourner 19 Mch 17$\frac{29}{30}$ to 14 July 1732, **M.** 19 Mch 17$\frac{29}{30}$ age 17, **Sar. 1732**, vac. 1762; B.A. 9 Ap. 1736, M.A. 9 July 1737, B.D. 12 Nov. 1748, D.D. 10 July 1761, Master of Aylesbury sch., d. 1771.

Joseph Atwell (Fellow 1718), el. **Rector** 17 Feb. 173$\frac{2}{3}$, res. 3 Mch 173$\frac{6}{7}$.

William **Score** (s. George and Joan), bap. Barnstaple 1 Oct. 1710, battellar 2 Mch 172$\frac{7}{8}$ to 12 July 1733, **M.** 8 Mch 172$\frac{7}{8}$, **Petr. 1733**, res. 21 June 1737, having been pres. by the University to the R. of Whitstone, Cornwall 25 May 1736, d. 1787; B.A. 13 Oct. 1731, M.A. 19 June 1734; Coll. Corn. 882.

Richard **Bryan** (s. Richard), b. Southmolton, Devon, battellar 1 Mch 172$\frac{8}{9}$ to 17 July 1733, **M.** 3 Mch 172$\frac{8}{9}$ age 16, **Petr. 1733**, res. 3 Nov. 1748 on marriage; B.A. 11 Oct. 1732, M.A. 6 June 1735, B.D. 7 July 1746; el. C. of Merton, Oxon 9 Oct. 1736 for the next year; held a cure in Glouc. 1739, and then the V. of E. Worlington, Devon, d. 1780.

John **Tapson** (s. Robert, of Ilsington), b. Ingsdon, Ashburton, **M.** 30 Mch 1731 age 17, **Dev. 1733**; B.A. 14 Mch 173$\frac{6}{7}$, M.A. 10 June 1737, M.B. 28 Nov. 1741, d. Devon 27 Jan. 174$\frac{6}{7}$.

John **Coryton** (s. John, pleb.), b. E. Antony, battellar 28 Feb. 17$\frac{29}{30}$ to 13 July 1733, **M.** 12 Mch 17$\frac{29}{30}$ age 18, **Corn. 1733**; B.A. 25 Oct. 1738, M.A. by decree (he being Chaplain in the navy) 4 July

1746 (but see Reg. 4 July 1746), d. 24 July 1746, news sent by Mr. Hodge, R. of S. John in Cornwall.

John **Andrew** (s. John, of S. Erme), **M**. Queen's 31 May 1727 age 17; **Corn. 1733**, vac. by m. Exeter Cathedral 14 May 1744 Isabella 5 d. of Sir W. Courtenay of Powderham; B.A. 2 Nov. 1731, M.A. 17 June 1734, M.B. 9 Feb. 17$\frac{39}{40}$, M.D. 11 Feb. 174$\frac{2}{3}$; on 26 Ap. 1735 had leave from Lord Petre to travel, and went abroad 6 June 1735, returning Ap. 1738, he was at Leyden 10 Sep. 1737; physician in Exeter, bur. S. David's Exeter 15 Mch 1772; Bibl. Corn. 655, 1029, Polwhele v. 67, 128–29; N. and Gleanings iii. 48, 64, W. Antiq. iv. 252.

Thomas **Broughton** (s. Thomas), b. Carfax, Oxford, **M**. Univ. Coll. 13 Dec. 1731 age 19; **Petr. 1733**, res. July 1741, m. Miss Capel 1742, by whom he had 15 children; his d. Anne m. 29 May 1793 the Rev. William Agutter (Nat. Biog.); B.A. 22 Mch 173$\frac{4}{5}$, wrote when C. at the Tower of London 1737 a sermon on *The Christian Soldier*; R. of Wotton, Surrey 1752; see the interesting life of him in Tyerman's *The Oxford Methodists* p. 334–60; d. 21 Dec. 1777; N. and Q. 6. iii. 288, Nat. Biog.

George William **Harris** (3 s. James, of the Close, Salisbury, by Elizabeth 3 sister of Anthony Earl of Shaftesbury, author of the *Characteristics*; she d. 1743 age 62, Cassan's *Bishops of Salisbury* ii. 109, 110, 121), **M**. Wadham 22 Mch 173$\frac{0}{1}$ age 17; **Sar. 1733**, res. 25 Ap. 1741 for a living in Cornwall; B.A. 4 Mch 173$\frac{4}{5}$, M.A. 10 June 1737, preb. of Sarum, R. of Egglescliffe, Durham, d. 23 Aug. 1777; Hutchins iii. 595.

Thomas **le Marchant** (s. Elisha, of the Castle, Guernsey), **M**. Pemb. 30 Mch 1731 age 15; **Guer. 1733**, B.A. 4 Mch 173$\frac{6}{7}$, M.A. 10 June 1737, appointed 1 July 1738 to help the Dean in teaching Logic and hearing Repetitions and Disputations; chaplain to garrison of Guernsey July 1739 in place of Bonamy deceased, Gent. Mag. ix. 217; d. 5 Dec. 1739.

John **Boughton** (s. Nathaniel, of Charles Church, Plymouth), b. Plymouth, battellar 16 June 1729 to 10 July 1734, **M**. 8 June 1729 age 14, **Petr. 1734**; B.A. 2 May 1733, d. 10 Feb. 173$\frac{4}{5}$, bur. in the Chapel; Gutch iii. 120.

John **Elworthy** (s. William), b. S. Stephen's, Exeter, **M**. 23 Feb. 17$\frac{29}{30}$ age 16, **Petr. 1735**, res. 2 Aug. 1746 for V. of Southmolton; B.A. 13 Oct. 1733, M.A. 25 June 1736, el. C. of Merton, Oxon 3 Oct. 1737 for a year, but res. 15 Nov.; V. of Colebrooke, Devon, and of S. Issey, Cornwall 25 Feb. 1769, d. 8 Mch 1794; wrote *The Influence of the Spirit* 1753.

Thomas **Granger** (s. Edmund, Fellow 1698), b. Cruwys Morchard, battellar 26 Feb. 173½ to 14 July 1735, **M.** 5 Ap. 1731 age 19, B.A. 12 Oct. 1734, **Chaplain** 31 Jan. 173⅚, res. 21 June 1737, having taken the V. of Widdecombe in the Moor 24 Ap. 1736, P.C. of Teignmouth, ? d. 1780.

James Edgcombe (Fellow 1727), el. and adm. **Rector** 11 Ap. 1737; d. 16 May 1750.

Edmund **Granger** (brother of Thomas), b. Cruwys Morchard, battellar 26 Feb. 173½ to 7 July 1737, **M.** 5 Ap. 1731 age 18, **Petr. 1737**, res. June 1751 having become R. of Sowton in Devon 16 Feb. 175⁰⁄₁; B.A. 12 Oct. 1734, M.A. 10 June 1737, B.D. 13 July 1747; C. of Merton, Oxon 1737; Preb. of Exeter 1771, d. 25 Aug. 1777 age 64; his widow Anne d. Exeter 4 Sep. 1812 age 82; Eccl. Ant. ii. 46, iii. 9.

James **Fortescue** (1 s. George, of Ford in Milton Abbot, Devon, by Mary d. of John Barrett of S. Tudy, Cornwall, Fortescue Family ii. 76, 77, Visit. Devon 360), b. Ford, bap. 21 July 1716, battellar 15 Feb. 173⅔ to 13 July 1737, G.C. 1 July 1765 to 24 Jan. 1766, and 23 Ap. to 8 July 1768, **M.** 9 Feb. 173¾, **Petr. 1737**, vac. 1765; B.A. 14 Oct. 1736, M.A. 22 June 1739, B.D. 11 Ap. 1749, D.D. 20 Jan. 175⁰⁄₁, Proctor 174⅞; el. C. of Merton, Oxon 29 Sep. 1738, 5 Oct. 1743, 27 Dec. 1746; pres. to R. of Wootton, Northants 29 June 1764 (the last day of the two calendar months within which the presentation was to be made, see legal opinion in Reg.), d. (? July) 1777; wrote *Essays Moral and Miscellaneous, Poems*, 2 vol. 1759 (part i. 1754, ii. 1752); *View of Life* 1749, *Science, an Epistle* 1750, *Sacred Harmony* 1753; took Le Marchant's duty as Sub-dean in 1739 (*see* Reg.)

James **Ibbetson** (s. Ebenezer, of S. Martin's, Ludgate, d. 1743), b. Ludgate Hill, sojourner 28 Sep. 1734 to 1 July 1737, **M.** 22 Oct. 1734 age 16, **Petr. 1737**, res. 6 Sep. 1749 on instit. 6 Sep. 1748 to Bushey in Herts (bought by the College, Ibbetson's family contributing; on 10 Nov. 1740 the College paid for conveying the books to Bushey which Mr. Nichols the Rector had left to the parish; the College bought 2 copyhold tenements at Bushey 1825); B.A. 14 July 1740, M.A. 23 Ap. 1741, B.D. 14 June 1748, D.D. 11 July 1752; C. of Merton, Oxon 1 Oct. 1747 (when a question arose whether Bray [*see* 1731] could vote for himself to be appointed); Archdeacon

of S. Albans 13 Feb. 1754, preb. of Lincoln 1757, d. 10 Aug. 1781;
Clutterbuck's Hertfordshire i. 340–2.   His sermon for the sons of the
Clergy 20 Ap. 1758 was printed in 4°.

Samuel **Gurney** (s. John, V. of S. Merryn, Cornwall, d. 13 Dec.
1764), **M.** 21 Mch 173⅔, named **Chaplain** 19 Oct. **1737**, res. 16 Sep.
1741; held Mastership of Tregony sch. in Cornwall and a neighbouring
cure by means of repeated leave of absence, Fortescue doing the
Chaplain's work for him and receiving the Chaplain's commons, &c.;
R. of Warleggan 1746, and V. of Colan 1762; Coll. Corn. 305.

William **Tonkin** (s. Uriah), b. Penzance 1718, sojourner 13 Feb.
173⅘ to 10 July 1739, **M.** Feb. 173½ age 17, **Corn. 1739**, vac. 1771
on pres. to R. of Broad Somerford, Wilts 2 Aug. 1771; B.A. 25 Oct.
1738, M.A. 30 June 1741, lic. to practise medicine 31 Mch 1748,
B.D. 11 Ap. 1749; el. C. of Merton, Oxon 1763; pres. to Wittenham
20 May 1765, res. 2 Aug. 1771 for Broad Somerford; d. Penzance
1 Nov. 1798; Coll. Corn. 1012.

Daniel **Dumaresq** (s. Elias, Jurat of Jersey, by Elizabeth de
Carteret), b. S. Trinity in Jersey, **M.** Pemb. 16 Mch 17²⁹⁄₃₀ age 17,
B.A. 19 Oct. 1733, M.A. 7 July 1736; **Jer. 1740** (the Dean and
Jurats of Jersey sent the names of Dumaresq and of Philip le Hardy
B.A., both of Pembroke, for the College to choose between them),
res. 18 Sep. 1763 for R. of Yeovilton, Som.; B.D. 24 Ap. 1745,
D.D. by diploma 28 Ap. 1752, being chaplain to the English Factory
at St. Petersburg since July 1747, after having been chaplain to
Sir C. H. Williams, our ambassador; el. C. of Merton, Oxon 27 Sep.
1744 for a year; preb. of Sarum in Ap. 1766, and Wells 24 Aug.
1770 (Hutchins ii. 107), R. of Limington 1790, d. Bath 28 Oct.
1805; Gent. Mag. lxxv. pt. ii. 1802; Biog. Brit. v. John Brown ii.
663.   He superintended making the walk up Headington Hill.

John **Weston** (s. Rhodes, pleb., of Kingsbridge), b. Exeter,
battellar 24 June 1737 to 6 July 1741, **M.** 30 Aug. 1736 age 18,
Dev. 1741, res. at Exeter 1 May 1745; B.A. 7 June 1740, M.A.
9 July 1743; kept a school at S. Thomas', Exeter; a John Weston,
V. of Whitchurch, R. of S. Leonard's, Exeter 16 May 1755, d. 8 Oct.
1767; Eccl. Ant. i. 167.

Robert **Wells** (s. Rev. Nathaniel), b. Remenham near Henley,
battellar 17 Dec. 1736 to 6 July 1741, **M.** 17 Dec. 1736 age 17, **Sar.**
30 June 1741 (where see Reg.), res. at Newington 22 June 1745 on
his marriage; B.A. 3 Mch 174⁰⁄₁; held a living in Glamorgan, Penmaen
and Ilston in deanery of Gower, d. 28 Feb. 1804.

Francis **Upton** (s. Rev. James, of Bishop's Hull, Som.), b. Taunton, sojourner 18 Feb. 173⅞ to 8 July 1741, **M.** 6 July 1737 age 19, **Petr. 1741**; B.A. 30 June 1741, M.A. 13 Ap. 1744, B.D. 9 Dec. 1755; el. C. of Merton, Oxon 5 Oct. 1745, 25 Oct. 1748, 28 Sep. 1759; V. of Wittenham 1771, and R. of Seavington with Dinnington about 1765 (in succession to his brother John), having leave to hold Wittenham with them, d. 30 Mch 1778 age 58, bur. in the Coll. Chapel; Gutch iii. 121; wrote *Vernonis Laudes* 1742.

James **Andrew** (s. James, pleb.), b. Probus, Cornwall, poor scholar 6 Ap. 1738 to 3 Dec. 1741, **M.** 23 Mch 173⅞ age 20, named **Chaplain** 3 Oct. (certificate to Dean and Chapter 21 Nov.) **1741**, had a year's leave of absence, Dumaresq taking the Chaplain's duty, the leave was prolonged several times, res. 17 Oct. 1752; m. Elizabeth sister of Sir J. Vanhatten; B.A. 17 Nov. 1741, M.A. 28 June 1745, B. and D.D. 5 Feb. 1766, preb. of Rochester 28 Mch 1765, res. 1775; V. of Ashford, Kent 13 Dec. 1765, res. 1774; V. of Lower Winchenden and of Ilmer, Bucks 13 Aug. 1746; V. of Eynesford, Kent Feb. 1784, ?d. 1790; Polwhele v. 67, Bibl. Corn. 1028.

Hugh **Fortescue** (s. Joseph, of Warwick Court, London), b. Middlesex, sojourner 8 June 1738 to 9 July 1742, **M.** 9 June 1738 age 17, **Petr. 1742**, res. 10 Jan. 174⅞; B.A. 7 May 1742, M.A. 4 Ap. 1745; R. of Filleigh and E. Buckland, Devon 1794 (Lysons' Devon 240), of Challacombe to 1815; Hist. of Fortescue Family ii. 46.

Edward **Morshead** (s. William), b. Menheniot, sojourner 6 July 1742 to 7 July 1744, **M.** 8 July 1742 age 17, **Corn. 1744**, vac. 1760 by having taken V. of Quethiock 19 Sep. 1759–1801; R. of Little Petherick; B.A. 11 July 1747, M.A. 11 Ap. 1749; el. C. of Merton, Oxon 8 Sep. 1749 for the next year; d. Bath 15 Nov. 1811 unm.; Maclean i. 82; Lake iii. 313.

John **Ramsey** (s. Rev. John), b. Abbots Langley near Watford, Herts, sojourner 7 Ap. 1742 to 18 Jan. 174⅘, **M.** S. Mary H. 13 Oct. 1741 age 17; **Shi.** 26 Dec. **1744**, vac. 1782; B.A. 27 Jan. 174⅞, M.A. 4 Feb. 1752, B.D. 28 Nov. 1763, D.D. 6 Dec. 1781; ord. deacon at Grosvenor Chapel, Westminster, by Bishop of Winchester 21 Dec. 1746, V. of Abbots Langley 1761, pres. to Bushey 4 and instit. 24 Jan. 1782, d. 17 June 1785.

John **Gardner** (s. Rev. William), b. Walton on Thames, **M.** Lincoln 11 Ap. 1739 age 13, battellar 22 Sep. 1744 to 11 Jan. 174⅘; **Shi.** 26 Dec. **1744**; B.A. 17 Dec. 1743, M.A. 28 June 1745, B.D. 15 Dec.

1756; deacon by Bishop of Winchester 14 June 1747 in chapel of Winchester House, Chelsea, d. Ap. 1765.

John **Fowell** (s. Richard, Fellow 1715), b. Hilperton, Wilts, sojourner 7 July 1741 to 12 July 1745, M. 3 July 1741 age 16, **Sar. 1745**, vac. 27 Nov. 1764; B.A. 29 Ap. 1745, M.A. 14 Mch 174$\frac{7}{8}$, B.D. 17 Dec. 1759, D.D. 2 Nov. 1762, Proctor 1756, Prof. of Moral Philosophy 1757-61; m. Susanna d. of Thomas Atkin of Canterbury; C. of Merton, Oxon 4 Oct. 1750 and 1 Oct. 1757; R. of Bishopsbourne and Chartham and Orpington, Kent; chaplain to Archbishop Secker; R. of the sinecure of Eynesford, Kent, d. 30 Oct. 1803.

Samuel **Cholwich** (s. John), b. Farringdon near Exeter, sojourner 8 Ap. 1742 to 11 July 1745, M. 8 Ap. 1742 age 15, **Dev. 1745**, vac. by marriage Feb. 1754: B.A. 11 July 1748, M.A. 22 Ap. 1749, B. and D.D. 28 June 1762 as grand compounder; V. of Ermington, Devon, and held the sinecure Rectory as well, V. of Bickleigh 9 June 1755, Preb. of Exeter 1758, V. of Sturminster Marshall, Dorset 21 Feb. 1753, d. 1775; Lysons' Devon cxli, 55, 177; Hutchins iii. 366, W. Antiq. Feb. 1888 p. 214.

Thomas **Pyne** (s. Hugh), b. Crowndle near Tavistock, sojourner 27 Feb. 174$\frac{1}{2}$ to 9 July 1746, M. 6 Mch 174$\frac{1}{2}$ age 18, **Dev. 1746**; had leave from Lord Petre 21 Dec. 1747 to study civil law and medicine at foreign universities for four years; B.A. 12 Oct. 1745, M.A. 1 July 1748, d. 1753.

John **Pering** (s. John), b. Blackawton near Dartmouth, sojourner 3 Feb. 174$\frac{3}{4}$ to 14 July 1747, M. 14 Feb. 174$\frac{3}{4}$ age 17, **Dev. 1747**; B.A. 19 July 1750, M.A. 2 May 1751, studied physic, had leave from Lord Petre to travel 6 Ap. 1751, d. 1754.

Robert Burnett **Patch** (s. John), b. Exeter, sojourner 9 Mch 174$\frac{4}{5}$ to 11 July 1747, M. 13 Mch 174$\frac{4}{5}$ age 18, **Dev. 1747**, vac. by marriage 175$\frac{9}{1}$; B.A. 22 Mch 175$\frac{9}{1}$; Schoolmaster at Crewkerne.

Benjamin **Kennicott** (s. Benjamin, parish clerk of Totnes), b. Totnes 4 Ap. 1718, master of the Charity School there; drew up the *Regulations* for the Totnes ringers, given in Polwhele. By the assistance of friends (dedication to his 'Two Dissertations on the Tree of Life in Paradise' 2 ed. 1747) he M. Wadham 6 Mch 174$\frac{3}{4}$ age 25; **Petr. 1747**, res. 9 Jan. 1771 on m. Anne (sister of Mr. Edward Chamberlaine of the Treasury, she d. 1830 [Gent. Mag. liii. pt. ii. 718, 744]. She founded two scholarships for the study of Hebrew at Oxford, see Encycl. Brit. ed. 8, xiii. 63-64; Hodgson's Life of Bishop Porteus 5 ed. 1821 p. 256); B.A. by decree 20 June

1747 without fees, M.A. 4 May 1750, B.D. 4 Dec. 1761, D.D. 10 Dec.
1761, when the King gave him a pension of £200 a year; Radcliffe
Librarian 1767 (negligent as a Librarian, Johnson's Letters ii. 77); el.
C. of Merton, Oxon Oct. 1751 for the next year; preb. of Westminster 1770 but exchanged for a canonry of Christ Church 19 Oct.
1770, instit. to Menheniot 18 Nov. 1771, res. Dec. 1781 ; preacher
at Whitehall, V. of Culham, Oxon, d. Oxford 18 Sep. 1783, his
gravestone is at Christ Church; in 1769 concluded his great task of
collating the Hebrew MSS. of the Bible; wrote *State of printed
Hebrew Text of the Old Testament* 2 vols 8° 1753-9, *Annual Accounts
of his Collections*, and his edition of the Hebrew Bible in 2 vols folio
1776 and 1780; Gutch iii. 476; Lysons' Devon 535, Harding's
Tiverton iv. 89, Polwhele v. 180, Wordsworth 94, 169, Nichols ii.
408 ; Devon. Assoc. for Science and Lit. 1878 p. 215-22 ; Chalmers'
Biog. Dict., Misc. Gen. Sep. 1884 p. 146, Boswell's Johnson 1884 iv.
211, 285, 288, State Papers 1770 p. 143, Hist. Comm. 1885 p. 310,
387 letter May 1765 to Edward Weston, 389, 406, his portrait is in
the Coll. Hall ; Nat. Biog.

Thomas **Horndon** (s. Thomas, of Kea), b. Callington. **M.** Ch. Ch.
28 Ap. 1744 age 19; **Corn. 1747**, vac. 1752 by having taken the R.
of S. Dominick 27 Feb. 1752, and m. May 1752 Elizabeth d. of John
Hickes of Saltash, widow of John Clarke of Halton in S. Dominick ;
B.A. 26 Feb. 175⁰⁄₁, M.A. 2 May 1751; R. of Merton, Devon, res.
1794 to his son David, Fellow 1779 ; d. Bath 8 Jan. 1800; Gent.
Mag. lxx. 1800, pt. 1, 90, Coll. Corn. 390.

Francis **Travell** (s. John, of Addlesthorp, Glouc.; it was certified
21 June 1747 that Lord Petre held land in Gloucestershire), sojourner
13 Feb. 174⁵⁄₈ to 7 July 1748, **M.** 29 Nov. 1745 age 17, el. ('from
Swerford, Oxon'), **Petr. 1748**, vac. Jan. 1764 being then an officer in
the Guards and not having taken his B.D.; his mother had d. 16 Jan.
1763 and the estate had come to him; B.A. 13 July 1751, M.A.
23 June 1752.

Robert **Ewings** (s. Rev. Christopher), b. Feniton near Honiton
28 May 1728, sojourner 22 Mch 174⁵⁄₈ to 5 July 1749, **M.** 22 Mch
174⁵⁄₈, **Dev. 1749**, B.A. 10 Nov. 1752, M.A. 30 May 1753, B.D. 23
Oct. 1764; el. C. of Merton, Oxon 30 Sep. 1752 for the next year,
R. of S. Ebbe's, Oxford, C. of Plymtree, Devon 1759, d. 1771;
Peshall 164.

Francis **Webber** (Fellow 1728), el. **Rector** 5 June 1750. d. 29
Sep. 1771.

George **Carwithen** (s. George), b. Exeter, sojourner 17 Mch 174⅞ to 21 July 1750, M. 20 Mch 174⅚ age 17, **Petr. 1750**, vac. 1757 ; B.A. 27 Mch 1754, R. of Ashprington 1757, of Manaton 1766, d. 2 Oct. 1794.

George **Stinton** (s. Thomas, V. of Ilfracombe, Eccl. Ant. ii. 139), b. Ilfracombe, M. Queen's 24 May 1748 age 18 ; **Dev. 1750**, vac. 1767 ; B.A. 8 Feb. 1754, M.A. 18 Ap. 1755, B.D. 18 Ap. 1765, D.D. 22 Ap. 1765, Proctor 1764 ; V. of All Hallows, Barking, Chancellor of Lincoln 1766, Preb. of Peterborough 1776, Chaplain to the Archbishop, R. of Newington, Oxon to 1781, and of Wrotham, Kent Sep. 1781, F.R.S. and F.S.A. 1776, ed. Secker's *Sermons and Charges* 1770–1, d. Great George St., Westminster 30 Ap. 1783 ; J. Maskell's *All Hallows, Barking* 107, 156, 157 ; London and Middlesex Archæol. Soc. Trans. ii. 138–9 ; for his sermons see Darling's Cyclopædia Bibliographica ; Hodgson's Life of Bishop Porteus 5 ed. 1821 p. 21–23, Boswell's Johnson 1884 iii. 288, Polwhele v. 182, T. Langley's *Hist. of the Hundred of Desborough* 287–8, *Letters of Radcliffe and James* (O. H. S.) 156.

Edward **Marshall** (s. Rev. William), b. Ashprington, sojourner 18 Mch 174⅚ to 4 July 1751, M. 18 Mch 174⅚ age 18, **Dev. 1751**, vac. 1758 by having taken the V. of Breage with Germoe, Cornwall ; B.A. 26 June 1754, M.A. 25 June 1755 ; el. C. of Merton, Oxon 22 Sep. 1753 for the next year ; V. of St. Eval, Cornwall 1782, d. Breage 3 May 1803 ; m. Loveday 2 d. of Richard Sandys, she d. 28 Jan. 1804 ; Lake i. 135 ; Polwhele v. 71–72, Coll. Corn. 535.

Bickham **Escott** (s. Bickham, R. of Kittisford, Som.), b. Kittisford, sojourner 1 May 1749 to 5 July 1751, M. 5 May 1749 age 17, **Petr. 1751**, vac. 1757 by having taken R. of Kittisford ; B.A. 12 June 1754, M.A. 9 Dec. 1755.

Thomas **Baker** (s. Archdeacon George), b. E. Allington, M. Merton 7 Nov. 1749 age 17 ; **Dev. 1751**, vac. 1760 by instit. to R. of Ringmore 3 Oct. 1759, pres. by John Baker B.D. of Corpus ; B.A. 12 June 1754, M.A. 28 Ap. 1756, B. and D.D. 13 Mch 1778 ; R. of S. Martin's, Exeter, V. of Staverton, preb. of Exeter 1757, of S. Asaph 1777, d. before April 1803 ; Lysons' Devon cxv.

Hender **Mountsteven** (4 s. Hender, d. 1774), b. Bodmin, bap. 1729, M. 30 June 1752, **Corn. 1752**, vac. by m. 1776 ; incorp. as B.A. from Pemb. Hall, Camb. 11 July 1752, M.A. 18 Ap. 1755, B.D. 9 July 1766, adm. to practise in medicine 11 July 1792 ; el. C. of Merton, Oxon 5 Oct. 1754 for the next year ; R. of Little Petherick, Cornwall in 1782, d. 1812 ; Coll Corn. 599.

Nicholas **Andrew** (s. James, pleb.), b. Probus, Cornwall, battellar 26 May 1748 to 9 Jan. 1753, M. 24 May 1748 age 18, adm. **Chapl**. 30 Dec. **1752**, B.A. 22 Jan. 1756, d. Dec. 1757.

Samuel **May** (s. Emanuel), b. Fremington near Barnstaple, bap. 1 Aug. 1732, sojourner 15 Dec. 1750 to 11 July 1753, M. 16 Oct. 1750 age **17**, **Dev. 1753**, res. 1 July 1755, m. 1756 ; B.A. 1 July 1755, d. 1782 ; Lysons' Devon 242.

William **Terry** (s. William), b. Norton in Townstal, Stoke Fleming, sojourner 16 Mch 1752 to 9 July 1754, **M**. 16 Mch 1752 age 17, **Dev. 1754**, vac. 1778 by pres. to Wootton, Northants 10 Oct. 1777 ; B.A. 30 June 1757, M.A. 25 May 1759, B.D. 27 Oct. 1770, D.D. 31 Oct. 1770, d. 26 Ap. 1805.

James **Stooke** (s. William), b. Exeter, sojourner 2 May 1752 to 13 July 1754, **M**. 12 May 1752 age 19, **Dev. 1754**, vac. by m. 22 Ap. 1765; B.A. 8 Mch 1758, M.A. 28 June 1759 ; el. C. of Merton, Oxon 10 Oct. 1755, held a living in Exeter; Lysons' Devon 538.

Emanuel **May** (s. Emanuel), b. Fremington, bap. 11 June 1735, sojourner 18 May 1753 to 16 July 1756, **M**. 22 May 1753, **Dev. 1756**, vac. 1774 by pres. to Baverstock in Wilts ; B.A. 5 Feb. 1760, M.A. 25 June 1760, B.D. 6 July 1761 ; el. C. of Merton, Oxon 24 Sep. 1758; V. of Ilfracombe 29 Jan. 1771 (certificate from Bishop Keppel 25 Oct. 1773 of its being under £80); bur. there 20 Mch 1804 : Phillipps ii. 87, **104**.

Richard **Hammett** (s. Richard), b. Clovelly, bap. Woolfardisworthy 4 Aug. 1736, sojourner 3 Ap. 1754 to 18 July 1757, **M**. 29 Mch 1754, **Petr. 1757**, res. 25 Dec. 1773 ; B.A. 3 Feb. 1761, M.A. 30 June 1762, R. of Clovelly and of Heanton Punchardon, m. Clovelly 30 Sep. 1777 Priscilla d. of William Henley of Gore Court, Kent, by whom he had Wilhelmina Dorothea, Richard, James, and Priscilla; d. 24 Aug. 1796; Lysons' Devon cxvii. 122, Drake 220.

John **Tickell** (s. William, of Sampford Courtenay, Devon), **M**. Merton 23 June 1755 age 18; **Petr. 1757**, vac. 1770 by instit. to E. Mersey, Essex 25 Mch 1769; B.A. 3 Feb. 1761, M.A. 22 Ap. 1762, R. of Gawsworth, Cheshire, d. 2 July 1802 'of Wargrave near Henley,' left (by will dated 22 June 1801) £500 to the College on the death of his wife (who d. Wargrave 4 Nov. 1816), to be accumulated for buying an advowson; the sum actually received was £468 7s. ; Lysons' Devon 431 ; letters in Reg. from Dr. Budd the executor 16 Nov. 1816, 8 Mch 1817.

Sampson **Newbery** (s. Sampson, of Zele in Tawton, Devon),

sojourner 22 May 1750 to 28 May 1756, **M.** 26 May 1750 age 19, adm. **Chapl.** 6 Feb. **1758**, vac. 1786 by pres. to Bushey in Herts 23 June and instit. 6 July 1785; B.A. 26 Feb. 1754, M.A. 30 June 1757, B.D. 19 May 1768, testimonials for deacon's orders 6 July 1754, el. C. of Merton, Oxon 28 June 1765, and 30 June 1766; V. of Long Wittenham 1778–85; d. 7 Mch 1794.

Edward **Michell** (s. John), b. Diptford near Totnes, battellar 29 Mch 1755 to 28 Sep. 1758, **M.** 7 Mch 1755 age 18, **Dev. 1758**, res. 24 Aug. 1763, m. 1764; B.A. 23 Feb. 1762, Master of Kingsbridge sch., then of Bruton, Som., R. of Witham Friary, Som.. d. 1799.

John **Kingdon** (s. Roger, by Judith d. of John Cory), b. Holsworthy 1735, sojourner 27 Oct. 1755 to 6 July 1759, **M.** 29 Oct. 1755 age 19, **Dev. 1760**, vac. 1765 by m. Jane d. of John Hockin V. of Okehampton; B.A. 13 June 1759, M.A. 21 Ap. 1762, V. of Bridgerule, Devon (to which he annexed the great tithes) and R. of Pyworthy 1781—both livings in his own gift; d. Bridgerule 25 Mch 1808; Lake iv. 320, Lysons' Devon 71, 425, Coll. Corn. 460, Athenæum ed. Dr. Aikin 1808 iii. 491.

John **Stackhouse** (2 s. Dr. William, R. of St. Erme, by Catherine d. of John Williams of Trehane in Probus), b. Trehane, bap. 15 Mch 1741, sojourner 23 June 1758 to 14 June 1761, **M.** 20 June 1758 (with his brother William age 17); **Corn. 1761**, vac. 1764 by succeeding to the estate of Pendarves, m. 21 Ap. 1773 Susanna o. d. and h. of Edward Acton of Acton Scott, Salop, she d. Bath 1834; d. Bath 22 Nov. 1819; Stemmata Chichleana No. 446; Lake iv. 46; Bibl. Corn. 681; Fellow of the Linnean Society, his *Illustrationes Theophrasti* 1811, and edition of *Theophrastus de historia plantarum, Critical remarks on Ælian and other authors*, and Works on British plants and algæ had some reputation. He also published *Dei Cataclasmi*, a poetical sketch of the revolutions which have happened in the natural history of our planet, Bath 1786, and *Nereis Britannica* fol. 1801 with coloured plates of Fuci, Algæ, and Confervæ, ed. 2 1816 4°; Coll. Corn. 923.

Thomas **Webber** (s. Charles), b. Exeter, sojourner 19 Nov. 1759 to 3 July 1761, **M.** 20 Nov. 1759 age 17, **Dev. 1761**, B.A. 20 June 1764, M.A. 18 June 1766, d. 13 May 1768; Polwhele's Devonshire ii. 25.

John **Radford** (s. Rev. William, of Nymet Rowland), b. Lapford, battellar 25 Feb. 1758 to 8 July 1762, **M.** 27 Feb. 1758 age 17,

Dev. 1762, vac. in his probation year; B.A. 5 Feb. 1762, R. of Lapford 1763; Lysons' Devon 310.

Thomas **Baker** (s. Rev. Thomas, of Hungerford), **M.** Merton 16 Nov. 1757 age 18, B.A. 2 June 1761, **Sar. 1762**, vac. 1766; M.A. 9 May 1764, R. of Buttermere, perhaps also of Combe Bisset, both in Wilts, d. 1789.

Arundel **Radford** (s. Rev. William), b. Lapford, battellar 19 Feb. 1760 to 5 July 1763, **M.** 19 Feb. 1760 age 17, **Dev. 1763**, vac. 1783 by having taken V. of Gwennap, Cornwall 28 June 1782; B.A. 27 Feb. 1767, M.A. 24 May 1769, B.D. 31 May 1780, R. of Nymet Rowland, d. 30 Oct. 1805.

Charles Tyrrell **Morgan** (s. Charles), b. Fairford, Glouc., sojourner 8 Dec. 1759 to 11 July 1764, **M.** 17 Dec. 1759 age 16, **Petr. 1764**, vac. by m. 1775; B.A. 3 June 1763, M.A. 11 July 1767, Proctor 1771, Prof. of Moral Philosophy 1772; barrister L. I. 1769.

Francis **Cole** (s. Francis), b. Treffry in Lanhydrock, sojourner 7 Mch 1761 to 11 July 1764, **M.** 8 Mch 1761 age 18, **Corn. 1764**, res. 13 June 1774, having taken V. of Luxulyan 1773–1796 (where John Cole preceded him 1728–73); B.A. 20 Nov. 1769, M.A. 2 July 1771; P.C. of Lanhydrock 1782.

George **Rhodes** (s. George), b. Modbury 1743, sojourner 14 Mch 1761 to 11 July 1764, **M.** 14 Mch 1761 age 17, **Dev. 1764**, vac. 1769 by instit. to South Pool, Devon 21 Sep. 1768; B.A. 12 Feb. 1768, M.A. 3 May 1768, m. in 1774, V. of S. Erth and of Uny Lelant, Cornwall 10 May 1776, res. them 1781 for V. of Colyton, Devon 4 Jan. 1782, R. of Stockleigh Pomeroy to death, d. 15 Mch 1798; Clark i. 58, Davies Gilbert i. 354.

Francis **le Couteur** (s. John, of St. Mary's, Jersey, by Elizabeth Payn), b. St. Sauveur's, Jersey, **M.** Jesus 6 July 1762 age 17; **Jer. 1764**, Guernsey having no candidate; vac. 1772 by m. Elizabeth Perrochon; B.A. 19 June 1767, V. of St. Sauveur's, d. 1808; wrote treatise on Cider.

Francis **Milman** (s. Francis, R. of E. Ogwell), b. there 1746, sojourner 4 July 1760 to 6 July 1765, **M.** 5 May 1760 age 13, **Dev. 1765**, had leave 25 Feb. 1772 from Lord Petre to travel for four years, vac. by m. 1780 Frances only child of William Hart, of Stapleton, Glouc.; B.A. 9 May 1764, M.A. 14 Jan. 1767, M.B. 7 July 1770, M.D. 23 Nov. 1776, B.D. 10 Nov. 1778: one of Dr. Radcliffe's travelling physicians 1771–80, fellow of the Coll. of Phys. 30 Sep. 1778 (afterwards President 1811–13; Croonian lecturer 1781,

Harveian lecturer 1782); physician to George III, bart. 28 Nov. 1800, F.R.S., d. 27 June 1821; Dean Milman was his youngest son; Sir Francis wrote on dropsy, and scurvy, and putrid fever; Gent. Mag. xci. pt. ii. p. 88 (1821); Lysons' Devon cxvii; Munk ii. 269.

Thomas Pearce **Hockin** (s. Rev. John), b. Okehampton, sojourner 22 June 1763 to 10 July 1765, **M.** 19 May 1763 age 17, **Petr. 1765,** res. 29 June 1770, having been instit. to Lydford 1 Dec. 1769, B.A. 9 June 1768, M.A. 31 May 1770; V. of Okehampton, d. 1789; Bibl. Corn. 248, Coll. Corn. 373.

John **Sarraude** (s. John, of Farringdon, Berks, and R. of Elvington, Yorks. 21 Dec. 1754. d. Sutton, Sep. 1800 age 89, by Sarah), b. Farringdon, **M.** Merton 27 May 1762 age 17; **Sar. 1765,** res. 14 Oct. 1789, having taken R. of Tollard Royal, Wilts 1788, res. 1796; B.A. 30 June 1768, M.A. 11 May 1769, B.D. 2 Nov. 1780, disp. from taking D.D. 1788; Proctor 1779, V. of Long Wittenham (under £70) 19 July 1785–1788; Preacher at Whitehall 1785 *vice* Thomas Stinton; V. of Bossall, Yorks. 14 Oct. 1796, instit. 14 Ap. 1798 to R. of Sutton upon Derwent, on his father's resignation; m. Hannah (bur. Sutton 21 Ap. 1810 age 44), d. Sutton 30 July 1808; Phillipps ii. 94, 99; Gent. Mag. 1808 p. 756.

Francis **Haultain** (s. James), b. Banstead, Surrey, **M.** Pemb. 11 Dec. 1764 age 17; **Shi. 1766,** vac. by m. 1775 Miss Stainsforth niece to the Bishop of London; B.A. 27 Jan. 1770, M.A. 6 July 1771, B. and D.D. 12 Nov. 1794; R. of Hornsey near Highgate, V. of Eastham, Essex, and of Weybridge, Surrey 1794, d. 28 Aug. 1827.

Henry **Richards** (s. Robert), b. Tawstock Mch 1747, ed. Barnstaple, battellar 26 Jan. 1764 to 24 July 1767, **M.** 14 Oct. 1763 age 16, **Dev. 1767,** res. 29 June 1794, having been pres. 13 and instit. 19 Mch 1794 to Bushey, Herts; B.A. 19 June 1767, M.A. 26 Ap. 1770, B.D. 9 Nov. 1781, D.D. 9 Nov. 1797; m. d. of Mr. Badcock, manciple of Pembroke; R. of S. Ebbe's, Oxford 1771; pres. to Long Wittenham 2 Dec. 1788 and instit. 8 Ap. 1789; Commissioner for the College under the Act for Lighting and Paving, in place of Sarraude, 2 Nov. 1789; Whitehall preacher 1787: el. Rector 23 July 1797, Vice-Chancellor 1806–7, d. of a paralytic seizure 19 Dec. 1807, bur. in the Chapel in his wife's grave 24 Dec.; Peshall 164; Gent. Mag. 1807 p. 1181–82; Dr. Richards left his money to the College (Reg. 24 Dec. 1807 and 2 Nov. 1810), either to buy advowsons or to improve the Domus fund; it was applied to the former purpose, and 22 Oct. 1833 the R. of Woodleigh near Kingsbridge, Devon was bought for £5,000, including the redeemed land tax. In 1841 the College bought two plots of ground adjoining the Rectory, and annexed them to the living; Cox 190, 239; Dr. Parr's Letter dated Exeter College, in Johnston's Parr i. (about White's Bampton Lectures). His portrait is in the Coll. Hall.

Robert **Campbell** (s. John), b. Sutton Benger, Wilts, sojourner 21 June 1765 to 8 July 1767, **M.** 22 June 1765 age 17, **Sar. 1767**, B.A. 30 June 1770, M.A. 1 July 1773, lieut. in 119 Foot, and capt. in the Guards; vac. 1776 by having taken V. of Much Marcle, Herefs.; V. of Mordiford and Doure, Herefs.

Thomas **Stinton** (s. Rev. Thomas, of Ilfracombe), b. 21 Dec. 1747, sojourner 28 June 1765 to 8 July 1767, **M.** 26 June 1765 age 17, **Dev. 1767**; B.A. 30 June 1770, M.A. 27 Jan. 1772, B.D. 18 Ap. 1782, D.D. 4 May 1785; V. of Great Carlton, Lincs. Ap. 1776, Whitehall Preacher 1775–85, preb. of S. Paul's 1795; el. Rector 15 Ap. 1785, d. 6 July 1797, bur. by his own desire close to 'the outside of the north wall of the chapel between two buttresses, which are next to the west door eastwards' Gutch iii. App. 245; J. Maskell's *All Hallows, Barking* 107, 156–7, London and Middlesex Archæol. Soc. Trans. ii. 138–9. On his kindness to (Sir) John Stoddart, see Leigh Cliffe's *Anecdotal Reminiscences* 1830 p. 172. His portrait is in the Coll. Hall.

Stephen **Weston** (1 s. Stephen, by Elizabeth Oxenham of South Tawton; Hearne 11 Dec. 1711), grandson of Stephen, bishop of Exeter, b. Exeter 1747, ed. Tiverton, sojourner 4 July 1764 to 7 July 1768, **M.** 7 June 1764 age 17, **Dev. 1768**, vac. by m. 1784 Penelope y. d. of James Tierney (she d. Caen 1789 of consumption, age 32); B.A. 29 Jan. 1768, M.A. 14 Nov. 1770, B.D. 2 May 1782; F.R.S. 1792, F.S.A. 1794, R. of Mamhead, Devon 29 Mch 1777–1790; pres. by the Commissioners of the Great Seal 1783 and instit. 17 Jan. 1784 to Hempston Parva, Devon, res. 1823, d. London 8 Jan. 1830; mem. in Gent. Mag. Ap. 1830 p. 370–3 and Ap. 1784, and in (W. Upcott's) Biog. Dict. of Living Authors 1816; Eccl. Ant. iii. 69; N. and Gleanings v. 6; published *Viaggiana* 1776, *Hermesianax* 1784, *A sermon at the Bishop's Visitation at Totnes* 1785, *Horatius cum Græcis collatus* 1801, *Werneria* 1805, and contributed notes to Bowyer's New Testament ed. 3; some of his Chinese studies are remarkable: Hist. Comm. 1885 p. 406, Polwhele v. 191, W. Antiq. x. 153. His portrait is in the Coll. Hall.

Joseph Atwell **Small** (s. Joseph), b. Cirencester, sojourner 4 July

1764 to 13 July 1770, **M.** 4 July 1764 age 16, **Petr. 1770**, vac. by
m. 1778; B.A. 30 June 1768, M.A. 2 July 1771, B. and D.D.
22 June 1781; R. of one moiety of Burnsall in Craven, Yorks.;
V. of Congresbury; el. 1781 P.C. of S. James', Bristol, by the
Corporation; chaplain to the King 1792, preb. of Glouc. 1794,
d. Bristol 12 Ap. 1814.

John **Toms** (s. Lewis), b. Bishop's Nympton, sojourner 24 May
1766 to 12 July 1770, **M.** 15 May 1766 age 18, **Dev. 1770**; B.A.
23 Feb. 1770, M.A. 16 Oct. 1772, B.D. 24 Feb. 1782, disp. from
taking D.D. 1790, d. Bishop's Nympton 9 May 1800.

Peter **Fisher** (s. Rev. Thomas and Elizabeth, of Little Torrington,
he was bur. 22 Mch 1772, she 17 June 1792), bap. 19 Ap. 1749,
sojourner 20 Mch 1769 (? previously) to 12 July 1770, **M.** 17 June
1766, **Petr. 1770**, res. 14 Mch 1774 having become R. of Little
Torrington; B.A. 26 Ap. 1770, R. of Thornbury, Devon 1781,
d. Torrington 1 June 1803 leaving a widow and nine children, mon.
in S. aisle of church, his widow Jane d. 1 Nov. 1832 age 82;
of their sons, Richard d. 20 Mch 1796 age 19, John 18 Ap.
1791 age 4.

William **Salkeld** (s. Robert, of Southampton Buildings, London),
b. S. Andrew's, Holborn 1749, ed. Eton, Reynolds exhibitioner 1767,
M. 16 Oct. 1767 age 18, **Petr. 1771**, vac. by m. 1781; B.A. 30 May
1771, M.A. 9 July 1774, M.B. 13 Nov. 1777, bur. 24 Feb. 1812;
Hutchins i. 270–1.

Thomas **Bray** (Fellow 1731), el. **Rector** 22 Oct. 1771, d. 28 Mch
1785.

William **Smith** (s. Henry, of S. Stephen's, Bristol), b. Bristol
25 Dec. 1749, ed. Eton, **M.** 26 Oct. 1769 age 19, Reynolds exhibitioner 1770; **Petr. 1772**, vac. by m. 1780; B.A. 17 June 1777,
M.A. 19 July 1783; R. of W. Worlington 1783, of Bideford 13 Oct.
1783, res. 1804, of Kingswinford 1804, d. 8 Ap. 1814; Gent. Mag.
1814 i. 516.

John **Jago** (s. John, V. of Tavistock, by Ann d. of Nathaniel
Beard, V. of Tavistock 1701–31), b. there 1751, sojourner 30 Mch
1770 to 14 July 1772, **M.** 29 Mch 1770 age 18, **Petr. 1772**, vac.
1782; B.A. 20 Feb. 1776, M.A. 17 July 1777, B.C.L. 22 Nov. 1781,
B. and D.D. 9 July 1793 : R. of Whimple and V. of Rattery 1781,
both in Devon; exchanged Whimple for V. of Milton Abbot 1786,
which he res. to his s. John 1818 but, his s. dying before him, he was
reappointed and held it till his death 28 Nov. 1835; m. Lamorran

23 Sep. 1786 Lucretia Bedford d. of Edward Stephens of Plymouth (b. 8 Sep. 1764, d. Plymouth 17 Nov. 1840) ; Coll. Corn. 410.

John **Dupré** (1 s. John, R. of S. Heliers, by Mary Millais), b. S. Heliers, **M.** Pemb. 13 Mch 1769 age 16; **Jer. 1772,** vac. by m. 1783 Eleanor; B.A. 16 Feb. 1776, M.A. 17 May 1776, B. and D.D. 17 Dec. 1790, V. of Mentmore, Bucks 1784–1834, of Toynton All Saints, Lincs. 1824–34; Master of Tringhead and then of Berkhampstead schools, d. Wyke cottage near Weymouth 12 Dec. 1834, his wife d. 12 Nov. 1827 in her 70th year, both bur. at Wyke Regis, Dorset; Hutchins ii. 852; he published 2 volumes of sermons 1782 and 1787; European Mag. Mch 1782 i. 201.

Edmund **Herring** (s. William, R. of Botus Fleming, Cornwall and Newton S. Petrock, Devon, who d. 5 May 1783 age 78, by Susanna Spettigue, m. Bickleigh 23 Jan. 1739, d. 14 Nov. 1800 age 77), b. Botus Fleming 18 Ap. 1752, sojourner 4 Ap. 1770 to 3 July 1773, **M.** 3 Ap. 1770, **Corn. 1773,** B.A. 8 Feb. 1777 : vac. by m. 27 Mch 1779 Elizabeth d. of George Warmington Bewes of Launceston, she d. 18 June 1811 age 65; R. of Newton S. Petrock 1783; d. 12 Dec. 1822; Lysons' Devon 387; W. Antiq. iv. 263, Coll. Corn. 352.

Richard **Clarke** (s. John), b. Totnes, sojourner 7 Mch 1771 to 5 July 1774, **M.** 7 Mch 1771 age 20, **Petr. 1774,** vac. by m. 1784 Miss Wise ; B.A. 28 May 1777, M.A. 23 May 1778 ; R. of Bedale in the N. Riding 1783–97, d. there 10 Jan. 1797.

Richard **Vivian** (3 s. Thomas, by Mary d. of John Hussey of Truro, Bibl. Corn. 836), b. Cornwood 1 Aug. 1754, **M.** 10 May 1771, Eliot exhibitioner; **Petr. 1774,** res. 21 June 1798, having been pres. 11 and instit. 25 Nov. 1797 to R. of Bushey; m. Bushey 7 Aug. 1798 Mary Catherine d. of E. J. Willshire Emmett of Dalton, Herts, she d. 22 Oct. 1843 ; B.A. 28 Feb. 1778, M.A. 11 July 1778, B.D. 3 Mch 1789, Proctor 1787 ; V. of Mullion, Cornwall 1780 (under £80), res. 26 Nov. 1797 ; d. suddenly in the Strand, of angina pectoris, 13 May 1825, Gent. Mag. 1825, i. 571.

John **Penrose** (1 s. John, V. of Gluvias, by Elizabeth d. of Rev. John Vinicombe of Exeter), b. Gluvias 15 Aug. 1753, ed. Truro, **M.** 16 May 1771, Eliot exhibitioner; **Corn. 1774,** B.C.L. 6 Mch 1778, vac. by m. 2 Ap. 1778 Jane 2 d. of Rev. John Trevenen (she d. 15 July 1818); R. of Cardynham 1777–82, of Perran-Uthnoe 1782, V. of Constantine; R. of Fledborough, Notts 1783 (mentioned 1788 in will of Elizabeth Duchess of Kingston), V. of Thorney, Notts 9 May 1803, d. Fledborough 14 Sep. 1829; Bibl. Corn. 457, Coll. Corn. 712.

Robert **Butler** (s. Rev. Joseph), b. S. Clement Danes, London, sojourner 10 Oct. 1772 to 3 July 1775, **M.** 10 Oct. 1772 age 19 as of Langley, Bucks, **Petr. 1775**, vac. 1780 by taking the R. of Inkpen, Berks; B.A. 25 June 1778, B.C.L. 2 June 1779.

John **Harding** (s. Thomas, of Pilton), b. Marwood, sojourner 14 Dec. 1772 to 6 July 1775, **M.** 17 Dec. 1772 age 17, **Dev. 1775**; B.A. 1 Feb. 1779, M.A. 28 Ap. 1779, B.D. 26 Oct. 1790, d. 28 Dec. 1816.

Robert **Laxton** (s. Rev. Robert), b. Leatherhead, Surrey, **M.** Pemb. 2 Ap. 1773 age 18; **Shi. 1775** as of Croydon, Surrey; B.A. 16 Feb. 1779, d. 1783.

Thomas Cary **Leach** (s. Philip, R. of Boconnoc and Bradock; Lake i. 122), b. Boconnoc 1753, sojourner 25 Ap. 1771 to 8 July 1775, **M.** 26 Ap. 1771 age 18, **Corn. 1776**; B.A. 23 Feb. 1775, M.A. 3 Ap. 1778, B.D. 9 June 1784, d. 1 June 1785, bur. 4 June in the south part of the Chapel; Gutch iii. App. 247; Bibl. Corn. 308; Hist. Comm. ii. 127.

Isaac **Frowd** (s. Edward), b. Longbridge Deverill, Brixton, Wilts, **M.** Merton 9 Ap. 1772 age 18; **Sar. 1776**, vac. 1779 by having taken V. of Bishop's Castle, Salop; B.A. 16 Feb. 1776, M.A. 13 Feb. 1779; R. of Shrawardine, Salop 1782 by dispensation, d. 3 Dec. 1835.

James **Gould** (s. William), b. Southmolton, sojourner 24 Oct. 1774 to 10 July 1778, **M.** 10 Oct. 1774 age 17, **Dev. 1778**; vac. by m. Southmolton 24 Feb. 1789 Elizabeth d. of Joseph Palmer, (Palmer Pedigree 1892 p. 1); B.A. 17 June 1778, M.A. 27 June 1782, d. of fever Nov. 1793.

John **Cole** (2 s. Humphry, by Phillis d. of Francis Maugham), b. S. Hilary 8 June 1758, **M.** 23 May 1775 Eliot exhibitioner; **Corn. 1778**; B.A. 26 June 1783, M.A. 22 May 1788, B.D. 20 Ap. 1795, D.D. 10 July 1800, Proctor 1794; Chaplain to William Duke of Clarence, through whom he was pres. to the V. of Gulval in Cornwall 1790; el. C. of Merton, Oxon 30 June 1792 for a year, pres. 29 Mch 1803 to V. of South Newington (then under £80); R. of Yaverland, I. of Wight 1809; el. Rector 7 Jan. 1808, Vice-Chancellor 1810, d. Marazion 13 Oct. 1819; Lake iv. 45, Bibl. Corn. 76, Cox 192, Memoir of Rev. John Russell 1878 p. 17. His portrait by Opie is in the Coll. Hall.

William **Holwell** (s. Edward, by Isabella Newte), b. Exeter 1758, bap. St. Martin's, Exeter 4 Ap. 1759 and named after his uncle William Holwell V. of Thornbury, Glouc., sojourner 4 Mch 1776 to

10 July 1778, **M.** 2 Mch 1776, **Petr. 1778**, allowed to travel 30 Ap. 1781, res. 14 Jan. 1793 having been pres. to Menheniot 17 Nov. 1791 and instit. 3 Jan. 1792, where however he did not reside; B.A. 5 June 1783, M.A. 6 May 1784, B.D. 20 Feb. 1790 though not in orders; F.R.S. 1806; changed his name 20 Nov. 1798 (London Gazette p. 1101) to Holwell Carr on property devolving on his wife Lady Charlotte Hay, 1 d. of James 14 Earl of Erroll, whom he m. London 18 May 1797, and who d. London 9 Feb. 1801 in her 38 year (mon. in Menheniot). He d. London 24 Dec. 1830, bur. Withecombe Raleigh, Exmouth. He bequeathed his fine pictures, mostly of the Italian school, one of which is 'Christ disputing with the Doctors,' (collected in France and Italy 1780) to the National Gallery; Gent. Mag. ci. part 1 (1831) p. 370; Misc. Gen. 1877 p. 416; Lake iii. 313, Nat. Biog. ix. 177. He gave the College Library the Editio Princeps of Homer, Florence 1488, and the publications of the Roxburgh Club. Some one remarked of his portrait (he was a sceptical art critic) that it looked as if in the act of saying 'Yes, but the original is in the Borghese gallery,' Fred Locker's Patchwork 1879 p. 140.

Stephen George Francis Triboudet **Demainbray** (o. s. Dr. Stephen Triboudet, astronomer to George III. at Kew, in which office his son succeeded him and held it 1782–1840), b. Ealing 7 Aug. 1759, ed. Harrow (Thornton's Harrow 167), sojourner 27 Oct. 1776 to 16 Oct. 1778, **M.** Ch. Ch. 26 May 1775; **Petr. 1778**, vac. 1799 by pres. to Broad Somerford 4 Feb. 1799, Reg. 18 Dec. 1823; B.A. 21 June 1781, M.A. 2 May 1782, B.D. 9 July 1793; Whitehall Preacher 1784, Chaplain to the King at Kew 1801, chaplain at S. James' 1802; V. of Wittenham 9 Aug. 1794; d. Broad Somerford 6 July 1854 age 94; his s. Francis **M.** Pemb. 1 Nov. 1809 age 14, his father had concealed his marriage from Exeter College for several years before 1799. He was one of the first promoters of the allotment system, and wrote *The Poor Man's Best Friend* 1830; Nat. Biog. xiv. 330.

David **Horndon** (s. Thomas, Fellow 1747), b. St. Dominick 2 Dec. 1759, sojourner 13 May 1777 to 10 July 1779, **M.** 2 May 1777, **Corn. 1779**, res. 29 June 1794, his father having resigned Merton *alias* Martin, Devon to him 1793; B.A. 30 May 1782, M.A. 1 July 1784; m. Bath 23 June 1802 Mary Ann d. of John Glubb, R. of Bicton, she d. 6 Mch 1836; R. of Bicton 4 Mch 1811, d. 6 Ap. 1845; Coll. Corn. 390.

George Avery **Hatch** (s. George), b. Windsor, **M.** Merton 3 July

1775 age 18; **Sar. 1779**, res. 14 Ap. 1792 on instit. 19 Ap. 1791 to Rectories of S. Matthew's in Friday Street and S. Peter's in West Cheap, London; B.A. 20 Ap. 1779, M.A. 6 July 1782; V. of Weekley, Northants (under £80) 1786, d. 15 Jan. 1837.

Samuel **Lane** (s. Thomas), bap. Totnes 9 May 1759, at Winchester 1770, sojourner Nov. 1776 to 12 July 1780, **M.** 26 Nov. 1776, **Dev. 1780**, res. at Totnes 26 May 1794; B.A. 25 May 1780, M.A. 9 May 1783, R. of Hook, Dorset (under £80) 2 Feb. 1791, d. 1827; Hutchins ii. 184.

Robert Palk **Welland** (s. Richard), b. Topsham, Devon, sojourner 28 Mch 1777 to 11 July 1780, **M.** 21 Mch 1777 age 18, **Petr. 1780**, res. May 1787 on instit. to R. of Shottesbrook and V. of White Waltham, Berks May 1786; B.A. 23 Feb. 1784, M.A. 26 Ap. 1785; R. of Talaton Oct. 1787, of Dunchideock with Shillingford 26 Oct. 1793 (patron his uncle Sir Robert Palk), d. Shillingford 24 June 1841 age 84; Lysons' Devon 470: Eccl. Ant. ii. 12, iii. 10.

Thomas Smyth **Glubb** (2 s. Thomas, by Elizabeth 4 d. of Christopher Cunningham, of Okehampton), b. Nether Stowey, Som., **M.** 10 May 1777 age 18, Symes scholar 30 June 1778; **Petr. 1780**; B.A. 20 Feb. 1784, M.A. 26 Ap. 1785, B.D. 16 Dec. 1795; el. C. of Merton, Oxon 10 July 1787 for the next year; pres. to Wittenham (under £80) 30 June and instit. 20 Aug. 1799, d. 4 Ap. 1823 at the house of his relative Coryndon Luxmoore, R. of Bridestowe, Devon (N. and Gleanings iv. 161): held office of Bursar nearly 20 years and his accounts were in such disorder that the College suffered considerable loss. For some time after this no one was bursar for more than two years; Allen's Liskeard 527.

Thomas **Jackson** (s. William, of S. Stephen's, Exeter), b. Exeter, **M.** 18 Feb. 1777 age 17, Reynolds exhibitioner 1779; **Petr. 1781**, vac. by marriage 21 Oct. 1806; B.A. 23 Feb. 1781, M.A. 4 May 1786, B.D. by decree 23 Nov. 1796 (Reg. 23 Nov. 1804, 29 June 1805); Secretary 22 Feb. 1783 to Hon. John Trevor English Minister at Turin; he was himself Minister Plenipotentiary at Turin 13 Ap. 1799 to 1807; Gent. Mag. 1799 i. 538.

John **Phillips** (1 s. Joseph, by Eulalia 3 d. of Abraham Barnfield of Mambury in E. Putford near Bideford; m. 14 Mch 174⅘, he was bur. 19 Mch 1781 age 79, she 2 Ap. 1788 age 79, both at E. Putford), b. Mambury 21 July 1751, **M.** 2 Dec. 1779, **Petr. 1782**, res. 8 July 1791: B.A. 24 Mch 1786, M.A. 16 May 1786, d. unm. 13 Mch 1828; wrote the *Glossary of Devonshire Words* published 1839 by

Mrs. Gwatkin, to whom he gave it; Lysons' Devon 424, Bibl. Corn. 200; great-uncle of E. A. Dayman, Fellow 1828.

Richard Hawkin **Hitchins** (1 s. Rev. Malachi), bap. Bideford 21 Oct. 1764, sojourner 23 Ap. 1781 to 5 Mch 1783 as of S. Hilary, Cornwall, **M**. 2 Ap. 1781, Reynolds exhibitioner 1781 ; **Dev. 1783**, vac. 6 July 1805 on pres. to Baverstock, Wilts 22 June and instit. 6 July 1804, where he only resided his last three years (Reg. 8 Mch 1823); B.A. 19 Mch 1787, M.A. 12 June 1789, B.D. 20 June 1799, d. 21 Feb. 1827 ; for 33 years Curate of Falmouth ; Lake i. 395 ; Bibl. Corn. 243, Coll. Corn. 369.

Joshua le **Marchant** (s. Rev. Joshua, of Guernsey, who d. 12 June 1794, by Rachel Carey Dobrée), b. St. Peter's Port 16 Nov. 1763, at Winchester 1777, **M**. Pemb. 3 Dec. 1779; **Guer. 1783**, vac. by m. 26 Mch 1792 Sarah Susanna d. of John Glubb, R. of Bicton, she was b. 1772, d. 1843 ; B.A. 18 June 1783, M.A. 4 May 1786, in orders, lived at Sidmouth.

Henry **Belfeild** (s. Henry), b. Studham, Herts, **M**. Pemb. 11 May 1780 age 18 ; **Shi. 1783**; B.A. 31 Jan. 1788, M.A. 12 July 1788, d. Berkhampstead Feb. 1789.

William **Griffiths** (s. Rev. John), b. Chiswick, ed. Eton, Reynolds exhibitioner 1780, **M**. 19 Oct. 1780 age 18 as of S. James', Westminster; **Petr. 1784**, vac. by marriage 10 Mch. 1794, B.A. 9 June 1784, M.A. 26 Ap. 1787; collated by Bishop Douglas to R. of S. Edmund's, Salisbury May 1793, V. of S. Issey, Cornwall 10 May 1794, fell over a precipice 30 July 1802, left a widow and five young children.

Thomas **Duncumb** (s. Rev. Thomas), b. Shiere, Guildford, **M**. Magd. H. 24 Mch 1779 age 18 ; **Shi. 1784**, vac. 10 Feb. 1806 by pres. to Shiere 1805 ; B.A. 28 Feb. 1783, M.A. 16 May 1786, B.D. 15 July 1797 (both as Duncomb); d. Shiere 9 Mch 1843 ; Gent. Mag. 1843 xix. 544.

Thomas **Stinton** (Fellow 1767), el. **Rector** 15 Ap. **1785**, d. 6 July 1797.

John **Vye** (s. Rev. John; a John Vye was V. of Ilfracombe 1770–1), b. and bap. S. David's, Exeter 5 Jan. 1764, Reynolds exhibitioner, **M**. 1 Nov. 1781, **Dev. 1785**, B.A. 25 May 1785, M.A. 5 Mch 1791, B.D. 22 Oct. 1801 ; V. of Morthoe, Devon (under £60) Mch 1795, res. 22 Feb. 1805 ; pres. to Wootton in Northants 27 June 1805 but, in consequence of his claim being disputed by Heyes (Reg. 13 and 19 June 1805, 2 Feb. 1810), his fellowship was not declared vacant till Feb. 1810; d. Teignmouth 28 June 1833; Gent. Mag. 1806 lxxvi. p. 1240, and 1833 pt. 2 p. 185.

Edward **Morshead** (4 s. William, by Olympia d. of John Treise), b. Cartuther, Menheniot, bap. 29 June 1764, **M.** 16 Dec. 1782, **Corn. 1785**, vac. 13 Jan. 1797 by pres. 12 Jan. 1796 to R. of Calstock; B.A. 23 Mch 1789, M.A. 22 May 1789; R. of Hascombe, Surrey 1791, of St. Dominick 12 June 1800–1803, of Little Petherick 27 Ap. 1801, V. of Quethiock 28 Ap. 1801, all in Cornwall, R. of Beaworthy 9 Nov. 1807, of Kelly 30 Dec. 1823–1833, both in Devon; Chaplain to Prince of Wales and Duke of York, Special Vice-Warden of the Stannaries, d. Calstock 17 Sep. 1852; m. Kelly, Devon 12 Ap. 1798 Mary 1 d. of Arthur Kelly, she d. June 1832; Maclean i. 80, 83; Gent. Mag. 1852 xxxviii. 545.

Robert Hele **Selby** (s. Robert Hele), b. Marazion, bap. 24 June 1765, **M.** 2 June 1783, **Corn. 1785**, vac. by m. 18 May 1791 Felicia 1 d. of George Horne bishop of Norwich; B.A. 12 July 1788, M.A. 10 Oct. 1789; el. C. of Merton, Oxon 11 July 1788 for the next year, instit. to R. of Colmworth, Beds, Jan. 1791, R. of Brede, Sussex 1822; took name of Hele at the wish of his uncle John Hele (London Gazette 1791 p. 287), d. Hastings owing to his chaise overturning 18 Nov. 1839; Gent. Mag. 1840 xiii. 103.

Samuel **Hart** (s. Samuel, V. of Crediton), b. Crediton 1762, **M.** 27 Ap. 1780 age 17, named **Chaplain** 29 July and adm. 3 Aug. **1786**, vac. by m. 12 May 1806 his 2 cousin Anne o. child and h. of Henry Cory of Holsworthy, who survived him; B.A. 20 Feb. 1784, M.A. 19 Oct. 1786, B.D. 7 Nov. 1798; pres. to V. of Merton, Oxon 2 May 1796; nominated by Archdeacon George Moore and pres. by Chapter of Exeter to V. of Alternon, Cornwall, instit. 30 Jan. 1806, res. Sep. 1841, d. *s.p.* Holsworthy 27 Oct. 1845; Lake i. 18; Mem. Gent. Mag. 1846 xxv. 214.

John Neville **Freeman** (s. Robert), b. Uxbridge, bap. 1 May 1764, **M.** 14 Dec. 1782; Reynolds exhibitioner 1782; **Petr. 1787**, vac. by m. 14 Feb. 1792 Miss H. M. Arthenius of Charlotte St., London; B.A. 15 June 1786, M.A. 5 July 1791, V. of Hayes, Middlesex May 1792, d. Hayes 16 Dec. 1843; Gent. Mag. 1844 xxi. 213.

Samuel **Teed** (s. Samuel), b. E. Budleigh, bap. 16 June 1768, **M.** 14 Mch 1785, Reynolds exhibitioner 1787; B.A. 12 June 1789, **Dev. 1789**; M.A. 5 July 1791, in orders, d. Exmouth 13 Jan. 1792, bur. E. Budleigh.

John Lea **Heyes** (s. Rev. Richard, of Rissington Magna, Glouc.),

b. White Waltham, Berks 1763, **M.** Queen's 17 Jan. 1781 age 18, B.A. Pemb. 6 Ap. 1785, M.A. 15 June 1787; **Sar. 1790** ; B.D. 7 Nov. 1798 ; pres. to V. of Merton, Oxon 3 July 1806, to R. of Bushey 7 June and instit. 8 Oct. 1825, d. Merton 4 Dec. 1825.

Edward **Rodd** (2 s. Francis, by Jane Hearle), b. Trebartha in Northill, **M.** Oriel 18 Nov. 1785 age 17, **Corn. 1791**, vac. 17 Mch 1805 by pres. Mch 1804 to St. Just in Roseland; B.A. 12 June 1789, M.A. 20 Ap. 1792, B.D. 22 Ap. 1803, D.D. 12 Mch 1816 : Proctor 1802 ('he was said to be a disciplinarian worthy of his name' ; Cox 204) ; allowed by the Visitor (see the previous case of Bray 1748) to hold the living of Dittisham near Dartmouth (for a minor, Robert Sparke Hutchins, son of the late Rector) with his fellowship 1802 : V. of Lamerton, Devon 1816, d. 23 July 1842 ; m. 25 Ap. 1805 Harriet 1 d. of Charles Rashleigh ; Lake i. 41, iv. 9; Bibl. Corn. 580.

Willshire John **Emmett** (o. s. John), b. Redburn, Herts 30 Nov. 1770, bap. 21 Dec.; at Westminster 1781, of Trinity, Cambridge ; **M.** 4 Dec. and el. **Shi.** 26 Dec. **1791**, vac. by m. 5 Jan. 1800 Miss Smith of Watford; B.A. 14 Jan. 1795, M.A. 12 May 1795 ; legatee of Hugh Smith M.D. of Hatton St. London, who d. 26 June 1789 at East Barnet, where he had a large estate; R. of Latimer, Bucks, d. 5 Ap. 1860.

Joseph **Rosdew** (s. Richard, Lysons' Devon 415, 578), b. Yealmpton, Devon, bap. 15 July 1768, **M.** 31 May 1786, **Petr. 1792** (the election was contested, Gent. Mag. 1792 lxii. 667), vac. 1827 by instit. to Bushey 19 May 1826 ; B.A. 16 Mch 1790, M.A. 28 June 1793, B.D. 26 Jan. 1804 ; el. C. of Merton, Oxon 30 June 1795 for a year, V. of South Newington 6 Ap. 1808 on resignation of Dr. Cole, res. 16 May 1818 ; d. Bushey 1 June 1835. There is a silhouette of him in the Common Room.

Thomas **Best** (s. Rev. Thomas), b. Newbury, Berks, bap. 4 May 1768, **M.** 1 June 1786, **Sar. 1792**, B.A. 12 Feb. 1790, M.A. 30 June 1794, B.D. 17 Feb. 1804 ; d. 11 Aug. 1830 ; tombstone in churchyard of Shaw, near Newbury, where he was Curate 28 years.

James **Reed** (s. James), b. Barnstaple, bap. 6 July 1768, **M.** Merton 20 Oct. 1787 and held an Eton postmastership : Reynolds exhibitioner 1789 ; **Dev. 1792**, res. 15 Ap. 1811, the mother of his pupil the Marquis of Downshire having pres. him to the R. of Eversholt, Beds, instit. 16 Ap. 1810 ; the Marquis pres. him to V. of Hampstead Norris, Berks 1819 ; chaplain to her Majesty at S. James' 1803 : B.A.

22 June 1791, M.A. 30 June 1794; B.D. 22 Jan. 1803; el. C. of Merton, Oxon 30 June 1793 for the next year; d. Eversholt 10 Jan. 1843; Gent. Mag. 1843 xix. 327.

John Collier **Jones** (s. Richard), b. Plympton Earle, Devon 7 Oct. 1770, ed. Truro, **M.** 10 Oct. 1788, **Petr. 1792**; B.A. 6 June 1792, M.A. 30 June 1796, B.D. 1 July 1807, D.D. 12 Nov. 1819, C. of Mortlake, Chaplain to H.M.S. Namur 29 Jan. 1796, Temeraire 16 Nov. 1799, on half-pay 5 Oct. 1802, was one of the English imprisoned by Napoleon after the breach of the Peace of Amiens, and detained 2 years at Verdun; Tutor 1808, Public Examiner 1812-14, el. Rector 6 Nov. 1819, select preacher 1820-1, Delegate of Accounts 1824, Vice-Chancellor 1828, d. Oban 7 Aug. 1838, bur. there 21 Aug.; m. Plympton 6 Jan. 1825 Charlotte 3 d. of Duke Yonge V. of Cornwood, widow of capt. George Crawley R.N., she d. 8 Ap. 1836, bur. in south aisle of Chapel. The College gave £1,000 to furnish the Rector's lodgings for him, and £500 to put up buildings on the Vicarial Estate at Kidlington. He left the furniture (given him by the College) and his books to the College by will, and some money after the death of his sisters; and also his plate and glass, but the latter were taken away by some relatives to Canada after the death of Miss Jones at Plymstock 17 Jan. 1873; Reg. 29 Ap. 1823 and pp. 65, 343, 347, and 25 Ap. 1855; Gent. Mag. 1838 x. 560; Cox 124, 198, 246, Coll. Corn. 1309; Hist. of Kidlington (O. H. Soc.) 58, 157, 159, 316, C. H. O. Daniel *Our Memories* 1893 p. 79.

Michael **Dupré** (s. John, and brother of John fellow 1772), b. S. Heliers, **M.** Pemb. 14 Dec. 1780 age 13; named **Jer.** Fellow by Dean and Jurats in May and el. 30 June **1792**, B.A. 9 June 1784, M.A. 10 Oct. 1791, B.D. 22 Jan. 1803, R. of S. John's, Jersey 1808-18 (under £120, Reg. 1809), master at Berkhampstead gr. sch. 1806, chaplain of a regiment of Foot, d. of apoplexy Southampton 19 Oct. 1818; Gent. Mag. 88 pt. ii. p. 571; his brother Edward was Dean of Jersey 1802; *Life of W. W. Phelps* i. 220.

Charles **Marshall** (s. Rev. John, master of Exeter sch.), b. Exeter, bap. 24 Aug. 1770, **M.** 23 Oct. 1788, Reynolds exhibitioner 1789; **Petr. 1793**, vac. by m. 26 Oct. 1797 Ann y. d. of W. Speke preb. of Wells, and niece to the dowager Countess of Guildford, she d. Lyme Regis 11 Mch 1858 age 86; B.A. 6 June 1792, M.A. 26 Nov. 1795, R. of Lawhitton, Cornwall 1798, built the parsonage 1801, d. there 24 July 1826; Gent. Mag. 96 pt. ii. p. 1806, Coll. Corn. 534.

John Haydon **Cardew** (s. Cornelius, D.D.), b. Truro 16 Feb. 1773,

M. 25 Mch 1790, Eliot exhibitioner; **Corn. 1794**, res. 6 June 1797 having been instit. to R. of Curry Mallet, Som.; V. of Salcombe-Regis, Devon 1813; B.A. 4 Mch 1794, M.A. 1 June 1797, B.D. 12 May 1813, d. Curry Mallet 8 Nov. 1853; m. Liskeard 4 Sep. 1798 Anne Pallet, she d. 14 Jan. 1851 age 72; Bibl. Corn. 55; Polwhele v. 64.

Stephen Peter **Rigaud** (s. Stephen, Observer to the King at Kew, by Mary Triboudet Demainbray, half-sister of the fellow of 1778), b. Richmond 12 Aug. 1774, **M.** 15 Ap. 1791, **Petr. 1794**, res. 29 Dec. 1810 on becoming Savilian Professor of Geometry; Observer at Kew 1814–27; B.A. 9 Nov. 1797, M.A. 21 Nov. 1799, Public Examiner 1801–2, 1804–5, 1825, Proctor 1810 but resigned his office to Prust; Savilian Professor of Astronomy 1827, Delegate of the Press 1824, of Accounts 1825, Radcliffe Observer 1827, F.R.S. (Vice-President 1837–8); d. 16 Mch 1839 at Mr. Vulliamy's house in Pall Mall, bur. in churchyard of S. James', Piccadilly; printed *Bradley's Works* 1831, *Harriot's Papers* 1833, *the Arenarius of Archimedes* 1837, *Notices concerning Newton's Principia* 1838; selected and transcribed the contents of *Correspondence of Scientific Men*, 1706–41, 2 vols. 1841, but only saw the first volume through the press, the second being edited by his son (see 1838); m. 8 June 1815 Christian Walker 1 d. of Gibbes Walter Jordan, colonial agent for Barbados, she d. 1827; Gent. Mag. 1839 xi. 542–43, Agnew's *Protestant Exiles from France*, Index volume p. 235; *Stephen Peter Rigaud, a memoir by his son J. Rigaud fellow of Magdalen*, Oxford 1883. A silhouette of him is in the Common Room.

Thomas Hockin **Kingdon** (5 s. John, Fellow 1760), b. Bridgerule 1 Feb. and bap. 3 Ap. 1775, ed. Kilkhampton, **M.** 6 June 1791, **Dev. 1794**, vac. by m. 24 July 1804 Caroline 1 d. of Samuel Nicholson of Ham Common, Surrey, formerly of Finsbury; B.A. 5 July 1797, M.A. 28 June 1800, B.D. 25 May 1808, succeeded his father at Bridgerule 1806 and Pyworthy 1808, d. Pyworthy 31 Jan. 1853; Gent. Mag. 1853 xxxix. 328, N. and Gleanings ii. 177. He resigned Bridgerule in 1844 in favour of his eldest s. Samuel Nicholson Kingdon; for his d. Emmeline Maria see Mod. Eng. Biog.

Theophilus **Barnes** (s. Ralph, archdeacon of Totnes), b. the Close, Exeter, bap. 9 Sep. 1775, **M.** 25 June 1791, Reynolds exhibitioner; **Dev. 1794**, vac. 24 Nov. 1804 on pres. to Castleford, Yorks. by the Chancellor of the Duchy of Lancaster; B.A. 6 Feb. 1798, M.A 10 May 1798, R. of S. Petrock's, Exeter 1800 (under £60 clear), R. of

Stonegrave in N. Riding 1815–55, preb. of York 6 Ap. 1826, d.
Castleford 9 Feb. 1855 age 79; Gent. Mag. 1855 xliii. 326.

James **Kevill** (s. Thomas, steward to Lord de Dunstanville), b.
Camborne, **M.** 19 May 1795 age 17, G. C. 22 June 1795 to 1797,
Corn. 1797, vac. by m. London 5 June 1815 Anne Isabella d. and h.
of Somerset Davis of Croft Castle, Herefs., she d. Bath 27 July 1826;
B.A. 2 July 1800, M.A. 29 Ap. 1802, B.D. 17 June 1813, d. Croft
July 1831 age 52; Gent. Mag. ci. pt. 2 p. 377, Coll. Corn. 452.

John Pomeroy **Gilbert** (s. Rev. Edmund), b. Constantine, Cornwall,
M. 30 June 1795 age 16 as of Bodmin, **Corn. 1797**, vac. by m. 11 Dec.
1807 Mary d. and h. of Mathew Storm of Ilfracombe, she d. 1829 age
47; B.A. 6 Nov. 1800, M.A. 2 July 1806, V. of S. Wenn 28 Aug.
1810, preb. of Exeter 25 Nov. 1815, d. at his son's residence, Barnstaple 29 Sep. 1853; Maclean i. 303, ii. 13; Gent. Mag. 1853 xl.
536, Bibl. Corn. 1195.

Henry **Richards** (Fellow 1767), el. **Rector** 23 July 1797, d. 19
Dec. 1807.

Thomas **Blackall** (s. Rev. Theophilus, and great-grandson of
Ofspring, bishop of Exeter 1707), b. S. Mary Major, Exeter, **M.** 28
June 1793 age 17, **Petr. 1798**, vac. 3 Ap. 1816 by instit. to V. of
Tardebigg, Worcs. 3 Ap. 1815, patron the Earl of Plymouth, to whom
he was tutor; B.A. 26 Ap. 1797, M.A. 7 Mch 1800, B.D. 9 May
1811.   His brother John, a celebrated physician in Exeter, d. 10 Jan.
1860, Nat. Biog.

George **Stinton** (s. Rev. William), b. Barnstaple, **M.** 4 June 1794
age 18, **Petr. 1798**, res. 5 Jan. 1809 on coming into property, B.A.
6 Feb. 1798, M.A. 16 July 1803, capt. in Militia 1801, in the 3 W.
York 1804, Major of Armagh 1811; ? of Elston, Notts, d. London
6 Sep. 1818 age 43.

John David **Macbride** (o. s. Vice-Adm. John David), b. Plympton
28 June 1778, G. C. 28 Mch 1795 to 3 July 1800, **M.** 28 Mch
1795 age 16, **Petr. 1800**, vac. by m. 19 July 1805 Mary 2 d. of
Sir Joseph Radcliffe; B.A. 23 May 1799, M.A. 18 Feb. 1802, B.C.L.
21 Nov. 1811, D.C.L. 22 Nov. 1811, Principal Magd. H. 1813–68,
Delegate of the Press 1813, Lord Almoner's professor of Arabic
1813–68, F.S.A. 1805, d. Oxford 24 Jan. 1868; his wife d. 10 Dec.
1862 in her 92 year, both bur. in Holywell cemetery; author; Gent.
Mag. 1868 v. 393–94, Mod. Eng. Biog.

Thomas **Melhuish**, junior (s. Rev. Thomas), b. Ashwater, **M.**
7 May 1796 age 18, **Dev. 1800**, vac. by m. 10 Aug. 1809 Elizabeth

Walter (N. and Gleanings i. 25); B.A. 25 Feb. 1800, M.A. 26 May 1803, R. of Ashwater 14 Nov. 1811 (patron); 'Thomas Melhuish clerk, of Ashwater, widower and Elizabeth Mill widow of Little Torrington, d. of Robert Hamlyn, married by license 12 July 1848' (Little Torrington Reg.). He d. 28 Oct. 1861; Lysons' Devon 18.

Boughey William **Dolling** (s. Rev. Robert, of 3 Vine St., Westminster Abbey), b. Aldenham, Herts, **M.** 27 Ap. 1796 age 13, commoner 17 Aug. 1796 to 27 Dec. 1800, **Shi. 1800**, vac. by m. 28 July 1806; B.A. 30 Ap. 1800, M.A. 5 July 1805, precentor of Dromore, R. of Maghralin, d. 13 Jan. 1853.

John James **Lake** (s. John, R. of Lanivet 1770, bur. there 4 June 1805), b. Lanivet 1 Sep. 1781, ed. Truro, **M.** 30 May 1797, Eliot exhibitioner 1799; **Corn. 1805**; B.A. 26 Feb. 1802, M.A. 5 July 1805, Examiner in Classics 1807–8, d. Bodmin 31 Jan., bur. Lanivet 3 Feb. 1809; Gent. Mag. 1809 lxxix. i. 278; Lake iii. 15, Coll. Corn. 469.

Joseph Prust **Prust** (1 s. Rev. Joseph who **M.** as Hamlyn), b. Woolfardisworthy 3 Nov. 1780, bap. 5 Jan. 1781; **M.** 30 Ap. 1799, **Dev. 1805**, vac. 22 Oct. 1823 by instit. to Langtree near Torrington 22 Oct. 1822; B.A. 22 Feb. 1803, M.A. 8 May 1806, B.D. 24 May 1817, Proctor on Rigaud's resignation 1810, pres. to W. Worlington, Devon 1804 (under £120); R. of Virginstow 1811–39, d. Langtree 6 May 1839 age 58 (tombstone Woolfardisworthy); Gent. Mag. 1839 xii. 96, Lysons' Devon clxxxi.

George **Barnes** (s. archdeacon Ralph), b. Harberton, **M.** 30 Oct. 1799 age 15, Reynolds exhibitioner; **Dev. 1805**; vac. by m. at S. Thomas', Bombay 19 Aug. 1817 Harriet Penelope Carnac, witnesses Evan Nepean &c. (see the Archdeacon's letter of 22 Sep. 1817 in Reg.); B.A. 8 June 1803, M.A. 22 May 1806, B.D. 23 May 1814, D.D. by decree (absent as archdeacon of Madras from 1814) 28 May 1818; R. of S. Mary Major, Exeter 1809–14 (under £120, see Reg. 1810), of Sowton 23 May 1826, archdeacon of Barnstaple 10 Mch 1830, d. Sowton 29 June 1847; Gent. Mag. 1847 xxviii. 548, 661; Mod. Eng. Biog. v. Barnes, G. Carnac.

George Peloquin **Cosserat** (s. Nathaniel Elias), b. Exeter, **M.** 19 June 1798 age 18; adm. **Chapl. 14 June 1806**, vac. by marriage 27 June 1809; B.A. 16 June 1802, M.A. 14 Jan. 1808; R. of S. Martin 13 Oct. 1827, of S. Pancras 25 Oct. 1830, both in Exeter.

Thomas **Darke** (s. John, R. of Kelly, Devon), b. Kelly, **M.** 10 Oct. 1801 age 18, **Petr. 1806**; his election was appealed against by

William Bradford of S. John's who was born in Yorkshire and had 9 votes against Darke's 8, but Darke's election was confirmed by Bishop Fisher the Visitor, because Bradford gave no proof that Lord Petre held any heritable property in Yorkshire; vac. by marriage 3 July 1816; B.A. 12 June 1805, M.A. 23 June 1808, Proctor 1817; d. Lew-Trenchard 14 May 1822, N. and Gleanings iv. 167.

John **Moore** (s. Thomas, V. of Bishop's Tawton 11 Jan. 1782, V. of Frithelstock 1794–1801, bur. Torrington, who m. Frithelstock 31 Oct. 1779 Christiana d. and h. of Henry Stevens of Cross), b. Torrington 7 Sep. 1784, ed. Tiverton, **M.** 31 May 1802, **Dev. 1806**, vac. 4 Aug. 1811 by instit. to R. of Langtree 4 Aug. 1810; B.A. 7 Mch 1806, M.A. 27 Nov. 1808; tutor to Lord Curzon; archdeacon of Exeter 1820 and canon 16 Nov. 1821, V. of Otterton 1 Oct. 1822 (on resigning Langtree), ? V. of Alrewas, Staffs. 13 June 1832; took surname of Stevens 17 July 1832, on succeeding his brother Thomas Stevens of Winscott (who d. 14 Jan. 1832, London Journal 1817 p. 1389, Gent. Mag. 102, i. 82–83); m. in the chapel of Eton 31 Dec. 1817 Anne Eleanor, 1 d. of Rev. William Roberts vice-provost of Eton; d. 30 Mch 1865 at the Chantry, Exeter, bur. Petersmarland; Lysons' Devon 386.

James Thomas **Holloway** (s. Jeremiah), b. Newington, Surrey, ed. Rugby, **M.** 27 June 1797 age 16, **Shi. 1806**, vac. by marriage 13 Sep. 1813; B.A. 20 May 1802, M.A. 12 June 1807, B.D. 6, and D.D. 7 May 1818; V. of Stanton on Hineheath, Salop 1819–55, d. Hackney 7 Aug. 1855 age 75; Gent. Mag. 1855 xliv. 439; wrote *The Analogy of Faith* 1838, *Baptismal Regeneration and Sacramental Justification not the doctrine of the English Church* 1842, ed. 2, 1843; *Eucharistia* 1845.

Humphrey Waldo **Sibthorp** (4 s. Humphrey Waldo, of Canwick near Lincoln, and grandson of Dr. Henry Sibthorp Professor of Botany, Bloxam vi. 228, 318), b. Skimpans, N. Mims, Herts 1786, **M.** Univ. Coll. 2 July 1804 age 17; **Shi. 1806**, vac. by m. 6 Jan. 1818 his 1 cousin Mary Esther, 1 d. of Henry Ellison of Beverley; B.A. 3 Mch 1810, M.A. 14 Feb. 1811, R. of Washingborough 9 May 1817, of Hatton 1824, both in Lincs., d. 4 Nov. 1865; gave a silver snuff-box to the Common Room.

Charles **Chichester** (2 s. Robert, V. of Chittlehampton), b. Sherwell, bap. 6 Aug. 1785, **M.** 31 Oct. 1803, **Petr. 1807**; B.A. 7 July 1810, M.A. 8 June 1812, B.D. 19 Feb. 1820, preb. Exeter 1817, R. of W. Worlington June 1822 (in succession to Prust, holding it for a minor), deprived of his fellowship 1840 because his living was over the value allowed, but reinstated by the Visitor 29 Ap. 1841; at Chittlehampton 1835, d. Stowford in Swymbridge 13 Ap. 1842, bur. Atherington 21 Ap. 1842 age 56; Gent. Mag. 1842 xviii. 103; Visit. Devon 178, Drake 275.

John Cole (Fellow 1778), el. **Rector** 7 Jan. **1808**, d. 13 Oct. 1819.

William Edward **Hony** (2 s. William, V. of Liskeard), b. Liskeard 7 Feb. 1788, **M.** 13 July 1805, **Corn. 1808**; vac. by m. Oxford 3 July 1827 Margaret y. d. of Nicholas Earle, R. of Swerford, Oxon; 3 Classics 1810, B.A. 4 July 1811, M.A. 8 June 1812, B.D. 26 June 1823; V. of South Newington 24 Oct. 1818, R. of Baverstock 4 June 1827, preb. of Sarum 1841, archdeacon of Sarum 1846, d. Salisbury 7 Jan., bur. Baverstock 12 Jan. 1875; Stemmata Chichleana No. 275; Lake iii. 139; Bibl. Corn. 252.

Peter **Johnson** (s. John Tossel, R. of Ashreigney, Devon), b. 17 Ap. 1787, **M.** Oriel 10 Oct. 1805; **Dev. 1808**, vac. by m. Timsbury, Hants 10 Ap. 1824 Gratiana Samborne d. of Samborne Palmer of Timsbury House by Gratiana d. of Richard Stukeley, she d. 12 Ap. 1845; 2 Classics 1810, B.A. 8 Feb. 1812, M.A. 20 May 1812, B.D. 26 June 1823, Proproctor 1815, V. of Long Wittenham 1823 (then worth by survey of the Vicarial estate £137 16s. 8½d.), res. 28 May 1825, C. to his father at Wembworthy, Devon 1827, preb. of Exeter 1843–1858, d. 16 July 1869, bur. with his wife at Wembworthy; his d. Elizabeth Anne m. 1850 John Curzon Moore-Stevens, son of archdeacon Moore-Stevens Fellow 1806; Lysons' Devon 551.

John **Jago** (s. John, Fellow 1772), b. Milton Abbott, bap. Tavistock 3 Aug. 1787, **M.** 8 July 1806, **Petr. 1809**, vac. 16 Ap. 1819 by instit. to V. of Milton Abbott 16 Ap. 1818; ? V. of Rattery; 3 Classics 1810, B.A. 27 Feb. 1813, M.A. 26 June 1813, d. Penzance 12 June 1824; Coll. Corn. 410.

Charles **Dayman** (s. John, of Poughill, who m. E. Putford 9 Dec. 1777 Mary d. of Jos. Phillipps, in presence of Jos. Phillipps and Lucretia Phillipps), b. 18 Sep. 1786, **M.** Balliol 3 July 1805, 2 Classics 1809, B.A. 4 May 1809; **Corn. 1809**; M.A. 12 May 1814, chaplain to the army in Portugal Sept. 1811, taken prisoner, m. 7 Ap. 1817 Flavie Restitude d. and h. of M. Delmaire of Lillers, she d. 1847; V. of Great Tew, Oxon 1830–44, Select Preacher 1838, d. Great Tew 19 Aug. 1844 age 57; Gent. Mag. 1844 xxii. 438, Maclean iii. 226, Coll. Corn. 199.

John **Williams** (s. Charles, C. of Shebbeare, Devon, who was bur. 18 Nov. 1806, by Margaret), **M.** 30 May 1797 age 23, Bible-Clerk Mich. 1799; adm. **Chapl.** 23 Oct. **1809**, vac. by m. S. Aldate's 20 June 1826 Anne y. d. of Sir William Elias Taunton, Town-clerk of Oxford; B.A. 16 June 1802, M.A. 10 Oct. 1808, B.D. 4 May 1820, V. of Probus, Cornwall 1826, d. 16 Mch 1828.   Bibl. Corn. 882; Gent. Mag. 98 i. 646.

John **Spurway** (s. William, of Barnstaple, R. of Clare Portion, Tiverton, who d. 1 July 1837, after being R. of Alwington 70 years, by Avice Cutcliffe of Barnstaple, who d. 19 Feb. 1856 age 98), **M.** 13 July 1807 age 17, **Dev. 1810**, vac. by m. 5 Oct. 1822 Elizabeth Hole; 1 Classics 1811, B.A. 2 July 1813, M.A. 16 June 1814, instit. to Pitt Portion in Tiverton 29 Nov. 1821 on his father's presentation; d. 17 Aug. 1874; in 1816 he was appointed ' Inspector of the Compositions of Undergraduates.'   He m. (2) Margaret Weston, d. of Charles Osmond, c. of Clare Portion, Tiverton.   (In Harding's Tiverton iv. 42 line 7 from foot *read* Alwington for Buckland-Brewer.)

William **James** (s. William, of Exeter), **M.** Corpus 7 Mch 1804 age 16; **Dev. 1810**, vac. 15 Ap. 1815 by having taken the R. of South Moreton, Berks 15 Ap. 1814–1855, V. of S. Mary's, Oxford 24 Dec. 1819; B.A. 24 May 1810, M.A. 17 Dec. 1812, Vice-Principal Magd. Hall 5 Nov. 1813; d. Lympstone, Devon 21 Dec. 1855; Gent. Mag. 1856 xlv. 432.

William **Dalby** (s. Thomas, capt. R.N., of Plymouth Dock), **M.** 28 Mch 1808 age 15 as of Bath, **Dev. 1811**; vac. by m. Frome 1 June 1826 Harriet 1 d. of George Byard Sheppard, she d. 17 Mch 1840; 2 Classics and 1 Math. 1811, wrote *English Poem recited at Reception of the Allied Sovereigns* 1814, B.A. 4 July 1814, M.A. 5 Ap. 1815, Public Examiner 1818–19, Proctor 1825, V. of Warminster, Wilts 27 Dec. 1825–1841, R. of Compton Basset 1841–66, preb. of Salisbury 23 Mch 1832, d. 3 Dec. 1861; wrote *Lectures on the Life of Samuel* 1834, and several sermons; Sir C. Lyell's Life i. 130.

Edward **Eliot** (1 s. late Richard, V. of Maker and of St. Teath in Cornwall, by Anna d. of Edward Pearce), b. Maker in Devon 22 May 1789, ed. Lostwithiel, **M.** 7 Ap. 1808 as of Camelford, Eliot exhibitioner 1810, 2 Classics 1811, **Petr. 1811**, vac. by m. Miss Skeet of Barbados 10 July 1826; B.A. 4 July 1814, M.A. 17 May 1815, B.D. 3 Feb. 1825, archdeacon of Barbados 1825–37, preb. of Salisbury 30 Dec. 1848, pres. 1837 to Norton Bavant, Wilts, where he died 1 Nov. 1861; Bibl. Corn. 1171.

John Taylor **Coleridge** (s. Captain James, by Frances Duke d. of
Bernard F. Taylor), b. Tiverton 9 July 1790, ed. Ottery S. Mary and
Eton, **M.** Corpus 21 Ap. 1809, scholar, Vinerian Law Scholar 1812;
Dev. 1812. vac. by m. 7 Aug. 1818 Mary 2 d. of Gibb Buchanan
R. of Woodmansterne, Surrey; B.A. 4 July 1815, M.A. 27 June 1817,
D.C.L. 1852; Latin Verse 1810, 1 Classics 1812, English and Latin
Essays 1813, *English Poem recited at Reception of the Allied Sovereigns*
1814; Serjeant at Law Feb. 1832, Recorder of Exeter 1832, Justice
of King's Bench 27 Jan. 1835 to 28 June 1858 when he retired,
knighted 1835, entertained at a public dinner in the College Hall
7 Mch 1835 on his first going on Circuit; d. 11 Feb. 1876. He
published an edition of Blackstone 1825, a *Life of John Keble* and
other works, and edited the Quarterly Review for 1824 (Sir Walter
Scott's *Journal* 1890); Reminiscences of Oxford (O. H. Soc.), 247–53,
Sir C. Lyell's Life i. 163. Mod. Eng. Biog., Nat. Biog. His portrait
is in the Coll. Hall.

John Thomas **Lys** (s. James, Comte de Lys in France, said to be
descended from a brother of Joan of Arc), b. Guildford, Surrey, **M.**
22 June 1809 age 17 as of Brighton, **Shi. 1813**; 3 Classics 1812,
B.A. 28 Ap. 1813, M.A. 24 Jan. 1816, B.D. 18 Dec. 1826, V. of
Merton, Oxon 3 Ap. 1826, res. it for Waterperry 2 Dec. 1833,
d. 4 Oct. 1871.

James Lampen **Harris** (s. John, of Radford, Plymouth), ed. Eton,
M. 2 Dec. 1811 age 18, **Dev. 1815.** vac. by marriage at Plymstock,
Devon 23 June 1829; 2 Classics 1815, B.A. 3 May 1815, M.A.
25 June 1818, P.C. of Plymstock, C. of Ringmore 1819–26; seceded
from Church of England, and wrote an *Address to the parishioners of
Plymstock* 3 Sep. 1832 (Rev. Robert Cox publ. *Recent Secession considered* in reply, Plymouth 13 Oct. 1832, see *Plymouth Brethrenism
examined* by John Cox, London 1845); *The carved stone altar at St.
Andrew's Church, Plymouth* 1841; *A Letter to the Christians meeting
in Mr. Hingston's loft, Kingsbridge* 1847; *The Confessional* 1852:
Worth's *Three Towns Bibliotheca* 70.

Thomas Trevenen **Penrose** (s. John, Fellow 1774), b. Carwythe-
nack in Constantine 6 May and bap. 18 June 1793, **M.** Corpus 5 Feb.
1811; **Corn. 1815.** vac. by m. 7 Sep. 1824 Susanna Mary 2 d. of
Joshua Brooke R. of Gamston, Notts; B.A. 7 Feb. 1815, M.A. 1 July
1819, R. of Weston, Notts 1834–62, V. of Coleby, Lincs. 1828–62,
preb. of Lincoln 1834–1862, d. Coleby 5 July 1862; Bibl. Corn. 458.

John **Blackmore** (s. Rev. John; Lysons' Devon 98), b. Charles,

Devon, **M.** 10 Oct. 1812 age 18, 2 Classics 1816, **Petr. 1816**, vac. by marriage 2 Feb. 1822; B.A. 5 June 1816, M.A. 25 June 1819; C. of Culmstock and Ashford near Barnstaple; d. Nottage-court, Glamorganshire 24 Sep. 1858, Gent. Mag. 1858 v. 535.

James **Yonge** (2 s. Rev. James, of Puslinch in Newton Ferrers, by his 2 wife Anne d. of Edmund Granger of the Castle, Exeter), **M.** Balliol 29 Ap. 1811 age 18, 2 Classics 1815, B.A. 4 Feb. 1815; **Dev. 1817**, M.A. 25 June 1818, vac. by m. 10 Mch 1823 Jane d. of Rev. Roger Mallock of Cockington, Devon; R. of Stockley Pomeroy 22 July 1826, P.C. of Tor Mohun and Cockington 12 June 1828, d. 15 Ap. 1830; one of his two volumes of Sermons was published after his death; Eccl. Ant. i. 210, Coll. Corn. 1311.

Walter Henry **Burton** (o. s. Michael, of Milding, Suffolk), **M.** 5 Aug. 1814, **Petr. 1817**, B.A. 1 July 1820, M.A. 7 July 1821; Vinerian Scholar 6 Oct. 1818, 1 Classics and 1 Math. 1818, Latin Verse 1816 *Druidae*, published *Compendium of Law of Real Property* 1828, 8 ed. 1856, d. of consumption at Sudbury, Suffolk 25 Aug. 1828 age 32; Gent. Mag. 1828, 98 ii. 468.

Robert Bateman **Paul** (s. Richard, V. of Mawgan in Pyder, by Frances d. of Robert Bateman, R. of S. Columb Major, she was bap. 16 Mch 1768, m. 8 Feb. 1797), b. S. Columb Major 21 Mch 1798, **M.** 10 Oct. 1815, Eliot exhibitioner; **Corn. 1817**; vac. by m. 11 Jan. 1827 Rosa Mira d. of Richard Twopeny R. of Casterton Parva, Rutland; 2 Classics 1819, B.A. 1 July 1820, M.A. 16 Feb. 1822, Examiner in Classics 1826, pres. to Long Wittenham 30 June 1825 and instit. 7 Feb. 1826, res. 1 Aug. 1829 on preferment to Llantwit Major in Llandaff; Archdeacon of Waimea, and afterwards of Nelson, New Zealand; preb. of Lincoln 1867, R. of S. Mary's, Stamford 1864–72, Confrater of Browne's Hospital, d. Stamford 6 June 1877; Bibl. Corn. 431–33.

Joseph Loscombe **Richards** (s. Rev. Joseph, of Penryn), b. Tamerton Foliot 21 Feb. 1798, ed. Ottery S. Mary under Dr. G. Coleridge and Dr. J. Warren, **M.** 21 Oct. 1815 as of Stoke Damerel, **Dev. 1818**, B.A. 30 June 1821, M.A. 17 Ap. 1822, B.D. 13 Dec. 1832, D.D. 6 Dec. 1838; 2 Classics 1819, Select Preacher 1828, 1839, Examiner in Classics 1828–29; vac. 11 July 1836 by being presented to R. of Bushey in Herts 1 and instit. 11 July 1835 (when an urn worth £100 was presented to him), res. 27 Sep. 1838 on being el. Rector 1 Sep.; Chaplain to Prince Albert, who was entertained at lunch in the Hall at the meeting of the British Association 24 May 1847; d. Bonchurch.

I. of Wight 27 Feb. 1854, bur. Ex. Coll. Chapel 7 Mch; his wife
Frances Elizabeth d. of J. W. Baugh, R. of Ripple, Worcs., b. 1812,
m. 28 Sep. 1837, d. 10 June 1840, bur. 16 June in the south part of
the Chapel. He gave £1,000 towards the new Chapel; J. B. Mozley's
Letters 113, 126. Bibl. Corn. 566, Coll. Corn. 804, Cox. His
1 sister Ann, b. Tamerton 12 Aug. 1797, d. St. German's 22 Ap. 1874,
m. Stoke 17 Aug. 1827 Tobias Furneaux, P.C. St. German's 1828, he
was b. Swilly 19 Ap. 1794, d. St. German's 19 Aug. 1874. A younger
sister Harriet Elizabeth b. 1807, d. St. German's 22 May 1859. The
last surviving sister Arabella Symons Richards b. Tamerton 7 Feb.
1803, d. the Vicarage St. German's 20 Nov. 1878; Pusey's Life ii. 173.

Samuel **Grover** (s. Henry, of Hemel Hempstead, Herts), **M.** Univ.
Coll. 7 Feb. 1815 age 19, **Shi. 1818**; B.A. 26 Nov. 1818, M.A.
12 Mch 1822, d. Hemel Hempstead 13 Sep. 1822 age 27; Gent.
Mag. 1822, 92 i. 380.

Josiah **Forshall** (1 s. Samuel), b. Witney 29 Mch 1795. M. 14 Dec.
1814 as of Northop, Flints., Reynolds exhibitioner 1816; **Petr. 1819**,
vac. by m. Edgbaston 13 July 1826 Frances o. d. of Richard Smith
of Harborne Heath, Warwicks., she was b. 1795, d. Woburn Place,
London 7 Feb. 1865; Cansick's *Epitaphs of Middlesex* 1872 ii. 250;
B.A. 10 Oct. 1818, M.A. 15 Jan. 1821; 2 Classics and 1 Math.
1818, Tutor 1822, F.R.S. and F.S.A. 1828; Assistant Keeper of
MSS. Brit. Mus. 1824, Keeper 1827, Secretary of Brit. Mus. 1828–51,
edited Wiclif's Bible 4 vol. 4° 1850 with Sir F. Madden; published
Catalogues of Arundel and Burney and Oriental MSS. 1838–39, 1834,
1840; Chaplain of Foundling Hospital for 34 years, d. Woburn Place
18 Dec. 1863; Gent. Mag. 1864 xvi. 391–92, Pusey's Life i. 181, 241,
Mod. Eng. Biog., Nat. Biog.

Thomas **Kitson** (s. Rev. William, of Shiphay in Marychurch),
b. Shiphay, ed. Westminster 1808, **M.** Balliol 3 Ap. 1816 age 17;
Dev. 1819, vac. by m. 7 June 1824 Mary d. of Capt. T. Ley of Little
Bradley, Highweek, Devon, she d. 23 Nov. 1882 age 77; 2 Classics
1819, B.A. 9 May 1823, M.A. 2 July 1824, C. of Combeinteignhead,
and of W. Ogwell 1840–47, of Haccombe 1847–68, d. Shiphay
5 Ap. 1880.

John Collier Jones (Fellow 1792), el. **Rector 6 Nov. 1819**,
d. 7 Aug. 1838.

Carré William **Tupper** (2 s. Daniel, of Hauteville House, Guernsey,
by Catherine, 1 d. of John Tupper), b. 1797, **M.** 26 May 1814
age 16, then exhibitioner Pemb. 1816; **Guer. 1820** (a case as

between him and Havilland Durand of Pembroke, s. of the Dean of
Guernsey, was sent to the Visitor 4 July 1819, Reg. 8 June 1820);
vac. 1 Dec. 1832 by not proceeding to degree of B.D.; B.A. 10 Dec.
1818, M.A. 24 May 1820, d. Guernsey 26 Mch 1881; m. 9 Jan.
1833 Eliza Jane 5 d. of Thomas Priaulx of Montville, Guernsey, she
d. 16 Ap. 1880 age 77.

George Nutcomb **Oxnam** (1 s. Rev. William, who d. 22 Nov.
1809, by his 2 wife Anne d. of George Nutcombe Nutcombe, Chancellor of Exeter), b. Paul near Penzance 17 Nov. 1799, **M.** Wadham
11 Dec. 1816, 2 Classics 1820, B.A. 24 May 1820; **Corn. 1820**, vac.
by m. 12 May 1830 Caroline 1 d. of Dr. Warwick Young Churchill
Hunt, V. of Bickleigh, Devon, she d. Kensington 10 Dec. 1849, bur.
Bickleigh; m. (2) Hamburg 1852 Mary Emma sister of his first wife,
she d. Kensington 18 Dec. 1854, bur. Brompton Cemetery; m. (3)
7 Jan. 1858 Charlotte Ellis 6 d. of John Milligen Seppings, of Culver
house, Chudleigh, Devon, b. 2 Mch 1822, d. 17 Earl's terrace,
Kensington 17 July 1880 age 58; M.A. 13 June 1823, barrister
L. I. 22 Nov. 1825; d. Kensington 15 Dec. 1873, bur. Brompton
Cemetery; Pedigree of Boase ed. 2 1893 p. 115.

Sidney William **Cornish** (s. Robert, by Frances Ann d. of Joseph
Squier), b. Exeter, ed. Ottery, commoner 8 June 1818 to 13 May
1862, **M.** 9 June 1818 age 17, Acland exhibitioner; **Petr. 1822**, vac.
23 Nov. 1828 by instit. to V. of South Newington 13 Nov. 1827, res.
Ladyday 1836; 2 Classics 1822, B.A. 20 June 1822, M.A. 17 Dec.
1825, B.D. 30 June 1836, D.D. 1 July 1836; Master of Gr. sch. at
Ottery 1824-63, V. of Ottery 18 Nov. 1841-74, d. Seaton 1 Aug.
1874 age 73; wrote *Clavis Homiletica* 1834, *Faith in the efficacy of
the means of grace*, Visitation Sermon 1842, *Short Notes on the church
and parish of Ottery S. Mary* 1869; m. Exeter 30 May 1829 Jane
1 d. of S. Kingdon of Southernhay.

James Charles **Clutterbuck** (2 s. Robert and Marianne), b. Watford, Herts 11 July 1801, ed. Harrow, commoner 15 Dec. 1820 to
11 Ap. 1859, **M.** 15 Dec. 1820, **Shi. 1822**, vac. 19 Jan. 1831 by
instit. to Wittenham 14 Jan. 1830; contributed largely to the new
parish schools; B.A. 23 Feb. 1826, M.A. 6 Dec. 1827, C. of Watford,
Herts, Rural Dean of Abingdon 1869, d. 8 May 1885, wrote several
works on Geology and the Drainage of the Thames Valley; Burgon's
Twelve Good Men ii. 115, 249-50.

Edward **Coleridge** (brother of Sir J. T. Coleridge), b. Ottery,
M. Corpus 21 Feb. 1818 age 17, exhibitioner, 2 Classics 1821. B.A.

16 Feb. 1822; **Dev. 1823**, vac. by m. Eton 3 Aug. 1826 Mary 1 d. of
Dr. Keate the Head Master; m. (2) Mary Caroline d. of Rev. Mr.
Bevan; M.A. 1 Feb. 1827; instituted and inducted to R. of Monk-
silver, Som. 30 Oct. 1825, Assist. Master at Eton 1824–50, Lower
Master 1850–57, Fellow 1857, V. of Maple Durham, Berks 1862,
d. 18 May 1883.

Henry Bellenden **Bulteel** (s. Thomas, of Plymstock), b. Bellevue
near Plymouth 1800, M. Brasenose 1 Ap. 1818, B.A. 30 May 1822;
Dev. 1823, vac. by m. 6 Oct. 1829 Eleanor sister of C. J. Sadler,
alderman of Oxford, she d. Plymouth 25 Sep. 1878 age 88 : M.A.
9 June 1824, C. of S. Ebbe's, Oxford 1826, d. Plymouth 28 Dec.
1866.   He published a sermon on 1 Cor. ii. 12, preached at S. Mary's
6 Feb. 1831.   Dr. Burton wrote some Remarks on it, and Bulteel
wrote a Reply; Gent. Mag. 1867 iii. 258; Mozley i. 228, 350, Life of
W. W. Phelps ii. 110, Jas. J. Moore's *Nonconformity in Oxford* 1875
p. 14, Cox 244, 248, Bodl. Cat. v. Anti-Osiander, J. B. Mozley's
Letters 25, 27, Pusey's Life i. 197, Nat. Biog.

James Thomas **Duboulay** (1 s. Francis Houssemayne, by Elizabeth
d. of John Paris of Wanstead, Essex), b. Walthamstow, Essex 5 Mch
1801, commoner 16 June 1818 to 17 May 1834, **M.** 16 June 1818,
B.A. 20 June 1822, **Petr. 1823**; vac. by m. 1 June 1825 Susan Maria
d. of Seth Stephen Ward, she m. (2) 2 May 1839 Rev. G. J. Majendie,
and d. 13 June 1875; M.A. 11 Nov. 1824, R. of Heddington,
Wilts 1828–36, d. Ventnor 13 June 1836 ; Gent. Mag. 1836 vi. 218.

Richard **Martin** (6 s. Rev. Joseph, of Ham Court, Worcs.), b. Exeter
3 Aug. 1802, M. Oriel 14 May 1819, 1 Classics 1823, B.A. 9 May
1823; **Dev. 1824**, vac. by m. 5 July 1831 Charlotte 1 d. of J. W.
Baugh, R. of Ripple, Worcs., b. 3 July 1809, d. 16 Jan. 1881 ; M.A.
15 June 1826, Classical Examiner 1830–1, instit. to Menheniot 19 Feb.
1831, res. 1883, canon of Truro 17 Jan. 1878, d. 3 Feb. 1888.

John Prideaux **Lightfoot** (1 s. Nicholas of Crediton, afterwards R.
of Stockleigh Pomeroy, by Bridget d. of Roger Prideaux), b. Crediton
23 Mch 1803, ed. Crediton, M. 28 June 1820, 1 Classics 1824, B.A.
5 June 1824, **Dev. 1824**, res. on pres. 28 June 1834 to R. of Woolton,
Northants ; M.A. 1 Feb. 1827, B. and D.D. 18 May 1854 ; Tutor,
Proctor 1833 ; hon. canon of Peterborough 1853, el. Rector 18 Mch
1854, member of first Hebdomadal Council 1854, Vice-Chancellor
1862–66, entertained the Prince and Princess of Wales at dinner in
the Hall 17 June 1863, d. 23 Mch 1887, bur. Kidlington.   He m. (1)
Elizabeth Anne 2 d. of Lieut.-Col. Henry Le Blanc, she d. 21 Nov.

1860 age 50, bur. Kidlington; m. (2) 7 Jan. 1863 Louisa o. d. of Sir
George Best Robinson, widow of Capt. Charles Robert George
Douglas, she d. 9 Dec. 1882 age 52 ; their only child Mary Frances
was born at the Rectory 13 Feb. 1864. Mrs. Lightfoot's only child
by her first marriage, Louisa Margaret Anne Douglas, m. in College
Chapel 14 Jan. 1875 Frank Willan. The Rector's 1 d. Emily
Singleton m. in the Chapel 30 Dec. 1875 the Rev. Edward Tindal
Turner, Registrar of the University. Both these marriages were by
special license. Cox 437, Rep. Comm. on Sci. Instruction 1872, i.
257–65, Hist. Kidlington 157. The Rector's eldest sister d. 12 July
1882.

Francis **Fulford** (2 s. Baldwin, of Fulford Magna in Dunsford, by
Anna Maria 1 d. of William Adams M.P. Totnes), b. Sidmouth 3 June
1803, bap. Dunsford 14 Oct. 1804, ed. Tiverton, **M.** 1 Feb. 1821,
3 Classics 1824, **Dev. 1824**, vac. by m. 18 Oct. 1830 Mary 1 d. of
Andrew Berkeley Drummond of Cadland, Hants ; B.A. 15 Nov. 1827,
M.A. 10 Oct. 1838, D.D. 1850 ; R. of Trowbridge 1832–41, pub-
lished Sermons 1837, V. of Croyden, Camb. 1841–45, Minister of
Curzon chapel, Mayfair 1845–50, Bishop of Montreal 29 June 1850,
consecr. 25 July, Metropolitan of Canada 1860; d. 9 Sep. 1868, bur.
Mount Royal Cemetery, Montreal 12 Sep. ; life in Fennings Taylor's
(of Ottawa) *The last three bishops appointed by the Crown for the
Anglican Church of Canada* 1869; Hutchins ii. 699. Men of the
Time 1868, Illust. London News xl. 576, 587 (1862), liii. 307 (1868),
Burke ed. 1868 p. 521.

John **Bramston** (2 s. Thomas Gardiner, of Skreens near Chelmsford, by Maria Ann d. of William Blaauw of London), b. Waltham
Magna, Essex 1804, **M.** Oriel 25 Ap. 1820 age 17, 2 Classics 1823,
B.A. 28 Feb. 1824; **Petr. 1825**, vac. 1831 by instit. to V. of
Great Baddow, Essex 15 Jan. 1830, which he held for a minor ; as he
had not given a bond of resignation, the Visitor decided that he had
vacated his fellowship ; M.A. 19 Oct. 1826, Master of the Schools
1828, B.D. 1872 ; res. Baddow 1840, V. of Witham, Essex 1840–72,
Dean of Winchester 26 Nov. 1872, res. 1883, d. Winchester 13 Nov.
1889; m. (1) 1832 Clarissa Sandford o. d. of Sir Nicolas Trant, (2)
Anna 2 d. of Osgood Hanbury of Holfield Grange, Essex.

John Griffith **Cole** (o. s. Samuel, scholar 1788, and nephew of
Rector J. Cole, and of Sir Christopher Cole, K.C.B., D.C.L. 10 June
1812, whose property he inherited), b. Gulval, ed. Ottery and Charterhouse, **M.** 7 Dec. 1821 age 16. **Corn. 1825**, res. 24 Dec. 1839;

3 Classics 1826, B.A. 23 Oct. 1828, M.A. 10 May 1832 ; d. Marazion 1868.

Henry Duke **Harington** (3 s. Rev. James Eyre), b. Salisbury 30 Jan. 1808, bap. privately 1 Feb. and received publicly 24 July at Woodford, Salisbury, ed. Rugby, **M**. 27 Jan. 1824, Symes Scholar, **Sar. 1826**, vac. by m. 1 June 1836 Harriet Daniel widow, of Dereham, Norfolk; 3 Classics and 2 Math. 1827, B.A. 2 July 1829, M.A. 2 June 1830, Master of the Schools 1831–32, C. of Kidlington 1833, instit. to South Newington 7 May 1836, exchanged it 1864 for Knossington, Leics. with George Candy (who d. 31 Jan. 1869) ; d. 15 Aug. 1875 age 68; wrote *A Manual for the use of Sponsors* 12° London 1842. His 2 wife Mary, d. of Jupp of Cobham and widow of F. Ashby, survived him ; Misc. Gen. iv. 295.

Benjamin Wills **Newton** (o. s. Benjamin Wills), b. Devonport 1808, **M**. 10 Dec. 1824 age 16, **Dev. 1826** age 18, vac. by marriage 15 Mch 1832 ; 1 Classics 1828, B.A. 2 July 1829 : C. M. Davies' *Unorthodox London* 1873 p. 183–91 : one of the early Plymouth Brethren ; for his publications see Worth's *Three Towns Bibliotheca* 70 : and Bibl. Corn. *v.* Tregelles S. P. and Dingle E. ; Coll. Corn. 614, 1169, Nat. Biog. v. 398, xiv. 44 ; resides Wickliffe Villa, Newport, I. of Wight 1893.

John Whittington Ready **Landon** (s. Whittington, dean of Exeter, by the o. d. of John Ready of Oakhanger Hall), **M**. Worcester 7 May 1818 age 16 ; B.A. 14 Jan. 1822, M.A. 9 June 1824, adm. **Chapl.** 16 Oct. **1826**, vac. 7 Nov. 1827 by inst. to Braunton, Devon 7 Nov. 1826 and to Bishopstone, Wilts 1826 ; d. 14 Feb. 1880 ; m. Bishop's Tawton 22 May 1828 Jane 2 d. of Charles Chichester of Hall ; see Reg. on question of Chaplain's year of probation, and Visitor's decision 5 Jan. 1827 on a probationer taking a College living ; a resolution was passed 30 June 1827 that the succession to College livings should be open to Lay Fellows.

William **Falconer** (1 s. Rev. Thomas, by Frances o. child of Lieut.-Col. Robert Raitt), b. Corston, Som. 27 Dec 1801, **M**. Oriel 10 Dec. 1819 ; 3 Classics and 1 Math. 1823, B.A. 2 Dec. 1823, **Petr. 1827**, res. 18 July 1839, having been pres. to Bushey, Herts 26 Jan. and instit. 1 Mch 1839 ; M.A. 25 Oct. 1827, Math. Examiner 1832–33, 1836–38; translated Strabo 1857, the text of which his father had edited in 1807 ; d. 10 Feb. 1885 ; m. 1840 Isabella d. of J. Robinson and widow of W. S. Douglas, she d. 7 Feb. 1869 ; his sister m. John Arthur Roebuck, who was bur. at Bushey Dec. 1879 ; Thomas Falconer's *Bibliography of the Falconer family* 1866. W. Antiq. iv. 215.

NOTE.—In 1879 the College consented to part of Bushey being made a separate parish, and allowed £50 to be deducted from the income of Bushey on Falconer's death or cession. In 1884 the advowson of Bushey was sold to Mrs. Gregory.

Hubert Kestell **Cornish** (3 s. George, of Salcombe Regis, by Sarah o. child of John Kestell of Ottery), b. Ottery 19 June 1803, **M**. Oriel 14 June 1821, exhibitioner of Corpus 1821, 2 Classics 1825, B.A. 5 May 1825, **Dev. 1827**, vac. by m. Cheddon, Som. 28 Feb. 1833, Louisa 2 d. of Rev. Dr. Warre of Cheddon; M.A. 19 June 1828; pres. to Merton, Oxon 8 Mch 1834, res. 2 July 1840, C. of Lewannick in Cornwall; V. of Bakewell, Derbys. 1840–69, R. of Hitcham, Oxon 1869–73, d. 1873; transl. part of S. Chrysostom's *Homilies on the First of Corinthians* (Library of the Fathers), publ. fourteen Sermons on *The Lord's Supper* 1834, *Family and Private Prayers* 1839. His 2 wife Theophania Lucy Vernon d. E. Grinstead 17 Mch 1892 aged 64.

George **Dawson** (2 s. Robert, architect, of Bangor), b. Liskeard, ed. Bangor Free sch., **M**. 17 June 1822 age 18, 3 Classics and 1 Math. 1826; B.A. 16 Nov. 1826, **Corn. 1827**, res. 7 Oct. 1841, having been pres. to R. of Woodleigh, Devon 26 Jan. 1841; M.A. 5 Feb. 1829; d. 7 Mch 1888.

William **Sewell** (2 s. Thomas, of Newport, I. of Wight), b. Southampton 23 Jan. 1804, ed. Winchester, **M**. Merton 2 Nov. 1822, Postmaster of Merton, 1 Classics 1827, B.A. 2 June 1827; **Petr. 1827**, English Essay 1828, Latin Essay 1829, M.A. 2 July 1829, B.D. 17 June 1841, D.D. 1857; Classical Examiner 1832–33, Tutor 1831; Incumbent of S. Nicholas in the Castle, Newport 1831–74, Prof. of Moral Philos. 1836–41, Select Preacher 1852, Preacher at Whitehall 1850; founded the Colleges of S. Columba in Ireland, opened 26 Ap. 1843, and Radley near Oxford 6 Mch 1847, Warden of Radley 1852–60, d. Litchford Hall, Manchester about 1 in the morning Nov. 13–14, 1874; bur. S. Andrew's, Blackley; wrote *Christian Morals* 1840, *Christian Politics* 1844; *Lectures on Plato* 1841, *Hawkstone* ed. 2, 1846, *Journal of a residence at St. Columba* 1848, *The University Commission, or Lord John Russell's Postbag* (anon.) 1850, and translated the Agamemnon, the Georgics, the Odes of Horace &c.; he ed. his sister's *Amy Herbert*, and other stories, only said to be 'by a lady'; Men of the Time 1872, Annual Reg. 1874 p. 175; *Memoirs of Samuel Clark* 1878 p. 147, Mozley ii. 23–28, J. B. Mozley's Letters 40, 71, 120, Church's Oxford Movement 130, Reminiscences of Oxford (O. H. Soc.) 351, Qu. Rev. April 1891 p. 403; Pusey's Life, index; Crockford 1860 p. 551 and 1874 p. 777. There is a memorial window in the Chapel. A biography is given in his sister's *Some last words of Dr. Sewell*, and a list of his writings in his posthumous *Microscope of the New Testament* 1878.

James **Fisher** (1 s. James), b. S. Mary le Bow 1807, ed. Winchester, M. Brasenose (*John* in matric. reg.) 22 Jan. 1824 age 17 ; **Petr. 1827**, res. by letter dated Nottingham 27 May 1837 on account of his father's ill health throwing much management on him; 2 Classics 1828, B.A. 27 Jan. 1831, M.A. 28 May 1834, at Inner Temple 1827.

William **Heberden** (3 s. Thomas, canon of Exeter, by Mary d. of Joseph Martin banker of Lombard St., N. and Gleanings iv. 161), b. 16 Jan. 1804, ed. Westminster 1817, **M**. Oriel 23 May 1821, 3 Classics 1825, B.A. 13 May 1825; adm. **Chaplain** 17 June **1828**, vac. 7 Jan. 1830 by instit. to Broadhembury, Devon 7 Jan. 1829, res. 1874; M.A. 19 June 1828, d. London 17 Aug. 1890; m. Littleham, Devon 1 July 1835 Susanna Catherine 9 d. of James Buller of Downes. His 3 s. Charles Buller became Principal of Brasenose 1889.

Edward Arthur **Dayman** (3 s. John, d. 1859, m. 1801 Jane o. d. of Nicholas Donithorne Arthur of S. Columb), b. Padstow 11 July 1807, ed. Tiverton, **M**. 14 Ap. 1825, **Corn. 1828**, vac. by m. Tiverton 7 July 1842 Ellen Maria 1 d. of William Dunsford of Ashley Court near Tiverton, she d. 27 Ap. 1890 age 79 ; 1 Classics 1829, B.A. 20 Oct. 1831, M.A. 20 May 1832, B.D. 13 May 1841 ; Tutor 1834, Subrector 1839, Proctor 1840 ; Classical Examiner 1838–39, 1841–42, pres. to Shillingstone, Dorset 21 Jan. and instit. 7 June 1842, hon. Canon of Sarum 1862, Proctor in Convocation 1852, d. 30 Oct. 1890 ; Hutchins iii. 448, 450 ; published *Modern Infidelity* 1861, *Essay on Inspiration* 1864, was joint editor of the Sarum Hymnal 1868 and contributed to the Hymnary 1872 ; Newman's Letters ed. Miss Mozley, Pusey's Life ii. 173, Bibl. Corn. 1153.

William **Jacobson** (o. s. William), b. Great Yarmouth 1803, ed. Homerton and Glasgow Univ., **M**. Edmund H. 5 May 1823 age 19, scholar of Lincoln ; 2 Classics 1827, Ellerton Prize 1829, B.A. 14 June 1827 ; **Petr. 1829**, vac. by m. S. Nicholas', Great Yarmouth 23 June 1836 Eleanor Jane y. d. of Dawson Turner; hon. Fellow 1882 ; M.A. 15 Oct. 1829, Vice-Principal Magd. H. 1832–48, Select Preacher 1833, 1842, 1869, Master of the Schools 1834–35, Public Orator 1842–48, Reg. Prof. of Divinity 1 Ap. 1848–1865, D.D. 15 Ap. 1848, Theological Examiner 1870 ; C. of S. Mary Magdalene, Oxford 1830–32, P.C. of Iffley 1839–40, R. of Ewelme

1848–65, consecr. Bishop of Chester 24 Aug. 1865, res. 1884, d. 13 July 1884; ed. *The Apostolic Fathers* 1840, and *Bishop Sanderson's works* in six volumes 1854; portrait in Illust. London News 1865 xlvii. 217; Mozley ii. 26, Burgon's *Twelve Good Men* ii. 238–303, Mod. Eng. Biog.

St. Vincent Love **Hammick** (3 s. Sir Stephen Love, surgeon of R. Naval Hosp., Stonehouse, by Frances o. d. of Peter Turquand of London, W. Antiq. xi. 95), b. Plymouth 9 July 1806, ed. Ottery, **M.** 2 Feb. 1824, 2 Classics and 2 Math. 1828, B.A. 12 June 1828, **Dev. 1829**, vac. 6 Jan. 1837 by instit. to V. of Milton Abbott, Devon 6 Jan. 1836; M.A. 1 July 1830, succeeded to baronetcy 15 June 1867, d. 20 Feb. 1888; m. 6 Ap. 1837 Mary 2 d. of Robert Alexander; Mod. Eng. Biog.

Richard **Croft** (3 s. Sir Richard, of S. James', London), b. Old Burlington St. 1808, **M.** Balliol 20 May 1825 age 16, 2 Classics 1829, B.A. 27 May 1829, **Petr. 1829**, vac. by m. Exeter 15 Oct. 1839 Charlotte Leonora d. of Lieut.-Col. Russell, she d. 1854; m. (2) 1856 Louisa d. of Samuel Holland of Dumbleton, Glouc.; M.A. 9 Feb. 1832, M.B. 30 Mch 1833; R. of North Ockenden, Essex 1840–45, V. of Hartburn, Durham 1845–56, of Hillingdon, Middlesex 1856–69, d. 17 Feb. 1869; on 22 July 1835 gave a dinner to the Judges in the College Hall; Denman's Life ii. 24; Doyle's *Reminiscences* 15.

Marwood **Tucker** (3 s. Marwood, V. of Harpford, Devon 1817, by Charlotte Jane d. of William Davy Foulkes), b. 24 Aug. 1804, **M.** Balliol 8 Dec. 1821, scholar 1822–9; 3 Classics 1825, B.A. 25 May 1825, M.A. 4 Dec. 1828; adm. **Chapl.** 29 Ap. **1830**, vac. by m. 18 Aug. 1831 (when C. of Honiton) Ann Cranmer Miller d. of Edmund Nagle one of the two coheiresses of the Beauchamps of Pengreep and Trevince in Cornwall; R. of S. Martin's, Exeter 1840–54, of Widworthy 7 Ap. 1862; Bibl. Corn. 809, N. and Gleanings iv. 37.

Edward Fanshawe **Glanville** (3 s. Francis by his 2 wife Elizabeth 2 d. of Robert Fanshawe of Plymouth, R.N.), b. Catchfrench, St. German's 16 Ap. 1807, **M.** 28 Feb. 1824, B.A. 19 June 1828, **Corn. 1830**, vac. by m. 25 July 1835 Mary Anne 4 d. of Sir Scrope B. Morland, widow of Rev. F. C. Spencer of Wheatfield, she d. Oxford 21 Jan. 1882 age 84; M.A. 1 July 1830, Proproctor 1833; R. of Wheatfield 1836–54, P.C. of Tideford, Cornwall 1854–56, resident Stoke Damerel 1856–65, C. of S. Mary Magdalene, Oxford

1866, R. of Yelford, Oxon 1869–77, d. Oxford 9 Aug. 1878, bur. at Jericho Cemetery.

Charles Lewis **Cornish** (3 s. Robert, by Frances Ann d. of Joseph Squier), b. Exeter 16 June 1809, **M.** Queen's 2 Feb. 1827, Michel Scholar; **Dev. 1830**, vac. by m. Marylebone 30 Dec. 1841 Eleanor 1 d. of E. T. Monro M.D. of Harley St., London; 1 Classics 1831, B.A. 6 July 1833, M.A. 28 May 1834; Tutor 1834–41, P.C. of Littlemore, Oxon 1847–48, V. of Compton Dando, Som. 1859–69, held a school at Walton in Gordano near Clevedon, d. there 3 Jan. 1870 age 60; Church's *Oxford Movement* 66.

Horatio Nelson **Dudding** (o. s. Edward Barr, of St. Martin's in London), b. Marylebone 21 Sep. 1808, ed. Charterhouse, **M.** 8 May 1826, 1 Classics 1830, B.A. 21 Oct. 1830, **Petr. 1831**, vac. by m. 25 Oct. 1837; M.A. 10 Feb. 1835, Lecturer Ex. Coll., C. of S. Ebbe's, Oxford 1836–37, instit. R. of Little Stonham, Suffolk 12 June 1837, res. 1842 for V. of S. Peter's at St. Albans.

George Frederic **Fowle** (4 s. William), b. Chute, Wilts 20 Oct. 1809, **M.** Balliol 2 Ap. 1827, 2 Classics 1830, B.A. 28 Ap. 1831; **Sar. 1831**, res. 28 Ap. 1841; M.A. 27 June 1833, barrister M. T. 24 Nov. 1843, d. Chute Lodge, Wilts, the residence of his brother, 8 Jan. 1863; Gent. Mag. 1863 xiv. 260.

Reginald Edward **Copleston** (3 s. Rev. John), b. Offwell, Devon, **M.** 24 Mch 1828 age 17, **Dev. 1831**, vac. by m. New Windsor 29 Dec. 1840 Anne Elizabeth d. of Thomas Sharpe; 2 Classics 1832, B.A. 13 Nov. 1834, M.A. 30 June 1837, R. of Barnes, Surrey 13 Jan. 1840, res. 1863 for V. of Edmonton, Middlesex, d. there 10 Jan. 1878. His s. Reginald Stephen is Bishop of Colombo.

John **Ley** (2 s. Jacob, R. of Ashprington, Devon 1794–1859, previously master at Ottery S. Mary, and C. of Talaton, by Caroline d. of Rev. John Hill), b. Ashprington 12 Sep. 1805, ed. Ottery, commoner 1822 to 5 Dec. 1859, **M.** 20 June 1822, B.A. 1 Dec. 1826, M.A. 18 June 1829, adm. **Chapl.** 20 Oct. 1831, Bursar and then Subrector; vac. 4 July 1851 by pres. 7 June 1850 to R. of Waldron, Sussex, res. 1882; B.D. 17 June 1841; C. of S. Aldate's, Oxford 1840–47; m. Harriet d. of A. Collett: d. Beechcroft, Torquay 26 Mch 1891 in 87 year; edited *Beveridge on the Catechism*, and *Nicholson on the Catechism*, and published an *Account of Waldron, its church, mansions and manors* in Sussex Archæol. Coll. 1861 xiii. 80–103; his sister m. Robert Hussey, Regius Prof. of Eccles. History.

Ernest **Hawkins** (6 s. Henry, Major E.I.C., by Ann o. child of John

Gurney of Bedford), b. Lawrence End, Kimpton, Herts 25 Jan. 1801, M. Balliol 19 Ap. 1820, 2 Classics 1824, B.A. 28 May 1824, M.A. 8 Feb. 1827; **Shi. 1831**, vac. by m. 29 July 1852 Sophia Anna d. of J. H. G. Lefroy, R. of Ashe, Hants; B.D. 14 June 1839, C. of S. Aldate's, Oxford, Select Preacher 1839, Secretary S.P.G. 1838–64, canon of Westminster 5 Dec. 1864, minister of Curzon chapel, Mayfair 1850–68, d. 5 and bur. 12 Oct. 1868 in the cloister of Westminster Abbey. Wrote *Documents relating to the erection of bishoprics in the Colonies* 1844, ed. 4 1855, *Manual of Prayer for Working men and their families* 1855, ed. 4 1856, *The Book of Psalms with explanatory notes* 1857, ed. 3 1865, and 14 other books : organized the *Gospel of S. John revised by five clergymen* 1857 ; Nat. Biog., Mod. Eng. Biog.

Nutcombe **Oxnam** (4 s. Rev. William), b. Exeter 1810, ed. Harrow, Peel Medallist 1828, **M.** Oriel 19 Mch 1828 age 17, scholar of Trinity 1829, 1 Classics 1832; **Dev. 1832**, vac. by m. Pitminster, Som. 9 Jan. 1834 his cousin Jane Georgina d. of John Gould, she was b. Mylor, Cornwall 1799, d. Torquay 13 Sep. 1871 ; B.A. 13 Nov. 1834, M.A. 17 Dec. 1839; V. of Modbury, Devon 1834, preb. Exeter 26 Jan. 1850, d. Modbury 13 Sep. 1859 ; Gent. Mag. 1859 vii. 535.

Robert Jefferies **Spranger** (1 s. Robert, R. of Toynton, Lincs. and V. of Tamerton Foliot, Devon, pres. by Lord Eldon), b. Tamerton, ed. Charterhouse, **M.** 10 Mch 1830 age 18, first open scholar 1831 ; **Dev. 1832**; Tutor 1839; res. 26 Mch 1841 ; 1 Classics 1834, B.A. 2 July 1835, M.A. 9 June 1836 ; d. Southampton 29 Aug. 1888; wrote *Faith of Apostles as delivered by S. Irenaeus* 1861 ; *Lectures on First Chapter of Genesis* 1863 ; *Studies from the Fathers—The Exodus—*1866 ; and other single sermons. J. B. Mozley's Letters p. 223.

John **Carey** (2 s. James, of Guernsey), B.A. Trin. Camb. 1833, incorp. B.A. Oxford 14 Jan. 1833; **Guer. 1833**; d. 25 Dec. 1836 age 25 ; Gent. Mag. 1837 vii. 216.

Gustavus Townsend **Stupart** (1 s. Gustavus, capt. R. N.), b. Starcross 25 July 1813, ed. Ottery, **M.** 30 June 1830, **Dev. 1833**, vac. 20 Dec. 1841 by instit. to V. of Merton, Oxon 20 Dec. 1840, res. Aug. 1863; 2 Classics 1834, B.A. 30 June 1837, d. 10 June 1868; translated S. Chrysostom's *Homilies on S. John, part i, Homilies* 1–41 in Library of the Fathers 1848.

John Philip **Hugo** (2 s. Thomas), b. Crediton, **M.** Wadham 23 June 1829 age 17 ; 4 Classics and 1 Math. 1833, B.A. 15 May 1833, Math. Scholar 1834, **Dev. 1834**, vac. by m. Crediton 15 Nov. 1842 Maria

Cleave 2 d. of John Smith of Crediton; M.A. 13 Ap. 1837, instit. to
Exminster 8 Dec. 1841, d. there 29 Oct. 1862 ; Gent. Mag. 1862 xiii.
786.

William Wyatt **Woollcombe** (1 s. William M.D., of Plymouth, by
Anne Elford d. of W. Wyatt R. of Framlingham, Suffolk, Misc. Gen.
1882 p. 287), b. Plymouth Ap. 1813, **M.** 10 June 1830 age 17,
3 Classics 1834, **Dev. 1834**, res. 27 June 1854 on instit. to R. of
Wootton, Northants, res. 1882 ; B.A. 30 June 1837, M.A. 8 Mch
1838, B.D. 21 June 1850 ; P.C. of Iffley, Oxon 1840–54 ; d. 25 Nov.
1886.

William Charles **Buller** (2 s. Sir Antony, puisne Judge at Calcutta,
by his cousin Isabella Jane 7 d. of Sir William Lemon), b. Gluvias
1812, **M.** Oriel 9 Dec. 1830 age 18, 1 Math. 1835, B.A. 14 May 1835,
Corn. 1836, vac. 1 Dec. 1851 by not taking the degree of B.D. ; M.A.
20 Nov. 1838, barrister L. I. 7 May 1840, d. 26 Aug. 1875 age 62 ;
Visit. Corn. 58, Coll. Corn. 120.

William **Andrews** (3 s. William, of Salisbury J.P. by Mary Theresa
d. of J. Allan of Salisbury), b. Salisbury 26 Feb. 1812, **M.** 27 Jan.
1831, then exhibitioner at Queen's 1832 ; 2 Classics 1835, B.A. 6 June
1835, **Sar. 1836**, vac. 6 Nov. 1855 by instit. to R. of Broad
Somerford, Wilts 6 Nov. 1854, m. 15 Jan. 1856 Mary Anne y. d. of
William Croome J.P. of Glouc. ; M.A. 8 Feb. 1838, B.D. 16 May
1849 ; Master of the Schools 1840–41, Proctor 1848, d. 24 Sep. 1887.

John Brande **Morris** (1 s. Rev. John, Michel fellow of Queen's,
D.D., of Brentford, Middlesex, by Anna Frederika d. of Augustus
Everard Brande ; and nephew to the distinguished chemist William
Brande), b. New Brentford 4 Sep. 1812, **M.** Balliol 17 Dec. 1830 ;
2 Classics 1834, B.A. 20 Nov. 1834, **Petr. 1837**, res. 24 Jan. 1846
on becoming a Roman Catholic ; M.A. 8 July 1837, d. Hammersmith
9 Ap. 1880 ; trans. *S. Chrysostom on the Romans* 1841, and *Select
Homilies of S. Ephrem from the Syriac* 1846 ; wrote prize essay on the
Conversion of the Hindus 1843 ; *Nature, a parable* 1842 ; *Taleetha
Koomee, or the gospel prophecy of our Lady's Assumption, a drama in
verse* 1858 ; *Jesus the Son of Mary* 2 vols. 1851 ; *Introduction to the
Eucharist* 1878 ; Oliver's *Collections illustrating the history of the
Catholic religion in the Western Counties* 1857 pp. 357–59, Cox 311,
Mozley ii. p. 10 ; J. H. Newman's Letters, ed. Miss Mozley ; N. and
Q. 1888 p. 48, Church's *Oxford Movement* 205, Pusey's Life ii. 413,
504, 507, Nat. Biog.

William Corbet **le Breton** (o. s. William), b. S. Helier's, **M.** Pemb.

23 Feb. 1831 age 15, Morley Scholar, 3 Classics 1835, B.A. 26 Nov. 1835; **Jer. 1837**, vac. by m. S. Luke's, Chelsea, 8 July 1842 Emilia Davis y. d. of William Martin; M.A. 26 Oct. 1837, Dean of Jersey 1850, R. of S. Saviour's, Jersey 1850–75, of S. Helier's 1875, d. London 28 Feb. 1888; Pycroft i. 64, 67, 114.

Louis **Woollcombe** (2 s. Rev. Henry, d. 1861, m. 18 Ap. 1812 Jane Frances 2 d. of Sir Thomas Louis), b. Broadhembury 1814, M. Wadham 9 Feb. 1832 age 17, scholar of Pembroke, 2 Classics 1835, B.A. 3 Dec. 1835, **Dev. 1837**, vac. 14 Jan. 1846 by instit. to R. of Petrockstow, Devon 14 Jan. 1845; V. of Menheniot 1883–7; M.A. 6 June 1838, d. 19 Ap. 1889; m. 1854 Augusta Rundell d. of Rev. Charles Brown, she d. 17 Ap. 1892; Misc. Gen. 1882 p. 288.

Philip **Mules** (1 s. Philip, by 2 d. of Col. Vibart of Amberd House, Som.), b. Honiton 8 Nov. 1812, ed. Eton 1829, M. Brasenose 10 Oct. 1832, 2 Classics 1836, B.A. 24 Nov. 1836; **Dev. 1837**, vac. by m. 26 Ap. 1855 Anne d. of William Egerton of Gresford Lodge, Denbighs.; M.A. 10 Ap. 1839, B.D. 1851; examining chaplain to Bishop of Gibraltar 1842–47, chaplain to Duke of Rutland at Belvoir Castle 1848, d. there 26 Ap. 1892; wrote in the Christian Remembrancer and Fraser's Magazine; Lysons' Devon ci.

Thomas Henry **Haddan** (1 s. Thomas, solicitor, by Mary Ann d. of John Haddan), b. City of London 1814, ed. Finchley, M. Brasenose 2 July 1833 age 18, 1 Classics and 1 Math. 1837, B.A. 5 May 1837; **Petr. 1837**, res. 11 Jan. 1843; English Essay 1838, Eldon Scholar 1840, M.A. 25 June 1840, B.C.L. 28 Nov. 1844; Vinerian Fellow 1847, barrister I. T. 11 June 1841; m. Southampton 3 Oct. 1861 Caroline Elizabeth y. d. of Capt. James Bradley R.N.; C. F. Trower was his brother-in-law; he d. Vichy 5 Sep. 1873; originated the *Guardian* newspaper 1846; published *Remarks on Legal Education* 1848, *Limited Liability Act* 1855, *Outlines of Administrative Jurisdiction of Court of Chancery* 1862; Nat. Biog.

Stephen Jordan **Rigaud** (1 s. Stephen Peter, Fellow 1794), b. Westminster 27 Mch 1816, ed. Greenwich, M. 23 Jan. 1834, 1 Classics and 1 Math. 1838, **Petr. 1838**, vac. by m. 6 July 1841 Lucy F. S., o. d. of Benjamin Lewis Vulliamy of Pall Mall; S.C.L., B.A. 1 July 1841, M.A. 6 Ap. 1842, B. and D.D. 1854; Math. Examiner 1845–46, Select Preacher 1856, Master at Westminster 1846–50, Head Master Ipswich 1850–57, F.R.S., consecr. Bishop of Antigua 2 Feb. 1858, d. there of yellow fever 17 May 1859; published sermons 1852 and

1856; Gent. Mag. 1859 vii. 83; Agnew's *Protestant Exiles from France*, Index vol. p. 236.   N. and Q. 5. xii. 495.

Joseph Loscombe Richards (Fellow 1818), el. **Rector** 1 Sep. 1838, d. 27 Feb. 1854.

George **Rawlinson** (3 s. Abram Thomas, by Eliza Eudocia d. of H. Creswicke of Camden, Glouc.), b. Chadlington, Oxon 23 Nov. 1812, ed. Ealing, **M.** Trinity 7 Nov. 1834, in University Eleven 1836, 1 Classics 1838, B.A. 21 June 1838; **Petr. 1840**, vac. by m. Oxford 8 July 1846 Louisa Wildman 2 d. of Sir Robert Alex. Chermside; treasurer and president Union Soc. 1840, M.A. 21 Ap. 1841, tutor 1841, Denyer prize 1842 and 1843, Classical Moderator 1852–53, Classical Examiner 1854, 1856–57, 1868–69, Theol. Examiner 1874–75, Bampton Lecturer 1859, Camden Professor of Ancient Hist. 1861–89, F.R.G.S., corresponding member of the Royal Academy of Turin, and the American Philosophical Society; C. of Merton, Oxon 1846–47, Canon of Canterbury 1872, Proctor in Convocation since 1873, R. of Allhallows, Lombard St., June 1888; published *Translation of Herodotus* 4 vol. 8° 1858–60, *The Five Great Monarchies of the Ancient World* 4 vol. 1862–7, *Hist. of Parthia* 1873, *Hist. of Egypt* 2 vol. 1881; contributor to *Aids to Faith*, to the *Speaker's Commentary*, to Smith's *Dictionary of the Bible*, to Dean Spence's *Homiletic Commentary*; Cox 374, Pycroft ii. 89, 95, 114, J. C. Mozley's Letters p. 223.

Charles Francis **Trower** (4 s. John, of Weston Grove, Hants, and half brother of Bishop Trower), b. S. George's, Hanover Sq., 1817, ed. Winchester, **M.** 18 Feb. 1835 age 17, scholar of Balliol Nov. 1835, in the University Eleven 1838, 1 Classics 1838, Latin Verse 1838, B.A. 24 Jan. 1839, **Petr. 1840**, vac. by m. Southampton 27 Dec. 1843 Frances Mary 1 d. of Capt. Bradley R.N.; Vinerian Scholar 1840, M.A. 21 Ap. 1842; Barrister I. T. 18 Nov. 1842, d. 3 June 1891: Guardian 17 June 1891 p. 952; wrote a legal novel called *Hutspot* 1852, *Anomalous Condition of English Jurisprudence* 1848, *The Web of Love* 1856, *The law of debtor and creditor* 1860, *The law of the building of Churches and divisions of Parishes* 1867, ed. 2 1874, *A manual of the Prevalence of Equity* 1876.

Robert Shuttleworth **Sutton** (1 s. Robert, by Susan Elizabeth Schuyler, both of Flushing), b. Flushing 23 Nov. 1818, ed. Tiverton, **M.** Brasenose 15 Ap. 1837; **Corn. 1840**, vac. 17 Feb. 1854 by instit. to R. of Rype, Sussex 17 Feb. 1853, res. 1888; m. Hellingley, Sussex 14 Sep. 1854 Henrietta d. of Thomas Woodward; 4 Classics 1841,

B.A. 30 June 1843, M.A. 22 May 1845, Preb. of Chichester 12 Aug. 1876; Coll. Corn. 937.

John **Rendall** (2 s. Charles Henry, by Harriet d. of Harry Salmon, of Bath), b. Oxenwood, Berks 21 Feb. 1819, ed. Charterhouse, **M.** Balliol 11 May 1837, 2 Classics 1841, B.A. 9 June 1841; **Sar. 1841,** vac. by m. 11 May 1854 Fanny d. of Laurence Desborough, of Grove Hill, Surrey; Ellerton Essay 1842, M.A. 22 May 1845, barrister I. T. 31 Jan. 1845; resident Westworth, Cockermouth 1892.

Paul Augustine **Kingdon** (3 s. Thomas Hockin, Fellow 1794), b. Bridgerule 10 Mch 1820, How exhibitioner 27, and **M.** 29, May 1837, 3 Classics and 1 Math. 1841, B.A. 28 May 1841, **Dev. 1841,** vac. by m. Shebbear 16 Sep. 1854 Elizabeth Fortescue 1 d. of late Peter Davy Foulkes V. of Shebbear; Math. Scholar 1843, M.A. 22 May 1845, barrister L. I. 24 Nov. 1846; N. and Gleanings ii. 177.

James Peers **Tweed** (1 s. Rev. James, of Dunmow, Essex), b. Writtle near Chelmsford 28 Mch 1819, **M.** Pemb. 15 Feb. 1838, Bible Clerk; **Petr. 1841,** vac. 9 July 1863 by instit. to R. of Little Waltham, Essex 9 July 1862; m. Yarpole, Hereford 5 July 1864 Annie Mary 2 d. of Joseph Edwards, preb. of Hereford; Ireland Scholar 1841, 1 Classics 1842, B.A. 6 July 1844, M.A. 2 May 1845; wrote pamphlets on *The Educational Question at Oxford*: d. 5 Dec. 1889; Cox 413.

Matthew **Anstis** (1 s. Matthew, solicitor, by Anne Gully), b. Liskeard 4 Nov. 1815, ed. Tiverton, **M.** 29 Oct. 1834, 3 Classics 1839, B.A. 21 Nov. 1839, M.A. 28 Ap. 1842, **Corn. 1842,** vac. by m. Longdon, Staffs. 1 Oct. 1853 Maria Elizabeth 1 d. of Sir George Chetwynd, and widow of Henry Grimes, she d. London 3 June 1882; C. of Menheniot 1840, C. of Kidlington 1843–51, V. of Cubbington, Warwicks. 1854–65, d. 5 May 1882; Bibl. Corn. 1032, Coll. Corn. index p. 1606.

James Antony **Froude** (y. s. Archdeacon Robert Hurrell), b. Dartington 23 Ap. 1818, ed. Westminster 1830, **M.** Oriel 10 Dec. 1835, 2 Classics 1840, English Essay 1842, B.A. 28 Ap. 1842, **Dev. 1842,** res. 27 Feb. 1849 (see Letter to Lord J. Russell, on *The Constitutional Defects of the University and Colleges of Oxford, by a member of the Oxford Convocation* 4° London 1850 p. 38); M.A. 2 Mch 1843, hon. Fellow Ex. Coll. 1882; Regius Prof. of Mod. Hist. and Fellow of Oriel 1892; wrote *A History of England from the Fall of Wolsey to the death of Elizabeth* 1856–70; *Short Studies on Great Subjects* 1867 seq., *The English in Ireland* 1871–4; *Biography and Letters of*

Thomas Carlyle 1881–2, *Oceana* 1886; *The Spanish Story of the Armada* 1892; Rector of S. Andrews 19 Mch 1869 and hon. LL.D., Commissioner at Cape of Good Hope 1874–5; editor of Fraser's Magazine to 1881; relinquished Deacon's Orders 1872; m.(1) S. Peter's Belgrave Sq. 3 Oct. 1849 Charlotte Maria 5 d. of Pascoe Grenfell, M.P. Marlow, she d. near Bideford 21 Ap. 1860; (2) 12 Sep. 1861 Henrietta Elizabeth d. of John Ashley Warre of West Cliff House, Ramsgate, she d. 12 Feb. 1874 age 49; Cartoon Portraits 1873 pp. 126–27; Illust. Review v. pp. 215–22; Illust. London News 1871 lix. 62–63 and 69, 9 Ap. 1892 (portrait); Mozley ii. 28–36, Revue des Deux Mondes Sep. 1887 p. 68; The Galaxy, New York Sep. 1872 pp. 293–303 (by Justin Macarthy); A. K. H. Boyd's *Twenty-five Years of S. Andrews.*

Frederick **Fanshawe** (4 s. gen. Edward, by Frances Mary d. of gen. Sir Hew Whiteford Dalrymple, and grandson of R. Fanshawe R.N., Commissioner of Plymouth Dockyard), b. Devonport 14 Feb. 1821, **M.** Balliol 28 Mch 1838, scholar, Latin Verse 1841, 1 Classics and 3 Math. 1842, B.A. 6 May 1842, **Dev. 1842**, vac. by m. 20 Dec. 1855 Mary Louisa y. d. of gen. Sir Henry Goldfinch; M.A. 30 May 1844, Tutor, Hebrew Lecturer, Senior Bursar, and Librarian; Master of the Schools 1851–52, Master of Bedford gr. sch. 1855–74, d. Cheltenham 27 Mch 1879.

Richard Cowley **Powles** (2 s. John Diston, by Emma d. of Lieut. Col. Ogle), b. City of London 21 May 1819, ed. Helston and King's Coll. London, **M.** 1 Feb. 1838, scholar 1839–42; treasurer 1840, president 1841, librarian of Union Soc. 1842; 1 Classics 1842, **Petr. 1842**, vac. by m. Leamington 13 June 1850 Mary d. of George Chester, of I.C.S.; B.A. 4 Dec. 1845, M.A. 22 Ap. 1846, tutor 1846, Classical Examiner 1849–50, kept a school at 9 Eliot Place, Blackheath 1850–69, then at Eversley in Hants 1869–80; preb. of Chichester, and examining Chaplain to Bishop of Chichester 1887; *Letters and Memoirs of C. Kingsley* ed. 4 pp. 23–28, 95, 130, 137–144; ed. *Sermons of Lousada* 1860, and published some single sermons; resides Priory House, Chichester; Burgon's *Twelve Good Men* ii. 272, 315.

George **Butler** (1 s. George, Dean of Peterborough, by Sarah Maria d. of John Gray of Wembley Park), b. Harrow 11 June 1819, ed. Harrow, kept 4 terms at Trinity, Camb., adm. Oxford *ad eundem* 1840, **M.** 16 Oct. 1840, Hertford Scholar and open scholar Ex. Coll. 1841; **Petr. 1842**, vac. by m. 3 Jan. 1852 Josephine Elizabeth 4 d. of John Grey of Dilston; 1 Classics 1843, B.A. 4 Dec. 1845, M.A. 30

Ap. 1846, Tutor of Durham, hon. D.D. Durham 1882, Principal of Butler's Hall, Oxford 1856-8, Vice-Principal of Cheltenham Coll. 1857-65, Principal of Liverpool Coll. 1866-82, canon of Winchester 7 Aug. 1882, d. London 14 Mch 1890 ; wrote *Principles of Imitative Art* 1852, *Descriptio Antiqui Codicis Virgiliani* (priv. p.) 1854, *The Raphael Drawings in the University Galleries* (Oxford Essays), *Village Sermons at Tyneside* 1857, *Family Prayers* 1862, *Sermons preached in Cheltenham College Chapel* 1862, and edited several Atlases; *Recollections of George Butler, by Josephine E. Butler* 1892 ; Cox 373, 390.

John Duke **Coleridge** (1 s. Sir John Taylor), b. S. Pancras 3 Dec. 1820, ed. Eton 1832-8, **M.** Balliol 29 Nov. 1838, scholar, B.A. 10 Nov. 1842, president of Oxf. Union Soc. 1843, librarian 1844; **Petr.** 1843, vac. by m. 11 Aug. 1846 Jane Fortescue 3 d. of Rev. George Turner Seymour of Farringford Hill, I. of Wight, she d. 6 Feb. 1878; m. (2) 13 Aug. 1885 Amy Augusta Jackson 1 d. of Henry Baring Lawford of Bengal C. S., and of Upton Park, Slough, Bucks, she was b. 1853 ; M.A. 26 Nov. 1846, hon. D.C.L. 13 June 1877, barrister M.T. 6 Nov. 1846, Recorder of Portsmouth 1855-1866, Q.C. 22 Feb. 1861, M.P. Exeter 1865-73, knighted at Windsor Castle 12 Dec. 1868, Serjeant-at-Law 12 Jan. 1874, Solicitor General 1868-71, Attorney General 1871-73, C.J. Common Pleas 21 Nov. 1873-1880, Privy Councillor 12 Dec. 1873, Lord Chief Justice 1 Dec. 1880, created Baron Coleridge of Ottery S. Mary 10 Jan. 1874; F.R.S. 3 May 1877; the College entertained him at a public dinner 5 Mch 1874 on his first coming as Judge to the Oxford Assizes; hon. fellow 1882; spoke in the Tichborne case 1872 for 25 days, the longest speech in any legal case on record; Daily News 16 July 1892.

Frederic Hookey **Bond** (4 s. late Rear Adm. Francis Godolphin, by Sophia d. of Thomas Snow), b. Alphington, Exeter 1821, ed. Winchester, **M.** 21 Feb. 1839 age 18, Gifford Exhibitioner 1841, 2 Classics 1843, B.A. 3 June 1843, **Dev.** 1843, vac. by m. 8 July 1852 Mary Isabella d. of Major Henry De la Fosse, Bengal Artillery; M.A. 26 June 1845, Master of Marlborough Free Gram. Sch. 1853-78.

Edmund **Boger** (1 s. Richard, capt. R.M., captain and paymaster R. Cornwall Militia, by Eliza d. of J. Squire, R.N.), b. Lanlivery 9 Nov. 1822, ed. Lostwithiel gr. sch. 1831-41, **M.** Magd. H. 13 May 1841; **Corn.** 1843, vac. by m. 15 Jan. 1850 Charlotte Gilson 3 d. of John Allen, Master of Ilminster gr. sch. and R. of Knowle ; 3 Classics 1845, B.A. 26 Nov. 1846, M.A. 1859, Master of Helston gr. sch. 1850-55, P.C. of Knowle S. Giles 1855-9, and of Kingstone 1857-9, both in

Som., master of Queen Elizabeth's gr. sch., Southwark 1859, C. of All Saints, Walworth, London 1876, hon. Canon of Rochester 24 Dec. 1877, wrote *Outlines of Roman History* 1861; Bibl. Corn. 30, 1080.

William **Lempriere** (2 s. Philip Raoul, by Elizabeth d. of John Poigndestre), b. Jersey 3 June 1818, ed. Rugby, **M.** Ch. Ch. 22 Oct. 1835; B.A. 14 Nov. 1839, M.A. 18 May 1843 ; adm. **Jer.** 2 Nov. **1843**, not el. full Fellow 1844 (he appealed to the Visitor, who decided against him) ; C. of Brockenhurst with Lymington, of Wolverstone, Suffolk 1852–5; Chaplain of Rozel Manor Chapel, Jersey 1869; m. 15 May 1850 Julia Ann y. d. of Thomas Moore Wayne of the Manor House, South Warnborough, Hants.

John Fielder **Mackarness** (1 s. John, of Elstree House, Bath, by Catherine d. of George Smith Coxhead, M.D.), b. S. Mary's, Islington 3 Dec. 1820, ed. Eton 1832–40, **M.** Merton 22 Oct. 1840, Postmaster there, 2 Classics 1843, B.A. 30 May 1844; **Petr. 1844**, vac. 11 Aug. 1846 by instit. to V. of Tardebigg, Worcs. 11 Aug. 1845, res. 1855; M.A. 22 May 1847, D.D. 1869 : R. of Honiton 1855–69, preb. of Exeter 1858–69, chaplain to Lord Lyttelton 1855–69, proctor in Convocation 1865–91, V. of Monkton near Honiton 1867–69, consecr. Bishop of Oxford 25 Jan. 1870, res. June 1888; Select Preacher 1870, Chancellor of the Order of the Garter 5 Feb. 1870, d. Eastbourne 16 Sep. 1889; m. Ottery 7 Aug. 1849 Alethea Buchanan y. d. of Sir John Taylor Coleridge; *Memorials of the Episcopate of J. F. Mackarness*, by C. C. Mackarness (his son) 1893.

Henry **Low** (5 s. John, and descended from Admiral Villeneuve), b. S. Aubin, Jersey 9 Dec. 1807, **M.** S. John's, Camb., 24 Wrangler 1834, B.A. 1834, M.A. 1837, incorp. M.A. Oxford 26 June 1845; **Jer. 1845**, Mathematical Lecturer 1848–64, B.D. 28 June 1849, vac. by m. 28 July 1864 Catharina Duke Crawley, she d. Bath 22 Jan. 1885 age 80; d. Ventnor 18 Nov. 1864, bur. Holywell Cemetery, Oxford; Gent. Mag. 1864 xvii. 797.

Thomas Blackmore **Colenso** (2 s. John William, an officer of the Duchy of Cornwall at Lostwithiel, by Mary Anne d. of Richard Blackmore of Devonport ; and brother of Bishop Colenso), b. Devonport, **M.** Trinity 26 Oct. 1843 aged 20; **Dev. 1846**; 2 Classics 1847, B.A. 7 July 1849, d. Lostwithiel 28 Sep. 1849; memorial window in the College Chapel; Gent. Mag. 1849 xxxii. 553.

Wharton Booth **Marriott** (7 s. George Wharton, barrister M.T.), b. S. George's, Bloomsbury 7 Nov. 1823, ed. Eton 1838–43, **M.** Trinity 12 June 1843 ; **Petr. 1846**, vac. by m. Bletchingley 22 Ap.

1851 Julia y. d. of William Soltau of Clapham; 2 Classics 1847, B.C.L. and B.A. 1851, M.A. 1856, B.D. 1870; Select Preacher 1868, Grinfield Lecturer 1871, F.S.A. 1857 and member of the Council 1871, Assistant Master Eton 1850–60, d. 16 Dec. 1871, his wife d. 1872; wrote Ειρηνικα 1864–5, *Vestiarium Christianum* 1868, *The Testimony of the Catacombs* 1870, and contributed to Smith's *Dictionary of Christian Antiquities*; Memorials of W. B. Marriott by F. J. A. Hort 1873, Proc. of Society of Antiquaries v. 309 (1870–71), Eton Portrait Gallery 1876 p. 195, Nat. Biog.

William **Ince** (1 s. William, by Hannah Goodwin Dakin), born S. James', Clerkenwell 7 June 1825, ed. King's Coll. sch., M. Lincoln 12 Dec. 1842, scholar 1842–6, 1 Classics 1846, B.A. 26 Nov. 1846; **Petr. 1847**, vac. 6 Ap. 1878 by becoming Regius Prof. of Divinity and Canon of Ch. Ch.; m. Alvechurch, Worcs. 11 Sep. 1879 Mary Anne y. d. of John Rusher Eaton; M.A. 26 Ap. 1849, D.D. by decree 7 May 1878; Tutor 1850–78, Subrector 1857–78, Proctor 1856, Select Preacher 1859, 1870, 1875, Whitehall Preacher 1860–62, hon. Fellow of King's Coll. London 1861, Classical Examiner 1866–68, Examining Chaplain to Bishop of Oxford 1870; hon. Fellow Ex. Coll. 1882; published *Aspects of Christian Truth, Advent Sermons at Whitehall* 1862, *A plea for definite Christian doctrine* 1865, *Religion in the University*, read in the Church Congress at Stoke-upon-Trent 1875, and several College and University Sermons.

George Herbert **Curteis** (1 s. George), b. Canterbury 3 Ap. 1824, ed. Winchester, M. Univ. Coll. 26 Nov. 1842, scholar, 2 Classics 1846, B.A. 26 Nov. 1846, **Petr. 1847**, vac. by m. Sherborne 7 Feb. 1863 Elizabeth Anna 1 d. of Edmund Robert Ball of Dublin, she publ. 1878 a Life of G. A. Selwyn, bishop of Lichfield; M.A. 28 June 1849, tutor 1855, Subrector 1856–7, Select Preacher 1857, 1866, 1875, 1888, H.M. Chaplain of the Savoy 1890; Fellow of S. Augustine's, Canterbury 1851–5, first Principal of the Theol. Coll. at Lichfield 1857–80, R. of Turweston, Bucks 1870–73, canon of Lichfield 1858–73, examining chaplain to Bishop of Lichfield 1880, pres. by the College to Waldron 1880, res. 1882; Prof. of New Testament Exegesis, King's Coll. 1882, chaplain Royal chapel Savoy 1890; wrote *Spiritual Progress, Sermons preached in Exeter College Chapel* 1855, *Cathedral Restoration, two sermons*, 1860, and *Dissent in relation to the Church of England* 1872, Bampton lecture 1871; *See Which is Right, the Established Church or the Liberation Society? correspondence between G. H. Curteis canon of Lichfield, and J. G.*

Rogers, B.A. Congregational minister, Clapham 1877; *The Scientific Obstacles to Christian Belief, Boyle lectures* 1884, 1885, *Life of Bishop Selwyn* 1889.

Francis Turner **Palgrave** (1 s. Sir Francis, by Elizabeth d. of Dawson Turner), b. Great Yarmouth 28 Sep. 1824, ed. Charterhouse 1838–43, scholar of Balliol Nov. 1842, **M.** 1 Dec. 1842; 1 Classics 1847; **Petr. 1847**, S.C.L. Ex. Coll. 1848, B.A. 1856, M.A. 28 May 1856; vac. by m. 30 Dec. 1862 Cecil Grenville Milnes 1 d. of J. Milnes Gaskell of Wakefield, M.P.; hon. LL.D. Edinburgh 23 Ap. 1878; Vice-Principal of Kneller Hall, secretary to Earl Granville, Assist. Secretary in Education Office to 1884; Professor of Poetry 26 Nov. 1885; published *Preciosa* 1852 (anon.), *The Passionate Pilgrim* 1854 (pseudonym H. J. Thurstan), *Idyls and Songs* 1854, *Hymns* 1867, *Lyrical Poems* 1871, among other volumes of poetry ed. *Poems of A. H. Clough* 1862, *Selections from Wordsworth* 1865, Life of Scott, prefixed to his *Poetical Works* 1866; *The Golden Treasury* 1861, 1881, 1891, *The Children's Treasury* 1875, *Selections from Herrick* 1877, *Visions of England* 1880 (pr. pr. 50 copies) reissued 1881, 1889, *Treasury of Sacred Song* 1889, *Amenophis* 1892.

Frederic Thomas **Colby** (1 s. Thomas, capt. R.N., by Mary 1 d. of Rev. John Palmer of Great Torrington), b. S. Andrew's, Plymouth 21 Sep. 1827, ed. Shrewsbury, **M.** 29 Jan. 1846; Gifford scholar 1849, 2 Classics 1849; **Dev. 1849**, B.A. 4 Nov. 1852, M.A. 20 Oct. 1853, B.D. 1868, D.D. 1875; Bursar 1856–69; V. of South Newington 1869–70; F.S.A. 10 Feb. 1870; R. of Litton Cheney, Dorset 9 Feb. 1875, res. 1 May 1893, resides 12 Hillsborough Terrace, Ilfracombe; vac. by m. Tiverton 6 Ap. 1875 Theophila Margaret 1 d. of George Hadow R. of Tidcombe Portion, Tiverton, b. 21 Sep. 1843, d. 1 July 1876; m. (2) 1 Aug. 1877 Louisa Margaret Anne 1 d. of George de Carteret Guille R. of Little Torrington, b. 12 Aug. 1849; wrote *Sermon on the Inward Epiphany* 1867, Oxford, *Heraldry of Exeter* in Archæol. Instit. 1873, *Catalogue of the Portrait Exhib. Exeter* 1873, on *Hist. of Great Torrington,* Devonshire Assoc. 1875; ed. *Visitations of Devon and Somerset* for the Harleian Society 1872 and 1876; the *Visit. of Devon* 1564, 1881; and *Addenda to the Visit. of Dorset* 1620, 1888; *Pedigree of Colby of Great Torrington,* ed. 2 1878; *Pedigrees of Five Devonshire Families* 1884, and *Appendix* 1885.

William **Hichens** (1 s. Robert of East Dulwich, d. 1865, by

Jane Snaith), b. Camberwell 1825, **M.** S. John's 6 Dec. 1842, 1 Classics 1847, B.A. 22 May 1847; **Petr. 1850**, d. 17 Aug. 1850 while C. of Feock, Cornwall; his Sermons were published 1851; memorial brass in S. Ives Church; Lake ii. 254.

Charles William **Boase** (1 s. John Josias Arthur, J.P. Penzance, by Charlotte 2 d. of Robert Sholl of Truro), b. Penzance 6 July 1828, and bap. 19 Sep. at S. Mary's, ed. Penzance gr. sch. to 1841, and Truro gr. sch. 1841–46, where he gained Lord Falmouth's medals 1841, and Dr. Cardew's prize 23 Sep. 1842, and Lord Falmouth's prize of books the same year; **M.** 4 June 1846 as Eliot exhibitioner, open scholar 1847–50, 2 Classics 1850, B.A. 18 May 1850, **Corn. 1850**; proximè for Arnold Historical Essay 1851 on 'Carthage,' and received a prize of books; M.A. 27 Jan. 1853; ordained 4 Mch 1855; Tutor or lecturer 1853–94, Lecturer in Hebrew 1859–69 and 1878–93, Librarian since 1868; Master of the Schools 1856, Examiner in Law and Modern History 1857–58, 1865–67, 1869–71, Classical Examiner 1862–63, Examiner in Modern History 1872–74; University Reader in Foreign History 1 May 1884 for 5 years, re-elected 31 Jan. 1889, Delegate of Privileges 25 Ap. 1885; member of Committee for nominating Examiners in School of Modern History; Delegate of Common University Fund; one of the joint translators and editors of Ranke's *History of England* for the Clarendon Press, 6 vols. 1875; wrote many articles for Smith's *Dictionary of Christian Biography* (Lives of Celtic Saints), and article on *Macedonian History* for Encycl. Brit. ed. 9; and *Oxford* in Longman's Historic Towns; and the present volume (ed. i. 1879, ii. 1893); *The Register of Exeter College, an annotated list of all the members of the College* (vol. ii. of previous work); *Register of the University of Oxford* i (O. H. Soc. 1885); *Exeter College*, in *The Colleges of Oxford* by A. Clark 1891; *An account of the families of Boase or Bowes*, Exeter 1876 pr. pr., ed. 2 1893, ed. 3 1894; and contributed to the Academy and other Literary Journals.

Henry Fanshawe **Tozer** (o. s. Aaron, capt. R.N., by Mary d. of Henry Hutton of Lincoln), b. Charles, Plymouth 18 May 1829, ed. Winchester 1842, **M.** Univ. Coll. 5 Mch 1847; Gifford Scholar Ex. Coll. 1848, 2 Classics 1850, **Dev. 1850**, vac. by m. Clapton 29 Aug. 1868 Augusta Henrietta d. of H. D. C. Satow of Sidmouth; re-elected 30 June 1882 for 7 years, and again 15 Mch 1889 for 5 years, res. 1893, hon. Fellow 1893, ordained 1852, B.A. 20 Oct. 1853, M.A. 10 May 1854, Librarian 1855–68, Tutor 1855–93,

Classical Moderator 1866–68, 1873, 1878–9, 1882–4, Curator of Taylor Institution from 1869; Vice-president of Soc. for Hellenic Studies 1879, Corresponding Member of United Armenian Educational Societies of Ararat 1881 and of Historical and Ethnographical Society of Greece 1882; wrote *Researches in the Highlands of Turkey* 1869, *Lectures on the Geography of Greece* 1873, *Primer of Classical Geography*, ed. Finlay's *Greece*, 7 vols. 1877, *Turkish Armenia and Eastern Asia Minor* 1881, new ed. of Wordsworth's *Greece* 1882, ed. Childe Harold 1885, *The Church and the Eastern Empire* 1888, *The Islands of the Ægean* 1890, *Selections from Strabo* 1893; wrote articles on *Attica*, *Eubœa*, *Mediæval Greek History*, *Macedonia*, *Thessaly*, &c., in Encycl. Brit. ed. 9.

Hans William **Sotheby** (o. s. late Hans, E.I.C.S., d. Park Place 27 Ap. 1827), b. S. George's Hanover Sq. 17 May 1827, ed. Charterhouse, **M.** 19 May 1845, 1 Classics 1849, B.A. 6 Dec. 1849 of Alban H., to which he went to avoid a rule that the Examination must be passed by the sixteenth term, which, as men did not then usually reside the first year after matriculation, acted unfairly, as other colleges had not the rule; the real rule, passed 5 Jan. 1819, was not so strict, see 9 Mch 1822 in the Book of College Orders, **Petr.** 1851, vac. by m. 8 Sep. 1864 Charlotte 1 d. of Charles John Cornish of Salcombe Regis; English Essay 1852, M.A. 30 June 1854; d. 93 Onslow Square, South Kensington 25 Sep. 1874.

George **Ridding** (3 s. Charles Henry, Fellow of Winchester, by Charlotte d. of Archdeacon Stonhouse), b. the College, Winchester 16 Mch 1828, at Winchester 1840, **M.** Balliol 30 Nov. 1846, 1 Classics and 2 Math. 1851, B.A. 1851, Craven scholar 1851, **Petr.** 1851, vac. by m. 20 July 1858 Mary Louisa 2 d. of George Moberly, Head Master of Winchester, she d. Winchester 20 July 1859; Latin Essay 1853, M.A. 28 Ap. 1853, D.D. 1869; Tutor 1853–63, Master of the Schools 1855, Classical Moderator 1856–57, Proctor 1861, Select Preacher 1863, Second Master of Winchester 1864–68, Head Master 1868–84; m. (2) 26 Oct. 1876 Laura Elizabeth Palmer 1 d. of Lord Selborne; first Bishop of Southwell 1884; has written on the educational improvements in which he has taken a leading part.

Thomas Henry **Sheppard** (8 s. Edward, of Firgrove in Dudmaston, by Mary o. d. of John Darke of Alstone, Worcs.), b. The Ridge near Wotten-under-Edge, Glouc. 9 Nov. 1814, ed. Rugby 1830–32, **M.** Oriel 13 Dec. 1832 age 18, 2 Classics 1837, B.A. 13 May 1837, M.A.

29 Ap. 1840, Master of the Schools 1849, 1851, adm. **Chaplain** 21
Oct. **1851,** B.D. 1852; Bursar to 1878; Sub-editor of the new English
Dictionary for letters U and V; instrumental in Mr. Gladstone's defeat
at Oxford; d. Canterbury 9 Ap. 1888, bur. S. Martin's, Canterbury,
memorial brass in Ex. Coll. Chapel.

Joseph William **Chitty** (2 s. Thomas, d. London 13 Feb. 1878 aged
76, by Eliza d. of A. Causton), b. 5 Calthorpe St., Gray's Inn Road,
London 1828, ed. Eton 1844–7, in the Eton Eleven 1844–47, captain
1847; **M.** Balliol 23 Mch 1847 aged 18, rowed No. 2 in Oxford
Eight 29 Mch 1849, and No. 4, 15 Dec. 1849, and stroke 3 Ap. 1852,
in University Eleven 1848–49, captain 1849, umpire of the Inter-Uni-
versity Boat Race 23 years to 1880; 1 Classics 1851, B.A. 1851,
Vinerian scholar 1852; **Petr. 1852,** vac. by m. Hanworth, Middlesex
7 Sep. 1858 Clara Jessie d. of late Lord Chief Baron Sir F. Pollock;
Major of Inns of Court Volunteers 1869-77; chairman of the University cricket jubilee dinner 1877, of the University boatrace commemo-
ration dinner 1881; M.A. 26 May 1855, barrister L.I. 30 Ap. 1856,
and Q.C. 5 Feb. 1874, Bencher of Lincoln's Inn 1875, M.P. Oxford
City 1880–81, Judge of High Court of Justice, Chancery Division, 6
Sep. 1881, knighted Windsor 7 Dec. 1881; photograph in Foster's
Oxford men 1880–92; resides 33 Queen's Gate Gardens, London S.W.

Richard Marrack **Rowe** (3 s. John), b. Ragennis in Paul near Penzance, bap. Paul 11 Oct. 1829, ed. Truro, **M.** Magd. H. 29 Ap. 1847,
3 Classics 1851, B.A. 1851; **Corn. 1852,** M.A. 16 Mch 1854, Theological Tutor at Queen's Coll. Birmingham 1859–60, British Chaplain
at Alexandria 1860–61, d. 17 Dec. 1861, bur. Paul 21 Dec.; wrote
Memorial Sermons at Queen's College, Birmingham 1860; Bibl. Corn.
604.

George Robert **Baker** (2 s. Col. George), b. Bayford, Herts, **M.**
Wadham 18 Oct. 1848 age 18, B.A. 12 Nov. 1852, **Shi. 1852;** in
orders 1855, d. of consumption Bath 8 Feb. 1856; Gent. Mag. 1856
xlv. 543.

Richard Corbett **Pascoe** (1 s. Major Richard, of Falmouth), b.
Stonehouse, **M.** Magd. H. 25 Nov. 1847 age 18, 3 Classics 1851,
B.A. 1851; **Dev. 1853,** M.A. 15 June 1854, C. of Harberton, Devon
1856–58, Vice-principal of Theol. Coll. Lichfield 1858–61, first Principal of Theol. Coll. Exeter 1861–67, R. of S. Stephen's Exeter
1862–63, d. The Close, Exeter 9 June 1868 aged 38; published several
sermons.

John Prideaux Lightfoot (Fellow 1824), **Rector** 18 Mch 1854, d. 23 Mch 1887.

John **Kempe** (o. s. John Arthur, Col. E.I.C., by Elizabeth d. of John Penhallow Peters), b. Philleigh 1827, and bap. 13 July, ed. Truro, **M.** 17 Ap. 1845, Eliot Exhibitioner 1846, scholar 1846, 2 Classics 1849, B.A. 14 June 1849, **Corn. 1854**, vac. 30 June 1869 by lapse of time ; M.A. 15 Mch 1855, writer for London press ; d. London 14 Nov. 1883 ; Graphic 17 Nov., Academy 24 Nov. 1883, Coll. Corn. 444.

Henry Carew **Glanville** (2 s. Francis, of Catchfrench in S. German's, by Amabel 6 d. of R. P. Carew of Antony, and nephew of E. F. Glanville Fellow 1830), b. Hexworthy in Lawhitton 1 Jan. 1830, ed. Bedford, **M.** 3 Feb. 1848, 3 Classics 1851, B.A. 1851, **Corn. 1854**, vac. 23 Jan. 1857 by instit. to R. of Sheviocke, Cornwall 23 Jan. 1856; M.A. 15 Mch 1855.

Arthur **Kekewich** (2 s. Samuel Trehawke, M.P. South Devon, by Agatha Sophia Maria 4 d. of J. Langston of Sarsden, Oxon), b. Peamore, Exminster 26 July 1832, ed. Eton, **M.** Balliol 21 Mch 1850, 2 Math. Mod. 1852, 1 Classics 1853, 2 Math. 1854, B.A. 22 June 1854 ; **Dev. 1854**, vac. by m. Reigate 23 Sep. 1858 Marianne 1 d. of James William Freshfield; M.A. 22 May 1856, barrister L. I. 7 June 1858, Q.C. May 1877, bencher 1881, Judge of High Court of Justice, Chancery division, 12 Nov. 1886, knighted 26 Nov. ; resides 19 Park Crescent, Portland Place, London.

James Thomas Houssemayne **Du Boulay** (2 s. James Thomas, Fellow 1823), b. Heddington, Wilts 26 July 1832, ed. Winchester 1845, **M.** 23 Jan. 1850, Exh. 17 May 1850; 1 Classics Mod. 1852, hon. 4 Classics and 4 Hist. 1854, B.A. 15 June 1854 ; **Sar. 1854**, vac. by m. Algiers 9 Feb. 1860 Alice Mead y. d. of George J. Cornish, V. of Kenwyn, Cornwall, b. Kenwyn 13 Feb. 1841 ; M.A. 12 June 1856, Tutor Ex. Coll. 1854–60, Master at Winchester 1862–93 ; Agnew's *Protestant Exiles from France*, Index volume p. 248; he published *Pedigree of Ward of Middleton Cheney* 1890.

William Monro **Wollaston** (6 s. Henry Septimus Hyde by his 3 wife Maria Frances d. of Charles Monro of London, and nephew of William Hyde Wollaston the famous chemist), b. S. David's, Exeter 19 Oct. 1831, ed. Eton 1844–51, **M.** Trinity 11 Mch 1851, Blount scholar; 1 Classics Mod. 1853, 1 Classics 1855, B.A. 7 June 1855 ; **Dev. 1855**, vac. by m. 24 May 1864 Constance Sophia d. of James MacGregor M.P.; M.A. 3 June 1857, tutor 1857–63 ; Conduct of

Eton 1863, V. of Merton, Oxon 5 Dec. 1863, res. 1 Sep. 1874, Chaplain of S. Paul at Cannes 1874, canon of Gibraltar 1892 ; m. (2) 15 Ap. 1890 Mary d. of late Rev. William and Lady Maria Brodie.

Charles Arthur **Turner** (1 s. John Fisher, R. of Winkleigh 1856–72, d. 1872), b. Exeter 1833, ed. Exeter, **M.** 12 June 1851 age 18, Gifford Scholar 1852, 2 Classics Mod. 1853, 2 Classics 1855, **Dev. 1855**, vac. by m. Wells Cathedral 8 Mch 1866 Emily Ayscough 1 d. of William Sampson Hodgkinson of Wookey Hole, Som., B.A. 30 Oct. 1856, M.A. 14 Jan. 1858 ; president of the Union 1856, barrister L. I. 30 Ap. 1858, Puisne Judge H. C., N. W. P., 1866–79, C. J. H. C. Madras 1879–85, and knighted by patent 23 Ap. 1879, Member of Indian Council 1888, C.I.E. 1 Jan. 1878, Knt. Bach. 23 Ap. 1879, K.C.I.E. 2 Jan. 1888, resides 24 Ashburn Place, Cromwell Road, London.

NOTE.—From this date the Fellowships became Open.

George **Miller** (4 s. Sir Thomas, V. of Froyle, Hants, by Martha 1 d. of Rev. John Holmes of Bungay, Suffolk), b. Froyle 7 July 1833, ed. Harrow, el. scholar and **M.** 12 June 1851 ; 1 Classics Mod. 1853, 1 Classics 1855, 4 Mod. Hist. 1856, B.A. 22 May 1856 ; el. **1857**, vac. by m. 25 July 1865 Mary Elizabeth d. of Peter Aubertin R. of Chipstead, Surrey ; M.A. 3 June 1858, barrister L. I. 1863, Examiner in the Education Office, London 1865–84, assist. Secretary 1884.

Thomas Erskine **Holland** (1 s. Thomas Agar, R. of Poynings, Sussex, by Madalena d. of Major Philip Stewart), b. Brighton 17 July 1835, ed. Brighton Coll., **M.** Balliol 23 Mch 1854, Demy of Magdalen 25 July 1855 ; 2 Classics Mod. 1856, 1 Classics 1858, B.A. 10 June 1858 ; el. **1859**, vac. by m. 12 Aug. 1871 Louise Henriette d. of M. Jean de Lessert, she d. 1891 ; M.A. 14 June 1860, B.C.L. 1871, D.C.L. 1876 ; English Essay 1860, barrister L. I. 26 Jan. 1863 ; Law Examiner 1868, 1873–75, 1880–2 &c., in Univ. of London 1871–5, for Inns of Court 1878–81 ; Vinerian Reader in English Law 22 Mch 1874, Chichele Professor of International Law 28 July 1874 ; Fellow of All Souls 30 Oct. 1875, Assessor of the Chancellor's Court 1876 ; Associé de l'Institut de Droit International 1875, member 1878 ; Knight (afterwards Officer) of Order of Crown of Italy Oct. 1876 ; hon. LL.D. of Universities of Glasgow 1884, of Bologna 1888, hon. member of Univ. of S. Petersburgh 1887, of Juridical Society of Berlin 1890, hon. D.C.L. Dublin 1892 ; wrote *An Essay on Composition Deeds* 1864 ; *A Plan for the Formal Amendment of the Law of England* 1867 ; *Essays upon the Form of the Law* 1870 : *The*

Institutes of Justinian, edited as a recension of the Institutes of Gaius,
1873, ed. 2 1881; *Albericus Gentilis, an Inaugural Lecture* 1874;
—— *tradotto da Aurelio Saffi* 1884; *The Brussels Conference of*
1874 and other diplomatic attempts to mitigate the rigour of warfare
1876; *The Treaty Relations of Russia and Turkey* 1774 *to* 1853,
with an Appendix of Treaties 1877; *Alberici Gentilis de Iure Belli*
Libri Tres 1877; *Select Titles from the Digest of Justinian* edited, with
C. L. Shadwell, 1874–1881; *The Elements of Jurisprudence* 1880, ed.
5 1890; *The European Concert in the Eastern Question, a Collection of*
Treaties and other Public Acts, edited, with introductions and notes
1885; *A Manual of Naval Prize Law, issued by authority of the*
Lords Commissioners of the Admiralty 1888.

Charles Edward **Hammond,** (1 s. Thomas John major E. I. C.,
d. 1878, by Anne d. of Dawson Warren V. of Edmonton), b. Walcot,
Bath 24 Jan. 1837, ed. Sherborne, **M.** Balliol 8 Dec. 1854, el. Symes
scholar Ex. Coll. same day, 1 Classics and 1 Math. Mod. 1857, 3 Classics
and 1 Math. 1858, B.A. 17 Dec. 1858, el. **1859,** vac. by m. 3 July
1873 Florence Jane d. of George Stallard V. of East Grafton; M.A.
10 Ap. 1861, Math. Moderator 1862–63, Proctor 1867, Bursar 1869–
82, Master of the Schools 1875–6, precentor of Keble 1876–9, Pass
Moderator 1880–1, Chaplain of Oxford Penitentiary 1870–82, pres. by
College to Wootton, Northants 1882, to Menheniot 1887, R.D. of East
1889; wrote *Outlines of Textual Criticism applied to the New Testament*
1872, *Liturgies Eastern and Western* 1878, and *Appendix (Ancient*
Liturgy of Antioch) 1879.

William Walrond **Jackson** (1 s. William Walrond, Bishop of
Antigua, by Mary Shepherd d. of Conrade Pile of Barbados), b. Port
of Spain, Trinidad 17 May 1838, ed. Codrington College, Barbados,
M. Balliol 8 Ap. 1856, 1 Classics Mod. 1858, 2 Classics 1860, B.A.
14 June 1860; el. **1863,** M.A. 10 Oct. 1863, B. and D.D. 28 Ap.
1892; Master of the Schools 1865, el. Proctor 1872 by Balliol;
Classical Moderator 1874–75; Select Preacher 1880; Censor of
Unattached Students 1883; Tutor Ex. Coll. 1864, Hebrew Lecturer
1869–78, Subrector 1878, el. Rector 15 Ap. 1887; translated a volume
of Ranke's History of England for the Clarendon Press; m. S. Mary's
Bryanston Sq., London 13 Sep. 1887 Amelia o. child of Francis
William Staines of S. Leonard's, and widow of Augustus Burke
Shepherd of Brasenose M.D.

Ingram **Bywater** (o. s. John Ingram, by Emma Marshall), b.
Islington 27 June 1840, ed. Univ. Coll., and King's Coll. schs. London,

M. Queen's 7 Oct. 1858, Taberdar 1858–63, 1 Classics Mod. 1860, 1 Classics and hon. 4 Math. 1862, B.A. 4 Dec. 1862, librarian Oxf. Union Soc. 1863; el. **1863,** vac. by m. 19 Aug. 1885 Charlotte 1 d. of Charles John Cornish, widow of Hans William Sotheby, fellow 1851; re-elected 1885, and 1889; M.A. 19 Ap. 1865, Pass Moderator 1868, Proproctor 1872, Proctor 1873, Classical Examiner 1874–5, 1881, Curator of Taylor Institution 1878–85, Delegate of Press 1879, Sub-librarian of Bodleian 1879–80, Curator of Bodleian 1884, University Reader in Greek 26 Oct. 1883, re-elected 1888 ; corresponding member of Royal Prussian Acad. of Sciences 1887 ; hon. D. Litt., Dublin 1892; published *Heracliti Ephesii Reliquiae* 1877, *Prisciani Lydi quae extant* Berlin 1886, *Aristotelis Ethica Nicomachea* Oxford 1890, *Textual Criticism of the Nicomachean Ethics* Oxford 1892; printed for private circulation 1878 sixty copies of a *Gnomologium Baroccianum*, and 1879–80 two specimens of a projected edition of Diogenes Laertius : contributor to Journal of Philology, Hermes, Rheinisches Museum, and Archiv f. Gesch. der Philosophie.

Charles James Coverly **Price** (2 s. Henry, by Mary Ann o. d. of William Wallace), b. S. Martin's, Ludgate 17 Jan. 1838, ed. Tiverton, **M.** Balliol 16 Oct. 1856, scholar; 1 Math. Mod. 1858, 1 Math. and 1 Nat. Sci. 1860, Johnson Mathematical Scholar 1861, B.A. 7 Feb. 1861, M.A. 30 June 1864; el. **1864,** vac. by m. 3 Aug. 1881 Sarah Octavia 3 d. of late Thomas Edward Scott J. P. of Carbrooke, Norfolk; re-elected for 7 years 30 June 1882, and again from 30 June 1889; Math. Moderator 1866–7, 1871, 1873–4, 1880, 1887, Math. Examiner 1877, Examiner for Univ. Math. Schol. 1869, 1871; wrote *Trilinear Coordinates* 1865.

Henry Walter **Moore** (1 s. John Walter, scholar 1833, by Frances Marianne); **M.** Merton 9 July 1859 age 17, postmaster 1860–4, 2 Classics Mod. 1861, 2 Classics 1863; el. **1864,** B.A. 10 Oct. 1864, M.A. 28 June 1866, d. 4 Oct. 1866 of fever at Hordley Rectory, Salop; Gent. Mag. 1866 ii. 703.

Paul Ferdinand **Willert** (o. s. Paul Ferdinand, d. 1879, by Susan Preston d. of Thomas Hanway Beale), b. Chetham, Manchester 29 May 1844, ed. Eton 1859, **M.** Balliol 20 Oct. 1862, scholar of Corpus 1864–7, Taylorian scholar 1863; 2 Classics Mod. 1864, 1 Classics 1866, B.A. 21 Feb. 1867, el. 1 July **1867,** vac. by m. Adel, near Leeds 5 July 1881 Henrietta d. of John Crofts; re-elected for 5 years 30 June 1882, and again 1887 ; his d. Dorothy bap. in the Chapel 20 Mch 1886 ; M.A. 22 Ap. 1869, barrister I. T. 1870, Assist. Master at

Eton; repeatedly Examiner; Dean to 1892, Tutor; wrote *The Reign of Lewis XI* 1876, *Henri IV* 1893.

George **Nutt** (1 s. George, V. of Shaw and Whitley, Wilts), b. Erlestoke, Wilts 12 Jan. 1846, ed. Winchester 1858, M. New Coll. 14 Oct. 1864, scholar 1864–9, proximè for Hertford 1865, 1 Classics Mod. 1866, Gaisford prize for verse 1866, 1 Classics 1868, Craven Scholar 1869, B.A. 4 Feb. 1869; el. **1869**, vac. by m. Weston-super-mare 26 July 1877 Diana Elizabeth d. of late Francis Reynolds archdeacon of Bombay; classical lecturer 1869, M.A. 22 June 1871, Master at Cheltenham 1870–4, at Rugby 1874.

Henry Francis **Pelham** (1 s. John Thomas, bishop of Norwich, by Henrietta Tatton), b. Bergh Apton, Norfolk 19 Sep. 1846, ed. Harrow 1860–4, M. Trinity 22 Ap. 1865, scholar 1865–69; 1 Classics Mod. 1866, 1 Classics 1869, B.A. 17 June 1869; el. **1869,** vac. by m. 30 July 1873 Laura Priscilla 3 d. of Sir Edward North Buxton; re-elected for 7 years 30 June 1882, and for 5 years 1889, tutor 1882–9, University Reader in Ancient Hist. 28 May 1887, vac. fellowship by being el. Camden Professor of Ancient History 29 Oct. 1889, and fellow of Brasenose; English Essay 1870, M.A. 7 Mch 1872, Proctor 1879, Member of Hebdomadal Council 1881–7; Classical Examiner 1878, 1881, 1884; Curator of the Parks 1879, of University Galleries 1885, of Bodleian 1892: F.S.A. 1890; a governor of Harrow; wrote in Encycl. Brit. ed. 9, articles *Roman History, Livy, Polybius, Nero, Otho, Nerva*; in Dict. Ant. ed. 2, *Princeps, Principatus, Senatus; The Imperial Domains and the Colonate* 1892, *Outlines of Roman History*, 1893.

Arthur Edward **Donkin** (2 s. Prof. William Fishburn), b. S. Peter's Port, Guernsey 19 July 1847, ed. Eton, M. Univ. Coll. 14 Ap. 1866 age 18, scholar, 1 Math. Mod. 1867, 1 Math. 1869, B.A. 17 June 1869; el. **1870,** vac. by m. 22 Dec. 1875 Mary Florence d. of Bridges Taylor and granddaughter of Sir Hugh Halkett; M.A. 28 Nov. 1872, tutor Keble 1874–5, Math. Master at Rugby 1875 and Housemaster 1884.

Edwin Ray **Lankester** (s. Edwin M.D. of London, by Phebe Pope), b. 15 May 1847, ed. S. Paul's sch. 1858, minor scholar of Downing, Camb. 1864; junior student of Ch. Ch. 1866, 1 Phys. 1868, B.A. 5 Nov. 1868; Burdett-Coutts scholar 1869, Radcliffe Travelling Fellow 1870; el. **1872,** under special statute as Teacher of Biology, vac. by lapse of time 2 May 1879; hon. fellow 1889; M.A. 6 July 1872, F.R.S. 3 June 1874; Royal medallist of the Royal

Society 1885; Professor of Zoology and Comparative Anatomy in University College, London; Deputy Linacre Professor (in Moseley's place) June 1890, Professor Dec. 1891 and fellow of Merton; edited transl. of *Haeckel's History of Creation* 2 vols., and of *Gegenbaur's Comparative Anatomy*; published monograph on the *Cephalaspidian Fishes* for Palaeontographical Society; in 1890 *The Advancement of Science, occasional Essays and Addresses*; and *Zoological Articles* (from Encycl. Brit. ed. 9); for numerous papers see Catalogue of Scientific Papers published by the Royal Society. From 1870 he has edited the Quarterly Journal of Microscopical Science.

Henry **Broadbent** (1 s. John, surgeon, by Alice Sophia d. of Thomas Smith Woolley), b. South Collingham, Notts 8 Feb. 1852, ed. Newark, **M.** 29 Jan. 1870, scholar 1869; el. 2 Feb. **1869** under special statute, full Fellow 1874; 1 Classics Mod. 1871, 1 Classics 1874: Ireland scholar 1873, Craven scholar 1874, Derby scholar 1875, Latin Essay 1875; B.A. 18 June 1874, M.A. 3 June 1876; Master at Eton 1876, m. Sessay, Yorks. 28 Ap. 1886 Alice Jane 1 d. of George Richard Dupuis R. of Sessay.

Henry Nottidge **Moseley** (1 s. Henry, F.R.S., V. of Olveston and canon of Bristol, by Harriet Nottidge), b. Wandsworth 14 Nov. 1844, ed. Harrow, **M.** 2 Feb. 1864, el. **1876** under special statute to a fellowship for Physical Science; 1 Phys. 1868, B.A. 18 June 1868, M.A. 6 July 1872; Radcliffe Travelling Fellow 1869, Member of the Eclipse Exhibition to Ceylon 1871, Naturalist to the Challenger Expedition 1872–6, on which he published 'Notes' 1879, ed. 2 1892 (with memoir by Gilbert Charles Bourne of New Coll.); F.R.S. 7 June 1877, Croonian Lecturer to the Royal Society 1878; Deputy Registrar of London University 1879–81; m. S. George's Hanover Sq. 24 Feb. 1881 Amabel Nevill y. d. of J. Gwyn Jeffreys LL.D., of Ware Priory; Linacre Professor of Anatomy Oxford 25 Nov. 1881 and fellow of Merton June 1882, d. Clevedon 10 Nov. 1891; for his papers see Philosophical Transactions, Quarterly Journal of Microscopical Science, Journal of Anthropological Institute, Annals and Mag. of Nat. Hist. Transactions of Linnean Society; he also wrote a small work on *Oregon* 1878; Nat. Biog. An etching of him is in the Common Room.

Lewis Richard **Farnell** (2 s. John Wilson, by Harriet d. of John Pritchard), b. Salisbury 19 Jan. 1856, ed. City of London sch., **M.** 17 Oct. 1874, 1 Classics Mod. 1875, 1 Classics 1878, B.A. 10 Oct. 1878, M.A. 10 Oct. 1881; el. **1880**, subrector 1883–93, tutor 1884, dean

1893; curator of Univ. Galleries; m. S. Peter's, Cranley Gardens, London 29 June 1893 Sylvia y. d. of capt. Christopher Baldock Cardew, of E. Liss, Hants, by Eliza Jane 1 d. of Lord Westbury, b. 14 Jan. 1872; wrote on *The Religion of the Greek States.*

William Mitchell **Ramsay** (3 s. Thomas, by Jane d. of William Mitchell of Alloa), b. Glasgow 15 Mch 1851, ed. Alloa, and Aberdeen Univ., **M.** S. John's 12 Oct. 1872, scholar 1872–77, 1 Classics Mod. 1874, 1 Classics 1876, B.A. 1879; el. **1882** under conditions of archaeological research, M.A. 23 Oct. 1884; Lincoln Professor of Archaeology and fellow 7 Feb. 1885, Prof. of Humanity at Aberdeen 1886; m. 28 Oct. 1878 Agnes Dick d. of Rev. William Marshall of Kirkintilloch; he described his repeated journies to Asia Minor in the Journal of Hellenic Studies and other archaeological journals, and *On the early historical relations between Phrygia and Cappadocia* 1883, *The historical geography of Asia Minor* 1890 (R. Geog. Soc. Suppl. Papers vol. iv), *The Church in the Roman Empire before* A. D. 170, 1893.

William **Sanday** (1 s. William, by Elizabeth d. of George Mann of Scawsby, Doncaster), b. Holme Pierrepont, Notts 1 Aug. 1843, ed. Repton, **M.** Balliol 1 Feb. 1862, scholar of Corpus 1863–6, 1 Classics Mod. 1863, 1 Classics 1865, B.A. 1866, fellow of Trinity 1866–74, president Oxf. Union Soc. 1867, M.A. 1868, lecturer in Theology 1875–6; Tutorial fellow Ex. Coll. for 5 years 6 July **1883,** re-elected 30 June 1888; Ireland Professor of Exegesis 1882, Bampton Lecturer 1893; V. of Great Waltham, Essex 1872–3, R. of Barton on the Heath, Warwicks. 1873–6, Principal of Hatfield Hall, Durham, 1876–83; Theol. Examiner Oxf. 1876–7, Exam. chaplain to Bishop of Durham 1879–81, Select Preacher Camb. 1880, Whitehall Preacher 1889; D.D. Edinburgh 1877, Durham 1882, hon. LL.D. Dublin 1887; m. 10 July 1877 Marian Charlotte Amelia 1 d. of Warren Hastings Woodman Hastings, J.P. of Twyring, Tewkesbury, grandson of only sister of Warren Hastings; wrote *Authorship and Historical Character of the Fourth Gospel* 1872, *The Gospels in the Second Century* 1876, *Romans and Galatians* (in Ellicott's Commentary) 1878, joint editor of *Variorum Bible* 1880–9, joint editor (with Bishop of Salisbury) of *Old Latin Biblical Texts,* ii. 1886.

Archibald Barwell **How** (2 s. William, by Louisa d. of Rev. R. Ardill), b. London 29 Mch 1860, King's scholar Eton 1872–9, **M.** 15 Oct. 1879, scholar 1879–84, 2 Classics Mod. 1880, 1 Classics 1883, B.A. 10 Oct. 1883, M.A. 28 Ap. 1886; lecturer 1884, Tutorial fellow **1886,** dean to 1892, bursar 1892.

William Walrond Jackson (Fellow 1863), el. Rector 15 Ap. 1887.

Charles Henry **Roberts** (1 s. Albert James, of Tidebrook, Sussex, by Ellen d. of Rev. H. R. Wace), b. Tidebrook 22 Aug. 1865, ed. Marlborough, M. Balliol 15 Oct. 1884, scholar, 1 Classics Mod. 1886, 1 Classics 1888, 2 Hist. 1889, B.A. 1890; Tutorial fellow Ex. Coll. 17 Mch **1890**, M.A. 1892, vac. by m. Lanercost 7 Ap. 1891 Lady Cecilia Howard 2 d. of Earl of Carlisle; lecturer at Balliol 1893.

Robert Ranulph **Marett** (o. s. Sir Robert Pipon Marett, Bailiff of Jersey), b. S. Brelade 13 June 1866, ed. Victoria Coll., M. Balliol 22 Jan. 1885, senior exhibitioner 1884, at Inner Temple 1885, 1 Classics Mod. 1886, mentioned for the Hertford 1886; Latin Verse 1887, 1 Classics 1888, B.A. 1889; proximè for English Essay 1889; Tutorial fellow Ex. Coll. **1891**, M.A. 1891, Dean 1892–3, Subrector 1893; Green Essay 1893.

HONORARY FELLOWS.

Besides six ex-fellows, Lord Coleridge, Jas. A. Froude, W. Ince, Bishop Ridding, Edwin Ray Lankester, H. Fanshawe Tozer, these include

Edward Coley Burne Jones (o. s. Edward Richard), b. S. Philip's, Birmingham Aug. 1833, ed. King Edward's sch., M. 2 June 1852, D.C.L. 22 June 1881, hon. Fellow **1882**, A.R.A. 1885, res. 1893; President of Royal Birmingham Society of Artists 1885. Dublin Univ. Mag. xciv. 40 (portrait). *Edward Burne Jones, a Record and Review*, with 100 illustrations, by Malcolm Bell 1892. He painted for the Chapel a picture of the Visit of the Magi, which has been executed in tapestry by William Morris; resides The Grange, W. Kensington Road, London W.

William Morris (1 s. late William, d. 1884), b. S. John's, Walthamstow, Essex 24 Mch 1834, ed. Marlborough, M. 2 June 1852, B.A. 1856, M.A. 1875, poet and artist, hon. Fellow **1882**; resides Kelmscot house, Upper Mall, Hammersmith.

Frederick Temple (3 s. Octavius, by Dorcas Carveth), b. Santa Maura, Ionian Islands 30 Nov. 1821, ed. Tiverton, M. Balliol 12 Oct. 1838, 1 Classics and 1 Math. 1842, B.A. 18 May 1842, fellow 1842–8, M.A. 11 Mch 1847, B. and D.D. 1858; bishop of Exeter 1869–85, of London 1885, hon. Fellow 24 Ap. **1885**; Coll. Corn. 975.

Adolf Neubauer, b. 13 Mch 1832, ed. Univ. Munich, Sublibrarian of Bodleian 1873, M.A. Ex. Coll. by diploma 18 Feb. 1873, hon. Fellow **1890**; Reader in Rabbinical Literature 1884, D. Phil. Leipzig,

Hon. D. Phil. Heidelberg 1890, Member of the Academia de l'historia Madrid; wrote *Hist. of Hebrew Geography* in French 1862, *Aus der Petersburger Bibliothek* in German 1866, *Hist. of the Karaites*; *La Géographie du Talmud* (couronné par l'Académie des Inscriptions) 1868, *The Earliest Samaritan Chronicle with an Arabic and a French translation* 1872, *Jewish Interpretation of* 53 *Isaiah*, (1) texts, Hebrew, Arabic, Persian, Spanish, Portuguese, (2) Dr. Driver's translation 1876, *Rabbins Français du xiii Siècle* (Hist. Litt. de la France 27) 1876, *Tobit Chaldee text*, Clarendon Press 1878, *Abul Walid's Hebrew Dictionary* in Arabic (book of roots) Clar. Press 1876, *Catalogue of Hebrew MSS. in Bodleian with Palaeographical Atlas* 1886, *Jewish Mediaeval Chronicle* (Anecdota Oxoniensia) 1889; Contributions to Studia Biblica (1) *Language of the Jews in the time of Christ*; (2) *Headings and Authorship of the Psalms*; (3) *On the square character introduced in the place of the Aramaic character, and the history of the earliest Hebrew MSS. of the Bible*; *The Jews in Oxford* (O. H. Soc., Collectanea ii) 1890.

PERPETUAL RECTORS.

1566 John Neale	1733 Joseph Atwell
1570 Robert Newton	1737 James Edgcumbe
1578 Thomas Glasier	1750 Francis Webber
1592 Thomas Holland	1771 Thomas Bray
1612 John Prideaux	1785 Thomas Stinton
1642 George Hakewill	1797 Henry Richards
1649 John Conant	1808 John Cole
1662 Joseph Maynard	1819 John Collier Jones
1666 Arthur Bury	1838 Joseph Loscombe Richards
1690 William Paynter	1854 John Prideaux Lightfoot
1716 Matthew Hole	1887 William Walrond Jackson
1730 John Conybeare	

SCHOLARS, EXHIBITIONERS, AND BIBLE CLERKS[1].

Scholar originally meant Fellow. Scholars in the modern sense do not occur till a late period (Shadwell's *Reg. Orielense*, pref.). We find exhibitioners perhaps earlier. A bible clerk is mentioned in 1403, 1529, and 1621.

Sir John Acland, besides contributing to the New Hall, gave £16 a year to two scholars at the College, Izacke's Register 1736 p. 11; and William Jesse, fellow 1639, is called *pensionarius Aclandianus* in 1632.

Robert Vilvaine, fellow, founded in 1637 4 exhibitions of £32 each yearly, to be paid through the Rector and Subrector; 2 from the High School and 2 from the Free Grammar School at Exeter, to be held for 7 years during residence without other preferment.

On 20 June 1877, in reply to the Visitor, the College did not oppose the Acland Exhibitions being made tenable at any University or other place of higher education; but, if the exhibitioner should come to Oxford, required that he should enter at Exeter College. It took no action as to the Vilvaine Exhibitions.

In 1622 (State Papers 27 Sep.) Thomas Stevens' sister was to pay £330 for her husband's legacies, viz. £100 to maintain poor scholars at Exeter College, £100 to the University Library, £100 to S. Michael's, where his son lay buried, £20 for a scaffold for scholars in that church, £10 to Dr. Prideaux.

Samuel Hill in 1634 gave £100, to relieve poor scholars and servitors, including at least 2 from Devon and 2 from Cornwall, by gifts of 30 shillings a year; Gutch iii. 106.

Robert Michell founded by will, 28 Mch 1641, an exhibition for which he gave the rent of 6 acres called Wild Arish in Withecombe Raleigh, 'the profits to be divided at Michaelmas among such poor scholars of the College as be servitors and apply themselves to the study of divinity.'

John Darell or Darrell, s. Edward of West Retford, Notts, **M.** Lincoln

---

[1] The letters B.C., Ch. I., Exh., Hist., Nat. Sci., Nat. Sci. Exh., Org., Stap., stand respectively for Bible Clerk, Channel Islands, Open Exhibition, Modern History, Natural Science, Natural Science Exhibition, Organist, Stapeldon; O. after another symbol means 'Open *pro hac vice*.'

24 Nov. 1637 age 16, B.A. 3 July 1641. He founded by will, dated 11 Nov. 1664, 'out of the lands which he himself had purchased,' an exhibition for 'some ingenious scholar whose father hath not above £30 per annum in land or estate, to be chosen out of Lincolnshire and Notts, upon the election of the Master of Retford Hospital [now the Subdean of Lincoln] and the Archdeacon of Nottingham, the same scholar to be admitted and educated in Exeter College, Oxford'; it is for Lincoln and Notts alternately; the property is quite distinct from the property of Retford Hospital, see Reg. 15 May 1793. It was long before the property was so applied. The first exhibitioner noticed is in 1705. The present rental is £75 10s., chiefly from 6 houses in a court at Retford, and a few acres of land in W. Retford parish.

Meriel Symes of Barwick, Som., y. d. of Sir John Horner of Mells, Som. by Ann Speke, b. 1635, d. 1717 (Misc. Gen. 1882 iv. 163), widow of Thomas Symes and mother of John Symes (who d. 6 July 1687 age 20, and was buried in the south aisle of the College Chapel), founded an exhibition for the maintenance of a poor scholar at Exeter College by deed dated 7 Nov. 1710; open to members of the College being of the kindred of John Symes, or, in default of such, to poor scholars born in Somerset or Dorset; in default of such, to natives of those counties at any other College; in default of such, to any poor scholar of Exeter College; the scholar must be examined touching his learning and abilities, and must intend to study divinity, and may hold the scholarship for eight years, unless otherwise provided for, but must reside without being absent above forty days in any one year, except in case of sickness, and even then the Rector must approve the cause of his absence; each scholar is to have the sums accruing during a previous vacancy, but, if the scholar becomes a Fellow of any College, he receives half the sums accruing during his year of proba-tion, the other half going to the College Treasury. But if the scholar at the end of five years is not able to render any chapter of the Greek Testament into Latin and also any chapter in the Hebrew Pentateuch (upon examination by the Bishop of Bath and Wells, or some one appointed by him), the scholarship shall be void. The College may make leases of the lands for 21 years, but it must be at the full value &c. Meriel's own kin, the Horners, were included (see the Horner pedigree in Hutchins ii. 667); and, as her sister Ann married John Harington of Kelston near Bath, the Haringtons were admitted, though John Harington seems to have only had a daughter Ann (who married Sir Robert Chaplyn) by Ann Horner, and the rest of his children were by his three other wives, Misc. Gen. 1881 p. 23. Meriel (who d. 30 Mch 1813 age 78), great granddaughter of Meriel Symes' brother Sir George Horner, married John Williams of Herringstone, and their granddaughter Elizabeth Williams married R. A. Burney, which admitted the Burneys. Meriel Symes herself named the first scholar; the land she gave consisted of three undivided parts in ten of Norwood Park called Shortwood, a mile from Glastonbury, containing by estimate 142 acres, together with the tithes thereof. The scholarship is now held for 5 years (since 1875), and is divided into two.

John Reynolds, 1 s. of John Reynolds (d. 1692), and uncle of Sir Joshua Reynolds, b. 9 July 1671, fellow of King's Camb., B.D. Oxford 7 Oct. 1718, Master of Exeter sch. 1713–33, fellow of Eton 1734, canon of Exeter 1743, d. 27 June 1758, his will is dated 27 Feb. 1756, W. Antiq. iv. 24, v. 113. He founded 6 exhibitions, 3 from Eton, and 3 from Exeter School, nominated alternately by the Chapter and Chamber of Exeter, tenable till the holders were 24 : the words of his will are ' that are designed for Clergymen to complete their education at Exeter College, preferably to all others if they can be accommodated there.'

The Rev. St. John Eliot founded 2 exhibitions of £30 each for candidates from Truro gr. sch.; the electors, after the death of his trustees, to be the Schoolmaster and the Vicars of Kenwyn, Gluvias and Veryan. The money was in the 3 per cents. Candidates were to have been 3 years at Truro School and to be members of Exeter College. The arrangements were settled by decree in Chancery 14 Mch 1767, see Allen's Liskeard 174–8, R.I.C.x. 423, Coll. Corn. 234, 1388, 1393. Latterly the money has been given in small sums to boys at the school or at parish schools with little beneficial result.

William Gifford in 1827 founded 2 Gifford Exhibitions of £30 each, Reg. 1827 p. 12, and 25 June 1832. By his will he left for this purpose £2000 in the 3 per cents. The exhibitions were to be given to youths educated at Ashburton gr. sch. or, in default of such, to youths of the County of Devon. On the evidence of Dr. Ireland Dean of Westminster, Gifford's friend and executor, Chancery by decree dated 8 Nov. 1831 settled the preference given to mean 'born, or educated (in part or wholly) in Devon.' There is no limitation of age or standing, under the degree of B.A. The exhibitions are tenable for four years, and dividends accumulated during vacancies are to be invested for the fund.

Thomas How of Balliol, R. of Huntspill, Som., who d. 15 Mch 1819, founded an exhibition at Balliol. On Balliol declining the gift, it was transferred to Exeter by decree of Chancery 4 Mch 1831. It was for sons of Clergy resident in Somerset and Devon, alternately, provided they were actually members of the College, and under 19, and was tenable till the holders were of standing for M.A., or were elected Fellows of the College, or ceased to be members of the College. The sum given was £2400 in the new 3½ per cents. The exhibition was divided into two in 1863.

Joseph Loscombe Richards, Rector 1838, left by will £350 in 3 per cent. bank annuities to found a divinity prize (Reg. 1836 p. 46–48 his letter and extract from his will, and p. 197); and the reversion, after his sister's death, of some fields in Kidlington (Hist. of Kidlington 137) to found an exhibition for a poor scholar, already matriculated at the College. His friends subscribed £644 18s., which bought £707 8s. 11d. in the funds, to found an exhibition for any poor scholar.

Mr. George Redsull Carter of Deal, who d. 13 Feb. 1879, founded, by will dated 11 Ap. 1873, proved 24 Mch 1879, a scholarship of the value of £80 a year, for which persons born in the County of Kent, who are already members of the College, have a preference *ceteris paribus*. Subject to this reservation the scholarship is open. He made a similar bequest to S. Peter's Cambridge, and the sum divided between the two Colleges was £4139 1s. 2d.

Miss Marianne Hasker, of 61 Eversfield Place, S. Leonard's-on-Sea, founded 2 Hasker Scholarships in 1883 for divinity students. She gave these and a stained glass window Jan. 1855, in memory of her father the Rev. George Henry Hasker who d. 26 Sep. 1881, and her mother Sarah Anne Hasker (1 d. James Jell Chalke, of Sheppey), who d. 9 Jan. 1883. George Henry Hasker, o. s. Thomas of Loughton, Essex, b. 10 Ap. 1794, ed. Winchester, M. 9 Dec. 1813, 2 Classics 1816, B.A. 24 Ap. 1817, at Lincoln's Inn 1815.

In 1831 the Bible Clerkship was suspended (Reg. 9 Feb.; and 7 Ap. 1841). It was restored 13 Nov. 1841, when an anonymous gift of £50 was made through Robert Jefferies Spranger. In 1862 it was made into two open exhibitions for poor scholars. The clerk used to dine off the joint that came from the High Table.

There were no open scholarships till 1831, when the College founded 4 of £30 a year each, tenable for 4 years, and open to all candidates above the age of 16. But the University Commission of

1854 threw the fellowships open, and (Reg. p. 205, New Ordinance of 9 Oct. 1855) suppressed 10, partly to found scholarships, 10 Open, 10 Stapeldon for (in the first place) the diocese of Exeter, and 2 for the Channel Islands; the first election of scholars under the new Ordinance was held 1856. In 1882 the numbers were made 12 Open and 8 Stapeldon. The College besides gives some scholarships or exhibitions for Modern History and for Natural Science.

Only a few names occur before 1705. William Jesse, fellow 1639, is called *pensionarius Aclandianus.* As the College does not appoint to some of the exhibitions, no list was kept; in fact, the authorities have not always been informed who hold the exhibitions. Unfortunately the schools also have no complete lists.

William **Rowland** (s. Griffin, pleb., of Worcester), at Ex. Coll. 1627 age 17, **B.C. 1631, M.** 3 Feb. 163½ age 21, B.A. 24 Mch 163½, M.A. 5 Dec. 1634, C. of S. Margaret's, Westminster under the Commonwealth, seceded to Rome, d. Vambre near Paris 1659; Prideaux' *Survey*, Athenae iii. 486, 649–50.

Gervis **Raynes** (s. Edward, of Ordsall, Notts), poor scholar 12 Mch 169⁴⁄₈ to 12 July 1699, **M.** 4 Dec. 1694 age 16, B.A. 1 Feb. 169⁹⁄₈, **Darell 1705.**

John **Lacy** (s. James, V. of Sherborne, Hutchins iv. 264), sojourner 25 June 1713, caution repaid 10 Dec. 1719, **M.** 25 June 1713 age 16, **Symes** 30 June **1713,** appointed by the Foundress; B.A. 10 May 1717, d. 23 Mch 1719 age 23; see Reg. 2 Oct. 1862; Gutch i. 119.

George **Lacy, Symes** 14 Ap. **1719** in place of his brother John; sojourner 10 Dec. 1719 to 20 Jan. 172⅔, **M.** 14 Dec. 1719 age 16, B.A. 13 June 1723, M.A. 28 June 1726; ? instit. to R. of Melbury Sampford and to Melbury Osmond 19 Nov. 1726; and V. of Stinsford 15 Jan. 1739, all in Dorset; R. of Silverton, Devon 1750; d. 1761; Hutchins ii. 442, 569, 681.

Robert **Westley** (s. Rev. Thomas, of Berkley, Som.), **Symes** 30 June **1727,** battellar 7 July 1727 to 14 July 1732, **M.** 3 July 1727 age 13 ; deprived 29 Ap. 1733, a notice fixed on the College gates 15 Mch summoning him to return into residence having proved fruitless.

George **Widdowson** (s. George, pleb., of Tuxford, Notts), **Darell** **1729,** poor scholar 26 June 1729 to 28 Mch 1734, **M.** 1 July 1729 age 20, vac. 1742 : B.A. 13 Ap. 1733.

George **Upton** (s. Rev. James, of Bishopshull, Som., and brother of Francis, fellow 1741), b. Taunton, sojourner 1 Ap. 1731 to 21 July

1740, and 24 Jan. to 3 Feb. 1752, **M.** 1 Ap. 1731 age 17; **Symes** 30 June 1733, res. 18 June 1741; B.A. 12 Oct. 1734, M.A. 10 June 1737; R. of Seavington with Dinnington, Som. 28 Feb. 1737 on cession of John Upton, patron John Lord Poulet.

Neville **Wells** (s. Dr. Thomas, V. of Frome), bap. 9 July 1724, ed. Winchester 1737, battellar 23 June 1741 to 22 July 1748, **M.** 26 June 1741, **Symes** 30 June 1741, B.A. 3 May 1745, M.A. 23 Mch 174⅞; res. 20 June 1749: Hutchins ii. 667; Master of Farley Hospital, and R. of Grinstead, Wilts 1768 till his death in 1801; Phillipps ii. 83, 102.

John **Frost** (s. John, pleb., of Granby, Notts), b. Barnston, Notts, **M.** Lincoln 19 May 1740 age 21; sojourner 28 Oct. 1740 to 30 May 1750, **Darell 1742,** named by archdeacon of Notts; B.A. 26 Jan. 174¾, M.A. 11 Oct. 1746.

John **Harington** (s. John, of Corston, Som.), b. 26 Mch 1732, sojourner 11 May 1749 to 4 July 1754, and 15 Nov. 1754 to 17 Ap. 1756, and 2 to 5 Jan. 1759, **M.** 11 May 1749, **Symes** 30 June 1749; res. 1756; m. Rachel 1 d. of H. Hawes R. of Bemerton, Wilts; B.A. 10 Ap. 1753, M.A. 8 Ap. 1756, B. and D.D. 17 Ap. 1771, perhaps V. of Bickleigh, Devon 14 June 1756, res. 1760, W. Antiq. vii. 214; R. of Chalbury, Dorset 1766, of Thruxton near Andover, preb. of Yatesbury, d. Thruxton, bur. S. Edmund's, Salisbury 10 June 1795; Hutchins iii. 118; Maclean iii. 260; Misc. Geneal. Nov. 1882 p. 275; see 1791.

Edmund **Brown** (s. Paul, of Butterwick, Lincs.), b. Lincoln, sojourner 24 May 1754 to 7 Mch 1758, **M.** 25 May 1754 age 18, adm. **Darell** 25 May 1754, named by George Reynolds, Master of Retford Hospital, and subdean of Lincoln; B.A. 7 Feb. 1758; testimonials for orders 9 Feb. 1758.

Samuel **Horner** (s. Samuel, of S. George's, London), b. Frome, Som., battellar 18 Mch 1755 to 1 Mch 1760, **M.** 19 Mch 1755 age 20, el. **Symes** 30 June and adm. 5 July 1756; d. 1760; Hutchins ii. 667.

John **Comyns** (s. John, of Bishops Teignton), **M.** Balliol 18 Mch 1758 age 19; sojourner Ex. Coll. 30 Mch 1759 to 23 May 1766, **Reynolds 1758,** named by the Chapter of Exeter, B.A. 4 Dec. 1761.

Samuel **Cooke** (s. John, of Exeter), sojourner 20 Mch 1758 to 29 Dec. 1761, **M.** 18 Mch 1758 age 18, **Reynolds 1758,** named by the Chamber of Exeter 8 Mch 17⅝⁹₆₀, B.A. 17 Dec. 1761, R. of Cottisford, Oxon 11 Ap. 1769, V. of Great Bookham, Surrey 1770–1820, d. Bookham 30 Mch 1820.

John **Wood** (s. Joseph, of Milton, Som.), sojourner 2 July 1760 to 5 July 1764, **M.** Balliol 29 Nov. 1758 age 17; **Symes** 30 June 1760; B.A. 18 June 1762, d. 1767.

James **Watts** (s. John, of London), b. Middlesex, sojourner 1 Nov. 1760 to 6 Jan. 1762, adm. **Reynolds** 1 Nov. 1760, **M.** 10 Nov. 1760 age 20, left 6 Jan. 1762.

Joshua **Sampson** (s. Rev. Joshua, of Retford), sojourner 13 Dec. 1762 to 26 June 1766, adm. **Darell** 6 and **M.** 9 Nov. 1762 age 20; B.A. 28 May 1766, M.A. 11 July 1769, M.B. 13 July 1772, M.D. 18 June 1776; R. of South Otterington, Yorks. 1796–1828; m. 29 Jan. 1793 Mary d. of Thomas Bramley of South Otterington.

Charles **Rugge** (s. William, of Westminster), ed. Eton, adm. **Reynolds** 10 Dec. 1762, **M.** 15 Dec. 1762 age 20, sojourner 19 Feb. 1763 to 24 July 1767, B.A. 6 June 1766; d. 1773.

Charles **Churchill** (s. John, of Exeter), adm. 24 and **M.** 28 Feb. 1763 age 17, **Reynolds** 12 Mch 1763, named by Chapter of Exeter, battellar 28 Feb. 1763 to 6 Dec. 1768, B.A. 23 Mch 1771.

John **Gibbons** (s. Alexander, of Hatherley), **M.** 10 Oct. 1763 age 17, named by Chamber of Exeter 3 and adm. 12 Oct.: battellar 26 Jan. 1764 to 15 June 1768, B.A. 19 June 1767, M.A. 27 June 1770; testimonials for orders 15 June 1768.

Robert **Westcott** (s. Rev. John, of Lyng and of Hatch Beauchamp, Som.), battellar 21 Mch 1765 to 14 Nov. 1777, **M.** 21 Mch 1765 age 17, **Symes** 11 Mch 1767; B.A. 1 Feb. 1769; testimonials for deacon's orders 16 Feb. 1769.

William **Salkeld,** named **Reynolds** 27 July and adm. 16 Oct. **1767,** Fellow 1771.

Robert **Pugh** (s. Hugh, pleb., of Dolgelley), ed. Truro, battellar 26 Mch 1768 to 23 May 1772, **Eliot; M.** 26 Mch 1768 age 19, B.A. 29 Feb. 1772, C. of Weston, P.C. of Lee Brockhurst, Salop, V. of Donnington, Lincs. 1794–1825, d. Whixhall near Wem, Salop 16 Feb. 1825 age 77; Gent. Mag. 1825 i. 474.

James **Ferris** (s. John, of Truro), battellar 26 Mch 1768 to 7 Nov. 1771, **Eliot; M.** 26 Mch 1768 age 19.

John Cope **Westcott** (s. Rev. John, of Lyng, and of Hatch Beauchamp), battellar 30 Mch 1770 to 23 Feb. 1774, **B.C., M.** 26 Mch 1770 age 18, B.A. 12 Feb. 1774; R. of Ruddington, Notts, and of Hatch Beauchamp, Som. 1784.

William **Smith,** sojourner 20 Oct. 1769 to 9 July 1772, named **Reynolds** 26 Feb. 1770; Fellow 1772.

Thomas **Donnithorne** (s. Richard, of Truro), sojourner 30 Mch 1770 to 23 Feb. 1774, **Eliot, M.** 26 Mch 1770 age 18 ; B.A. 12 Feb. 1774, V. of Cuckney, and R. of Holmepierrepont, Notts July 1797, m. Mary 4 d. of John Penrose V. of Gluvias ; Gent. Mag. 1797, 67 ii. 626.

John **Penrose,** sojourner 18 May 1771 to 7 July 1774, **Eliot 1770 ;** Fellow 1774.

Ames **Crymes** (s. Rev. Ames, of Buckland Monachorum), b. Oxford, sojourner 30 Mch 1770 to 23 Feb. 1774, **M.** 29 Mch 1770 age 20, named **Reynolds** 7 July 1770, B.A. 12 Feb. 1774.

John **Hodge** (s. John, of Clyst-Honiton), sojourner 17 Dec. 1770 to 10 Ap. 1772, **Reynolds, M.** 17 Dec. 1770 age 18, V. of Cullompton 12 June 1830, d. 10 Oct. 1833.

John **Cole, Eliot 1771,** Fellow 1778, Rector 1808.

Richard **Vivian, Eliot 1771,** Fellow 1774.

Francis **Moore** (s. of Rev. William, of South Tawton), named **Reynolds** 7 Nov. 1772, sojourner 13 Mch 1773 to 20 Feb. 1778, **M.** 13 Mch 1773 age 17, B.A. 8 Feb. 1777, M.A. 18 Nov. 1779, R. of Inwardleigh, d. 25 Aug. 1795.

John **Blake** (s. Nicholas, pleb., of N. Molton, Devon), battellar 21 June 1773 to 31 Jan. 1777, **B.C., M.** 21 June 1773 age 18.

Robert **Dodge** (s. Rev. Robert, of Plymouth), named **Reynolds** 12 Mch 1774, sojourner 18 June to 1 Sep. 1774, **M.** 18 June 1774 age 16 ; B.A. Queen's 7 May 1778, M.A. 31 May 1781.

John **Pearson** (s. Rev. Robert, of Crewkerne and W. Camell, Som.), **M.** Wadham 27 May 1773 age 18 ; **B.C.,** battellar 11 May 1775 to 22 Ap. 1777, B.A. 14 Mch 1777, chaplain of Piddington, Oxon, ed. bishop Pearson's *Twelve Sermons* Buckingham 1803.

Samuel **Johnson** (s. William, pleb.), b. Great Torrington, **M.** Pemb. 23 Mch 1771 age 17 ; sojourner 4 Nov. 1775 to 4 Feb. 1777, and 6 July 1783, named **Reynolds** 19 Aug. 1775 ; see Pedigree of Colby 1884 p. 26.

Buckland **Bluett** (s. Gilbert), b. Taunton, battellar 5 Ap. 1773 to 4 Aug. 1777, commoner 22 Ap. to 4 Aug. 1777, and 10 May 1794 to 10 Mch 1795, **M.** 3 Ap. 1773 age 19, **Symes** 30 June 1775 ; B.A. 10 Oct. 1776, M.A. 10 Mch 1795, R. of Church Staunton 1784–1837, C. of Otterford 1817, d. Haygrass near Taunton 13 June 1837 age 83.

John **Cutler** (s. Roger, of Eton), sojourner 4 Nov. 1775 to 18 June 1779, **Reynolds, M.** 1 Nov. 1775 age 19; B.A. 9 June 1779 :

Master of Dorchester, and then of Sherborne, school; Hutchins iv. 290.

John **Comins** or Comyns (s. Thomas, of Witheridge, Devon, by Johanna), b. 28 Jan. 1759, **M.** Balliol 18 Oct. 1777; named **Reynolds** 24 and el. 28 Feb. 1778; B.A. 26 Ap. 1781.

Thomas' Smyth **Glubb,** sojourner 13 May 1777 to 11 July 1780, **Symes,** named 7 Aug. 1777, el. 30 June 1778, Fellow 1780.

John **Arthur** (s. John, of Truro, by Judith d. of Thomas Pellew), b. 1759, ed. Truro, sojourner 13 Ap. 1778 to 11 Mch 1782, and 16 May 1791, **Eliot, M.** 10 Ap. 1778, B.A. 9 Feb. 1782; V. of Little Colan, Cornwall 1790–1836, of S. Neot's, Hunts 1 Nov. 1806–1836, d. Little Colan 12 Dec. 1836; Polwhele's Biography, Bibl. Corn. 1036.

William **Gifford** (s. Edward; W. Antiq. x. 187, see his letters in Smiles' Life of John Murray ii. 163; ? great grandson of Roger Giffard sen. of Halsbury), b. Ashburton Ap. 1756, **B.C., M.** 16 Feb. 1779 age 21, 'but was excused from putting in any caution on account of his place,' B.A. 10 Oct. 1782, editor of the Antijacobin 1798, and the Quarterly Review from 1809 to 1824, trans. Juvenal, ed. Ben Jonson; d. London 31 Dec. 1826; Nat. Biog.

William **Rawlings** (s. William, of Padstow, who d. 1795, by Catherine), bap. S. Columb Major 3 June 1761, sojourner 13 Mch 1780 to 10 Mch 1784, **Eliot, M.** 11 Mch 1780; B.A. 26 Nov. 1783, V. of Padstow 1790–1836, m. Padstow 14 May 1787 Susanna d. of Peter Salmon; their d. Mary was bap. S. Columb Major 12 Sep. 1788. He d. 20 Dec. 1836 age 76, monu. at Padstow; his wife d. 3 Jan. 1821 age 57; Lake iv. 15, 16, Bibl. Corn. 550, Coll. Corn. 787, 1394.

Thomas **Jackson,** sojourner 20 Feb. 1777 to 5 July 1781, named **Reynolds** 25 Sep. 1779, Fellow 1781.

John **Whalley** (s. Daniel), b. Aldgate Without, London, ed. Eton, **M.** 14 July 1780 age 19, el. **Reynolds** July 1780, sojourner 2 Dec. 1780 to 12 Feb. 1785, B.A. 13 May 1784, M.A. 5 Feb. 1788; V. of Rushall, Staffs. 1807–1839, d. 12 July 1839.

William **Griffiths,** el. **Reynolds** Oct. 1780 from Eton, Fellow 1784.

William **Hayne** (s. Richard), b. Exeter, sojourner 22 Dec. 1780 to 28 June 1784, and 8 Mch 1811 to 26 June 1816, **M.** 9 Dec. 1780 age 17, el. **Reynolds** Dec. 1780, named 9 Jan. 1783 (?), B.A. 9 June 1784, M.A. 20 June 1811.

Henry **Parsons** (s. Rev. Francis, of Yeovil and Bridgwater), sojourner 13 Oct. 1781 to 17 Aug. 1787, el. **Symes** and **M**. 10 Oct. 1781 age 16, B.A. 21 June 1785; Fellow of Oriel 1787, M.A. 21 May 1788, R. of Goathurst 1789–1845, V. of Wembdon 1791, both in Som.; chaplain to Earl Poulett, preb. of Wells 20 Aug. 1791 *vice* Francis Crane Parsons; d. Goathurst 9 Jan. 1845 aged 80.

Richard Hawkin **Hitchins**, sojourner 23 Ap. 1781 to 4 July 1783, named **Reynolds** 25 Aug. 1781, Fellow 1783.

John **Vye**, named **Reynolds** 22 Mch 1783, sojourner 11 Mch 1782 to 9 July 1785, Fellow 1785.

Richard **Paul** (s. William), b. Trevarth house, Gwennap 1763, sojourner 11 Ap. 1781 to 24 Mch 1785, **Eliot, M**. 3 Ap. 1781 age 18; B.A. 3 Feb. 1785, R. of Mawgan in Pyder, Cornwall 1804, d. 7 Dec. 1805 age 42. His widow Frances d. of Robert Bateman M.D., of Queens', Camb., R. of S. Columb Major and of Mawgan in Pyder, d. 25 Oct. 1819 age 51; Lake iii. 291, 293; Coll. Corn. 662.

John Neville **Freeman**, adm. **Reynolds** 13 Dec. 1782, Fellow 1787.

Thomas **Roberts** (s. Thomas, of Denbigh), b. Llanbedrog, Carnarvon, ed. Eton, **M**. Jesus 16 May 1782 age 19; adm. **Reynolds** 19 July 1783, commoner Mich. 1783 to 12 Mch 1790, B.A. 18 Dec. 1786, M.A. 12 June 1789, testimonials for priest's orders 11 May 1789.

Henry **Dillon** (s. Henry, of Penryn), commoner 20 Mch 1782 to 11 July 1786, **Eliot, M**. 20 Mch 1782 age 18; B.A. 28 Feb. 1786; Coll. Corn. 207.

William Huntridge **Moore** (s. Samuel, druggist and alderman), b. S. Stephen's, Exeter, **M**. 30 Mch 1784 age 17, named **Reynolds** 29 Sep. 1783 and adm. 26 Mch 1784, commoner 6 Ap. 1784 to 12 Mch 1788, B.A. 16 Feb. 1790.

Richard **Reed** (s. John, pleb., of Buckland and Tavistock), **M**. Queen's 8 Ap. 1783 age 19; battellar 21 Feb. 1784 to 12 Ap. 1787, **B.C.** 1784, testimonials for orders June 1786, B.A. 19 Oct. 1786.

Anthony **Pyne** (s. John, of Charlton Mackerel, Som., 'and brother in law of Mr. J. Michell'), bap. W. Charlton 14 Feb. 1768, **M**. 10 Nov. 1786, **Symes** 4 Nov. 1788, res. 1791; B.A. 3 June 1790; R. of Pitney and Kingweston, d. 1819.

John **Tothill** jun. (s. John, of Exeter), **M**. 16 Oct. 1784 age 20, commoner 26 Nov. 1784 to 21 May 1788, named **Reynolds** 20 Dec. 1786, B.A. 21 May 1788.

Edward **Tippet** (s. Peter, by Elizabeth d. of Edward Collins, V. of S. Erth), b. Truro 10 July 1769, commoner 29 Dec. 1786 to 6 May 1791, **Eliot, M.** 13 Dec. 1786, B.A. 4 Mch 1791, M.A. King's, Camb. 1802, V. of S. Allen, Cornwall 23 Ap. 1833, d. there 17 Sep. 1840; Lake i. 13, Bibl. Corn. 722, Coll. Corn. 997.

Samuel **Teed** jun., named **Reynolds** 11 Sep. 1787, Fellow 1789.

James **Harvey** (s. Rev. Edmund), b. Radwell, near Baldock, Herts, ed. Eton (superannuated for King's, Camb.), commoner 6 Mch 1787 to 17 Mch 1791, **Reynolds, M.** 16 Mch 1787 age 18; B.A. 11 Mch 1791, in orders.

Joseph **Worgan** (s. John, Mus. D., of S. Andrew Undershaft, London), b. Marylebone, ed. Eton, commoner 30 Oct. 1787 to 3 Jan. 1795, **Reynolds, M.** 26 Oct. 1787 age 19, B.A. 22 June 1791, testimonials for orders June 1791, V. of Pebworth, Glouc. 1822, d. 1825.

Charles **Marshall**, commoner 29 Oct. 1788 to 10 July 1793, named **Reynolds** by the Chapter 12 Mch 1789, Fellow 1793.

David **Williams** (s. Morgan, pleb., of Llanrhystid, Cardigan), **M.** Wadham 3 May 1786 age 19; battellar Ex. Coll. 29 Dec. 1786 to 29 Nov. 1790, **B.C.** 1788, B.A. 14 Jan. 1790, ordained 30 May 1790 on a title to C. of Merton, Oxon, Chaplain of Ch. Ch., d. 15 Dec. 1791.

Samuel **Cole** (5 s. Humphry), b. Marazion 18 Nov. 1766, commoner 4 June 1785 to 28 June 1789, and 17 June to 7 July 1791, and 8 Dec. 1821 to 24 Ap. 1839, **M.** 17 Mch 1785, **Eliot** 1788, B.A. 10 June 1789, M.A. 10 June 1811, B. and D.D. 12 Nov. 1819, Chaplain to Duke of Clarence, Chaplain at Calcutta 1799, V. of Sithney, Cornwall 1819–39, Chaplain of H.M. Fleet; senior Chaplain of Greenwich Hospital; George IV ordered that all books for religious instruction in the navy should be submitted for his sanction; d. Greenwich Hospital 25 Nov. 1838; m. Jane d. of John Griffith; Bibl. Corn. 76.

James **Reed**, ed. Eton, **Reynolds**, commoner 6 Ap. 1789, Fellow 1792.

John **Wolvey-Astley** (s. Edward), b. S. Dunstan's in the West, London, **Reynolds**, commoner 7 Nov. 1789 to 19 June 1801, **M.** 10 Oct. 1789 age 18, B.A. 17 Feb. 1795, M.A. 6 June 1798.

John Collier **Jones, Eliot** 1789, Fellow 1792.

Frederick **Croker** (s. Richard, of Liskeard and Truro, capt. in the army, then in the Custom House, London), **B.C., M.** 18 May 1790 age 18, B.A. 29 Jan. 1794.

James Eyre **Harington** (4 s. Dr. John, of Sarum), b. 16 June 1774, Misc. Geneal. Nov. 1882 p. 276, and iv. 294; el. **Symes** and **M.** 9 Nov. 1791, B.A. 3 June 1795, M.A. 4 Mch 1799, R. of Chalbury, Dorset 1815, of Sapcote, Leics. 1815; m. Margaret d. of James Moffat; d. 16 Aug. 1836; Hutchins iii. 117, 118.

John Warren **Plowman** (s. John, M.A., V. of Toller Porcorum, Dorset; and nephew of John Warren, M.D., of Taunton, Hutchins ii. 712), b. Dorset, **M.** Oriel 20 May 1790 age 18; **Reynolds**, commoner Mch 1791 to 5 May 1794, B.A. 4 Mch 1794, V. of Toller Porcorum, d. Milton Abbas, Dorset 7 Nov. 1798.

Theophilus **Barnes**, named **Reynolds** 28 May 1791, Fellow 1794.

Robert **Lukin** (3 s. George William, of Felbrigg and Metton in Norfolk, afterwards Dean of Wells, by sister of William Windham of Felbrigg; the brother of Robert Lukin inherited the Windham property by will of William Windham, on condition of his taking the name, London Gazette 1824 p. 700, Gent. Mag. 1803 i. 269–70, Nichols' Illust. vi. 720–21); b. Metton, ed. Eton, **Reynolds, M.** 13 July 1791 age 18, Demy of Magdalen July 1792–1802, B.A. 15 Ap. 1795, M.A. 4 Ap. 1799, Fellow of Magdalen, First Clerk in War Office 1831, secretary to the Tennis Club, and a very fine player; Bloxam vii. 126, Parr's Works vii. 648, Misc. Gen. 1893 p. 332.

John Haydon **Cardew, Eliot 1791**, Fellow 1794.

William **Smith** (s. William Edward, clerk in the Treasury), b. Hammersmith, ed. Eton, commoner 22 Oct. 1792 to 5 May 1794, **Reynolds, M.** 16 Oct. 1792 age 20, B.A. 23 Nov. 1796.

Charles **Vaughan** (s. Rev. Henry, of Brecknock), ed. Eton, commoner 15 Oct. 1793 to 4 June 1801, **Reynolds, M.** 5 July 1793 age 18, B.A. 13 Mch 1798, M.A. 3 June 1801.

Henry **Moon** (s. Peter, priest vicar, and then preb. Lincoln 1780), b. Lincoln, commoner 31 May 1793 to 10 Ap. 1801, **Darell, M.** 15 May 1793 age 18; B.A. 26 Ap. 1797, testimonials for orders Aug. 1797, V. of Chippenham, Camb. 1808, d. Ap. 1815.

Henry **Nicholls** (s. Henry, of Gerrans, Cornwall), commoner Mich. 1791 to 3 July 1800, **M.** 13 Dec. 1791 age 18, **Eliot 1793**; B.A. 9 Feb. 1796, M.A. Peterhouse, Camb. 1808, V. of Payhembury and of Rockbeare 1831–60, d. 5 Jan. 1860 age 87.

John **Davis** (s. William, of Cheselborne and Dewlish, Dorset), **B.C.** at Midsummer 1794, commoner 12 Nov. 1796 to 23 Feb. 1798, **M.** 4 June 1794 age 18, B.A. 15 Feb. 1798, testimonials for orders 16 Nov. 1797, diocese of Bristol.

George Thomas **Plummer** (s. William), b. Truro, commoner 24 Mch 1795 to 28 Mch 1800, **Eliot, M.** 25 Mch 1795 age 18, B.A. 5 Feb. 1799, Chaplain of Bodmin Gaol to 1812, R. of Northill 31 May 1821, d. Plymouth ? Dec. 1828 ; Coll. Corn. 742.

Charles Trevanion **Kempe** (s. Admiral Arthur, by Mary d. of Christopher Warrick of Park near Truro), b. Penzance, **Eliot**, commoner 5 Dec. 1795, as of Polsue near Tregony, to 9 Dec. 1802, **M.** 4 Dec. 1795 age 18, B.A. 23 May 1799, M.A. 24 Ap. 1805, R. of S. Michael Caerhayes, S. Dennis and S. Stephens in Brannel 20 Jan. 1806–1851, V. of Grade 1813–23, d. Caerhayes 23 Dec. 1851 ; m. Elizabeth 3 d. of Edward Marshall V. of Breage, she d. Falmouth Aug. 1857 age 72 ; Coll. Corn. 443, 535, 1394.

Gilbert **Hancock** (s. George, of Exeter), **B.C., M.** 9 Nov. 1796 age 17, commoner 3 July 1800, B.A. 7 July 1809, testimonials for orders 19 Mch 1810, diocese of Exeter.

Robert **Maunder** (s. Robert, of Tiverton), b. Tiverton, commoner 4 June 1794 to 2 Jan. 1802, **M.** 4 June 1794 aged 19, **Reynolds** 1796, B.A. 15 Feb. 1798, testimonials for orders Dec. 1797, C. of N. Molton 1798.

Thomas **Law** (s. John, of Barnstaple), b. Bishop's Tawton ; named **Reynolds** 12 Nov. 1796 by Chapter of Exeter, commoner 14 Dec. 1796 to 29 Dec. 1803, **M.** 15 Dec. 1796 age 19, B.A. 12 June 1800, R. of Newton Tracey 1814–32, d. 18 Feb. 1832.

John **Salter** (s. John), b. Exeter, named **Reynolds** 7 Feb. and **M.** 3 May 1797 age 15, commoner 26 May 1797 to 3 Nov. 1819, B.A. 4 Mch 1807, M.A. 10 Oct. 1808, R. of Stratton S. Margaret, Wilts, 1801–33, P.C. West Teignmouth, preb. of Sarum 1814, d. 19 Mch 1833 ; Phillipps ii. 106, Le Neve ii. 683.

Gilbert Henry **Langdon** (s. Rev. Gilbert, of Piddletown and Milton Abbas, Dorset), b. Piddletown, commoner 29 May 1797 to 27 June 1806, **M.** 26 May 1797 age 17, **Symes** 30 June 1797, civilian Lent 1801, R. of Weston Patrick 1813, of Athelhampton 1818, both in Dorset, and of Rotherwick, Hants, d. 28 Sep. 1840.

Richard **Ellicombe** (s. William, R. of Alphington), b. Exeter, **Reynolds**, commoner 29 Nov. 1798 to 2 Mch 1803, and 27 Oct. 1807 to June 1818, **M.** 29 Nov. 1798 age 18, B.A. 16 June 1802, M.A. 24 Ap. 1811, preb. of Exeter 1812–51, R. of Alphington 1831–51, d. 4 Aug. 1851 ; m. Eliza., 1 d. of Rev. John Swete of Oxton house, Devon ; Gent. Mag. 1851 xxxvi. 328.

Edward Arthur **Bush** (s. James), b. S. George's, Hanover Sq., commoner 13 Oct. 1798 to 16 Mch 1805, **Reynolds, M.** 11 Oct. 1798 age 18, B.A. 16 June 1802, M.A. 31 Jan. 1811, R. of S. Andrew and S. Mary Bredmore, Canterbury 1808.

William **Cardew** (s. Rev. Cornelius, of Truro), commoner 12 Nov. 1798 to 2 June 1803, **Eliot, M.** 10 Nov. 1798 age 17, B.A. 22 Feb. 1803, brother of J. Haydon Cardew, Fellow 1794.

John James **Lake**, **Eliot 1799**, Fellow 1805.

George **Barnes**, named **Reynolds** 19 Oct. 1799, Fellow 1805.

John **Williams**, commoner 29 May 1797 to 5 Nov. 1798, **B.C.** Mich. 1799, Fellow 1809.

John **Hewes** (s. Rev. James, of Woodborough and Burton Joyce near Nottingham), **Darell**, commoner 18 Nov. 1801 to 22 July 1803, **M.** 18 Nov. 1801 age 16; 2 lieut. R.M. 4 July 1803, lieut.-col. 12 Feb. 1842, ret. on full pay 17 Dec. 1846, d. Epperstone, Notts 22 Jan. 1852; Gent. Mag. Ap. 1852 p. 425.

Thomas (Hunt) **Ley** (s. John, of Exeter), named **Reynolds** 6 Ap. 1802, **M.** 31 May 1802 age 16, 3 Classics 1812, B.A. 26 Nov. 1812, M.A. 23 June 1813.

Francis **Swan** (s. Francis, preb. of Lincoln), b. 1786, **Darell**, commoner 5 Dec. 1803 to 30 July 1807, **M.** 26 Nov. 1803 age 16, Demy of Magdalen 1807, B.A. 10 Oct. 1808, M.A. 4 May 1810, B.D. 25 Feb. 1818, V. of Blyton 1811–24, ? R. of Swerford with C. of Showell 22 Mch 1824, R. of Sausthorpe 1819–28, R. of Bennington 1833–69, preb. of Lincoln 1825–78, d. 5 Jan. 1878; Le Neve ii. 146, Foster's *Index Ecclesiasticus*.

John **Baron** (s. James, lieut. R.N., of Lostwithiel, Cornwall), bap. 4 Mch 1783, commoner 8 Ap. 1802 to 1805, **M.** 8 Ap. 1802, **Eliot 1803**, V. of Lostwithiel 1807–16, of Walsall 1822–37; Coll. Corn. 53.

Matthew **Lowndes** (s. Matthew, V. of Buckfastleigh, Devon), **B.C.**, **M.** 7 Nov. 1804 age 17, B.A. 22 Nov. 1810, V. of Buckfastleigh 1825.

John **Bower** (s. late James, of Lostwithiel), commoner 24 Mch 1804 to 10 Feb. 1811, **Eliot, M.** 23 Mch 1804 aged 18, 2 Classics 1808, B.A. 25 May 1808, M.A. 18 Mch 1815, V. of Lostwithiel 2 Aug. 1816, d. there 21 Dec. 1872; Bibl. Corn. 39, 1091; Davies Gilbert's Cornwall iii. 29.

Henry **Cutler** (s. Rev. John, see above 1775), b. Dorchester, Dorset, commoner 25 Ap. 1805 to 22 Oct. 1811, **M.** 25 Ap. 1805 age 17, **Symes** 30 June 1805; left Mich. 1811.

Hugh **Bent** (s. Rev. George, of Sandford near Crediton), b. Bow near Crediton, commoner 20 Nov. 1805 to 24 Feb. 1815, **Reynolds, M.** 20 Nov. 1805 age 19, B.A. 25 May 1809, M.A. 28 Ap. 1813, R. of Highbray and of Jacobstow, and P.C. of Sandford 1814, d. Sandford 8 June 1836 aged 49; Gent. Mag. 1836 vi. 218, N. and Gleanings v. 36.

John **Jope** (s. Rev. John), b. S. Cleer near Liskeard 12 Mch 1787, **Eliot,** commoner 16 Jan. 1805 to 27 June 1811, **M.** 16 Jan. 1805, B.A. 21 Feb. 1809, M.A. 28 June 1811, C. of S. Ive, Cornwall, Mch 1810–1814, d. Lisbon 2 Ap. 1815 age 27; his spirit haunted the church and vicarage at S. Cleer, Gent. Mag. 1815 i. 571, Coll. Corn. 437, N. and Q. 6. vii. 305.

William **Carter** (s. Richard, of Duke St., Westminster, and Foxley near Malmesbury), commoner 9 Ap. 1807 to 29 Oct. 1834, **Reynolds, M.** 9 Ap. 1807 age 18, B.A. 26 Feb. 1811, M.A. 28 May 1817; C. of Quedgeley, Glouc.

Thomas Hardwicke **Rawnsley** (s. Thomas, of Bourn, Lincs.), ed. Eton, commoner 23 Ap. 1807 to 31 March 1819, **Reynolds, M.** 23 Ap. 1807 age 17, B.A. 14 Feb. 1811 (*collector*), M.A. 2 Dec. 1814, R. of Falkingham 1814, of Halton Holgate 1825–61, both in Lincs., d. Halton 2 July 1861 age 71; Gent. Mag. 1861 xi. 213.

Nathaniel **Cole** (s. Nathaniel, of Moreton Hampstead), b. Exeter, commoner 11 May 1807 to 23 Feb. 1832, named **Reynolds** 14 Mch and **M.** 9 May 1807 age 18; 3 Classics 1811, B.A. 5 June 1811, M.A. 16 June 1814, V. of South Brent, Devon, 1845–66.

Joseph **Howard** (s. Joseph, of Heavitree), named **Reynolds** 28 Ap. 1807, **M.** 9 May 1807 age 16.

William Charles **Hill** (s. William), b. Bedminster, Som., **B.C., M.** 27 May 1808 aged 18 as resident at Swansea; B.A. 30 Ap. 1812, C. of Buckland Brewer 1821–28, and V. of Fremington 1829, both in Devon, d. 5 Mch 1855 age 65.

John Trehane **Symons** (s. John, of S. Ervan, V. of S. Gennys, and of Feock near Truro), b. Feock 1786, commoner 16 Jan. 1805 to 30 Sep. 1812, **M.** 16 Jan. 1805 age 17, **Eliot** 1808; B.A. 25 May 1809, R. of Trevalga 30 Nov. 1832–1867, d. 1867; m. Elizabeth Bowen, d. of James May, R. of Trevalga (who d. 12 Mch 1831 age 64); Coll. Corn. 545, 949.

Sampson **Harris** (1 s. Peter Bown, d. 12 March 1830 age 64), b. Rosemerryn, Falmouth, commoner 22 Mch 1809 to 2 Dec. 1819, **M.** 22 Mch 1809 age 18, named **Reynolds** 27 Ap. 1811, B.A.

11 Feb. 1813, M.A. 27 Oct. 1830, d. Sancreed Vicarage 16 Mch 1832 age 41; Coll. Corn. 323. Was he also a Stephens exhibitioner?

Edward **Eliot**, **Eliot 1810**, Fellow 1811.

John Martyn **Collyns** (s. Charles, of Exeter), named **Reynolds** 28 Ap. **1810**, **M.** 28 May 1810 age 17, commoner 31 May 1810 to 17 June 1830, 3 Classics 1813, B.A. 19 Feb. 1814, M.A. 24 May 1817, V. of Sancreed, Cornwall 1851, d. 31 Dec. 1878; Coll. Corn. **157.**

William **Dansey** (s. John), b. Blandford 1792, commoner 5 July 1810 to 26 Mch 1819, **M.** 4 July 1810 age 18, **Symes** 30 June **1811**, res. 1812; 2 Classics 1814, B.A. 12 May 1814, M.A. 12 June 1817, M.B. 1 Ap. 1818, R. of Donhead S. Andrew 1820, preb. of Salisbury 10 Aug. 1841–1856, d. Weymouth 7 June 1856; transl. *Arrian on Coursing* 1831, ed. *A Brief Account of the Office of Dean Rural* (by J. Priaulx) 1832, and wrote *Horae Decanicae Rurales*, 2 vols. 1835, ed. 2, 1844; Nat. Biog. xiv. 35.

William **Potticary** (s. late William, of Wiley, Wilts), chorister Magdalen 1802–11; **B.C.**, **M.** Ex. Coll. 2 Nov. **1811** age 17, migrated to Alban H. 10 Oct. 1813, with a *liceat* only; at Edmund H. 1815.

Richard **Cutler** (s. Rev. John), b. Sherborne, commoner 27 June 1811 to 3 Dec. 1819, **M.** 22 June 1811 age 15, **Symes** 30 June **1812**, vac. 1819; 3 Classics 1815, B.A. 13 May 1815, M.A. 9 Ap. 1818; Master of Dorchester gr. sch., Maye's *Bibl. Dorset.* 148.

John Matthew **Glubb** (s. Peter Goodman, of Liskeard, by Jane d. of Philip Matthew of Chudleigh), b. Liskeard 1792, commoner 9 Ap. 1810 to 29 Aug. 1816, and 1822 to 27 Aug. 1823, **M.** 9 Ap. 1810, **Eliot 1812**, 3 Classics 1813, B.A. 19 Feb. 1814, M.A. 7 Nov. 1822; C. of S. Petrock at Dartmouth 1821, R. of S. Kerian and S. Petrock at Exeter 1822, of Shermanbury, Sussex 1836–71, Diocesan Inspector of Schools, d. 27 Sep. 1871 age 80; m. 1821 Mary James d. of Rev. Richard Lyne, she d. Cowfold, Sussex 26 May 1876 age 83.

Joseph **Thorne** (s. Rev. John), b. 15 Dec. 1797, **Eliot and B.C.**, **M.** 10 July **1813** age 15, B.A. 6 Feb. 1817, M.A. 1859. V. of Bishop's Nympton, Devon 1835–71; Lake iv. 213; ?d. 1871; Maclean iii. 410, 416, Coll. Corn. 987.

David **Jenkins** (s. Francis, V. of S. Clement's, Cornwall), b. S. Clement's 2 June 1797, commoner 15 Dec. 1814 to 15 Mch 1882, **Eliot, M.** 10 Oct. **1814**, B.A. 13 May 1818, V. of S. Goran 1824–69, d. there 17 Mch 1869 age 72 ; Coll. Corn. 424.

John **Russell** (s. Rev. John), b. Dartmouth 21 Dec. 1795,

Reynolds, M. 9 Nov. **1814** as of Crediton, B.A. 17 Dec. 1818, P.C. of Swymbridge 1832, R. of Black Torrington 1880, known throughout Devon as 'Jack Russell,' Life publ. 1878, and *Out-door Life of J. Russell* 1883, d. 28 Ap. 1883; Coll. Corn. 852.

Robert Hodgson **Fowler** (s. Rev. Charles, of Southwell, Notts), commoner 15 Dec. 1815 to 7 June 1823, **Darell, M.** 15 Dec. **1815** age 17, B.A. 14 Dec. 1819, M.A. 9 July 1825, V. of Rolleston, Notts, 1841, minor canon of Southwell, d. 2 Jan. 1858.

Josiah **Forshall**, named **Reynolds** May **1816**, Fellow 1819.

George Parker **Cleather** (s. Edward, capt. R.N.), b. Stoke Damerel, Devon, ? ed. Military Coll. Sandhurst; **M.** Pemb. 21 May 1816 age 17; **B.C. 1816**, commoner to 27 Jan. 1823, B.A. 3 Feb. 1820, M.A. 14 Jan. 1824, V. of Aldbourne 1852, Preb. of Sarum 1868, d. 2 Aug. 1881.

Robert Bateman **Paul**, **Eliot 1817**, Fellow 1817.

John **Law**, (y. s. John, of Tawton), b. Barnstaple, ed. Exeter, commoner 13 Dec. 1817 to 14 May 1824, **M.** 15 Nov. 1817 age 18; named **Reynolds** Dec. 1817; B.A. 29 Nov. 1821; M.A. 13 May 1824; V. of Bradworthy, Devon 1823; d. 12 Jan. 1845.

John **Pyke** (s. John, of Barnstaple), named **Reynolds** Dec. **1817**, **M.** 14 Jan. 1818 age 19, B.A. 4 Dec. 1821; M.A. 2 June 1825; R. (and patron) of Parracombe 1826, d. 25 Jan. 1868; m. (2) Elizabeth d. of John Nott, of Bydown (Byndon) near Barnstaple.

William Windsor **Berry** (s. William), b. S. Mary's, Lambeth, commoner July 1818 to 18 June 1819, and Ap. 1823 to 14 Feb. 1843, **B.C.**, **M.** 9 July **1818** age 16, 2 Classics 1822, B.A. 17 Dec. 1824, M.A. 18 Mch 1826; R. of Wadingham, Lincs. 1853, resides Morden Place, E. Greenwich.

Richard **Hill** (2 s. Peter, of Helston, by Jane Penneck, y. d. of Rev. William Robinson of Nansloe, of Carwythenick), b. and resident Helston, commoner 14 Jan. 1818, **Eliot, M.** 14 Jan. **1818** age 18, B.A. 20 June 1821, d. London 11 March 1880 age 81; m. Henrietta Amelia d. of G. Soltau, of Ridgway, Devon, she d. 3 Ap. 1880 age 70; Coll. Corn. 365.

Sidney William **Cornish**, **Acland 1818**, Fellow 1822.

James Moffat **Harington** (1 s. Rev. James Eyre), b. Caversham, Oxon, ed. Oakham, commoner July 1819 to 30 Mch 1832, **M.** 29 June 1819 age 17, **Symes** 30 June **1819**, res. 11 Ap. 1824; B.A. 2 May 1823, M.A. 8 June 1826, instit. to R. of Chalbury, Dorset, on his father's death 1836, d. 18 Aug. 1861 age 59; m. Mary Rebecca

d. of Rev. H. J. Maddock; Hutchins iii. 117, 118.   Misc. Geneal. iv. 295.

William **Churchward** (o. s. Rev. William), b. Goodleigh, Barnstaple, ed. Exeter, named **Reynolds** Sep. **1819, M.** 19 Oct. 1819 age 17, B.A. 25 June 1824.

Richard Caddy **Thomas** (o. s. Richard, of Helston, by Jane d. of Captain Jas. Caddy, of Manaccan), b. Manaccan 5 Oct. 1800, **M.** Magd. H. 25 Nov. 1820 age 20; **Eliot**, commoner 24 Feb. **1821** to 29 June 1824, 3 Classics 1824; Chaplain in the West Indies; afterwards of Haverland in Norfolk; Lake iii. 260, Coll. Corn. 983.

William **Polwhele** (8 s. Rev. Richard), b. Manaccan; **Eliot**, commoner 12 Ap. **1821** to 22 Mch 1825, **M.** 12 Ap. 1821 age 18, B.A. 12 Feb. 1825, V. of S. Anthony, Meneage 1828–58, d. 24 July 1858; m. 1831 Georgiana d. of John Roskruge, of Trenevas, she d. 5 Jan. 1884 age 73; Coll. Corn. **747.**

Cecil James **Lucas** (o. s. Carr Ellison, M.D.), b. Hatfield, Herts, ed. Eton, commoner 1 Nov. 1821 to 18 Dec. 1823, **Reynolds, M.** 25 Oct. **1821** age 18, left Lent 1824.

Charles **Wollaston** (3 s. Rev. Henry John, of Scotter near Gainsborough, Lincs.), ed. Ripon, **Darell, M.** 23 Oct. **1823** age 17, left 25 Feb. 1826 and went as military cadet to India, lieut.-col. E.I.C.S., d. 13 Jan. 1882.

John Hockin **Cartwright** (3 s. Thomas, of Okehampton), **M.** 6 May 1822 age 17, **B.C. 1823,** B.A. 20 Nov. 1828, P.C. of Winterborne Earls, Wilts 1851.

Henry Vere **Hodge** (1 s. late Rev. John Davy), b. Chard, ed. Ilminster and Exeter, commoner 1822 to 11 June 1844, **M.** 20 May 1822 age 18, named **Reynolds** 25 Jan. **1823,** B.A. 4 Feb. 1826, M.A. 7 Nov. 1828, V. of Middleton, Warwicks. 1836–84, d. 25 Dec. 1884.

Edward **Marshall** (3 s. Charles, Fellow 1793), ed. Tiverton and Exeter, **M.** 16 Ap. **1823** aged 18, named **Reynolds** 11 June.

Henry Duke **Harington, Symes** 30 June **1824,** Fellow 1826.

Francis John Hext **Kendall** (2 s. Rev. Charles), b. Lansallos, Cornwall, ed. Exeter, **M.** 28 Ap. 1824 age 18, **Vilvaine 1825,** B.A. 12 June 1828, M.A. 30 May 1844, V. of Lanlivery 1844–62, of Talland 1862, d. 16 Ap. 1873; Exeter Flying Post 30 June 1825.

Rufus **Hutton** (5 s. Rev. James Harriman), b. Teignmouth, **M.** 25 Feb. 1825 age 18, **B.C. 1826**–28; 3 Classics 1828, B.A. 16 Oct. 1828, V. of S. Nicholas near Teignmouth 1834–76, d. 6 Aug. 1876.

Hugh **Polson** (1 s. Rev. John Hugh Paysley), b. and ed. Exeter, **M.** 9 Nov. 1825 age 18, named **Reynolds** 4 Nov. **1826**, B.A. 10 Dec. 1829.

Edward **Carlyon** (4 s. Rev. Thomas), b. Truro, ed. Exeter, **Eliot**, **M.** 11 Feb. **1826** age 17, B.A. 19 Nov. 1829, V. of Lamerton 1840–60, R. of Dibden, Hants 1860; Crockford 1870, 1890.

John Stuart Hippesley **Horner** (2 s. col. Thomas Strangways, of Mells Park, Som.), b. 9 Oct. 1810, ed. Charterhouse, **M.** 11 May 1827, **Symes** 2 Nov **1827**, res. 1831, B.A. 17 May 1834, M.A. 29 Oct. 1835, R. of Mells 1835, preb. of Wells 24 May 1842; d. 9 Ap. 1874; m. 22 Sep. 1840 Sophia Gertrude d. of W. Dickinson, M.P., of Kingweston, Som.; Hutchins ii. 667.

Edward (John) **Wilcocks** (1 s. Edward), b. S. Sidwell's, Exeter 8 May 1809, ed. Exeter, named **Reynolds** Ap. 1828, **M.** 23 Ap., scholar Lincoln 1830, 4 Classics 1831, B.A. 26 Jan. 1832, M.A. 18 May 1842, took name of Treffry 4 May 1850, B.C.L. and D.C.L. 1864, V. of Fowey 1863–7, R. of Lansallos 1871–2, both in Cornwall, d. 10 July 1880; Bibl. Corn. 738, 1346.

James Buller **Kitson** (2 s. Rev. John Lane), b. Crediton, ed. Exeter, named **Reynolds** 31 Dec. **1828**, **M.** 4 Mch 1829 age 17, B.A. 15 Nov. 1832, M.A. 1869, V. of S. Veep 1836, of Pelynt 1841, of Morval 1858, d. 13 July 1870; Coll. Corn. 464.

Thomas Price **Jones** (o. s. Walter, of Llanio in Llandewi Brefi, Cardigans.), ed. Lampeter, **M.** 18 Ap. 1828 age 18, **B.C. 1831**, B.A. New Inn H. 25 May 1833.

Robert Jefferies **Spranger**, el. 6 June **1831**, first **Open** scholar, Fellow 1832.

Henry Skinner **Templer** (1 s. late John, V. of Cullompton, Devon 1819, R. of Teigngrace 1832), ed. Shrewsbury, **M.** Wadham 9 June 1831 age 18; **How** 30 June **1831**, at New Inn H. 1835, 3 Classics 1836, B.A. 20 Nov. 1845, M.A. 25 Feb. 1847, R. of Thornton with Nash, Bucks 1853–61, V. of Great Coxwell, Berks 1861–77, d. 26 Oct. 1877.

Charles Henry **Spragge** (1 s. Rev. Francis Roche, of Comb S. Nicholas near Chard, Som.), b. Brighton, **M.** 17 June 1831 age 18, **How** 30 June **1831**; 2 Classics 1835, B.A. 21 May 1836, d. 3 July 1837.

Arthur **Lowth** (7 s. Rev. Robert Henry, and grandson of bishop Lowth), b. Hinton, Hants 10 Nov. 1813, at Westminster 1825, **M.** 27 Jan. **1831**, **Exh.**, B.A. 20 Nov. 1834.

Edward **Geare** (3 s. John), b. and ed. Exeter, **M.** 4 Mch 1831 aged 17, named **Reynolds** 5 Ap.; 3 Classics 1835, B.A. 19 Nov. 1835, M.A. 8 Mch 1838, V. of Wolverhampton 1872.

Henry **Burney** (founder's kin, o. s. Richard Allan, R. of Kympton, near Sherborne, by Elizabeth d. of John Williams V. of Merston Magna), ed. Dr. Burney's, Greenwich, **M.** 29 June 1831 age 17, **Symes** 30 June 1831, vac. 1835 by non-residence; B.A. 18 June 1835, ? M.A. 1836; R. of Wavendon, Bucks 1847, R.D. of Bletchley 1866, d. Wavendon 16 July 1893.

Henry **Barne** (4 s. John), b. and ed. Tiverton, **M.** Trinity 17 Feb. 1831 age 17, exhibitioner; **Gifford 1832**, 2 Classics 1835, B.A. 27 May 1835, M.A. 17 May 1837; V. of Farringdon, Oxon 1851–80, Chaplain to Earl of Radnor, Minister of Memorial Church, S. James', Clifton 1884–86, d. Clifton 14 Oct. 1886 age 73. His wife d. of severe burns 1878.

John **Woolley** (2 s. John, surgeon, 8 Brompton Row, London), b. Petersfield, Hants, ed. Western gr. sch., Brompton, and London Univ., **M.** 26 June 1832 age 16, **Open** 25 June 1832; 1 Classics 1836, Fellow of Univ. Coll., Oxford; B.A. 9 June 1836, M.A. 28 Feb. 1839, D.C.L. 26 Ap. 1844, D.D., Head Master of Rossall sch., and of King Edward's sch. at Norwich, Professor in Univ. of Sydney, Australia 1852; m., Frankfort, Mary Margaret 1 d. of capt. William Turner; drowned in the *London* 11 Jan. 1866, Gent. Mag. 1866 p. 440; wrote *Sermons preached at Rossall* 1847, *Social use of Schools of Art* 1860.

Henry Bawden **Bullocke** (2 s. John, lieut. R.N.), b. Falmouth 3 May 1814, ed. Truro, **Eliot, M.** 10 May 1832, B.A. 25 May 1836, M.A. 23 Nov. 1848, Principal of Ex. Dioc. Females Training College Truro 1849–51, V. of Mullion 1853–65, R. of Truro 1865–75, V. of Clyst-Honiton, Devon 1875, d. there 3 Dec. 1892. Bibl. Corn. 1105.

John Charles **Carwithen** (2 s. of Dr. William, of S. Thomas, Devon), named **Reynolds 1833**, **M.** 31 Oct. 1833 age 17, B.A. 9 Nov. 1837, M.A. 1861, R. of Manaton 1841–8, of Challacombe 1848–61, V. of Stokenham 1861, d. 2 Feb. 1884.

Walter John **Moore** (3 s. William), b. S. George's, Hanover sq., London, ed. Plymouth, **M.** Trinity 25 May 1831 age 18; **Gifford** 10 June 1833, 2 Classics 1835, B.A. 26 Nov. 1835, M.A. 7 July 1838, R. of Hordley, Salop 1839, published several tracts and pamphlets anonymously.

David **Anderson** (1 s. Archibald), b. Hans Place, Chelsea 10 Feb.

1814, ed. Edinburgh, **M.** 9 Feb. 1832 age 17, **Open** 10 June **1833**, 4 Classics and 3 Math. 1836, B.A. 10 Nov. 1836, M.A. 28 June 1838, B. and D.D. 16 May 1849; Vice-Principal of S. Bees 1841–47, first Bishop of Rupert's Land 1849–64, consecrated Whit-tuesday 1849; R. of Clifton 1864–81, wrote charges and sermons; *Notes of the flood at the Red River* 1852, *Journal of a Visit to Moore and Albany* 1854; m. 21 July 1841 Ellen 1 d. of James Marsden of Everton near Liverpool, she d. 30 Nov. 1847; he d. 5 Nov. 1885.

George **Moyle** (s. Richard, M.D. of Bodmin by Jane Baron, widow of William Hichens), b. Marazion 9 Ap. 1815, ed. Exeter, **Reynolds, M.** 7 Feb. **1833**; scholar Lincoln 25 Mch 1835, 2 Classics 1836, B.A. 24 Nov. 1836, M.A. 31 Oct. 1839, ordained 1840, Master of Chudleigh gr. sch. Devon July 1850, d. London 22 Nov. 1861; m. 28 Dec. 1850 Fanny Day d. of Francis Newcombe by Elizabeth Day.

Robert **Milman** (2 s. of Sir William George, by Eliz. Hurry o. d. of Robert Alderson, recorder of Ipswich), b. Easton in Gordano, Som. 25 Jan. 1816, ed. Westminster 1824, **M.** 9 May 1833, **Open** 2 June **1834**; 2 Classics 1837, B.A. 2 June 1838, M.A. and D.D. 30 Jan. 1867; V. of Chaddleworth 1840–1851, of Lambourne 1851–62, both in Berks, of Great Marlow, Bucks 1862–7; consecr. Bishop of Calcutta 2 Feb. 1867, author; d. Rawul Pindee 15 Mch 1876; Times 20 Mch 1876 p. 5 col. I, Illust. London News li. 313 (1867) lxviii. 267 (1876). Memoir by his sister Frances Maria Milman 1879.

Charles John **Maddison** (founder's kin, 1 s. Rev. John George), b. Swallowfield, Wilts, ed. Exeter and in Germany, **M.** 18 June 1835 age 18; **Symes** 30 June **1835**; V. of Stottesdon, Salop 1846.

George Peloquin Graham **Cosserat** (1 s. Rev. George Peloquin, of Brampford Speke), **M.** 14 May 1835 age 19, named **Reynolds** Nov. **1835**, B.A. 21 Feb. 1839, M.A. 3 June 1846, R. of Winfrith Newburgh, Dorset 1851.

William Duckworth **Furneaux** (2 s. James, of Swilly, Plymouth), b. Calcutta 2 Aug. 1815, ed. Tiverton, **M.** 23 Jan. 1834 age 18, **Gifford** 7 June **1836**, 2 Classics 1837, B.A. 23 Nov. 1837, M.A. 10 June 1840; R. of Berkeley, Som. 1860, d. there 9 Dec. 1874; m. 13 Aug. 1846 Louisa 1 d. of W. Dickins of Cheriton, Devon: published *Sermon on anniversary meeting of Blundell's School* 1847; *Glory of God promoted by the memory of the just*, two sermons by R. Seymour and W. D. Furneaux 1848; Coll. Corn. 266.

Thomas **Phinn** (1 s. Thomas, of Bath, by Caroline d. of R. Dignell of Banbury), b. Exeter, ed. Eton, **M.** 29 Oct. 1834 age 20, **Open** 7 June **1836,** 1 Classics 1837, B.A. 28 June 1838, barrister I.T. 20 Nov. 1840, Q.C. 1854, Recorder of Portsmouth 1848–52, of Devonport 1852–55, M.P. Bath 1852–55, but contested Bath unsuccessfully 1859, second Secretary and Counsel to the Admiralty, known in society as 'Tom Phinn'; d. suddenly Pall Mall 31 Oct. 1866.

John Dobree **Dalgairns** (1 s. William), b. Guernsey 21 Oct. 1818, ed. Elizabeth Coll., **M.** 4 Feb. 1836, **Open** 27 May **1837,** 2 Classics 1839, B.A. 28 Nov. 1839, M.A. 30 June 1842; joined church of Rome 29 Sep. 1845, d. 6 Ap. 1876; Cox 334; Church's Oxford Movement 206; for his works see Nat. Biog., Mod. Eng. Biog. i. 802.

Paul Augustine **Kingdon, How** 27 May **1837,** Fellow 1841.

Augustus Archer **Hunt** (1 s. Richard Burges), b. Plympton Earle, Devon, ed. Winchester, **Gifford** 27 May **1837, M.** 29 May age 17; 4 Classics 1841, B.A. 28 May 1841, M.A. 26 Jan. 1844, V. of Tipton, Devon 1845, d. 26 Nov. 1889.

Alfred James **Lowth** (8 s. late Rev. Robert), b. Chiswick, Middlesex 27 July 1817, at Winchester 1829, **M.** 21 Oct. 1836, **Symes 1838,** res. 1841; in Univ. Eleven 1841, B.A. 13 May 1841, M.A. 8 Feb. 1844; m. Miss Cobbold; R. of Harsworthy, Dorset 1860–2, of S. Swithun, Winchester 1865–85; Misc. Geneal. Nov. 1882 p. 277.

Matthew Calley **Morton** (1 s. Henry, of Lambton, Chester le Street, Durham), b. Kirknewton, Northumb., **M.** 20 Ap. 1837 age 18, **Open** 18 June **1838,** 3 Classics 1841, B.A. 28 May 1841, M.A. 29 Feb. 1844; Warden of S. Columba, Ireland, d. 25 Ap. 1850.

Richard Cowley **Powles, Open** 17 May **1839,** Fellow 1842.

Allan **Cowburn** (took name of Smith-Masters 1862; 1 s. William, of 10 Lincoln's Inn Fields, London), b. S. Pancras, ed. Winchester, **M.** 17 May 1838 age 18, **Open** 4 June **1840,** in Univ. Eleven 1841, 2 Classics 1842, B.A. 26 May 1842, M.A. 17 Oct. 1844; V. of Tidenham, Glouc. 1854–62, d. 8 Oct. 1875.

Lewis **Gidley** (1 s. Lewis, by Frances d. of Robert Cornish), b. Honiton 18 Ap. 1822, ed. Ottery, **M.** 10 Ap. 1839, **Gifford** 4 June **1840**; English Verse 1840 *The Judgment of Brutus,* 3 Classics 1843, B.A. 3 June 1843, M.A. 20 Nov. 1845, Chaplain of S. Nicholas' Hospital, Sarum 1868, d. 28 Ap. 1889; published *Poems* 1857, ed. 2, 1884, *Morven Devonshire Legends and other poems* 1864, *Aletes a poem,* 1865, *Faith a poem* 1868; *Disputed Points of Theology; Stonehenge viewed by the light of ancient history* 1873; translation of *Bede's Ecclesiastical History* 1870; translator of *Epigrammata* 1848;

Fasciculus [selections from English poets translated into Latin verse], ediderunt L. Gidley, et Rev. Robinson Thornton et M. J. Baker 1866; Acad. 4 May 1889 p. 305, Bibl. Corn. 1194.

Charles **Garvey** (4 s. Richard, minor canon of Lincoln), b. Faldingworth, Lincs., ed. Wakefield, **Darell**, appointed 18 July **1840**, M. and adm. exhibitioner 6 May 1841 age 20, B.A. 24 Ap. 1845, M.A. 14 June 1848, V. of Manthorpe, Lincs. 1851.

Frederick Hookey **Bond, Gifford 1841**, Fellow 1843.

Edward Herbert **Harington** (1 s. William, Madras C.S.), b. Arcot, India, ed. Sherborne, **Symes** 30 June **1841**; M. 1 July 1841 age 16; in Madras Army, d. unmarried.

George **Butler, Gifford 1841**, Fellow 1842.

Henry Wilson **Tweed** (1 s. late Henry), b. Romford, Essex 1824, M. 28 Ap. 1842, **Michell** 27 June **1842**, B.A. 14 May 1846, M.A. 1 Feb 1849, V. of Bridstow, Ross 1858, d. 27 Jan. 1892.

De Courcy **Meade** (3 s. Rev. Richard John, of Keyford, Frome), b. Marston Bigot Rectory 7 Nov. 1824, ed. Winchester 1836, M. 13 May 1842, **How** 30 June **1842**, 2 Classics 1846, B.A. 3 June 1846; R. of North and South Barrow, Som. 1870, Diocesan Inspector of Schools 1876, R. of Tokenham, Wilts 1878.

Benjamin Fuller **James** (2 s. John Haddy), b. and ed. Exeter, M. 11 Nov. 1841 age 17, named **Reynolds** June **1842**, 2 Classics 1846, B.A. 30 May 1846, M.A. 22 June 1848, in orders, master at Westminster 1846-84, d. Tonbridge Wells 29 Jan. 1892 age 67; Mod. Eng. Biog.

Robert **Tweed** (4 s. Rev. James, of Dunmow, Essex), b. Ongar, Essex, M. and appointed **B.C.** 20 Jan **1843** age 17, B.A. 3 Dec. 1846, M.A. 22 June 1849, V. of Ascot-under-Wychwood, Oxon 1860–74.

James **Godley** (2 s. John, of Killigar House, Carrigallen, Leitrim, by Catherine d. of Rt. Hon. Denis Daly of Dunsandle, Galway), ed. Winchester, and Trin. Dublin; M. Trinity, Oxford 7 June 1841 age 20; **Open** 19 June **1843**, 2 Classics 1844, B.A. 25 May 1844, M.A. 4 Feb. 1847; incumbent of Carrigallen 1866; m. Elizabeth d. of Peter La Touche of Bellevue, Wicklow.

Richard Seymour Conway **Chermside** (founder's kin, 1 s. Sir Robert Alexander, M.D. by Jane Merriel d. of Robert Williams of Cerne Abbey, Dorset), b. Marylebone 1823, ed. the Sorbonne in Paris, M. 6 May 1841 age 17, **Symes** 30 June **1843**, B.A. 2 May 1844, M.A. 18 Mch 1847, R. of Wilton 1848-67, Preb. of Sarum 1857; m. 9 July 1846 Emily d. of John Dawson of Regent Sq.,

S. Pancras, London; d. Wilton 30 July 1867; Gent. Mag. 1867 iv. 402.

Thomas **Whitehead** (2 s. late Rev. Edward), b. East Ham, Worcs., ed. Bridgenorth, **M.** 27 Oct. 1842 age 17, **Open 1843**; 3 Classics 1846, B.A. 4 Feb. 1847, M.A. 26 Ap. 1849; m. 16 Ap. 1857 Frances 2 d. of John Webb of Chigwell, Essex; C. of Water Eaton, Kidlington 1850–52, of Kidlington 1852–63, of Wimbledon, Surrey 1863–70, V. of South Newington, Oxon 1870–86, of Shustoke, Birmingham 1886.

Richard James **Hayne** (1 s. Richard, C. of Pilton, Barnstaple), b. S. Helier's, Jersey, ed. Eton, **M.** Wadham 20 Oct. 1842 age 17; **How** 30 June **1843**, B.A. 12 Nov. 1846, M.A. 1851, V. and Patron of Buckland Monachorum, Devon 1855, preb. of Exeter 1889.

Richard Doddridge **Blackmore** (2 s. John, Fellow 1816, of Torre, Torquay), b. Longworth, Berks 1825, ed. Bruton, Som., and Tiverton, **M.** 7 Dec. 1843, **Gifford 1844**, 2 Classics 1847, B.A. 2 Dec. 1847, M.A. 19 May 1852, barrister M.T. 7 June 1852, resident at Teddington, Middlesex 1878, eminent as a writer of fiction. His best work is *Lorna Doone* 1869; he also wrote *The Farm and Fruit of Old*, a translation of the first and second Georgics 1862, a translation of the Georgics 1871; *see* Men of the Time, Foster's Men at the Bar.

Thomas **Jones** (2 s. Thomas), b. Bryn Owen, Cardigan 1826, ed. Bridgenorth, **Open 1844**, **M.** 25 May 1844 age 18, drowned while bathing at Aberystwith 17 July 1847.

Charles Edward Shirley **Woolmer** (2 s. Edward), b. and ed. Exeter, **M.** 6 June 1844 age 16, held Stephens, **Reynolds** (named Jan. **1846**) and Acland exhibitions from Exeter, 4 Classics 1849, B.A. 30 May 1849, M.A. 1851, R. of S. Andrew's, Deal 1866–80, V. of Ramsgate 1880–87, of Sidcup 1887; m. Walcot, Bath 7 Feb. 1860 Cordelia Charlotte d. of Charles Worthington of Bath; author, *see* Crockford.

Reginald William **Cleave** (2 s. Rev. Thomas), b. Totnes, ed. Ashburton, **Gifford**, **M.** 11 Ap. **1845** age 17; 3 Classics 1849, B.A. 24 Ap. 1850, C. of Alwington, Devon 1852–55, and of Ivybridge, d. Exeter 21 Jan. 1865.

Maurice **Day** (2 s. late Rev Henry Thomas, LL.D.), b. Wickham Market, Suffolk 26 Feb. 1827, ed. King's Coll. sch., el. **Open**, and **M.**, 10 May **1845** age 18; B.A. 18 May 1850, M.A. 1855; Hertford Scholar 1847, scholar of Univ. Coll. 1847, Ireland Scholar 1849, 2 Classics 1850; Head Master of King's sch., Worcester 1860–79, and R. of S. Swithin's 1865–79, Librarian of Worcester Cathedral 1872, V. of Wichenford, Worcs. 1679, d. 28 Mch 1890; see *The Vigornian*, July 1890 p. 270.

John Robert **Nankivell** (3 s. John Thomas, wine merchant), b. Truro 1826, ed. Truro, **Eliot 1845, M.** 17 Ap. 1845 age 18, B.A. 18 Feb. 1849, M.A. 1852, chaplain of Holy Cross, Crediton 1867, d. The Chantry, Crediton 5 Nov. 1833; Coll. Corn. 611, 1394–5.

John **Kempe, Open 1846**, Fellow 1854.

Henry **Algar** (3 s. late Joseph, V. of Christchurch, Frome), b. Frome 2 May 1825, ed. Rugby, **M.** 25 May 1844, **Symes** 27 Feb. **1846**, B.A. 18 May 1848, C. of Barnardiston near Bury S. Edmunds 1869–71, and Rector 1871–72, C. of Butterton, Staffs. 1883–6, of Yatesbury, Wilts 1886–7; wrote *Notes on Galatians* 1882, and *on Philippians*.

Richard John Howard **Rice** (o. s. John Howard, lieut. E.I.C.S.), b. S. Mary le Bow, ed. Kingsbridge, **B.C. 1846–9, M.** 20 May 1846 age 18, 4 Classics 1850, B.A. 30 May 1850, M.A. 1852, V. of Sutton Courtney, Abingdon 1856.

Charles William **Boase, Open 1847**, Fellow 1850.

George Frederick **Wilgress** (o. s. late George Weatherell, Commissariat Department), b. Kennington, Surrey, ed. Tonbridge 1841–6, **M.** 19 Nov. 1846 age 18; **Open 1848**, 3 Classics 1851, B.A. 1851, M.A. 2 June 1853; C. of S. Mary's, Oxford 1854–6, of Garsington, Oxon 1857–66, P.C. of Headington Quarry, Oxon 1866–7, Hebrew Lecturer in Cuddesdon Theol. Coll. 1867–71, V. of S. Mary, Cadmore End, Oxon 1871; d. there 4 Jan. 1878 aged 49.

Henry Fanshawe **Tozer, Gifford 1848**, Fellow 1850.

Frederick Thomas **Colby, Gifford 1848**, Fellow 1849.

Henry Hughes **Still** (1 s. Rev. Peter), b. Harley St. London, ed. Eton, **Reynolds, M.** 11 May **1848** age 19, B.A. 1854, M.A. 1855, R. of Cattistock, Dorset 1855, d. 9 Oct. 1859.

Francis John **Poynton** (2 s. Thomas, of Sheffield and London, by Hannah Mary d. of John Hall, V. of Chew Magna, Som.), b. Chew 16 June 1827, ed. Shrewsbury 1841–1846, **M.** 29 May 1846, **Symes** 7 Mch **1849**, B.A. 22 May 1850, M.A. 1853; Rector's theol. prize 1851; C. of Ducklington, Oxon 1851–52, in charge of R. of Slapton, Bucks 1852–53, of C. of Burmington, Warwicks. 1853–58; R. of Kelston near Bath 1858, member of Palaeontological Society, contributed to Miscellanea Genealogica, wrote 1874 *Memoranda of the Yorkshire Blackburnes*, 1878 *Memoranda &c. of Kelston* (see there

ii. 20), contributed to B. and G. Archæol. Soc. 1885 *Genealogy of Haynes of Westbury*, 1887 *Hicks of Beverston*, 1888 *Early Registers of Aust and Henbury*: to Som. Archæol. Soc., 1887 *Roman burial place at Northstoke, Som.*: to Bath Lit. Club (not printed), *on W. Prynne the antiquary*, *on a find of Roman bronze coins at Lower Easton, Bristol 1874, on Hinton Charterhouse and its Cell on Mendip*; m. (1) Hurst 1 Sep. 1852 Mary Matilda Anne y. d. of Thomas Morris P.C. of Twyford, Berks (b. 2 Feb. 1829, d. 20 Mch 1863), (2) 9 May 1866 Frances Mary d. of Thomas Billinge of Weston, Som.

George Francis **Coke** (o. s. George, R. of Piddle Hinton, Dorset), b. Munsley, Herefs., ed. Eton, **Reynolds, M.** 24 Oct. **1849** age 19, 2 Classics Mod. 1852, 4 Classics 1853, B.A. 1854, V. of Titley, Herefs. 1877, d. 13 Feb. 1885.

John George **Gresson** (6 s. late Rev. George L.), b. Ardnocker, King's County Feb. 1832, ed. Bromsgrove, appointed **B.C.** 19 and **M. 20** Dec. **1849**; 2 Classics Mod. 1852, 4 Classics 1853, B.A. 1854, M.A. 13 Nov. 1856, deacon 1858, priest 1859, resident W. Mansion, W. Worthing 1878, ? dead.

Charles Henry **Pearson** (4 s. Rev. John Norman, of Tonbridge Wells), b. Islington 7 Sep. 1830, ed. King's Coll., **M.** Oriel 14 June 1849; **Open 1850**; 1 Classics 1852, Sacred Poem 1857; B.A. 21 Ap. 1853, M.A., Fellow of Oriel 1854–73, Professor of Modern History at King's Coll., London 1855–65, Lecturer on Modern History at Trinity Coll., Camb. 1869–71, edited National Review in 1862–63, Principal of Ladies' Presbyterian Coll. Melbourne, Australia, Professor of History in University of Melbourne 1873; took a considerable part in colonial political life, was Minister of Education in Victoria; published a *History of England during the Middle Ages* 2 vols. 8° 1867, *Historical Maps of England during* 13 *centuries* fol. 1867, *English History of the* 14*th century* 12° 1876; *National Life and Character, a Forecast* 1893; hon. LL.D. St. Andrews, Secretary to London Agency of Victoria 1892; Heaton's Australian Dictionary of Dates 1879 p. 163.

Samuel Harvey **Reynolds** (1 s. Samuel, M.D.), b. Stoke Newington, London, ed. Radley, **M.** 17 Ap. 1850 age 18, **Gifford** Easter **1850**, 1 Classics Mod. 1852, Newdigate 1853, 1 Classics 1854, English Essay 1856; B.A. 15 June 1854, M.A. 1857: Fellow Brasenose 1855–72, Classical Examiner 1866–68, V. of East Ham, Essex 1871; published *System of Modern History* 1865, *The first* 12 *books of the Iliad* 1867, *Notes on the Iliad* 1871, *Bacon's Essays with Notes* (Clarendon Press).

James Thomas Houssemayne **Du Boulay**, **Open 1850**, Fellow 1854.

Francis Charles **Hingeston** (afterwards Hingeston-Randolph; o. s. Francis and Jane, of S. Ives), b. Truro 31 Mch 1833, ed. Truro, where he gained Dr. Cardew's prize and Lord Falmouth's prize of books, **Eliot 1850**, **M.** 12 Nov. 1851, hon. 4 Classics and hon. 4 Math. and B.A. 1855, M.A. 3 June 1858, C. of Holywell, Oxford 1856–58, P.C. of Hampton Gay, Oxon 1858–60, R. of Ringmore, Devon 1860; preb. of Exeter 1885; m. 26 July 1860 Martha Jane o. child and h. of Rev. Herbert Randolph (whose name he assumed); published *Specimens of ancient Cornish Crosses* 1850, *Capgrave's Chronicle* 1858, *Capgrave's The Illustrious Henries* 1859, *Letters during the reign of Henry IV* 1860—the last three in the Rolls series. He is now editing the Episcopal Registers of Exeter, (1) Stafford 1886, (2) Bronescombe and Quivil 1889, (3) Stapeldon 1892, (4) Grandisson, in the press; Allibone Suppl.

James Bellett **Richey** (o. s. Rev. James, of Stoodleigh, Tiverton), b. Culmstock, Devon, ed. Bromsgrove, **M.** 12 June 1851 age 17, **How** 30 June 1851, 2 Classics Mod. 1853, 4 Classics 1855, B.A. 12 June 1856, First Assistant Collector and Magistrate at Panch Máhál, Bombay, C.S.I. 25 May 1878.

William George **Pedder** (1 s. William Newland, V. of Clevedon), b. Clevedon 1832, **M.** Worcester 21 Nov. 1849; **How 1851**, 2 Classics Mod. 1852, 4 Hist. 1854; B.A. 15 June 1854, M.A., Bombay C.S. 1855; m. 1863 Julia Frances d. of Lieut.-Col. Cyril Jackson Prescott; Collector and Magistrate at Katadgi, Bombay 1856, see Report presented to Parliament by him; Municipal Commissioner for City of Bombay, retired from the service 1879, Secretary to Revenue Commerce and Statistics department India office 1879, C.S.I. 29 May 1886, d. Nov. 1888.

James Augustus **Atkinson** (3 s. James, Inspector General of Hospitals, Bengal), b. Boulogne 8 Mch 1831, ed. Eton, **M.** 23 Jan. 1850, **Open 1851**, 1 Classics Mod. 1852, 3 Classics 1853; B.A. 9 Dec. 1853, M.A. 5 June 1856; m. 5 July 1855 Charlotte Adelaide d. of Viscount Chetwynd; C. of S. Mary's, Dover 1855–56, of Kirtlington, Oxon 1856–58, P.C. of Hollingwood, Manchester 1858–61, R. of Longsight, Manchester 1861, hon. Canon of Manchester 1884, V. of Bolton 1887–93. He recited the prize Latin alcaics at the installation of Lord Derby as Chancellor 1853, printed in Palatine Notebook Sep. 1883; author.

George **Miller, Open 1851**, Fellow 1857.

Thomas Sikes **Hichens** (2 s. Robert), b. E. Dulwich 20 Feb. 1834, ed. King's Coll. sch.; **Open** 4 Mch, **M.** 5 Mch **1852** age 18, 2 Classics Mod. 1853, 3 Classics 1856, B.A. 22 May 1856, M.A. 9 Dec. 1858; m. S. Giles' Camberwell 4 Feb. 1862 Mary d. of Rev. John Oldham; V. of Guilsborough, Northants 1864; Coll. Corn. 358.

Charles Arthur **Turner, Gifford 1852**, then **Reynolds** 16 Feb. **1852**, Fellow **1855**.

Morgan George **Watkins** (1 s. late Morgan, V. of Southwell, Notts), b. Southwell 1 Feb. 1835, ed. Southwell; **Darell, M.** 2 June **1852**, 2 Classics Mod. 1854, 2 Classics 1856, B.A. 17 Dec. 1856, M.A. 20 Oct. 1859, 2 Master of gr. sch. and C. of Ottery 1858–61, R. of Barnoldby le Beck, Lincs. 21 Ap. 1861, of Kentchurch, Herefs., with Llangua, Mon. 1885; m. 27 June 1866 Edith Alethea d. of Sidney W. Cornish Fellow 1822, V. of Ottery; Bibl. Corn. 854; author, *see* Crockford.

Plumpton Stravenson **Wilson** (1 s. Plumpton, R. of Knapton), b. Northborough near Ilchester 1 May 1831, **M.** 30 May 1849, **Symes** **1852**, B.A. 1853, M.A. 1854, vac. on ordination 1854, V. of Horbling, Lincs. 1876.

Robert Ingham **Salmon** (4 s. Thomas, solicitor), b. S. Hilda, South Shields 23 Sep. 1834, ed. Durham; **Open**, and **M.** 25 Feb. **1853**, 2 Classics Mod. 1855, 3 Classics 1857, B.A. 10 Dec. 1857, M.A. 17 Dec. 1859; in Univ. Eight 1856; C. of Kidlington 1858–61, of Morchard Bishop, Devon 1861–2, senior C. of S. Michael's, Paddington 1862–72, C.F. at Preston Cavalry barracks 1872, V. of S. Martin's, Brighton 1875–87, R. of Barcombe, Lewes 1887; published several sermons.

Benjamin Smith **Dawson** (1 s. Richard Henry), b. Boston, Lincs. 24 Nov. 1835, ed. Exeter, named **Reynolds** 4 Nov. **1853**; **M.** Oriel 6 Dec. 1853; **Gifford** 7 Dec. 1855; 2 Classics Mod. 1855, 3 Classics 1857, B.A. 28 Jan. 1858, M.A. 21 June 1860; C. of S. Teath, Cornwall 1859–64, Chaplain to Legation at Madrid, assist. civil chapl. Gibraltar 1871, R. of Hempstead near Gloucester 1879.

Henry **Benwell** (o. s. Rev. Henry), b. S. Peter's Port, Guernsey, ed. Elizabeth Coll., **B.C. 1853**, **M.** 19 Jan. 1854 age 19; 2 Classics Mod. 1856, 3 Classics 1858; B.A. 9 Dec. 1858, M.A. 19 Ap. 1865; 2 Master Ystrad Mewrig gr. sch. 1859–61, C. of S. Michael's, Aberystwith 1862–6, C. of Merton, Surrey 1866–8; Chaplain Convalescent Hosp. Wimbledon 1868–72, Head Master of Horncastle gr. sch., Lincs. 1872–78, R. of Langton and V. of Woodhall, Lincs. 1878–90.

Roderick Bain **Mackenzie** (3 s. John, of Civil Service), b. Malta 14 Sep. 1834, **Darell, M.** 18 May **1853**, B.A. 1858, M.A. 1860, chaplain at Spezia 1855, V. of S. Peter at Gowts, Lincoln 1868–74, R. of Sudbrooke, Lincs. 1874.

Frederick Harrison **Hichens** (5 s. Robert), b. Camberwell, E. Dulwich, ed. King's Coll.; **Open, M.** 23 June **1854** age 18; 3 Classics Mod. 1857, B.A. 14 June 1860, M.A. 21 Feb. 1867; m. Abigail Smyth; V. of S. Stephen's near Canterbury 1885; Coll. Corn. 358.

George Collyer **Harris** (o. s. Joseph Hemmington, D.D., by Charlotte Anne 3 d. of archdeacon John Bedingfeld Collyer of Hackford Hall, Norfolk, she d. 1834), b. Toronto, resided at Torquay 1839, ed. Harrow, **M.** 5 Mch 1852 age 18; **Gifford 1854,** 3 Classics 1856, B.A. 11 Dec. 1856, M.A. 17 June 1858; C. of Tormohun, Torquay 1859–69, Preb. of Exeter 1865, V. of S. Luke's, Torquay 1869–74, d. 4 May 1874; m. S. Paul's, Knightsbridge, London 26 Ap. 1865 Percy 2 d. of Hon. Francis Ward Primrose; for his works see Sermons 1875 by late G. C. Harris, with a memoir by Charlotte Mary Yonge.

John Hocking **Hocking** (1 s. Samuel, surgeon), b. S. Ives, ed. Truro, **M.** 25 Feb. **1853** age 18, **Eliot 1854**, B.A. 1858, M.A. 1861, V. of Debenham, Suffolk 1883; Bibl. Corn. 1232, Coll. Corn. 378.

Denis Times **Moore** (1 s. Francis, surgeon), b. Much Hadham, Herts, ed. Eton, **Reynolds, M.** 21 Oct. **1854** age 18, 3 Classics Mod. 1857, B.A. 1859, M.A. 1861, V. of Woolton Hill, Hants 1873–84.

Charles Edward **Hammond, Symes 1855**, Fellow 1859.

Philip Edgar **Pratt** (1 s. Philip Proks, bank manager), b. Walsall, ed. Beaumaris, **M.** 15 June 1855 age 18; 2 Classics Mod. 1857, 3 Classics 1859, B.A. 8 Dec. 1859, M.A. 3 July 1862; C. of S. Margaret's, Leicester 1859–61, of Ross, Herefs. 1861–5, P.C. of Minsterley, Salop 1865–70, V. of Diddlebury, Salop 1870–80, V. of Madley, Herefs. 1880.

Thomas Henry **James** (o. s. Rev. Thomas George), b. Elmswood, Burnley, Lancs. 1838, ed. Aldenham, Herts, **M.** 15 June 1855 age 17, **How** 30 June **1855**, 1 Classics Mod. 1857, 3 Classics 1859, B.A. 8 Dec. 1859, M.A. 6 Nov. 1862; barrister L. I. 11 June 1862, revising barrister N. and E. Lancs. 1873–83, practised 13 Harrington St., Liverpool 1878, d. Bakville, Birkenhead 8 Aug. 1883.

William Frederick **Gibson** (2 s. Rev. Henry), b. Fyfield, near

Ongar, Essex, ed. Rossall, **Open** 15 Nov. **1856**, **M.** 23 Jan. 1857 age 19; 1 Classics Mod. 1858, 2 Classics 1861, B.A. 6 June 1861, died young.

George **Graham** (1 s. Peter, by Margaret d. of George Arrowsmith), b. Kensington 26 Jan. 1839, King's Scholar Eton July 1851; **Open** 15 Nov. **1856**, **M.** 23 Jan. 1857; 3 Classics Mod. 1858, B.A. 8 Dec. 1859, M.A. 27 June 1867, E.I.C.S. July 1859, Postmaster at Dacca, Bengal, retired Oct. 1875; published *Life in the Mofussil* 1878; ?dead.

Thomas Smyth **Abraham** (1 s. Richard Thomas), b. St. Peter's, Exeter, ed. Exeter, **M.** 27 June 1856 age 18, **Stap.** 15 Nov. **1856**, 2 Classics Mod. 1859, 3 Classics 1860, B.A. 7 Nov. 1861, barrister L. I. 9 June 1865, d. 14 Dec. 1873.

Charles Mackworth **Drake** (o. s. Charles Digby Mackworth, R. of Huntshaw, N. Devon, bur. there 28 Mch 1874), bap. Huntshaw 1 July 1838, ed. Cheltenham; **How, M.** 18 Jan. **1856** age 17; B.A. 23 June 1859, M.A. 12 June 1862, V. of Chittlehampton Dec. 1864–1867, of Seaton 1867–9, of Veryan, Cornwall 6 Sep. 1869, d. Veryan 17 Dec. 1873: m. 4 Jan. 1866 Georgina 4 d. of Owen Wethered of Remnanty, Marlow; N. and Gleanings v. 117.

Henry Aldrich **Cotton** (1 s. W. Aldrich), b. Ellesmere, Salop, ed. Bedford, **M.** 18 May 1853 age 17, **Michell** 15 Nov. **1856**, 2 Classics Mod. 1856, B.A. 1858, M.A. 1860; V. of Haynes, Beds. 1869–76, minor Canon of Westminster 1876, priest in ordinary to Chapel Royal 12 June 1878.

Feltrim Christopher **Fagan** (3 s. Christopher Sullivan), b. Southampton, ed. Tiverton, **Richards** 15 Nov. **1856**, **M.** 23 Jan. 1857 age 18; Michell Exhibitioner 21 Nov. 1857, B.A. 13 Dec. 1860, M.A. 30 June 1864, P.C. All Saints, Guernsey 1865, Chaplain Allahabad 1868–71, d. 22 Aug. 1872.

Arthur **Weekes** (1 s. late Arthur), b. Hurstpierpoint, ed. Harrow, **M.** 7 Feb. 1857 age 18, **Open** 21 Nov. **1857**, 2 Classics Mod. 1859, B.A. 13 Dec. 1860, M.A. 5 Nov. 1863, Indian Civil Service 1860, barrister L. I. 1888.

Frank Fortescue **Cornish** (2 s. Sidney William, V. of Ottery), b. Exeter 28 Dec. 1837, **M.** 13 May 1856, **Gifford 1857**, 1 Classics Mod. 1858, 2 Classics 1860, B.A. 1861, M.A. 10 Oct. 1863; m. 1869 Margaret Gertrude d. of Thomas Garnier dean of Lincoln: C. of S. Mark's, Victoria Docks, London 1863–6, of Greenhill, Harrow 1867–8, H.M. Inspector of sch. 1868, contributor to Proceedings of English Goethe Society.

Robert John **Tomes** (1 s. Robert, V. of Coughton, by Sarah Washbourne d. of Thomas Perry of Kidderminster), b. 14 May 1838, ed. Rugby, **M.** Wadham 20 May 1857; **Richards** 21 Nov. **1857**, How 23 Feb. 1860; 2 Classics Mod. 1859, 3 Classics 1861, B.A. 6 June 1861, M.A. 19 Ap. 1865, Master in Bishop Stortford Congregational sch. 1864–76, d. Baschurch, Shrewsbury 12 Aug. 1893; Misc. Geneal. iii. 277.

John **Turner** (3 s. George), b. Barton, Exminster, ed. Exeter, **M.** 29 May 1855 age 18, named **Reynolds** 15 Oct. **1857**, 2 Classics Mod. 1857, B A. 1860.

Charles Adams **Houghton** (2 s. Rev. John), b. Matching, Essex 23 Dec. 1837, **M.** 13 May 1856, **B.C.** 21 Nov. **1857**, 2 Math. Mod. 1858, 2 Math. 1860, Theol. Essay 1862; B.A. 1860, M.A. 19 Feb. 1863; V. of E. Harnham, and chaplain to Alderbury Union 1868–75, R. of S. Peter, Marlborough 1875–87; preb. of Sarum 1881, V. of W. Alvington, Kingsbridge, Devon 1887, commissioner under Pluralities Act for Archd. of Wilts 1884–7; m. 1868 Mary Josephine d. of W. Mayo, R. of Folke; wrote *Christian Burial* 1880, *Plea for the use of Means of Grace* 1882, *Life and Revelation* 1891.

John **Simpson** (2 s. Joseph, chemist), b. and ed. Newark, **M.** Queen's 11 June 1857 age 18; **B.C.** 21 Nov. **1857**, drowned in the Cherwell 20 June 1859; Gent. Mag. 1859 vii. 198.

Godfrey **Kingdon** (3 s. Cory, M.D., of Poughill, and Stamford Hill, Stratton, Cornwall, by Elizabeth d. of James Buckingham, V. of Burrington, N. Devon), b. 8 Ap. 1837, ed. Exeter, **M.** Pemb. 25 Oct. 1856 age 19; **Vilvaine** exh.; named **Reynolds** Jan. **1857**, B.A. 13 Dec. 1860, M.A. 1863, V. of St. James', Taunton 1885; m. 15 Jan. 1863 Frances d. of Thomas Adams, J.P. of Lenton Firs, Notts.

Samuel James Banner **Bloxsidge** (1 s. Samuel, land agent), b. S. Nicholas', Warwick, ed. Warwick, **Open** Nov. **1858**, **M.** 28 Jan. 1859 age 17; 1 Classics Mod. 1860, 1 Classics 1863, B.A. 17 Dec. 1863.

Alfred Woodley **Croft** (3 s. Charles Woodley), b. Plymouth 7 Feb. 1841, ed. Manna Mead, **Stap. O.** Nov. **1858**, **M.** 28 Jan. 1859, 1 Math. Mod. 1860, 2 Classics and 2 Math. 1863, B.A. 10 June 1863, M.A. 8 July 1871, Prof. at Presidency Coll. Bengal 1866, Director of public instruction, Bengal 1877, C.I.E. 23 May 1884, K.C.I.E. 15 Feb. 1887; fellow Calcutta Univ. 1867, member of Legisl. Council of Bengal 1887–92, President of Asiatic Soc. of Bengal, 1891–2; *Review of Education in India* 1888.

John Bond **Lee** (1 s. Thomas), b. Crediton, **M.** 29 June 1858 age 17, **Stap.** Nov. 1858, 2 Classics Mod. 1860, 2 Classics 1862, B.A. 11 Dec. 1862, M.A. 9 Feb. 1865, assist. master Bedford gr. sch. 1865–75, Master of Barnet gr. sch. 1875; in orders 1870.

Frederick Aylmer Pendarves **Lory** (4 s. William, R.N., of Mylor near Falmouth), b. Mylor 14 July 1839, ed. Truro, **Eliot, M.** 16 Ap. 1858, B.A. 1861, C. of Par, Cornwall 1871–75, V. of Bagshot 1875; m. at S. Peter's Port, Guernsey, Emily Jane Burton d. of Robert Thornton; Coll. Corn. 510.

William Henry **Bliss** (2 s. John), b. S. Mary's, Oxford, **Org., M.** 22 Oct. 1859 age 25, B.A. 1862, Mus. Bac. 1863, M.A. 8 July 1871, chaplain in ordinary to the Queen 1876, V. of Kew 1885.

Francis Alston **Channing** (o. s. Rev. William Henry, of Boston and Liverpool, by Julia Maria d. of W. Allen; and nephew of Dr. W. E. Channing), b. Cincinnati, Ohio 21 Mch 1841, ed. Liverpool, **M.** Queen's 22 Oct. 1859 age 18; **Open** 5 Nov. 1859, 2 Classics and 2 Math. Mod. 1861, 2 Classics and 4 Math. 1863, English Essay 1865, Arnold Essay 1866; B.A. 10 Dec. 1863, M.A. 1866, Fellow of University College 1866–70; m. 1869 Elizabeth 1 d. of H. Bryant of Boston; barrister L. I. 21 June 1882, M.P. Northants (E. division) Dec. 1885, re-elected 1886 and 1892.

Charles Marriott **Hayward** (3 s. Rev. George Christopher), b. Nympsfield, Stonehouse, Glouc., ed. Sherborne, **Open** 5 Nov. 1859, **M.** 21 Jan. 1860 age 19, left soon.

Charles Coleridge **Pode** (3 s. Thomas Julian, surgeon, by Anne Duke y. d. of Duke Yonge V. of Otterton), b. Plympton Earle 3 Ap. 1841, ed. Winchester 1854, **Stap.** 5 Nov. 1859, **M.** 21 Jan. 1860, 2 Classics Mod. 1862, 1 Phys. 1864, Radcliffe Travelling Fellow 1867–9, B.A. 10 June 1863, M.B. 22 Dec. 1868, M.A. 30 May 1872; d. Castle cottage, Plympton 25 May 1873, age 32.

Ebenezer **Lethbridge** (1 s. Ebenezer), b. Plymouth 23 Dec. 1840; el. **Gifford** and **M.** 1 Feb. 1859 age 18, **Stap.** 2 Nov. 1860; 1 Math. Mod. 1861, 4 Classics 1862, 2 Math. 1863, B.A. 10 June 1863, M.A. 3 May 1866; m. 12 July 1865 Eliza 4 d. of Washington Finlay; Principal of Kishnaghur College, Bengal 1868, Fellow of Calcutta University and Secretary of Simla Educational Commission 1877, Political Agent of the First Class, Press Commissioner 1878, editor of Calcutta Qu. Rev. 1871–8, C.I.E. 1878, K.C.I.E. 1890; knighted by patent 14 Sep. 1885 (as Sir Roper L.), barrister I. T. 9 June 1880, M.P. North Kensington 1874, 1885–92; wrote *The Vernacular*

Press in India (Contemp. Rev. Mch 1880), *A short manual of the History of India* 1881, ed. 2, 1893, *The Golden Book of India* 1893.

Frederick George **Scrivener** (s. Frederick Henry Ambrose, R. of Gerrans, Cornwall 1861–76), b. Sherborne, **Symes** 5 Nov. 1859, M. 21 Jan. 1860 age 18, 3 Classics Mod. 1862, B.A. 26 May 1864, V. of Lakenheath, Suffolk 1874.

Francis Nelson **Wright** (2 s. Rev. William, of Huddersfield), ed. Eton, M. Queen's 22 Oct. 1859 age 18 ; **B.C.** 5 Nov. 1859, B.A. 11 Dec. 1862, Settlement Officer at Cawnpore, now Commissioner of Revenue and Circuit Allahabad division.

Edward **Wilkinson** (6 s. George, solicitor of North Walsham, Norfolk), ed. Bradfield, M. 12 Oct. 1860 age 18, **Open** 2 Nov. 1860, 1 Classics and 3 Math. Mod. 1862, 2 Classics 1864, B.A. 1864, M.A. 27 Nov. 1873 ; barrister L. I. 27 Jan. 1868, conveyancer at 10 New Sq. Lincoln's Inn 1878.

Francis Porten **Beachcroft** (1 s. Samuel, architect), b. Putney, ed. Rugby, M. Corpus 20 Oct. 1860 age 19 ; **Open** 2 Nov. 1860, 1 Classics Mod. 1862, 4 Classics 1863, 4 Hist. 1864, B.A. 26 May 1864, Assist. Commissioner, Kangra, Punjab ; Civil Annuitant 1891.

John Nott **Pyke** (1 s. Rev. John ; took name Pyke-Nott on succeeding to the property of his uncle John Nott of Bydown, Swymbridge, Devon, London Gazette 1863 p. 4285 ; and descended from Thomas Kaynes of Winkleigh who m. Joan sister of Bishop Stapeldon, and from Sir Richard Stapeldon), b. Barnstaple 26 Mch 1841, ed. Winchester, M. 29 May 1860, **Stap.** 2 Nov. 1860, 1 Classics Mod. 1862, B.A. 15 June 1865 ; lord of manor of Parracombe and Rowley ; m. Bishop's Tawton 25 Ap. 1867 Caroline Isabella d. of Frederick Ward of Gillhead, Westmoreland ; wrote *The White Africans, The Æonial* 1887, *Stapeldon, a tragedy* 1892.

Edward Russell **Bernard** (1 s. Rev. Thomas Dehany), b. Marylebone, ed. Harrow, **Open** 2 Nov. 1860, M. 14 Oct. 1861 age 18, Hertford Scholar 1863, 1 Classics Mod. 1863, 2 Classics 1865, Craven Scholar 1866, B.A. 24 Mch 1866, M.A. 30 Ap. 1868, Fellow of Magdalen 1868, V. of Selborne 1875, canon of Salisbury 1889.

Alfred **Plummer** (3 s. Rev. Matthew, by Louisa d. of John Diston Powles), b. Heworth, Durham 17 Feb. 1841, ed. S. Nicolas College, Lancing, M. 14 June 1859 ; **Gifford** 2 Nov. 1860, 1 Classics Mod. 1861, 2 Classics 1863, B.A. 17 Dec. 1863, M.A. 1866, Fellow of Trinity 1865, Tutor 1867–74, Master of Univ. Coll., Durham 1874 ;

m. **Exeter** 29 Dec. 1874 Bertha Katherine d. of Frederick William Everest of Bodmin, now hon. canon of Truro : translated a volume of Ranke's *History of England* for the Clarendon Press, Döllinger's *Fables respecting the Popes* 1871, *Prophecies in the Christian Era* 1873 ; *see* Crockford.

Robert William **Burnaby** (o. s. Rev. Robert), b. and ed. Leicester, **Richards** 2 Nov., **M.** 8 Nov. **1860** age 18, Choral Scholar of New College 1861, B.A. 1863, M.A. 1867, V. of S. Barnabas, Marylebone 1876–81, of E. Cowes, I. of Wight 1881.

Charles Donald **Macleane** (1 s. Rev. Arthur John, of Bath), b. S. Michael's, Cambridge, capt. of Shrewsbury sch.; **Open, and M.** 19 Oct. **1861** age 18 ; Mus. Bac. 3 July 1862, Org. Ex. Coll. 1863, Indian Civil Service 1864 ; B.A. 8 June 1865, Mus. D. 16 Nov. 1865 ; Organist Eton 1872–5, M.A. 27 Nov. 1879 ; composed Two Pastorals for the Piano 1864, a Scherzo 1864, and other pieces; published *Latin and Greek verse translations* .1880 ; Magistrate in Madras Presidency 1891.

Richard Goodall **Gordon** (5 s. capt. Robert Cumming Hamilton), b. S. Peter's, Worcester, ed. Cheltenham, **Open** 19 Oct. **1861, M.** 24 Jan. 1862 age 16, 2 Classics Mod. 1864, 3 Classics 1866, B.A. 25 Oct. 1866, M.A. 30 May 1868, assistant master in King's sch., Canterbury, d. Rothie-Norman, Aberdeenshire 22 July 1892 age 49.

Peter Burrowes **Hutchins** (4 s. late Samuel), b. Dawlish, ed. Sherborne, **Stap.** 19 Oct. **1861, M.** 18 Oct. 1862, 2 Classics Mod. 1864, 3 Hist. 1866, B.A. 7 Feb. 1867, barrister I. T. 26 Jan. 1870.

Osborne William **Tancock** (2 s. Dr. Osborne John, Master of Truro School, V. of Tavistock 1857), b. Truro 25 June 1839, **M.** 2 Feb. 1858, **How** 19 Oct. **1861**, 2 Classics Mod. 1859, 2 Classics 1862, B.A. 11 Dec. 1862, M.A. 2 June 1864, master at Sherborne Nov. 1862 ; wrote *An English Grammar*, for the Clarendon Press; Head Master of Norwich gr. sch. 1879 ; pres. by the College to Little Waltham, Essex 1890 ; Crockford, Bibl. Corn. 702, 1342.

Charles Edward **Cornish** (1 s. Charles Lewis, fellow 1830), b. Harley St., London 9 Oct. 1842, ed. Uppingham, **M.** 29 May 1860, **Richards** 19 Oct. **1861**, 3 Classics Mod. 1862, 2 Classics 1864, B.A. 13 May 1864, M.A. 3 June 1869 ; Master at Uppingham 1864–70, V. of South Petherton, Som. 1875–82, of S. Mary Redcliffe, Bristol 1882, hon. Canon of Bristol.

George **Moore** (2 s. George, solicitor), b. and ed. Warwick, **M.** 23 May 1861 age 18, **Michell** 19 Oct. **1861**, 3 Classics Mod. 1863,

3 Classics 1865, B.A. 1865, M.A. 3 June 1869; V. of Denham, Suffolk 1886.

Samuel Gilbert **Beal** (2 s. William, V. of Brooke, Norwich, d. 20 Ap. 1870, Nat. Biog.), b. Tavistock, ed. Rossall, **Gifford** 19 Oct. **1861, M.** 24 Jan. 1862 age 19, 3 Classics Mod. 1864, B.A. 7 June 1866, M.A. 5 June 1873; R. of Romaldkirk, Darlington 1889; wrote *Recitation of the Daily Office* 1870, and other works.

Edward **Walker** (2 s. John), b. York 1843, ed. York, **Open** 10 Oct. 1862, **M.** 24 Jan. 1863 age 20, 2 Math. Mod. 1865, 3 Math. 1867, B.A. 6 July 1867, M.A. 15 May 1869; barrister L. I. 17 Nov. 1868.

William Henry Atkinson **Emra** (1 s. John, R. of Biddeston, Wilts), b. Charlton, Wilts 17 Dec. 1843, ed. Marlborough, **Open** 10 Oct. **1862, M.** 24 Jan. 1863, 2 Classics Mod. 1865, 3 Classics 1867, B.A. 27 June 1867, M.A. 8 June 1878; R. of Great Blakenham, Ipswich 1871–6; Head Master Salisbury sch. 1877–81; published *The Death of Ægeus and other poems* 1875; m. Bruton, Som. 15 Aug. 1871 Anna Louisa d. of late H. E. Dibdin of London.

William Daniel **Pitman** (1 s. William Parr, R. of Aveton-Gifford, Devon), b. Tiverton 1 Ap. 1844, ed. Repton, **Stap.** 10 Oct. **1862, M.** 24 Jan. 1863, 3 Classics Mod. 1865, B.A. 21 June 1866, M.A. 15 May 1869; C. of Chippenham 1867–70, of Aust with Northwick, Glouc. 1870–74, Patron and R. of Aveton-Gifford 1874.

Walter **Cornish** (2 s. Charles Lewis, fellow 1830), b. Bushey, Herts 6 Sep. 1844, ed. Uppingham, **How** 10 Oct. **1862, M.** 17 Oct. 1863, Symes scholar 10 Oct. 1863, 2 Classics Mod. 1865, 2 Classics 1867, B.A. 1867, M.A. 20 Ap. 1870; master at Lancing sch. 1868–9, at Clevedon sch. 1869–73; d. at sea 24 Feb. 1873.

George **Ekin** (3 s. Thomas), b. Grantham, Lincs., **M.** 19 Oct. 1861 age 18, **Exh.** 10 Oct. **1862**, d. 28 Mch 1865.

James **Avery** (3 s. Thomas), b. Honiton 1844, ed. Honiton, **M.** 11 Oct. 1862, **Stap.** 10 Oct. **1863**, 1 Classics Mod. 1864, 2 Classics 1866, Denyer and Johnson scholar 1867; B.A. 17 Dec. 1866, M.A. 1 Ap. 1871, master at Honiton gr. sch. 1868–74, V. of Merton, Oxon 26 Oct. 1874, d. 7 July 1880.

Robert John **Beadon** (3 s. William), b. Taunton 1844, ed. Sherborne, **M.** 17 Oct. 1863 age 19, **Stap. O.** 10 Oct. **1863**, 2 Classics Mod. 1865, 2 Classics 1867, B.A. 27 Feb. 1868, M.A. 30 Nov. 1876, barrister I. T. 17 Nov. 1870.

Richard Monsell **Waller** (4 s. late John, barrister), b. S. Peter's,

Dublin, ed. Marlborough, **Open** 10 Oct. 1863, **M.** 4 Oct. 1864 age 19; B.A. 6 July 1867, Assist. Magistrate at Bancoorah 1867, Collector of Land Revenue at Purneah, Bengal.

Richard **Abbay** (3 s. Thomas, of Great Ouseburn, Yorks.), b. Hunday Field near Aldborough, **Open** 10 Oct. 1863, **M.** 9 Ap. 1864 age 20, 1 Math. Mod. 1865, 1 Math. 1867, B.A. 6 July 1867, Fellow of Wadham 1869–79, M.A. 22 June 1871, F.G.S., F.R.A.S.; Chaplain Kandyan province, Ceylon 1872, R. of Earl Soham, Essex 1880.

John Henry **Wilkinson** (2 s. Rev. Matthew), **M.** New Coll. 10 June 1863 age 18; **How** 10 Oct. 1863, Demy Magdalen 1863, B.A. 1870, M.A. 1872, master at S. Paul's Coll., Stony Stratford 1871–2, resident Durdam Down, Clifton 1878.

George Osmond Lees **Thomson** (2 s. late Rev. Henry Thurston, by Agnes Elizabeth Phipps), b. Kentisbeare, Devon 29 June 1842, ed. Hurtspierpoint, **M.** Magdalen H. 1 Nov. 1861, Lucy exhibitioner Magd. H.; **How** 3 Dec. 1863, 2 Classics 1865, B.A. 18 Dec. 1865, M.A. 2 Dec. 1869, Master at S. John's Coll., Hurtspierpoint, Fellow of S. Nicholas Coll., Lancing, Sussex 1867–80; in orders, Head Master of King's Coll., Taunton 1880.

Charles Henry Cecil **Ward** (2 s. Rev. Edward Langton), b. Blendworth, Hants 1844, ed. Tonbridge 1856–63; **How O.**, and **M.** 3 Dec. 1863 age 19, B.A. 7 Nov. 1867, resides at Lausanne.

Robert **Hutchinson** (1 s. Robert Pender, C. of Christchurch, Camberwell), b. Portsea, Hants 4 June 1845, ed. Merchant Taylors; **Open** 8, and **M.** 11 Oct. 1864, 1 Classics Mod. 1866, 3 Classics 1868, B.A. 22 Dec. 1868, M.A. 10 Oct. 1871, tutor at Cumbrae College 1869–70, master at S. Edward's sch., Summertown, Oxford 1873–75, R. of Woodeaton, Oxon 1881.

Richard Allin **Robertson** (2 s. Rev. James, of Bristol), b. Southsea, ed. Crewkerne, **Open** 8 Oct. 1864, **M.** 28 Jan. 1865 age 18, scholar Peterhouse, Camb. 1867.

Edward **Armstrong** (2 s. John, first bishop of Grahamstown, by Frances d. of Edward Whitmore), b. Tidenham, Glouc. 3 Mch 1846, ed. Grahamstown gr. sch., and Bradfield, **Open** 1864, **M.** 28 Jan. 1865, 1 Classics Mod. 1866, 1 Classics 1869, B.A. 10 June 1869, M.A. 15 June 1871; Fellow of Queen's 1869, Lecturer and Senior Bursar, delegate for the Examination of Schools, Curator of the Botanic Garden, and of the Park; m. 2 Oct. 1879 Mabel d. of J. W. Watson; wrote *The Duty of the University with relation to the Modern Languages* (pr. pr., anon , no date); *Elizabeth Farnese, the Termagant of*

Spain 1892; *The French Wars of Religion in their Political Aspects* 1892.

John Maitland **Reid** (o. s. Edward Maitland), b. Marylebone 1846, ed. Cheltenham, **Stap. O**. 8 Oct. **1864, M**. 28 Jan. 1865 age 19, 1 Classics Mod. 1866, 1 Classics 1869, B.A. 4 Nov. 1869, M.A. 17 May 1872; barrister L. I. 18 Nov. 1872, on the Stock Exchange.

John Morgan **Ley** (3 s. Col. John Morgan, d. Exeter 15 Feb. 1864); **Stap.** 8 Oct. **1864**, d. Penge, Surrey 19 Jan. 1866, bur. 26 Jan. S. David's, Exeter. Memorial window in chapel of Sherborne School: Coll. Corn. 499.

Alfred **Messervy** (3 s. George, merchant), b. S. Helier's, Jersey 1845, ed. Victoria College; **Ch. I**. 10 Dec. **1864, M**. 14 Oct. 1865 age 20, Taylorian scholar 1867, 1 Classics Mod. 1867, 3 Classics 1869, B.A. 9 Ap. 1870, M.A. 3 Feb. 1881 in absence, Master of modern languages at Haileybury, teacher in Mauritius.

William Torry **Scott** (1 s. Rev. William Langston, of Dunmow, Essex), b. S. Giles', Northampton 1845, **M**. 16 Jan. 1864 age 19, **Richards** 8 Oct. **1864**, 1 Classics Mod. 1866, 2 Classics 1867, B.A. 17 Dec. 1867, d. Dunmow 5 Nov. 1877.

Alfred Beaven **Beaven** (o. s. John), b. Bristol 1847, ed. Bristol; **Exh.** 8, and **M**. 18 Oct. **1864** age 17; scholar Pemb. 1865, 2 Classics and 2 Math. Mod. 1866, second in I. C. S. Exam. 1866, 4 Classics and 2 Hist. 1868, B.A. and S.C.L. 1868, M.A. 16 Ap. 1873, master at Ch. Coll., Finchley 1868, at Bruton 1871, 2 master Worcester Cath. sch. 1872–4, master of Preston gr. sch. 1874, resides Avenham house, Preston; *see* Crockford.

Erasmus **Wilkinson** (3 s. Matthew, D.D., of W. Lavington, Devizes), b. Marlborough 1846, ed. Eton, **Gifford O**. Oct. **1864, M**. 28 Jan. 1865 age 19, vac. 1868; 2 Classics Mod. 1867, B.A. 14 Dec. 1876, M.A. 31 May 1879.

John Lancaster Gough **Mowat** (3 s. Rev. James, of Frome, by Elizabeth d. of John Wilmot Lancaster), b. S. Helier's, Jersey 25 Sep. 1846, ed. Taunton; **Ch. I**. 17 June, and **M**. 14 Oct. **1865**, 1 Classics Mod. 1867, 2 Classics 1869, B.A. 22 Dec. 1869, Fellow Pemb. 1871, M.A. 1872, Proproctor 1877, 1879, el. Proctor by Ex. Coll. 1885, Curator of Bodleian, edited *Latin Glossary called Sinonoma Bartholomei* in Anecdota Oxoniensia, *A walk along the Teufelsmauer and Pfahlgraben* 1885, *Notes on the Oxfordshire Domesday* 1892.

Edgar **Wharton** (3 s. John), b. Scarborough, ed. S. Peter's school, York, **Open** 30 Sep. **1865, M**. 19 Jan. 1866 age 20, 1 Math.

Mod. 1867, 1 Math. 1870, B.A. 30 June 1870, M.A. 6 Feb. 1873, V. of S. Mary le Wigford, Lincoln 1878.

Alfred Vivian **Jones** (2 s. Alfred, of Bedford), b. S. Kitts, W. Indies, ed. Bedford; **Open** 30 Sep., and **M.** 14 Oct. **1865** age 19, 1 Classics Mod. 1867, 3 Classics 1869, B.A. 24 Mch 1870, M.A. 2 June 1876, Master at Haileybury.

William **Mogg** (1 s. Frederick George, of Brecon), b. Pilmore, Durham, ed. Sherborne, **Stap. O.** 30 Sep. **1865**, **M.** 19 Jan. 1866 age 18, 1 Classics Mod. 1867, 3 Classics 1869, B.A. 10 Feb. 1870, M.A. 31 Oct. 1872, master in Loretto sch., Edinburgh, V. of Locking, Som. 1880.

George Aubrey William **Thorold** (1 s. Rev. William, by Frances Elizabeth 1 d. of James Gould of Knapp, Devon), b. Warkleigh, Devon, ed. Rugby, **M.** 19 Jan. 1865 age 19, **Stap.** 30 Sep. **1865**, 2 Classics Mod. 1868, 2 Hist. 1870, B.A. 18 June 1870, M.A. 12 June 1873, solicitor London.

Charles Edward Thornes **Roberts** (3 s. William, solicitor), b. and ed. Oswestry, **M.** 11 Oct. 1862 age 19, **Exh.** 30 Sep. **1865**; 1 Classics Mod. 1864, 3 Classics 1866, B.A. 17 Dec. 1866, M.A. 24 May 1883 ; Subwarden of S. Paul's sch., Stony Stratford 1865-9, master at Ely gr. sch. 1869-74, V. of Brinsley, Notts 12 Mch 1874-1881, P.C. S. Clement's, Notting Hill 1886.

Charles Edward **Leeds** (1 s. Edward Thurlow), b. Eye, Northants, ed. Warwick, **M.** 16 Jan. 1864 age 18, **Michell** 30 Sep. **1865**, 1 Math. Mod. 1866, 2 Math. 1868, B.A. 22 Dec. 1868, M.A. 23 June 1870, Whitworth engineering scholar; solicitor 1873, in practice at 5 Victoria St., Westminster, ? d. 1876.

Geoffry **Hill** (7 s. Rev. Richard Humphry, of Britford, Salisbury), b. Coombe Bisset, Wilts, ed. Beaumaris ; **Exh.** 30 Sep., and **M.** 19 Oct. **1865** age 19, 2 Classics Mod. 1867, 2 Hist. 1869, B.A. 3 Nov. 1870, M.A. 16 Ap. 1879, C. of S. Columba, Edinburgh 1883.

Edward Chorley **Lutley** (2 s. Samuel Baker), b. and ed. Exeter, named **Reynolds** Mich. **1865, M.** 14 Oct. 1865 age 18, B.A. 1869, M.A. 5 June 1873, C. in charge of Oake, Taunton 1882.

Frederick Scotson **Clark** (1 s. Michael), b. Southwark 16 Nov. 1840, ed. King's Coll., London ; **Org.**, and **M.** 13 Oct. **1865** age 24, Mus. Bac. 1867, founded London Organ School 1865, C. of S. Michael's, Lewes 1868-9, assist. chapl. Stuttgart 1870-4, chapl. Amsterdam 1874-8, chapl. Paris 1879, d. 5 July 1883 ; Nat. Biog. x. 401, Mod. Eng. Biog.

Geoffrey **Hughes** (4 s. late Rev. Henry), b. All Saints, S. Pancras, ed. Canterbury, **M.** 19 Jan. 1866 age 18, **Stap. O.** 2 June 1866, 1 Math. Mod. 1867, 2 Math. 1869, B.A. 16 June 1870, M.A. 13 Dec. 1877, C. of Milverton, Som. 1871–2, of Dorking 1872, Chaplain of Dorking Union 1875.

William **Lovell** (3 s. Charles Henry, solicitor), b. S. Pancras, ed. Islington, **M.** 19 May 1866 age 17, **Open** 1 Dec. 1866, 2 Classics Mod. 1868, 3 Classics 1870, B.A. 17 Dec. 1870, M.A. 5 Ap. 1873; C. of Wantage 1874–6, joined Church of Rome 1876, solicitor.

Thomas Alexander Ashburnham **Chirol** (1 s. Rev. Alexander), b. Enfield, ed. Hurstpierpoint, **M.** Ch. Ch. 23 May 1866 age 19; **Open** 1 Dec. 1866, 1 Math. Mod. 1868, Junior Math. Scholar 1868, 1 Math. 1870, B.A. 30 June 1870, M.A. 6 Feb. 1873; master at King's sch., Canterbury 1872–3, 2 master S. Chad's sch., Denstone 1873–5, chaplain of S. Chad's gr. sch. 1873–5, master at Kelly Coll., Tavistock 1876, at Harrow 1877–8, at Uppingham 1879–84, at Shrewsbury 1885–90.

William Gregory **Walker** (2 s. Giles; and nephew of Plumpton S. Wilson 1852), b. North Lynn, Norfolk 1848, ed. Tonbridge 1860–7, **Stap.** 1 Dec. 1866, **M.** 19 Oct. 1867 age 18, 2 Classics Mod. 1869, 3 Classics 1871, B.A. 22 Dec. 1871, barrister L. I. 7 June 1873, wrote *The Partition Acts* 1868 *and* 1876, ed. 2 1882; *A Compendium of the Law of Executors* 1880, ed. 2 1888, *The Law and Practice of Administration Actions* 1883 (both with E. J. Elgood), *The Practice in Equity* (Sydney); practising 1885 at Sydney, N. S. Wales, Chancellor of the Diocese under Bishop Barry.

John Rainforth **Walker** (1 s. Frederick John, R. of Eaton-Hastings near Lechlade), b. Teignmouth, ed. Exeter, named **Reynolds** Mich. 1866, he held also the **Vilvaine** exhibition, **M.** 1 Dec. 1866 age 18, 2 Math. Mod. 1868, 2 Math. 1870, B.A. 15 Dec. 1870.

Alfred John **Pound** (2 s. Rev. William), b. Norton, near Malton, Yorks., ed. Eton; **Reynolds, M.** 29 May 1866 age 19, 3 Law and Hist. 1869, B.A. 1869, M.A. 1875, magistrate Guiana 1875–6.

Arthur Wollaston **Hutton** (7 s. Henry Frederick, R. of Spridlington Lincs., by Louisa d. of H. J. Wollaston, R. of Scotter), b. Spridlington 5 Sep. 1848, ed. Bury S. Edmunds, Brussels, and Cheltenham, **Stap.** 1 Dec. 1866, **M.** 26 Jan. 1867, 2 Classics Mod. 1869, 1 Theol. 1871, B.A. 15 June 1871, M.A. 31 May 1873; C. of S. Barnabas, Oxford 1871–73, R. of Spridlington 1873–76, at the Oratory, Birmingham 1876–83, Librarian of Gladstone Library, National Liberal Club 1887; wrote 1872 *Our Position as Catholics* *in the Church of England*, 1879 *The Anglican Ministry*, with preface by Cardinal Newman, 1892 *Life of Cardinal Manning*; edited 1892 Arthur Young's *Tour in Ireland*, and *The Speeches and Public Addresses of the Right Hon. W. E. Gladstone.*

Edwyn Reynolds **Massey** (3 s. Thomas, R. of Hatcliffe, by Mary d. of William Heywood of Broughton, Lincs.), b. Hatcliffe 28 Ap. 1847, ed. Newark, **M.** 14 Oct. 1865, **How O.** 2 June **1866**; **Darell** 1865–70, 1 Classics Mod. 1867, 4 Classics 1869, B.A. 24 Mch 1870, M.A. 2 May 1872; C. of Summertown, Oxford 1871–74, Viceprincipal Lichfield Theol. Coll. 1875; m. 28 Ap. 1879 Jessie Margaret d. of Charles Titian Hawkins of Summertown; V. of Merton, Oxon, 1880–93, R. of Marsh-Gibbon, Bucks 1893, R.D. of Claydon 1893.

Edward **Symonds** (1 s. George Edward, V. of Thaxted, Essex), b. Kingskerswell, Devon, ed. Eton 1859, King's scholar, **M.** 13 Mch 1866 age 19, **Gifford** 2 June **1866**, vac. end of 1868; 3 Classics Mod. 1868, B.A. 25 Nov. 1869, M.A.; V. of Stoke by Nayland, 1891.

Lewis Taswell **Lochée** (1 s. Alfred, physician), b. Canterbury 1849, ed. Tonbridge 1861–7, **Exh.** 1 Dec. **1866**, **M.** 19 Oct. 1867 age 18, 2 Classics Mod. 1869, 3 Classics 1871, B.A. 22 Dec. 1871, M.A. 22 May 1874; R. of Barnes, London 1885, d. there 26 Jan. 1891.

George Purnell **Merrick** (1 s. William), b. Clifton, **M.** 27 June 1865 age 23, Mus. Bac. Edmund H. 28 June 1865; **Org.** 1867–71, B.A. 8 July 1871, M.A. 1878, Chaplain Milbank Prison 1883.

William John **Stewart** (1 s. William Goldfinch, collector of customs), b. and ed. Liverpool, **M.** 12 June 1867 age 18, **Open** 22 Feb. 1868, 2 Classics Mod. 1869, 3 Classics 1871, B.A. 8 Feb. 1872, barrister L. I. 13 June 1877.

William **Grey** (o. s. Rev. William, d. 1872), b. S. John's, Newfoundland 18 Ap. 1850, ed. Bradfield, **Open** 22 Feb. **1868**, **M.** 16 Jan. 1869, 1 Classics Mod. 1870, 2 Classics 1873, B.A. 26 June 1873, M.A. 15 May 1875, lay reader in dioc. London, and lic. to lecture on foreign missions: Professor of Classics and Philosophy at Codrington Coll., Barbados: 9 Earl of Stamford 1890, claim to sit in Upper House admitted May 1892: portrait in Figaro 11 May 1892 p. 9.

Sidney Thomas **Irwin** (4 s. late Col. Irwin), b. Perth, W. Australia, ed. Wellington College, **M.** Worcester 14 Oct. 1867 age 19; scholar Lincoln 1867–8; **Open** 22 Feb. **1868**, 1 Classics Mod. 1869, 2 Classics 1871, B.A. 2 May 1872, M.A. 15 Ap. 1880, master at Clifton College.

Walter Churchill **Perry** (4 s. John, V. of Perranzabulo, Cornwall, by Sophia d. of Rev. Thomas Stabback), b. 4 Feb. 1849, ed. Sherborne, **Stap.** 22 Feb. **1868, M.** 30 May 1868, 1 Classics Mod. 1870, 3 Classics 1872, B.A. 31 May 1873, M.A. 12 June 1886, master at Uppingham, now has a preparatory school at W. Malvern; Coll. Corn. 721.

William Charles **Warner** (2 s. John, barrister), b. S. George's, Bloomsbury, ed. Eton, **Stap. O.** 22 Feb. **1868, M.** 30 May 1868 age 19; 2 Classics Mod. 1870, 2 Classics 1872, B.A. 24 Dec. 1872, M.A. 8 Ap. 1876; C. of Herstmonceaux, Sussex, d. 28 Ap. 1876.

Joseph Henry **Ayre** (1 s. Rev. Joseph Watson), b. South Lambeth, ed. Harrow, **How** 22 Feb. **1868, M.** 16 Oct. 1868 age 19; scholar of Trinity 1869, d. 22 Nov. 1872.

Henry **Chettle** (1 s. Henry Hulbert, governor and chaplain of Woodhouse Grove Wesleyan sch., Leeds), b. Manchester, ed. Shrewsbury; **Richards** 22 Feb. **1868, M.** 30 May 1868 age 20, 2 Classics Mod. 1870, 2 Classics 1872, B.A. 6 Feb. 1873, M.A. 29 Ap. 1875; Master of Tottenham sch., then of Stationers' sch., Fleet St., London.

Henry **Broadbent, Open** 6 Feb. **1869,** Fellow 1874.

Samuel **Wood** (1 s. Edwin Henry), b. Waltham, ed. Christ's Hospital, **Open** 6 Feb. **1869, M.** 15 Oct. 1869 age 19, 1 Math. Mod. 1871, 3 Math. 1873, B.A. 5 Feb. 1874, d. 21 Feb. 1879.

Edward Theodore **Gibbons** (o. s. George Buckmaster, P.C. of Laneast, Cornwall, by Anne 3 d. of Sir W. L. S. Trelawny), b. Launceston 31 July 1850, ed. Sherborne; **M.** 5, and el. **Stap.** 6 Feb. **1869,** 1 Classics Mod. 1870, 1 Classics 1872, Ellerton Essay 1875, B.A. and S.C.L. 24 Dec. 1872, M.A. 10 June 1875, a Senior Student of Christ Church 18 Dec. 1872, deacon 1874, d. Madeira of consumption 28 July 1876; Bibl. Corn. 171, Oxf. Undergraduates' Journal 26 Oct. 1876 p. 25 a brief memoir.

Edgar John **Elgood** (4 s. John G.), b. Marylebone 26 May 1850, ed. Harrow, **Stap. O.** 6 Feb. **1869,** also held scholarship from Harrow; **M.** 18 Oct. 1869, 1 Classics Mod. 1871, 2 Classics 1873, 2 B.C.L. 1874, B.A. 5 Feb. 1874, B.C.L. and M.A. 15 June 1876, barrister L. I. 17 Nov. 1875, J.P. Kent, resides 8 New Court, Carey St., London W.C.; m. 23 Nov. 1875 Margaret Cooper d. and coh. of Robert Milnes Wright of South Collingham, Notts, and stepdaughter of John Broadbent; joint author, with W. G. Walker, of *Law of Administration Actions* 1883 and *Law of Executors* 1888; ed. *Simpson on Infants,* ed. 2 1890.

George Herbert **Engleheart** (1 s. late George Edward, barrister M.T.), b. S. Peter's Port, Guernsey 25 Ap. 1851, ed. Elizabeth Coll.; **Ch. I.** 10 Dec. **1869, M.** 29 Jan. **1870,** B.A. 3 Dec. 1874, M.A. 25 Oct. 1877, master at Lucton gr. sch., Leominster 1874, V. of Chute Forest, Dorset 1881 ; m. Bredon 2 July 1878 Mary Isabel 1 d. of William Henry Evans of Bredon Old Hall, Worcs.

James Alexander **Balleine** (2 s. George), b. S. Helier's, Jersey, ed. Victoria Coll.; **Ch. I.** 10 Dec. **1869, M.** 29 Jan. 1870 age 19, 3 Math. Mod. 1872, 3 Math. 1874, B.A. 3 Dec. 1874, M.A. 29 June 1876, V. of Yarnton, Oxon, 1878–90, of S. Mary's, Acock's Green, Birmingham 1890.

Sydney Hamilton **Little** (10 s. John, solicitor), b. Stewartstown, Tyrone, ed. Trinity Coll., Dublin; el. **Symes,** and **M.** 6 Feb. **1869** age 19, B.A. 5 Dec. 1872, M.A. 7 June 1878; C. of S. John's, Waterloo road 1872–4, of S. Peter's, Bournemouth 1874–5, V. of Hordle, Hants 7 Sep. 1875, res. 9 Oct. 1877, joined the Church of Rome 1881.

Richard John **Milner** (2 s. Edward, architect), b. Liverpool, ed. Dulwich College, **M.** 2 June 1868 age 18, **Michell** 6 Feb. **1869,** 1 Math. Mod. 1870, 3 Math. 1872, B.A. 17 Dec. 1872, M.A. 28 Jan. 1875, R. of Stock-Gaylard, Dorset 1883.

John Wood Deane **Comins** (1 s. Rev. John, of North Huish, Ivybridge), b. E. Budleigh, ed. Exeter, named **Reynolds** Mich. **1867**; el. 6 Feb. 1869, obtained Gifford exhibition 1869 and Vilvaine 1871 ; **M.** 17 Oct. 1867 age 18, became a Non-Coll. student, B.A. 1873.

Charles Coleridge **Mackarness** (1 s. J. Fielder, Fellow 1844), b. Tardebigge, Worcs. 22 July 1850, ed. Winchester 1863, **M.** 17 May 1869, **How** 19 May 1869, res. when his father became Bishop of Oxford ; 3 Classics Mod. 1871, 2 Classics 1873 ; B.A. 17 Dec. 1873, M.A. 8 Ap. 1876, C. of S. Mary's, Reading 1874, chaplain to Bishop of Oxford 1875, examining chaplain to Bishop of Argyle 1876, V. of S. Martin's, Scarborough 1889.

Arthur **Reynolds** (2 s. Patrick H., LL.B., V. of S. Stephen's Birmingham 1854), b. Waterhead, Lancs. 12 Ap. 1851, ed. King Edward's sch. Birmingham, sch. exhibitioner, **Open** 5 Feb. **1870, M.** 4 June 1870, 2 Classics Mod. 1872, 3 Classics 1874, B.A. 22 Dec. 1874, M.A. 15 Jan. 1877, master at Honiton gr. sch. 1875–8, at Merchant Taylors 1878 ; resides 41 Nevern sq., S.W. ; m. 30 July 1886 Jeannie Marianne 2 d. of late C. T. Bell, of Freemantle, Southampton.

James Saumarez **Mann** (o. s. James Saumarez, lieut. R.N., d. Guernsey 15 Sep. 1851 age 30), b. S. Peter's Port, Guernsey 11 Oct. 1851, ed. Elizabeth Coll.; **Open** 5 Feb. **1870**, **M.** 15 Oct. 1870, 2 Classics Mod. 1872, 1 Classics 1874, B.A. 22 Dec. 1874, M.A. 21 Mch 1878, fellow of Trinity 29 Sep. 1879; translated Schömann's *Antiquities of Greece* (with E. G. Hardy), vol. i 1880; m. London 7 Aug. 1890 Amy Gertrude d. of late Rev. T. Bowman of Clifton.

Charles Coverdale **Tancock** (3 s. Dr. Osborne John), b. Truro 1 Dec. 1851, ed. Sherborne, **Stap.** 5 Feb. **1870**, **M.** 15 Oct. 1870, 1 Classics Mod. 1872, 1 Classics 1874, B.A. 22 Dec. 1874, M.A. 18 May 1877, master at Charterhouse 1875, at Rossall 1886, in orders; Bibl. Corn. 1342.

Francis Hardwicke **Manley** (o. s. major Henry John), b. Jubbulpore, India, ed. Tiverton, **Stap.** 5 Feb. **1870**, **M.** 15 Oct. 1870 age 18, 1 Math. Mod. 1872, 1 Math. 1874, B.A. 18 June 1874, M.A. 19 May 1877, master at Felstead sch. 1877, pres. by the College to R. of Broad Somerford, Wilts Dec. 1887.

· Frederick Gordon Bluett **Campbell** (1 s. late capt. William Wilson, by Jane Bluett), b. S. Helier's, Jersey 21 Aug. 1851, ed. Cheltenham; **Ch. I.** 6 Dec. **1870**, **M.** 21 Jan. 1871, 3 Classics 1873, 4 Law 1875, B.A. 10 June 1875, M.A. 25 Oct. 1877, incorp. M.A. Trinity, Camb. 1877, LL.D., barrister I. T. 11 May 1881; lecturer under Board of Legal Studies, Cambridge.

Edward James **Campbell** (4 s. late John), b. Looe, ed. Mannamead, Plymouth, **M.** 15 Oct. 1869 age 19, **Gifford** 5 Feb. **1870**, 1 Math. Mod. 1871, 2 Math. 1873, B.A. 17 Dec. 1873, M.A. 19 Ap. 1877, master at United Service Coll., Westward Ho, Bideford 1874, and chaplain 1875, master at King's sch., Canterbury 1879, d. Looe 14 Aug. 1891.

Edwin Augustus **Deacon** (6 s. George Edward, V. of Leek, Staffs.), b. Ottery, ed. Marlborough, **How** 5 Feb. **1870**, **M.** 23 Ap. 1870 age 19; 3 Classics Mod. 1872, 3 Law 1874, B.A. 18 June 1874, M.A., of Chinese Imperial Maritime Customs, d. Swatow, China 31 Oct. 1881 age 31.

Frederick Eden **Pargiter** (1 s. Rev. Robert), b. Jaffna, Ceylon, ed. Taunton, **How** 5 Feb. **1870**, **M.** 25 Ap. 1870 age 18; 1 Math. Mod. 1871, Boden Sanskrit scholar 1872, 1 Math. 1873, B.A. 26 June 1873, Assist. Collector and Magistrate at Chittagong, Bengal 1875.

Francis Edward **Pitman** (2 s. Rev. Henry Rogers), b. Basford, Notts, **Darell 1870**, **M.** 30 May 1871 age 19, 4 Theol. 1874, B.A. 17 Dec. 1874, naval chaplain 1882, chaplain H.M.S. Serapis 1888.

Arthur Russell **Baker** (o. s. John Russell, M.A. barrister), b. S. Gerrans, Cornwall, ed. Marlborough, **Open** 21 Jan. 1871, M. 13 Oct. 1871 age 19, 2 Classics Mod. 1873, 2 Classics 1875, B.A. 3 Jan. 1876, M.A. 24 Ap. 1879, C. of S. James', Devonport 1876, d. 6 Ap. 1885; Coll. Corn. 47.

Samuel Blackwell **Williams**, Guest-Williams 1873 (1 s. John Guest), b. Frodsham, Cheshire, ed. Shrewsbury, **Open** 21 Jan. 1871, M. 13 Oct. 1871 age 19, 1 Classics Mod. 1873, B.A. 2 Dec. 1875, M.A. 24 Ap. 1878, master at Durham sch. 1877.

Ernest George **Hardy** (1 s. George, I.C.S.), b. Hampstead, ed. Highgate, **Stap.** 21 Jan. 1871, M. 25 Jan. 1871 age 19, 1 Classics Mod. 1872, 1 Classics 1874, B.A. 22 Dec. 1874, M.A. 1877, Fellow of Jesus Dec. 1874–8, m. 1876; Master of Grantham sch. 1879, edited Plat. *Republic I*, 1882; *see* p. 242.

Augustus Jameson **Miller** (2 s. Joseph Augustus, V. of Ile Brewers, Taunton), b. New Windsor 5 July 1852, ed. Tiverton, **Stap.** 21 Jan. 1871, M. 14 Oct. 1871 age 19, 2 Math. Mod. 1873, 1 Theol. 1875, junior Septuagint prize 1875, Denyer and Johnson 1876, senior Septuagint prize 1877; B.A. 12 June 1875, M.A. 2 May 1878, C. of Puckington, Som. 1875–7, assist. lecturer at the Clergy sch., Leeds 1877–8, C. of Bramley near Leeds 1878–80, V. of Middleton, Leeds 1880, presented by Ex. Coll. to Wootton, Northants 1887, R.D. of Preston (1) 1890; m. S. James', Tonbridge 1 Oct. 1879 Kate Alice d. of Henry Matthews of Southsea; wrote *The Three Mirrors, an allegory* 1882.

Lewis Boyd **Sebastian** (o. s. Lewis and Helen Sarah), b. London 15 Feb. 1851, ed. Winchester 1863, M. 15 Oct. 1869, **Richards** 21 Jan. 1871, 2 Classics Mod. 1871, 1 Law 1873, Vinerian Law scholar 1874, B.A. 11 Dec. 1873, 1 B.C.L. 1874, B.C.L. and M.A. 2 June 1876; barrister L. I. 26 Jan. 1876, wrote *The Law of Trade Marks* 1870, ed. 3 1890.

Edward Vernon **Collins** (2 s. John Basset, by Elizabeth Avis Scobell, 1 d. of Richard Cunnack of Penzance), b. Bodmin 25 Dec. 1849, ed Exeter, M. 2 June 1868, **Vilvaine 1871**, B.A. 30 May 1872, M.A. 28 Jan. 1875, master in All Saints' sch., Bloxham near Banbury 1872–9, V. of Caldicot, Monmouth 1885.

Joseph Cox **Bridge** (3 s. John P., professor of music, d. Chester 1893), b. and ed. Rochester; **Org., M.** 14 Oct. 1871 age 18, 4 Hist. 1875, B.A. 10 June 1875, Mus. B. 26 Oct. 1876, M.A. 24 Ap. 1878, Mus. D. 22 May 1885, org. Chester Cathedral.

William Ramsay **Sparks** (1 s. William, merchant, Glasgow, by
Isabella d. of Jas. Irvine, merchant, Demerara), b. Dunoon, Argyles.
22 May 1850, **M.** 15 Oct. 1869 age 19, **Stap.** 18 Ap. **1872**, 2 Theol.
1872, B.A. 12 Dec. 1872, Denyer and Johnson 1873; C. of Folkestone
1873–4, incumbent of S. John's, Aberdeen 1874–7, C. of Nottingham
1878–80, V. of Carrington, Notts 1883; m. S. Matthias', Richmond,
Beatrice d. of Josiah Greene, shipowner, King's Lynn; wrote *Our
Village Mission* 1882.

Frederick Arthur **Clarke** (1 s. late Fred. Ricketts, by Elizabeth d. of
William Woodford), b. Taunton.   Bishop's Hull, 24 May 1853, ed.
Taunton, **Open** 3 Feb. **1872**, **M.** 8 Feb. 1872 age 18, 1 Classics Mod.
1873, 1 Classics 1875, Ellerton Essay 1878, B.A. 3 Feb. 1876, M.A. 1878.
Fellow of Corpus 20 Mch 1876, lecturer at S. John's 1877, Chaplain
to Legation at Athens 1884–87, Vice-Principal of Wells Coll. 1888.
R. of Duntisborne Rous, Glouc. 1893.

William **Foord-Kelcey** (2 s. late William Foord), b. Mersham,
Kent, ed. Ramsgate, **Open** 3 Feb. **1872**, **M.** 21 May 1872 age 18,
1 Math. Mod. 1873, 1 Math. 1876, B.A. 22 June 1876, master at
Woolwich Acad. 1877; barrister I. T. 9 June 1880: took name
Kelcey 1872, under will of Stephen Kelcey of Lyminge, Kent.

Thomas Alford **Rogers** (4 s. Richard Cogan, barrister), b. Stonehouse, ed. Christ's Hosp. (A. W. Lockhart's *Exhibitioners of Christ's
Hospital*, 9 twice, 21, 29, 33, 34); **Stap. O.** 3 Feb. **1872**, **M.** 11 Oct.
1872 age 19. 1 Math. Mod. 1874, 2 Math. 1876, B.A. 7 July 1877.

Henry Stacy **Skipton** (3 s. Henry Stacy), b. Londonderry, ed.
Cheltenham, **Stap. O.** 3 Feb. **1872**, **M.** 14 Oct. 1872 age 19, 3 Classics
Mod. 1874, 3 Classics 1876, 3 Hist. 1877, B.A. 26 Oct. 1876.

William Knapman **Willcocks** (4 s. Roger), b. Teignmouth 20 Sep.
1852, ed. King's Coll., London, **M.** Lincoln 18 Oct. 1871; **Exh.**
12 Dec. **1871**, 2 Classics Mod. 1873, 3 Classics 1875, B.A. 24 Dec.
1875, M.A. 24 Ap. 1878, master in King's Coll. sch., London 1876,
barrister M. T. 17 Nov. 1879, wrote *Devonshire Men at the Inner
Temple* 1547–1660 (Devonshire Assoc. 1885), resides 17 Scarsdale
villas, Kensington.

Frederick Sanders **Pulling** (1 s. Frederick William, V. of Pinhoe,
Exeter, by Sarah Caroline d. of Rear Adm. Thomas Sanders), b.
Modbury, Devon 22 June 1853, ed. Bradfield, **Gifford** 12 Dec. **1871**,
M. 19 Jan. 1872, 1 Hist. 1875, B.A. 10 June 1875, M.A. 24 Oct.
1878, Prof. of History at the Yorkshire College, Leeds 1877, d.
Pinhoe 6 July 1893; m. 24 Sep. 1877 Edith Louisa d. of Richard

William Geldart, R. of Clyst S. Laurence, Devon; wrote *Life of Sir Joshua Reynolds* 1880, *Life and Speeches of the Marquis of Salisbury* 2 vols. 1885; joint ed. of *The Dictionary of English History* 1884.

Stuart Oliver **Ridley** (1 s. Oliver Matthew, V. of Cobham, Gravesend, by Louisa Pole d. of William Stuart), b. Marylebone 8 June 1853, ed. Haileybury, **M.** Magdalen 20 Jan. 1872; **Nat. Sci.** 3 Feb. **1873**, 1 Nat. Sci. 1875, B.A. 17 Dec. 1875, M.A. 19 May 1881, master in Friars sch., Bangor; Assistant in Brit. Mus. 1878, C. of Maryport, Cumberland 1887–90, of Wareham 1891; wrote Report on the *Monaxonida* (spunges), in Scientific Results of the Challenger expedition 1873–6, with A. Dendy; Articles *Alcyonaria* and *Spongida* in Zoological Collections made by the Alert 1881–2; articles on *Polyzoa, Corals,* and *Spunges,* in Proc. Zool. Soc., Journ. Linn. Soc., Annals and Mag. of Nat. Hist., and Zoologist (with H. N. Ridley).

Robert Edward **Newport** (5 s. Rev. Henry, Master of Exeter gr. sch.), b. and ed. Exeter, **M.** 21 May 1872, **Acland** and **Vilvaine** **1873**; at Alban H. 1875; Abbott scholar 1872.

William **Warry** (1 s. William), b. W. Coker, Som., ed. Sherborne, **Open** 3 Feb. **1873**, **M.** 31 May 1873 age 19, 1 Classics Mod. 1875, 3 Classics 1877, B.A. 7 July 1877, M.A. 1880, Interpreter in Civil Service, Siam 1878, Political officer Public Works department, India.

George Gidley **Robinson** (3 s. Samuel Henry), b. Howrah, Bengal 27 Oct. 1854, ed. Crediton, **Stap.** 3 Feb. **1873**, **M.** 31 May 1873, 1 Classics Mod. 1875, 2 Classics 1877, B.A. 7 July 1877, M.A. 14 May 1880.

Thomas Northmore **Hart-Smith** (1 s. William, V. of S. Minver, Cornwall, by Charlotte Pierce 1 d. of N. H. P. Lawrence), b. S. Minver 9 June 1854, ed. Marlborough 1868, **Stap.** 3 Feb. **1873**, **M.** 10 Oct. 1873, 1 Classics Mod. 1875, 2 Classics 1877, B.A. 25 Oct. 1877, M.A. 29 Ap. 1880, master at Marlborough 1879–89, deacon 1881, Head Master Epsom Coll. 1889.

Frederick Some **Hewson** (1 s. Frederick, solicitor), b. Brentford 4 July 1853, ed. Winchester 1866, **M.** 21 May 1872 age 18, **Michell** 3 Feb. **1873**, 1 Classics Mod. 1874, 2 Classics 1876, B.A. 8 July 1876, M.A. 5 May 1881; master at Marlborough 1877–8, C. of Alton, Hants 1882–4, V. of Combroke with Compton-Verney, Warwicks. 1884.

John Edward **Gill** (1 s. lieut.-col. Charles, Madras army), b. India, ed. Harrow, **Exh.** 3 Feb. **1873**, **M.** 10 Oct. 1873 age 18, B.A. 13 Dec. 1877, I.C.S. 1877, magistrate Azamgarh, N.W. Provinces, India.

Edward Martyn **Venn** (1 s. late Rev. Edward S. German), b.

Langham, Norfolk, ed. Sherborne, **Symes** 3 Feb. **1873, M.** 31 May 1873 age 19, vac. Easter 1875, B.A. 5 July 1884, incumbent of Kilkenny West, Westmeath 1886.

Edward Geoffrey **O'Donoghue** (o. s. Rev. Francis Talbot, V. of S. Paul's, Devonport, by Ellen Catherine 1 d. of William Pascoe of Tregembo in S. Hilary), b. Sennen, Cornwall 22 July 1854, ed. Manchester, **Stap.** 12 Dec. **1873, M.** 16 Oct. 1874, 2 Classics Mod. 1876, 4 Classics 1878, B.A. 20 July 1878, Head Master Kensington gr. sch. 1886, chaplain Bethlehem Royal Hosp., London 25 Ap. 1892; Coll. Corn. 634.

Arthur Sampson **Napier** (1 s. George Webster, by Martha Bridgwood), b. Wilmslow, Cheshire 30 Aug. 1853, ed. Rugby 1867, and Owen's College, B. Sci. London Univ. 1873; **Open** 14 Feb. **1874, M.** 23 May 1874, 1 Phys. 1877, B.A. 8 June 1878, M.A. 9 Ap. 1881, Reader of English at Berlin 1878, Professor of Anglo-Saxon at Göttingen 1882, Professor of English Language and Literature, Oxford 27 May 1885, Fellow of Merton 1885; has written much on Early English.

Lewis Richard **Farnell,** **Open** 14 Feb. **1874,** Fellow 1880.

Marcus Synnot **Crawford** (1 s. Francis, R. of Cookstown, Tyrone), b. Portadown 25 Ap. 1855, ed. Sherborne, **Open** 14 Feb. **1874, M.** 22 Oct. 1874, 1 Classics Mod. 1876, 2 Classics 1878, B.A. 20 July 1878, writer in Civil Service, Ceylon 1878.

Sidney **Davies** (3 s. Thomas, Independent minister), b. Darwen, Blackburn, Lancs. 15 Ap. 1855, ed. Manchester, **Stap.** 14 Feb. **1874, M.** 17 Oct. 1874, 1 Math. Mod. 1876, 3 Math. 1877, 2 Nat. Sci. 1878; B.A. 14 June 1877, M.A. and M.B. 14 June 1883, M.D. 27 June 1889, doctor in Egypt 1883, physician Burrage road, Plumstead, Kent 1889.

John **Bennett** (3 s. William, M.A.), b. and ed. Plymouth, **Gifford** 14 Feb. **1874, M.** 16 Feb. age 19, 1 Math. Mod. 1875, 2 Math. 1877, B.A. 17 Dec. 1877, M.A. 10 July 1880, master of a school at Plymouth.

Edward Hagarty **Parry** (2 s. Rev. Edward St. John), b. Toronto 24 Ap. 1855, ed. Charterhouse 1868, exhibitioner; **Richards** 14 Feb. **1874, M.** 17 Oct. 1874, 2 Classics Mod. 1876, 3 Hist. 1878, B.A. 12 Dec. 1878, M.A. 14 Jan. 1882, master at Felstead sch., head m. prepar. sch., Stoke house, Slough.

William Evans **Hoyle** (1 s. William Jennings, of Manchester), **Nat. Sci. Exh.** 14 Feb. **1874,** junior student at Ch. Ch. for Physical Sci. 1874-9, **M.** 16 Oct. 1874 age 19, 1 Nat. Sci. 1877, B.A. 1877, M.A. 1882.

Charles **Phillips** (3 s. Henry), b. Rugby 14 Aug. 1856, ed. Rugby 1867, **Open** 1 Feb. **1875**, **M.** 16 Oct. 1875 age 19, 2 Classics Mod. 1877, 2 Classics 1879, 4 Law 1880; B.A. 11 Dec. 1879, M.A. 22 May 1885, solicitor 29 Aug. 1882, in firm of W. H. and C. Phillips at Manchester 1883.

Henry Robinson **King** (2 s. Rev. Henry), b. Kirkby Stephen, Westmoreland 6 July 1855, ed. Clifton; **Ch. I. O.** 1 Feb. **1875**, **M.** 16 Oct. 1875, 2 Classics Mod. 1877, 3 Classics 1879, B.A. 10 Oct. 1179, M.A. 25 Oct. 1883, assist. master Sherborne.

Stephen Montagu **Burrows** (2 s. Prof. Montagu), b. S. Giles', Oxford 26 Dec. 1856, ed. Eton 1871–4; **Stap. O.** 1 Feb. **1875**, **M.** 19 May 1875, 2 Classics Mod. 1877, 3 Classics 1879, B.A. 13 Nov. 1879, M.A. 31 Jan. 1884; in Civil Service, Ceylon.

Thomas O'Hara **Horsman** (1 s. Thomas, of Leeds), b. Chelsea, ed. Leeds, **Open** 1 Feb. **1875**, **M.** 15 Oct. 1875 age 19, 3 Math. Mod. 1877, Non-Coll. Oct. 1877, B.A. Ex. Coll. 15 June 1882.

Arthur William **Upcott** (4 s. John Samuel), b. Cullompton, Devon 6 Jan. 1857, ed. Sherborne, **M.** 15 Oct. 1875, **Stap.** 18 Oct. **1875**, 1 Classics Mod. 1876, 2 Classics 1879, B.A. 10 Oct. 1879, M.A. 27 Ap. 1882, chaplain of S. Mark's sch., Windsor 1884, and Head Master 1886, Head Master Clergy Orphan sch., Canterbury.

Robert Holman **Peck** (o. s. late Robert William, solicitor), b. Fairfield, Manchester, ed. Cranbrook, **M.** New Coll. 16 Oct. 1874 age 18; **Nat. Sci.** 18 Oct. **1875**, 1 Nat. Sci. 1878, B.A. 28 Nov. 1878, M.A. 10 Oct. 1882, M.B. 19 June 1884, dead.

Reginald Theodore **Blomfield** (3 s. George John, R. of Aldington, Hythe, Kent), b. Bow, Devon 20 Dec. 1856, ed. Haileybury, **Stap.** 18 Oct. **1875**, **M.** 22 Jan. 1876, 2 Classics Mod. 1877, 1 Classics 1879, B.A. 5 Feb. 1880, M.A. 19 June 1884, architect 39 Woburn sq. London, wrote 1891 *English Architecture*, 1892 *The Formal Garden in England*; m. 13 Mch 1886 Frances d. of late Henry Burra of Rye, Sussex.

Charles **M'Rae** (3 s. late Gilbert), b. Limehouse, Middlesex 29 July 1851, ed. King's Coll., London, **Nat. Sci.** 18 Oct. **1875**, **M.** 3 June 1876, 2 Nat. Sci. 1879, B.A. 17 Dec. 1879, M.A. 7 July 1883, assist. inspector South Kensington.

Thomas Bainbridge **Eden** (2 s. Charles Page, V. of Aberford, Yorks.), b. Aberford 27 Ap. 1856, ed. Rugby 1869, **How** 1 Feb. **1875**, **M.** 18 Oct. 1875; exhibitioner of Oriel 1876, B.A. 1878, M.A. 1882.

Henry **Gee** (2 s. William), b. Freshford, Som. 24 July 1857, ed.

Clifton, **Symes** 18 Oct. **1875, M.** 22 Jan. 1876, 2 Classics Mod. 1877, 3 Theol. 1879, B.A. 17 Dec. 1879, M.A. 27 May 1882, proximè for junior Septuagint prize 1880, tutor S. John's Hall of Divinity, and C. of S. Augustine's, Highbury 1880–4, senior tutor 1885.

George Loraine **Hawker** (1 s. John Manley, preb. and treasurer of Exeter), b. Ideford, Devon 8 Nov. 1856, at Winchester 1870, **How** 18 Oct. **1875, M.** 22 Oct. 1875, 3 Nat. Sci. 1878, B.A. 6 July 1878, adm. solicitor 1881, in practice at Raydon house, Potter's Fields, Tooley st. London.

Richard Moody **Ward** (1 s. William Baker), b. Ashburton, ed. Ashburton and Taunton, **Gifford** 18 Oct. **1875, M.** 22 Jan. 1876 age 18, 3 Classics Mod. 1877, 3 Nat. Sci. 1879, B.A. 5 Feb. 1880, M.B. 18 June 1885.

Hugh **Brookbank** (1 s. Hugh, of Peterborough), **M.** New Coll. 20 Oct. 1873 age 19, Mus. Bac. 1874; **Org.** Easter **1876**—Mich. 1877, fellow of Coll. of Organists, Org. of Llandaff Cathedral.

Allen Henry **Powles** (1 s. Rev. Henry Charles, of the Chantry Dursley, Glouc.), b. Whitchurch, Herefs. 29 Ap. 1857, ed. Marlborough, **Open** 29 Jan. **1876, M.** 14 Oct. 1876, 1 Classics Mod. 1878, 2 Classics 1880, B.A. 10 July 1880, M.A. 28 Mch 1885.

Henry John **Tylden** (3 s. late William, V. of Stamford near Hythe, and of the Manor house, Milstead, Kent, by Eleanor Coates 2 d. of Rev. James W. Bellamy, V. of Sellindge), b. Hythe, Kent 14 Dec. 1856, ed. Uppingham 1869–76, captain of the school; **Open** 29 Jan. **1876, M.** 14 Oct. 1876, 1 Classics Mod. 1877, 1 Classics 1880, B.A. 11 Oct. 1880, M.A. and M.B. 1 July 1886, M.D. 17 Dec. 1891; M.R.C.P. 1888, physician 38 Harewood sq. London, d. of typhoid fever London 16 July 1892.

Matthew Henry **Peacock** (1 s. Matthew), b. Leeds 29 May 1856, ed. Leeds; **Ch. I. O.** 29 Jan. **1876, M.** 14 Oct. 1876, 1 Classics Mod. 1878, 2 Classics 1880, B.A. 28 Oct. 1880, proximè for junior Hall and Houghton prize 1881, M.A. 28 Mch 1883, Mus. Bac. 14 Nov. 1889, Master of Wakefield gr. sch., wrote *History of Wakefield School* 1891.

James Moullin **Lainè** (2 s. John Abraham), b. S. Sampson's, Guernsey 15 Oct. 1857, ed. Elizabeth College; **Ch. I.** 31 Jan. **1876, M.** 14 Oct. 1876, 2 Classics Mod. 1878, 2 Classics 1880, B.A. 10 July 1880, M.A. 12 May 1883, clerk General Post Office.

Joseph Baldwin **Nias** (1 s. Adm. Sir Joseph, K.C.B., by Caroline Isabella o. child of John Laing of Montague sq. London), b. Bath

13 Dec. 1857, ed. Winchester 1870, **M.** 16 Jan. 1875 age 18, **Nat. Sci.** 17 Oct. **1876,** 1 Nat. Sci. 1878, B.A. 30 Jan. 1879, Burdett-Coutts scholar 1881, Radcliffe Travelling Fellow 1882, M.B. 14 June 1883, M.R.C.P. 1883, physician 56 Montagu sq. London; M.D. 8 June 1893, his dissertation was on *Mastication in young children.*

Horace Ralph **Burch** (2 s. Arthur, solicitor, Registrar of the Diocese of Exeter), b. Exeter 15 Mch 1859, ed. Exeter, **M.** 14 Oct. 1876, **Vilvaine** and **Acland** exhibitioner Oct. **1876,** 2 Law 1880, B.A. 10 June 1880.

Raymond Mortimer **Latham** (1 s. Mortimer Thomas, V. of Tattershall, Lincs.), b. Coningsby, Lincs., ed. Lincoln, **M.** 15 May 1875 age 17, **Darell 1876,** B. and M.A. 18 Dec. 1882.

Henry Goldney **Baker** (1 s. Henry Goldney, solicitor), b. Axminster 23 Jan. 1858, ed. Honiton, **Stap.** 16 Oct. **1876,** **M.** 19 Jan. 1877, 3 Math. Mod. 1878, in N. Zealand.

Robert **Armitage** (1 s. Arthur, of Bridstow, Herefs.), ed. Marlborough, **Exh.** 29 Jan. **1875,** demy of Magdalen 1876, **M.** 16 Oct. 1876 age 19, 2 Classics Mod. 1877, 3 Classics 1880, B.A. 1880, M.A. 1883, chaplain Oxf. Military Coll. 1882–4, C. F. Aldershot 1887–90.

Andrew Oswald **Acworth** (4 s. William, V. of South Stoke, Bath), b. Plumstead, Kent 25 July 1857, at Winchester 1869, **M.** 14 Oct. 1876, **Exh.** 16 Oct. **1876,** 1 Classics Mod. 1878, 2 Classics 1880, B.A. 28 Oct. 1880, M.A. 4 Dec. 1884, barrister L. I. 21 June 1882, Judge Small Causes Court, Calcutta.

Carl Theodore Vaughan **Buch** (o. s. of late Dr. Carl, President of Bareilly College, India), b. Almorah, India, ed. Christ's Hospital; **Nat. Sci. Exh., M.** 3 June **1876** age 18; Junior Student of Ch. Ch. 1877.

D'Arcy **Power** (1 s. Henry, surgeon), b. Westminster 11 Nov. 1855, ed. Merchant Taylors 1870, **M.** New Coll. 16 Oct. 1874; **Nat. Sci. Exh.** 17 Oct. **1876,** 1 Nat. Sci. 1878, B.A. 27 June 1878, M.A. 23 June 1881, M.B. 15 June 1882, M.R.C.S. 1882, F.R.C.S. 1883, surgeon 26 Bloomsbury square, London.

Theodore William **Gould** (2 s. Joseph Henry), b. Newport, Barnstaple 16 Oct. 1858, ed. Cheltenham, **Open** 27 Jan. **1877, M.** 13 Oct. 1877, 2 Classics Mod. 1879, 1 Classics 1881, B.A. 2 Feb. 1882, M.A. 26 June 1883, master in S. Paul's sch., London.

Alfred Hull **Dennis** (1 s. John), b. Sutton Scotney, Hants 31 July 1858, ed. Marlborough, **Open** 27 Jan. **1877, M.** 13 Oct. 1877,

1 Classics Mod. 1879, 2 Classics 1881, B.A. 8 June 1882, M.A. 18 June 1885, barrister I. T. 29 April 1885.

Henry Leech **Porter** (1 s. Rev. John Leech), b. Shipley, Yorks. 25 Mch 1858, ed. King William's Coll., Isle of Man; **Stap.** 23 Jan. **1877**, **M**. 13 Oct. 1877, 3 Classics Mod. 1878, 3 Math. Mod. 1879, 3 Math. 1881, B.A. 2 Feb. 1882, C. of S. Cross Hospital and of S. Faith, Winchester 1883–90, resides Wellington House, Winchester 1892.

Thomas Herbert **Spinney** (3 s. Thomas Edward), b. Sturminster Newton, Dorset, ed. Salisbury Cathedral sch., **M**. Hertford 2 Feb. **1877**; **Org.** 12 Oct. **1877**–1883, B.A. 23 June 1881, M.A. 16 Ap. 1884, R. of Newborough, Derby 1885.

Horace Ayton **Hill** (2 s. Rev. John Spencer), b. Pendleton, Lancs. 31 Aug. 1857, ed. Manchester gr. sch., **Symes** 27 Jan. **1877**, **M**. 13 Oct. 1877, 2 Classics Mod. 1879, B.A. 15 June 1882, C. of Scilly 1884–6, of S. Just in Roseland 1886–8, of S. Sampson 1888–91, both in Cornwall, R. of W. Worlington, Devon 1891.

Thomas **Whittaker** (1 s. James), b. Higher Walton, Lancs. 25 Sept. 1856, ed. Royal Coll. of Science, Dublin, **Nat. Sci.** 16 and **M**. 17 Oct. **1877**, 2 Nat. Sci. 1880, B.A. 3 Feb. 1881; writer in 'Mind'; now editing Bentham's MSS.

Richard Stephen **Kindersley** (1 s. Rev. Richard Cockburn), b. Brampford Speke, Devon 27 Sep. 1858, ed. Clifton, **How** 16 Oct. **1877**, **M**. 26 Jan. 1878, 2 Classics Mod. 1879, 3 Classics 1881, in Univ. Eight 1880–2, B.A. 2 Feb. 1882, M.A. 12 June 1884, master at Radley, then at Eton.

William **Ellison** (o. s. late William), b. Folkestone 10 Oct. 1853, ed. Victoria College, Jersey, **M**. 17 Oct. 1874, **Michell** 23 Oct. **1877**, B.A. 19 June 1879, M.A. 24 Nov. 1881, chaplain Dera Ismail Khan, Punjab 1877–90, chaplain at Multan 1890.

Walter John **Barton** (3 s. Humphrey Conwell), b. Etchingham, Sussex 2 Jan. 1860, ed. Cranbrook, **Open** 2 Feb. **1878**, **M**. 8 June 1878, 1 Math. Mod. 1880, 1 Math. 1882, B.A. 8 July 1882, M.A. 12 Nov. 1885, assist. master Highgate school.

Douglas John **Byard** (2 s. Alfred John), b. Madras 8 Feb 1859, ed. Clifton, **Open** 3 Feb. **1878**, **M**. 12 Oct. 1878, 2 Classics Mod. 1880, 2 Classics 1882, B.A. 8 July 1882.

James **Mackintosh** (4 s. Lachlan), b. Edenkellie, Moray 26 Feb. 1858, ed. S. Andrew's, **M**. Balliol 20 Oct. 1877; **Stap. O.** 3 Feb. **1878**, 1 Classics Mod. 1879, 2 Classics 1881, B.A. 19 July 1881;

Scotch Advocate; wrote *The Roman Law of Sale*, with references to the Sale of Goods' Bill, Edinburgh 1892.

Arthur Silver **Murray** (6 s. late Col. Henry, R.A.), b. Douglas, Isle of Man 13 Aug. 1858, ed. King William's Coll., Isle of Man, **Stap. O.** 3 Feb. **1878, M.** 12 Oct. 1878, 1 Classics Mod. 1880, 2 Classics 1882, B.A. 26 Oct. 1882, M.A. 12 June 1886.

Alwyne Compton Howard **Rice** (1 s. Richard John Howard, V. of Sutton-Courtney), b. 1 Jan. 1859, ed. Elizabeth College, Guernsey, **Gifford** 3 Feb. **1878, M.** 8 June 1878, B.A. 18 Dec. 1882, M.A. 3 Dec. 1885, Chaplain R.N. 1886.

Arthur Stanley **Butler** (2 s. George, Fellow 1842), **M.** 24 Jan. 1874 age 19, 1 Math. Mod. 1875, 1 Math. 1877, B.A. 13 Dec. 1877, **Nat. Sci. Exh.** Feb. **1878,** M.A. 10 June 1880, Professor at S. Andrew's 1880.

Thomas Cunningham **Porter** (1 s. Christoper Waltham), b. Bristol Feb. 1860, ed. Bristol gr. sch., **Nat. Sci.** 12 Oct. **1878, M.** 31 May 1879, 2 Math. Mod. 1881, 3 Math. 1883, 2 Nat. Sci. 1884; B.A. 23 June 1883, M.A. 17 Ap. 1886; master at Eton 1883, in orders.

Edward Spry **Leverton** (1 s. Henry Spry, surgeon, by Fanny Parkyn), b. Truro 22 Sep. 1859, ed. Marlborough, **Stap.** 12 Oct. **1878, M.** 15 Oct. 1879, 1 Classics Mod. 1881, 3 Classics 1883, B.A. 31 July 1883, M.A. 17 Dec. 1886, master in Eastbourne Coll. 1888, R. of Mawnan near Falmouth 1890.

Isaac **Richards** (4 s. Isaac, of Tavistock, by Anne Maunder), b. 11 Feb. 1859, ed. Wesleyan Coll., Taunton, el. **Stap.** 12 and **M.** 16 Oct. **1878,** 2 Math. Mod. 1880, 2 Math. 1882, B.A. 26 Oct. 1882, M.A. 11 July 1885, R. of Remuera, Auckland, N. Zealand 1885.

William **Dawson** (2 s. Richard, J.P.), b. Bunratty, Clare 22 Ap. 1858, **Nat. Sci.** 12 Oct. **1878, M.** 25 Jan. 1879.

Thomas **Read** (s. Charles, by Sarah Jane d. of Thomas Avery), b. Honiton 22 May 1861, ed. Honiton, **Open** 3 Feb. **1879, M.** 15 Oct. 1879, 1 Classics Mod. 1880, 2 Classics 1883, B.A. 31 July 1883, M.A. 1 July 1886; assist. master in Cowbridge sch. 1884, C. of Llanblethian with Cowbridge, Glamorg. 1885.

Archibald Barwell **How, Open** 3 Feb. **1879,** Fellow 1886.

Alfred **Evans** (1 s. David, civil engineer), b. Aberdare Nov. 1859, ed. Aberystwith Coll., **Nat. Sci. 1879, M.** 15 Oct. 1879 age 19, 2 Nat. Sci. 1883, B.A. 14 June 1883, M.A. and M.B. 6 July 1889.

Percy **Morton** (1 s. William, landscape painter), b. Hulme, Lancs.

12 Sep. 1860, ed. Manchester, **Nat. Sci.** 1879, **M.** 15 Oct. 1879, 2 Nat. Sci. 1883, B.A. 17 Dec. 1883, M.A. 28 Ap. 1886.

Arthur Ernest **Leckenby** (1 s. Richard, of the Excise), b. Sible-Hedingham, Essex 24 May 1860, ed. Exeter, sizar S. John's, Camb.; **Stap.** 1879, **M.** 15 Oct. 1879, 2 Classics Mod. 1881, 2 Classics 1883, B.A. 31 July 1883, M.A. 17 Dec. 1886.

Thomas James Forbes **Haskoll** (1 s. late Rev. Joseph), b. E. Barkwith, Lincs. 21 July 1858, ed. Newark, **M.** Non-Coll. 12 Oct. 1878; **Darell** 1879, 3 Hist. 1881, B.A. 15 June 1882.

Percy John **Heawood** (1 s. Rev. John Richard), b. Newport, Salop 8 Sep. 1861, ed. Ipswich; **Open** Jan. 1880, **M.** 22 Oct. 1880, 1 Math. Mod. 1881, 1 Math. 1883, 2 Classics 1885, Junior Math. Scholar 1882, Senior Math. Scholar and Lady Herschell's prize 1886; B.A. 25 Oct. 1883, M.A. 23 June 1887, tutor Durham Univ. 1888.

Wilfrid Cotton **Sproule** (3 s. late Rev. Thomas Patterson), b. Messingham, Lincs. 21 Jan. 1863, ed. Canterbury sch., **Open** Jan. 1880, **M.** 22 Oct. 1880, 2 Classics Mod. 1882, 3 Classics 1884, vac. by marriage 1884, B.A. 2 Aug. 1884.

Joseph Rushton **Shortt** (1 s. Rev. Edward), b. Newcastle 17 Dec. 1860, ed. Christ's Hosp., London; **Open** Jan. 1880, **M.** 22 Oct. 1880, 2 Classics Mod. 1881, 1 Classics 1884, B.A. 10 Oct. 1884, M.A. 30 June 1887, Class. Lect. Durham 1887, Chaplain Univ. Coll., Durham 1888, Censor and Bursar of Hatfield Hall, Durham 1889–91.

Francis Henry **Gribble** (1 s. Henry, banker), b. Pilton, Barnstaple 15 July 1862, ed. Chatham house sch., Ramsgate; **Stap.** 16 Oct. 1880, **M.** 1 Nov. 1880, 2 Classics Mod. 1882, 1 Classics 1884, B.A. 2 Aug. 1884, journalist.

William John **Ward** (2 s. William Baker, merchant), b. Ashburton, Devon 23 Mch 1861, ed. Wesleyan Coll., Taunton, **Stap.** 16 Oct. 1880, **M.** 20 Oct. 1881, 2 Math. Mod. 1883, 2 Math. 1885, B.A. 17 Dec. 1885, C. of Ardingly, Sussex 1888–90, C.F. London 1890.

Henry George **Johnston** (1 s. Rev. Walker, of Magherlin, Ireland), b. Magherlin, ed. Merchant Taylors, **M.** Non-Coll. 18 Oct. 1880 age 20; **Richards** 18 Oct. 1880, 3 Classics Mod. 1882, 3 Classics 1884, B.A. 2 Aug. 1884.

Robert Shelton **Bate** (4 s. Robert, conveyancer), b. Bridgwater 30 Sep. 1862, ed. Bristol gr. sch.; **Open** 1 Feb. 1881, **M.** 4 June 1881 age 18, 2 Classics Mod. 1883.

Walter Baldwin **Spencer** (1 s. Reuben, J.P.), b. Stretford, Manchester 23 June 1860, ed. Old Trafford sch. and Owen's Coll.; **Nat.**

Sci. 20 Oct. 1880, M. 20 Oct. 1881, 1 Nat. Sci. 1884, B.A. 10 Oct. 1884, fellow of Lincoln 1 Feb. 1886 to 1887, Professor of Biology at Melbourne Univ. 1887.

Edward Francis **Johns** (2 s. late Rev. Charles Alexander), b. Rickmansworth, Herts 15 Ap. 1861, ed. Bradfield, M. 15 May 1880, **How 1881**, Abbott Scholar 1881, 2 Classics Mod. 1882, B.A. 17 Dec. 1884, M.A. 13 Ap. 1887, has a preparatory school at Winchester.

William Alexander **Shearer** (1 s. William Campbell, Independent minister), b. Soham, Cambs., ed. Bradford, **Open** 1 Feb. 1881, M. 20 Oct. 1881 age 18, 1 Classics Mod. 1883, 2 Classics 1885, B.A. 1 Aug. 1885, M.A. 27 Ap. 1893, assist. master Merchant Taylors sch., Crosby.

Henry Llewellyn **Higgins** (1 s. Henry, M.D.), b. Peel, I. of Man, ed. there at King William's Coll.; **Open 1881, M.** 20 Oct. 1881 age 19, 2 Math. Mod. 1883, 3 Nat. Sci. 1885, B.A. 18 June 1885, M.A. 31 July 1888.

William **Russell** (y. s. William, wine merchant), b. Walworth, ed. King's Coll. sch. London, **Exh.** 2 Feb. 1881, M. 20 Oct. 1881 age 19, 2 Classics Mod. 1883, 2 Classics 1885, B.A. 1 Aug. 1885, M.A. 18 May 1888.

David Purdy **Buckle** (1 s. Matthew, draper), b. Durham, ed. Durham gr. sch.; **Open** 2 Feb. 1881, M. 20 Oct. 1881 age 19, 3 Classics Mod. 1883, 3 Classics 1885, B.A. 1 Aug. 1885, M.A. 18 May 1888, C. of Queensbury 1887-91, of Earlsheaton 1891, both in Yorkshire.

Frederick **Ball** (3 s. William, shipowner), b. Torquay, ed. Newton Coll., Devon, and Queen's sch. Bayswater; **Stap.** June 1881, M. 20 Oct. 1881 age 19, 2 Math. Mod. 1883, 2 Math. 1885, B.A. 27 June 1885, M.A. 26 April 1888, chaplain H.M.S. *Boadicea* 1891.

Charles Probart **Whitaker** (2 s. late John, artist), b. Walcot, Bath 28 Jan. 1858, ed. Hermitage sch., Bath; **Symes** June 1881, M. 20 Oct. 1881, 2 Classics Mod. 1883, 1 Theol. 1885, Richards Theol. Prize 7 July 1884, B.A. 12 June 1884, M.A. 21 June 1888, R. of High Bray, Devon 1890; N. and Gleanings v. 37.

Thomas Hatheway **Dodson** (1 s. George, surveyor of taxes), b. Rotherham, Yorks. 11 May 1862, ed. Merchant Taylors; **Exh.** June 1881, M. 20 Oct. 1881, 3 Classics Mod. 1883, 1 Theol. 1885, B.A. 11 July 1885, M.A. 26 Ap. 1888, C. of Kidlington 1885-7, fellow of S. Augustine's Coll, Canterbury 1887-9, Principal of S.P.G. College, Trichinopoly 1889, fellow of the University of Madras.

Arthur Frank **Kerry** (3 s. Henry, builder), b. S. Ebbe's, Oxford 28 July 1862, ed. Wesleyan sch. Oxford; **Nat. Sci.** Oct. **1881, M.** 18 Oct. 1882, 2 Nat. Sci. (Physiol.) 1886, B.A. 27 Jan. 1887, M.A. 5 July 1890, resides in Oxford.

Thomas Herbert **Harvey** (1 s. Aaron, master at Handel Coll., Southampton), b. All Saints, Southampton, ed. Handel Coll.; **Richards 1881, M.** 20 Oct. 1881 age 20, 1 Theol. 1884, B.A. 5 July 1884, M.A. 30 June 1888, C. of Portsea, Hants 1884–8, mission. and master in Ch. Miss. Soc. Coll., Ningpo, dioc. Mid China 1888, dead.

John Howard **Palmer** (2 s. John, engineer), b. Lincoln, ed. Christ's Hosp.; **Open** 20 Jan. **1882, M.** 18 Oct. 1882 age 19, 1 Math. Mod. 1884, 2 Math. 1886, B.A. 7 Aug. 1886.

James Vernon **Bartlet** (o. s. Rev. George Donald, M.A. Aberdeen, minister U.P., by Susan McNellan), b. Scarborough 15 Aug. 1863, ed. Highgate; **Open** 31 Jan. **1882, M.** 18 Oct. 1882, 1 Classics Mod. 1883, 2 Classics 1886, 1 Theol. 1887, Hall and Houghton Prize 1889; B.A. 11 Nov. 1886, M.A. 10 Oct. 1889, fellow Mansfield Coll. Oxford 1889.

John Arthur Ruskin **Munro** (1 s. late Alexander, sculptor), b. S. George's, Hanover sq. London 24 Feb. 1864, ed. Charterhouse 1876, **Open** 31 Jan. **1882, M.** 18 Oct. 1882, 1 Classics Mod. 1883, 1 Classics 1886, B.A. 21 Oct. 1886, M.A. 1889, fellow of Lincoln 10 Ap. 1888, explorer in Cyprus.

Gerard Chilton **Bailey** (2 s. Anthony Winter, V. of East Stoke, Newark), b. Panton Wragby, Lincs., ed. Newark, **M.** 20 Oct. 1881 age 18, **Darell** Feb. **1882,** B.A. 30 June 1887, M.A. 18 May 1888, C. of S. Luke's, Leeds 1888–9, of Durban 1889, of Newcastle 1891, both in Natal.

Charles **Sadler** (6 s. Michael Ferrebee, R. of Honiton), b. Bedford 9 Oct. 1864, ed. Honiton, **Stap.** June **1882, M.** 18 Oct. 1883, 2 Classics Mod. 1885, 2 Classics 1887, B.A. 10 Oct. 1887, M.A. 9 Ap. 1890, assistant master at Honiton.

Arthur Henry **Lemon** (3 s. William George, barrister L. I. 1866, F.G.S.), b. Blackheath 23 Aug. 1864, ed. Merchant Taylors 1874, **Open** 30 Jan. **1883, M.** 18 Oct. 1883, 2 Classics Mod. 1885, 3 Classics 1887, B.A. 17 Nov. 1887.

Humphrey Marett **Godfray** (1 s. Walter Bertram, Greffier of the Royal Court of Jersey), b. Jersey 2 Oct. 1863, ed. Victoria Coll.; **Ch. I. Exh. 1882, M.** 18 Oct. 1883, 2 Law 1887, B.A. 9 July 1887, treasurer and president of the Union 1887; at Inner Temple 1883, Greffier of Jersey, d. there 17 Jan. 1892.

Julian Hilton **Sargent** (1 s. William, assist. master Rugby), b. S. Petersburgh 8 Ap. 1864, ed. Rugby 1875–83, **Open** 30 Jan. 1883, **M.** 18 Oct. 1883, 1 Classics Mod. 1885, 2 Classics 1887, B.A. 8 Dec. 1887, Latin Essay 1888, d. Costebelle near Hyeres 6 Mch 1891.

Frederick **Tracey** (4 s. late John, R. of Lesnewth, Cornwall), b. Dartmouth 10 Mch 1858, ed. Honiton, and Uppingham 1872–3, **M.** Lincoln 30 Jan. 1882; **Michell** 20 June **1882**, res. Oct. 1883, 3 Math. Mod. 1883, B.A. 4 Dec. 1884, M.A. Sydney Univ. 1885, Vicewarden S. Paul's Coll., Sydney Univ. 1885–6, 2 master Colston's sch. Bristol 1886–8, Principal of All SS. College, Bathurst, New South Wales 1888, chaplain to Bishop of Bathurst 1891.

Henry Oliver **Minty** (1 s. Oliver), b. Cheltenham, ed. R. Coll. of Science, Dublin; **Nat. Sci. Exh.** Nov. **1882, M.** 18 Oct. 1883 age 20, 1 Nat. Sci. (Chem.) 1886, B.A. 23 June 1887, M.A. 23 May 1890, clerk in Patent Office 1892.

Lionel Richard **Stert** (2 s. Rev. Arthur Richard), b. Lamarsh, Essex 25 Feb. 1865, ed. Cheltenham, **Exh.** 30 Jan. **1883, M.** 18 Oct. 1883, 3 Classics Mod. 1885.

William Charles **Gough** (1 s. Charles), b. Oxford 9 Ap. 1864, chorister New Coll. 1876–79; **M.** Non-Coll. 15 Oct. 1881; **Exh.** 30 Jan. **1883**, 2 Classics Mod. 1883, 2 Classics 1885, B.A. 10 Oct. 1885, M.A. 18 June 1891.

Francis Pritchett **Badham** (o. s. Rev. Francis, fellow S. John's, by Gertrude Anne d. of Capt. Fitzpatrick of Ossory, of 39 Reg.; she was Principal of the Girls' Coll. sch. Folkestone 16 years, and d. there 14 July 1893), b. Charlton, Kent 16 Mch 1864, ed. Merchant Taylors 1874, **Hist.** 30 Jan. **1883, M.** 18 Oct. 1883, 2 Hist. 1887, B.A. 9 July 1887, M.A. 23 June 1892, barrister I. T. 1893, at 6 Crown Office Row, **Temple**; wrote *The Formatiom of the Gospels* 1891, ed. 2 1892.

Alexander James **Carlyle** (2 s. Rev. James Edward, of Free Church of Scotland, by Jessie Margaret d. of Robert Milne; he was b. 22 Aug. 1821, d. 5 May 1893), b. Bombay 24 July 1861, ed. Glasgow Univ. 1876–8 and London Coll. of Divinity; **M.** 18 Oct. 1883 age 22, **Hist.** 8 Dec. **1884**; 1 Hist. 1886, 2 Theol. 1888; B.A. 21 Oct. 1886, C. of S. Stephen's, Westminster 1888–90, General Secr. of S.P.C.K. 1890–1, chaplain fellow Univ. Coll. Jan. 1893.

Henry Eden **Smith** (1 s. Henry Robert, hon. Canon of Carlisle),

b. Grange-over-Sands, Lancs. 1864, ed. Bruton, and Charterhouse 1878; **Carter** 30 Jan. **1883, M.** 18 Oct. 1883 age 19, 2 Classics Mod. 1884, 2 Classics 1887, B.A. 8 Dec. 1887, M.A. 9 Ap. 1890, master at Bruton 1889–90, assist. master Sedbergh sch., Yorks. 1891.

Ernest Henry **Cartwright** (o. s. Henry Edmund, barrister), b. S. John's, Paddington, ed. Charterhouse; **Nat. Sci.** 13 Oct. **1883, M.** 18 Oct. 1883 age 18, 2 Nat. Sci. (Physiol.) 1887, B.A. 23 June 1887, B.M. (Organic Chem.) 1888, M.A. and M.B. 23 June 1892; M.R.C.S. 1892.

William Caldecott **Ridding** (2 s. Rev. William, late fellow of New Coll.), b. Winchester 27 Feb. 1864, ed. Winchester 1877, **Stap.** 30 Jan. **1883, M.** 18 Oct. 1883, 2 Classics Mod. 1884, 2 Classics 1887, B.A. 2 July 1887, M.A. 9 Ap. 1890, C. of E. Retford 1889.

Harry Chalmers Gray **Morice** (4 s. James, bank manager), b. Brixton, ed. Bedford; **Stap. O.** 10 Dec. **1883, M.** 16 Oct. 1884 age 18, 1 Classics Mod. 1886, 2 Classics 1888, B.A. 16 May 1889, M.A. 23 Ap. 1891, C. of Churchstow with Kingsbridge, Devon 1890.

James Garden Blackie **Sutherland** (2 s. Peter Cormack, M.D., Surgeon General of Natal), b. Pietermaritzburg, Natal; ed. Fettes Coll., **Ch. I. O.** 30 Jan. **1883, M.** 18 Oct. 1883 age 19, left 1885.

William **Marsh** (o. s. William Hobson) b. Clayton, Yorks., ed. Hemsworth gr. sch., and Durham Univ.; **Hasker** 10 Dec. **1883, M.** 24 Jan. 1884 age 21, Junior Septuagint prize 21 Mch 1885, 1 Theol. 1887, proximè for Ellerton 1888, Hall and Houghton prize 1889; B.A. 27 Oct. 1887, M.A. 16 May 1891, C. of S. Andrew's, Huddersfield 1889–90, Vice-Princ. Glouc. Theol. Coll. and assist. missionary dioc. G. and B. 1890, C. of S. Catherine's, Glouc. 1891.

Hubert Henry **Cox** (5 s. Rev. Thomas of Monksilver, Som.), b. Taunton, ed. Aldenham gr. sch.; **How** 30 Jan. **1883, M.** 18 Oct. 1883 age 19, 2 Classics Mod. 1885, 4 Theol. 1886, B.A. 10 July 1886.

Reginald Thomas **Talbot** (3 s. late John Thomas), b. Leamington 1862, ed. Clifton, **M.** 20 Oct. 1881 age 19, **Michell** 10 Dec. **1883; Symes** 1884; 1 Theol. 1885, B.A. 11 July 1885, M.A. 26 Ap. 1888, C. of Gateshead 1885–9, hon. Canon of Durham 1889, and lecturer on church doctrine in the diocese, V. of Millfield, Sunderland 1893.

Alfred Herbert **Brewer** (1 s. Alfred, of Court of Probate), b. Gloucester 21 June 1865, ed. Coll. sch. Glouc.; **Org.** Dec. **1883** to 1887, **M.** 24 Jan. 1884, Org. of S. Michael's, Coventry 1886–92, Org. and teacher of music Tonbridge sch. 1892.

Sydney Gwenffrwd **Mostyn** (2 s. John, minister), b. Braintree,

Essex, ed. Ipswich gr. sch., **Open** 18 Jan. **1884, M.** 16 Oct. 1884 age 18, hon. mentioned for jun. math. sch. of the Univ. 20 Mch 1886, 1 Math. Mod. 1886, 1 Math. 1888, 1 Nat. Sci. (Phys.) 1889; B.A. 10 Oct. 1888, M.A. 19 May 1892, lecturer at Lampeter 1890–92, assist. master at S. Paul's sch. London 1892.

Thomas Herbert **Harvey** (1 s. Aaron, schoolmaster) b. All Saints, Southampton 12 July 1861, ed. Handel Coll. Southampton, **M.** 20 Oct. 1881, **Richards** 28 Jan. **1884,** 1 Theol. 1884, B.A. 5 July 1884, M.A. 1888; C. of Portsea 1884–88, master in C.M.S. Coll., Ningpo, China 1888; married Ningpo 13 Aug. 1890, d. at sea 19 Aug. 1890.

Herbert Louis **Wild** (1 s. Robert Louis, C. of Uffington, Salop, by Mary d. of Robert Vaughan), b. Shrewsbury 2 July 1865, ed. Charter-house, **Open** 28 Jan. **1884, M.** 16 Oct. 1884, 1 Classics Mod. 1886, 2 Classics 1888, B.A. 25 Oct. 1888, M.A. 17 Dec. 1891, lecturer at Durham Univ. 1888.

John Russell **Larkins** (o. s. Frederick), b. Greenwich, ed. Ch. of E. gr. sch. Auckland, N. Zealand, and King's College sch., London, **Stap. O.** 28 Jan. **1884, M.** 16 Oct. 1884 age 18, d. Remuera, N. Z. 31 May 1886.

Robert Garland **Plumptre** (1 s. Robert William, R. of Corfe Mullen, Dorset), b. Corfe Mullen 8 June 1865, at Winchester 1878, **Open** 28 Jan. **1884, M.** 16 Oct. 1884, 2 Classics Mod. 1886, 3 Classics 1888, 1 Theol. 1889, prize of books for Hall Gr. Test. prize 1889, B.A. 25 Oct. 1888, M.A. 23 Ap. 1891, Vice-princ. of Edmund H. July 1889–1893, lecturer of Queen's, chaplain to Bishop of Southwell 1893.

John **Dowsett** (2 s. John, merchant), b. West Ham, Essex, ed. Christ's Hospital; **Exh.** 28 Jan. **1884, M.** 16 Oct. 1884 age 19, 2 Classics Mod. 1886, 3 Classics 1888, B.A. 31 July 1888.

John **Carter** (1 s. John, prof. of music), b. Toronto, ed. Trinity Coll. Toronto, **M.** 18 Oct. 1883 age 21, **Richards 1884,** 3 Classics Mod. 1885, 2 Classics 1887, B.A. 10 Oct. 1887, M.A. 5 Ap. 1893; C. of S. Anne's, Limehouse, London 1888–9, at Pusey House, Oxford 1890, assist. chaplain Ex. Coll. 1890.

John Nicholson **Dobie** (1 s. William, Mus. D.), b. Temple Sowerby, Westmoreland, ed. Bingley gr. sch., Leeds, **Nat. Sci.** 30 Oct. **1884, M.** 16 Oct. 1884 age 18, at Caius, Camb. 21 Oct. 1885, 3 Nat. Sci. Tripos 1888, B.A. 1888.

William Henry Granger **Southcomb** (1 s. Henry Granger, R. of Roseash, Devon 1882), b. Newton Abbot 15 Ap. 1866, ed. Sherborne,

Stap. 10 Oct. **1884, M.** 23 Oct. **1885,** 2 Classics Mod. 1887, 4 Classics 1889, B.A. 24 Oct. 1889; see Plumptre's *Bishop Ken* ii. 166.

Bower **Marsh** (2 s. Bower, solicitor), b. S. Nicholas, Rochester 25 Jan. 1866, ed. Christ's Hosp., **Open** 19 Jan. **1885, M.** 23 Oct. **1885,** 2 Math. Mod. 1887, transferred to **Richards Exh.** Oct. 1887, 2 Hist. 1889, B.A. 2 Aug. 1889.

Rupert Charles **Clarke** (5 s. late Frederick Ricketts, printer), b. Taunton 4 July 1866, ed. Taunton Coll. sch., **M.** Balliol **15** Oct. 1884; **Stap.** 8 Dec. **1884,** 2 Classics Mod. 1886, 2 Classics 1888, B.A. **25** Oct. 1888, M.A. 28 Ap. 1892; at Brit. Archæol. sch. Athens 1887, C. of S. Mary's, Reading, 1889.

Frederick Wilfrid **Walters** (5 s. Rev. Alfred Vaughan), b. Wyke, Winchester 11 Oct. 1863, **M.** Non-Coll. 13 Jan. 1883; **Hasker** 8 Dec. **1884,** 2 Theol. 1886, B.A. 10 July 1886, M.A. 26 June 1890, C. of All Hallows, Southwark 1887-8, of S. Luke's, Camberwell 1888-91, of S. Philip's, Sydenham 1891, M.R.C.S. and L.R.C.P. 1892, missionary at Isandlana 1893.

Samuel **Swire** (3 s. Rev. Frederick), b. Newark 2 May 1866, ed. S. Paul's; **Open** 8 Dec. **1884, M.** 23 Oct. **1885,** 2 Classics Mod. 1887, 2 Classics 1889, B.A. 10 Oct. 1889, M.A. 3 June 1892, C. of S. Stephen's, Westminster 1890, V. of S. Thomas', Huddersfield 1893.

Reginald Herbert **Ferard** (4 s. Charles Cotton, barrister, by Emily Jane, d. of Thomas Dale, dean of Rochester), b. Winkfield, Berks 21 June 1886, ed. Eton, **Open** 8 Dec. **1884, M.** 23 Oct. **1885,** 1 Classics Mod. 1887, 2 Classics 1889, B.A. 2 Aug. 1889, M.A. 10 Oct. 1892, lecturer at Keble 1892.

Herbert George **Belcher** (5 s. late Charles), b. Farringdon, Berks 10 Aug. 1866, ed. Bedford, **Open** 8 Dec. **1884, M.** 23 Oct. **1885,** 2 Classics Mod. 1887, 2 Classics 1889, B.A. 2 Aug. 1889, master at High sch., Oxford 1890, M.A. 28 Ap. 1892.

Frederick Arnold **Overton** (1 s. Rev. Samuel Charlesworth), b. Hackness, Yorks. 15 July 1862, ed. King's Coll., London, **M.** Non-Coll. 13 Oct. 1884; **Richards** 8 Dec. **1884, Michell** 16 Oct. **1885,** 2 Theol. 1887, B.A. 9 July 1887, M.A. 23 Ap. 1891; C. of Headington, Oxon 1887-93, assist. chaplain Ex. Coll. 1890, V. of High Cross, Herts 1893; m. 16 June 1891 Ella, y. d. of Rev. Alfred Edersheim.

Vernon **Holt** (1 s. Joseph, by Frances Emily, d. of late C. A. Martin, of Pontefract), b. Brooklands, Cheshire 10 July 1866, ed. Bedford, **Hist.** 8 Dec. **1884, M.** 23 Oct. **1885,** 4 Hist. 1888, B.A. 31 July 1888,

M.A. 28 Ap. 1892, C. of Deddington, Oxon 1889, of Ruan-Lanihorne, Cornwall 1893; m. Oct. 1889 Mary Monckton, 1 d. of Major-Gen. Brownlow Hugh Buckley-Mathew-Lannowe, R.E., now of Trematon Castle, Cornwall; Visit. Corn. 313.

Edward **Schönberg** (2 s. Rev. Moritz), b. Wolverhampton 3 Jan. 1863, ed. Manchester gr. sch. and Owen's Coll., **Exh.** 8 Dec. 1884, **M.** 23 Oct. 1885, drowned in the Isis 18 Feb. 1886.

Henry John **Smale** (1 s. John Jackson, barrister), b. S. Pancras, London 18 Mch 1866, ed. Exeter, **M.** 8 Dec. 1884, named **Reynolds** Easter 1885, 2 Nat. Sci. (Chem.) 1888, B.A. 30 June 1888, M.A. 18 June 1891, C. of S. Mark's, Worsley, Lancs. 1891.

Edward Henry **Fox** (1 s. late Rev. Edward William), b. W. Allington, Dorset 14 Aug. 1867, named **Reynolds** 11 Sept. 1885, **M.** 21 Oct. 1886.

Henry Rivington **Chappel** (3 s. Rev. William Pester, by Susan Jane d. of William Rivington), b. Camborne, Cornwall 13 Ap. 1867, ed. Marlborough, **Stap.** 16 Oct. 1885, **M.** 21 Oct. 1886, 2 Classics Mod. 1888, 3 Classics 1890, 2 Theol. 1891, B.A. 10 Oct. 1890, M.A. 8 June 1893; C. of S. Antholin, Nunhead, for Cheltenham Coll. Miss. 1891; Coll. Corn. 138.

Denys Edward **Shorto** (o. s. Edward Henry), b. S. Sidwell's, Exeter 21 May 1868, ed. Exeter, **Stap.** 16 Oct. 1885, **M.** 21 Oct. 1886, held Huish Exhibition from Ex. sch., 1 Math. Mod. 1887, 1 Math. 1890, 2 Nat. Sci. (Physics) 1891, B.A. 31 July 1890, M.A. 20 May 1893, master at King Edward's sch., Birmingham.

Isidor **Goldstein** (o. s. Abraham), b. Simno, Suwalki, Poland 29 Sept. 1862, **M.** Non-Coll. 26 Jan. 1885, **Symes** 16 Oct. 1885, Pusey and Ellerton 1885, drowned in the Isis 2 Dec. 1885, body not found till 5 Jan. 1886.

Ernest Augustus **Glover** (2 s. Frederick Augustus R. of Withern, Lincs.), b. Shepton Mallet 5 Ap. 1866, ed. Christ's Hosp., London; **Darell, M.** 23 Oct. 1885, B.A. 17 Dec. 1888, M.A. 3 June 1892, C. of S. Paul's, Brentford 1888–91, of Quebec Chapel, London 1891.

Henry Hesse Johnston **Gompertz** (1 s. Henry James Colley, Inspector Revenue Survey India), b. Nundyal, India 31 Aug. 1867, ed. Bedford, **Open 1885, M.** 21 Oct. 1886, 2 Classics Mod. 1888, 2 Classics 1890, B.A. 10 Oct. 1890, 2 in Indian Cadets Exam. 1890, at Chao Chow fu, China.

John Matthew **Hallam** (o. s. John Winfield, architect), b. Oxford 4 May 1867, ed. Magd. Coll. sch., **Open 1885, M.** 21 Oct. 1886, 2

Classics Mod. 1888, 3 Classics 1890, 2 Theol. 1891, B.A. 10 Oct.
1890, M.A. 5 Ap. 1893, C. of Upton with Chalvey, Bucks 1891.

George Slythe **Street** (2 s. Samuel Philip, by Sarah d. of Thomas
Chignell), b. Wimbledon 18 July 1867, ed. Charterhouse, **Open 1885**,
M. 21 Oct. 1886, 1 Classics Mod. 1888, 2 Classics 1890, B.A. 4 Dec.
1890, wrote *Miniatures and Moods* 1893, resides in London.

Harold Worthington **Curjel** (2 s. William, clerk), b. Manchester
18 Mch 1868, ed. Warrington gr. sch., **Open 1885**, **M.** 21 Oct. 1886,
1 Math. Mod. 1887, 1 Math. 1890, B.A. 5 July 1890, master at
Shrewsbury 1890, Math. Lect. at S. David's Coll., Lampeter 1893.

Thomas William **Tidmarsh** (1 s. Thomas), b. Steeple Claydon,
Bucks 25 Dec. 1859, ed. S. Mark's Coll., Chelsea, **M.** Non-Coll.
13 Oct. 1883; **Symes** 7 May 1886, 2 Theol. 1887, B.A. 9 July 1887,
M.A. 23 Oct. 1890, C. of Sutton Courtney, Berks 1887–9, of Plympton
S. Mary, Devon 1890, of Harbridge, Ringwood 1893.

William Loring **Kindersley** (6 s. Rev. Richard Cockburn), b.
Brampford Speke, Devon 7 Sep. 1868, ed. Marlborough, **Stap.**
16 Oct. **1886**, **M.** 19 Oct. 1887, 2 Classics Mod. 1889, 3 Classics
1891, B.A. 9 Ap. 1892, Eastern student interpretership 1892.

Archibald Steele **Thomson** (1 s. Arthur Henry, by Caroline d. of
Henry and Emma Steele), b. Plymouth 20 June 1868, ed. Mannamead sch. Plymouth 1879–81, and Charterhouse 1882–5, **Stap.**
16 Oct. **1886**, **M.** 21 Oct. 1886, 2 Classics Mod. 1888, 3 Classics
1890, 2 Theol. 1891; B.A. 23 Oct. 1890, M.A. 27 Ap. 1893, classical
master Plymouth Corp. gr. sch. Jan. 1892.

John Maurice **Schulhof** (o. s. late Maurice, M.D.), b. S. George's,
Hanover Sq. 23 Aug. 1858, ed. S. Paul's sch. 1868, Pauline exhibi-
tioner, capt. of the school 1876–7, **M.** Univ. London June 1878,
scholar Trinity, Camb. 1877, 12 Classic and B.A. 1881, assist. master
S. Paul's 1882, **M.** Non-Coll. 13 Oct. 1884, 1 Classics Mod. 1886;
Exh. 1886, Ireland and Craven scholar 14 Dec. 1886, 1 Classics 1887,
B.A. 2 Aug. 1887, lect. Ex. Coll. 1889–90, has sch. at Bayswater.

Maurice William **Keatinge** (2 s. Maurice), b. Monkstown, Dublin
25 Feb. 1867, ed. S. Mark's sch. Windsor, **Gifford 1886, M.** 21 Oct.
1886, 2 Classics Mod. 1888, 2 Classics 1890, B.A. 17 Dec. 1890,
master at King William's Coll., I. of Man 1891–3.

Francis Cunningham **Woods** (2 s. Alfred, Indian Agent), b.
S. George's, Hanover Sq. London 29 Aug. 1862, ed. City of London
sch., studied music at National Training sch. for Music 1877–81,
under Sir Arthur Sullivan, Sir John Stainer, &c., **M.** S. Mary H.

22 Oct. 1883, Org. of Brasenose 1884–6, **Org**. of Ex. Coll. 18 Jan. **1887**, B.A. 6 July 1889, M.A. 1 May 1890, Mus. Bac. 12 Nov. 1891, Conductor of Oxford Choral Union 1893.

James **Forbes** (o. s. Archibald, manufacturer), b. Carlisle 14 Aug. 1868, ed. Carlisle gr. sch., **Open** 26 Jan. **1887**, **M**. 19 Oct. 1887, 2 Math. Mod. 1889, 3 Math. 1891, B.A. 1 Aug. 1891, assist. master Warrington, and C. of S. Paul's 1891, ord. priest 20 Dec. 1892.

Harold Buchanan **Ryley** (1 s. Rev. George Buchanan), b. Bocking, Essex 18 July 1868, ed. S. Olave's gr. sch., Southwark, **Open** 7 July **1887**, **M**. 19 Oct. 1887, 2 Classics Mod. 1889, 4 Classics 1891, B.A. 1 Aug. 1891, ordained in Colorado 1892.

John Leonard **Burbey** (1 s. Robert, tea merchant), b. Edmonton, Middlesex 20 Feb. 1869, ed. Clifton, **Open** 7 July **1887**, **M**. 19 Oct. 1887, 2 Classics Mod. 1889, 3 Classics 1891, B.A. 3 Dec. 1891, master at Clifton Coll. 1893.

Roland D'Arcy **Preston** (3 s. John D'Arcy Warcop, R. of Ch. Ch., Freemantle, Southampton), b. Sandgate, Kent 1 July 1867, ed. Marlborough, **M**. 21 Oct. 1886, **How 1887**, and then 7 July **Carter**, 2 Classics Mod. 1888, 2 Classics 1890, 2 Theol. 1891, B.A. 10 Oct. 1890, M.A. 27 Ap. 1893; C. at Marlborough Mission, Tottenham.

Arthur Rollo **Warburton** (4 s. of William Parsons, hon. canon of Winchester), b. S. Maurice, Winchester 14 Oct. 1868, ed. Honiton, **Stap.** 7 July **1887**, **M**. 19 Oct. 1887, 2 Classics Mod. 1889, 3 Classics 1891, B.A. 1 Aug. 1891.

Willoughby Charles **Allen** (3 s. Rev. Charles Fletcher), b. S. Werburgh, Derby 7 Oct. 1867, ed. Clergy Orphan sch., Canterbury, and Cambridge, **M**. Non-Coll. 21 Oct. 1886; **Hasker** 7 July **1887**, 1 Theol. 1890, B.A. 10 Oct. 1890, Pusey and Ellerton scholar 1890, prize of books in Kennicott examination 1891, Syriac prize 1892, 1 Semitic languages 1892, Kennicott scholar 1892, highly commended for Senior Greek Testament prize 1893 and had prize of books; assist. chaplain and lecturer Ex. Coll. 1893; ordained 28 May 1893, C. of South Hinksey, Berks 1893.

Henry Beresford **Herbert** (3 s. late Rev. Samuel Asher), b. Gateshead, Durham 19 Jan. 1869, ed. Leamington Coll., **Exh.** 7 July **1887**, **M**. 19 Oct. 1887, 2 Math. Mod. 1889, 3 Math. 1891, B.A. 2 July 1891.

George Ridley **Theobald** (2 s. Rev. Charles), b. Chale, I. of Wight 19 Oct. 1868, ed. Radley, **How** 7 July **1887**, **M**. 19 Oct. 1887, 3 Classics Mod. 1889, 3 Classics 1891, B.A. 1 Aug. 1891.

Joseph Louis **Whitehead** (1 s. Joseph Whiston, merchant), b. Quebec 17 July 1854, ed. Queen's Coll. Belfast, **M.** Non-Coll. 17 Oct. 1885, at New Coll. 1887 ; **Hist. Ex. Coll.** 7 July **1887**, Stanhope Essay 1888, 2 Hist. 1889, B.A. 2 Aug. 1889, M.A. 31 July 1893.

Robert Francis Chiappini **de Winton** (6 s. Henry, archdeacon of Brecon), b. Boughrood, Radnors. 6 Sep. 1868, ed. Marlborough, **How** Nov. **1887**, **M.** 19 Oct. 1887, in Rugby Union Fifteen, 2 Classics Mod. 1889, 4 Classics 1891, B.A. 3 Dec. 1891.

James Newland **Newland-Smith** (1 s. late Rev. James, by Emma d. of late Rev. Dr. Smithers), b. Maze Hill, Greenwich 7 Dec. 1867, foundation scholar S. Paul's sch. 1881–6, **M.** 19 Oct. 1887, **Exh. 1887**, **Hasker** 22 Mch. **1888**, 2 Classics Mod. 1889, 2 Theol. 1891, B.A. 1 Aug. 1891, C. of Ch. Ch., Battersea 1891.

Francis Joseph **Stevens** (5 s. Thomas, barrister), b. Enfield, Middlesex 27 Ap. 1862, ed. Kensington Catholic sch., S. Bartholomew's, and King's, Camb. 28 Jan. 1885, **M.** Ch. Ch. 16 June 1887 ; **Exh.** 24 Nov. **1887**, 3 Nat. Sci. (An. Physiol.) 1890, B.A. 31 July 1890, M.R.C.S., assist. med. officer of Health, Camberwell 1893.

William Thomas **Southern** (1 s. William, schoolmaster), b. Kenton, Devon 22 Ap. 1869, ed. Exeter, **Open** 21 Jan. **1888**, **Reynolds** 21 July, **M.** 17 Oct. 1888, 2 Math. Mod. 1890, 2 Math. 1892, B.A. 30 June 1892, Phillpotts exhibitioner 1892.

Philip **Lance** (3 s. lieut.-col. William Henry Joseph), b. Kuch-Behar, India 28 Sep. 1869, ed. Vict. Coll. Jersey, **Ch. I.** 10 Feb. **1888**, **M.** 17 Oct. 1888, 3 Classics Mod. 1890, B.A. 17 Dec. 1892.

George Herbert **Trepté** (1 s. George Frederick, schoolmaster), b. Chelsea 25 Ap. 1869, ed. Bedford, **Open** 22 Mch. **1888**, **M.** 17 Oct. 1888, 2 Classics Mod. 1890, 3 Classics 1892, B.A. 3 Aug. 1892.

William Ffloyd **Watson** (2 s. Hickman Barratt, farmer), b. Elsham, Lincs. 11 June 1869, ed. Clifton, **Open** 22 Mch **1888**, **M.** 17 Oct. 1888, 2 Classics Mod. 1890, 3 Classics 1892, B.A. 10 Oct. 1892.

Herbert Theodore **Knight** (o. s. William Angus, professor St. Andrew's), b. Dundee 23 Mch 1869, ed. Fettes ˙Coll., Edinburgh, **Exh.** 22 Mch. **1888**, **M.** 17 Oct. 1888, 3 Classics Mod. 1890, 4 Classics 1892, B.A. 3 Aug. 1892, ordained 1893.

Alfred Thomas **Powell** (2 s. William, R.M.), b. E. Stonehouse, Devon 19 Ap. 1869, ed. Paignton sch., **Stap.** 25 Ap. **1888**, **M.** 17 Oct. 1888, 1 Math. Mod. 1890, 2 Math. 1892, B.A. 30 June 1892, 2 Nat. Sci. (Phys.) 1893, master at S. Peter's Training Coll., Peterborough 1893.

Thomas **Hamilton** (1 s. Thomas, of Manchester), b. Chorlton upon Medlock's Lane 19 July 1865, ed. City of London sch., **M.** Non-Coll. 23 Jan. 1886 ; **Symes** 2 Ap. **1888,** 4 Theol. 1889, B.A. 6 July 1889, M.A. 9 July 1892, C. of S. German, Roath, Cardiff 1890, of S. Mary Magdalen, Chiswick, 1892.

Armine Wodehouse **Fox** (2 s. Rev. William Charles), b. Weston-super-Mare 7 Ap. 1869, ed. Wellington Coll., **Exh.** 25 Ap. **1888, M.** 17 Oct. 1888, 3 Classics Mod. 1890.

Ernest William Mundy **Mundy** (2 s. James Terry Mundy, late Patch), b. Weston-super-Mare 26 June 1869, ed. Exeter, named **Reynolds** July **1888, M.** 17 Oct. 1888.

William Alfred **Norton** (o. s. William), b. Allhallows on the Walls, Exeter 13 May 1870, ed. Exeter, named **Reynolds** 9 Jan. **1889, M.** 16 Oct. 1889, 3 Classics Mod. 1891, 3 Classics 1893, B.A. 26 Oct. 1893, Phillpotts exhibitioner 1893.

Montague Charles **Eliot** (2 s. Col. the Hon. Charles George Cornwallis, brother of Lord S. Germans), b. London 13 May 1870, ed. Charterhouse, **Open** 21 Jan. **1889**–91, **M.** 16 Oct. 1889, 2 Classics Mod. 1891, 3 Law 1893.

John Charles **Miles** (1 s. John, solicitor), b. S. Peter's, Bayswater 29 Aug. 1870, ed. Shrewsbury, **Open** 21 Jan. **1889,** res. 1891 : **M.** 16 Oct. 1889, 2 Classics Mod. 1891, 1 Law 1893, B.A. 31 July 1893.

Theodore Hayes **Robinson** (1 s. Rev. Richard Hayes, d. 1892), b. Walcot, Bath 22 June 1870, ed. Bath Coll., **Stap. O.** 21 Jan. **1889, M.** 16 Oct. 1889, 2 Classics Mod. 1891, 3 Classics 1893, B.A. 10 Oct. 1893.

Alexander **Ramsbotham** (2 s. Samuel Henry, M.D.), b. S. Paul's, Leeds 28 June 1870, ed. Charterhouse, **Stap. O.** 21 Jan. 1889, **M.** 16 Oct. 1889, 2 Classics Mod. 1891, 3 Classics 1893, President of University athletic club.

Horace John **Gibbins** (1 s. John George, architect), b. Brighton 24 July 1870, ed. Brighton Coll., **Hasker** 21 Jan. **1889, M.** 16 Oct. 1889, 1 Classics Mod. 1891, 3 Classics 1893, B.A. 10 Oct. 1893.

Percy Holland **Lester** (2 s. Rev. Edward), b. Kirkdale, Lancs. 20 Jan. 1871, ed. Merchant Taylors, and Great Crosby near Liverpool, **Open** 21 Jan. **1889, M.** 16 Oct. 1889, 2 Math. Mod. 1891, 2 Math. 1893, B.A. 8 July 1893, Phillpotts exhibitioner 1893.

George Alfred Travers **Nettleton** (2 s. Harry Thomas, R.N., M.C.R.S., by Julia Louisa Browne), b. Weymouth 30 Mch 1871, ed. Merchant Taylors, **Michell** 21 Jan. **1889, M.** 16 Oct. 1889, 2 Classics Mod. 1891, 2 Theol. 1893, B.A. 31 July 1893.

William George **Cruft** (o. s. William John, V. of Edwalton, Notts., by Mary d. of Thomas Steel), b. Nottingham 7 June 1871, ed. High sch. Nottingham; Darell, **M.** 21 Mch **1889**, **Exh. 1891**, 2 Theol. 1892, B.A. 9 July 1892, at S. Stephen's house, Park St., Oxford 1893.

Lewis Jones **Roberts** (2 s. late Lewis), b. Aberayron, Aberath, Cardigans. 25 May 1866, ed. S. David's Coll., Lampeter, **Hist.** 24 June **1889**, **M.** 7 Dec. 1889, 2 Hist. 1892, master at S. David's sch. 1892.

Walter **Hudson** (1 s. John, by Mary Jane Burrows), b. Brierfield, Lancs. 22 Oct. 1865, ed. Univ. Coll., Liverpool; **Hist.** 24 June **1889, M.** 16 Oct. 1889, 1 Hist. 1892, B.A. 3 Aug. 1892.

Hamilton **Rose** (1 s. John Henry, V. of S. James', Clerkenwell), b. Islington 28 Sep. 1870, ed. Merchant Taylors; **Symes** Oct. **1889, M.** 13 Oct. 1890, Pusey and Ellerton scholar 1893.

John Loveband Langdon **Fulford** (1 s. Rev. John Loveband Langdon), b. Woodbury, Devon 2 Jan. 1871, ed. Exeter, named **Reynolds** 12 Sep. **1889, M.** 16 Oct. 1889, 3 Classics Mod. 1891, 3 Classics 1893, B.A. 31 July 1893.

George Herbert Wippell **Mallett** (2. s. William George, R. of S. Mary Major, Exeter), b. Jaunpore, Bengal Feb. 1872, named **Reynolds** 12 July **1890, M.** 16 Oct. 1890, went to Emmanuel, Camb. 1892.

Henry Ernest **Atkinson** (1 s. Rev. Francis Home), b. Exmouth 21 July 1871, ed. Victoria Coll., Jersey, **Ch. I.** 8 Mch **1890, M.** 13 Oct. 1890.

John Herbert **Withers** (3 s. Rev. Bigland), b. S. Paul's, Bury, Lancs. 3 June 1872, ed. Bury gr. sch., **Open** 8 Mch **1890, M.** 13 Oct. 1890, 2 Classics Mod. 1892.

Frank **Anderson** (3 s. William, director general of Ordnance factories), b. Christchurch, Erith, Kent 22 Nov. 1871, ed. Marlborough, **Open** 8 Mch **1890, M.** 13 Oct. 1890, 2 Classics Mod. 1892.

Frederick Percival **Dixon** (1 s. Percival Ridyard), b. Manchester 25 July 1871, ed. Manchester gr. sch., **Open** 8 Mch **1890, M.** 13 Oct. 1890, 2 Classics Mod. 1892.

Sydney Charles **Gayford** (3 s. John), b. Wicken Bonhunt, Essex 28 Oct. 1871, ed. Felstead sch., **Open** 8 Mch **1890, M.** 13 Oct. 1890, 1 Classics Mod. 1892.

William Inskip Digby Shuttleworth **Read** (2 s. William, naval instructor in H.M.S. Britannia), b. S. Saviour's, Dartmouth 18 Ap. 1871, ed. Tiverton, **Stap.** 8 Mch **1890, M.** 27 May 1890, 2 Classics Mod. 1892.

John Wilfred **Jenkinson** (2 s. William Wilberforce), b. Norwood, Surrey 31 Dec. 1871, ed. Bradfield, **Carter** 8 Mch **1890**, **M**. 13 Oct. 1890, 2 Classics Mod. 1892.

Henry Alban **Smith** (2 s. Rev. Henry, inspector of schools; and nephew of P. H. Wilson, see 1852), b. Tattenhall, Cheshire, June 1871, ed. Rossall, **Gifford** 8 Mch **1890**, **M**. 13 Oct. 1890, 2 Classics Mod. 1892.

Frank Douglas **Simpson** (3 s. Alexander, advocate), b. Aberdeen 18 Oct. 1870, ed. Aberdeen Univ., **Richards** 18 Oct. **1890**, **M**. 13 Oct. 1890, fifth in I. C. S. Exam. 1893.

Herbert Fuller Bright **Compston** (4 s. Rev. John), b. Barnsley, Yorks. 17 Oct. 1866, ed. Ilminster, **M**. Non-Coll. 13 Oct. 1888, at Ex. Coll. 16 Oct. 1889, **Richards** 18 Oct. **1890**, 1 Theol. 1891, B.A. 11 July 1891, C. of Totnes 1893.

Frederic William **Pearson** (1 s. William), b. Wrenthorpe, Yorks. 28 Mch 1873, ed. Wakefield gr. sch., **Open** Jan. **1891**, **M**. 22 Oct. 1891, 1 Classics Mod. 1893.

Charles Robert Loraine **McDowall** (1 s. Charles, D.D., Master of Highgate sch.; Mod. Eng. Biog.), b. Malvern 9 June 1873, ed. Marlborough, **Open** Jan. **1891**, **M**. 22 Oct. 1891, 1 Classics Mod. 1893.

Walter Reginald **Kirby** (2 s. Thomas Frederick, barrister), b. London 5 Mch 1872, ed. Charterhouse, **Open** Jan. **1891**, **M**. 3 Nov. 1891, 2 Classics Mod. 1893.

Oswyn Alexander Ruthven **Murray** (4 s. James Augustus Henry), b. Hendon, Middlesex 17 Aug. 1873, ed. Oxford high sch., **Stap.** Jan. **1891**, **M**. 22 Oct. 1891, 1 Classics Mod. 1893.

John Christian **Pringle** (2 s. Robert, W.S.), b. Edinburgh 27 Aug. 1872, ed. Winchester, **Stap.** Jan. **1891**, **M**. 22 Oct. 1891, 1 Classics Mod. 1893.

John Hubert **Smith** (3 s. Rev. John Nathaniel), b. Clapton 2 Ap. 1872, ed. King's sch., Canterbury, **Hasker** Jan. **1891**, **M**. 22 Oct. 1891, 2 Classics Mod. 1893.

Edward Hibbert **Binney** (8 s. Douglas Belcher, R. of Limington, Ilchester), b. Clifton Hampden, Oxon 26 Oct. 1874, ed. Charterhouse, **How** Jan. 1891, **M**. 22 Oct. 1891, 2 Classics Mod. 1893.

John Francis Gore **Little** (1 s. Major Francis Gore, R.A., Chief Constable of Preston), b. Leitrim 8 Jan. 1872, ed. Magdalen Coll. sch., **M**. Trinity Oct. 1890 ; **Richards** Jan. **1891**, 2 Classics Mod. 1892.

David **Thomas** (3 s. Jenkin, insurance agent), b. Ystalyfera, Glamorgans. 15 Mch 1873, ed. Llandovery, **Open** Jan. 1891, **M.** 22 Oct. 1891, 2 Math. Mod. 1893.

Walter Aubin **Le Rossignol** (1 s. John Mauger, governor H.M. prison, Jersey), b. S. Helier's, Jersey 3 Ap. 1873, ed. Victoria Coll., Jersey, **Ch. I.** Feb. **1891, M.** 22 Oct. 1891, 1st selected candidate I.C.S. 1891.

Godfrey Mohun **Carey** (3 s. Thomas Godfrey, solicitor), b. S. Peter's Port, Guernsey 17 Aug. 1872, ed. Sherborne, **Ch. I.** Feb. **1891, M.** 22 Oct. 1891, in University Rugby Union football fifteen, 3 Classics Mod. 1893.

Sydney Harcourt Dunsford **Holton** (3 s. late Francis, Surgeon-General), b. Kingstown, Dublin 7 Dec. 1869, ed. Bradfield, **Hist.** 30 May **1891, M.** 22 Oct. 1891, 2 Classics Mod. 1893.

William Thomas Webb **Baker** (1 s. Henry Laurence, solicitor), b. Abergavenny 6 Dec. 1873, ed. Rugby, **Open** 23 Jan. **1892, M.** 18 Oct. 1892.

Victor Edwin Grove **Hussey** (1 s. John Fraser, M.R.C.S., of Dorchester, Dorset), b. Melcombe Regis, Dorset 16 June 1873, ed. S. Paul's sch., W. Kensington, **Open** 23 Jan. **1892, M.** 18 Oct. 1892.

Alfred Edmund **Lynam** (7 s. Charles, architect), b. Stoke-on-Trent 27 Mch 1873, ed. Rossall, **Open** 23 Jan. **1892, M.** 18 Oct. 1892.

Sidney Robert **Hignell** (2 s. Thomas Evans, of Keynsham, Bristol), b. Thornbury, Glouc., 3 June 1873, ed. Malvern Coll., **Open** 23 Jan. **1892, M.** 18 Oct. 1892.

John Hall **Barron** (s. late David James), b. Inverurie, Aberdeensh. 15 Ap. 1873, ed. Aberdeen Univ., **Stap. O.** 23 Jan. **1892, M.** 18 Oct. 1892.

Edward Arthur **Selby-Lowndes** (o. s. late capt. William Seymour Selby, of S. Margaret's, Westminster), b. Paddington 22 May 1873, ed. Merchant Taylors, **Hasker** 23 Jan. **1892, M.** 18 Oct. 1892, Pusey and Ellerton sch. 1892.

Ernest **Cleave** (4 s. William Oke, LL.D., R. of Graveley, Hunts), b. S. Helier's, Jersey 27 May 1873, ed. S. John's sch. Leatherhead; **Ch. I** Feb. **1892, M.** 18 Oct. 1892.

Benwell Harold **Bird** (1 s. Rev. Benwell, Wesleyan minister), b. Birmingham 28 June 1872, ed. Plymouth Coll., **M.** 13 Oct. 1890, 2 Classics Mod. 1892, **Exh.** 18 June **1892.**

Percival Robert Nepean **Carleton** (1 s. major William Henry), b. Londonderry 25 Feb. 1874, ed. Tiverton, **Stap.** 5 Nov. **1892, M.** 17 Oct. 1893.

Frederick John **Richards** (1 s. John Ward, cashier L. and Westm. bank), b. Stoke Newington, London N., 26 June 1875, ed. Merchant Taylors, **Open** Jan. **1893**, **M.** 17 Oct. 1893.

Wilmot Peregrine Maitland **Russell** (3 s. capt. Theodosius Stuart, chief Constable W. Riding, Yorks.), b. Rochdale 6 June 1874, ed. Rugby, **Open** Jan. **1893**, **M.** 17 Oct. 1893.

Edward Stuart **Mills**, (3 s. Robert John), b. S. Sidwell's, Exeter 30 Ap. 1874, ed. Exeter, **Open** Jan. **1893**, **M.** 17 Oct. 1893.

Oswald Addenbrooke **Holden** (2 s. Oswald Mangin, V. of Gailey, Staffs.), b. Kingswinford, Staffs. 9 Ap. 1874, ed. Rossall, **Open** Jan. **1893**, **M.** 17 Oct. 1893.

Lewis Albert **Abbott** (1 s. Lewis Lowe, metal merchant), b. Chicago, Illinois 8 June 1874, ed. Uppingham, **Ex.** Mch **1893**, **M.** 17 Oct. 1893.

Ernest William Harry **Parker** (o. s. Samuel Compigné, by Emma Charlotte Giles), b. Camden Town 24 July 1874, ed. King's Coll. sch. London, **Hist. Exh.** 28 Ap. **1893**, **M.** 17 Oct. 1893.

Francis **Colmer** (1 s. John William, merchant, by Mary Scudamore d. of William Taylor), b. Bayswater 22 Oct. 1873, ed. Merchant Taylors, **Hist. Exh.** 28 Ap. **1893**, **M.** 17 Oct. 1893.

Reginald William Dawson **Stephenson** (2 s. Jacob, V. of Forton, Gosport), b. London 10 Sep. 1874, e Felstead, **How** May **1893**, **M.** 17 Oct. 1893.

BENEFACTORS' BOOK.

AFTER mentioning Stapeldon, Stafford, Petre, and Charles I, it enumerates other benefactors[1] of the College as follows (in Latin) :—

Nicolas Goss Chancellor of Exeter, Walter Windsor subdean, and John Lynden dean of Crediton acquired the rectory of Menhinnet for the College, A.D. 1478; and the executors of Henry Webber dean of Exeter, of James Hamlin and of Richard Mounceaux canons gave £60 for the expenses of the appropriation[2].

Nicolas Goss also gave £15 towards buying our Inn (domus Pandoxatoria)[3].

Solomon Firstthorp 10 marks.

The executors of Cardinal Bewford 50 marks.

Edward Hawley Bachelor of Decrees 20 marks.

John Harris[4] bedell of theology 100s. in gold and a tenement in the Great Baily 2 Ap. 1460.

Thomas Pydington and Alice his wife gave Carole Hall in the Little Baily 12 Rich. II.

[1] The older Benefactors' Book gives the following :—'Exsequiae celebrandae Benefactorum nonnullorum nomina ab ea oblivione vindicarunt quae ipsorum beneficia obruit, viz., John Pyttys, Robert Lydford, Edmund de la Beche, William Wellys, John and Baldwin Shillingford canons of Exeter, Thomas Freyma (?); Fulk Bourchier and Elizabeth his wife, Edward Courtenay and Elizabeth his wife, Halnatheus Maleverer and Joan his wife—the original patrons of Minhinnet; William Palmer, Philip Copleston, Thomas Carew and Elizabeth his wife, Elizabeth Cheselden, Walter Lyhert, John Parhous, William Bristow for whose obit John Harris bedell made provision ; John Goldon priest and sometime fellow gave to the use of the Masters and Fellows that sang the mass Pretende in divers parcels £20, and upon trust to have a cotidian memory of him hereafter nominatim in the cotidian memento of or in the said cotidian Pretende mass other £20, whereof £10 2s. 6d. he bestowed upon a chalice of silver to be used at the said Pretende mass principally—the other £10 to be bestowed to prepare a room for an altar in the south side of the Chapel for the cotidian mass of Pretende, and hereupon Mr. Philip Bale Rector, M. Edmond Fletcher, M. Thomas Lake, M. William Slade, M. John Moxay, M. Bartholomew Michel, M. John White, M. John Bere, M. John Colyns, M. John Toker, M. John Cunnere, M. Stephen Carsleigh, Sir Euryn Cocks, Sir Thomas Forde, and Sir John Pekyns, Masters and Fellows of Exon College have granted and decreed &c. to register the name &c., sealed 10 May 1524.'

[2] John Colyforde gave £50, John Lyndon £20, N. Gosse and T. Copleston sojourners each lent £5, to procure letters patent for a mortmain licence.

[3] On 9 Feb. 154⅜ our Inn in S. Giles' was let to Edmund Iryshe for 15 years.

[4] An attempt was made in 1462 to murder John Harris by Roger Bride of Ex. Coll., and Laurence his accomplice ; Anstey 696 and index.

William Palmer £100 in 1432 to build four chambers west of the North Tower, and the Tower and Gateway itself, and the Rector's Lodge adjoining.

Dionysius de Orleigh prior of St. John's at Exeter £40 in 1485.

John Goldon, formerly fellow, £20 in 1524.

Sir William Petre left us £40 by will, and Anna his wife the same, and their son John £20.

Bishop William Bradbridge collected for us £250 among the ministers of Devon and Cornwall.

Andrew Scutt of Cheriton Fitzpain in Devon left us £70 by will.

Henry Dotin left us £20.

John Peryam of Exeter, 1616, built the rooms north of the Hall next the garden for £560.

Sir John Acland gave £800 to build the Hall and beer cellar underneath.

George Hakewill, Rector, gave £1200 to build the new Chapel in 1624, and £30 that a sermon might be preached annually on 5 October. To these three buildings the College contributed £600.

Richard Sandis fellow £20.

Robert Vilvain formerly fellow £20.

William Orford fellow £20.

William Helme fellow £20.

Luke Eaton [1] formerly cook 40 shillings annually for ever.

Sir John Maynard £20 to a Praelector of Theology, and £12 to a Praelector of Hebrew, for ever.

George Hall bishop of Chester left us a gold cup and land at Trethewin in S. German's [2].

Samuel Cosins fellow in 1668 left £120 to buy books for the Library.

Thomas Matthews left £5 to the Library.

John Barbon M.A. 50 shillings to buy silver Patens for the Eucharist.

Richard Eastchurch M.A. sojourner in this College (1652–59) left £20 to the Library.

William Paynter, now Rector, gave £100 in 1685.

Thomas Rowney, seneschal of the College, gave the Rectory of Wootton, Northants, 1685.

---

[1] He gave a bakehouse in Magdalen parish 1621; it was sold to Worcester College, and the money laid out in purchase of land tax.

[2] *Gilda Aurifabrorum* by W. Chaffers 1886 p. 16.

Richard Hutchins fellow gave the Rectory of Sommerford Magna, Wilts 1704, and left his books to the College in 1718, and £500 to buy a living, with which Baverstock was bought 1720.

Lady Elizabeth Shiers of Slyfield in Surrey, d. 14 Aug. 1700; her will was set aside for informality, but the Rev. Hugh Shortridge her executor gave the College her lands as she intended, and added two fellowships for Herts and Surrey.

William Earl Cowper gave a silver cup weighing 167 oz. in 1721.

Edward Richards Esq. of Compton Beauchamp in Berks, formerly fellow commoner, gave his choice collection of Greek and Latin authors to the Library in 1729.

Matthew Hole, Rector, left £100 in 1730.

Lawrence Horner gave £45 to adorn the Chapel in 1731.

Charles Talbot Esq., Solicitor General and afterwards Chancellor, gave 50 guineas in 1731.

William Talbot his son, fellow commoner, afterwards Earl Talbot, gave 20 guineas in 1731.

Lady Moyle of Bake in Cornwall sent £50 in 1733 as a memorial of her son Walter late fellow.

Thomas Secker gave £20 in 1733, when archbishop he gave £100 in 1763.

Samuel Norris, formerly fellow, in 1739 gave £50 a year due from the Exchequer till 1804[1].

George Talbot, son of Chancellor Talbot, fellow commoner, gave £50 in 1740.

John Conybeare, Dean of Christ Church, gave £50 in 1741.

Robert Jocelyn, afterwards Lord Roden, gave £20 in 1743.

Thomas Blackall of Hasely Magna, Oxon, fellow commoner, gave a fine orrery 1757.

Francis Webber, Rector, left £500 in 1771.

Joseph Sandford, fellow commoner, left his books and manuscripts to the Library in 1774.

John Ratcliffe, M.A. of Pembroke, son of Robert Ratcliffe (once fellow), left £400 in 1775.

George Viscount Parker, son of Thomas Earl of Macclesfield, gave a silver cup weighing 83 oz.

Benjamin Langley, formerly fellow, gave £105, to buy a silver vase, in 1777.

Henry Harford Esq. M.A. of the College gave £50 in 1779.

[1] Exchequer annuities of £50 for 99 years from 1704.

William Peters Esq., fellow commoner, gave a picture of Walter de Stapeldon in 1780.

William Holwell fellow gave a picture of Sir William Petre, painted by himself, in 1785.

Thomas Bray, Rector, left £500 in 1785.

Thomas Stinton, Rector, left £50 in 1797.

For erecting the buildings north of the front gate and up to the chapel (begun in 1672 but not finished till 1682, Gutch iii. 111), Lord Clifford the Lord Treasurer gave £50, William Helyar, Esq., of East Cokar, Som., £20, John Cabel, Esq., of Brook, Devon, £20, Richard Duke, Esq., of Otterton, Devon, £10, Thomas Rowney, Steward of Ex. Col., £10, Richard Newte of Tiverton, once Fellow, £10, William Jesse, once Fellow, £5, John Beauford, R. of S. Columb Major in Cornwall, £5, William Harding, cook of Ex. Coll., £12, John Wauchop £10, Joseph Squire, once Fellow, £5, John Wilcox, barber of Ex. Coll., £5, John Tuckfield, Esq., of Cree, Devon, £10, Thomas Isaak, Esq., of Heavitree, Devon, £6, Francis Chichester, £6, Josua Tucker, Archdeacon of Barnstaple, £10, Bernard Gealard of Poltimore, once Fellow, £10, Richard Coffin, Esq., of Devon, £10; 36 Fellow commoners gave £8 each; and contributions were made by Sir Walter Yong, Bart., Sir Henry Carew, Sir John Chichester, Bart., Sir Sandys Fortescue, Bart.

Arthur Bury, Rector, gave over £700 towards these buildings and towards enlarging the Rector's lodgings, building a stable, constructing an organ, &c.

For building the front gate with a tower over it, and the buildings between it and the hall (begun 2 July 1700, finished 2 Nov. 1703), Narcissus Marsh Archbishop of Armagh and formerly fellow gave £300; Sir George Treby fellow commoner now C. J. of the Common Pleas £100; Henry Hatsell once a sojourner in the College and now a Baron of the Exchequer £40; Sir Nicolas Morice baronet of Werrington in Devon, formerly fellow commoner, £200; John Wauchop R. of Bratton-Fleming in Devon £110; Hugh Shortridge of Slyfield in Surrey, once fellow commoner, £30; Samuel Norris formerly fellow £20; John Ellis V. of Chudleigh in Devon £3; John Conant of Kidlington, LL.D., £10; Samuel Conant formerly fellow £10; Thomas Smith Esq. of Kidlington ten guineas=£10 15s.; Ames Crymes of Crapston in Devon formerly fellow £40; George Snell formerly fellow £40; Sir Francis Drake baronet of Buckland Monachorum £50; Elizabeth Conant widow of John Conant late Rector £5; John Ceely canon of Exeter £20; George Musgrave Esq. of Nettlecombe in Somerset £20; William Williams Esq. of Bodinnick in Cornwall £30; Laurence Lord of Fritwell in Oxon £5; Denys Glin Esq. of Glinford in Cornwall £10; Edward Richards Esq. fellow commoner £50; Charles Tarleton V. of Bicton in Devon £10; Francis Strode R. of Ideford in Devon £10; Gilbert Yard Esq. of Bradley in Devon £30; Nicolas Kendall R. of Sheviocke and Canon of Exeter £10; Thomas Hurrell R. of Beer Ferrers in Devon £5; William Holloway R. of Bremor in Hants £5; Matthew Attwell R. of Morton Hampstead in Devon £5; Francis Paynter Esq. of Trelistick in Cornwall £10; Thomas Pine M.D. of Tamerton in Devon £10; William Stawell Esq. of Bovey Tracey in Devon £40; Richard Osborne Esq. of Clis S. George in Devon £10; William Cornish R. of Bigbury in Devon £10; John Pendarvis R. of Dittisham in Devon £5; Richard Rotherick S.T.P., V. of Blandford in Dorset £5; John Combs R. of Lindlinck in Dorset £5; William New, Promus of the College, £10; Daniel Osborne fellow £10; Benjamin King S.T.P., V. of All Saints at Northampton £5; John Speccott Esq. of Penhele in Cornwall £50; Sir Richard Vyvyan baronet of Trelowarren in Cornwall £50; Sir William Scawen of Molinnick in Cornwall £50; Roger Crews R. of Creed in Cornwall £5; William Mitchell V. of Kenwin in Cornwall £5: George Fowler R. of Filly in Cornwall £3; Joseph Trewinnard R. of Mawnan in Cornwall £5; William Tonken V. of Mullian in Cornwall £2; Henry Seyntaubyn V. of Crowan in Cornwall £5; John Ralph V. of S. Erth in Cornwall £2; John Hawkins V. of Uny-Lelant in Cornwall £4; Jonathan Trelawny Esq. of Coldrennick in Cornwall 50s.; James Bishop of Guenap in Cornwall £1; George Hawkins Vicar of Sithney in Cornwall £1; Richard Scaddon V. of Treneglos in Cornwall £2 3s.; James Fincher R. of Duloe in Cornwall £10; Thomas Pendarves R. of S. Columb in Cornwall £10; Robert Hoblyn R. of Ludgvan in Cornwall £10; Benjamin Archer R. of Quainton in Bucks £10; John Walker fellow £5 7s. 6d.; James Praed Esq. of Trevethow in Cornwall £30; Louis Stephens V. of Minhinnett in Cornwall £20; Henry Kingsmill Esq. of Sandleford in Berks £10; Richard King Esq. of Exeter £10; John Snell R. of Heavytree £10; Gilbert Geer R. of Kenn in Devon £5; Thomas Snell V. of Bampton in Oxon £10; John Hippisly Esq. of Lamborn in Berks £15; Edward Southby of Carswell in Berks £5; Thomas Granger V. of Lamerton in Devon £5; Richard Dodwell, Seneschal of the

College, £5 7s. 6d.; Samuel Adams fellow £10 15s.; John Arscott Esq. of Tetcott in Devon £20; Nicolas Morrice Esq. of Werrington in Devon £50; Gilbert Yard Esq. Alderman of Exeter £20; John Copleston R. of Tedburn S. Mary in Devon £1 1s. 6d.; Edward Waldo Esq. of Harrow in Middlesex £10; George Mullins gentleman of Sarum £5; George Parker Esq. of Burrington in Devon £50; Joseph Quash gentleman of Exeter £5; Charles Harward R. of Tallaton in Devon £5 7s. 6d.; John Gay Esq. of Frithle-Stoke in Devon £8; Mainard Colchester Esq. of Westbury in Gloucester £20; Martin May gentleman of Kidlington in Oxon £5 7s. 6d.; Robert Rous fellow £5; John King S.T.P., R. of Chelsea £5; Henry Southcott M.D. of Devon £1 1s. 6d.; Robert Manley M.A. £10; Nicolas Hicks R. of Cheriton in Devon £5 ; Nicolas Rook R. of Dartington 40 shillings; William Jane Regius Professor and Dean of Gloucester £10 15s.; John Burrington Esq. of Sandford in Devon £10; Henry Levett M.D. of London £20; Richard Vyvian R. of S. Ervan in Cornwall £2 3s.; Thomas Hawkey R. of Marum (Marham-church) in Cornwall £10 15s.; Joseph Coryndon R. of Kilhampton in Cornwall £10; John Jago of Egloskerry in Cornwall 40 shillings; Joseph Dill R. of S. Just in Cornwall £5; William Bedford V. of Tregony 20 shillings; Francis Carswell V. of Bray in Berks £10; Nicolas Trist of Halberton-Ford in Devon £5 7s. 6d.; Walter Getsius V. of Brixham in Devon £10; Francis Duncombe Esq. of Broughton in Bucks £10 15s.; John Furse of Upex in Devon £10; William Crab R. of Child Ockford in Dorset £5 ; Joseph Carveth R. of Luxulian in Cornwall £3; John Ross R. of Gittisham in Devon £2 3s.; Robert Ratcliffe R. of Stonehouse in Gloucester £5; Henry Northcott M.D. £10.

For the buildings opposite the front gate eastwards, from 1708 to 1710, Narcissus Marsh Archbp. of Armagh gave £1,000; William Mervin formerly fellow, R. of Tawstock in Devon £6 9s.; William Wright Esq. Recorder of Oxford (at the time his two elder sons were admitted to the Sojourners' table) £10 15s.; George Verman senior fellow £10; Humphrey Smith Esq. of Kidlington £10 5s.; Laurence Horner 'tonsor' of the College £10 15s.; Francis Duncombe, son of Francis Duncombe of Broughton in Bucks, fellow commoner £10 15s.; George Goodall R. of Padworth in Berks left £20, paid by his executor Rev. M. Goddard; Joseph Davy Esq. fellow commoner £20; Edward Richards Esq. of Compton in Berks fellow commoner £50; John Lagett 'promus' £10 15s.; Joseph Coryndon R.

of Kilhampton £21 10s.; Edward Herle Esq. of Landew in Cornwall fellow commoner £10; Walter Moyle Esq. of Bake in Cornwall £5; Sidenham Burgh M.A. of the College £2 3s.; Edward Richards Esq. gave £50 additional, spent in repairing Peryam Buildings. (See Gutch ii. 111.)

Afterwards follow the names of Benefactors during this century.

LIST OF THE PICTURES IN THE HALL, AND LISTS OF ARMS.

Beginning with the East end of the Hall, and proceeding round the South, West and North sides, the order of the pictures is as follows, the upper row being given first, and the rows separated by semicolons: **East** side, 1 J. Prideaux, rector 1612, 2 A. A. Cooper, Earl of Shaftesbury; 3 Walter de Stapeldon, 4 J. C. Jones, rector 1819–38; 5 H. Richards, rector 1797–1807, 6 Sir C. Lyell; **South** side, 7 Stephen Weston, fellow, d. 1830; 8 J. L. Richards, rector 1838–54, 9 J. Conybeare, rector 1730–3; 10 Sir J. Maynard, d. 1690, 11 G. Hall, Bishop of Chester, d. 1668; 12 W. Noy, attorney general 1631, 13 Sir J. T. Coleridge, judge; 14 J. Selden, 15 G. Bull, Bishop of S. David's; 16 Sir W. Morrice, d. 1676, 17 Luke Milbourn, d. 1720; **West** side, 18 Thomas Lord Ducie, d. 1840, 19 Walter de Stapeldon, 20 Charles I; 21 Narcissus Marsh Archbp. of Armagh, 22 Sir W. Petre; 23 G. Parker, son of Earl of Macclesfield, picture given by him to rector Bray 1777, 24 T. Bray, rector 1771–85, 25 Sir J. Acland 1618; **North** side, 26 Lady Elizabeth Shiers, d. 14 Aug. 1710, 27 (name lost); 28 J. Periam 1616, 29 F. Webber, rector 1750–71; 30 H. Shortridge, d. 1720, 31 G. Hakewill, rector 1642–9; 32 J. Cole, rector 1808–19 (by Opie), 33 T. Secker, Archbishop of Canterbury, d. 1768; 34 T. Stinton, rector 1785–97, 35 B. Kennicott.

On the wainscot behind the High Table are these arms of Benefactors, running from North to South: 1 Charles I, 2 J. D. Macbride (? impaling Radcliffe), 3 P. Orchard, 4 Viscount Parker, Earl of Macclesfield, 5 J. S. Enys, 6 Hon. R. Jocelyn (Earl of Roden), 7 Archbishop Secker, 8 Lord Talbot, 9 Lady Elizabeth Shiers, 10 Sir G. Treby, Knt., 11 Sir F. Drake, Bart., 12 Dr. Arthur Bury, 13 T. Rowney (impaling St. Lowe), 14 Bishop Hall (impaled with see of Norwich), 15 J. Pulteney, 16 Dr. J. Hakewill, 17 Sir W. Petre, 18 Walter de Stapeldon, 19 Sir J. Peryam, Knt., 20 Sir J. Maynard, Knt., 21 J. Prideaux (impaled with see of Worcester), 22 G. Bull (impaled with see of S. David's), 23 J. Halse, Bishop of Lichfield, 24 R. Hutchins, B.D., 25 Narcissus Marsh (impaled with see of

Armagh), 26 Sir N. Morrice, Bart., 27 Earl Cowper, 28 Dr. Radcliffe, 29 J. Conybeare (impaled with see of Bristol), 30 H. Webber, Dean of Exeter, 31 Earl Ducie, 32 Dr. Cole, 33 Dr. J. C. Jones.

The arms carved on the stalls of the Chapel are (1) on the South side, Stapeldon, Stafford, Courtenay, Palmer, Acland, Maynard, Shiers, Cowper, Webber, Bray, N. Marsh, Richards, Reynolds, Phillpotts, Hasker; (2) on the North side, Petre (ancient coat), Charles I, Bishop Bradbridge, Periam, Hakewill, Hall, Hole, Talbot, Radcliffe, Bury, Morice, Symes, J. L. Richards, Ridding, Tozer.

The University Almanack for 1739 gives busts of Stapeldon, Stafford, Petre, Charles I, Dr. Hakewill, Sir J. Acland; and whole lengths of Primate Marsh, Bishop Bull, Chancellor Shaftesbury, George Treby, and Henry Pollexfen, Judges; Sir J. Maynard; arms of Sir F. Drake of Buckland, Sir W. Morice of Werrington, Sir R. Vyvyan of Trelowarren, Edward Richards, Treby of Devon, Gilbert of Devon, the principal contributors, after Primate Marsh, towards building the Tower, &c., about 1700.

For arms that once existed in the old buildings and windows, see Gutch iii. 110, seq.

The windows in the Chapel given *in memoriam* are as follows: **North** side (the antechapel and first window blank), two to Dr. Lightfoot, given by old members; one to Rev. G. H. Hasker and his wife, by Miss M. Hasker; **Apse**, 1 S. Marshall (undergraduate, d. 1860), by the undergraduates; 2 T. B. Colenso fellow, by members of the College; 3 and 4, centre, J. L. Richards rector, by members of the College; 5 given by Old Fellows at dedication of Chapel; **South** side, Mrs. Lightfoot, by Dr. Lightfoot; Mr. and Mrs. Tozer's parents, by Rev. H. F. and Mrs. Tozer; H. W. Moore fellow, by old members; Dr. Sewell, by old members; (antechapel blank).

There are tablets in the antechapel to **Rectors** Jones and Lightfoot, **Fellows** S. P. Rigaud and his son S. J. Rigaud (one tablet) and T. H. Sheppard; other members, W. E. Maynard (d. India 1887), J. F. White (d. 1871), J. W. Barne (accidentally shot 1868), W. P. Barnes (drowned in the Isis 1877), A. L. Burleigh (d. 9 May 1872), Gerald Evans and W. R. Harvey (d. 1889 and 1890; one tablet), H. T. Hope (d. 1892), Isidor Goldstein (drowned in the Isis 1885), H. L. H. ffolkes (drowned at King's Weir, Oxford, 12 Feb. 1892, in trying to save a friend).

For inscriptions in the old chapel *see* Gutch, 118–21: some of the Prideaux ones are still visible.

COLLEGE PLATE[1].

GUILT PLATE.—i. *Bowles.* ii. *Tankerds.*

	oz.	dwt.

Bowle and cover; *inscription:* 95 3

Haeredi Crookus Thomae dum triste parentat
Nec satis ad luctum marmor et aera putat,
Exonides, dixit, gratum tumulastis alumnum,
Nec leve erit pretium, sit memor urna calix.

Bowle and cover, Ex dono Francisci Henrici Lee Baronetti
1632 . . . . 45¾

Bowle and cover, Ex dono Philippi Whartoni Baronis de
Wharton hujus collegii commensalis 1626 . . . 31¾

Bowle and cover, Ex dono Francisci Godolphin armigeri
collegii hujus commensalis et filii natu maximi Guilelmi
Godolphin equitis aurati Cornubiensis 1622 . . 26¾

Bowle and cover, Ex dono Gulielmi Wrey equitis aurati filii
unigeniti et hujus collegii commensalis . . . 20½

Bowle and cover, Ex dono Johannis Tracy . . . 15½

Bowle and cover, Ex dono Roberti Oxenbridge filii Roberti
Oxenbridge equitis aurati hujus collegii commensalis . 20 1

Bowle, Ex dono Henrici Rivers filii Marcelli Rivers armigeri
natu maximi et hujus collegii commensalis . . . 12½

Bowle, Ex dono Johannis Bolney armigeri Ex. Coll. commensalis 12

2 Bowles, Ex dono Philippi Papillon in artibus magistri, in
usum battellariorum collegii Exoniensis . . . 12½

Bowle, The gift of Rainold Mohun to Exceter Colledge
1622 . . . . 12¼

Tankerd, Ex dono Henrici Carey Exon. coll. commensalis . 30¼

Tankerd, Ex dono Thomae Carey Exon. coll. commensalis 31¼

Tankerd, Ex dono D. Lionelli Cary Baronis de Lepington
filii natu maximi Henrici Comitis Monmothiae . . 30½

Tankerd, Hoc est donum Richardi Prideaux filii Jonathae
Prideaux armigeri Devon 1622 . . . . . 20 1

Dish, A dish marked with W. W. in the bottome . . . 21

Tankerd, Ex dono Johannis Reynell, Georgii Reynell equitis
aurati filii tertii et hujus collegii commensalis 1627 . 18½

[1] A list of the plate in Rector Glasier's time is given at the beginning of the
Computus Book marked H. See South Kensington Museum Art Handbooks,
College and Corporation Plate 1881, pp. 81, 92, 103, 115, 117.

1. *Bowles.*

	oz.	dwt.
Ex dono Carew Reynell Georgii Reynell Equitis Aurati filii natu maximi et hujus collegii commensalis . . .	12½	4
Ex dono Gulielmi Godolphin hujus collegii commensalis et filii Gulielmi Godolphin equitis aurati	12¾	
Ex dono Petri Speccot Johannis Speccot equitis aurati filii natu maximi; Johannes Coningesby	18¾	
(Battlers Bowle), Ex dono Oliveri Morton Magistri in artibus; Richardi Spicer, Rogeri Jope, Humphr. Jenkins, Johannis Maynard, Johannis Arden, Hugonis Baunton, Johannis Horsome Baccalaureorum in artibus; in usum Battellariorum in aula publica 1616 . . .	17¾	3
(Battlers Bowle), Ex dono Humphredi Smith, Gulielmi Coles, Gulielmi Kinge Magistrorum in artibus; in usum Battellariorum in aula publica 1637	15½	
Ex dono Gualteri et Thomae Chetwind 1626 . . .	17	
Ex dono Hugonis Portman Johannis Portman equitis et baronetti filii secundi hujus collegii commensalis . .	22¼	
Ex dono Francisci Whiddon filii Francisci Whiddon armigeri hujus collegii commensalis	15	
Ex dono Johannis Mohune equitis aurati filii collegii hujus commensalis 1606	12½	
Ex dono Johannis Strode Gulielmi Strode equitis aurati filii et hujus coll. commensalis	13¾	
Ex dono Ferdinandi Mohun filii Reginaldi Mohun equitis et baronetti, et hujus collegii commensalis 1630 . .	15¾	
Ex dono Jacobi Huyshe Rowlandi Huyshe armigeri filii unigeniti et hujus collegii commensalis 1622 . .	23¾	
Ex dono Gulielmi Morrice hujus collegii commensalis et filii Evani Morrice doctoris et olim cancellarii Exoniensis .	17¾	
Ex dono Thomae Dod Edvardi Dod armigeri et baronis Scaccarii Cestrensis filii natu maximi et hujus collegii commensalis 1620	19	
Ex dono Thomae Glanvill Johannis Glanvill unius e Justitiariis de banco Regis filii, collegii hujus commensalis	14½	
Ex dono Richardi Spencer equitis et baronetti filii natu tertii hujus collegii commensalis 1633 .	17¼	

	oz. dwt.
Ex dono Johannis Arundell filii natu maximi Thomae Arundell equitis aurati, et hujus collegii commensalis 1624 .	16¼
Ex dono Samuelis Peyton filii Thomae Peyton equitis aurati, commensalis 1606	17¼
Ex dono Johannis Conocke Johannis Conocke armigeri filii natu maximi et coll. Exon. commensalis 1618 . .	12½
Ex dono Edmundi Fortescue filii natu maximi Johannis Fortescue armigeri Devoniensis et hujus collegii commensalis 1629	20¾
Johannes Dowrish	11
Ex dono Johannis Harrison filii natu maximi Johannis Harrison armigeri Londinensis et hujus collegii commensalis	12 4
Ex dono Johannis Trevanion filii unigeniti Caroli Trevanion de Carhease Cornubiensis armigeri, hujus collegii commensalis	20¼
Ex dono Johannis Syms filii natu maximi Johannis Syms armigeri et hujus collegii commensalis 1616 .	17¾
(Wine bowle), Ex dono Jacobi Manninge	10¼ 3
(Wine bowle), Ex dono Nicolai Byrch magistri artium; in usum Battellariorum in a ! publica .	5 4

2. *Eard Pots.*

Ex dono Johannis Powlet domini Johannis Powlet baronis de Hinton St. George filii natu maximi 1631 . .	34¾ 4
Ex dono Francisci Powlet domini Johannis Powlet baronis de Hinton St. George filii natu secundi 1631 . .	35
Ex dono Philippi Stanhope filii Philippi Stanhope comitis de Chesterfield	33
Ex dono Georgii Stanhope filii Philippi Stanhope comitis de Chesterfield	38½
Ex dono Thomae Wharton equitis de Balneo hujus coll. commensalis 1626 . .	24
Ex dono Roberti Caulfield . .	18¼
Henrici Brien	17
Ex dono Johannis Chichesteri collegii commensalis 1599 .	13½
Ex dono Johannis Chichesteri Johannis Chichesteri armigeri filii natu maximi, et hujus collegii commensalis .	17¼
Ex dono Johannis Pine Armigeri 1614. Ex dono Johannis Flemminge .	34½

	oz.	dwt.
Ex dono Thomae Chaloneri filii Thomae Chaloneri equitis aurati	19	3
Ex dono Roberti Tracy Johannis Tracy equitis aurati filii natu maximi	$15\frac{1}{2}$	
Ex dono Henrici Champernoune hujus collegii commensalis et filii natu maximi Arthuri Champernoune armigeri Devoniensis 1619	$14\frac{3}{4}$	
Ex dono Richardi Southcot Georgii Southcot equitis filii secundi	16	
Ex dono Hugonis Clifford hujus collegii commensalis et filii natu maximi Thomae Clifford armigeri . . .	$14\frac{1}{2}$	
2 pots, Coll. Exon. Ex dono Raimundi Westlake scholaris ejusdem collegii 1580	$29\frac{1}{2}$	
Ex dono Roberti Napier armigeri filii natu maximi Roberti Napier militis ac baronetti et hujus collegii commensalis 1619	17	
Ex dono Henrici Bromely equitis aurati filii tertii hujus collegii commensalis	14	
Ex dono Arthuri Wise commensalis hujus collegii 1607 .	$11\frac{3}{4}$	
Ex dono Thomae Williams hujus collegii commensalis et filii unici Thomae Williams armigeri 1618 . .	14	
Ex dono Richardi Seymour hujus collegii commensalis et filii Edvardi Seymour Baronetti	$14\frac{3}{4}$	
Ex dono Antonii Dormeri filii Roberti Dormeri equitis aurati et hujus collegii commensalis. Ex dono Thomae Carminow filii natu maximi Thomae Carminow armigeri, collegii Exoniensis commensalis	$23\frac{5}{4}$	2
Ex dono Hugonis Pollard filii natu maximi Lodovici Pollard armigeri et hujus collegii commensalis . .	$14\frac{3}{4}$	
(Battler's pot) Ex dono magistrorum in artibus Jobi Kirkland, Thomae Buckland, Anthonii Bonner, Nicolai Tooker, Roberti Buckland, Gualteri Jackman, in usum Battellariorum in aula publica 1611	$13\frac{1}{4}$	3
(Battler's pot). Ex dono Bacchalaureorum in artibus Gulielmi Roweston, Roberti Petifare, Johannis Bury, Tho. Stafford, Martini Blake, Anthonii Standerd, Thomae Browne, in usum Battellariorum in aula publica 1613 . .	16	
Ex dono Gulielmi Mohune equitis aurati filii, collegii hujus commensalis 1606	$23\frac{1}{4}$	
Ex dono Dionisii Prideaux Thomae Prideaux equitis aurati filii natu secundi et hujus collegii commensalis 1613 .	$14\frac{3}{4}$	

3. *Tankerds.*

	oz.	dwt.
Ex dono domini Anthonii Ashley Couper baronetti hujus collegii commensalis 1637	$44\frac{1}{4}$	
Ex dono Johannis Pulteney armigeri Leycestrensis et hujus collegii commensalis 1626	$40\frac{1}{4}$	
Ex dono Roberti Rolle filii natu maximi Samuelis Rolle equitis aurati, et hujus collegii commensalis 1640 .	$27\frac{1}{2}$	1
Ex dono Bevilli Greynvile filii Bernardi Greynvile equitis aurati et hujus collegii commensalis 1611 . . .	34	3
Ex dono Henrici Tothill filii unici Gulielmi Tothill Devoniensis armigeri, et hujus collegii commensalis 1642 . .	$31\frac{3}{4}$	
Ex dono Richardi Vyvian Francisci Vyvian equitis aurati filii natu maximi, et hujus collegii commensalis 1628 . .	28	1
Ex dono Johannis Pye filii Gualteri Pye equitis aurati Herefordiensis hujus collegii commensalis 1640 . .	22	
Ex dono Willielmi Kingsmill Henrici Kingsmill equitis aurati Hantonensis filii natu maximi et hujus collegii commensalis 1628	$21\frac{3}{4}$	
Ex dono Andreae Henley hujus collegii commensalis 1640 .	$21\frac{3}{4}$	
Ex dono Johannis Jesop armigeri et hujus collegii commensalis 1619	17	
(2 Tankerds), William Herbert	$41\frac{1}{2}$	1
Ex dono Gulielmi Helyar filii Henrici Helyar armigeri de East Coker in comitatu Somersett, hujus collegii commensalis 1637	$22\frac{1}{2}$	
Ex dono Henrici Ford armigeri Devoniensis et hujus collegii commensalis 1632	$21\frac{1}{2}$	3
Ex dono Edmundi Brawne Hugonis Brawne equitis aurati filii quarti, et hujus collegii commensalis 1629 . .	$20\frac{1}{2}$	1
Ex dono Johannis Treffry hujus collegii commensalis 1611	$27\frac{3}{4}$	4
Ex dono Tobiae Chauncii equitis aurati filii natu maximi et Exoniensis coll. commensalis	$19\frac{3}{4}$	3
Ex dono Gulielmi Tyringham equitis aurati filii et hujus collegii commensalis 1637	21	
Ex dono Sidney Godolphin hujus collegii commensalis et filii Gulielmi Godolphin equitis aurati	$17\frac{1}{2}$	
Ex dono Thomae Dacres Thomae Dacres equitis aurati filii natu maximi, in artibus magistri, et hujus collegii commensalis 1629	$24\frac{1}{2}$	

Ex dono Edvardi Parker Devoniensis Edmundi Parker armigeri filii natu maximi et hujus collegii commensalis 1628 . . . . $19\frac{3}{4}$

Ex dono Willielmi Bowyer filii natu maximi Willielmi Bowyer equitis aurati Staffordiensis de Knypersley et hujus collegii commensalis . . . . . . $15\frac{1}{2}$ 4

Ex dono Johannis Copleston filii unigeniti Amiae Copleston armigeri Devoniensis 1626 . . . . . . 20 1

Ex dono Johis Chichester hujus collegii commensalis filii unici Roberti Chichester equitis Balnei Devoniensis . 36 3

Ex dono Johis Chichester armigeri filii et haeredis Johannis Chichester de Hall in comitatu Devoniensi equitis aurati $17\frac{1}{2}$

Ex dono Johannis Lovet Roberti Lovet equitis aurati filii primogeniti et hujus collegii commensalis . . . 18

The gift of Edmund Lambert sonne of Thomas Lambert of Boyton in Wilts Esqre. . . . . $17\frac{3}{4}$

Ex dono Johannis Walcot filii natu maximi Humphrici armigeri et hujus collegii commensalis . . . $26\frac{3}{4}$

Ex dono Johis Wolstenholme Johannis Wolstenholme equitis aurati filii primogeniti hujus collegii commensalis 1636 $27\frac{1}{2}$

Ex dono Lorenzo Cary Vicecomitis de Falkland filii secundi et hujus collegii commensalis 22

Ex dono Theobaldi Michell hujus collegii commensalis et filii natu maximi Edvardi Michell armigeri . . . $18\frac{1}{4}$ 3

Ex dono Elizaei Crymes Devoniensis armigeri hujus collegii commensalis 1634 . . . . $20\frac{1}{2}$ 1

Ex dono Thomae Hatch Devoniensis Arthuri Hatch armigeri filii natu maximi et hujus collegii commensalis 1619 . . . . $18\frac{3}{4}$

Ex dono Francisci Trentham Thomae Trentham equitis aurati Staffordiensis filii unigeniti et hujus collegii commensalis 1638 . . . . $20\frac{1}{4}$ 3

Ex dono Gulielmi Farmor Hatton Farmor equitis aurati filii natu maximi et hujus collegii commensalis 1637 . . $27\frac{1}{4}$

Ex dono Gulielmi Button Gulielmi Button militis et baronetti filii natu maximi et hujus collegii commensalis 1629 $20\frac{1}{2}$ 3

Ex dono Francisci Vincent filii unigeniti Anthonii Vincent equitis aurati et collegii Exon. commensalis . . $17\frac{3}{4}$ 3

Ex dono Gulielmi Jones Isaaci Jones armigeri Salopiensis filii natu maximi et hujus collegii commensalis 1632 . $22\frac{1}{2}$

Ex dono Thomae Raynell filii natu maximi Richardi   *oz. dwt.*
Reynell equitis aurati Devoniensis et hujus collegii commensalis 1640 . . . . 24½

Ex dono Essexii Powlet Gulielmi Powlet equitis aurati filii,
et hujus collegii commensalis 1637 . . . . 21¾

4. *Beakers.*

2 Beakers, Ex dono Johannis Bamphield Devoniensis equitis
filii collegii hujus commensalis 1604 . . . . 15½

In usum Battellariorum in aula publica, ex dono Thomae
Quinten, Nicolai Whitaker, Philippi Jermyn, Christo-
phory Sprey 1611 . . . . 9¼

In usum Battellariorum in aula publica, ex dono Gulielmi
Cake, Michaelis Dollinge, Christoph. Sadbury, Roberti
Standerd 1617 . . . . 8¾

In usum Battellariorum in aula publica, ex dono Bacchalaureorum in artibus Gualteri Searle, Johis Pitts, Nathan.
Norrington, Thomae Hele 1613 . . . . 9¼

In usum Battellariorum in aula publica, ex dono Bacchalaureorum in artibus Edvardi Clarke, Gregorii Heyman,
Johis Gee, Andreae Blackwell 1617 . . . . 8¾

Ex dono Bacchalaureorum in artibus Bartholomaei Parre,
Johannis Fley, Antonii Manington, Johis Baker 1613 . 8¾   4

Ex dono Bacchalaureorum in artibus Gualteri Cowling,
Thomae Benson, Samuelis Cosens, Johis Conant 1611   9   1

Ex dono Ferdinandi Carpenter magistri in artibus, Johannis,
Johannis, Gulielmi, in usum Battellariorum in aula
publica 1617 . . . . 8½   4

Ex dono Thomae Harris hujus collegii battellarii 1610 . 7

In usum Battellariorum in aula publica, Franciscus Durant,
Johannes Hodges, Antonius Salter, Georgius Newton . 9

5. *Flagons.*

(2) Ex dono Caroli et Philippi Herbert illustrissimi
Philippi Comitis Pembrokiae et Montgommeri filiorum
1632 . . . . . 94 oz. and 94¼

6. *Basons and Ewers.*

	oz.	dwt.
Bason, Ex dono D. Jacobi Hamiltoune Arraniae Comitis illustrissimi Marchionis Hamiltonis Comitis Arraniae et Cantabrigiae, baronis Evennae et Inerdaliae, et filii et haeredis 1622	88½	
Ewer	41½	
Randall's Ewer . .	23	4

7. *Dishes.*

Matthaeus Hele 1635 .	23½	
2 College dishes .	22¾	

8. *Salts.*

Ex dono Gulielmi Glanvill filii primogeniti Johannis Glanvill de Lincolnes Inne armigeri	28¾	
2 College salts . . . 21 oz. 3 dwt. and	11	2

9. *Bowles.*

Ex dono Peryami Reynell filii natu maximi Richardi Reynell armigeri Devoniensis et hujus collegii commensalis 1631	21½	1
Ex dono Burrough Reynell filii natu secundi Richardi Reynell armigeri Devoniensis, et hujus collegii commensalis 1631	21	1
Ex dono Hastingi Ewens filii natu maximi Matthaei Ewens armigeri et hujus collegii commensalis 1618 . .	12¼	3
Townsend 2 wine bowles . .	7	4

DOCUMENTS.

HART HALL.

(1) HEC est convencio facta ad festum S. Michaelis anno regni regis Henrici filii regis Johannis quinquagesimo primo inter Henricum Punchard carnificem Oxon ex una parte et Priorissam de Stodle et conventum eiusdem loci ex altera: videlicet quod dictus Henricus dimisit et tradidit dictis Priorisse et Conventui quandam placeam terre sue ad caput curie sue iacentem in eadem curia sua in parochia S. Petri in oriente Oxon, que placea continet in longitudine octodecim ulnas cum pulicis et in latitudine ad superius caput decem ulnas et dimidiam ulnam et unum quartum unius ulne cum policis. Tenendam et habendam dictam placeam terre cum pertinenciis dictis Priorisse et Conventui et suis assignatis, usque ad finem decem annorum proximo subsequencium libere et in pace. Et predictus Henricus et heredes sui warantizabunt acquietabunt et defendent predictam placeam terre predictis Priorisse et Conventui et suis assignatis usque ad finem termini predicti plenarie complete contra omnes homines, mares et feminas: pro hac autem dimissione tradicione warantizacione acquietacione et defencione dederunt predicta Priorissa et Conventus predictus predicto Henrico duas marcas sterlingorum pre manibus. Et post decursum dicti termini dicta placea soluta et quieta ad dictum Henricum et heredes suos vel suos assignatos revertatur. Ad hanc autem convencionem fideliter inter se observandum, fidem suam affidaverunt et huic in modum cyrographi confecto alternatim sigilla sua apposuerunt. Hiis testibus Ada Feteplace tunc maiore Oxon, Johanne de Colleshull et Philippo de O. tunc ballivis, Johanne Kepeharm, Willelmo Kepeharm, Laurencio Kepeharm, Jacobo clerico et multis aliis (29 Sep. 1267).

(2) Henry Punchard grants and quitclaims to Joan widow of H. de Stocwell a messuage lying between the land of the University on the west and the land of the prioress of Stothle on the east, Joan paying him 24*s*. Witnesses N. de Kingeston mayor, P. de Eu and Andrew de Durham bailiffs, John de Coleshulle, Geoffrey de Hengseie, Geoffrey aurifaber, Geoffrey le mercer, H. Oweyn, Giles de Stocwell, Thomas clerk, &c. (1283).

(3) I J. de Hancketon and Edith my wife have granted to Walter de Grandon mercer the mesuage between the land of the University on the west and that of the Prioress of Stodle on the east, and an adjoining area which H. Punchard let to farm to the Prioress, in S. Peter's in the East; giving me yearly a clove at Easter; and we warrant the land against all, males and females, Christians and Jews. For this, Walter gave us 13 marks. Witnesses N. de Kingeston mayor, Geoffrey aurifaber and J. de Eu bailiffs, H. Oweyn, Walter aurifaber, W. le Espicer, Geoffrey le mercer, J. Culvert, Andrew de Durham, J. de Ardern, T. clerk and others (? 1269).

(4) I Walter de Grandon mercer have given to Elias de Hertford and Johanna Barenger ('Hareng' Wood) his wife and Elias their son a mesuage between the land of the University of Oxford on the west and the land of the Prioress of Stodle on the east, and an area which Henry Punchard leased to the Prioress near the said tenement in S. Peters in the East. Habendam &c. Hiis testibus Nicholao de Kyngeston tunc maiore Oxon, Andrea de Durham, Johanne de Eu tunc ballivis eiusdem, Henrico Oweyn, Waltero aurifabro, Willelmo le Espicer, Philippo de Eu, Nicholao de Coleshulle, Egidio de Stokwell, Johanne Filekyinger, Thoma clerico et aliis (1283).

(5) Elias de Hertford quitclaims to his son Elias, Wycombe 10 May 1301.

(6) Elias filius Elie de Hertford dat et concedit Johanni de Doke-lyngton burgensi Oxon totum illud messuagium suum cum pertinentiis quod vocatur le Herthalle situatum in parochia S. Petri orientalis Oxon inter tenementum Universitatis Oxon quod vocatur le Blackhalle ex parte occidentali et tenementum priorisse et conventus de Stodleye quod vocatur le Micheldhalle ex parte orientali, habendum sibi heredibus et assignatis suis in perpetuum de capitalibus dominis feodi per servitia inde debita, cum clausula de warrantia contra omnes gentes : pro predicta concessione et warrantia dedit predictus Johannes viginti libras sterlingorum pre manibus in gersumam : sigillatum hiis testibus Johanne de Ew tunc majore Oxon, Ricardo le Especer et Johanne Wyth tunc ballivis ejusdem ville, Roberto le Notour, Simone ligatore librorum, Ricardo clerico et multis aliis. Datum apud Oxon die sabbati in festo S. Botulphi abbatis anno regni regis Edwardi filii regis Henrici vicesimo nono (17 June 1301). Oblong seal, S. ELIE DE HERTFORD, a hart's head with a cross between the horns.

(7) Agatha widow of Walter de Grendon quitclaims to J. de Doke-linton for any right to dowry &c. in Herthalle, lying between the

University tenement called Blakehalle on the west and the Stodley tenement called Scheldhalle on the east (26 Jan. 130½).

(8) Agnes widow of John de Staunton gives J. de Dokelington the tenement which she had from Alice wife of Giles de Stokwelle, between the tenement of the abbot of Osney on the east and the tenement of Adam de Spalding on the west (25 Ap. 1308: *see* Bodleian Charters 287).

(9) Elyas filius Elye de Hertford remittit et quietum clamat Johanni de Dokelington de Oxon totum jus quod habuit vel habere potuit ratione hereditatis in toto illo tenemento cum pertinentiis, quod idem Johannes habuit ex dimissione predicti Elye patris sui, situato in parochia (as before). Datum apud Oxon die Veneris proxima ante festum S. Michaelis anno regni regis Edwardi filii regis Edwardi secundo. Hiis testibus Willelmo de Burcestre et Johanne de Hampton tunc ballivis Oxon &c. (27 Sep. 1308). Seal like the former but smaller.

(10) Margery widow of Elias le Quilter quitclaims for the same tenement as (8), viz. Arthurhalle (12 Ap. 1312: Bodleian Charters 287).

(11) Ego Johannes de Dokelington de Oxon dedi concessi et hac presenti carta mea confirmavi magistro Waltero de Stapeltone dei gracia Exon. episcopo et magistro Ricardo de Wodeslade clerico unum mesuagium cum pertinenciis suis vocatum le Herthalle quod habui ex dono et concessione Elye filii Elye de Hertford et quod situatur in parochia Sancti Petri Orientalis Oxon inter tenementum Universitatis Oxon quod vocatur le Blakehalle ex parte occidentali et tenementum Priorisse et Conventus de Stodleye ex parte orientali. Dedi etiam et concessi prefatis magistris Waltero et Ricardo aliud mesuagium cum pertinenciis suis, illud videlicet quod habui ex dono et concessione Agnetis que fuit uxor quondam Johannis de Stauntone de Oxon et quod situatur in parochia S. Petri predicta inter tenementum Abbatis et conventus Osen. ex parte orientali et tenementum Ade de Spalding ex parte occidentali : Habendum &c. Money paid 80 marks. Datum apud Oxon die Jovis proxima post festum S. Leonis Pape anno regni regis Edwardi filii regis Edwardi quinto (12 Ap. 1312; Bodl. Charters 287)

(12) Ricardus de Wydeslade precentor ecclesie de Criditon remittit et quietum clamat domino suo Waltero Exon episcopo totum jus in duobus messuagiis cum eorum pertinentiis situatis in parochia S. Petri orientalis Oxon, quorum unum vocabatur Hurthalle et modo vocatur Stapeldonhall, et aliud vocatur Arturhalle, de quibus predictus pater et

ipse per Johannem de Dokelington de Oxon prius fuerant conjunctim feofati : habenda predicto Waltero heredibus et assignatis suis de capitalibus dominis feodorum per servitia inde debita : Hiis testibus domino Ricardo de Merton, Ricardo de Stapuldon, Johanne de Treiagu militibus &c. Datum Oxon septimo Aprilis A. D. 1314 et regni regis Edwardi filii regis Edwardi septimo (7 Ap. 1314). Large seal with image of the Virgin.

(13) Conventio inter Walterum de Stapelton Exon episcopum et priorem et conventum Sancte Frydeswyde Oxon, quod cum dictus Walterus teneat de dictis priore et conventu unum messuagium in Oxon vocatum Stapeltone halle, situatum inter tenementum universitatis Oxon quod vocatur Blakehalle ex parte occidentali et tenementum priorisse de Stodleye ex parte orientali infra portam de Smythgate, per certum servitium duorum solidorum eisdem priori et conventui annuatim debitum, concedunt dicti prior et conventus quod predictus Walterus illud tenementum dare et assignare possit duodecim scolaribus in universitate dicte ville studentibus, habendum dictis scolaribus et successoribus suis de predictis priore et conventu et successoribus suis in perpetuum, salvo servitio annuali duorum solidorum debito et consueto : quod si a retro fuerit, licebit priori et conventui in dicto tenemento distringere. Concedunt etiam prior et conventus quod in dicto tenemento ratione assignationis predicte per aliquod beneficium Statuti de comuni consilio regni editi quo provisum est ne terre aut tenementa ad manum mortuam deveniant, nihil de cetero exigere seu clamare poterint ullo modo nisi servitium duorum solidorum ut predictum est. Datum Oxon die Veneris proxima post festum S. Jacobi apostoli A. D. 1314 (26 July 1314). Seal of prior and convent in green wax : a half figure on a seat, under it a figure in a doctor's dress with a book in his left hand.

(14) Conventio facta inter Rectorem et Scolares domus de la Stapeldonhalle in Oxon et Walterum de Plescye rectorem ecclesie de Westwardon, cui ad firmam dimittunt Aulam cum cameris et curtilagio adjacente que vocatur Arthurhalle in parochia S. Petri in oriente a festo S. Michaelis anno regni regis Edwardi tertii octavo usque ad terminum decem annorum sibi et assignatis suis, reddendo inde annuatim novem solidos sterlingorum ad quatuor anni terminos principales solvendos per equales portiones. Et predictus Walterus sustentabit Aulam predictam in bono statu, et clausuram circa predictum curtilagium faciet competentem et in statu competenti sustentabit. Et ad istam conventionem fideliter tenendam partes supradicte

condemnationi domini cancellarii Oxon se submiserunt. Sigillatum hiis testibus M. Ricardo de Evesham, M. Johanne de Aylesbure, M. Thoma Bradwardine, Petro de Aynho universitatis Oxon bedello, Nicholao de Seintefey et aliis. Datum Oxon in vigilia Omnium Sanctorum anno regni regis Edwardi supradicto (31 Oct. 1334). Walter's seal in red wax, S. Michael treading down the dragon, the shield in his left hand has a cross engraved on it.

(15) Robert Newton Rector of Excyter College and the Fellowes demise to Philip Randall M.A. then Principall of Hart Hall their tenement or house ordained for the advancement of learning comenly called Hart Hall, to have to him and his assigns from the Annunciation before the date to the end of 21 years, paying yearly 33s 4d, the said Philip from 5 years to 5 years to put in sufficient security before the Chancellor. The Rector and Fellowes covenant to make all outward repairs in slatt and slatting, and the said Philip the inward reparations of particyons windowes doors flooring and glazeing, except it shall please the Rector and Fellowes of their benevolence to give lime boards stones clay nayles, as they had accustomed to do before the making of this lease: the Rector &c. to pay all rents and other dutyes goeing out of the said tenement to the University. The said Philip shall not let &c. to any but one of the foundation of the said College (10 June 1559). A bond of £6 13s 4d is added to secure this, by P. Randell and John Collens M.A. and B.M.

(16) Similar lease to John Evelighe M.A. 10 Oct. 35 Eliz. (1593): a bond of £40 is added, and a letter of attorney to Thomas Merser to deliver &c.

THE CHAPEL.

(1) Nono die mensis Julii A.D. MCCC decimo nono &c. in mei &c. presencia constitutus personaliter Johannes Parys Rector aule que vocatur Stapeldon halle Oxon.—in ecclesia beati martini oxon., coram officiali archidiaconi Oxon tunc ibidem de mandato Roberti Lincoln episcopi per rectores et vicarios ecclesiarum inquirente si in capella infra septa domus de Stapeldon halle predicta infra parochiam S. Mildrede construendâ canteria haberi valeat absque matricis ecclesie prejudicio—prefatus M. Johannes Parys in presencia dicti officialis ac domini Johannis rectoris ecclesie S. Mildrede et cuiusdam canonici de conventu canonicorum regularium Prioratus S. Fredeswyde patronorum ecclesie S. Mildrede, necnon rectorum et vicariorum decanatus Oxon. per quos officialis inquisivit, optulit &c. et promisit

nomine suo et scolarium se velle cavere Rectori S. Mildrede &c. quod canteria, si quam idem Rector aule de Stapeldon et scolares in capella construendâ habere valeant, in nullo cedet in prejudicium ecclesie S. Mildrede &c. sed quod ius &c. in percipiendis decimis oblacionibus et quibuscunque aliis iuribus parochialibus ab ipso Rectore et scolaribus conservetur integrum et illesum, et quod Rector et scolares ecclesiam S. Mildrede ut suam parochialem ecclesiam, non obstante dicta Canteria, si concedatur, in decimis oblacionibus &c. agnoscent et ipsam ecclesiam diebus solempnibus exercebunt et facient eidem ecclesie ac Rectori quicquid facere tenentur de consuetudine &c.   Rogavit idem M. Johannes Parys &c. acta sunt hec &c., presentibus magistris Ricardo Noreys, Henrico Bloyou, Stephano Pyppcote, Johanne de Sovenasche &c. (9 July 1319).   Et ego Willelmus Beare clericus Exoniensis diocesis publicus S. Romani Imperii auctoritate notarius &c. scripsi.

(2) Henricus, Lincoln. episcopus, dilectis filiis Rectori et Scolaribus &c.; precibus inclinati ut oratorium seu capellam [? valeatis] construere et divina officia per perpetuum sacerdotem, cui de vite necessariis teneamini congrue providere, alta voce vel submissa celebranda cum familiaribus vestris et hospitibus audire, vobis concedimus licenciam et liberam facultatem.   Ita tamen quod de oblacionibus &c. ecclesie parochiali faciatis prout ius exigit quodque singuli capellani in primo adventu de huiusmodi iuribus et oblacionibus vicario seu Rectori ecclesie &c. fideliter persolvendis sacramentum prestent corporale. Datum apud Newenton iuxta London ix Kal. Sept. A.D. MCCC vicesimo primo (24 Aug. 1321).

(3) Decanus et Capitulum ecclesie cathedralis Lincoln, Noveritis nos literas Henrici Lincoln. Episcopi inspexisse, formam que sequitur continentes &c., nos que acta sunt rata habentes &c. approbamus. Datum in capitulo nostro Lincoln ultimo die mensis Maii A.D. MCCC vicesimo secundo (31 May 1322).

(6) Waltero Exon. episcopo Henricus Lincoln. episcopus &c. ad dedicandum et consecrandum maius altare capelle de Stapeldon hall Oxon. nostre diocesis in honorem beate Marie virginis beati Petri Apostoli et beati Thome martiris constructe, una cum aliis super-altaribus portabilibus, si que tempore dedicacionis altaris ad vos deferri contigerit consecranda, Eo non obstante quod dicta capella in nostra diocesi fuerit situata, vobis concedimus vices nostras; Ita tamen quod, per dedicacionem seu consecracionem huiusmodi, ecclesie parochiali infra cuius parochiam dicta capella situata est preiudicium

non fiat aliqualiter. Datum apud parcum Stowe tercio Idus Aprilis A.D. MCCC vicesimo sexto (3 Ap. 1326).

(7) Anno MCCC xxvi^{to} xxv. die mensis Aprilis, in mei &c. presencia constitutis personaliter infra mansum parsonatus S. Mildrede Oxonie M. Johanne de Sovenassh Rectore domus de Stapeldon halle et domino Willelmo de Ponte in capella seu oratorio eiusdem domus tunc temporis capellano ex parte una et domino Johanne Rectore ecclesie S. Mildrede ex altera. Idem rector domus de Stapeldon hall proposuit quod, cum per Henricum Lincoln. Episcopum Rectori et Scolaribus ut infra septa eiusdem oratorium seu capellam construere valeant et divina officia per perpetuum sacerdotem celebranda &c. audire, Ita tamen quod singuli capellani &c., licentiam dignaretur admittere. Qui quidem Johannes &c. gratanter admisit. Acta sunt hec &c., presentibus M. Willelmo Bere baculario iuris civilis, dominis Roberto Kary, Henrico Wall, Henrico de Tiverton, Roberto de Middellond scolaribus tunc temporis Universitatis, ac Waltero de Hamme, Ricardo de Burcestre, Willelmo Russel, Simon de Bristowe eiusdem ecclesie parochianis (25 Ap. 1326).

Et ego Jacobus Ricardi dicti Coleman de Hanont Wint. dioc. clericus apostolica auctoritate notarius publicus &c.

(8) Walterus de Stapeldon Exon. episcopus Aulam nominatam Stapeldon hall pro duodecim scolaribus et uno capellano in municipio Oxonie fundavit, nos Rector et scolares ordinamus quod singulis annis pro anima Fundatoris &c. die S. Michaelis circa tumbam (*i. e.* 16 Oct.) Placebo et Dirige cum missa in crastino celebretur . . . in termino estivali. (imperfect.)

(12) Although the Rector and Fellows have had a chapel &c. from their foundation, yet Thomas Bp. of Lincoln, at the instigation of Roger de Faryngs calling himself Rector of S. Mildred's, has put an interdict on the chapel without any cause being heard and refused to listen to the College, I the procurator of the College appeal to the Apostolic See and the Court of Canterbury. (? 1342–7).

(16) Robertus Rygge S. T. P. Cancellarius Universitatis Oxon., Johannes Landreyn S. T. P. et Thomas Chylyngdon decretorum doctor, Willelmi archiepiscopi Cantuariensis commissarii, Rectori et Scolaribus collegii aule de Stapuldon. Ad officium capellani per amocionem M. Willelmi Serche nuper dicti collegii capellani auctoritate metropolitica factam vacans et ad presentacionem dicti Patris hac vice spectans M. Willelmum Talkarn capellanum Exon. diocesis vobis prefecimus et eciam presentamus. Datum Oxonie

octavo die mensis Decembris A.D. MCCC octogesimo quarto. (8 Dec. 1384.)

(17) A.D. M. quadringentesimo septuagesimo septimo mensis Novembris die vicesimo quinto in domo habitacionis mei Willelmi Marke notarii publici infra villam Taunton in vico vulgariter nuncupato Forstrete constitutus personaliter M. Johannes Harrow A.M. sacreque theologie scolaris necnon capellanus capelle S. Thome martiris in Collegio Exon. M. Walterum Wyndesore S.T.B. ecclesie cathedralis Exon. canonicum suum fecit procuratorem per presentes, deditque potestatem dictam capellam in manus Ordinarii resignandi, et licet M. Johannes Harrow penes M. Ricardum Bradle Rectorem collegii Exon. pluries institit ut idem Rector resignacionem recipere dignaretur, ipse tamen Rector resignacionem recipere recusavit absque causa racionabili. Acta sunt hec &c. presentibus Johanne Osbren et Johanne Marchaunt literatis Bathon. et Wellen. dioc. (25 Nov. 1477). Et ego Willelmus Marke &c.

TERRA WYDONIS[1].

Notum sit omnibus presentibus et futuris quod ego Thomas filius Beatricis[2] concessi et dimisi et liberavi Willelmo filio Widonis hoseri totam terram meam que iacet inter terram Roberti filii Oweni et terram Henrici Chaudre, illi et heredibus suis, habendam et tenendam de me et heredibus meis in feodo et hereditate libere et quiete,

---

[1] In College Chest. The land may have been near Bedford Hall, as the Wido family held land on the opposite side of Brasenose Lane viz. Winchester Hall, which lay East of S. Mildred's church, with only Little Deep Hall between.

[2] Thomas son of Beatrice held land in S. Mildred's 1180-90, Bodleian Charters 309; Wood D. 2 p. 88 Thomas son of Beatrice, with the consent of Cristina de Sandford his wife, gave Hamo mercer of Oxford unam placeam terre ejus ad caput curie ejus, sicut murus camere ejus ex utraque parte condonat in longum ipsius Hamonis, et in latum inter terram que fuit Roberti filii Seman et terram ejusdem Thome filii Beatricis ; witnesses Torold Cordwaner, Thomas and Henry sons of Edwin [Henry Edwyne occurs in a Lincoln deed, Wood D. 2 p. 65], Thomas son of Wydo and William his brother, Ambr. pistore, W. Specer, Gregory mercer, R. cuteler, H. Socham and Elias his brother. Wood says 'about 1174—but no, it can't be so soon, because Hamo mercer lived 1243 : ? written about 1200.' Thomas Fitzwido m. Agatha temp. R. I and John, Wood D. 2 p. 490 ; Agatha widow of Thomas Fitzwido occurs when N. Stockwell was mayor, i.e. 1208. See Wood's City i. 121, ii. 357-8 ; a Wydo of S. Walery, and Reynold Fitzwydo occur in Godstow documents, Dugdale iv. 360. Lincoln has a deed of about 1243 by which Geoffrey son of Henry Bodin sells his father's land in All Saints parish to Robert Bodin and Robert filius Widonis ; it lay between Richard Bodin's land, and land formerly Walter Bilet's. The *selds* built underneath, *versus vicum*, are not included in the sale. Thomas filius Widonis is a witness.

honorifice et integre, Reddendo inde annuatim mihi et heredibus meis sex solidos ad duos terminos anni pro omni servicio et pro omni exaccione, videlicet tres solidos in dominica palmarum et tres solidos ad festum sancti Michaelis, et fidelitatem fecit mihi de predicto tenemento et de predicto redditu reddendo ad prescriptos terminos. Et pro concessione mea et dimissione et liberatione et warentizacione mea et heredum meorum predicte terre Willelmus prenominatus dedit mihi sex marcas argenti de recognicione, et Cristine uxori mee dedit unum bisantium. Et quia volo quod sepedicta terra de me et heredibus meis sepedicto Willelmo et heredibus suis perpetuo firma et inconcussa permaneat hac mea carta presenti et sigilli mei impressione confirmavi. Hiis testibus Laurencio Kepeharm[1], Henrico filio Simco (?), Thoma filio Eilrici, Willelmo filio Radulphi de Oxon., Turold Cordwaner, Johanne le Stiword, Henrico Chaudre, Lamberto fratre ejus, Thoma filio Widonis, Rogero filio Erlewini, Radulpho filio Sundi (?), Ricardo de Boteleia, Johanne Kari, Rogero filio Stephani, Rogero Sodeknave. (Seal of Thomas fil. Beatricis, and of Cristina his wife.)

WARLIGE[2].

Sciant &c. quod ego Milicencia relicta Willelmi de Whytefeld de Warlge in pura viduitate et propria potestate mea concessi et tradidi Henrico Cuyet (?) de Warlge ad cap. partem lucrand. unam acram terre mee arabilis cum pertinenciis que iacet in campo de Warlge in Wordylonde inter terram Abbatisse de Godestowe et terram Willelmi Levesone (?) Et se extendit versus austrum et aquilonem, Habendam et tenendam &c. a proximo festo S. Michaelis post diem confeccionis hujus . . . usque ad finem viginti annorum proximo sequencium plene conpletorum, nichil inde per annum reddendo. Ita scilicet quod predictus Henricus per totum terminum predictum predictam acram terre arabit serabit et liciabit ad custus suos proprios, et medietatem bladi ejusdem acre metet et quo loco voluerit cariabit.

Et ego predicta Milicencia aliam medietatem bladi ejusdem acre quolibet anno infra predictum terminum metam et cariabo quo loco voluero . . . . quod eidem . . . . Henrico vel suo attornato hoc scriptum ostendenti . . . . [ster]lyngor. de predicta medietate bladi me tingentis infra . . . . annos predictorum viginti annorum, videlicet quolibet anno duos solidos argenti ad festum S. Michaelis archangeli prout scriptum obligatorium eidem Henrico inde confectum preportat

---

[1] Laurence Kepeharm was Mayor of Oxford 1178.
[2] See Pat. Roll 7 Edward II part 2 memb. 10.

et testificatur. (Warranted) sub pena viginti solidorum argenti in subsidium terre sancte solvendorum.

In cujus rei testimonium huic scripto bipartito sigilla nostra alternatim apposuimus. Datum apud Warlige die dominica in crastino festi exaltacionis sancte crucis anno regni regis Edwardi octavo. Hiis testibus Johanne Stoyl Willelmo le Cocere Johanne Daleber Waltero le Bone Willelmo clerico Thoma Batayle Johanne Coppe et aliis. (15 Sep. 1280.)

FRAGON HALL.

(1) I William de Tauton with consent of Agatha my wife have given to M. Peter de Skelton clerk for his life a tenement in S. Mildred's parish between the tenement of the Abbess of Godstow on the west and Fragon Halle on the East, near the City Walls, at a rent of 4 shillings. Oxford, Sunday before S. Lucia the Virgin 1313. Witnesses William de Berncestre mayor of Oxford, Richard Cari Roger Mymecan bailiffs of Oxford, Robert de Wormenhale, Philip de Wormenhale, Henry de Lynne, John de Colesille and others. (9 Dec. 1313.)

(2) We William de Tauton and Agatha my wife have given &c. to M. Peter de Skelton clerk &c. 2 tenements with 2 curtilages, and buildings on them, in S. Mildred's parish, between a tenement of the said Peter on the west, and S. Hugh's Hall on the east, within the Walls of the City, at a rent of 12 shillings. Oxford, Wednesday the Vigil of S. Lucia the Virgin, A.D. 1313. Witnesses William de Burcestre mayor of Oxford, Richard Cari Roger Mymcan bailiffs of Oxford, Robert de Worminhale, Philip de Worminhale, Henry de Lyne, John de Colleshul, and others. (12 Dec. 1313.)

(3) Ego Agatha filia Henrici Oweyn de Oxon in pura viduitate mea et legia potestate dedi concessi et hac presenti carta mea confirmavi Rectori et Scolaribus de Stapeldonhall Oxon et eorum successoribus imperpetuum duo mesuagia coniuncta cum pertinenciis in Oxon. situata in parochia S. Mildrede Virginis inter tenementum Scolarium de Baliole hall ['i.e. S. Hugh's hall,' Wood] ex parte orientali et tenementum dictorum Rectoris et Scolarium de Stapeldonhall, quod quondam fuit tenementum Abbatisse et Conventus de Godestowe ex parte occidentali, et abuttant se usque ad regiam stratam que ducit de Northgate usque Smithgate, et extendunt se in longitudine a predicta regia strata usque ad tenementum Petri le Fitz Johan et Alicie uxoris eius quod communiter vocatur la Scothall, que duo mesuagia

michi accidebant in purpartiam meam post mortem Henrici Oweyn patris mei. Pro hac autem donacione et concessione dederunt michi predicti Rector et Scolares quandam summam pecunie pre manibus. In cuius rei testimonium huic presenti carte sigillum meum apposui et, quia sigillum meum pluribus est incognitum, sigillum Maioratus Oxon. apponi curavi. Hiis testibus Johanne de Hampton tunc maiore Oxon., Johanne Culvard Stephano de Adynton tunc ballivis eiusdem ville, Johanne de Dokelyngton, Willelmo de Burcestre, Ricardo Cary, Willelmo Pennard et aliis. Datum apud Oxon. die veneris in festo S. Johannis ante portam Latinam, anno regni regis Edwardi filii Regis Edwardi sextodecimo (6 May 1323; 'on the dors of the duplicat is writ Fragun hall' Wood).

SCHOOLS.

. . Robertus de Grymmeston et Magister Willelmus Dobbe dedimus concessimus, et hac presenti carta nostra confirmavimus . . . Rectori domus scolarium de Stapeldon halle Oxon. et eiusdem domus scolaribus duas scolas . . . Scolestrete situatas inter scolas Priorisse et Conventus de Stodleye ex parte una et scolas Magistri et scolarium Aule de Balliolo Oxon ex parte altera, et quas nuper habuimus ex concessione et reddicione Willelmi Attehole et Katherine uxoris ejus . . . Oxon maiore ballivis eiusdem ville per finem inter nos inde levatum . . . scolaribus predicte domus de Stapelton halle et eorum successoribus (mutilated).

Hec est finalis concordia facta in Hustengo Oxon. die lune proxima post festum S. Gregorii Pape anno regni regis Edwardi tercii post conquestum septimo coram Ricardo Kary maiore, Henrico de Stodlegh et Johanne Blundel ballivis, Willelmo de Burcestre, Andrea de Wormenhale, Johanne Culverd et Simone de Gloucestre Aldremannis ville Oxon. et aliis domini Regis fidelibus tunc ibidem presentibus inter Willelmum Dobbe et Robertum de Grymeston querentes et Willelmum Atte Hole et Katerinam uxorem eius deforciantes de uno mesuagio cum pertinenciis in Oxon unde placitum terre sum. fuit inter eos in eodem Hustengo per breve domini Regis de Recto, scilicet quod predicti Willelmus Dobbe et Robertus recognoscunt quod predictum mesuagium cum pertinenciis esse ius ipsius Katerine. Et pro hac recognicione iidem Willelmus atte Hole et Katerina concesserunt predictum mesuagium cum pertinenciis predictis Willelmo Dobbe et Roberto et illud eis reddiderunt in eodem Hustengo : Habendum et tenendum predictis Willelmo Dobbe et Roberto et heredibus

ipsius Roberti de capitali domino feodi illius per servicia quae ad predictum mesuagium pertinent imperpetuum. Et preterea iidem Willelmus atte Hole et Katerina concesserunt pro se et heredibus ipsius
Katerine quod ipsi warantizabunt predictis Willelmo Dobbe et Roberto
et heredibus ipsius Roberti predictum mesuagium cum pertinenciis
contra omnes homines imperpetuum (15 Mch 1333; Wood 'note
that all those tenements that were between Mildred lane and Exeter
lane were scooles, of which these were 2').

CATSTREET.

(1) John Wytewong son and heir of Stephen Wytewonge alias
Stephen Somnor of Oxford grants to John Dolle of Oxford bookbinder
and Joan his wife a tenement *cum shopis* in the parish of S. Mary in
Catstreet between the tenement of the Prior of S. Frideswide on the
north and the tenement of Godstow on the south, 6 Feb. 3 H. vi
W. Offord mayor, W. Aston and W. Somerset bailiffs (6 Feb. 142⅘).

(2) (Thomas le clerk), Nicholas Spragot alut. Oxon grants Thomas
lee cler. a tenement in S. Mary's in Cattestrete, between the tenement
of S. Frideswide on the north and of Godstow on the south and
Einsham on the south and Catestreete on the east, 28 Nov.
14 Edw. iv; W. Dagvyle mayor, W. Plompton and N. Warden
bailiffs, J. Clerk, J. Dobbys, J. Seman aldermen (28 Nov. 1474).

(3) Hec indentura facta vicesimo die mensis Aprilis anno regni
regis Edwardi quarti quintodecimo inter Ricardum Spragat et
Johannam uxorem ejus ex parte una et Johannem Bray et Johannam
uxorem ejus ex parte altera testatur quod cum nuper dictus Ricardus
Spragat teneatur Jacobo Benett clerico et dicto Johanni Bray per
scriptum suum obligatorium in viginti libris sterlingorum, cujus datum
est undecimo die mensis Octobris anno regni regis Edwardi quarti
quartodecimo ut in eodem plenius apparet; predicti tamen Jacobus et
Johannes volunt et concedunt quod si dicti Ricardus et Johanna uxor
ejus annuatim durante termino sex annorum proxime sequencium
post datum presencium de dictis Johanne et Johanna uxore ejus aut
eorum heredibus pro et de eorum tenemento in Catstrete in quo modo
ipsi inhabitant et quod de predicto Ricardo et Johanna uxore ejus
nuper iidem Johannes et Johanna perquesierunt sibi heredibus et
assignatis suis imperpetuum, non amplius pro aliquo redditu ipsorum
Johannis et Johanne uxoris ejus aut heredum suorum de eodem
tenemento quam sex solidos et octo denarios, durante predicto termino
sex annorum, annuatim solvendos ad duos anni terminos viz in festo

S. Michaelis archangeli et Annunciacionis beate Marie Virginis per equales portiones exigerint seu levaverint, aut alter eorum exigerit seu levaverit, et si dicti Ricardus et Johanna uxor ejus istas indenturas et condiciones in eisdem contentas coram Majore ville hic in Oxon cognoverint esse factum ipsorum Ricardi et Johanne uxoris ejus citra festum nativitatis S. Johannis Baptiste proxime futurum post datum presencium, Quod tunc dictum scriptum obligatorium pro nullo habeatur: sin autem, in suo robore permaneat et effectu.   In testimonium premissorum partes suprascripte sigilla sua alternatim apposuerimus.   Hiis testibus Willelmo Dagvyle tunc majore ville Oxon, Johanne Clerk Johanne Seman tunc ejusdem ville aldermannis, Willelmo Plompton et Ricardo Warton tunc ipsius ville ballivis et multis aliis.   Datum Oxon die et anno supradictis (20 Ap. 1475).

Hoc presens scriptum indentatum recognitum fuit per Ricardum Spraget et Johannam uxorem ejus coram Willelmo Dagvile majore die lune xii die Junii anno regni regis infrascripti xvº.   Et sic irrotulatur in Rubro libro inter Recorda anni illius folio cxxviiº.

(4) Thomas Pate, son and heir of Richard Pate, gave Catstreet tenement to Exon. Coll. 22 H. VIII (1530–1).   Richard Pate was bedell (Turner 22).

In winter 1531 10s was received from Catstrete.   In Nov. 1560 'our house in Catstrete with a small one next to it was let to M. Baylye M.D. for 63 years'; and in autumn 1566 Baylye pays 14s as a year's rent for the 2 houses.

PEYNTOUR'S HALL.

Peyntour's hall (called Culver hall in Henry IV's time) came to Exeter College in 1478 with these title deeds.   John de Bereford (Wood's City i. 359) gave it to Henry Malmesbury, who left it 1361 to Alice his wife, 'without north gate, near to Gose Court on the south.'   On 18 Aug. 1407 John Abel gave John Sutton and Alice his wife a messuage called Peyntour hall or Culver hall, in S. Giles' street, between the tenement once belonging to John Hartwell on the north and the tenement called Gosecourt once belonging to John Bereford on the south, which messuage Abel lately had from the feoffment of John Southam; given at the Hundred outside the north gate.   On 30 Ap. 1421 John and Alice Sutton grant to their son Stephen their tenement in the North Hundred, lying between the garden of Thomas Daggevill on the south and the tenement of John Spicer senior on the north, except a shop with a chamber over it on the north of the tenement, which they reserve for their lives, with access to the fountain in the tenement for drawing water; Stephen to have the reversion of the shop with all belonging to the 'bracina' there.   On 5 Feb. 143½ Stephen grants the tenement and reversion to William Thomas of Abberbury, Oxon.   On 6 Feb. 143⁹⁄ William Thomas *alias* Thomlyn granted it to John Bailly mason of Oxford; witnesses W. Brampton mayor, Robert Tretherf and Robert Watford bailiffs, T. Coventre, W. Herbfeld, T. Daggeville, J. North aldermen etc.   On 8 Mch 144⅘ Bailly granted it to John Say Esq., William Brown [? Brome], William Bruges, and Walter Baron; but on 16 Jan. 145⁸⁄₉ Bailly granted it to Nicholas Robyns brewer of Oxford; and on 17 Jan. William Brome of Halton [Holton, Visit. Oxon. 104, 230] in Oxon gentleman quitclaimed to Robyns at Halton.   On 12 Feb. 146½ Robyns granted it to Richard Andrew, James Andrew, and John Harrys.   On 6 Mch 147⅞ James Preston clerk and John Harrys bedell granted it to the Rector and Scholars of Exon College, 'which we lately had jointly with Richard Andrewe clerk now dead'; and on the same day they named John Stapulhille and John Bradeston their attorneys to deliver seisin; on 8 Mch Robyns and his wife Agnes quitclaimed; while on 1 Ap. 1478 the College granted Robyns and his wife for their lives a 'Parlour sette on the north side of the tenement of the College in which Robyns now dwelleth, with all from the hay dore into the fylde, and with 2 palasses with all within them, beryng yerely therfor at the fest of Seynt John Baptist a rede rose.' An indenture follows, 30 Nov. 1478, between John Orell rector and Nicholas Gosse chancellor of Exeter, who gave £15 for the purchase, by which the College is to spend 13s 4d on the day of his obit annually.   Lastly on 28 Jan. 148⁷⁄ Edmund Gille grants Thomas Ruer rector, and the scholars, a garden in S. Giles.

GARDEN.

Leave of a garden and stable from Robert Roper, Master of Baliol, and the fellows, to John Neale, Rector of Exeter College, and the fellows, 19 Mch 156⅝; adjoining the Divinity School on the north, and abutting to Exeter College wall on the west, with Brasenose lane on the south, and abutting upon Baliol and Exeter Schools on the east; from Ladyday 1581 (at the expiring of a lease to Mr. John Lewes), for 41 years, at a rent of 20s, and a fine of 3s 4d for every time they neglect necessary repairs, and Exeter shall not make any bowling allee or tennisse court which may be noisome to students, or any hogsty or dunghill or any other filthy savour.   If the University should build schools on this ground by virtue of any commandment of the Queen or her successors during the lease, Exeter is to pay such rent for the remaining part as four honest men, two for either party, determine.

Exchange 6 Oct. 1572 of 3 garden grounds belonging to Baliol, in the occupation of Walter Bailie M.D., Garbrand Harks, and Richard Hanson, lying west of School Street [as above], for a messuage and garden, lately occupied by Thomas Kerialls doctor of law, lying north of the way that leads from Baliol to Magdalen church, on the west of the wall of Baliol, and on the east of certain Baliol tenements; but Hanson is to hold for the remainder of his lease, on which the rent of 2s 6d is reserved; and Exeter grants Baliol a rent of 12s 6d, issuing out of a house in Magdalen parish, now occupied by John Sommersbye, with power of distraint on that house; Witnesses[1] William Germin, Jasper Best, John Roscarrocke, Trevenor Roscarrocke, William Connocke, William Kyrckham.   A Bond of £200 is attached from Adam Squire, Master of Baliol, to Robert Newton, Rector of Exeter, to secure observance of the conditions.

CAROLE HALL.

(1) I William Blauet of Oxford senior and Dyonisia my wife have given to Ralph de Nottingham cordwainer Oxford a mesuage near the land which Osbert le Cutiller once held in the parish of S. Peter in the West, Oxford; which mesuage William our son once held, Et acquietavit pro nobis de Judaismo Oxon, at a rent of 8s to Richard our son.   For this grant Ralph has given 3 marks of silver to us and 7 to Richard.   Hiis testibus Galfrido de Stokwell, Petro filio Toroldi, Philippo molendinario, Henrico filio Henrici, Thoma filio Walteri Pentecost, Adam Cruste, Hugone Fane, Thoma Cruste, Johanne de Kingestun, Laurencio With, Willelmo de Lisewis, Laurencio Log, Simone fratre eius, Hagone le Cordwaner, Johanne Mazelin, Willelmo Londun, Milone de Kokesham, Willelmo de Mildecumbe clerico et aliis (1230 or 1240).   Seal 1. S(igillum) Will. Blevet (round 8-spoked star or wheel).   Seal 2. S(igillum) Dionisie Blavet (round sheaf or thunderbolt).

---

[1] William Germyn was M.A. Ex. Coll. 1572; John Roscarrock, B.A. (probably Ex. Coll.) 1577; Trevenor Roscarrock was son of Richard Roscarrock by Isabel d. and coh. of Richard Trevenor (Visit. Corn. 400, and see 93 for William Connock). See Wood's City i. 112 for Baliol property here, Savage's *Balliofergus* pp. 34, 80.

(2) Dionisia widow of William Blauet confirms the grant to Ralph de Notingham of the land between the land of Philip de Leycestre baker and the land of Geoffrey de Heynesh baker in S. Peter's in the West, at a rent of 7s: for this, Ralph gave her 20s *in garsumma*. Witnesses Laurence Wyth mayor, Adam Feteplace and John Curcy bailiffs, Peter Fitztorald, John With, N. de Kingeston, William . . . , Henry cordwaner, Henry Lisewis, Robert Bonvalet, Walter de Mideltun, Robert clerk and others (1241-2).

(3) I Dyonisia Carpin widow have granted to Philip de Leycestre baker the land and buildings which are on the east next to the land of Adam Feteplace in the parish of S. Peter's in the West, at the rent of a penny at Easter to me, and to Adam Feteplace 7s, and to Lady Mabilia de Bildewyk 3s and *breugavel*. For this Philip gave me 20s for my great affair. Witnesses Laurence Wyth mayor, Adam FitzWalter and J. Curcy bailiffs, N. de Kingestun, W. Lowdin, R. persona, Roger Noif, J. Achard, Simon de London, Robert clerk and others (1241-2).

(4) I Dionisia widow of W. Blauet of Oxon have quitclaimed to Ralph de Notingham cordwainer my right in the land between the land of P. de Leycestre baker and the land of Geoffrey de Heynesh baker in the parish of S. Peter's in the West, reserving a rent of 7s. Witnesses Laurence Wyth mayor, Adam FitzWalter and J. Curcy bailiffs, Peter FitzTorold, Laurence Log, Adam Crust, N. de Kingeston, W. Lowdin, Hugh cordwainer, H. Lisewis, Robert Bonvalet, Walter de Mideltun, Robert clerk and others (1241-2).

(5) Ego Dyonisia que fui uxor Willelmi Blauet senioris concessi et hoc presenti scripto confirmavi et me fide mea adhibita spontanea uoluntate mea obligavi Radulpho de Notingham cordewanerio Oxon. sub pena decem librarum eidem sine contradiccione et dilacione reddendarum si transgrediar, quod nunquam movebo eidem Radulpho vel heredibus suis questionem vel calumpniam de illo mesuagio cum pertinenciis quod Willelmus Blauet filius meus aliquando tenuit iuxta terram quam Osebertus le Cutiler aliquando tenuit in parochia S. Petri occidentalis Oxon., quod quidem mesuagium idem Willelmus acquietavit pro nobis de Judaismo Oxon. sub hac forma, scilicet quod volo quod hec sit mea super hec ultima voluntas nullo modo revocanda, quod si contigerit me aliquo motu vel consilio aliorum vel proprio contra istam obligacionem venire, quod nullam habeam personam standi in iudicio nec per me nec per procuratorem, scilicet quod exiudicata semper permaneam quousque eidem Radulpho de

predictis decem libris nomine pene satisfecero et de custu quem apposuerit in eiusdem pene acquisitione, dato manente iure eiusdem Radulphi in eodem mesuagio per cartas quas inde haゝuerit et ad hec omnia fideliter et sine dolo tenenda subieci me sponte districcioni Baillorum Oxon. et iurisdiccioni Decani Oxon. qui pro tempore fuerint, ad me compellandum ad omnia prescripta observanda, renunciando privilegio fori et appellacioni et cavillacioni et excepcioni et omni iuris remedio et Curie Regie prohibicioni et omni impetracioni et consilio et auxilio unde prescripta possint aliquatenus infirmari, et In huius rei testimonium huic scripto patenti sigillum meum apposui. Hiis testibus Thoma Cruste Ada Cruste Laurencio Log Simone Log Johanne Pille Milone de Cokesham Willelmo de Mildecumb clerico et aliis (? 1242)   S(igillum) Dionisie Blavettes.

(6) I J. Blouet have granted and quitclaimed to Ralph de Notingeham 7s of rent which Ralph pays to Dyonisia my mother for the land between the land once belonging to P. the baker and the land once belonging to Osbert le Cutiller in S. Peters in the West, reserving only a penny at Michaelmas.   For this grant Ralph gave me 6 marks. Witnesses N. de Stokewell mayor, W. le Seinter and Geoffrey son of Geoffrey the goldsmith bailiffs, Laurence Wyth, Hugh son of Philip cordwainer, Ralph de Graundpunt, Laurence Log, William Loudin, Robert Bonvallet, Adam Ornfer ('Crust' Wood), N. de Kingestun and others (1246-7).

(7) I N. son of R. le Bone[1] of Oxford have granted and quitclaimed to T. le Macoun of Oxford and Elena his wife my sister my messuage in S. Peter in the West between the messuage of J. de Falleye on the east, and the messuage of T. de Pyrie and Joan his wife on the west.   Witnesses W. de Burncestre mayor, R. Carye and J. de Bischopeston bailiffs, H. de Lenne, J. de Colushull, W. Pennarth, J. Culverd, Reginald Yve, W. de Eynesham, J. de Aston clerk and others. Oxford, Friday after the Translation of S. Thomas the Martyr 9 Edward II (11 July 1315).

(8) I Alice d. of Ralph de Notingham have granted to Elena my sister my share in a messuage in S. Peter in the West, between the messuage of J. de Falleye on the east, and the messuage of T. de Pyrie and Joan his wife on the west; witnesses W. de Burncestre

---

[1] Richard le Bone married Elena, d. of Ralph de Notingham, and had 2 children, Nicholas, and Elena who married Thomas le Macoun.   Thomas le Masun married Margery and had 2 children, Alice and Matilda: Thomas m. (2) Agnes and had 2 children, Richard and Cristina.

mayor, R. Cary and J. de Byschopeston bailiffs, H. de Lenne, W. Pennarth, J. Culverd, W. de Eynesham, J. de Aston and others. Oxford, Friday after the Translation of S. Thomas the Martyr 9 Edw. II (11 July 1315).

(9) I Elena widow of R. le Boun of Oxford have granted to T. le Macoun a messuage in S. Peter's in the West between the messuage of Isolda de Weston widow of J. de Weston on the north and the messuage of Emma widow of J. de Oseneye on the south. Witnesses W. de Burncestre mayor, R. Cary and J. de Byschopeston bailiffs, J. de Dokelingtone, H. de Lenne, W. Pennarth, J. Culverd, W. de Eynesham, W. de Perye, J. de Aston clerk and others. Oxford, (? Tuesday) next before Feast of S. Margaret the Virgin (9) Edw. II (8 July 1315).

(10) I Elena widow of R. le Bone have granted to T. le Macoun and Elena my daughter his wife my messuage in S. Peter in the West, between the messuage of J. de Falleye on the east and the messuage of T. de Pyrie and Joan his wife on the west. If they die without heirs, then to my son N. Witnesses W. de Burncestre mayor, R. Cary and J. Byschopeston bailiffs, J. de Dokelington, H. de Lenne, W. Pennarth, J. Culverd, Roger Mymekan, W. de Eynesham, J. de Aston clerk and others. Oxford, Tuesday before S. Margaret the Virgin 9 Edw. II (8 July 1315).

(11) We Thomas le Macoun and Elena my wife have granted to Elena Bone for her life a messuage in S. Peter in the West, between the messuage of J. de Falleye on the east and that of T. de Pyrie and Joan his wife on the west, at a rent of a penny on S. John Baptist's day, we doing the repairs. Witnesses W. de Burncestre mayor, R. Cary and J. de Byschopeston bailiffs, H. de Lenne, Roger Mymekan, J. Culverd, Reginald Yve, W. de Eynesham, J. de Aston clerk and others. Oxford, feast of S. James the Apostle 9 Edw. II (25 July 1315).

(12) I Elena Dewy of Oxford have quitclaimed to T. le Masun and Margery his wife, Alice daughter of T. le Masun and Matilda sister of Alice, for all actions and demands &c. for a transgression against me for which I had a royal Breve against them. Seal of Dean of Christianity at Oxford. Oxford, the feast of S. Vincent the martyr A.D. 1315, 9 Edw. II (22 Jan. 131⅝).

(13) We Robert de Crundon cissor of Oxford and Alice my wife have granted to T. le Macoun half of our stone wall between our two tenements, viz. the half nearer his tenement, our tenements being in

S. Peter in the West. Witnesses J. de Dokelington mayor, Robert de Wattlington and J. Culverd bailiffs, H. de Lenne, Roger Mymekan, Gilbert de Wynchecoumbe, W. de Eynesham, J. de Aston clerk and others. Oxford, Sunday before the Nativity of the Virgin 10 Edw. II (5 Sep. 1316).

(14) I John son of Philip de Ew have granted to John son of Thomas de Durham of Oxford a messuage in the Little Bailey in S. Peters in the West, between the tenement of the Hospital of S. John on the south and the tenement of the same John son of Thomas on the north. For this he gave me 20 marks. Witnesses W. de Burncestre mayor, R. Cary and Gilbert de Grensted bailiffs, J. de Dokelinton, Andrew de Pyrie, J. de Coleshull, H. de Lenne, Roger Mymekan, J. Culverd, T. Somer, J. de Loughteburgh, T. clerk and others. Oxford, Friday the morrow of the Conception of the Virgin 11 Edw. II (9 Dec. 1317).

(15) I N. Bone of Oxford have quitclaimed to T. le Mason and Agnes his wife a messuage in S. Peter in the West beween the tenements of J. de Fallee on either side. Witnesses J. de Dokelyngton mayor, Andrew de Wormenhale and J. de Gonewarderby bailiffs, W. de Burcestre, R. Cary, W. Pennard, J. Culverd, Nigel de Godwynston, R. le Hoppe, Hugh Tychmersli, T. de Legh clerk and others. Oxford, 1 Feb. 15 Edw. II (1 Feb. 132½).

(16) We T. le Mason and Agnes my wife have granted to N. Bone our house in S. Peter in the West between our tenements on both sides, for his life. Witnesses J. de Dokelyngton mayor, Andrew de Wormenhale and J. de Gonewarderby bailiffs, Walter Aylmer, N. de Glecton, Roger Pyron, T. de Legh clerk and others. Oxford, 6 Feb. 15 Edw. II (6 Feb. 132½).

(17) I Philip son of J. de Eo have quitclaimed to J. de Durham in a messuage in S. Peter in the Baily called Karolehalle [1] and other lands and tenements which J. de Durham has in the city and suburbs. Witnesses R. Cary mayor, H. de Stodle and J. Blundel bailiffs, W. de Burcestre, Andrew de Wormenhale, Simon de Gloucestre, J. Culverd, Peter de Eu, J. de Langrisshe clerk and others. Oxford, Sunday after S. Dyonisius 6 Edw. III (11 Oct. 1332).

---

[1] Wood's City i. 206 ' la Carol Hall reddit per annum 40s ' (temp. Edward II): the antientest mention is in a complaint of a clerk thereof, 12 Edward I (1284) against another for defaming him. Richard le Noreys of Brehull (Brill) conveyed 1325 to John de Brehull and Isolda his wife 3s annual rent from it by the name of a tenement of John Derham called Karol Hall.

(18) We W. de Herdwyk and Agnes widow of T. le Mason, executors of Thomas' will have granted to R. son of T. le Mason a messuage for his part of the third part of the goods of his father Thomas, according to the custom of England, in S. Peter in the Baily, between the tenements of J. de Brehull on either side. If R. dies without children, then to Cristiana his sister. Oxford, Sunday after S. Katherine the Virgin 7 Edw. III. Witnesses W. de Burncestre mayor, J. Blundel and Stephen de Adynton bailiffs, H. de Stodleye, J. de Gonewardby, Peter de Eu, N. de Pebbesbury, W. atte More, E. le goldsmyth and others (28 Nov. 1333).

(19) I J. de Durham son and heir of Thomas de Durham of Oxford have granted to M. John de Wyldelond and Joan his wife a messuage called Carolehalle in S. Peter in the West in a street called le litle-bailly between the tenement of the Hospital of S. John and a tene-ment of J. de Durham. Witnesses H. de Stodelegh mayor, R. de Selewode and J. Peggy bailiffs, J. de Norton, J. de Legh, Robert le gryndere, J. Cosyn, T. de Legh clerk and others. Oxford 1 Sep. 12 Edw. III (1 Sep. 1338).

(20) I Hugh de Saundresdon R. of S. Peter in the Baily have granted to H. Rolf of Oxford and Joan his wife a messuage in S. Peter's parish, between the tenement of the Fraternity of the Chantry of S. Mary in All Saints church Oxford on the north, and the tenement of the Hospital of S. John on the south. Witnesses J. de Stodle mayor, W. Hunte and W. Bergaveny bailiffs, J. de Bedeford, J. Hertwelle, R. Wodehay, N. de Thornele and others. Oxford, 12 Mch 36 Edw. III (12 Mch 136½).

(21) Thomas son of Thomas de Pydynton, and Alice his wife. Joan widow of H. Rolfe [and previously widow of John de Wyldelond] holds of us and of Alice's inheritance a messuage in S. Peter in the Baily, in the Little Bailly between the tenement of the Hospital of S. John on the south and the tenement of the Brothers of the Chantry of S. Mary in All Saints church on the north, called Karolehall, at a rent of 3s. Joan has paid us the rent for 40 years from Michaelmas next. Witnesses R. de Wodehay mayor, J. de Wyndesore and T. de Couele bailiffs, J. de Stodle, J. de Bedeford, J. de Hertwelle, J. Denham, J. de Norhampton clerk and others. Oxford, 1 Aug. 37 Edw. III (1 Aug. 1363): acknowledged before the mayor and bailiffs at the Hustings held Monday after S. James the Apostle 38 Edw. III (29 July 1364). Alice wife of Thomas son of Thomas consented.

(22) On 18 Sep. 1382, 6 Rich. II. I Joan Wildelond make my

will as follows . . I leave to my executors the messuage I live in
in S. Peters in the Baily, to sell, and with the money provide fit
chaplains in S. Peter's church to celebrate for my soul &c.; item to
Alice daughter of W. Aunger a garden in S. Ebbe outside the little
gate towards the Friars Preachers on the Thames: item to Alice my
sister 2½ acres of meadow in a meadow behind Osneye. I appoint
J. Croydon, Robert Hasele and N. Kent executors. Witnesses Walter
Nettelham, N. Chipper and T. de Sarter (18 Sep. 1382): (she made
another will, see 2 Mch 138⅚).

(23) I N. Chipir parmunter of Oxford have quitclaimed to J. Croidon
executor of the will of Joan Wyldelend widow of H. Rolf of Oxford
all my right in a messuage in S. Peter in the Baily, in the South
Baily, in which Joan lived. Witnesses J. Gibbes mayor, T. Baret and
Peter de Welyngton bailiffs, W. Godeshale, W. Dagevyll, R. de Garston,
J. Hicks aldermen, J. Dadyngton, J. Northampton clerk and others.
Oxford, 3 Mch 8 Rich. II (3 Mch 138⅘).

(24) I John Croidon executor of Joan Wildelond widow of H. Rolf
have sold to Bartholomew Bysshop of Oxford tavener a tenement in
S. Peter in the Baily, in which Joan lived, called Carole hall in a street
called le Little Bailly between the tenement of the Hospital of S. John
on the south and a tenement of W. Codeshalle (formerly belonging
to J. de Durham son and heir of Thomas de Durham of Oxford) on
the north. Witnesses W. Dagevyll mayor, Alan Lekenesfeld and
Edmund Kenyon bailiffs, W. Codeshalle, J. Gibbes, R. de Garston,
J. Hickes aldermen, J. de Dadyngton, J. Lope, J. Page, J. Northampton clerk and others. Oxford, 3 Mch 9 Rich II (3 Mch 138⅝):
Wood D. 2 p. 92 'from Bishop it seemeth it came to Thomas
Pedyngton.'

(25) Court of W. Dagevyll mayor Friday feast of S. Cedda 9
Rich. II. Will was proved of Joan Wyldelond widow of H. Rolf by
oath and witness of Walter Nettelham and Ralph Pakenhull, the lessor
as follows: 23 Nov. Monday the feast of S. Clement the Pope
A.D. 1383 7 Rich. II. I Joan Wyldelond widow of H. Rolf . . . leave
to Alice my sister a toft in S. Ebbe between a tenement of that church
on the west, and a garden once belonging to W. Couper on the east,
and 2½ acres of meadow behind Oseney near the meadow of J. Shaw,
for Alice's life, and after her death my executors are to sell the toft
and 2½ acres for the good of my soul &c. And I leave to J. Croidon
. . . and (N.) Chipper my executors the tenement I live in in S. Peter
in the Baily, to sell ¼ to pay chaplains for the same purpose: the said

N. is to have a preference in buying on offering the same price as others (2 Mch 138⅚).

(26) I N. Chipper skynner have quitclaimed to Bartholomew Bisschoppe of Oxford my right in a tenement in the Little Baily formerly belonging to Joan Wyldelond which Bartholomew bought of J. Croydon executor of Joan's will. Oxford, feast of All Saints 10 Rich II (1 Nov. 1386).

(27) Ego Willelmus Gyngyure dedi concessi et hac presenti carta mea confirmavi domino Willelmo Curtenay archiepiscopo Cantuariensi et totius Anglie primati unum mesuagium cum omnibus edificiis et pertinentiis suis in Oxon in Balliolo situatum inter mesuagium domine Johanne Wyland ex parte orientali et mesuagium Henrici Schethore ex parte occidentali. Quod quidem mesuagium cum edificiis et pertinentiis suis predictis Walterus Burnom et Felicia uxor ejus tenent ad terminum annorum ex dimissione mea et Alicie nuper uxoris mee jam defuncte, videlicet a festo S. Michaelis anno regni regis Ricardi secundi quinto usque ad finem viginti annorum extunc proxime sequencium, prout in quibusdam indenturis inde confectis plenius continetur, et quod post terminum illum ad me prefatum Willelmum Gyngyure et heredes meos reverti deberet, volo et concedo per presentes quod idem mesuagium cum edificiis et aliis pertinentiis suis universis prefato archiepiscopo post terminum illum remaneat, Habendum et tenendum prefato archiepiscopo heredibus et assignatis suis de capitalibus dominis feodi per servicia inde debita et consueta imperpetuum. Et ego predictus Willelmus Gyngyure et heredes mei predictum mesuagium cum edificiis et aliis pertinenciis suis universis prefato archiepiscopo heredibus et assignatis suis et assignatis assignatorum suorum contra omnes gentes warantizabimus imperpetuum. In cuius rei testimonium huic presenti carte mee sigillum meum apposui. Datum in festo Translationis S. Martini anno regni regis Ricardi secundi undecimo (4 July 1387).

(28) I William Gyngyure have given W. Curtenay archbp of Cantorbury a mesuage in the Baily between the mesuage of Dame Joan Wyland on the East and the mesuage of H. Schethere on the West, which Walter Burnom and his wife Felicia hold for a term of years from me and Alice my late wife viz. from Michaelmas 5 Ric. II, for the next 20 years, on the condition that Alice should have a solar for herself and husband over the well in the mesuage with free access during the term, and that Walter and Felicia should provide meat and drink for W. Gyngyure for a week or

fortnight a year; and, if Alice should die before William, he might choose between receiving meat and drink and *amiciam cum capucio* fitting his condition, or 26*s* 8*d*: but if Walter and Felicia should die during the term, it was to revert to W. and Alice.   Given on the feast of the translation of S. Martin 11 R. II (4 July 1387).

(29) I W. Gyngere have deputed M. J. Gardener fellow of the college of Merton hall to deliver to W. Courtenay archbp a mesuage in the Baily, between the mesuage of Dame Joan Wyland on the East and the mesuage of H. Schethere on the West.   Given at Lambheth on the feast of S. Gregory the pope 11 R. II (12 Mch 138$\frac{7}{8}$).

(30) The archbishop deputes M. John Wendore Warden of the college of Merton halle to take possession (12 Mch 138$\frac{7}{8}$).

(31) Presens scriptum factum inter Rogerum Forde vicarium ecclesie de Bampton ex parte una et Bartholomeum Bisschopp de Oxon taverner ex altera testatur quod predictus Rogerus dimisit et tradidit prefato Bartholomeo heredibus ac assignatis suis liberum ingressum et egressum in mesuagium ipsius Rogeri, quod mesuagium cum pertinenciis idem Rogerus nuper habuit ex dono et feoffamento predicti Bartholomei, et in qualibet parte ejusdem per totum terminum mansionis sive occupationis Johannis Croydon de Oxon et Margerie uxoris ejus in predicto mesuagio sive in aliqua parte ejusdem . . . quadraginta dies postea et quod quoddam gardinum ipsius Bartholomei eidem mesuagio adjacens quod idem Bartholomeus tenet per indenturam de Willelmo . . . ad supervidendum quedam vasa dicti Bartholomei et pro eisdem . . . vasa predicti Johannes et Margeria de predicto Bartholomeo tenent ad . . . et pro redditibus dictorum vasorum et gardini in predicto mesuagio et in qualibet parte ejusdem distringendum et districiones retinendum et ad removendum asportandum et cariandum predicta vasa fixa et non fixa et lapides circa predicta vasa dum tamen . . . existunt alicujus domus.   Preterea predictus Rogerus vult et concedit pro se et heredibus suis quod in *vasis* et in gardino predicti Bartholomei pro redditu predicti mesuagii nec pro alia causa quacunque . . . districionem non faciet per se vel per alium, nec aliquod jus vel clameum in dicto gardino tanquam pertinens ad mesuagium vel . . . predicto . . . et assignatis suis per totum terminum mansionis dictorum Johannis et Margerie in dicto mesuagio vel . . . quadraginta dies . . . libere in dictum mesuagium intrare, et pro redditu vasorum et gardini a retro fuerit . . . et dictum gardinum cum ei placuerit cum muro vel sepi obturare et a dicto mesuagio

totaliter separare . . . assignatorum suorum vel . . . eorum nomine quorumcunque. Et predicti Johannes Croydon et Margeria uxor ejus habebunt dictum mesuagium cum pertinenciis salvo . . . nuper . . . Bartholomeum et Johannem et Margeriam uxorem ejus de dimissione mesuagii predicti confectarum. In cujus rei testimonium partes predicte sigilla sua alternatim apposuerunt. Hiis testibus Ricardo Gerston majore ville Oxon, Waltero Bowne Johanne Berford tunc ballivis ejusdem ville, Willelmo Dagevyll Johanne Hykkes Nicholao Saundresdon Thoma Somerset Johanne Actce (?) Hamundo Croyden et aliis. Datum apud Oxon secundo die Julii anno regni regis Ricardi secundi post conquestum Anglie duodecimo (2 July 1388).

(32) We Thomas Pedyngton and Alice my wife have granted to Roger Forde[1] one of the Vicars of Bampton power to assign over a mesuage (in S. Peter in Ballio Oxford, called Carolehall, in a street called Lytelebaly, between the tenement of the Master and Brothers of the Hospital of S. Johns outside the East gate of Oxford, on the south, and on the north the tenement lately belonging to William Codeshale but formerly to John de Durham) to the Rector and Scholars of Stapeldon Hall. Hiis testibus Ricardo de Gerston tunc maiore ville Oxon &c. Datum apud Oxon die martis proxima post festum S. Martini anno regni regis Ricardi secundi post conquestum Anglie duodecimo (17 Nov. 1388).

(33) Quitclaim (1388, ? 1389).

(34) . . . Johannem . . . The Rector and Scholars let to John (? Croydon) and Margery the tenement in the Little Baily which Joan Wyldelond widow of H. Rolf lived in, for the lives of John and

---

[1] Statutes iii, App. p. 40 licence to Roger Forde, one of the Vicars of Bampton, John Nymet, and John Chamberleyn to give a messuage in S. Peter in the Bailey to the Rector and Scholars of the House of Stapeldon, Oxford 22 July 1388. Computus autumn 1388 'iis viiid pro expensis in die Enquestus, viis ixd ob pro expensis unius socii laborantis London in negociis domus, iiis iiiid pro conductione equorum eadem vice, iiiis viiid pro expensis circa homines in Cancellaria tempore consilii, vis viiid pro compositione cuiusdam carte Regie, xxiis iiiid pro sigillo eiusdem carte'; winter 1388 'vis viiid datis uxori Thome Pedyngton, xid pro prandio Thome Pedyngton et Alicie uxoris eius quando habuimus licenciam ad mortizandum Karolehall, iis pro sigillo Majoris quando habuimus seisinam in Karolehall, id pro cera rubea eadem vice, iiis Ballivis pro feodis suis, viiis iiiid pro emptione cuiusdam redditus capitalis viz trium solidorum de Karolehall, iis pro sigillo majoris quando relaxacio de predicto redditu fuit sigillata'; winter 1390 'iiiid circa Bartholomeum Tavernere pro munimentis habendis, id in visitacione munimentorum apud Croydon, id in capiendo possessionem in Carolhall, iid pro vino ad Johannem Salveyn, iiiid pro scriptura indentarum inter Domum et Simonem Byslegh de Carollhall.' For Croydon see Gutch i. 456, Bloxam iv. 85.

Margery and either of them, at a rent of 40s, John and Margery to do all the repairs and pay the dues to the chief lords of the fee. Witnesses R. Garston mayor, Bartholomew Bysshop and John Forster bailiffs, W. Dageville, J. Hykkys, N. Sandresdon aldermen, J. Leper, J. Croydon and others. Oxford, Friday after the Conception of the Virgin 12 Ric. II (11 Dec. 1388).

(35) Hec indentura facta inter Willelmum Colton de Oxon draper et Margaretam uxorem eius ex una parte et magistrum Willelmum Penbugule Rectorem aule sive Collegii de Stapulton halle alias dicti de Excestre hall in Oxon et eiusdem collegii socios et scolares ex altera parte testatur quod dicti Willelmus Colton et Margareta concesserunt tradiderunt et ad firmam dimiserunt prefatis magistris Willelmo rectori sociis et scolaribus totam illam vacuam placeam terre iacentem ad finem australem tenementi eorundem Willelmi Colton et Margarete in parochia S. Petri in Balliolo Oxon inter idem tenementum ex parte boriali et tenementum dictorum Rectoris et Scolarium collegii predicti ex parte australi, et inter tenementum praepositi et scolarium collegii del Oryel in Oxon ex parte occidentali et tenementum Thome Forshall ex parte orientali, Habendum &c. a die confectionis presencium usque ad finem termini nonaginta et octo annorum &c., Reddendo inde annuatim duodecim denarios argenti &c. Hiis testibus Iohanne Sprunt maiore ville Oxon; Iohanne Spycer et Iohanne Lodelowe ballivis eiusdem ville; Ricardo de Garston, Iohanne Merston, Ed. de Kenyan, Waltero Daundeseye aldremannis; Nicholao Norton clerico et aliis. Datum apud Oxon in festo nativitatis S. Iohannis Baptiste anno regni regis Henrici quarti post conquestum Anglie octavo (24 June 1407).

(36) I William Robekyn of Redyng have granted to J. Harrys and Sibil(ina) his wife a messuage in S. Peter in the Baily between the tenement of J. Keepe on the West and the tenement of J. Boseworth on the East with a little area of land lying between the land of J. Keepe on the North. . . .

Witnesses Robert Walford mayor, J. Clarke and H. Philippes bailiffs; T. Dagfeld, J. Northe, T. Wythuges, R. Spragete aldermen: W. Briggs clerk, and J. Walker and many others (17 Oct. 1445).

(37) Quitclaim by W. de Robekyn of Redyng in Berks for lands and tenements which I and Sibil had from feoffment of W. Ripkyn alias W. Ropkyn of Redyng (1 Dec. 1445).

(38) Robert Ropkyns alias Mason clerk and J. Ropkyns Mason quitclaim to J. Harrys bedell and Sibil his wife. Witnesses R.

Spragot mayor, T. Dagfeld, J. North, Robert Walford, T. Wythiges aldermen : J. Barton, T. Wymond bailiffs : W. Bruges, J. Hauslape and others (8 Ap. 1448).

(39) Ego Johannes Harrys valect. bidell. facultatis sacre theologie Universitatis Oxon dedi concessi et hac presenti carta mea confirmavi Johanni Trevylian [deleted lower down] armigero Nicholao Gosse et Johanni Ward clericis totum illud mesuagium meum cum suis pertinenciis situatum in parochia S. Petri in Balliolo Oxon inter tenementum Johannis Kepe ex parte occidentali et tenementum Johannis Boseworth ex parte orientali cum parvo fundo seu area terre jacente inter fundum predicti Johannis Kepe ex parte occidentali et fundum Henrici Philipp ex partibus orientalibus et australibus et pertin. super mesuagium prefati Johannis Boseword ex parte boriali. Habendum &c. Witnesses R. Spragot mayor, Robert Walford, T. Wythygg, J. FitzAleyn, Robert Attewood aldermen : Oliver Viry one of the bailiffs : J. Walker, J. Hauslapp and many others (2 Aug. 1449).

Omnibus Christi fidelibus ad quos hoc presens scriptum pervenerit sit notum quod ego infrascriptus Johannes Harrys continue habens dictum scriptum in manibus meis usque ad dampnacionem et cancellacionem ejusdem, quam cancellacionem approbo et ratifico testibus manu mea propria ac sigillo meo in dorso dicti scripti apposito.

(40) Nos Nicholeus Gosse et Johannes Warde clerici tradidimus dimisimus et hac presenti carta nostra confirmavimus Willelmo Mogys clerico Rectori collegii Exon in Oxon et Scolaribus ejusdem collegii ac dictorum Rectoris et Scolarium successoribus unum tenementum situatum in parochia S. Petri in magno Balliolo Oxon inter tenementum Ricardi Spragot alderman ex parte orientali et tenementum Johannis Kepe ex parte occidentali, unde unum caput abuttat super altum vicum versus boriam, et alterum caput abuttat super terram dicti Ricardi et Johannis Kepe versus austrum, quod quidem tenementum cum suis pertinenciis nuper habuimus ex dono et feoffamento Johannis Harrys valect. bedelli sacre theologie Universitatis Oxon. Habendum &c. Witnesses J. Clerke mayor, R. Spragot, Robert Atte Wode, W. Dagvile, J. Dobbys aldermen : J. Seman and J. Dudley bailiffs, and others (1 Ap. 1460).

(41) Quitclaim by J. Harrys bedell junior of Theology to W. Moges and the Scholars &c. Datum in collegio predicto (2 Ap. 1460).

(42) Hec indentura facta inter magistrum Willelmum Mogys Rectorem collegii Exon in Oxon et ejusdem loci Scolares ex parte

una, et Johannem Harrys bidellum inferiorem facultatis sacre theologie universitatis Oxon ex parte altera testatur quod dictus Rector et Scolares ac eorum successores tenebunt obitum domini Willelmi Brystow quondam pincerne dicti collegii concurrentem cum obitu domini Henrici quondam cardinalis et episcopi Winton annuatim imperpetuum ac eciam obitum dicti Johannis Harrys cum ab hac luce migraverit cum obitu dicti domini Willelmi Brystow annuatim imperpetuum : Proviso quod communis serviens ville Oxon vulgariter dictus Belman in die exequiarum proclamet obitum dicti domini Willelmi ac eciam dicti Johannis cum ab hoc seculo migraverit per totam villam Oxon et suburbia ejusdem singulis annis imperpetuum, recipiendo annuatim pro labore per manus Rectoris dicti collegii qui pro tempore fuerit seu ejus vicemgerentis . . . . , et quilibet socius dicti collegii, sive Rector fuerit sive Scolaris, presens in exequiis predictis per manus Rectoris qui pro tempore fuerit seu ejus vicemgerentis recipiat ii*d*, et quilibet socius eciam presens ad missam ii*d*, et quod sacerdos celebrans missam in obitu predict. recipiat ii*d* ultra alios socios seu scolares presentes dicti collegii et hoc singulis annis imperpetuum. Et pro premissis fideliter observandis dictus Johannes Harrys per magistros Nicholaum Gosse et Johannem Warde feoffatos suos dedit et dimisit dicto magistro Willelmo Mogys rectori collegii antedicti ejusdemque loci scolaribus ac eorum Rectoris et Scolarium successoribus imperpetuum unum tenementum cum suis pertinenciis situatum in parochia S. Petri in magno Balliolo Oxon inter tenementum Ricardi Spraget aldermanni ex parte orientali et tenementum Johannis Kepe ex parte occidentali, unde unum caput abuttat super altum vicum versus boriam, et alterum caput abuttat super terram dicti Ricardi Spraget et Johannis Kepe versus austrum. Dedit eciam dictus Johannes Harrys predictis Rectori et Scolaribus centum solidos in aureo. In cujus rei testimonium tam sigillum commune dicti collegii quam sigillum dicti Johannis Harris hiis scriptis indentatis sunt appensa. Datum in collegio predicto secundo die Aprilis anno regni regis Henrici sexti post conquestum Anglie tricesimo octavo (2 Ap. 1460). (Wood D. 2. p. 92 ' Alderman Griffin's house.')

A SURVEY OF EXETER COLLEGE

Taken by Dr. Prideaux 29 Dec. 1631 ; beginning at the West Tower [built 1605], now the Fore Gate, and so circuiting on the right hand till it end where it began. [From a copy made by Rector T. Stinton, with some additions by Rector J. L. Richards. Stinton abridged in parts, and it is not easy to make out what he added.]

1. Of the Privy Kitchin Buildings[1]. In that place stood the ancient Privyes, from the foundation. In Processe of Tyme, when the Colledge became inlarged and the Company increased, these were found too straight, and have been so often drayned on all sides and within so short a space that the rottenness of the ground about admitted no more emptying. Wherefore necessity caused the burying of these and the building of new Privyes [1614].

These Buildings have in them five rooms. The 1st lower that hath a dore to the Colledg is allotted to the Bible-Clearke in lieu of his old chamber that was annexed to the old Chapel now the Library. An old bedstead without any covering, and a chest opening in the side, are implements [furniture] in it. It is now in possession of Wᵐ Rowland, Bible-Clarke. The chamber over it, with a chimney in it, hath in it, and another opposite to the same, house implements in them. In ye kitchen under, cockloft over, ye boards and ye luggage there belongs to ye Rector. In ye kitchen and larder under, ye dresser and larder boards are ye College's.

These buildings were erected at the Colledg charges, the Rector conferring about 40s to it. They belong to the Rector, in that they stand upon the ground which appertained to his Back Side and house of office before the alteration by reason of building the Chapel.

2. From that the space between the Walls, keeping of the same breadth to the City Walls, the ground was not consecrated, but was reserved so in case Benefactours might be led by God to build lodgings there[2]; which was also the consideration that the Chapel

---

[1] At the N.W. of the quadrangle. There are no cellars here, with good reason. This part was rebuilt about 1672, and the Chapel staircase N. of it finished 1682.

[2] Now the Chapel staircase, no. 8.

hath no west window. In that space the narrowe garden and *mound* were at the Rector's charge. The little Privye of 12 deepe was erected at the House-cost to remayne for the Rector's familye.

3. The new building [1] behind the Chaple erected at the Rector's charg (especially when the Earle of Carnarvan, Jo. Robarts sole son to the Lord Robarts, the Lord Wharton and Sir Tho. Wharton his brother, with Mr Lorenzo Carye the Lord Falkland's son, were togither pupills under him). Of the space [2] between the Chapel and Towne Wall yt is consecrated ground as runneth even in length with the Chapel, and noe more; as appeareth by the Instrument.

The Tower house standing between the butts, heretofore [3], before the Rector's stable was taken in lease from the Towne by Dr Holland, who builded it and left it to his wife Mrs Susanna Holland; she sold hir right therein to Dr Prideaux, the succeeding Rector, in whose possession it now remaynes, paying yearly for it 2s to the Cittye, until Dr Holland's lease be ended. This, being before a stable, was turned into a Kitching, with the Lodgings over it, at the charg of the sayd Rector Dr Prideaux; who, yielding up his lease which he had of Mrs Holland, took a new of the Colledg for 40 years, for the entrance of that lower rome and studye which stands on the *Mount.* The Colledge was at the most charge, as also for the rayles about the new part, and walling of it. The Dyall on the Mount is the said Rector's, given unto him by Richard Standish (?), mason, when he was Vicechancellour.

4. Without the Rector's Back side, ranging along by the Cittye Wall, stood 3 little gardens, which were demolished when the East part of the publique Library and Schooles were built. They belonged to the Colledg, but were let out to Principal Bradwell [4], widow Almond [5], and goodwife Hollyday. That next the Schools Principal Braddle was well paid for by the University. The 2 others rest yet to be reckoned for, both for the stones and lease.

All that space of ground upon part of which the Mount and our Chapel stand, and out of which we had our Bowling Alley [6], was

[1] Since demolished.   [2] Rector's Area, North side of the Chapel.
[3] The Bog there adjoining, to the South side of the City Wall, and on the North side of the Rector's courtyard, was emptied and cleansed, and the building over it renewed, in 1785.
[4] Ralph Braddyll, Principal of S. Mary Hall 1591–1632.
[5] Hist. of Kidlington (O. H. Soc.) 132.
[6] Afterwards the Rector s garden, in 1790.

formerly a common Cart-Waye[1], which we gott to be interrupted and inclosed, from the Citty, in a lease of 99 years, by King James's mandatory letters to the Maior and Aldermen, who before withstood us: which letters were procured by meanes of the now Marquesse of Hamilton, some tymes student of our Colledg, which we and our successors will acknowledge with thankfull Remembrance.

5. Ranging with the Bowling Alley, without the doore in the City-Wall stand our publique Privyes[2]. Builded at the Colledg charg (cost 200 li), in the dongeon of wch are left two Arches opposite East and West, about the midst: to be taken notice of by Posterity that may have occasion to empt them.

Of the 3 Roomes into the wch they are divided, that next the Wall with the Roome over it is only for the Rector's use. The second for the Fellowes: and the third for the Company of the House. Over these 2 Roomes are Woodhouses belonging to those that had their Woodhouses demolished at the building of the new Hall and Sellers. The tenement of one Davye Waters without it is part of the ground whereof we have a lease from the Cittye for [? 40] years, paying yearely for the whole.

6. Eastward from the Privyes, *the Tower in the Towne Walle* is a part of the mentioned ground lease of 99 years, but a lease of . . . with a garden before it was granted by the Cittye to one Thomas Almond for the Terme of 41, wch terme the Colledg is bound in their grand lease quietly to suffer to. . . . But, anno 1632, the interest of Almond was bought in by John Prideaux, Rector, for the summe of 30 li for 23 yeares, wch Almond had then in it: who renewed that lease to make it up 40 yeares, and so to pay 1sh yearely for it to the Colledg.

The Bowling Alley, Rayles, and the two Freestone Walls that bound it were erected and perfected at the Colledg charg, which was no small thing, to turne a place so deformed and incommodious (being a stinking unpitched Cartway before) to the Use it now serves: both for Recreation, Comlynesse, and benefit of the lower chambers that open their windows to it.

So much of the Outworkes or Suburbs.

---

[1] The street within the Wall of the City, connecting Ship Lane and New College Lane.

[2] A new Bog-house was built on the same site 1706, which cost £149 17s 9d. [The rebuilding in 1887 cost a large sum.]

Cap. 2. Of the mayne Buildings of the Colledg.

For Order's sake may be parcelled into
1. Rector's Row.
2. Library List.
3. Bentley's Nest.
4. Pyriam's Mansions.
5. Acland's Alleye.
6. Tower Range.

1. In *Chapel Row* (called before *Rector's Row*) the Chapel there erected was at the charg of Geo. Hakewell D^r of Divinitye, Chaplayne to his Maj^tye Charles the 1st both when he was Prince and King. He was an Exceter man, born of pious and worthy Parents: Fellow of this Colledg, wherein he took all his degrees: afterwards was Archdeacon of Surrye. His learning appears in his printed workes. But his piety and bounty in this, that having two sonnes of his owne to be provided for, he notwithstanding gave 1200^li by the least for the publique good of the Place he was bred in. For the waynscoting of and paynting the Sowther Isle the Colledg was at the charge of about 200^li, in regard the Building Plott by the Founder was by so much and more exceeded.

2. Adjoyning to the Chapel are the Rector's Lodgings: which howsoever indamaged by that neighbourhood in the loss of a garden and private walkes, with the stopping of three western windowes, the far best light to the roomes abutting that way, yet all these are more than recompensed by the Fitnesse of the place for his own private entrance to it, and the separated seates for his Familye.

To the Rector's Lodgings[1] there belong

1st Cellar, divided into two roomes.

---

[1] The part of the Rector's Lodgings looking eastward, and containing the Kitchen, the Dining Room over it, and the Long Garret over that, were built by Dr Arthur Bury in 1671, the House fronting northwards by Dr Prideaux himself, subsequently to this Survey in 1631. The windows of the Dining Room were new glazed in 1785; having been before glazed in 1733 by Dr Atwell in the manner of Italian Balcony-windows, which let in Pools of Water in rainy weather.

The south front of the Rector's Lodging towards the Quadrangle was new sashed together with all the other windows of the Quadrangle, and great West Front of the Coll. towards Jesus Coll. in long Vacation 1789 (Soluta Varia 3 Dec. 1789, 6 May 1790).

The same front cleansed, with a stone-coloured wash, and the windows and cornice new painted, early in June 1793. [In pencil] This front, or rather the whole Lodgings, taken down and rebuilt, being raised to a height corresponding with the rest of the College 1800-2.

The Stillings, Bynns, and Shelves, and old Table there standing, belong to the Colledg.

2d Waynescote Parler: which was so fitted at the Colledg charge, and these two ... windowes added to it to supply the Light taken from it by the Chapel.

3d Rector's Bedchamber: enlightened by the two larg windowes at the Howse charg by Dr Prideaux, who turned the passage, from it into the Dyning chamber, into a little studye. The waynscote Presse in it, with cubbords, is an House implement.

4th Entry: wch was before with open stayres to the Colledg, with much deformity and inconvenience: this altered by the appoyntement of the same Rector, and that division of ... with a door opening to the back side, for most of the materialls were at his own charg.

6th Studye gained from under the old Stayres, looking to the back side, conveniently shelved at the House cost.

7 Hall: much mended in the changinge. A table in it, 2 Formes, and a ... waynscote cubbord are House implements in it, togither with an old flat Chest.

8 Studye: lately gayned from an obscure Passage to the Tower, by breaking out the window to the Colledge.

9 Waynscoted great dyning Roome over it: wherein the cubbord of the same Worke, and Bench annexed, are House-implements.

10 Tower-Studye: at the Stayre-Foote of the Rector's Studye, with some shelves in it put up by Mr Hoffman[1] when he had it.

11 Treasury over; is only for the Colledg use: to the Doore are 3 Lockes, of wch the Rector, Subrector, and Deane, have alwayes the Keyes, as also of a Chest[2] in it, where the money is kept. The Waynscote Presse in it with distinct Boxes for Colledg Evidences, and a Roome for plate, was set up at the Colledg charge by Mr. Willm Helme when he was Subrector.

12 Cock-loft next eastward from the Towre: had the window added to it in Dr Holland's Tyme; the Chymny in Dr Prideaux's; together with the Stydye towards the Colledg by Mr John Robarts the Lord Robarts's only sonne; who there left the Hangings and Travasse [Traverse] to it to the Rector, at his going from it. In this Cock-loft the great Standing Bedsted with the old Court-Cubbord, belong to the Colledg.

---

[1] John Hoffman, from the Palatinate, M. 16 July 1625 age 23, wrote in the *Epithalamia* of 1625.

[2] This Chest is now in the muniment room, which also has 3 locks.

13 Middle Chamber next under it : having but one studye formerly in it, and another added in Dr P.'s Tyme, with the Dore and Stayres that descend from it to the lower Roome.

14 Lower Chamber : in wch the . . . Waynscote was at the charg of the Colledg, with the new building the Chymny and altering the Window.

15 Larg Grund-Studye within it : with the window altered and convenient shelves which belong to the House. This Ground-Chamber and Study, with that above it, and the 2 Studyes in it, were granted by a Decree of the Society to Dr Prideaux, to belong to his Lodging for his Tyme of Rectorship only, but not to his Successors but uppon a new Grant.

3. The next Under-Chamber eastward, belonging to the House, togither with a dark Woodhouse annexed, were turned into a Bursary by Dr P., with addition of the 4 windowes in it, newe flooring, and the Waynscote and Portall in it, with the Doore and Lock about it : the Table and Chayres in it are the sayd Rector's ; the Formes and Germane's Hutch in it, with 2 other Coffers, belong to the House. Then follows a Detail[1] of the rest of the Rooms in Rector's Row, viz : what are in the present Library Court in Staircases marked and named in the present Register [1792] of Chambers as no. 7, no. 10, no. 11[2]. These three Staircases were new-roofed and otherwise substantially renewed and repaired in the Time of the Rectorship of Drs Conybeare and Atwell 1732–3.

Cap. 3. Of the Library List.

The Library at this Time (1631–2) was the old Chapel of Bishop Stapleton turned into a Library, and having one Room (some Time the Bachelors or Junior Common Room), and two small Places, latterly used, the one for a Barber's Room, and the other a Hole for Ashes ; by means of which last the Library was burnt on Dec. 2. 1709. But being refitted, it was used as the College Library till 1778 ; when it was taken down. This old Chapel, afterwards a Library, being much too near to the Buildings of Rector's Row, being within 25 feet of them, the new Library was built farther off viz. near sixty feet south from those buildings, by which the windows in that Area, which were before much obscured by the height of the old Chapel or Library, and its steep Roof, are now much lighter and more chearfully situated,

---

[1] Stinton here abridges.
[2] These staircases were pulled down when the present Rector's House was built. They were popularly known as Hell Quad.

and open to the Air and Sunshine, making a decent oblong quad-
rangular Court, about 60 F. by 110. Dᴿ Prideaux remarks that the
Bible-Clerk was allowed a Room under the old Chapel, but on the
Building of Dᴿ Hakewell's Chapel, he had another Room assigned to
him nearer to that new Chapel. The Society have of late allowed
him one of the House-Rooms, of the inferior Class as to Rent, viz.
Kitchen Staircase or no. 3, 2 pair Stairs middle; or one of the Rooms
no. 11 at the East End of the Library Court viz. the North East
Corner next the Pump.

Cap. 4. Of Bentley's Nest[1].

Filling up the space between the West End of the Old Chapel (at
that time turned into a Library) and Periam's Buildings (the Common
Room Staircase) were Timber Buildings, made over the *oldest and
original Library*; for them see Loggan's Print, where the oldest
Library, and its Superstructure may be seen very distinctly. The
old Library was turned into a Fellow's Chamber with 8 Studyes:
called a Fellow's Right, but probably let to younger members, having
one Room in common, and the Studies or Closets severally. [Thomas]
Bentley was Butler of the College in Dᴿ Holland's Rectorship, and
a native of Plymouth.

Cap. 4. Of Peryam's Mansions.

The 4ᵗʰ Parcell of building termed Peryam's *Mansions* in regard of
the Firmenesse and Magnificence of it, in comparison of wᶜʰ Bentley's
wooden Stuffe may be termed a Nest. Mᴿ John Peryam, a merchant
of Exeter, gave 560ˡⁱ towards the erecting of it, which the Colledg
made up 700ˡⁱ to perfect it[2]. The Place where it stands was before
a Tennys Court. In digging of the Foundation, 12 Foote deepe in
the Earth was found a Stone mortar full of small Peeces of Silver, of
divers stamps, but about the same value, of 2ᵈ—whereof some were
distracted by the workemen, and others knew not what to make of
them at first. A Part of them were brought to the Rector, who
changed them for —ˡⁱ, wherewith the Brasen Candlestick wᶜʰ hangeth
in the Hall was purchased. The Arms uppon both sides of this

[1] Memorandum 1632 Feb. 18: 40ˢʰ yearely to be paid to the House out of the
Fellowes Right that hath the North Chamber in the higher Loft in Bentley's Nest:
and 40ˢʰ more of him that hath the highest Chamber in Peryam's Mansions North-
ward.

[2] In 1618. The senior Common Room, being the southern Ground Room of
Peryam's Building, was new-floored with Oak in the long Vacation of 1792, and
a new Window made in that, and the Room over it. New furnished and carpeted
1820.

Building are Peryam's, and Prideaux; his first wife being a Prideaux; who brought with her the Ground of his Estate. He never saw what he had done for us; nor required Account of the money he gave; neither conditioned with the Colledg in any sort for the disposing of the Lodgings, with Reference to himself or any of his. A worthy Benefactor. God rayse us many such to follow his example.

Here follows a Recital of 8 Chambers. It appears from Loggan's View that the original Building was a story higher than at present, and it was reduced probably to match the Armagh Buildings, and the rest of the Fabrick.

Cap. 5. Of Acland Alleye.

This may be diversed from the rest in Honour of that worthy Knight Sir John Acland of Devon who gave us 800 li to the erecting of our new Hall[1]; to wch the Coll. added 200li before it could be furnished as it is. The Hall before stood in the midst of the Quadrangle, having the Kitchen and Buttery[2] annexed to it. It was in latter Tymes augmented with Lofts at the West End over the screen (?), but never could conveniently intertayne the Company: Whereupon Sir John Acland (having formerly bene of this Colledg) uppon the Persuasion especially of Mr Isaiah Faringdon, Fellow sometyme and Bacchalaur of Divinitye of this House, was brought to take such an . . . Worke in Hand; which he never saw after it was built: and was so far from reserving any Interest to him or any of his for performing it, that he gave 16li yearely for a Pension to be payd unto 2 poore Scholars to be chosen out of Exceter Schoole, which at this Time fayleth, God knoweth by whose Fault. The Colledg affords them Roomes (?) in Honour of the Benefactor. In Tyme perchance the Cittye of Exceter will thinke uppon it to do some Good to Exceter Colledg, in wch it hath had . . . The Place where this new Hall stands was voyd, having in it only an old Worke-house and 2 patched Studyes to the Buttery-Chambers. The Pillars in ascending the Stayres are of . . . bestowed uppon us by the Dean and Chapter of Christ-Church from Oseney.

2. The Buttery adjoyning to the Hall[3] was heretofore a Fellow's Right.

[1] Built 1618. The Parts West of it 1701-3, and at the same Time the whole from thence to the great Western Gateway and that Gateway itself 1701-3.

[2] [30 June 1591 Jo. Eveleghe subrector: hoc anno extructa est cella in promptuario ad perpetuum et summum Collegii beneficium scholariumque utilitatem, et reparata est aula atque elevata eiusdem area.]

[3] Dimensions of the Buildings from the Hall to the Street westward. From the

3. The great Cellar under the Hall was made when the Hall was builded. But

4. The little Cellar within was formerly a vacant Place where dark Woodhouses stood wch belonged to the Fellowes, whereof the Larder within . . . is Part.

5. The Kitching also next to it was a Fellowes Chamber wch had 2 Studyes in it. The former Kitching stood in the midst of the Colledg very disgracefully, long after the Hall was down. Over it was a Fellowes Right, as also over the old Buttery, taken away with the old Hall, wch Rights were recompensed fully in the Colledg by other new Buildings. Seniors . . . of a private Garden paled in and annexed to the Kitching Chamber, with a Vine in it that took up a great Part of the Square, so that then the whole Colledg was but a confused number of blynd Streats.

This old Kitching was removed and the other finished 1632, Robt Vilvayne D^r of Physicke of the Cittye of Exeter and Mr William Orford Bacchalour of Divinitye Parson of Clyst-Hydon in Devon contributing to this Work 20^{li} a peece, to which the Rector added for the Tyme that wch finished it for Use. Under the Kitching is a fayre Sinke of 12 long and 4 foote broad, to receive the washing of it and the Larder, as Use shall require. The Pastry within was a Part of the next Chamber, formerly a Woodhouse.

The Water [1] comes from the Comduit at Carfoxe. It came to the old Kitching from a Cisterne in the Wall by the Chapel Doore, which Cisterne at the building of the new Kitching was taken away as not being of farder Use.

Then follows an Acc^t of the Rooms over these, demolished together with the Kitchen and Buttery under them, as above described by Dr Prideaux, in order to make Room for the Kitchen and Buttery substituted in their Room in the Rectorship of Dr Wm Paynter 1700-3.

---

coin of the Hall westward to Jesus College (i.e. to the Corner facing Jesus College) containing the Buttery and Kitchen; Length 62 Feet, Breadth 28 Feet, 2 Inches. The Buttery, and Passage from the Kitchen to the Hall; Breadth 23 F., Breadth of Buttery alone 18 F. (From an original in the handwriting of Dr Wm Paynter, in whose Rectorship that Part of the College was rebuilt 1701-3.)

[1] The Kitchen at the S.W. Angle of the Coll. was supplied only by a Pump in the said Kitchen till 1795, when a new Pipe for Water from the Hinxey Conduit was laid from ab^t the north Gate of Lincoln College, in order to supply the new Culinary Apparatus for which the Pump was not so well suited.

Cap. 6. Of Tower Range.

So denominated, says D[r] Prideaux, from the Tower [1] at the End of it. This was the Range of Building from the South-West Corner of the great Quadrangle to the West or principal Gateway of the College towards the Street. This Place was formerly the back-Gate [2], a poore Thing, and a stinking pissing Place. At the Entrynge in at the Right Hand before the lower Chamber was a Piece of an old Wall, and then an i . . . with . . . before the Tower Windowes, full of Bones Filth and Nettles. All which were taken away at the Building of the Towre w[ch] was done by the fore-mentioned M[r] Everard Chambers uppon his own Cost, who had an Interest of the Colledg in it for certayne (40) yeares, for w[ch] the Coll. afterwards compounded with him, as it appears by the Register-Booke.

OTHER LAND.

Some land was sold when the Theatre was built; Reg. 2 Sep. 1664 consensu Scholarium tunc domi petentium (?) decretum est ut major pars cujusdam areae posticae ad hoc collegium pertinentis a parte orientali sitae pro rationabili fine in usum Universitatis elocaretur, quo convenientius publici Theatri fundamina ponerentur.

The College perhaps had also a small slip of land projecting towards the Ashmolean; and part of the College was damaged in 1679 when some houses were being pulled down to make way for the Ashmolean; Hist. Comm. xii. 7, p. 158, Wood's Life ii. 452. In the summary at the end of Prideaux's Survey are the words ' 2 Towres which were formerly in the Rector's backyard and garden, now all demolished.' The Eastern of these, south of the centre of the Ashmolean, would seem from an old map (B) in the Rector's possession to have been Almond's (p. 313), and perhaps this was sold to the University. About the site of the other tower there is no doubt, as its site was clearly visible when the modern buildings were erected.

---

[1] Dimensions of Tower Range according to D[r] Paynter. From the North side to the Kitchen is 74 Feet. The wideness of the Chambers with the walls 25 F. 3 Inches; Chambers within the walls (clear) 18 F. 3 Inches.

[2] Old Western Gateway purchased by the Coll. of M[r] Everard Chambers who built it, in 1605: the same pulled down and a new one built 1701-3. The Parapet Wall and Balustrade at the top being decayed, were renewed about 1787, both the side Parapets, including 3 chimneys, and the like Parapets in the two Fronts without and within above the semicircular Pediments.

LIVINGS.

GWINEAR.

The earliest deeds connected with Gwinear are as follow :—

(1) Ralph abbot of S. Mary de Valle to all &c., 1267 Wednesday next after the Sunday on which Reminiscere is sung (16 Mch 1267), We have sent R. de Ponte canon as our proctor 'tam in Anglia quam in Cornubia,' to effect an exchange with the prior and convent of Merton, canons of St. Augustine, of our property in England and Cornwall, for what they hold in Normandy viz. at Kaignes in the diocese of Bayeux [S. Mary de Valle was on the river a little above Caen, there is a slight account of it in Gallia Christiana ix. 440. Gosselin de la Pommeraye and Petronilla were benefactors to it or perhaps founders about 1125; Dugdale vi. 246, 248; Whitaker's Cathedral of Cornwall ii. 51; Monast. Exon. xv. 33, 38, 41, 65, 188, Suppl. 5, 7 under 'Tregony']. (2) Brother R. de Ponte to all &c., Nemeton 4 Aug. 1267, I resign the priory of Treguny into the hands of Walter [Bronescomb] bishop of Exeter, the parish church of the same place, the parish church of Bery, with their rents possessions advowsons &c., held in England by S. Mary de Valle; that the said bishop, with the consent of Merton priory, may dispose of the same at his pleasure, only reserving the moveables belonging to the said abbey; witnesses the religious men Robert prior of Berliz of the order of S. Augustine in the diocese of Bath and Wells, R. his canon, Brother Vincent of the order of Preachers, Robert his confrater; M. John [de Bradlegh] archdeacon of Barnstaple, M. W. de Capella, M. Thomas de Bocland, M. R. Pace; dominis W. de Esse, Peter de Guldeford; presbyters Hugh de Plumpton, R. de Grangeys clerks: (printed in Monast. Exon. 7, where see the next document). (3) Brother Gilbert prior of Merton to all &c., at Merton the day of S. Margaret 1267, We have appointed Brother Roger of Norwich our canon, and dominus Roger de Eyta R. of Shirefeld our seneschal, as our proctors for the dioceses of Exeter and of Bath and Wells, to exchange &c., and assign over to Walter bishop of Exeter &c. (4) Brother Roger

of Norwich canon of Merton, and Roger de Ayeta R. of Shyresfeld, proctors of Gilbert prior of Merton, to all &c., at Nemeton 4 Aug. 1267. Since Ralph abbot of S. Mary de Valle &c. have exchanged their priory of Treguny and their church of Bery, together with the advowsons of the churches of Uppotery, Bokerel, Clystwyk, S. Laurence Exon, Stockleigh Pomeray, Ascumbe, and Aure, with all &c. in the dioceses of Exeter and of Bath and Wells—for the priory of Kaygnes belonging to our church of Merton in the diocese of Bayeux, with the assent of the Bishops of Exeter and Bayeux; we place the 'statum' of the priory of Treguny, and the parish churches of Treguny and Bery (to which the bishops of Exeter are said to present), 'alte et basse,' in the hands of the bishop of Exeter; witnesses M. John archdeacon of Barnstapol, Sir Ralph de Arundel, Alexander de Okeston; M. W. de Capella, Thomas de Bocland, Roger de Dertford, R. Pace, Walter de Lacking, W. de Braddon, Peter de Guldeford chaplains. (5) Henry de la Pomeray, Lord of Treguny and of Bery to all, &c., Nemeton 4 Aug. 1267, Since the Abbot of S. Mary de Valle had these places from the gift of our ancestors, we consent, &c., witnesses as before. (6) Walter Bishop of Exeter to all, &c. Crideton, 16 Aug. 1267, we consent to the exchange, and ordain that the parish church of Bery shall belong to Merton Priory, and they are to present to the vicarage. As to the manor of Teygne Canonicorum and the land of Worthy, which S. Mary de Valle held from the family of de la Pomeray, Henry de la Pomeray is to have Worthy in compensation for the attendance of one priest, whom the abbey had to send from among their canons to attend him continually, and for other services due; and Merton is to have Teygne in frankalmoigne, but is to admit a fit person presented by the family of Pomeraye to pray for their souls, &c., and he is to give them three acres in Bery to store their fruits on, &c.; and three priests are to be maintained in the Priory of Treguny to keep up divine service, reserving to ourselves, &c., as to Uppotery, &c., the usual rights; witnesses dominis W. deacon and Roger [de Thoriz] archdeacon of Exeter, M. John archdeacon of Barnstaple, Thomas de Hereford, J. Fitz Robert, J. of Exeter canons of Exeter; Robert Prior of Berliz; Sir Wydo de Novant, Sir Warin de la Stane, M. J. Wyger, M. W. de Capella, M. Roger de Derteforde, M. W. de Braddon, M. Peter de Guldeford chaplains; Hugh de Plympton, R. de Grangeis clerks.

Wittenham.

Nicholas Bishop of Sarum, in the visitation of his diocese 1292, ascertained these facts: clergy and laity say that M. Robert de Clifford R. of Earl's Wittenham[1] 60 years since held all the tithe of the demesnes now held by domini Hugh de Plecy, John de S. Elena, and Robert de Saunford parishioners of that church; and so his immediate successor dominus Drogo de Turbeville, and so for a long time his successor dominus Almaric de Plecy. But now the Prior of Longa Villa, through his agent in England, began to take the tithes under a fiction by the connivance of this last Rector, and so it has gone on. The Bishop then issued a commission to M. Thomas de Eadburbiry canon of York and M. Nicholas de Rudham clerks, at Remesbiry 17th Nov. 1292. Brother Philip prior de Longa Villa Giffardi had appointed Odo prior of S. Andrew, Norhampton, his proctor in England 15 May 1292. Odo on 6 Oct. 1292 named as his commissary before the bishop John de Appelford. On 10 or 17 Dec. 1292 in the parish church of Hungerford the Dean of Abendon certified that notice had been served on the prior to appear. The prior's agent appeared and said that he had a special privilegium to receive the tithe of Wittenham as an exception to the common right, and asked a further day to produce it, and he was allowed till Tuesday after Epiphany, and then till Wednesday after Purification. Then he produced nothing and went away contumaciously, and was allowed till the next Thursday. He did not appear then and was excommunicated. The Dean of Abendon announced this from Stakeburn 25 June 1294 to N. de Rudham, but added that the Prior of Longa Villa was allowed till the first lawday after S. James the Apostle (the message to the Prior of Longa Villa seems to have been dated Remesbiry 7 June 1294). As no one appeared in the Church of St. Nicholas at Abendon on the Monday after S. James, sentence was given that the prior had no right to the tithe, and that the present rector William de Braybroke should have it, witnesses dominus Nicholas V. of St. Nicholas at Abendon, William V. of Boklond, William V. of Pusie, Reginald de Ocby and John James deacons (diaconibus), Richard Michel, Richard de Stiventon, William de Sancta Wteford, Henry Loby clerks. In 20 Edward I the 'taxatio' of the parish is given as xxv marks, tenth xxxiii*s* iiii*d*, pensio of the Prior of Longa Villa c*s*, tenth ix*s*: and in the Computus of 1380 we read

[1] For list of rectors and vicars see ed. i. p. 193.

'xxii*s* ii*d ob* ad subsidium domini regis per clerum sibi concessum, et pro porcione Prioris de Longa Villa x*s*, x*d* uni homini qui portavit dictum subsidium domini regis ad monasterium de Malmesb. et pro acquietancia, iiii marcis pro uno libro inpignorato pro utilitate domus in cista August.' Prior Philip on 6 July 1320 says that considering the distance and difficulty of collection and the smallness of his portion of the tithe he gives it up to William de Braibrok the present Rector of West Wittenham and his successors. The same day he named William de Benefeld of Cambroun and William Russel of Methe (Methe near Torrington belonged to the Giffards), Rectors of churches in the Diocese of Exeter his agents in the matter of the Wittenham tithe. Sealed with his seal and that of Walter Bishop of Exeter. In another deed he grants Walter Bishop of Exeter the advowson of West Wittenham, witnesses Sir Martin de Fishacre, Sir Richard de Stapeldon, John de Ralegh, John de Caignes, John de la Pomeray; and in another deed, also dated 6 July 1320, he makes M. John le Knyght clerk and Roger de Morthoe his attorneys, to give seisin to Bishop Walter. Before William de Bereford and other Justices of the King's Bench in Michaelmas term 14 Edward II, rotulo xxxix 'Philippus Prior de Longa Villa Giffardi in Normannia summonitus fuit ad respondendum Waltero de Stapeldon episcopo Exoniensi de placito quod teneat convencionem inter eos factam de advocacione ecclesie de West Wittenham,' &c.; a fine is levied, and the bishop gives the prior 100 marks (stated in the king's Breve here recited, 28 July 14 Edward II); the prior named John de la Slo and John de Caneford his agents. On 12 April 1322, at Exeter, the bishop gave the advowson to the Rector and Scholars of Stapeldon Hall, witnesses Sir Richard de Merton, Sir Richard de Stapeldon, Sir William Hereward, John Caignes, John Prodhomme. Pat. Rolls 20 May 15 Edward II (1322) Pro Rectore et Scolaribus de Stapeldone Halle Oxonie (for the appropriation of West Wyttenham church). Teste Rege apud Ebor. On 1 Feb. 13$\frac{22}{30}$ at Poterne, Roger Bishop of Salisbury certifies that he found in the Register of his predecessor Nicholas Lungespeye that the Prior of S. Andrew, Norhamptone, agent of the Prior of Longa Villa, presented John de Sicheston to the Church of West Wittenham 21 July 1292 at Chardestok but owing to various defects his predecessor had not accepted the presentation, but gave that church to William de Braybrok deacon on Saturday after the Assumption of the Virgin, at Croel.

The following deeds show the enquiries made as to the presentation :
(1) The Official of the Archdeaconry of Berks to Robert Bishop
of Sarum, Abyndon, 6 April 1361, I have received your letter dated
Poterne 19 Mch 136⁰⁄₁, stating that the Rector and Scholars of
Stapeldon Hall have presented John Bremdon presbiter to the
vicarage of Wittenham, and ordering full enquiries to be made. The
vacancy is caused by John Folyot the late vicar holding the parish
church of Slyndefold (Slinfold in Sussex) in the Diocese of Chichester.
The vicarage is worth £10 a year. John Brindon is over 26, liber
et legitimus, &c. The Rector and Scholars presented John Folyot.
(2) Hugh Rector of Rugwyk to Robert Bishop of Chichester,
Sullyngton, 22 April 1361, I received your mandate dated Aldyng-
bene, 21 Dec. 1359, stating that you conferred Slyndefold, vacant by
resignation of the late Rector Reginald, on John Foliot, and ordering
me to induct him; I therefore inducted Foliot 24 Dec. 1360 in
presence of Godfrey sacrist of the said church, Gilbert Atte Hallond,
&c. (3) Robert Bishop of Sarum to John Bremdon, Maidenbrade-
leigh, 9 April 1361, We admit you to the Vicarage of West Wittenham
this day. (4) Robert Bishop of Sarum to all, &c., recites the presentation by the Rector and Scholars 'in our College Oxon' 7 Mch 136⁰⁄₁,
and the letter of the Archdeacon's Official, and a letter from the
Bishop of Chichester, and that of Hugh R. of Rugwyk, and a certificate
of the Dean of Abendon that John Foliot had held two incompatible
benefices together for a year, and was therefore now pronounced
deprived of Wittenham. (5) The Official of the Court of Canterbury
to the Rector of Staunton in the Diocese of Lincoln, and the perpetual
Vicar of Morton, and dominus Nicholas chaplain of the same place in
the Diocese of Sarum; John de Brendon V. of Wittenham has been
disturbed by the claims of John Foliot, you are to inhibit Foliot from
all such conduct; dated Ocleford 6 June 1361.

By a convention between dominus Richard Pyn Rector and Henry
le Hunt and Agnes his wife, 15 Mch 134¾, they granted him a 'placea'
of land for life at a rent of a quarter of barley. On 27 Dec. 1362
William le Blake of West Wyttenham and Agnes his wife daughter
of John Kemp of West Wyttenham give Robert Bossorn, Robert
Blakedon, John de S. Hillario and Robert le Ryche clerks a 'placea'
of land 6 perches long and at the end towards the public road 32 feet
broad and at the other end towards the cemetery 23 feet broad,
'which I Agnes lately had from Robert de Folham,' witnesses Thomas
Stoyl, John Tyso, John Waryn, John Brid, William Lepesofte (at the

back, 'West Wyttenham de quadam placea pertinente ad Rectoriam).
Some other deeds follow: (1) John Bishop of Sarum to the Rector
and Scholars, Sonnyng, 26 August 1381, We allow you to let out
Wittenham to farm for 5 years. (2) Henry Bishop of Sarum to the
Rector and Fellows, 6 Nov. 1607, This day John Best clerk, S.T.B.,
resigned Wittenham. (3) On 5 Feb. 161$\frac{9}{}$ William Prowse of Witnam
clerk, John Reston of Culnham alias Cullam yeoman and Gregory
Slade of Longe Witnam yeoman acknowledge being bound to John
Prideaux Rector of the College in £100. (4) Whereas the College
has granted William Prowse the present incumbent the next presentation of Wittenham, if it happens before Michaelmas 1622 by Prowse's
death, provided a Fellow of Exeter is presented, if he will take it, &c.

Summer 1520 'vis viii$d$ pro expensis magistrorum doctorum Wylton
et Powell procuratorum in Convocatione episcoporum facta A.D. 1517°.
Was this for Wittenham?

On 1 Feb. 154$\frac{7}{}$ the rule of 1541 about not letting Long Wittenham
and Gwinear before the end of a previous lease was relaxed for this
once, and on 10 Feb. Wittenham let to Thomas Perse of Hincksay
for 5 years from the Annunciation to 1551; 10 Feb. 154$\frac{8}{9}$ let to him
for 22 years, and on 27 Mch 1551 for 41 years. (Perse of South
Hinxey was father of John Pierse archbishop of York.) The land tax
was redeemed on the rectory, and the vicarage augmented by redeeming the land tax 9 Feb. 1804.

In magno rotlo de anno xv regis Henrici VIII in item Berks.
'Collegium vocatum Excet. College in Oxon debet xvi$d$ videlicet de
quarta decima quatuor decimarum regi a clero Cantuar. anno iiii^{to}
concessarum in Archidiaconatu Comitatus Cornub. pro ecclesia de
Manhinyett in decanatu de Estwylkshere: viii$d$ de secunda medietate
primae decimae duarum decimarum regi a clero Cantuar. anno vii°
concessarum in archidiaconatu predicto pro eadem ecclesia in decanatu predicto in comitatu predicto. Quae quidem ecclesia est dicti
Collegii sicut continetur in literis certificatoriis venerabilis in Christo
patris Ricardi episcopi Exon retornatis ad scaccarium anno ii° regis
Henrici VII quae sunt inter certificaciones episcoporum de nominibus
collectorum decimae dicto anno secundo concessae. Summa xxiiii$d$.
Sed non debetur inde summa eo quod quaecunque beneficia et possessiones omnium et singulorum Collegiorum Aularum sive Domorum
Collegiatarum, quibuscunque nominibus censeantur, in Universitate
Oxon et Cantab. existentium a concessione levacione et solucione
dictae decimae et cujuslibet partis ejusdem excipiuntur sicut continetur

in concessione dictae decimae irrotulata in memorandis hujus scaccarii videlicet inter recorda de termino S. Michaelis anno decimo regis hujus . . rotlo . . ex parte Remembranc. regis. Quiet. est. —Custos et scolares Collegii vocati Excet. College in Oxon debent x*d* videlicet de quarta decima iiii decimarum regi a clero Cantuar. anno iiii concessarum in archidiaconatu Berk. pro ecclesia de Witteham in decanatu de Abendon. Quae quidem ecclesia est dicti Custodis et Scolarium sicut continetur in quadam certificatione Ricardi nuper episcopi Sarum retornata hic ad scaccarium anno vi° regis Edwardi iiii. Sed non debetur inde summa eo quod bona, beneficia et possessiones omnium et singulorum Collegiorum sive Aularum Collegiatarum in Universitate Oxon et Cantabr. existentium a concessione levacione et solucione dictae decimae et cujuslibet partis ejusdem excipiuntur sicut continetur in concessione ejusdem irrotulata in memorandis anni quinti regis hujus videlicet inter recorda de termino S. Michaelis rotulo primo ex parte Remembranc. regis. Quieti sunt.

Clifton Ferry, in Long Wittenham[1].

A genealogy of a family in one of the lowest stations, given both in narrative and in the form of a pedigree, written so early as 1437, and reaching back a century farther, is a curiosity and a rarity. Such is the following copied from the earliest document the College possesses about Clifton Ferry. It is a small parchment, written on both sides by the same ancient hand; the pedigree is in roundlets. I have expanded some contractions.

Johannes Brouns senior, Hythewarde de Westwyttenham in comitatu Berk., habuit issu viz. duos filios Johannem et Ricardum, et quinque filias scilicet Matildam, Aliciam, Ysabellam, Rosam, et Cristinam. Johannes primogenitus hereditavit dictum Hythe et ipse obiit sine issu, et tunc descendebat Ricardo fratri suo jure hereditario; qui Ricardus habuit issu, viz. Johannem et Willelmum; et post obitum dicti Ricardi descendit Johanni filio suo, qui Johannes decessit sine issu; et postea descendit Willelmo fratri, qui Willelmus habuit unicum filium Johannem nuncupatum; qui Johannes obiit infra etatem et sine issu, et tunc descendit jure hereditario ad le issu predictarum duarum sororum viz. Alicie et Cristine, duabus sororibus predictarum quinque. Alicia fuit nupta cuidam J. nativo, et habuit

---

[1] Communicated by W. H. Black to Collectanea Topographica et Genealogica i 239 (1834). The Ferry was sold to Henry Hucks Gibbs Esqʳᵉ, who has built a bridge there; the College reserved a right for the parson to pass free of toll.

filiam Aliciam vocatam, que quidem Alicia filia fuit nupta Johanni
Frensh, et generit ex ea filium Thomam nominatum modo superstitem ;
et alia soror viz. Cristina desponsata fuit cuidam Johanni Stevenes,
qui genuit ex ea filium Johannem, de quo Johanne veniebat Emota
uxor Willelmi Seward. Et dictus Thomas Frensh, alias Kynge, et
Emota uxor Willelmi Seward, admissi fuerunt in plena curia pro
heredibus coram Johanne Hore ad tunc senescallo, hiis testibus
Ricardo Drayton armigero, Willelmo Borde, Johanne Stowe, et
Willelmo Felys, ibidem tunc presentibus. Hec docta et informata
fuerunt per Johannem Tubbe de Cliffton, etatis sexaginta annorum
et amplius, anno regni regis Henrici sexti post conquestum Anglie
xvi^mo.

Johannes Brouns de Westwitenham in com. Berks. Hytheward h'uit duos filios et
quinque filias legitime procreat. de corpore suo.

| Cristina filia d'ci Joh'is. Ista fuit uxorata cuidam Joh'i Stevenis, et h'uit ex eo filium Joh'em | Rosa moriebatur sine prole, vivente p're. Ysabella decessit sine sobole ante p'rem. | Alicia. Ista fuit nupta cuid' Joh'i North' nativo ex quo h'uit unu' filiu' et filia' Alicia' nativos. | Matilda defuncta est absq'e liberis p're superstite. | Joh'es. Iste hereditavit le hithe post morte' p'ris et decessit sine prole. un' Ric' fr' successit i' her'. | Ric'us h'uit duos filios legittimos vz. Joh'em et Will'm. |

| Joh'es filius Cristine qui h'uit filiam legittime procreat' viz. Emotam
Emota fil. Joh'is filii Cristine, adhuc superstes. | Henricus . . . Slypon iste h'uit filia' Matild'.
Will' fil' = Matris cognomento North. | Alic' filia d'ce Alicie soror Henrici nativi, Ista fuit nupta cuid' Jh'i Frensh, h'uit filiu' Thomam
Matill' fil' Henr' S. . . iste h'uit filiu' Will'm et filias duas | Thomas fil' Alic' et Joh'is Frenshe | Joh' filius Ric'i. Iste successit p'ri suo in her' et morieba'r abs. liberis, un' Will' fr' ejus successit in her'.
Joh'es fil' Joh'is. Iste morieba'r infra etatem et sic devolut' est duab' sororib' ; videl. Alic' et Cristine et hered' suis. | Will'm's fil' Ric'i. Iste Will'us h'uit filiu' Joh'em. |

This pedigree seems to have been designed to show that Thomas
Frenshe, *alias* Kynge, grandson of Alice the second daughter, and
(by failure of her brother's issue) co-heir of John Brouns, the hitheward or ferryman of Clifton, was one of the heirs-at-law to his
great-grandfather's estate. By what means he satisfied the other heirs
does not appear; but on Holyrood day 18 Henry VI (3 May 1440)
he conveyed, under the name of ' Thomas Kynge de Wittenam Abbatis,'

all his part of the 'hithe' and passage over the Thames at Clifton, with all chambers, houses, lands, meadows, pastures, ditches, waters, and fisheries, to Peter Shotesbroke Esq. of Newenham, John Shephard of Wittenham-Comitis clerk, and Thomas Haukyne of the same; one of the witnesses being John Tubbe, the old man from whose knowledge of the family the genealogy was drawn. These 3 persons re-infeoffed him and Joan his wife of the same estate, for their lives, and to the assigns of the said Thomas Kynge for ever, on Saturday in Easter week 19 Henry VI 1441. In 1483, 4 Nov. 22 Edward IV, Joan Goldry and John Frenshe alias John Kynge, of Redyng, (who seem to have been the widow and the son of Thomas Kynge) gave their half-part of the hithe to John Yonge of Watlyngton, his heirs and assigns; and on 30 Nov. the said J. F. alias J. K. released and quitclaimed to him, Sir W. Stoner being the chief witness to both deeds. John Yonge conveyed it to John Mercer clerk, William Buldry, and Roger Roper of Watlington, and to Roper's heirs and assigns, 12 Jan. 2 Ric. III (148⁴⁄₅); appointing, on 14 Jan., Chr. Swan bailiff of Abingdon, and John Gibon of Watlington, his attorneys, to give seisin; and on 31 Jan. he released the same with the same remainder. Eight years after, this Roger Roper 'draper' demised it to Ric. Panter rector of Exeter College, Will. Ford, Walter Kyngdone, John Philipe, Will. Brue, Will. Merifelde, John Frendshipe, Tho. Laurey, Walter Cowse, and John Hickys, clerks, Rich. Robertis, Walter Dudman, Will. Glovere, Tho. Tremayne, and Peter Druet *literatis*, and to their heirs for ever, Oxford 1 Aug. 8 Hen. VII 1493; and on 28 Nov. he quitclaimed to them 'then in full possession'; Tho. Larkyne, Robert and Reginald Curteys, and Roger Aleyne being witnesses to both deeds. This is the substance of the only (nine) ancient deeds relating to Clifton Ferry.

Merton was impropriated to the monastery of Ensham (form given in Kennett's *Parochial Antiquities* 481) temp. Edw. III and rated at 17 marks 10s, of which 10 marks were secured to the Vicar or Parochus. There is an Inspeximus of Richard II; and John, bishop of Lincoln, on 20 May 1380 confirmed an ordinance of Geoffrey abbot of Ensham, made 4 Aug. 1379, about payments to the parish. See Dugdale, Monasticon iii. In the Valor Ecclesiasticus of Henry VIII the Vicarage is stated to be worth £8 by perpetual composition. It was granted, with Kidlington, to Sir W. Petre, and by him to Exeter College, as 'rectory and church of Meryton with all lands glebes tithes oblations obventions profits &c.,' and stated to be part of the lands &c. granted to Cardinal Pole. We have a copy of the lease of the parsonage, made by Abbot Antony Dunstone to Richard Gunter, one of the Bailiffs of Oxford, on 21 Aug. 1530, for 99 years (beginning after a previous lease of 28 years granted to John Camby 23 Dec. 1514) at a rent of 40s, reserving £8 for the Vicar, and some other small payments, and Gunter was to have the right of cutting wood in the woods of Wood Eaton for housebote, ploughbote, hedgebote, and firebote.

The parish was enclosed under a private Act 1762 (3 George III, c. 34), and the Enclosure Act of 1763. On 17 Jan. 1763 the College petitioned the House of Commons against Sir Edward Turner's bill for enclosing the common field of Merton; on 23 Feb. the matter was referred to the award of Lords Harcourt, Talbot, Strange, and Sir R. Newdigate; on 16 Mch it was agreed to pay £250 to Sir E. Turner for surrendering his lease, which had still 3 years to run; on 9 Sep. it was agreed to exchange some land with Sir E. Turner under the Enclosure Act, and on 26 Sep. £162 11s 9d was paid him for timber, &c. Before the enclosure the Rectory appears to have consisted of old enclosures 137a. 3r. 14p., with a common field of 86 acres, total 223a. 3r. 14p., also the great and small tithes of about 654 acres, and certain rights of common pasture. An allotment was made of 168a. 2r. 35p. in lieu of tithes, common field, &c. This, added to 137a. 3r. 14p., makes 306a. 2r. 9p., valued in 1763 at £173 13s 9d, 1798 at £361 1s 7d, 1806 at £439 7s 6d, 1813 at £727 6s 2d, 1820 at £586 15s 3d. At first it was let on a fine system, and the fine on renewal in 1827 was £810.

Mete et bunde terrarum glebalium Rectorie de Meriton in comissione presentibus annexa mentionatarum capte et designate coram nobis Thoma Moyle Johanne Hawley armigeris et Jeronnimo Nashe generoso, sexto die Aprilis anno regni domini regis Jacobi Anglie &c. decimo, per sacramenta Willelmi Chapman, Edwardi Hopper, Edwardi Coxall, Willelmi Clare, Walteri Coxall alias Presson, Thome Hampson, Willelmi Derle alias Witham, Johannis Bull, Ricardi Jones, Johannis Spittle, Marci Bryan, Johannis Derle, Johannis Bowdon, Johannis Burnam, Johannis Borne, et Johannis Darling alias Brokes, virtute comissionis domini regis presentibus annexe, in presentia et ex assensu tam infranominati Jacobi Harrington militis quam Rectoris et diversorum Scholarium Collegii de Exon. infranominati.

In Claypill feild.

Imprimis, in the shorte stone furlonge eight Butts abbutting north-ward upon the Towne, and southward upon the hade land of the parsonage commonly called the long Land furlonge, and lying betwene the land of . . . Tame widowe on the west and Johane Cope widowe on the east.

Item one hade land in Long Landes furlonge abutting upon fower Leyes of the Parsonage on the west, and uppon a hade land of the widdowe Cope on the east, and lyeinge betwene an acre of the said widdowe Cope on the south, and crosseinge the ridges of the Shorte Stone upon the north.

Item foure shorte Leyes lyeinge togeather abuttinge upon dewes close on the west, and upon a hadelande of the Parsonage and one Lande of widdowe Copes, one other Lande of John Bull, and one other Lande of the Parsonage on the east, and lyeinge betwene the Lande of William Clare on the south, and the ridges of the Shorte Stone on the north.

Item foure Landes with hades and meeres in long Land furlonge shutinge on a hadeland of widdowe Cope eastward, and upon the widdowe Kinge and widdow Robins and William Clare, and a laye of the Parsonage on the west, and lyeinge betwene the lande of John Bull on the North, and a yeard of Henrie Kinge on the south.

Item the Parsonage Close in the west feilde conteyninge by estimacion tenne acres, abuttinge upon dewes close on the North, and upon the River on the South, and lyeinge betwene Claypitt feilde on the east, and Robert Paynes close on the west.

Item foure other landes with the meeres in Claypitt furlonge, abuttinge uppon a hadeland of Sir James Harrington some tymes called dewes on the north, and upon a hadeland of John Bowdon on the southe, and a lande of Robert Payne on the west, and a lande of Sir James Harringtons on the east.

Item in the Ray furlonge one acre butt, shutinge upon the Ray on the south and abuttinge upon a hade laye of widdow Cope on the north, and lyeinge betwene the landes of John Bull east and west.

Item in Beane furlonge twoe landes shutinge upon the Shorte Stone on the north, and upon a had waye on the south, and lyeinge betwene the landes of Mr George Danvers some tymes Withams on the east, and on the land of John Brokes on the west.

Item twoe other landes in Lambes earefurlonge abuttinge uppon beane furlonge on the north, and upon a had land of Edward Presson on the southe, and lyeinge betwene the lande of Mr George Danvers some tymes Wythams on the west, and William Crane on the east.

Item one lande in Lambe eare furlonge beinge the uttmost land towardes the east, abuttinge upon a butt of dewes on the north being of equal length with the other land of John Bull lyeinge next yt on the west.

Item one other lande adjoyninge to yt lyeinge in the shorte furlonge, shuteinge upon Burnams hadd land, beinge the utmost lande on the west.

Item one single lande in Raye furlonge, abuttinge uppon the River southward, and on Pressons had land on the north, and Richard Gurden on the west, and Joane Osborne on the East.

Item one Land in Gogmoye Leyes with halfe the mere on eyther side abuttinge uppon the hadd land of Robert Payne on the west, and upon a hadd of Greeneford parcell of dewes on the east, and lyeinge betwene the lande of John Brokes on the south, and one Carters on the northe.

Item seaven butts and one hade land in the Raye furlonge, the hadd land crossinge the butts on the north and abuttinge upon the River on the south, and lyeinge betwene the Landes of Robert Payne on the west and Alice Cope on the east.

Item one lande abuttinge upon Bornes foreshuter on the north, and on the Raye furlonge on the south, lyeinge betwene the Landes of Mr George Danvers on the west and John Burnam on the east.

Item twoe other landes in Hard land furlonge abuttinge upon the Hangle furlong on the north, and upon the Hill furlonge on the south, lyeinge betwene the Landes of Henrie Yale on the west and John Borne on the east.

Item a peece of meadow grounde at the hill called the Parsonage Hame with a hadd land adjoyninge hereunto on the north, and abbuttinge upon the River on the south and west, and shutenge upon the hadd lande of John Wytham on the east.

Item five landes in Hangle furlonge abuttinge upon Hardland on the south and one John Wythams haddeland and the Longe stone on the north, and lyeinge betwene the Landes of John Borne on the east and Kathern Kinge widdowe on the west.

Item foure Landes in the Longe stone furlonge, abuttinge uppon John Withames hadeland on the south, and upon the hedge towardes the towne on the north, and lyeinge betwene the landes of John Burnam on the west and Mathew Barett on the east.

Item twoe leyes lyeinge in Gogmoyre layes, the one a had ley, abuttinge upon a forshute of John Bull on the east, and a had lande of Robert Payne on the west, and lyeinge betwene the leyes of widdowe Robins and the ende of a leye of the Parsonage on the south and the Longe stone on the north.

Item the said ende of the Ley in Gogmoyre abuttinge upon the said foreshuter of John Bull on the east and the said Leaye of the widdow Robbins on the west, and the said Layes of the Parsonage on the north, conteyninge by estimacion sixe poles.

Item a lytle square of grounde in Gogmoyre lyeinge upon the ende of Robert Paynes hadeland on the south, and upon the Longe stone on the north and to the middle of the furrowe of John Bulls Ley on the west, and the lande of widdow Robbins on the east, conteyninge aboute sixe poles.

Item twoe other landes lyeinge in the Longe stone, abbuttinge upon parte of the said square on the south and the lane hedge on the north, and lyeinge betwene the land of John Brooke on the west and the land of widdowe Robins on the east.

In Ashley bridge feilde.

Item twoe landes in hadland furlonge abuttinge upon the Hangle on the north and upon Morgige furlonge on the south, and lyinge betwene the landes of John Bowdon on the west, and Thomas Gurden on the east.

Item foure butts with their hades and meares in long neck furlonge abuttinge upon the hadland of William Crane on the north, and the had of Thomas Gurden on the south, and lyeinge betwene the landes of John Bowdon on the east and widowe Cope on the west.

Item three whole eared acres lyeinge in Worgige furlonge abuttinge upon John Withams hadland on the south and Crabtree Leise on the north, and lyeinge betwene the landes of widdowe Kinge on the west and John Bull on the east, and Henrie Yates haremge one lande lyeinge betwene them.

Item twoe landes and a hadland in the reede, the hadland abuttinge upon long necke furlong on the west, and upon Lambcott furlonge on the east, and the twoe landes abuttinge upon the said hadland on the north, and upon Ashley Bridge butts on the south, and lyeinge betwene the landes of Sir James Harrington sometyme dewes on the west, and John Bull on the east.

Item two short ley butts lyeinge a niengest Ashley Bridge butts abuttinge upon dewes hame and leyes south and west and upon the lande of John Borne on the east beinge the uttmost butts towards the west.

Item twoe lands in short Lambcott furlonge, abuttinge upon long Lambcott on the north and the reede furlonge on the south, and lyeinge betwene the landes of John Borne on the east and John Bull on the west.

Item foure butts at Lappinge Ars furlonge, abuttinge on the old marshe on the north and upon Sturpitt Corner south and east and a parcell of meadow grounde conteyninge by estimacion twoe acres, and beinge compassed with the foure butts and Sturpitt ditch.

Sir John Maynard's letter to Prideaux about the lease of Merton,
1629.

Reverend Sir

I received your letters by Mr Tozer, with which he proffered me a fee from the Colledge, to which I must ever both in the behalfe of my selfe and my brother acknowledge that I am so much bounden as I could not accept therof, my poore abilitys being indetted for themselves to that House, and therfore I desire you to do me that favor as to suffer some small payment of my dett in acknowledging it. Touching the lease of Meriton parsonage, I was with Mr Tozer at Sir Edward Harrington's lodging, who very readily showed me his lease, of the making whereof being under the seale of the Abot of Enysham I thinke there is no doubt, but thereby I find the case to stand thus. The abbot and convent of Enesham in 6º H. 8 21 Decemb by indenture made a lease to one Camby for 28 yeares, then in 22º H. 8 the successor reciting that Camby had and did hold the said parsonage by demise for 28 years, he and the convent made a 2d lease to one Gunter to have and to hold for 99 yeares from thend of the said 28 years, for which 28 years the said Camby did hold the same, so that by the frame of the 2d lease it is implyed that the first lease was determined at the making of the 2nd; expired in tyme it could not be but determined by surrender or otherwise it might. But this if it were so can helpe you nothing, for then the case is this. A lease is made for xx years, tenne years expird, then the lessee surrenders, and the lessor reciting the old lease makes a new, to comence after the 20 years for which the first lessee did hold; this lease begins not till the 20 years expired, but it had bin otherwise if he had said to comence after the first lease, for in our law we distinguish inter Tempus annorum and Terminus annorum; the terme of years in our construction is the Interest which is in the lessee, and may determine within the tyme, but the tyme that cannot be . . . But I conseive that there may be some question on Sir Edward Harrington's [1] lease another way: for by his deed it appeareth that the lease for 28 years was made by such an Abot as at the same tyme was also Byshopp of Landaffe, and so he no Abot at that tyme, for if an Abot be made a Byshop the abby becomes void unlesse he have

for if a man make a lease to commence after another, and there was never any such, it comenceth forthwith.

a Comendam and Retinere, which must be lookt into. If it be otherwise, then the first lease was void in creation of yt, and then perchance the 2d lease will comence presently and then is now expired.

But this is but conjecture, because I know not whether there were a Comendam or no. You write that there is one lease inrolled, I pray send me a copy of yt and then I shall have more tyme to advise upon it, which now is no longer then the small space that I am in writing, and what I have out of Sir Edward's lease is but cursory, without the use of a penne but only my memory. My father remembers his service and love to you. As for my selfe I shall be very glad if I may expresse my selfe as I am

Your loving kinseman and
servant

London 4th of Dec. 1629. JOHN MAYNARD.

Postcr. I shal be able to give my selfe much more satisfaction if the coppy of that inrolled lease you write of were in my hands for an hower, and shall accordingly be able to give you further and more certaine satisfaction also. But for the inrolling or not inrolling of a lease, that makes no difference (as you write) for the inrolment is not a necessity of the conveyance, but security of the purchaser.

(outside) To the Right Worshipfull John Prideaux doctor of divinity Rector of Exon. Coll.

---

[1] Indenture 20 May 1635 between Rector Prideaux and Sir Edward Harrington: lease of rectory or parsonage of Merton for £120 down, for 10 years from the feast of the Annunciation last past, paying yearly rent of 33s 4d, one quarter of wheat, two quarters of malt. The Harringtons renewed the lease till beyond the middle of the 18th century.

Dr. Paynter in 1695 wrote to White Kennett, remonstrating on a passage reflecting on Exeter College in his 'Parochial Antiquities' p. 671; the following is an extract, 'You mention Long Wittenham as Sir William Petre's gift to Exeter College, but that appropriation belonged to it long before his time; neither did he give advowsons of Yarnton and Cudlington: there being no presentation institution or induction to the latter; and the former is in the gift of the Spencers, though we conceive the College wronged as to that matter' [but J. Patteson in 1820 gave an opinion against the College, thinking the V. of Yarnton was in gross, while that of Merton was appendant to the Rectory, see Reg. p. 333, 336]. 'Again you say, that none of late years have been presented to Merton, I believe you have given the true reason, viz, the poverty of the Vicarage. The College never refused any, willing to accept a presentation. In the mean time the College hath taken care of the place and added to the maintenance of the curate. The case is common to other Colleges as well as Exeter College; and the appropriation of the donor's will is now applied to other uses, which must be answered before better care can be taken to provide more largely for such cures. We have much exceeded the dues of the Vicarage in our allowance, I might add also the ability of the College.' White Kennett answers 13 July 1700 'I assure you that these reflexions were meant purely on the abuse of the thing and not upon your Body as authors or instruments of it, I am heartily sorry that I should be thought to cast any rash and unjust censure on so worthy a Society.' Subsequently the College gave considerable sums (Reg. 13 Ap. and 24 May 1796): £100 on 19 June 1817 to repair the Vicarage, £560 in 1827 for the same object; and in 1840 £1500 to augment the living (to meet £200 from Queen Anne's Bounty), with further temporary allowance to the Vicar and other smaller donations; and paid besides £157 17s 10d for extra work and the architect's fees; and in 1829 £30 was given towards a school; Reg. 19 Sep. 1730, 'M. Question electus ad curam ecclesiae de Meryton in annum sequentem, hac conditione, quod si officio suo hac in parte intra annum cedat, alius per Rectorem et Socios eligatur;' third Register p. 31 a. 1744, and 5 Oct. 1745.

Some of the parishioners of Merton were married in the College chapel, during the years 1741–50 (similar cases occur from Kidlington 1747–54; see Hist. of Kidlington 194).

1741 Sep. 5 Wm Smallbroke and Elizabeth Coles both of this Parish were married by Mr Hole in Exeter College Chappel.

1741 Oct. 4 William Powel and Ann Lipscombe both of this parish were married by Mr Webber.

Nov. 20 1742 Thomas Gurden of this parish & Anne Patchet of Fencot in yᵉ Parish of Charlton were married by Mr Bray in Exeter College Chappel.

Decʳ 27ᵗʰ 1743 Job Brown & May Wil . . . [torn edge] were married by Mr Fortescue in Exeter College Chapel.

April 21 1746 John Crips of Charlton & Catharine Coles of this parish were married by Mr Upton in Exeter College chappel.

Feb. 28 1746–7 Thomas Motley & Sarah Coles both of this parish were married in Exeter College Chappel by Mr Bray.

1747 Decemʳ 21ˢᵗ James Payne and Mary Young both of this Parish were married in Exeter College Chapel by Mr ~~Ramsay~~ [so corrected in reg.]. *Cosserat*

1748 June 29ᵗʰ Justinian Morse and Mary Bull both of this Parish were married in Exeter College Chappel by Mr Kennicott with License.

1748 Sepʳ 27ᵗʰ John Hattwell & Elizabeth Fr . . . [torn edge] both of this parish were married . . . Exeter College Chappel by Mr Kennicott.

Ocʳ 3ᵈ Edward Howlett & Mary Hall both of this parish were married in Exeter College Chappel by Mr Upton.

Novʳ 7ᵗʰ Thomas Cooper & Ann Lipscombe both of this parish were married in Exeter College Chappel by Mr Upton.

1750 Octob: 1ˢᵗ Jno Elford & Mary Preston both of this Parish were married in Exeter College Chapel by Mr Kennicott.

South Newington.

Reg. 13 June 1738, Peter du Bois M.A., Master of the school at New Woodstock, was el. V. of South Newington, Oxon, on a strong recommendation from the parishioners (Reg. 30 Sep. 1741 his widow); Andrew Wood the next Vicar, was instit. 3 and inducted 6 Aug. 1743 to R. of Headley in Surrey; James Williams, Fellow of Jesus, presented to succeed him 18 Oct. 1743, d. 11 Nov. 1802. For a list of the Vicars see 'History of Great Tew and South Newington' in the Transactions of the North Oxfordshire Archaeological Society 1875, printed 1877 by the University Printers. No Fellow took the living till John Cole 2 Ap. 1803. On 17 Oct. 1741 £10 or £12 was voted for measuring our manor of Little Tew, and having a map

z

made; this *Survey of Little Tew*, copied from an older map, gives the strips of each owner in the commonfields in the way described by Mr. Seebohm at Hitchin, and in the maps printed by Mr. Mowat, Oxford 1888; 28 June 1742,'constitutus est M. Ibbetson bursarius hujus Collegii qui, una cum seneschallo, Curiam Baron. intra manerium de Parva Tue teneat, nomine Rectoris et Scholarium, in qua Curia Eliz. Judge (quondam Ingram) sursum redditura est in manus dominorum manerii omne jus et titulum de et in uno messuagio virtute Rotulorum istius Curiae copiae'; 1 Oct. 1742 William Lord a tenant is appointed 'Viridarius' of the manor; 8 Jan. 1787 a gamekeeper. On the enclosure of the common at Little Tew, see 19 Nov. 1787, 14 Jan. 1788; an act was passed 1793 (Reg. 13 Mch 1793, 21 Ap. and 8 Oct. 1794); a manor court was held at Little Tew 17 May 1809, 13 June 1815, 19 June 1821, &c., the courts being held every three years. By the award under the Enclosure Act of 1794 the V. received land worth £10 a year, and the College was to pay him yearly £40. He now receives £78 from Queen Anne's Bounty, the Vicarage land of 13a. 1r. 30p. brings in £60 a year, and the Home field £10—the total from all sources is over £200. Originally, by old custom, the tenant of the Rectory had to pay the parish clerk 6s 8d, and to the parishioners yearly 12 bushels of mauslin corn or rye. On 27 May 1817 the College gave £200 and the materials of the rectorial house towards building a vicarage at South Newington, and on 29 June 1818 another £100 was given, and £40 a year added to the Vicar's stipend. For the lease of the estate allotted in lieu of tithes see Reg. 1819, p. 329; on 18 Dec. 1823 the Vicarage was augmented through an advance made by Mr. Hony, which the College repaid. In 1826 the College gave £1000 to augment the Vicarage, see Reg. 17 Nov. 1848. See Peshall Append. p. 16, Bodleian Charters p. 307.

APPENDIX.

COMPUTI RECTORIS.

THE Computi date from 1324. The first account is for a whole year, and probably implies 12 scholars and one vacancy[1]. The Academic year began on the morrow of S. Dionysius, i. e. October 10, but the Long Vacation usually extended from July 7 to October 18. Only 11 computi exist previously to 1354, 2 for complete years, 9 for single terms, and some are in a fragmentary state, so that sometimes the items slightly disagree with the total. Were the 17 years' computi 1337–54 destroyed in the riot of S. Scholastica's day 1355? Or is the Black Death responsible for this, and for 6 years and a term being missing between winter 1365 and summer 1372? The worst plague years were 1349, 1362, 1369–71, 1376. From the third outbreak Oxford suffered severely, and a similar cause may account for the year missing 1376–7[2]. Besides the terminal accounts, there was a final account for the whole year.

It is worth while inserting here, since it throws light on the rental

---

[1] The Latin of these and several other computi is printed in ed. i. p. 170.

[2] The missing terms are, for the latter half of the fourteenth century, winter 1355—summer 1356, summer 1357, summer and autumn 1360, winter 1362, winter 1364—summer 1365, Lent 1366—Lent 1372, winter 1372—winter 1373, autumn 1374, winter 1376—autumn 1377, winter 1381—autumn 1382, Lent and summer 1383, winter 1383—summer 1384, winter 1384—autumn 1385, summer and autumn 1386, winter 1387—Lent 1388, Lent 1389, Lent 1390, winter 1394—winter 1395, summer and autumn 1396, winter 1398—summer 1399, these dates being in all cases inclusive. From the winter of 1354 to the winter of 1399 therefore the computi of 107 terms are extant (besides the Library Computus of 1383) and 74 terms are missing. For the fifteenth century rather more than 70 terms are missing out of 400.

Arabic numerals begin to be used about 1374 (? the earliest date known, except two mentioned by Hunter, 'Archæol. Journal' vii. 84), and are often employed for purposes of distinction as in the computus of 1432; English words, such as 'strainer,' appear about 1365; see Rogers iv. 597, note in Hearne i. 370.

of the Halls, an account of the Inquiry at Oxford before Richard le Wayte, the King's Escheator[1], June 4, 1326; and the verdict of the jury that it will not be to the prejudice of the King to allow Walter bishop of Exeter to assign 5 messuages to the Rector and Scholars of Stapeldon Hall.

Copia inquisicionis capta Oxon' coram Escaetore domini Regis super ad quod dampnum impetratum per Episcopum Excestr', pro tenementis collegio suo in villa Oxon' appropriandis.

Inquisicio capta apud Oxon' coram Ricardo le Wayte, Escaetore domini Regis in comitatibus Suth', Wiltes', Berk', Bed', et Buk', iiii^{to} die Iunii A^o regni Regis E. f. Regis E. xix^o per breue domini Regis huic inquisicioni consutum, per sacramentum Iohannis de Gunwardeby, Henrici Ethrope, Willelmi de Wattele, Petri de E., Thome le irmonger, Galfridi de Shipton', Thome de Curtlyngton', Ricardi de Ethrope, Thome le maschen, Willelmi de Diere, Nicholai de Glatton', et Willelmi le Fourbour, qui dicunt super sacramentum suum quod non est ad dampnum nec preiudicium domini Regis nec aliorum si dominus Rex concesserit venerabili patri Waltero Episcopo quod possit assignare Rectori et Scolaribus domus de Stapuldon' v messuagia cum pert. in Oxon'. Dicunt eciam quod messuagium quod vocatur Scothall' reddet per ann. Pr. et Con. S. F. Oxon' et successoribus suis v*s* vi*d*. Item dicunt quod messuagium vocatum le Ledeneporche reddet per ann. Eccl. S. Michaelis vi*d*. Item dicunt quod predicta messuagia valeant per ann. secundum verum valorem c*s*. Item dicunt quod messuagium vocatum Bataylhall' reddet per ann. heredi de Stokewell' i*d*. In cuius rei, &c.

A later memorandum adds, Postea compertum est quod tenementa quondam Thome Bedford, Laurencii Wyth, et area vocata Wistle dimissa sunt Collegio de Excestrehall' per Philippum Littylmore, nichil inde reddendo, i. e. S. Frideswide's had given up the rent of 5*s* 6*d*.

COMPUTUS RECTORIS, 13 OCT. 1324—19 OCT. 1325.

Final account of Master Stephen de Pippecote, Rector of Stapeldonhalle, Oxford, given in to the Scholars of the House of Stapeldonhalle, from Saturday before the feast of S. Luke the Evangelist 1324 to Saturday after the feast of S. Luke, and he thus renders an account for 53 weeks.

---

[1] Cartulary of S. Frideswide (O. H. Soc.), no. 648.

	RECEIPTS.	£	s	d
Arrears from his account of last year		20	6	2¼
Rent of Hart Hall			60	
,, Ledeneporche			33	
(3s allowed out of 36s to the Principal, the Hall not being full)				
,, Bateylhalle			20	
(less than the full rent owing to the lack of scholars)				
,, Arturhalle (mostly unoccupied) . . .			18	2
From the Bishop, through *dominus* Gilbert de Keldis- hille		(22	15	6½)
,, ,, . . .		18 (10)		
,, ,, . . .			20	(½)
Total		69	2	11¼

	EXPENSES.	£	s	d
Commons for 53 weeks in 4 terms		25	15	10½
Payment for Fragon Hall			21	2
(5 marks still due to widow of William de Tauton who sold us the Hall)				
(? on repairs there)			77	5¾
On the Chapel and its tenements		(116)		7¼
On kitchen and stable of Ledeneporche, and repairs of all the out halls viz. Harthall, Arturhall, Scyldhall, Bateylhall		10	4	8
For timber (much still in store)		4	17	6¾
For slates [1], lime &c. (dearer in winter than summer) .			64	(10...)
Annual payments to Scholars		6	15	5½
Total		62		20½

He therefore owes the House £7 0 14¾. Memorandum that 15s 7½d of the annual payments were not allowed by the community, though paid by the Rector to *dominus* John de Nymeton chaplain, until the Bishop shall allow them.

COMPUTUS RECTORIS, 21 DEC. 1325—22 MCH 1326.

Account of Master John de Sovenayssh, Rector of the Scholars of Stapeldonhall, from Saturday the feast of S. Thomas the Apostle 1325 to Saturday after the feast of S. Cutbert in the same year.

[1] Slates cost from 4d to 7d a hundred and were used, instead of thatch, as a security against fire (Aula Tegulata); 1500 cost 10s autumn 1420; Wood's City i. 92, 189, 192, Peshall 172, Dict. Pol. Econ. i. 64.

RECEIPTS.		£	s	d
Arrears from his account, of last term		12	14	6½
From the Bishop, through Richard Pyn, 10 marks . .		6	13	4
From the Dean and Chapter (for Gwinear tithe) . .		11	6	8
17 marks, through Walter de Blaceheworthy bailiff of Bampton. The acquittance for £20 and 13 marks includes previous payments through Masters Richard de Bynescote and Walter de Lappeflod.				
Rent of Herthall . . .			24	
,, Ledeneporch . . .			14	6
,, Scothall (not received)			12	
,, Bataylhall (not received) .			?	
,, Schildhall (not received) .			10	8
,, Arturhall (mostly unoccupied) .			6	7
	Total	34	3	10½

EXPENSES.		£	s	d
Commons		6	9	7½
Expenses on Stapeldonhall .			20	1¾
,, Ledeneporch .			5	1¾
,, Schildhall .				14¼
,, Scothall .			5	4¾
,, Bataylhall .			2	5
	Total	8	3	11

He therefore owes the House £25 19 11½.

COMPUTUS RECTORIS, 22 MCH—12 JULY 1326.

Account of Master John Sovenassh, Rector of the Scholars of Stapeldonhall, from Saturday after the feast of S. Cuthbert the bishop 1325 to Saturday after the feast of Translation of S. Thomas the Martyr 1326.

RECEIPTS.		£	s	d
Arrears from his account of last term		25	19	11½
From the bailiff of Bampton 13 marks to complete the payment of £20 from the Dean and Chapter of Exeter .		8	13	4
From the Bishop, through *dominus* Gilbert de Kolshull 10 marks .		6	13	4
Rent of Harthall .			12	
,, Ledeneporch .			7	
,, Scothall . . .			6	
,, Bataylhall . . .			6	
,, Schildhall . .			5	4
,, Arturhall . .			3	3
	Total	43	6	2½

EXPENSES.	£	s	d
Commons	8	14	
In payment of Rents		8	6
On Stapeldonhall	25	1$\frac{3}{4}$	
Materials for a new building remaining in store	4	6	11$\frac{3}{4}$
On Herthall		7	11$\frac{1}{4}$
On Bataylhall		11	8$\frac{1}{2}$
On Ledeneporch, Arturhall, and Scothall		23	
On buying books		21	9
Total	16	17	11$\frac{1}{4}$

He therefore owes the House £26 8 3$\frac{1}{4}$, and asks for 8d to be allowed for two studies in Schildhall not occupiable in the summer term, and 6d for a study in Scothall not occupiable in the winter term, and 6d for a study in Ledeneporch not occupiable in Lent term, and 12d for a ruinous chamber in Bataylhall not occupiable in the summer term: total 2s 8d. If these are allowed, he owes £26 5 7$\frac{1}{4}$.

COMPUTUS RECTORIS, 20 DEC. 1326—11 AP. 1327.

Account of Master John de Kelly, Rector of the Scholars of Stapeldonhalle, for the second term of 1326, from Saturday the Eve of S. Thomas the Apostle to Saturday after the feast of S. Ambrose.

RECEIPTS.	£	s	d
Arrears from his account of last term	15	17	11
Rent of Ledeneporche		5	1
„ Bataylhalle		14	4
„ „ (again)		8	
„ Syldhalle		8	
„ Arthurhall, for Lent, as it was not occupied in the winter term		10	3$\frac{1}{2}$
„ Ledeneporche		7	
Borrowed from Chest of M. Ralph Germeyn [1] for Commons, &c.		36	
Total	20	6	7$\frac{1}{2}$

EXPENSES.	£	s	d
Commons	8	4	11
Repairs of the Houses, and 6s paid the agent of the Abbess of Godistouwe out of the rent due for Michaelmas term for 2 chambers opposite the Chapel		32	7$\frac{1}{4}$
Total	9	17	6$\frac{1}{4}$

He therefore owes the House £10 9 1$\frac{1}{4}$.

[1] instit. to Upton Pyne 3 Sep. 1283, collated to S. Ervan 13 Mch 128$\frac{4}{}$, preb. of Crediton 16 Jan. 128$\frac{9}{}$, archdeacon of Barnstaple till promoted to the Precentor-

LIBRARY BUILDING ACCOUNT, EASTER TO MICHAELMAS, 1383.

Account of Master William Slade, Rector of the College of Stapeldonhall, for the building of a Library.

RECEIPTS.		£	s	d
Arrears from last autumn term		25	5	8½
Gift from Thomas Bryntyngham, bishop of Exeter . .		10		
„ Master John More, rector of S. Petrock, Exeter		20		
	Total	55	5	8½

EXPENSES.	£	s	d
The carpenter for timber and his labour 14½ marks, his expenses 9d, gloves 6d	9	14	7
William the mason for stone from Teynton[1] 12 marks 7s	8	7	
a mason		2	
expenses on masons		2	6
stone bought at Watle	4	12	10½
expenses on Robert of Watle, from whom he bought the stone			12
carriage of stone from Watle		25	6
timber for scaffolding and carrying it . .		9	8
crates and carrying them		3	7
a labourer			8
a mason who was twice at Watle on business of the House			8
2 carpenters for 1 day			12
a cord			2
vessels for carrying cement .			9
nails			3
cheese for labourers			2
withies for the scaffolding . . .			1
Expenses of the Rector thrice at Watle . . .			7
carriage of stone from Teynton	7	0	10
a mason at Watle for a week 3s, another for 3½ days 21d, another for 4 days 2s, another for 2½ days 15d, another for a week at Watle and here 3s 3d, another here for a week 3s		14	3

ship of Exeter 28 Mch 1308 in succession to Stapeldon, d. 3 Dec. 1316. A commission occurs, in Stapeldon's Reg. 7 Feb. 131⅘ to Ralph Germeyn precentor of Exeter and John de Stok, R. of S. Melan. See Bronescombe's Reg. p. 347 for Lawhitton; Oliver's Bishops 50, Eccl. Ant. ii. 209, Hearne ii. 161, R. I. C. 1879 p. 246, Stapeldon's Reg. 164, 188, 210. He founded a Chest of £10 for making loans to poor scholars. See pp. xxxv, 45.

[1] Taynton, near Burford, Oxon; Rogers i. 258, iv. 700 earriage of stone from Teynton to Burford 3 miles, from Burford to Oxford 22½ miles, 1d a load per mile. Whatley is near Frome, Aldermaston is in Berks 8 miles E. of Newbury. Bricks only became common towards the end of the 15th century, iv. 434.

£ s d

First week after Easter; a mason's work 3s 4d, 2 others
6s, their servant 18d; David's commons 5d, and his
labour 8d[1] 11 11

Second; masons 9s 4d, their servant 18d, David's commons and labour 13½d 11 11½

Third; masons 9s 4d, their servant 18d, David's commons
and labour 10½d 11 8½

Fourth; masons 9s 4d, David's commons and labour 10½d 10 2½

Fifth; 2 masons 6s 4d, another 4½ days 2s 3d David's
commons 6d 9 1

Sixth; masons 3s 4d, David's commons 5½d . . . 3 9½

Seventh; masons 20d, David's commons 6d . . 2 2

Eighth; masons 2s 10d, David's commons 6d . . 3 4

Ninth; masons 3s 4d, David's commons 5½d . . 3 9½

Tenth; masons 3s 4d, David's commons 5½d, a mason for
one day 6d 4 3½

week before Michaelmas; masons 3s 4d . . . 3 4

next week; 2 masons for one day 12d, dinner to masons
on the last day 8½d, breakfasts (merendae) of masons,
and dinner and drink to those who carried stone, crates,
and timber 11s . . . .

Expenses of the Rector and one fellow riding to Alder-
meston for timber 17d, and for a horse hired 6d . . 1 11

Plumber for lead, and for covering the Library £13 13 4,
expenses on the plumber 22½d 13 15 2½

lime for the Library 3 4 5

red earth 2 6

wood for the lead (lignis ad lignandum plumbum) . . 12

expenses on the plumber for a week . . . 3 10½

iron fastenings (fermentis) 45 1

nails 3 11½

a mason for two days 12

hay 4

labour in repairing and whitewashing the Library . 6

breakfast (merenda) for the whitewashers . . . 7

mending a sieve (cribrum) 1

drink of the smiths (fabri) 4

Total 57 13 5½

The House therefore owes him 47s 9d.

Account of John Prideaux, Rector, from the morrow of All Saints
1638 to the same day 1639.

RECEIPTS. £ s d

In the chest, from last year, and from the legacy of Andrew
Scutt 232 8 4

[1] David was the foreman, there was no architect: so at Wadham in 1610,
Clark's Colleges of Oxford 391.

	£	s	d
a year's rent from our rectory of Guyniar, to last Michaelmas	60		
from our rectory of Long Wittenham	61	7	9
three quarters of the corntithe of our rectory of Minhinnet	20		
from our rectory of South Newington	58		
from our rectory of Kidlington	20		
from our rectory of Yarnton	10		
from our rectory of Meriton	6	4	8
from our close of Chasehill [in Hanborrowe]	13	6	8
yearly payment from our manor of Thrupp	5		
from our Vicarage of Kidlington	4		
rent of our manor of Little Tew, to Michaelmas	13	1	3
rent of 2 mills in Kidlington	10	2	3
rent of our tenement in Bampton	1		
rent of our tenement in Montacute			
rent of our tenement in Catstreet	1	8	
rent of our tenement in S. Martin's parish	1	13	
for Hart Hall	1	13	4
from our tenement of Leddenhall		2	
for 2 gardens, now demolished, between the North part of the College and the City walls		2	
for a tenement in S. Mary Magdalene	1	3	4
our tenement in Garsington	10	1	2
our tenement in Tingtenhull	4	7	9
a cottage there		10	10
tenement of Clifton-ferry	2	11	4
tenement at Bensington	3	18	10
for the Tower near the Chapel		2	
pro agello propter Collegium			6
our tenement in South Newington	1	10	10
our publichouse in S. Giles'	8	7	10
for house of John Robinson (from Luke Eaton)	2		
our tenements in the town ditch			
three cubicles of the Rector (belong to the Rector)			
lower cubicle near the front gate (belongs to the Rector)			
cubicle attiguo ad orientem (the Bursary)			
cubicles and studies (*musaeis*) prox. ad orient. (Le Barne Chambers)	1	6	8
lower cubicle in same place	3		
middle cubicle under the new Library	1		
last cubicle in same place	2		
first study at top of upper cockloft (*coclei*) in Bentley's Buildings	1		
second study		15	
fifth cubicle, with three studies	2		
sixth study		17	6
seventh study	1		
eighth study		17	6
ninth study	1		

	£	s	d
tenth study		15	
eleventh study	1		
twelfth study	1		
study A. in place of the old Library	1		
study B. there	1		
study K. there	1		
first cubicle under the old Library	3		
second cubicle	4		
cubicle and two studies in Pyriam's Building's, on the left as you go up	1		
second cubicle and two studies	4	10	
third cubicle and two studies	5	10	
fourth cubicle and two studies	2		
fifth cubicle and two studies	4		
sixth cubicle and two studies	4	10	
seventh cubicle and two studies	5		
study at top of stairs (*scalae*)	1		
cubicle A. over back gate in Chambers' Buildings	1	10	
cubicle B.	1	10	
cubicle C.	1	10	
cubicle D.	1	10	
cubicle E.	1		
cubicle F.	1		
cubicle G.	1		
received after the division of the rent of the farmer (*frumentarii*) of Kidlington for three quarters of a year	26	17	11¼
for the fourth quarter	9	14	6¾
Bursar's receipt for coals (*carbonibus*, i.e. charcoal)	35	2	
for admission of *Magister* Jesse	4		
for admission of *dominus* Parker	4		
for admission of Northcote	4		
pro Nota domus	1	4	11
Arrears, from widow Brunt for Thruppe	5		
Cullins for Montacute		5	
James Collins for Clifton Ferry	2	10	6
M. Denis Prideaux	26		
M. King for cubicle	14	5	
Summa	751	5	5½

PAYMENTS.

£ s. d.

Stipend and clothes, at £2 13 4 each, to the Rector, M. Maynard subrector, M. Tozer, M. Procter, M. Carpenter, M. Terry, M. Willet, M. Ackland, M. Squire, M. Dennys, M. Kendall, M. Conant, M. Goddard, M. Snow, M. Hackwell, M. Prideaux, M. Newte, M. Cotton, domino Fortescue, domino Polwheele : and at 13s 4d to M. Hall, M. Beard : £1 6 8 domino Hall. M. Jesse, domino Porter, Northcote *nil*   56

	£	s	d
M. Maynard subrectori, M. Kendall decano, M. Prideaux lectori, domino Porter subdecano	6		
Bursars for fellows' commons and decrements, pro Nota domus, for Bursars' stipends: first term . . .	26	9	2¼
second term . . .	42	2	8½
third term . . .	31	13	1½
fourth term . . .	36	2	11¼
Vicar of South Newington, stipend	12		
quit rent to Christ Church			4
payment to All Souls	4	12	4
quit rent to S. John's, for tenement at Clifton Ferry .		8	2
to Bailiol, chief rent for part of our garden near the Theology School		12	6
the City for our tenement in S. Magdalene . . .		1	8
for a parcel of land before the front gate . . .	1		
for tenements lately bought from Withers . . .	1		
the City for tenement of David Walters, and privies, and aqueduct through the City ditch		11	
tenement once belonging to Henry Carter . . .		6	8
M. Paynton for answering in the Hoystings Court . .		1	8
quit rent to John Bigger, due to the King . . .		6	4
quit rent to John Bigger, due from Godstow . . .		12	8
procurations for Kidlington and South Newington . .	1	4	4
procurations for Long Wittenham	1	3	4½
Cook, porter, gardiner, barber, library-keeper, tiler, washerwoman	8		
mariscallis mendicorum pro stipendio			
synodals for Kidlington and South Newington . . .		4	
mason (caementario), carpenter, workmen, glazier, blacksmith, plummer, tiler, payments about kitchen, tinner (stannario), coalman (carbonario), various expenses	300	13	2
dividends from Long Witnam	39	18	9½
dividends from rectory of Guyniar . . .	24		
	595	4	11½

	£	s	d
Receipts	751	5	5½
Payments	595	4	11½
Cash in the Common Chest	156	0	6

Jo. Prideaux Rector
Josephus Maynard Subrector
Henricus Tozer
Johannes Procter
Edwardus Carpenter
Rob. Snow

EXTRACTS FROM THE REGISTER.

'23 Oct. 1566, the Fellows being summoned to the Chapel, John Chardon on the completion of his year of probation was accused by many of many wrong acts and those not light ones, which he confessed and asked pardon for with many tears as having been lead away by others and especially a Frenchman M. Harcot a seditious man whose blandishments, counsels, threats and instigation had acted like an enchantment on his tender years. On this his admission was put off till the next day, when the Rector and majority of the Fellows admitted him, having good hope of amendment in his future life, especially as the Frenchman had been deservedly expelled.'

3 Sep. 1594 'decretum ut quicunque inter prandendum vel caenandum aliquem, absentem, publico huius regni iure non convictum, detrectaverit, a mensa statim ipso facto (vel cum ignominia) removeatur;' 30 Oct. 'quod omnes scholares suscepturi gradum bachalauriatus solvant decano, vel ei saltem plenarie satisfaciant, priusquam presententur, sin vero decanus propter nimiam suam incuriam et negligentiam tunc non acceperit, nihilominus eam pecuniam Collegio solvere tenetur;' 2 Nov. 'ut quicunque commensalis aut batelarius rus esset profecturus illud Rectori vel subrectori vel Bursariis indicet, ut communarum ratio habeatur;' 'ut unusquisque commensalis vel batelarius ad gradum bachalauriatus vel magisterii promotus, vel eundem quem habuit, vel alterum fideiussorem producat e sociis, ut ratio etiam communarum habeatur;' 29 Nov. 'quod tam battalarii quam socii et commensales habeant in unoquoque ferculo tempore caenae (exceptis diebus pisculentis) cibum qui constat sex denariis.'

23 July 1621 'decretum erat ut Guilielmus Hardinge Collegii nostri coquus primarius qui hactenus pro ligno carbonibus et aliis expensis minutioribus viginti tres libras et octo solidos annuatim recipere consueverat, haberet iam a nobis stipendium illud suum tribus libris quinque solidis et quatuor denariis auctius, adeoque a Bursariis nostris quadraginta marcas seu 26*l* 13*s* 4*d* posthac quotannis acciperet: Ea lege et conditione ut post idoneum semel a Collegio paratum patinarum numerum ille postea sumptibus propriis omne genus patinas nobis suppeditaret, veteres confractas seu imminutas reficeret, novasque quoties opus esset, sine aliquo Collegii damno aut sumptu, in eorum

locum perpetuo substitueret. Eodem tempore visum est decernere ut David Waters latrinarum purgator et janitoris vicem in Collegio implens quolibet prandii ac cenae tempore portam posticam seu occidentalem observaret, Boreali vero etiam clausae iisdem temporibus semper adstaret venientesque intromitteret vel excluderet, eoque nomine stipendii loco quadrantem a quolibet in Collegio commorante cujuscumque ordinis aut conditionis, etiam pauperibus scholaribus, hebdomadatim acciperet.'

27 Sep. 'decretum erat ut Bibliorum lector tempore disputationum presertim bacchalaureorum in aula habendarum scamna apte disponeret, et idoneum candelarum numerum suo semper sumptu parari curaret; stipendiique loco a quolibet commensali sociorum mensae adscripto, necnon suggenario, obolum; a quolibet autem battellario quadrantem, hebdomadatim acciperet.'

1 Oct. 'decretum erat ut (quia scholarium Juniorum cubicula habitationi minus apta censebantur) tria inferiora cubicula in infima stega aedificii Bentleiani cederent posthac in usum perpetuum sociorum hujus Collegii: tria autem alia cubicula quae ad hunc usque diem a sociis incolebantur commensalibus dehinc locarentur eorumque reditus in usum aerarii nostri converterentur.'

Nov. 1661 'decretum est magistros commensales aeque ac scholares perpetuos in posterum teneri ad disputationes in sacra theologia obeundas et sub eadem paena,' 11 Aug. 1663 'decretum est ut baccalaurei omnes qui ante vices suas disputandi intra quatuordecim dies praesentes in Academia fuerint teneantur vices istas praestare vel per seipsos vel alios baccalaureos.'

12 Dec. 1684 'decretum est ad utilitatem Bibliothecae in usum juniorum institutae, quod quilibet socio-commensalis solvet decem solidos, suggenarius 7s 6d, battelarius 5s, pauper scholaris 2s 6d, a Bursario recipiendos, in usum Bibliothecae impendendos ex arbitrio Sub-rectoris et Decani.'

20 Feb. 171⁸⁄₉ 'Agreed that every determining batchiler pay in lew of the accustomed breakfast in the Hall on Egg Saturday and the Stipulators dinner the same day and in lew of the Aristotle supper Ash Wednesday night to the Dean of the College the sum of fourty shillings to be disposed of in the manner following: to the House for the Library £1 1s 6d, to the Dean for treating his assistants Ash Wednesday 10s, to the Aristotle 5s, to the Stipulators 3s 6d.'

3 Ap. 1733 'Cum exercitia hujus Collegii ordinaria nimis hactenus neglecta fuerint, unde jacent literarum studia bonarumque artium

doctrina minus promovetur; cujus rei in causa sunt partim stipendia Officiariorum admodum exilia nec pro ratione conditionis illorum, vel laboris constituta; partim autem statutorum defectus et inopia prae-scriptorum, quorum ad normam exigantur Officiariorum labores, diriganturque praedicta exercitia; Nos Rector et Scholares Collegii Exoniensis in Universitate Oxoniensi in sacellum nostri Collegii solenniter convocati, re prius mature deliberata, et perlectis diligenter statutis perpensisque, ex unanimi nostro assensu et consensu, pro nobis et quantum in nobis est pro successoribus nostris Statuimus et sancimus Regulas et Ordinationes sequentes posthac observandas.

Primum statuimus et ordinamus quod nullum munus vel officium alicui scholari absenti, nec in Collegio personaliter residere in animo habenti, quo munus suum recte obire possit, quacunque de causa concedatur. Si vero contigerit quod scholaris in aliquod officium electus et ordinatus, idemque virtute juramenti Collegio olim in admissione sua praestiti capessens, fato vel aliter e sodalitio cedat, vel ob valetudinem suam minus firmam aliamve quamcumque causam juxta formam statutorum approbandam a dicto Collegio in tempus aliquod discedere cogatur, vel quovis alio modo minime aptus et idoneus ab Rectore, sive eo absente Subrectore et scholarium quorum interest Officiarium praedictum eligere, vel a majore parte eorundem inveniatur, ordinamus et statuimus quod praedicti Rector et Socii alium aliquem scholarem idoneum intra septem dies constituant, qui prioris munus gerat et mercedem accipiat, omne id tempus quo prius ille electus deerit officio suo.

Praeterea statuimus et ordinamus quod nullus scholaris (exceptis Subrectore et Theologiae Praelectore, uti infra pluribus exponetur) in officia duo vel plura eligatur; modo scholares ad munera singuli singula capessenda domi existentes inveniantur. Sin aliter per-mittimus et concedimus uni alicui scholari idoneo duo munera simul gerenda. Proviso tamen quod Officiarius ille cui minus incumbat laboris, quique minorem prioris sui muneris fructum speret, modo sit muneris istius secundi capax et ad id fungendum idoneus, Officiario alteri plus operae debenti plusque mercedis speranti anteponatur, adeo ut exinde labores et conditiones Officiariorum quantum potest inter se pares fiant.

Quoniam vero stipendium Subrectoris conditioni et loco ejus minus sit accommodatum, onus autem Hebraici Praelectoris satis leve; ordinamus et statuimus quod haec duo munera conjungantur; quodque praedictus Subrector virtute muneris Hebraici Praelectoris singulis anni terminis tres praelectiones portionem aliquam Veteris Testamenti ex natura Hebraicae linguae explicantes (ita tamen ut ne plures unâ in eadem septimana sint habendae) die martis tempore pomeridiano legere teneatur. Nihilominus si posthac contigerit Subrectorem non satis idoneum officio Hebraici Praelectoris eligi teneantur electores alium scholarem, modo reperiatur idoneus, huic muneri praeficere.

Quoniam autem Catechista stipendii nomine tantum viginti solidos annuatim habeat, nec ulla alia emolumenta percipiat; et cum officii sit in Christianae religionis elementis juventutem instituere, quod ad munus Theologiae Praelectoris merito attinere judicamus, nos ea consideratione moti haec duo munera semper esse connectenda volumus et sancimus. Ac insuper statuimus quod Theologiae Praelectori, singulis S. Michaelis et S. Hilarii terminis septem, Paschatis termino quatuor, et Trinitatis termino tres, praelectiones (quarum alternis saltem annis undecim continuas volumus esse Catecheticas) de argumentis theologicis vel de aliqua portione Novi Testamenti in diversis septimanis singulae praelectiones die jovis tempore antemeridiano sint legendae.

Praeterea volumus et ordinamus quod Dialectices, Philosophiae et Rhetorices Praelectores locis et temporibus per statuta constitutis sedulo praelegant vel a juventute ad audiendum destinata sedulo legi faciant eique exponant nempe Dialectices Praelector librum aliquem Aristotelis vel Porphyrii Dialecticam vel Georgii Diaconi Epitomen; Philosophiae Moderator librum aliquem Aristotelis Ethicum, Œconomicum vel Politicum, sed ut librum aliquem Physicum a recentioribus conscriptum alternis paribusque numero vicibus; Rhetorices autem Praelector Rhetoricen vel Poeticen Aristotelis, aliumve librum Rhetorum Graecorum Ciceronis vel Quintiliani rhetoricam artem tractantem; nisi magna sit Vacatio, qua durante alia argumenta tractari volunt statuta. Repetitiones quoque earundem praelectionum sexta quaque vice ab auditoribus exigant Praelectores praedicti.

Insuper etiam volumus et ordinamus quod singuli Praelectores videlicet Dialectices Philosophiae et Rhetorices librum aliquem cum consensu Rectoris et quinque scholarium maxime seniorum, vel majoris partis eorundem (quem quidem consensum in singulis necessarium decernimus) praelegere et explicare aggredientes eidem continuo insistant et ad finem usque perducant, priusquam eis vel eorum successoribus alium librum legere et explicare liceat. Cum vero qui ad auditionem destinati praelectionibus absint, vel praesentes minus decore et negligentius se gerant, ex antiquo more plecti pecuniaria mulcta soleant; quae poena patribus et cognatis ipsorum plus damni quam ipsis commodi inferre videtur; nos igitur juventutis ipsius bono consulentes et sumptus academicae disciplinae minuere pro viribus cupientes volumus et ordinamus quod in posterum penso aliquo literario, quale Rectori et Officiario visum fuerit, plectantur delinquentes; pecuniaria mulcta nunquam aut perraro irroganda. Hoc autem pensum ordinarie Dialectices, Philosophiae vel Rhetorices praelectionis quam neglexerint versionem esse ordinamus.

Insuper autem quo diligentius incumbant muneribus suis Officiarii atque operam majorem bonis literis et artibus promovendis navent, volumus et ordinamus quod omnes et singuli scholares commensales et battellarii, singulis anni quartis pro spatio quadriennii ab eorum admissione proxime numerandi, nisi forte intra id tempus a Collegio penitus recedant quinque solidos Officiariorum omnium mercedis causa solvant; ex qua pecunia Sub-rector Decanus et Philosophiae moderator decem denarios singuli accipiant, Rhetorices Praelector unum solidum et denarios duos, Dialectices autem Praelector unum solidum et denarios quatuor. Omnes vero bacchalaurei in Collegio residentes sive scholares sint sive alii et scholares non graduati quadriennio in Academia completo, singulis anni quartis Decano soli conferant duos solidos et sex denarios, remunerandi gratia laboris a Decano exercitationibus eorum impensi.

Quoniam autem jus designandi amovendique famulos dicti Collegii, arbitriumque omnium eorum ex statutis Rectoribus sit permissum, unde gravissima incommoda aliquando oriri possunt et jam olim orta fuerunt, quia nonnulli Rectores, reverendum virum Johannem Conybeare S. T. P. antecedentes, quem jure et honoris causa nominatim excipimus, contra leges hujus inclyti regni et piam fundatorum nostrorum voluntatem pecunia se suosve ambiri et corrumpi permittentes, famulos minus idoneos aut designarunt aut designatos continuarunt, nec postea delinquentes vel etiam manifesto scelere deprehensos punire commode et secure potuerunt: Nos, huic incommodo vel potius crimini remedium sedulo quaerentes, ultro et sponte sua proponente consentiente et instante ipso Rectore, volumus et ordinamus quod in omne posterum tempus Coqui Promi et Tonsores sive superiores sint sive inferiores, cum consensu Rectoris suffragium duplex habentis et septem scholarium ex domi existentibus maxime seniorum, vel majoris partis eorundem designentur. Per Rectorem vero solum peccantes vel minus idonei inventi amoveantur, nunquam in eundem aliumve Collegii locum quacunque de causa nominandi.

A a

Si tamen scholaris aliquis amotionem cujuscumque famulorum prae-
dictorum minus idonei aut providi justa de causa petierit, teneatur
Rector, modo in Collegio exstiterit et commode id facere potuerit,
intra triduum septem scholares praedictos in convenientem locum
cogere atque famulum delatum una cum delatore vel delatoribus
appellare ibique postulationi vacare. Et si causae sententia prac-
dictorum Rectoris et Scholarium vel majoris partis eorundem satis
probatae fuerint, tum volumus et ordinamus quod una alteraque
admonitione praemissa, praedicti Rector et socii famulum sic tertio
postulatum penitus amovere, aliumque idoneum mora quam minima
subrogare hoc scito in perpetuum astringantur.

7 May 1737 'Orta fuit contentio inter dominum Byrdall et
baccalaureos tunc temporis in Academia presentes, utrum dominus
Byrdall vices suas disputandi praestare teneretur, qui ad Collegium
rediit inter quatuor horas ante quaestiones traditas in proximis Disputationibus discutiendas. Delata est querela domino Rectori, qui
Decreto considerato et perpenso determinavit dictum dominum
Byrdall ex litera non vero proposito seu intentione istius Decreti vices
suas praestare teneri. Quoniam vero compertum est literam potius
quam propositum antehac observari, dominus Rector isti consuetudini
obediens quod pro hac vice etiam consuetudo observetur determinavit, Volens tamen quod in posterum nemo baccalaureorum ad
Collegium e rure regressus vices disputandi praestare tenebitur, nisi
qui per biduum saltem ante Quaestiones traditas in Collegio vel Academia praesens fuerit; N. B. Quaestiones sunt tradendae baccalaureis
proxime disputaturis immediate post priores peractas Disputationes.'

7 July 1739 at a meeting of the Rector and five Seniors, 'Whereas
by the intent of our Founders it appears that public lectures and
disputations should be kept up according to the form of our statutes,
and whereas by certain orders and rules enacted in the year 1733 an
augmentation of the salaries of the several officers was made in order
to encourage them to do their respective duties, and yet notwithstanding there appears to have been great neglect in the officers, sometimes by not attending at all, at others by staying up so small a time
as to render the exercise of little or no consequence, and whereas
the authority of the Rector and five Seniors hath been very much
slighted by the officers not consulting them, as the statutes direct,
what books shall be read in their several lectures; wherefore to
remedy these evils for the future, the Rector and five Seniors have
thought fit to order and it is hereby ordered—

1. That every Lecturer shall read such books only as shall be appointed by the Rector and five Seniors, excepting only the Subdean who is more properly under the sole direction of the Rector.

2. That during every long vacation the Lecturer in the classicks shall read (as the statutes require and as former Lecturers always did) either arithmetick or geometry, or the rudiments of cosmography at least four days in every week, unless such days are festivals.

3. That every Lecturer shall continue his lecture for the major part of an hour at least, that he shall require repetitions of the said lectures from his respective auditors at least every fifth lecture, and shall exact from those, who either absent themselves, or when present behave indecently or carelessly, translations of such lectures or parts of such books as shall be then explained, of which they shall provide two copies, one of which to be given to the Rector, the other to the proper officer.

4. That every person neglecting the ordinary disputations of the College shall be obliged to bring in *states* on the question or questions then disputed on and that all such disputations shall be continued for the major part of an hour at least, unless for the ease of young beginners the Subdean shall judge it proper (which should be but rarely done) to shorten the morning disputations in the Hall.

5. It is desired that the Rector, according to his oath, would be careful in exacting such mulcts or punishments from the respective Officers as the statutes require, and that no excuse may be admitted in bar of such punishments, allowing only in case of sickness an appearance by deputy to be approved of, by the Rector in case of the Subdean, by the Rector and five seniors in the case of the other officers.

6. That the Subdean shall be liable to the same penalties with the other Officers for neglect of duty, or for refusing to demand the punishment to be inflicted on those who shall not attend his exercise according to what is above required from the Lecturer and Moderator.

7. That the lecturer in the Greek Testament shall exact from all persons who do not attend, Translations or Collections from such commentators as he shall think it proper to advise them to consult and read upon those lectures.

8. That all persons neglecting to declame in their proper turns shall give up such declamations within three days at least, and to take the next turn of declaming.

9. That all other exercises of the College shall be kept up according to the true intent and meaning of the statutes, and that particularly the Hebrew and Divinity lectures, as they are called, shall be read according to the directions and penalties mentioned in the Injunctions of Lancelot Lord Bishop of Exeter, and the times settled in the Acts of 1733.

Lastly it is ordered these Acts of the Rector and five Seniors shall be entered in the College Register and signed by the persons making them, that copies of them be given to the respective Officers, and that they be strictly conformed to by all persons concerned.'

Reg. 24 July 1741 (on W. Tonkin being chosen to assist the Dean in Logic Lectures &c.) 'in hac re agenda electio facta est contra sententiam domini Rectoris, qui sentiebat se teneri aliquem ex baccalaureis nominare et eligere, et post maturam deliberationem dominus Rector nominavit et elegit M. Tonkin, et publice declaravit se in posterum baccalaureos solos in hoc officium nominare statuisse'; but on 30 June 1742 Tonkin was re-elected, there being no bachelor available.   It was found difficult to get the Fellows to reside.

30 June 1747 'decretum quod Praelector Theologiae, singulis diebus Martis Jovis et Saturni intra terminum, nisi festus dies inciderit, aliquam portionem Novi Testamenti ad scopum et literam textus originalis perlegat explicet et exponat hora nona matutina.   Auditores sunto omnes non Graduati post biennium ab adventu ad Academiam, ad tempus quo admitti possunt ad gradum A.B.'; see Reg. 30 June 1749 on renewing the theological Disputations ordered by the statutes for Regent Masters; 7 Aug. they were to be held in the Chapel every week in full term (except in Lent), between 1 and 3 o'clock; 9 July 1753 on keeping up Bachelors' Disputations in the order of Seniority.

Owing to the change in the value of money, it was resolved 17 Mch 174$\frac{7}{8}$ that the Caution money should be increased, those admitted to the Fellows' table were to pay £9, to the sojourners' table £8, to the battellers' table £7 ; it was further resolved that money due to the College must be paid before the end of Term ; on 28 Jan. 1758 it was ordered that the names of those who did not pay should be crossed in the Buttery Books on Crossing Day, 'and that after such crosses shall be affixed to their names they shall not be permitted to battel till all their former battels are discharged,' &c.

DATE-LIST OF BUILDINGS AND IMPROVEMENTS.

The authorities for the dates are given, in italics, just after the figures, in this form:—*ch.* Chalmers, *gu.* Wood as edited by Gutch, *ms.* Prideaux's manuscript survey, *re.* the College register; and the names of architects are placed at the end of the line, also in italics. Letters in square brackets refer to diagrams on pp. 360–1.

1312. Hert Hall bought by Walter de Stapeldon.

1315. Stapeldon Hall, afterwards Exeter College, founded (on site of S. Stephen's Hall); p. 366.

1316. Godstow tenement acquired; pp. ix, xvi.

1319. Agreement between the Rector and the vicar of S. Mildred's, about a chapel.

1320. Bataile Hall bought.

1321–6. The Chapel built [X]; licence from the Bp. of Lincoln, 1326, to consecrate the high altar.

1323. Fragnon Hall bought, p. 293.

1325. Sheld Hall bought.

1328. Scot Hall bought.

1333. Two Schools given by W. Dobbe, pp. lii, 294.

1335. Bedford Hall bought.

1353. Culverd Hall bought.

1358. Castel Hall bought.

1375 *re.* In Autumn, 'Straw . . . and for covering the library,' pp. xlvii, liv; was this first library attached to the chapel?

1380. Hambury Hall bought.

1383 *re.* Chapel with rooms below it rebuilt or modified [X. X]; and Library built.

*c*1404 *gu.* An entrance obtained toward the Turl [A], and porch built west of the Library (Bp. Stafford).

1406. Checker Hall bought.

1427. S. Hugh's or Baliole Hall sold to the University for the Divinity School.

1432 *gu. re.* College tower and gateway erected at the North [F].

1432 *re.* Chapel lengthened (Mr. Palmer).

1470. Peter Hall bought.

1483 *re.* Kitchen altered or rebuilt.

*c*1540. Buildings erected in the Turl [H. A].

1572. A Balliol garden, adjoining the Exeter garden, bought, p. xcix.

1595 *re.* Front opposite Jesus College heightened, 'Chambers' musea [H. A].

1597 *ch.* Bentley's 'nest' erected, Wood says, incorrectly, over the library [F. E in part].

1605 *ms.* West Tower gateway first built.

*c*1606 *ms.* Letters from James I about closing the lane joining S. Michael's lane and Cat street [betw. K and G].

1618 *re.* Buildings at east end of Hall and running north to Bentley's nest—'Peryam's Mansions' [D. E].

1618 *ms.* The present Hall and cellar below it, at the cost of Sir John Acland [C. D].

*c*1620. Prideaux puts a third story to Wright's house [X. X].

1623–4 *gu.* The second, double chapel, dedicated to S. James, mainly at cost of Dr. Hakewill [G. H].

1624 *re.* New chapel consecrated and the old one [X. X] fitted up as a library—Wood says the last was in 1625, Gutch iii. 115-6.

1632 *ms.* Mention of Tower House west of Prideaux's house, and Mount on south part of present Ashmole site. Wood's *City* i. 258 'two towers, one whereof is converted into chambers for scollers,' i. e. the second tower in map B. Was it a bastion? Is it concealed by a building as drawn in Loggan? See p. clvii.

1634. Lease to the University of ground, on which the west end of the Bodleian was built. See p. cxiii, Wood's *Life* iii. 53.

1644. Part of the site of Fragnon Hall sold to the University.

1671 *gu.* Rector Bury added to the Rector's lodgings, occupying the former cartway north of the College [G to K].

1671 *gu. ms.* The buildings north of the Turl entrance completed [south half A. H]. Loggan's view is in 1675.

1679. College damaged through clearing of site for Ashmolean.

1682 *ms.* The buildings further north, i. e. to the west of the chapel, completed [north half A. H].

1701–3 *ms.* Tower over the (Turl gateway) [A], and buildings south of it [A. B] rebuilt, and those west of the new Hall [B. C].

1708 *ms.* The (large) quadrangle closed at the north-east corner by the 'Armagh buildings' [E. F].

1709 *re.* Library burnt down, shortened, and patched up [X. X].

1740. Lamp put up to light the quadrangle.

1778 *re. ms.* The old library taken down [X.X].

1778 *ms.* A second library, Ionic in style, built south of the old site. *Crowe* (p. cliv) or *Townsend* [near S. T].

1780. Mount with 2 studies mentioned.

1789 *ms.* Front toward Jesus College fitted with sashes, and gables cleared away [A. H].

1795 *ms.* Hincksey water from the Conduit 'laid on' to the kitchen [B].

1798 *ms.* Front of Rector's lodgings rebuilt [F. G].

1800–2 *ms.* Rector's lodgings rebuilt (!) [F. G. K].

1820. Porch for the Hall, with new clock, constructed: and gas introduced.

1821. Strip of ground granted to the University for boiler house.

1832 *various.* New buildings in Broad Street, near the Ashmolean. [O. N]. *Underwood.*

1834–5 *various.* West front, Turl, refaced or Gothicized, groining to gateway not [H. B]. *Underwood.*

1854. West half of Broad Street front [N. M]. *Sir Gilbert Scott.*

1855. Chapel [G. H] and present Library [R. S. T]. *The same.*

1856. Part of Prideaux's house shifted from Canditch and placed in the Turl.

1856. New gateway, north, into Broad Street. *The same.*

1857. New Rector's lodgings. *The same.*

1859. Third chapel completed.

1881. East side of front quadrangle restored.

1887. Main drainage re-arranged.

1888. Small quadrangle and chapel re-slated, the Hall cleaned.

1890. North side of the Hall roof re-slated, and part of the cellar cut off for a larder.

1894. Electric Light introduced into kitchen and 3 next staircases.

DIAGRAMS TO EXHIBIT CHANGES IN THE BUILDINGS.

N.B.   There was no Turl-front to the College till after Elizabeth's days; previously to that, the main entrance was on the north side (it is now on the west), under Palmer's Tower. This tower and part of one set of rooms, to the east of it, are all the portions of the XV century College that remain, and they are indicated by **F** in all the diagrams which follow.

Court of Divin. Sch.

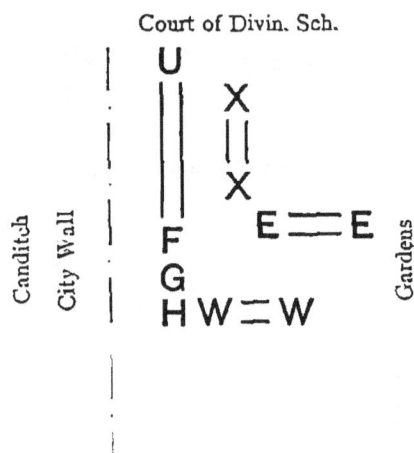

1. Bereblock's

In **Diag. 1**, **E. E** marks the position of the substructure of Bentley's 'Nest'; **F** of the earliest gateway tower; **F. G** and possibly **H** of the Rector's Lodgings; **F. U** is Rector's Row; **X. X** first chapel; and **W. W** is roughly the position of the first Hall of the College. Between the City wall and the College front Agas shows, 1588, a row of posts and rails to keep the cattle off.

Court of Divin. Sch.

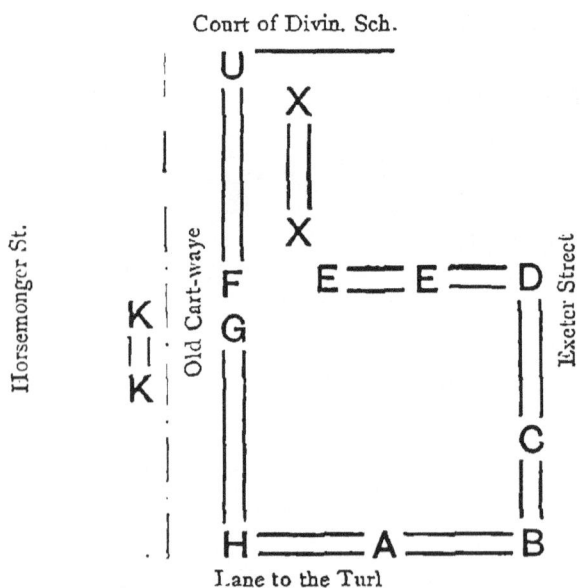

2. Loggan's

In **Diag. 2**, a quadrangle is nearly enclosed and the buildings have been extended westward to Turl Street and southward to the present Brasenose Lane. **A** is the main entrance; **A to B** Halls variously occupied; **B. C** the kitchen; **C. D** Acland's new hall; **D. E** Peryam's 'Mansions'; **E. E** Bentley's 'Nest' on walls of earlier date; **F. G** to **K** Rector's Lodgings; **K. K** Alderman Wright's House, now Prideaux's, with a bastion of the City Wall at its south-east angle; **G. H** Hakewill's double Chapel; **F. U** and **X. X** unchanged,—between these a Court, 110 feet by 25 ft, politely designated St. Helen's, which, later on, was widened by placing a new library, Palladian in style (**S. T**), 35 feet farther south. The first hall **W. W** has been removed.

In **Diag. 3**, the old Chapel-library has disappeared; Rector's Row, then called Chapel Row, has been removed, but a frontage to Broad Street has been inaugurated, and the old Cart-waye is now blocked up at its two ends. **M. O** is the Broad Street front; **F. P. N. M. L** a small quadrangle with the bastion still under its surface; between **F** and **G** passage to small quadrangle; **G. H** the New Chapel; and **K** a portion of Prideaux's House blocking up the old lane or road 'under the walls.'

Remarks on the Plan.

This attempt to construct a plan of the College differs considerably from any previous attempt in the same direction: first, the number of documents consulted has been more numerous; secondly, the originals of all of those in College possession have been carefully transcribed and compared in all instances with Wood's transcripts in MS. D. 2. The result is by no means encouraging:—the more the material accumulated, the more discrepancies were noticed, one with another, and frequently, too, with the hasty conclusions of Wood. To have made the plan at all resemble that in his *City* i. 113, would have been plainly in opposition to several charters he himself must have copied.

In a few cases measurements were obtained, but they have scarcely proved of so much value as was hoped.   Still, the *relative* positions of eleven of the tenements on the present site have been probably accounted for, but regarding a twelfth too little has been unearthed, and as regards ' St. Petir Hall on Wyger's land' its relative bearing to any of the known ones abutting on St. Mildred's Lane is nowhere given.   The references to this hall mainly occur in the rentals of Osney which seldom advert to position; this fact, and the obscurity elsewhere, are the key to the very peculiar statements in the plan by Wood before noticed.   It is almost clear that Wood omitted to notice that the wording in one instance is ' ex opposito ejusdem ecclesiae S. Mildredae,' but the position of that church still remains doubtful.   He regarded the body exhumed from the foundation of the south extremity of Peryam's ' Mansions' as indicating the site of the church, but the remains were found so near to the lane that we may easily imagine an encroachment by the tenement on which it was found, upon some part, perhaps the east, of the former churchyard. Nor had the discovery of human remains south of the present kitchen and of two more in the Turl, been then made.   These are probably interments in the west part of the churchyard, for it would never have occurred to our ancestors to bury on the north side of a church, and moreover there are good reasons for locating the site of the church well within the present limits of Lincoln College, near or on the site of the present Common Room.

It may be noticed that not one of the tenements toward the south-west of the Exeter site is described as *angulare* or *ad corneriam*; this is so unusual as to lead to the theory that some cottage, a priest's house or other structure, had grown up at the west end of the churchyard and obliterated that angle.

Mr. Clark's conclusions upon the question of sites have been generally followed, and a few particulars have been taken from an old map in the Rector's possession (B) which assisted indeed in some points, especially in the position of the earliest buildings, but added to the complexity by providing *two* apparent bastions in front of the College.   In making the north face of the early College to be out of the straight line, this map, because of a well-known propensity, is probably correct.   The eastern boundary has intentionally been left undecided; its variations at several periods would be these ;—1. Before the Divinity School was built ;—2. before the enclosure south of the same was obtained ;—3. after the site of the west wing of Bodley had been sold ;—4. before a portion of School Street at the east of the present garden was obtained ;—5 and 6, before and after part of the 'Lane under the walls' was obtained;—and 7, when a part of it (*n. n.*) south-west of the Sheldonian had been relinquished to the University. To have attempted all these would have resulted in a confused mass of lines.

To keep the plan distinct, letters only have been placed at certain angles of buildings, to which the following is a key.

References to letters in the Plan.

a. a. The north or new quadrangle. *b.* Land sold for site of the Ashmolean. *c. c.* The main quadrangle. *d. d.* The Rector's Lodgings at first. *e. e.* The first Hall of Stapeldon Hall. *f.* The Tower-entrance. *g. g.* Bentley's nest. *h. h.* Rector's Row. *L. L.* Full extent westward of the Bodleian Library. *nn.* Part of the old Lane, south-west of the Theatre, granted by the City at King James' solicitation, and afterwards leased or sold to the University. *r. r.* Sites of interments.

Tenants &c. of Halls at various times.

V is a MS. of Wood so entitled ; now D. 2.

The question of the ownership of a Hall at any fixed date must be considered quite as much as the various names given to the Hall; hence the use of the subjoined table.

Hambury Hall or Gramer Scooles.

John de Hankinton 1288.
Richard de Hamburia *c.* 1288.
John Leyre 1327, 1341.
Tho. de Wormenhale 1331.
John Martin, or of Daventry, 1343, 1344, 1351, 1353, 1361.
Will. of Daventry 1361.
Matthew of Daventry 1362.
John de Middleton 1364.
John Ottery 1366 (waste).

Culverd or Kylverd Hall.

Tho. de Radnor 1258, 1281.
Hugh Ruffus 1275.
John Culvert before 1296, 1327.
John Aldwynckle 1330.
Roger de Ludlow 1352.

Steph. Bantry 1353.
John Cerjeaux 1353.
(46 ft. broad in that year.)
(Waste in 1343, 1361, 1366, 1380.)

St. Stephen's.

Will Crompe 1275.
Geoffry de Merston 1281.
Tho.   ,,   ,,   1284.
Will. de Coudray 1286, 1296.
Hen. de Boveles 1297.
Hen. de la Grave 1294.
Will. de la Rode 1306, 1313.
John de Skelton 1315.

La Lavandrie.

Godstow Nunnery 1313.
Peter de Skelton 1316.
(Two rooms and area 1315.)

Godstow Tenement.

Peter de Skelton 1313.
Will. de Tanton 1313.
Tho. de Hengesey 1316.

*Fragon, Fragnon, Fragnum,
Fragonum, School of Arts.*

Tho. de Hengesey 1310, 1316.
Will. de Taynton 1313.
Peter de Skelton 1313.
Agatha Owen 1323.
  (Reached to Scot Hall, V. 83, 85.)

[*St. Hugh's or Baliole Hall.*

Walter de Saundford 1310.
Galf. de Horkstow 1310.
Juliana de Saundford 1313.
  Acquired by *Balliol* 1317.
  Reached south to Patrick Hall.
  Wood's *City* i. 112.]

Patrick Hall, Aula Hibernorum.

St. Frideswide's 1313, 1324, 1326, 1327.
  (Wood's *City* i. p. 112, on the *north*
  side of Divinity schools?)

Scott Hall.

Rich de Tekue 1325.
William de Brabanzoun 1325.
Walter Prodomme 1327.
  (Ten. of St. Frideswide—was south
  of the old Chapel 1360, V. 83.)

Castell Hall.

John de la Wyke 1325, 1330, 1345, 1348.
  his son John 1358.
John Hall 1358.
John Wyseburgh 1360.
  (The disportum.)

Bedford Hall.

St. Frideswide's (in capite).
John de Eu 1287.
Johanna de Bedford 1301.
Peter de Skelton 1301.
Emma de Bedford 1329.
Henry de Chalfunt 1330.
Walt. de Chalfont 1330, 1335.
Steph. de Hereweldesore 1335.
Hamo le Mercer 1344.

Peter Hall, Wyger's.

St. Frideswide's 1288.
Oseney 1348.
John Sewys and others 1395.
  (Faced St. Mildred's Church, V. 458,
  and was ' on Wyger's land.')

Chequer Hall, Aula Skakkarii.

John de Schepton 1384.
Thom.   „   „   1384.
Rob. le Draper 1391, 1395, 1396.
. . . Thyngden 1405.
  (Next to Bedford Hall 1287.)

St. Williams.

John Pershore 1323.
St. John's Hospital 1344.

Sheld Hall.

Hugh Ruffus 1275, 1288.
Will. de Parys 1285.
  „   le Sauser (? same) 1288.
Hillaria de Parys 1313, 1316, 1345.
Joanna   „   „   1316, 1324.
Rich.   „   „   1327.
John de Pershore 1316, 1323.
Will. Syward 1322.
Will. de Pershore 1344.

NOTES.

P. i. Merton, see *Social England* i. 430.

The English language was now recovering its place.

iii. Richard Hankford (s. and h. of Sir Henry, by Elizabeth d. and h. of Sir Richard Stapeldon; ? at Winchester 1409; see Foss 325), m. Elizabeth sister and heir of Fulk lord Fitzwarine (d. 1420), their dau. Thomasin m. William Bourchier; Cokayne's *Complete Peerage* iii. 377.

Thomas Kaignes or Keynes, of Winkleigh, Devon, m. Joan sister of bishop Stapeldon. She had a d. Joan, and a s. John who m. Isabel d. and coh. of John baron de Wake. Their s. Thomas m. Margaret d. of Sir John Beaumont of Youlston. Their s. John m. the d. and coh. of Nicholas Wainpford. Their 1 s. John left an heiress who m. Speke: the 2 s. Richard had a s. John, who had a s. Nicholas, whose heiress Margaret m. Richard Chichester of Raleigh, whose s. Richard m. Thomasin d. of Simon de Hall (Visit. Devon 176). The male line was continued by Margaret's brother John Keynes, whose s. John had a s. Humphry, who m. the d. and coh. of John Whiting. Of their 2 daughters, Elizabeth m. Sir John Acland, and Anne m. John Cruwys. A John de Kaignes occurs 1320–2 in Eyton's *Dorset* 76.

v. Pat. Rolls Edw. III, 26 Mch 1331, mortmain licence to Richard de Stapelton to found a Carthusian house to pray for the souls of Bishop Walter, Edward II, &c.; 9 Sep. 1332 for lands in Erniscombe, 26 Nov. lands in Brodwodewyger for a similar purpose, see p. viii; J. I. Dredge's *Frithelstock Priory* 1894 p. 1. See Pat. Rolls, Edw. II 16, 18 and 26 Dec. 1307, 8 July 1389, 3 Feb. 131⅘,

About Stapeldon's monument S. Hart, fellow of Exeter, writes from Exeter 17 June 1792 to rector T. Stinton as follows (Gough, Oxford 86), 'It is in a perfect state, though it has not undergone any repairs since 1733. Especially the two tablets of wood where the verses are (over the monument) are in high preservation. The word *feretra* in the 4th distich is *too plainly* legible. These tablets front the north Aile, their back is towards the chancel, and is hid by a wainscot screen ornamented with pillars and arches after the Grecian manner. It was this facing of wainscot which the Chapter wished to remove, meaning to put in its place something in the Gothic style, of a piece with the Fabric; but when Dean Buller left Exeter this design was dropped, and no alteration whatever has been made. Now that I am upon the subject of monuments, I am reminded of a gravestone in the church of Crediton, which records the death of John Lyndon, dean of the collegiate church of Crediton, who had been rector of Exeter College, and if I mistake not was a party in giving the advowson of Menhenniot. He died Dec. 16, 1482. The stone had been broken and the fragments lay in different parts of the church. I have had them put together.'

On the arms of the College, see *N. and Q.* 6. xii. 515.

vi. In our Book of Evidences fol. 141 (see Wood D. 2, p. 93) are the following royal grants :—

(1) 7 Edw. II, York 10 May (1314) for Hart Hall and Arthur Hall—see Bodleian Charters, p. 288. (2) Duplicate. (3) Inspeximus at Clipston 4 Nov. 1315 of Peter de Skelton's grant of S. Stephen's Hall on S. Faith's day 9 Edw. II =6 Oct. 1315. (4) Inspeximus 30 Oct. 1318 at York of Godstow deed of 23 Ap. 1318. (5) Licence at York 20 May 15 Edw. II (1322) to hold an advowson worth 40 marks, i. e. Wittenham. (6) Richard II at Westminster 24 July 1380 confirms the grant of the sites of Hambury Hall and Culverd Hall by John Otery, Lucas Holland, Robert Lydeford, and Richard Rouland. (7) Appropriation of Merton to Ensham, Richard II's Inspeximus at Woodstock 8 Aug. 1382 of Edw. III's grants of 15 July 1344 and at the Tower 22 June 1351. (8) 22 July 12 Edw. II (mistake for Richard), 1388, allows Roger Ford, V. of Bampton, to give a messuage in S. Peter le Bayly: refers to his *proavus* Edward II. (9) Henry IV at Westminster 19 June 1406 permits John Couling, Thomas Noreys, and John Gynne to grant Cheker Hall and Gyngyvere's Place. (10) Henry VI extends the mortmain licence, Coventry 12 Mch 35 H. VI = 1457. (11) Henry VI, on grant of Wyttenham Nov. 1466, through John Smyth M.D.

The Windsor grant was not carried out.

Sanctuary means the home farm with the buildings on it.

vii. Mahynyet. Brantingham's Reg. i. 19 gives 3 royal breves on the subject.

viii. Trejagu see ix ; Maitland, Parl. of 1305 (Rolls Series) p. cxv.

x. W. Crompe ; *S. Frideswide's Cart.* i. 325. Lucia la Rede, *S. Frideswide's Cart.* i. 372.

2¼ marks for a rent of 2*s* is 17 years' purchase.

xi. Andrew de Pyrie was M.P. for Oxford several times; Maitland, Parl. of 1305 (Rolls Series) p. cxviii.

xii. H. de Lynne, p. xvi ; *S. Frideswide's Cart.* i. 279.

xiii. The small houses were generally of two stories, a solar on the upper floor, which contained the dwelling-rooms, while the storerooms, &c., were on the ground floor. The access to the solar was often by steps outside; *Social England* i. 382, 468. On the look of the College in early times see p. 319 'a confused number of blynd streets.'

xvi. Dyne. Dugdale gives Dyve as her name; there is a similar doubt in Foss 227. See Nat. Biog. xvi. 301, Pat. Rolls Edw. II index.

xvii. There is a place Hambury in Worcs., Foss 324.

xviii. John de Middleton ; ? fellow of Oriel: Stapeldon's Reg. 289, Le Neve ii. 391, Gutch i. 387, 516, Rogers ii. 631, 635, 672, 674; called ' Linc. dioc. clerico et presbitero M.A. in theol. scolari' in a petition to the Pope.

xix. Culverd Hall was 'lately built' in 1352, it went to ruin in 30 years.

xx. J. de Littlemor, *S. Frideswide's Cart.* i. 279.

xxi. Seynt Holde. The R. of S. Aldate's in 1358 was 'Walter,' for in 1361 the next R. succeeds 'per mortem domini Walteri.' Walter's predecessor Roger de Pershore was instit. 1337. In 1341 Adam de Kemerton was instit. to a chantry in S. Aldate's.

xxiii. Tekne, ? Tekue (Tekew). There is a place Tekene in Yorkshire.

xxvii. John de Brayles was R. of S. Mildred's 1308-33.

xxviii. Note, see p. 289.

xxix. Edm. de la Beche, Close Rolls Edw. II i. 547.

xxii, line 2. E. g. p. 59, 9 Ap. 1530 to 9 Oct. 1543.

xxxi. *Determining,* see xl, Wordsworth 248, 251, 281, 314–6. Coleridge's *Life of Keble* ed. 2 ch. 5 *init. Collectors,* see cxv, Wordsworth 670.

xxxii. Battels, Wordsworth 657.

xxxv. Age at degree, Wordsworth 638.

xxxviii. So Univ. Statutes; Hearne 25 Nov. 1727.

xxxix. Pat. R. Edw. III, 20 Dec. 1300 price of wine in Oxford not to exceed the London price by more than $\frac{1}{4}d$ a *gallon*; see 16 Dec. 1333.

xl. Honey, Foss 228.

xli. See article on Medieval Cookery in Qu. Rev. Jan. 1894.

Th. Lentwardyn, Oriel muniments no. 39 and 41, 16 and 18 Ric. II; 30 Oct. 1417.

xliii. Never a fire at breakfast time, Wordsworth 658.

xliv. The windows of the rooms were fastened with *vertinelli,* Anglice *twysts,* see Rogers i. 500, Hist. Comm. ii. 136; Lent 1334 in una fenestra nova empta 1*d ob,* in quinque vertinellis emptis ad fenestras camerarum ii*d*; Lent 1337 vii*d* pro twyst et hok; 'twystys' occur winter 1392, 3 pair cost 6*d* in winter 1443, 2 pair of twysts and 2 pair of hooks cost 10*d* Lent 1444; and see summer 1496.

Chums, and trucklebeds, Wordsworth 635.

xlv. There is no list of the burials in the Chapel, which continued to a late date. Amy Cole, widow of Thomas Cresswell, major R. M., d. 2 Jan. 1807 age 45, was buried there. She was probably sister of rector J. Cole; Lake iv. 45.

xlvi. Siesta, John Inglesant 281.

Bevers, Wordsworth 215.

l, line 1. See Wordsworth 405, 407.

Carriage, *Social England* i. 366.

After 'Cosmography' *insert* 1637.

Thames, Wordsworth 174.

lxiv. Nineteenth Century Nov. 1890 p. 812 the Oxford movement of the 15th Century.

lxv, note 1, and H. Kaylle.

lxix. John Stanbury, V. of Barnstaple 9 Nov. 1451–1460, Chanter's *Barnstaple* 93. But John Stanbury, bishop of Hereford 1453, d. 11 May 1474 was probably the King's confessor; C. S. Gilbert's *Cornwall* ii. 196, 268, 558, Bibl. Corn. 683.

lxxvi. Penkyll, R. of Redruth, res. 1505; preb. of Hereford 1489.

John Kirkham. ? Sir John Kirkham of Blagdon, Devon, d. 11 July 1529.

lxxxvi. *For* 18 May, *read* 28 May.

lxxxix. *Insert* Lent 1556 'xixs viii*d* pro expensis meis cum ibam Exoniam ad conveniendum episcopum de nostris statutis, viii*s* pro conductione equi eo tempore, vs viii*d* pro duobus paribus chirothecarum exhibitis episcopo Exon ex communi consensu sociorum.' For horse hire, see notes on p. li, lxx, 56; the rate for horse provender (*prebendae*) was fixed by the Assize of Weights and Measures (and so for charcoal, dimensions of laths, timber, tiles, &c.), Dict. Pol. Econ. i. 64.

xc. On vacating fellowships, see Wordsworth 553–4, 565, 568, and on non-resident parsons. On expenses, see Wordsworth 413, 572 income of fellowships.

Some writers think the requirement of divinity degrees implies that the Colleges were ecclesiastical corporations. But those degrees were open to laymen

up to Laud's time, and the restriction to the clergy should now be abolished ;
see pp. xc, 133, 155.

xcvii.   The poor scholars are called the *scolares* or *scolastici* of some fellow.
Thus, p. 53, 'viii*d* a magistro Moremane pro scolari suo Baron pro stipendio
camere sue pro uno termino.' Men of rank often brought up a humble companion,
whose university expenses they paid ; thus in the matriculation of 1575 'John
Gerarde, Darbie, equitis filius, 13 ; William Eyton, Darbie, 22, serviens
M. Gerarde.' For an account of the different classes of undergraduates see
Boase's *Commoners of Exeter College* 1894, preface.

P. 1. Parys, John, ordained deacon at Exeter 19 Sep. 1321, *Magister*.
Another John Paris occurs in Stapeldon's Register.

2. Pippecote was probably fellow before 1322 : he is called *Magister* Stephanus
on 10 May 1323.

Sevenaysshe, probably fellow by 1319.

Lappeflod (Laployd is in Bridford), see Stapeldon's Reg. 23 June and 23 Sep.
1319, 28 Sep. 1321, 20 Oct. 1322, 24 Mch 132$\frac{2}{3}$; Eccl. Ant. ii. 129-30, iii. 70.

3. W. de Brokelond. Two deeds in the chest run thus : (1) I William Broclond
have put in my place Robert Passemere, to give my daughter Sarra seisin of
a *selva* in Chulmelegh, between the tenement of Robert Bristawe and that of
Ralph Prodomme. At Chulmelegh, Sunday after feast of S. Edward, in 19 (?)
year of King Edward. If this is Edward I, the date would be 7 Jan. 129$\frac{4}{5}$;
if Edward II, 132$\frac{5}{6}$. (2) I Sarra daughter of William Broclond of Chulmelegh
have given to William Broclond my father a *selva* in Chulmelegh, between the
tenement of Robert . . ., towards Goshmalok (?) ; witnesses Robert . . ., John . . .
At Chulmelegh 13 Edward III (?).

5. Master Godfrey Fromond was physician to Edward III, who recommended
him 8 June 1349 to Bishop Grandisson for a prebend at Exeter, but the Bishop
excused himself because of so many Papal Provisions, &c., Grandisson's Reg.
i. 307.

Landreyn, *Early muniments of Oriel* (ed. Shadwell) no. 26, and 18 Oct. 1366,
no. 37 Landreyn, Redruth, and the Chancellor to govern Oriel till the dispute as
to the provostship is settled, no. 38.

6, line 3. John Martyn, *of Davyntre*, see line 13, and p. xix.

8. R. Colshulle, ? related to Sir J. Colshull p. 7.

10. Boson, see p. 15.

11. Rygge, see *Cartulary of S. Frideswide* i. 87.

14. Tremayne, Visit. Devon 730.

18. Noe ; a son not unfrequently succeeded to his father's benefice ; Papal
Letters (Rolls Series) i. 11 Indult to deprive sons of clerks who have immediately
succeeded to the benefices of their fathers, and i. 23 and repeatedly ; 15 marriages
of clerks, &c.

19. Chylyndon, prior of Christ Church, Canterbury ; Gervase of Canterbury
ii. p. lii (p. xxvi Adam of Chylyndon), Gutch i. 534, Tanner 177 ; *Cart. of
S. Frideswide* i. 87. Chillenden is near Sandwich.

21. Sawyer, servant of Richard II.

22. Grostete ; Perry's *Life of Grostete* p. 47 ; Gascoigne (writing between 1433
and 1457) p. 43, 70 'illa epistola responsiva domini Lincolniae doctoris Roberti

Grosseteste est Oxoniae in Collegio Exoniae in libraria, et in monasterio Ordinis Sancti Salvatoris in Syon in Anglia : ' MS. no. 21 (Coxe) contains his *Dictamina Sermones* [24 per circulum anni] et mandata.

23. Helias Stoke, see p. 28 Helias.

24. A John Bowring was R. of Slapton chantry 24 Mch 14⁴⁸/₉₀.

29. H. Kaylle, Oriel muniments 30 Oct. 1417 and 3 Dec. 1421.

32. W. Lihert, Oriel muniments 16 July 1425, 4 June 1436, 22 Feb. 144⅝, 13 Aug. 1446.

33. J. Arundel, bishop of Chichester in place of Pecock, Gairdner's and Spelding's *Studies* 1881 p. 50.

The abbot of Nutley was probably residing in College rooms as a *sojourner*.

At Palmer's *obit* (read 25 July 1468) every scholar present was to receive 2*d* ; 20*s* was to be forfeited each time the obit was omitted.

34. J. Halse, Oriel muniments 22 Feb. 144⅘ ; for John Halse the justiciary, Foss 324.

36. Weye, *cantu organico*, perhaps = *descant* (Fr. déchant), a variation on plain-chant ; i.e. singing in parts, and combining several distinct notes in a single strain : said to have been suggested by the varied tones of the organ ; Lecky, *History of Rationalism* ii. 342. See the admirable description in *John Inglesant* ed. 1887 p. 255, 439.

37. Lyndon, d. 16 Dec. 1482, gravestone in Crediton church ; note on p. v.

Markewyke ; a Nathaniel Markwick occurs 1664–1735, Nat. Biog.

38. French and Codie did not reside on their livings, but preferred Oxford.

47. Stockton, ? John Stockton, B.A. 26 Feb. 152¼.

48. Trotte, the name occurs at Kidlington in the settlement of 1445.

T. Tremayne, Visit. Devon 730 *clerk in orders*.

50 rushes, see Charles I's *Declaration of Sports*.

53. Moreman, Reynolds' *Chapter Act Book* 20 Aug. 1528, 9 May 1530, 19 July 1544, June 1546, 21 Aug. 1554.

54. Ashely, ? William Ashley, M.A. 2 Dec. 1528.

56. Lacy, i.e. Dunstan Lacy, fellow of Lincoln 1525–30, and perhaps to his d. 1534.

Bensynton. The College held a farm at Bensington, Summer 1486 iiis viii*d* in expensis apud Bensyngton per Rectorem tempore quo pepigit cum Roberto Brey de Henley pro allodio in Bensyngton emendo ; liiis iiii*d* Brey apud Wallyngforde, pacto facto coram Maiore de Wallyngforde in partem solucionis xviii*li* xiiis iiii*d* pro dicto allodio ; iis viii*d* pro conductu duorum equorum per 3ᵒˢ dies alio tempore quo possessionem suscepi ; xvi*li* Brey eodem tempore in Bensyngton in plenam solucionem xxiii*li* xiiis iiii*d* pro dicto allodio ; iiis ix*d* in Bensyngton pro prandio nostro et pro prebendis equis ; vis xi*d* in Abyngdon pro prebendis equis per noctem et diem et pro refectione facta quibusdam hominibus in dicto allodio feofatis, pro eorum refeofatura ; ii*d* pro cera rubea ; vis viii*d* Nicholas Brey fratri Roberti Brey pro relaxacione iuris eius si quod habuerit ad dictum allodium quod tunc vendicabat ; iiis iurisperito pro diversis scriptis et munimentis de novo factis pro dicto allodio ; viii*d* Bredston pro equo et expensis equitanti apud Bensyngton tempore quo ibidem observabatur curia.

Rowland Barratt paid 31*s* in 1535 ; the tenant paid in 1578 half-yearly £28, 3 bushels and a peck of good wheat, and ½ quarter of good malt. A *Terrier* was taken 4 June 1604. It consisted of 2 yardlands, of 30 acres each; and 2 acres, 12 cowpastures (2 horse), 205 sheep, in Dr. Webber's time. A map by Kelsey 1802 gives the whole land as 60 a. 2 r. 15 p.; 'about 70 pieces, generally under an acre each, lying much dispersed over the common fields of Benson and Warborough.'

John Collins; one of this name was V. of Cumnor and d. 1559, when his sister Joan Poopes administered to his effects. The Collins executed with the Poles is described as 'late of Medmenham, Bucks, alias of London, clerk,' State Papers 153⁸, ii. p. 423.

58. W. Cholwell was *sojourning* in College 1554.

59. J. French was resident 6 Dec. 1555.

60. Maister Peverys, ? Richard Pever, M.A. 30 June 1505.

Thomas Yonge, of Broadgates Hall.

61. John Peter, ? pres. by Sir W. Petre to the preb. at Exeter vacated by the death of Moreman, pres. read 21 Aug. 1554 to the Chapter; *Chapter Act Book.*

65. M. Ley, sojourner 1553-4.

66. W. Peryam, Foss 513.

67. R. Tremayne, sojourner 12 Oct. 1550 and Oct. 1551.

70. Vidua Polkynhorne, ? Katherine, Visit. Corn. 374.

Shepereve, the name occurs at Kidlington in the settlement of 1445.

Somersbye, ? John; Turner 250.

73. W. Stocker, M.A. Broadgates Hall or All Souls; Foster 1425.

79. Th. Pawly and W. Huish the 2 first bursars, in 1588, Jo. Eveleghe subrector.

86. Alford, Henry.

T. Winniffe, Oriel muniments no. 83.

Richard Carpenter. There were 2 of this name, and the account of them is confused. Winslow Jones distinguishes the *fellow* thus; he was B.A. 8 July 1596 (in his *supplicat* he says that he was teaching boys in Cornwall), M.A. 7 Nov. 1598, instit. as M.A. 24 July 1605 to R. of Sherwell, Devon (Cotton's Reg. 82), resigned his fellowship 30 June 1606, B.D. 25 June 1611, instit. as S.T.B. 19 July 1611 to R. of Loxhore, Devon (Cotton's Reg. 95 b), preached a sermon 1612 or 1613 at Landkey at funeral of Sir Arthur Acland, published London; D.D. 10 Feb. 161⅘, held Sherwell and Loxhore till his death 18 Dec. 1627, age 52, buried at Loxhore. He was not R. of Georgeham.

91. Christopher Palmer, at Christ Church 160⅜.

92. N. Carpenter, part i. of his *Geography* was dedicated to William Herbert earl of Pembroke (Shakspere's 'W. H.', say some), ii. to Philip Herbert as earl of Montgomerie. In his remarks on 'Colonies transplanted,' he refers to 'Our Virginian colony in America.'

95. J. Prideaux, Hist. Comm. vi. 47.

99. James Bampfield, of Alban Hall.

101. T. Denys, Wood's Life iii. 57 Comp. Vice Canc. 1640-1 to Mr. Dennis of Exeter College for a sermon preached at S. Marie's Sep. 7, ex decreto praefectorum, 3 *li.*

102. The appendix to Kendal's Sancti Sanciti, 'A fescue for a Hornebook [against Mr. Horne's book] or an Apology for University Learning as necessary for country-preachers' contains many allusions, e. g. 'a late Examiner of the Universities pleas'd to call Reason the spawn of the old Serpent.'

105. P. Northcote, admin. granted by Prerogative Court 13 Aug. 1641.

107. A. Bury, his arms are over the doorway of the Chapel staircase.

114. N. Marsh, left books to the Bodleian.

125. H. Northcote, Lord Iddesleigh published extracts from his Notebooks in Blackwood Jan. 1894, p. 87.

126. Joseph Glanvill of Ex. Coll., the author of *Scepsis Scientifica*, writing about this time pronounced University education in general, and that of Oxford in particular, to be almost worthless; Lecky *Hist. of Rationalism* i. 124.

128. G. Stubbes, inscribed his poem *The Laurell and the Olive* to G. Bubb; Hearne ii. 386, 7 May 1710.

156. J. Phillips, P. C. of Frithelstock, 'had licence 13 May 1806 to be absent from his benefice of Frithelstock for 2 years, on account of there being no house of residence.' J. [Fisher, bishop of] Exeter. J. I. Dredge's *Frithelstock* 1894, p. 7 (from the parish chest).

162. J. D. Macbride (his father d. 1800); Pusey's Life ii. 102, Nat. Biog.

166. J. Spurway, Visit. Devon 724.

J. T. Coleridge, Foss 181; Pusey's Life, index.

168. J. L. Richards, Pusey's Life ii. 171, Newman's Letters ii. 330, 370, F. D. Maurice's Life i. 112, Burgon's *Twelve Good Men* 300; he proposed Mr. Gladstone as M.P. 1847.

170. J. C. Clutterbuck, Burgon's *Twelve Good Men* 303, 373.

E. Coleridge, Pusey's Life i. 12, ii. 414.

171. H. B. Bulteel, Pusey's Life ii. 450, Newman's Letters i. 215, 226, 245, ii. 297.

172. J. Bramston, Newman's Letters, i. 184, 223.

173. W. Falconer, Mozley i. 18, Nat. Biog.

174. W. Sewell, Burgon's *Twelve Good Men* 158, 187.

175. E. A. Dayman, Newman's Letters ii. 330.

W. Jacobson, b. 18 July, Burgon's *Twelve Good Men* 212, 367-401, 386. F. D. Maurice's Life i. 99, 111-3, 123, 131, 179, 356, Mozley ii. 25, Nat. Biog. The engraving of his portrait in Burgon's book (by Richmond) gives the very expression of his face as we knew him, a remark true of so few portraits.

177. C. L. Cornish, Newman's Letters ii. 323.

182. J. A. Froude, Mozley i. 347, F. D. Maurice's Life i. 516-8, 539, ii. 280, 322-3, Pattison's Memoirs 215, Burgon's *Twelve Good Men* 179.

185. J. F. Mackarness, Nat. Biog., Mod. Eng. Biog.

H. Low, see Burgon's *Twelve Good Men* 76.

W. B. Marriott, scholar Trinity 1843-6: Mod. Eng. Biog.

187. F. T. Palgrave, *Prothalamion* 1893. His wife d. 27 Mch 1890.

188. C. W. Boase, again reelected Reader Feb. 1894, but soon resigned owing to ill health. In last line but one *dele* 'ed. 3, 1894.'

193. I. Bywater, Reg. Prof. of Greek 30 Nov. 1893, and a Senior Student of Christ Church; portrait in S. James' Budget 17 Nov. 1893 p. 20, I. L. N. 18 Nov. p. 631, Graphic 18 Nov. p. 618; delivered Inaugural Lecture *Four Centuries of Greek Learning in England* 8 Mch 1894 in Exeter College Hall.

194. P. F. Willert, Curator of Taylor Institution 1893.

198. Sir R. P. Marett, see Mod. Eng. Biog.

E. C. Burne Jones, cr. bart. Feb. 1894; portrait in I. L. N. 10 Feb. p. 159, in Graphic 10 Feb. p. 150.

200. S. Hill, see Coll. Corn. 365, Boase's *Commoners* of Ex. Coll. 1894 p. 385.

Rob. Michell; Wild Arish (see Reg. 9 Feb. 1841) was sold for £1000 on 11 Oct. 1864, which bought £1136 7s 3d Consols.

J. Darell, see pedigree in *Roll Call of the Hospital of the Trinity*, West Retford 1894.

204. Richard **Carslake** (s. Richard, pleb., of Sidbury, Devon), **M.** 5 Ap. 1661 age 18, poor scholar 6 Ap. 1661 to 26 July 1664, **B.C.** 1661-4.

218. Hugh Polson, C. of Bourton on the Water, d. Monaco 23 Nov. 1872 m. Jan. 1831, Georgiana only child of George Crawley capt. R.N., and step-daughter of Rector J. C. Jones.

219. J. Woolley, b. 28 Feb. 1816, first head master of Rossall 1844-9; St. Vincent Beechey, *The Rise and Progress of Rossall* 1894, pp. 12-22 (portrait).

221. Dalgairns, Mozley ii. 13, Pusey's Life ii. 459.

223. M. Day, scholar of Univ. Coll. 1849, he was scholar of Ex. Coll. when he won the Ireland; m. 22 Mch 1856 Amelia Greaves Johnson.

224. H. Algar, has written further commentaries on S. Paul.

226. J. B. Richey, s. James, by Elizabeth d. of J. Bellett, of Sampford Arundel, Som.; b. 11 Dec. 1833; Chief Secretary Bombay 1884, member of Council 1887, retired 1890, K.C.I.E. 1890; m. 21 Mch 1872 Blanche d. of William Perkins, of Somerset, Louisiana.

233. O. W. Tancock, m. (1) Clifton 13 July 1865 Elizabeth Clara Kendall 1 d. of Col. George Girdwood Channer by Susan Kendall of Lanlivery, Cornwall, she d. Sherborne 6 Oct. 1867 age 26 (2) Sherborne 23 Ap. 1874 Isabella Poyntz 2 d. of Thomas Poyntz Wright of Tiverton, by Charlotte Anne Chilcott.

234. W. H. A. Emra, d. Twickenham of heart disease 10 Nov. 1893.

235. R. Hutchinson, *read* Hutchison; m. 6 May 1876 Clementina Stuart.

236. J. L. G. Mowat, el. a Councillor for City of Oxford 1893.

239. Symonds, b. 18 Nov. 1846, **Reynolds** 1866, barrister L. I. 1872, M.A. 12 May 1894, m. Dedham, Essex 21 June 1888 Mary d. of H. R. Edwards.

242. C. C. Tancock, head master of Rossall 1887 ; m. Godalming 26 Ap. 1886 Marion Alma d. of Robert Smith; St. Vincent Beechey, *The Rise and Progress of Rossall* 1894, p. 48.

247. C. M'Rae, assistant examiner and occasional inspector for Science, in Science and Art Department Jan. 1894 (permanent).

250. J. Mackintosh, Prof. of Civil Law, Edinburgh 1893.

252. W. J. Ward, M.A. 30 Nov. 1893.

254. T. H. Harvey, repeated 257, his wife Annie Louisa d. 9 Sep. 1891.

257. R. G. Plumptre, m. S. Peter's in the East, Oxford 28 Dec. 1893 Edith 1 d. of Rev. E. Moore, Principal of Edmund Hall.

260. A. S. Thomson, master at preparatory school, Moscow Road, Kensington Gardens 1894.

261. W. C. Allen, **M.** Non-Coll. Camb. 21 Oct. 1886; chaplain fellow 1894.

263. M. C. Eliot, B.A. 1 Mch 1894, at the bar.

A. Ramsbotham, B.A. 18 Dec. 1893.

264. L. J. Roberts, B.A. 15 Jan. 1894, assist. inspect. of sch. in Wales, Jan. 1894.

J. L. L. Fulford, Richards theol. prize Mch 1894.

266. W. T. W. Baker, 2 Classics Mod. 1894.

V. E. G. Hussey, 2 Classics Mod. 1894.

A. E. Lynam, 2 Classics Mod. 1894.

S. R. Hignell, 2 Classics Mod. 1894.

J. H. Barron, 2 Classics Mod. 1894.

E. A. Selby-Lowndes, Hall and Houghton Syriac prize 1894.

E. Cleave, 3 Classics Mod. 1894.

267. John Edgar **Langdon** (3 s. Alfred, V. of New Sleaford, Lincs.), b. High Bickington, Devon 20 July 1874, ed. Lincoln gr. sch., **M.** 17 Oct. 1893, **Darell** 1893.

Frederic Stephen **Hughes**, ed. Marlborough, **Open** Jan. 1894.

Ernest Edward **Yates**, ed. Rossall, **Open** Jan. 1894.

Francis Arthur **West**, ed. Merchant Taylors sch., Crosby, **Open** Jan. 1894.

Robert Ernest **Yates**, ed. Bolton gr. sch., **Open** Jan. 1894.

Robert **Hancock**, ed. Exeter gr. sch., **Open** Jan. 1894.

Richard **Nettell**, ed. Plymouth College, **Stap.** Jan. 1894.

Dudley William **Mortimer**, ed. Ashburton, **Gifford** Jan. 1894.

St. John **Trevor**, ed. Denston Coll., **Symes** Jan. 1894.

Frederick Burton Pendarves **Lory**, s. F. A. P. Lory (p. 231), b. 23 Mch 1875, ed. Marlborough, **Richards** 1894.

Edmund Spenser **Bouchier**, ed. Elizabeth Coll., Guernsey, **Ch. I** Feb. 1894.

Philip **Hartridge**, ed. Elizabeth Coll., Guernsey. **Ch. I** (Nat. Sci.) Feb. 1894.

W. Shepley Airy, s. Basil Reg., V. of S. John's, Torquay, b. 12 Nov. 1874, ed. Newton Coll., Devon, **Coll. Exh.** 1894.

268. Richard Mounceaux or Mounceys, R. of Widworthy, Devon 2 Mch 145$\frac{3}{4}$; N. and Gleanings iv. 35.

J. Pyttys, ? R. of Parkham 1467, ? d. 1472 : N. and Gleanings i. 12.

274. L. Milbourn, of Pemb., Camb., d. 15 Ap. 1720, wrote on Dryden's Virgil.

284. Geoffrey de Hengseie, S. Frideswide's Cart. i. 279.

287 (13). See S. Frideswide's Cartulary i. p. 386.

291, note 2. S. Frideswide's Cartulary i. no. 546 p. 392 William Fitzwydo of London 1230-40 ; see no. 613 ; no. 626-7-8 Winchester Hall in S. Mildred's, Thomas Fitzwydo 1215, and Agatha his widow 1240, 'inter terram Walteri Feteplace et terram Thome de Bedeford' ; no. 623 Walter Pilet 1180-90 ; no. 637 Robert Bodin ; no. 642 Patrick Hall ; no. 643 two schools ; no. 640-1 the *selds*.

293. Roger Mymecan, S. Frideswide's Cart. i. 280.

294. Steph. de Adynton, Bodl. Chart. p. 306, 309, 352, 356.

295 (2). S. Frideswide's Cartulary i. p. 325.

299. H. Lisewis, S. Frideswide's Cart. i. 348, 355.

321. Had Gwinear ever been dependent on Treagony, or on S. Mary de Valle? On 7 Mch 154$\frac{5}{8}$ Gwynner was let to John Vivian of Bodman for 18 years.

337. Old rent of Rectory £28, 3 quarters of good wheat, 52 quarters of good malt, as valued on the market day before Michaelmas, sold to the tenant for £30. Yeard land 4s, 1 bushel of wheat, 2 bushels of malt.

341. For slates see Rogers i. 493, 3500 slates cost 21s autumn 1401, 1500 cost 10s autumn 1420, 500 cost 3s 4d Lent 1421, 1000 cost 6s autumn 1444; for crests and tiles see i. 491, tiles were fastened as now by pins (Hist. Comm. vi. 548); for lime i. 468, 484, in 1432 17 quarters of lime cost 24s; for charcoal i. 422, 446, in 1566 29 quarters cost 33s 10d; winter 1416 'carbones pro igne ad solidandum plumbum'; 'colestone' is mentioned summer 1450; for the use of moss see Hist. Comm. ii. 136, v. 477.

344. Jackson's Wadham 31, 38 carriage of stone 1*s* 4*d* a cartload of a ton or more, a plow load 2 tons; 40 traffic to Oxford by water.

346. In 1578 Yarnton parsonage paid halfyearly £4 13*s* 4*d*, and a ½ quarter of wheat and 4 quarters of malt, but instead of this the tenant later on paid £10 yearly.

347. *For* Parker *read* Porter.

---

178. Spranger, m. 29 Dec. 1842 Mary Eliz. Elwin, d. 13 Ap. 1845.

185. Colenso, ed. Harrow, scholar S. John's Camb. 1842.

194. Moore, b. Oct. 1841, ed. Bradfield.

209. Tothill, C. of Cheriton Bishop, Dev. 1798, R. of Hittisleigh, Dev. 1800-44, d. 8 Dec. 1844.

213. Ley, d. 4 Mch 1866.

214. Howard, d. Heavitree Sep. 1810.

217. Wollaston, b. 18 Oct. 1806.

219. Moore, m. 30 Dec. 1840 Frances Marianne Yates, d. 1 Aug. 1886.

220. Cosserat, d. 28 July 1889.

221. Cowburn, m. 30 Oct. 1844 Phebe Mary d. of W. Jas. Randall.

222. Meade, d. Bath 6 Oct. 1890.

James, m. 13 Aug. 1862 Eliza Mary Heald.

224. Wilgress, m. 7 Ap. 1864 Mary d. of Ven. Walker King.

225. Pearson, m. 10 Dec. 1872 Edith Lucilla Butler; he d. London 31 May 1894.

Reynolds, m. 12 Ap. 1871 Edith Claudia Sandys.

226. Pedder, d. Dulwich 21 Nov. 1888, his widow d. 5 Jan. 1891.

227. Salmon, m. 7 July 1868 Emma Caroline d. of Lieut.-Col. Ch. Thorold Hill.

232. Wright, m. (2) 4 July 1893 Emily C., d. of Sir Douglas Forsyth.

Beachcroft, b. 7 May 1841.

Bernard, b. 12 July 1842, m. Privett, Hants 4 Sep. 1878 Ellen Isabel, 1 d. of William Nicholson, of Basing Park, Hants.

233. Cornish, m. 4 July 1867 Mary d. of H. G. Randall.

234. Avery, b. 11 Mch 1844, m. 29 Dec. 1874 Mary Anne Bond.

235. Abbay, m. 14 Sep. 1880 Jane 1 d. of C. Norman.

Wilkinson, b. 9 Nov. 1844, m. 4 Sep. 1873 Agnes Louisa d. of Rev. Jas. Guillemard.

236. Reid, b. 7 July 1845.

Wilkinson, b. 15 Sep. 1845, m. 31 July 1886 Catherine d. of Rev. T. B. Cornish.

237. Mogg, b. Oct. 1847, m. 20 May 1879 Edith Percival Clifton, and is now W. Clifton Mogg.

Leeds, his wife Agnes Maria d. 24 Jan. 1892.

238. Chirol, b. 19 Dec. 1846.

239. Stewart, b. 1 Jan. 1849, m. 24 Aug. 1880 Catherine J. Garnett.

240. Ayre, b. 25 June 1849.

241. Little, m. 28 Oct. 1874 Edith Stretton.

Comins, b. 7 June 1849.

Mackarness, m. 14 Sep. 1882 Grace Emily d. of Rev. R. N. Milford.

242. Campbell, E. Jas., b. 27 May 1850.

Deacon, b. 18 June 1850.

Pargiter, b. 28 Mch 1852.

Pitman, m. 8 June 1893 Myra Amy Florence Clarkson.

243. Baker, m. 24 Aug. 1880 Charlotte Thurman.

Williams, in orders; m. S. Margaret-at-Cliff 5 Aug. 1884 Katherine d. of William Gray, of York and Blackheath.

Hardy, m. 29 Mch 1877 Mary Rebecca d. of J. Mann.

Collins, m. 30 Aug. 1881 Caroline Susanna Maria Ward.

Bridge, m. 4 Aug. 1878 Mary Gibbous.

244. Sparks, m. 14 Ap. 1874.

Kelcey, b. 21 Ap. 1854, in Univ. Eleven 1874–5.

Skipton, b. 29 Jan. 1853.

245. Robinson, Master of Hill Side sch., Godalming; m. 12 Jan. 1892 Marian Eliz. Evans.

Hart-Smith, m. 27 Ap. 1886 Edith Mabel Wood.

Venn, m. 27 Sep. 1890 Ida Butler.

246. O'Donoghue, m. 13 Sep. 1880 Mary Louisa Birley.

Napier, Prof. of English Philology at Göttingen, Ph. D. Gottingen 14 Feb. 1882; m. Alderley Edge, Cheshire 11 Sep. 1879 Mary Ferrier d. of Jas. Hervey.

Davies, m. 16 Oct. 1886 Lucy Eccles.

Hoyle, b. 28 Jan. 1855.

247. Horsman, b. 10 Nov. 1856, barrister I. T. 18 Ap. 1894.

Upcott, m. 22 Aug. 1888 Sophia Madeleine Dalgairns.

Peck, d. London 31 Oct. 1888.

Eden, m. 27 Ap. 1889 Horatia Katherine Frances d. of Alf. Gatty D.D.

248. Ward, b. 8 Feb. 1857, d. 9 Nov. 1893; m. 16 Nov. 1891 Jessie Strode.

Powles, barrister I. T. 1892; m. 8 Ap. 1885 Lydia Laura Herklots.

Lainè, barrister M. T. 1893.

249. Armitage, b. 5 Mch 1857.

Acworth, m. 5 Dec. 1890 Ellinor Mary Wilson.

250. Porter, H. L., 1 s. John, by Sophia Mary d. of William Hill; m. S. John's, Yeovil 29 Dec. 1885 Ada Louisa d. of H. T. Beebe, V. of S. John's.

251. Butler, b. 17 May 1854, m. 8 Feb. 1886 Edith Rhoda Bolton.

Porter, T. C., m. 28 Oct. 1893 Helen Henriette d. of H. Allenby.

252. Heawood, m. 26 June 1890 Christina d. of H. B. Tristram, canon of Durham.

Shortt, m. 7 Ap. 1891 Georgina Woodman Hastings.

Spencer, m. 18 Jan. 1887 Mary Elizabeth Newman.

253. Dodson, m. 27 Dec. 1888 Ellen Amelia d. of Rev. G. S. Ward.

255. Tracey, m. 30 June 1890 Lilian Mary Elder.

256. Marsh, b. 6 Mch 1862; m. 8 Sep. 1890 Frances Mary 1 d. of J. C. Brockwell, V. of Owston, Doncaster.

Talbot, m. 15 Ap. 1891 Eleanor Maud, d. of late C. Waring, C.E.

258. Walters, m. 4 Oct. 1888 Helen Millicent Mansfield.

263. Lester, dele *and* after Merchant Taylors.

266. Rossignol, 7th in final competition 1893.

NOTE.—For most of these later additions I am indebted to the kindness of M. H. Green, Esq., fellow of Trinity.

INDEX.

The letters C E F G H J L N P R S T W stand invariably for Charles Edward Francis George Henry John Lewis Nicholas Philip Richard Samuel Thomas William. The names of Fellows are followed by their date in a parenthesis.

THE END

Oxford

HORACE HART, PRINTER TO THE UNIVERSITY

PLATE II

COLLEGIVM EXONIENSE.

FRITHCRS III COL 1566 COM IIII II IH

PLATE III

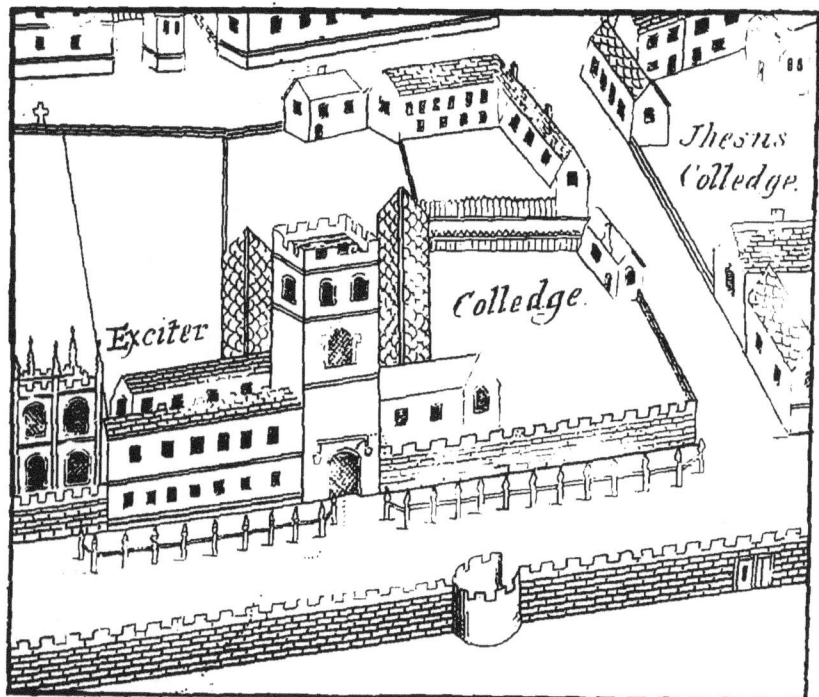

AGAS' VIEW, 1588, FROM THE NORTH

S T   O

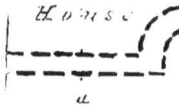

Alderman
Wright's
garden.
a

&

House

a

R   E   (

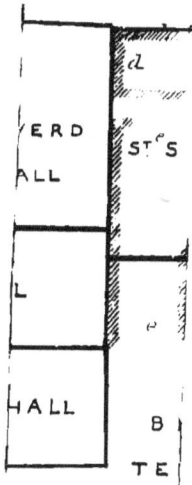

d

ERD

ST^e S

ALL

L

e

HALL

B

TE

ETER

H A

T   M

O L N

S MILDRED'S

www.ingramcontent.com/pod-product-compliance
Lightning Source LLC
Chambersburg PA
CBHW022125020426
42334CB00015B/760